A NEW HISTORY
OF THE ISLE OF MAN
Volume 1

Evolution of the Natural Landscape

A New History of the Isle of Man
VOLUME 1

Evolution of the Natural Landscape

Edited by
RICHARD CHIVERRELL
and GEOFFREY THOMAS

LIVERPOOL UNIVERSITY PRESS

First published 2006 by
LIVERPOOL UNIVERSITY PRESS
Liverpool L69 7ZU

© 2006 Liverpool University Press

The rights of Richard Chiverrell and Geoffrey Thomas
to be identified as the editors of this work have been asserted by them
in accordance with the Copyright, Designs and Patents Act, 1988

British Library Cataloguing-in-Publication data
A British Library CIP record is available

ISBN 0-85323-577-5 (hardback)
ISBN 0-85323-587-2 (paperback)
ISBN-13 978-0-85323-577-4
ISBN-13 978-0-85323-587-3

Typeset in 10.5/12.5pt Sabon by XL Publishing Services Tiverton
Printed by Henry Ling Ltd, Dorchester

This volume is dedicated to
DR LARCH SYLVIA GARRAD
1936–2005

Contents

Acknowledgements

The editors and contributors to this volume are indebted to numerous people who have helped at various stages in its production. Philippa Tomlinson would like to thank Betty Hopson, Terry Holt, Mil Millichap, Alan Hiscott and colleagues at the Isle of Man Meteorological Office, Nick Pinder from the Wildlife Park, Linda Moore from the Wildlife Office, Andrew Foxon from Manx National Heritage and members of Manx Wildlife Trust: Caroline Steel, Duncan Bridges and particularly Tricia Sayle. Special thanks go to Peter Davey and Nick Johnson, at the University of Liverpool's Centre for Manx Studies in Douglas, for giving unfailing help, advice and encouragement. Kate Hawkins would like to thank Mike Bates, Steve Crellin, Larch Garrad, Ben Jones, Martin Luff, Chris Sharpe, Phil Styles, Stella Thrower, Chris Wormwell and Jamie Wright for providing biological records.

Richard Chiverrell, Geoff Thomas, Jim Innes and Jeff Blackford thank the Scottish Universities Reactor Research Centre, NERC RCL (Allocation 1026.0403), the Quaternary Research Association, the British Ecological Society, the Gough Ritchie Trust, the Manx National Heritage and the Manx Heritage Foundation for providing or financing radiocarbon dates.

Geoff Thomas is indebted to generations of undergraduate students and to former postgraduate students Roger Dackombe and Mike Connaughton for help and assistance in the field over the years. He is also greatly indebted to the Manx National Heritage, the Manx Heritage Foundation and the Gough Ritchie Trust for generous financial assistance in supporting post-doctoral fellowships for Richard Chiverrell and Dave Roberts. Without their work filling important gaps in our knowledge of the island this volume would be a different book.

Much of the early work in planning the book was undertaken by Roger Dackombe of the University of Wolverhampton, and the editors are grateful for the head start given to them by his endeavours. Trevor Ford, formerly of the University of Leicester, and Rob Barnes of the British Geological Survey are thanked for reviewing early versions of the manu-script. Many of the maps produced in the volume are based upon the Isle of Man Government MANNGIS dataset and the Government and Juan Bridson (MANNGIS Project Manager Information System Division), in particular, are thanked accordingly. The editors are particularly indebted to Sandra Mather and Suzanne Yee of the Cartographics Unit at the Department of Geography, University of Liverpool, for the enormous amount of work they have undertaken in drawing, editing, amending and collating the large number of illustrations used in the volume. The editors are also very grateful for the patience of all the contributors while we have fought to juggle our commitment to the book with seemingly endless demands on our time to complete concurrent research projects and contracts and deliver heavy teaching loads.

Contributors

Jeff Blackford is Senior Lecturer in the Department of Geography, Queen Mary College, University of London

Dave Burnett is a geologist with Amerada Hess

Elizabeth Charter is Senior Wildlife Officer with the Wildlife Division of the Isle of Man Department of Agriculture, Fisheries and Forestry

Richard Chiverrell is Senior Lecturer in the Department of Geography at the University of Liverpool

Russell Coope is Emeritus Professor of Quaternary Palaeoecology at the Department of Geography, Royal Holloway College, University of London

Pat Cullen is an ornithologist, author, editor of *Peregrin* and bird recorder for the Manx Ornithological Society

Trevor Ford is retired from a senior lectureship in the Department of Geology at the University of Leicester

Mike Fullen is Reader in Soil Science in the School of Applied Sciences, University of Wolverhampton

Larch Garrad was Assistant Keeper of Natural History at the Manx Museum

Silvia Gonzalez is Reader in Biology and Earth Sciences at Liverpool John Moores University

Michael Hallett is Environmental Sciences Technician in the School of Applied Sciences, University of Wolverhampton

John Harris is retired from the post of Senior Agricultural Advisor with the Isle of Man Department of Agriculture, Fisheries and Forestry

Kate Hawkins is Curator of Natural History at the Manx Museum

Dave Huddart is Professor of Quaternary Geology at Liverpool John Moores University

Jim Innes is a research fellow at the Department of Geography, University of Durham

Edward Pooley is the vertebrate recorder for the Isle of Man

Dave Quirk is Senior Exploration Geologist with Amerada Hess and chairman of the Manx Geological Survey

David Roberts is Lecturer in Geography at the University of Durham

Chris Sharpe is Director of the Manx Bird Atlas

Geoff Thomas is Senior Lecturer in the Department of Geography at the University of Liverpool

Stella Thrower is a retired biology teacher and author

Philippa Tomlinson is Research Fellow at the Centre for Manx Studies, Douglas

1   Introduction

GEOFF THOMAS, RICHARD CHIVERRELL,
DAVE QUIRK and DAVE BURNETT

The original geological survey of the Isle of Man, undertaken by George Lamplugh[1] in the last decade of the nineteenth century, provided a wealth of geological data and the precision of his observations has long stood the test of time (Figure 1.1). The conceptual basis of the accompanying memoir[2], however, reflected the geological opinion of his times and a reinterpretation of the geology of the island, taking in developments in plate tectonic theory and climatic change, has been long overdue. This volume, the first in the five-volume series of the *New History of the Isle of Man*, is intended to provide a modern view of the geological history of the island and the evolution of its natural landscape. Its publication is timely in that it is published shortly after the release of the revised geological map (Figure 1.2) and memoir for the island undertaken by the British Geological Survey[3], upon which many of the contributors to this volume worked.

The geological history of the Isle of Man is immensely long, and the rocks and sediments that have accumulated on the island over time tell a fascinating story of drifting continents, changing climates and the evolution of life. The rocks record a history in which the area now occupied by the island was at any one time on the floor of a deep ocean basin, part of a Himalayan-scale mountain range caught between two colliding continents, one small corner of an immense sandy desert stretching across much of Europe, lost beneath the waters of a shallow tropical sea, buried by volcanic lava and, much later, overrun by an immense ice-sheet. At other times the island stood above the oceans and was subject to intense erosion that removed many of the rocks previously deposited. Over its long history the island has been torn apart by faults, shaken by earthquakes, heated by magma, covered with lava, and denuded by wind, water and ice. All these factors have contributed, in one way or another, to the physical landscape seen today. They have also contributed to the cultural landscape for geology is not just a dry record of rocks and changing environments over unimaginable timescales, but it is also about economic resources and their utilisation. The former importance of the mining industry on the island is one manifestation of this; the possibility of valuable hydrocarbon resources under the seas surrounding the island is, for the future, another.

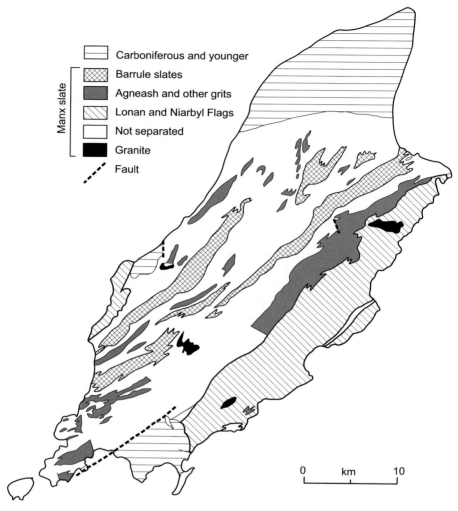

Figure 1.1 *Lamplugh's 1898 geological map of the Isle of Man.*

This book takes into account a broad spectrum of potential readership, ranging from the scientifically aware and educated layman, probably of Manx origin or living on or visiting the island, who wants to know more about the evolution of the Manx environment, to an academic readership. In recent years the island has seen a resurgence of earth science research and the resulting published work has had significance beyond that of simply unravelling the local geological history. Consequently, the book

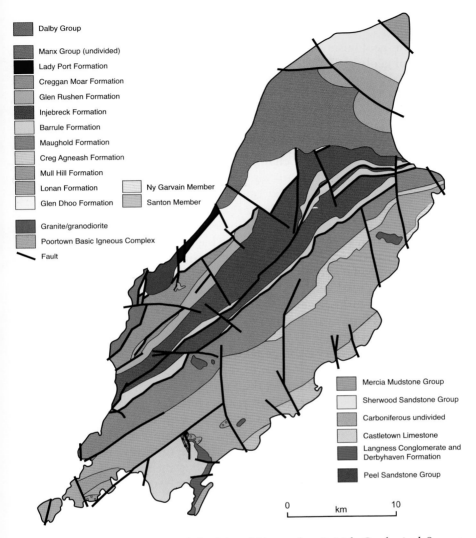

Figure 1.2 *Geological Map of the Isle of Man, after British Geological Survey (2001).*

attempts to provide a readable account for the general reader, on the one hand, and a review of present knowledge for the specialist, on the other. This dual purpose has presented some problems in presentation and, as a consequence, we start this introductory chapter with a brief treatment of some conceptual background designed for the general reader.

TIME, SPACE AND PLATE TECTONICS

Most non-geologists have two principal conceptual difficulties with the science of geology. The first is grasping the enormity of the timescale over which geological processes operate. The second is conceiving how dramatically environments can change over these timescales. Most of our measures of time relate to episodes in the span of a single human life. Thus, our own personal experience is limited to around 70 to 80 years. For comparison, the earth is estimated to be approximately 4.6 billion years old. Although we see evidence of natural change over our own lifetime, it is difficult to imagine to what extent it can change over thousands, let alone millions or billions of years. Some basic rates of contemporary denudation may provide some clue. The denudation rate of the modern Amazon River is equivalent to the lowering of its catchment surface by approximately 7 cm per 1,000 years, a seemingly imperceptible amount[4]. Multiplying by (say) 10 million years gives an amount of 700 m; enough to remove the whole of the Isle of Man were it located in the catchment of the Amazon River. The Amazon is relatively modest as an eroding agent and most of the major rivers of the world have rates that are double this; the Brahmaputra, draining the Himalayas, has the world's highest rate at nearly 10,000 m per 10 million years.

In geological history if things get worn down they also tend to get raised back up again and these long-term rates of denudation are compensated by tectonic uplift. For example, the European Alps are currently rising at a rate of about 300 m per million years whilst the Southern Alps in New Zealand are rising at the remarkable rate of up to 5,000 m per million years. Geological time therefore provides opportunity for great change and, given enough time, environments can change radically. At a more local level, one metre of cliff erosion per year along the northwest coast of the Isle of Man may seem high, but a visit each year hardly seems to notice any change. This rate, however, would remove the whole of the northern drift plain in 10,000 years – barely tomorrow in geological terms.

The nature of any environment is largely determined by climate, which in turn is basically determined by latitude. Thus, equatorial forest environments occur only in the tropics; hot, dry deserts only between the tropics and the temperate latitudes. If you wish to change your environment to a tropical one the only way of seemingly doing so is to move there. Geological processes and long periods of time can provide this option. The earth's surface is made up of a set of mobile tectonic plates, moving slowly by convection beneath the crust. Some plates are moving away from one another, like the Eurasian and the North American; some are moving towards one another, like the Eurasian and the African; some rift apart, like the African plate along the Great Rift Valley. Others collide, as the African and Eurasian plates and the Indian and Eurasian plates are doing, whilst others weld together.

Many of the world's plates are joined together in such a way that they move as a coherent whole. The margins of these plates are termed 'passive' (Figure 1.3) and are typified by areas such as the eastern Atlantic Ocean crust and the west coast of the African continent. However, other plate boundaries are 'active' and characterised by earthquakes and volcanoes due to movement of one plate relative to the other. When plates move towards each other at an active, 'destructive' margin, dense ocean crust is often pushed beneath thicker but lighter continental crust. As the oceanic crust descends beneath the continental crust, it begins to heat up and parts of it will eventually melt. The molten rock then rises towards the surface and may eventually erupt as a volcano. Where two plates comprising continental crust move towards each other, neither can be easily pushed beneath the other and instead, a crumple zone or mountain belt is formed, such as the Alps or the Himalayas (Figure 1.3).

The Atlantic Ocean is currently widening at an average rate of 50 mm

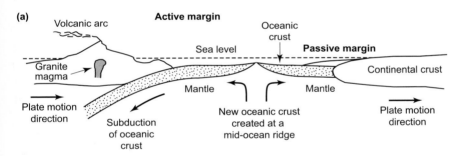

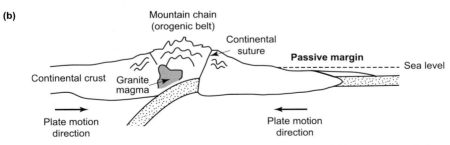

Figure 1.3 *Cross-sections through the earth's crust showing different types of plate margin. (a) Diverging. (b) Converging.*

per year[5] by sea-floor spreading across the mid-Atlantic Ridge as the North American plate moves west and the Eurasian plate moves, relatively, east. This rate is equivalent to 50 km in a million years, 500 km in ten million years and 5,000 km in 100 million years, providing neither of the plates involved collides with another plate in the process. These rates explain why different rock types found on the Isle of Man represent cool temperate, equatorial and desert environments, conditions that can all be met when a continent migrates from a position south of the equator, for example, to one north of the equator. This is essentially the geological story of the Isle of Man for the tectonic plate to which the island belongs has drifted over the last 500 million years from cool latitudes in the southern hemisphere, across the equator and up into the temperate, northerly latitudes of the present day. Thus the grey slates of the Manx Group were deposited in a deep, cold ocean in the southern hemisphere approximately 480 million years ago, the Castletown Limestone was formed in shallow, tropical seas around 330 million years ago at the equator and the offshore Permo-Trias was deposited in hot deserts at about 20° N around 248 million years ago. During its passage northwards the plate collided with a number of other plates to create a supercontinent during the Caledonian (423 to 413 million years ago) and the Variscan (320 to 290 million years ago) orogenies. The plate has also risen and fallen relative to sea level as it has stretched and crumpled and rifted over time.

The earth is approximately 4.6 billion years old but relatively few of the oldest rocks survive and the majority of those that make up the British Isles are younger than 550 million years old. This period of time, known as the Phanerozoic, is sub-divided into the Palaeozoic, Mesozoic and Cainozoic eras (Figure 1.4). These eras are, in turn, divided into periods. The oldest and most widespread rocks on the Isle of Man were formed during the early part of the Palaeozoic era. They belong to the Manx and Dalby Groups, deposited during the Ordovician and Silurian periods, respectively. Rocks formed in the Devonian (the Peel Sandstone), Carboniferous (the Castletown Limestone), Permo-Triassic (rocks buried beneath the northern plain) and Tertiary periods (solidified magma occurring in dykes) are also present. Overlying the solid geology is one of the thickest sequences of Quaternary deposits in the British Isles, formed by the passage of ice-sheets over the last million years or so. The island, consequently, has a very varied geology, encompassing a great variety of rock types formed in different environments at different times.

Geologists measure time in a number of ways. Relative time is established by the relationship of one rock unit to another through the laws of superposition and the science of stratigraphy. Normally, unless tectonic events have intervened, rocks are laid out one above the other in decreasing order of age, with the oldest at the bottom and the youngest at the top. The tracing of a sequence of rock units from area to area by correlation of their character thus enables a relative time-scale to be established. Rocks are also dated by the fossils they contain. Throughout geological time, and especially in the last 500 million years, life forms have evolved slowly from early primitive forms to later more complex forms. During the evolutionary process many forms have died out, or become extinct, as a result of competition from other forms or by their failure to adapt to changing environmental conditions. Fossils found in rocks can therefore be used to identify fossil zones that allow the relative age of the rock in which they occur to be determined (Figure 1.4). Absolute age can be determined by the use of dating techniques, such as potassium-argon and radiocarbon dating that utilise the rate of decay of naturally occurring radioactive isotopes contained within rocks. The geological time-scale used throughout this volume takes the age of all era and period boundaries from Gradstein and Ogg[6].

In this book dates older than a million years are shown in short form with the suffix Ma, for millions of years; for example 452 Ma or 452 million years ago. Dates between one million years and one hundred thousand years are shown in short form with the suffix ka, for thousands of years; for example 350 ka or 350,000 years ago. Dates younger than 100,000 years are shown in full. Most dates from the last 40,000 years have been obtained using radiocarbon dating methods. Any raw radiocarbon dates referred to in this volume carry the suffix ^{14}C yrs BP to distinguish them from calibrated dates. For radiocarbon dating the present is defined as AD 1950, so dates are in years before AD 1950. Direct quotation of radiocarbon dates requires reference to the standard error for each age determination, for example 22,350 ±350 ^{14}C yrs before present. Radiocarbon dates increasingly depart from calendar dates back from about 3,000 years. However they can be corrected to a calendar timescale using the relationship between ^{14}C years and calendar years identified by the radiocarbon dating of samples of a known age. Tree rings, where counting of the annual growth increment, and corals, where independent dating has been achieved by uranium series methods, provide these calibration datasets or curves. Calibration of radiocarbon dates does not produce a single unique age because the raw radiocarbon date and associated error have a zone of interception with the calibration curves. The majority of radiocarbon dates in this volume are referred to as a calibrated age range that reflects two standard deviations. Each age determination is shown with the suffix BP (for Before Present, or before AD 1950), for example 3,790 BP.

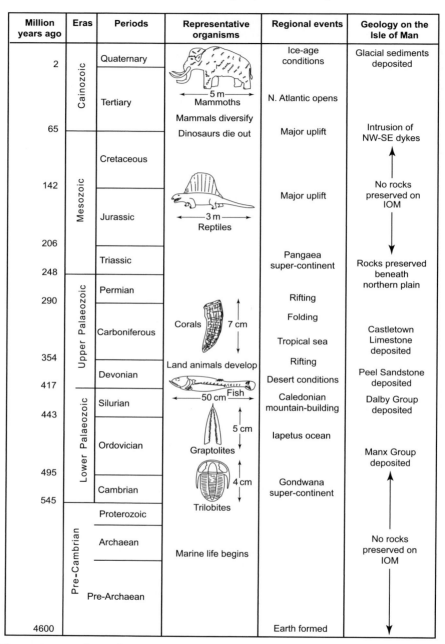

Million years ago	Eras		Periods	Representative organisms	Regional events	Geology on the Isle of Man
2	Cainozoic		Quaternary	Mammoths ←5 m→	Ice-age conditions	Glacial sediments deposited
65			Tertiary	Mammals diversify Dinosaurs die out	N. Atlantic opens Major uplift	Intrusion of NW-SE dykes
142	Mesozoic		Cretaceous		Major uplift	No rocks preserved on IOM
206			Jurassic	←3 m→ Reptiles		
248			Triassic		Pangaea super-continent	Rocks preserved beneath northern plain
290	Upper Palaeozoic		Permian		Rifting	
354			Carboniferous	Corals 7 cm	Folding Tropical sea Rifting	Castletown Limestone deposited
417			Devonian	Land animals develop 50 cm Fish	Desert conditions	Peel Sandstone deposited
443	Lower Palaeozoic		Silurian	5 cm Graptolites	Caledonian mountain-building Iapetus ocean	Dalby Group deposited
495			Ordovician			Manx Group deposited
545			Cambrian	4 cm Trilobites	Gondwana super-continent	
	Pre-Cambrian		Proterozoic			
			Archaean	Marine life begins		No rocks preserved on IOM
4600			Pre-Archaean		Earth formed	

Figure 1.4 *Geological timescale showing typical organisms, regional geological events and the equivalent rocks of the Isle of Man.*

ROCKS AND ROCK-TYPES

Rocks are divided into igneous, metamorphic and sedimentary types, each formed through separate processes and representing different stages of the geological cycle (Figure 1.5). Igneous rocks, such as the Foxdale Granite, form when molten magma or lava cools and solidifies into rock. Once a rock has formed it may become exposed at the Earth's surface where it is subject to weathering and erosion by the elements and is gradually broken down over time into sediment. Typically, rivers and wind transport the sediment into the marine environment where deposition is the dominant process. Over many millions of years sediment thicknesses of several kilometres can accumulate in areas where the Earth's surface is subsiding in

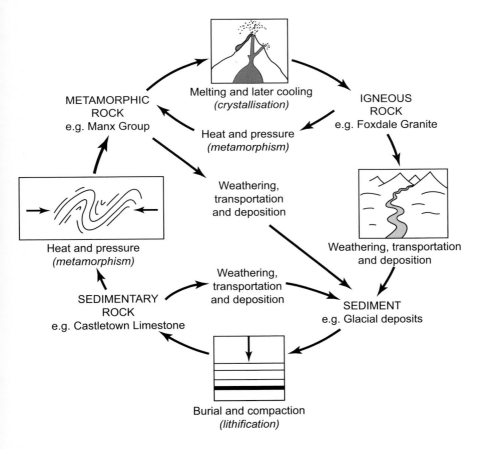

Figure 1.5 *The geological cycle.*

what are known as sedimentary basins. As the sediment is buried it becomes compressed beneath the overlying strata and the temperature increases causing the sediment to harden into rock in a process known as lithification (Figure 1.5). Examples of sedimentary rocks on the Isle of Man are the Peel Sandstone and Castletown Limestone. If the sedimentary rock continues to be buried and subjected to even greater pressures and temperatures it will eventually begin to recrystallise to form a metamorphic rock. The Manx and Dalby Groups of rock are composed of slightly metamorphosed sedimentary rocks such as slate. With a further increase in temperature and pressure the rocks begin to melt forming magma. Magma tends to move upwards where pressures are lower but the concomitant decrease in temperature will cause it to crystallise and solidify into an igneous rock. Any of these rocks can become exposed at the surface and are subject once more to weathering and erosion, thus continuing the geological cycle.

The Isle of Man is now surrounded by sea but its rocks do not stand in isolation. Similar rocks of the same age around the Irish Sea are thought to have formed in equivalent tectonic and environmental settings (Figure 1.6). The Manx Group, for example, has many similarities with rocks of the same age in the Lake District (the Skiddaw Group) and in Leinster. The Dalby Group is of the same age and was formed by the same processes as the Windermere Supergroup of the Lake District and also rocks in the Southern Uplands of Scotland. Devonian sediments (such as Peel Sandstone) are not common around the Irish Sea but do occur further north in Scotland. Lower Carboniferous sediments, like the Castletown Limestone, are present in the Lake District and over much of Ireland. Granite, analogous to that seen at Foxdale, is exposed in southeast Ireland and in the Southern Uplands. Large ice-sheets advancing south from the mountains of Scotland to cover the Isle of Man deposited most of the Quaternary deposits, and equivalent deposits are found in the surrounding regions of eastern Ireland and western England.

THE LANDSCAPE OF THE ISLE OF MAN

The island covers some 500 square kilometres, is mostly low upland and owes much of its form to the influence of the underlying geology. Dackombe and McCarroll[7] divided the landscape into a number of major landscape regions (Figure 1.7). Two upland massifs dominate the island and are separated by the central valley, which runs across the width of the island from Douglas to Peel. The *northern upland massif* is both larger and higher and includes the two highest points on the island, Snaefell at 621 m

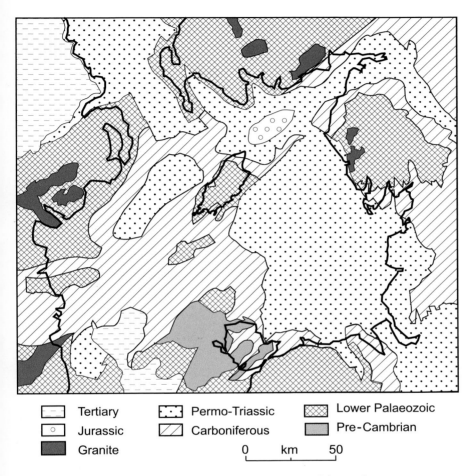

Figure 1.6 *Generalised Pre-Quaternary geology map of the Irish Sea.*

and the adjacent North Barrule at 565 m; *the southern upland massif* is more subdued reaching only 483 m at South Barrule. Both upland massifs are topographically controlled by the underlying geology and are dominated by two prominent ridges aligned north-north-east to south-south-west along the Caledonian structural trend, a belt of complex folding arising from the collision of two continents more than 400 million years ago. Except for the drift lowland of the north this trend also defines the elongated outline of the island. The westernmost of the two ridges runs from Mount Karrin, through Slieau Dhoo towards Beary Mountain. It is then cut by the central valley but extends south from St Johns via Slieau

Figure 1.7 *Map of the main landscape zones in the Isle of Man, after R.V. Dackombe and D. McCarroll (1990).*

Whallian and Dalby Mountain to the coast at Gob yn Ushtey. The higher, eastern ridge runs from North Barrule to Snaefell then on to Greeba Mountain. Cut again by the central valley the ridge continues via South Barrule, the highest point in the southern hills at 483 m, to the coast at Cronk ny Arrey Laa. Both ridges are flanked by a series of shallow upland basins and dissected high plateaux. These are mostly covered by thin glacial deposits, which blanket the landscape and impart a smoothly undulating topography displaying little exposed rock. The high plateaux are often incised by deep river valleys such as the Sulby, the Auldyn and the Dhoo and only one, Laxey, bears any suggestion of possible glacial erosion.

Around the periphery of the upland massifs are two narrow coastal plateaux. The *eastern coastal plateau* is divided into two major components. In the north is a roughly triangular area between Port e Vullen, Maughold Head and the Dhoon, lying in the shadow of the east flank of North Barrule. The topography is characterised by low rolling hills deeply incised by short streams draining steeply to the sea. Many of these streams are characterised by waterfalls along their lower courses and are indicative of immature rivers systems not yet adjusted to the present level of the sea. Other valleys are underfit and occupied by streams disproportionately small for the size of their valley. The Port Mooar valley, running between Maughold Head and the lower slope of North Barrule, is a case in point and is either a relic of a long vanished drainage system or, more probably, of glacial modification. Running from Laxey, through Douglas, Port Grenaugh towards Fleshwick Bay on the west coast is a second area of coastal plateau. Most of the drainage runs north to south and is probably a function of glacial diversion, the most notable being the diversions between Port Soderick and Port Grenaugh highlighted by Dackombe and McCarroll[8]. The western coastal plateau is far less extensive than the eastern and forms the coastal fringe from Dalby to the Peel Embayment and then northwards to Kirk Michael and Ballaugh. It is largely drift covered and cut by numerous short, steep streams descending directly to the coast and a number of distinctive drainage channels associated with glacial drainage diversion occur. The southwest extremity of the island forms a continuation of the coastal plateau, with Meayll Hill and the Calf of Man forming isolated hills of Manx slate separated from each other by the Calf Sound.

The *Peel Embayment* is a low-lying area with an undulating topography underlain by Devonian sandstones buried inland by thick glacial deposits. This is the only area along the west coast where foreign glacial deposits penetrate inland. The embayment passes eastwards into the Central Valley, the boundary with which is defined at the gravel fans where the Neb and Foxdale rivers meet. The morphology of the embayment features low-lying ridges and terraces; landforms that betray their glacial origins as ice marginal moraine ridges and glacial outwash plain. The deeply incised *Central Valley*, a relic of a long dormant geological fault generated during the Caledonian Orogeny, separates the northern and southern upland massifs. It runs from the Peel Embayment and the River Neb in the west to Douglas and the River Dhoo in the east. The valley has a broad open cross-section and a floor infilled with peats and alluvium of Holocene age.

Fans and terraces of fluvial gravel are relict features from the glaciation of the island. The valley is characterised along its length by areas of poor drainage and peat-filled basins, with thicker accumulations of peat at Greeba Curragh and Glen Dhoo.

The *Plain of Malew* in the south of the island is a low plain of gently undulating topography, mostly developed across the Castletown Limestones, that extends down to a more subdued coastal strip of gravelly bays, poorly drained back-beach lagoons, raised beaches, ancient cliff-lines and rocky shores. Glacial till covers much of the surface and is moulded into a swarm of drumlins, mostly rock-cored, around Ballasalla. Elsewhere the surface is diversified by narrow or gently sloping glacial outwash sandar systems running to the southwest and small areas of former lake sedimentation, especially around Colby and the airport.

The low-lying *northern plain*, extending from the steep scarp slope of the northern upland massif to the Point of Ayre in the far north of the island, is probably the most distinctive and different landscape region on the island. The plain is entirely underlain by a complex sequence of unconsolidated, glacial and post-glacial deposits up to 180 m thick, overlying deeply buried and unexposed Carboniferous and Permo-Triassic rocks. These deposits are exceptionally well exposed along both coasts and the surface of the plain displays a very diversified small-scale topography that includes a wide range of glacial deposition landforms including large moraine ridges, sloping sandur surfaces, shallow kettle basins, ice-front alluvial fans and lake basins. This topography is fronted across the Ayres by a prominent fossil-raised cliff running from Blue Point to Cranstal, cut during an episode of high sea level in the recent geological past. Both coasts are eroding very rapidly and longshore drift to the north has transported much of the sediment eroded from the cliffs and redeposited it as a series of gravel beach ridges and associated wind-blown sand dunes between the fossil cliff and the Point of Ayre.

STRUCTURE OF THE BOOK

The volume presents an account of what is currently known of the geology and natural history of the island, from its first appearance on the geological scene at the bottom of a faraway ocean, some 500 million years ago, through to the present day and this is reflected in the structure of the book. This devotes a chapter to each of the eras of geological time that have significance to the island and, as appropriate, describes the plate tectonic setting, the regional stratigraphic framework, the tectonic structure, the character of the rocks and any fossils they contain and an interpretation of their environments of deposition. The first chapter describes the Lower Palaeozoic Manx and Dalby Groups of rocks, which together underlie most of the island, and which were deposited in the southern hemisphere between 495 and 423 Ma. The next chapter describes their subsequent deformation in the Caledonian Orogeny between 420 and 410 Ma. These accounts are followed by a chapter describing the enigmatic red rocks of the Devonian Peel Sandstone, deposited in intermontane desert basins between 410 and 400 Ma by erosion of the mountains created by the Caledonian Orogeny. This account is followed by a description of the Carboniferous Castletown Limestone and associated volcanic rocks of the south of the island, formed in shallow tropical shelf seas between 300 and 330 Ma when Britain had moved north and was located within the equatorial zone.

Rocks younger than the Carboniferous are not exposed on the island, either because they were never deposited in the first place or because they were, but have subsequently been eroded away. Consequently, the geological events of the last 330 million years cannot be observed directly on the island. Much of the missing geological history, however, can be inferred from other areas around the margins of the Irish Sea basin or pieced together from data acquired during recent oil and gas exploration offshore from the island. The chapter on the 'Missing Periods' consequently summarises what probably happened on and around the island during the long period of time in which Britain moved progressively northwards from the equator in the Carboniferous towards its present northerly mid-latitude location. This long and complex period was associated with significant changes in climate, episodes of continental rifting, regional tectonic subsidence, the opening of the Atlantic Ocean by sea-floor spreading, intense volcanic activity and widespread erosion. Except for some Tertiary volcanic dykes occurring on the island any other rocks deposited during this 330 million year episode have been completely removed. The basic form of the Isle of Man and its surrounding shallow seas was etched out by the end of the Tertiary.

Major glacial episodes occur at intervals throughout the geological record and frequently last for millions of years. During the Tertiary the world climate slowly declined and just a few million years ago, at the start of the Quaternary Period, temperatures in the northern mid-latitudes passed below the threshold necessary for the growth and expansion of large, continental-scale ice-sheets. Because of its location in the northern part of the Irish Sea basin, astride the path of successive ice movements from source areas in western Scotland, the island has been dramatically influenced by repeated glaciation and a chapter is devoted to examining its effects. This chapter is followed by an account of the short but very complex period of rapid climatic and environmental change that occurred as the island recovered from the retreat of the last ice-sheet. Following this episode world climate ameliorated rapidly into the present interglacial and a further chapter examines the radical changes that took place as the sea level rose around the island, the natural fauna and flora returned and the environmental stage was set for the appearance of man. Exploitation of the island's geology by people is dealt with in a subsequent chapter on the economic geology and includes an account of both historic mine working and recent hydrocarbon explorations across the island's offshore areas. A final chapter examines in detail the current state of the contemporary natural environment and ecology of the island, including descriptions of the main semi-natural habitats, discussion of current conservation and land management policies and an assessment of current environmental threats to the island's fauna and flora.

Notes

1   G.W. Lamplugh, *Isle of Man, Solid and Drift Geology Map*, Geological Survey of England and Wales, Sheet 100 (1898).
2   G.W. Lamplugh, *The Geology of the Isle of Man*, Memoir of the Geological Survey of England and Wales (1903), 620.
3   R.A. Chadwick, D.I. Jackson, R.P. Barnes, G.S. Kimbell, H. Johnson, R.C. Chiverrell, G.S.P. Thomas, N.S. Jones, N.J. Riley, E.A. Pickett, B. Young, D.W. Holliday, D.F. Ball, S.G. Molyneux, D. Long, G.M. Power, and D.H. Roberts, *Geology of the Isle of Man and its offshore area*, British Geological Survey Research Report, RR/01/06 (2001), 143.
4   M.A. Summerfield, *Global Geomorphology*, Longman, New York (1991), 537.
5   M.A. Summerfield (1991).
6   F.M. Gradstein and J. Ogg, 'A Phanerozoic time scale', *Episodes*, 19 (1996), 3–4.
7   R.V. Dackombe and D. McCarroll, 'The Manx Landscape', in V. Robinson and D. McCarroll (eds), *The Isle of Man: Celebrating a Sense of Place*, Liverpool University Press (1990), 10–17.
8   R.V. Dackombe and D. McCarroll (1990), Figure 2.2.

2   The Lower Palaeozoic Rocks

DAVE BURNETT and DAVE QUIRK

The oldest rocks on the Isle of Man are informally known as the Manx Slates. These are composed of deformed sedimentary rocks originally deposited as layers of mud and sand in a deep water marine environment during the Lower Palaeozoic, an era stretching 545 to 417 Ma. They occur at surface across three-quarters of the island, form parts of the sea-floor immediately adjacent to the east and west coasts and underlie the Quaternary drift of the southern part of the Ayres. They make up most of the island's upland topography including the prominent ridge of mountains running northeast to southwest from North Barrule to South Barrule, parallel to the main structural grain of the rocks.

Lamplugh[1] defined the Lower Palaeozoic rocks as the 'Manx Slate Series' and identified four principal rock units. Following Lamplugh, little geological work was undertaken on the island until the 1960s when Simpson[2] revised Lamplugh's classification of the Manx Slates, subdividing it with additional units, and redefining it as the 'Manx Group'. Further work in the 1990s by Woodcock et al.[3], Quirk and Burnett[4], Burnett[5], Morris et al.[6] and the British Geological Survey[7] led to a complete reclassification of the different rock units and also showed that the rocks lying between Peel and Niarbyl, the 'Niarbyl Flags' of Lamplugh, were approximately 50 million years younger than the rest of the Manx Slates. Consequently, this unit was separated from the Manx Group (Early Ordovician age, 495–470 Ma) to be defined instead as the Dalby Group (early Silurian age, 428–423 Ma).

PLATE TECTONIC SETTING IN THE LOWER PALAEOZOIC

In early Ordovician times, around 495 Ma, the continental crust that now underlies the Isle of Man lay in the southern hemisphere. At this time the land area of the earth principally comprised two large continents: the supercontinent of Gondwana, centred around the South Pole, and the Laurentian continent, straddling the equator. The wide Iapetus Ocean separated these continents (Figure 2.1a). Gondwana was composed of what is now Africa, South America, India, Australia, Antarctica and most of Europe, including the southern part of the British Isles and southern Ireland, while Laurentia comprised present-day North America, Greenland, Scotland and the

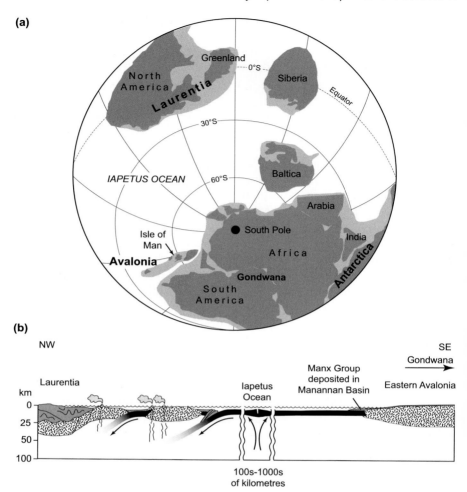

Figure 2.1 *(a) Reconstruction of the earth's continental plates, 480 million years ago during the Arenig epoch of the early Ordovician, after Cocks (2000). (b) Schematic cross-section through the Iapetus Ocean during the Arenig epoch, 480 Ma, redrafted from Watson and Dunning (1979).*

northern half of Ireland.

Attached to the northern edge of Gondwana, at a latitude of approximately 60°S, lay a long, narrow landmass or microcontinent known as Avalonia. The region that was later to become the Isle of Man formed part of the seabed north of this microcontinent and consequently Avalonia played a very significant role in the evolution of the geology of the island.

During early Ordovician times (*circa* 470 Ma), Avalonia began to split off from Gondwana and move northwards (Figure 2.1). By mid Ordovician times (*circa* 460 Ma) it had reached a latitude of 30°S. The Iapetus Ocean, to the north, had consequently diminished in size and a new ocean, the Rheic Ocean, had developed to the south between Avalonia and Gondwana (Figure 2.1b). By early Silurian times (*circa* 440 Ma) the Iapetus Ocean had closed up to a point where the western part of Avalonia had slid in against the North American portion of Laurentia in the vicinity of what is now Newfoundland. By *circa* 430 Ma, the eastern part of Avalonia had drifted further north, to a latitude of approximately 20°S, and collided with the European part of Laurentia. Complete closure of the Iapetus Ocean occurred at the onset of the late Silurian (*circa* 423 Ma) resulting in the formation of a mountain belt known as the 'Caledonides', which stretched from present-day eastern United States to Scandinavia. Compression and deformation associated with the collision (the Caledonian mountain-building event or 'orogeny') continued intermittently on into the early Devonian period (410 Ma).

The oldest rocks in the Isle of Man, the Manx and Dalby Groups, therefore record the deposition of ocean sediments off the northern continental margin of Avalonia, movement of the plate northwards and its eventual collision and uplift against the southern margin of Laurentia.

THE MANX GROUP

Origin of the sediments

The rocks of the Manx Group were originally deposited over a period of approximately 20 million years in water several hundreds or thousands of metres deep, several tens of kilometres offshore from the northern continental margin of Avalonia. The time period involved corresponds to the latest part of the Tremadoc epoch (*circa* 495–485 Ma) and all of the Arenig epoch (*circa* 485–470 Ma), subdivisions of the oldest part of the Ordovician period (Figure 2.2).

The sand and mud that make up the Manx Group were originally eroded from upland areas in Gondwana and Eastern Avalonia and transported northwards by major river systems. Much of this sediment may then have been temporarily deposited in shallow water on the margin of the Avalonian continental shelf where it was moved around by coastal currents and waves, large amounts of it eventually spilling down the continental slope and onto the ocean floor to accumulate in an area termed the

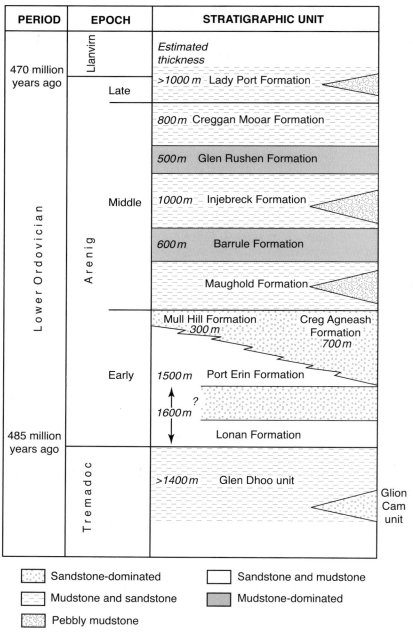

Figure 2.2 *Table showing subdivisions of the Manx Group relative to geological time and their estimated thickness.*

Manannan Basin[8] (Figure 2.1b). It is also likely that at times the rivers fed sand directly onto the ocean floor through submarine canyons similar to those that cut across most modern day continental shelves. Such canyons are most active in transporting sand into deep water during periods when sea level has fallen and the shelf is exposed. Such episodes of low sea level were common during the early Ordovician due to the effects of glaciation when large volumes of water were trapped in a continental ice-sheet on Gondwana around the South Pole.

The mechanism by which the sand and mud made their way into the deepest parts of oceans was through 'turbidity currents', literally a surging flow of turbid water carrying sediment. Turbidity currents are usually caused by collapse at the shelf edge or from the head or sides of a submarine canyon and may be set off by earthquakes. They then move rapidly down slope into deeper water similar to avalanches, often scouring channels into the seabed as they go. Where the seabed flattens out, the turbidity currents slow down leading to the deposition of material caught up in the flow; first the largest grains (sand) and eventually the finest material (mud). Therefore, where a turbidity current has come to rest, it is often recorded as a layer of sandstone overlain by a layer of mudstone (Figure 2.3a). Such an event may occur only once every hundred years or so but over millions of years a blanket of sediment can accumulate that is thousands of metres thick and tens of kilometres in extent. These blankets tend to be fan-shaped in plan view, spreading out from where the turbidity currents were fed down-slope, and are therefore known as submarine fans (Figure 2.4).

Essentially, the Manx Group is a stack of sand-prone submarine fans interspersed with intervals of predominantly mudstone. These intervals of mudstone are thought to represent prolonged periods when sea level was high, submerging the continental shelf, thereby trapping most of the sand. However, during such periods, the sea-floor became unstable and slurries of sediment slid down-slope to be deposited as muddy debris ('debrites') where they came to rest. On the Isle of Man, debrites are represented by beds of pebbly mudstones, the pebbles consisting of pieces of mudstone and siltstone that were broken and caught up in the slurry.

The sands within the Manx Group have left a number of clues as to the direction in which they moved ('palaeocurrent' evidence). Turbidity currents usually flow down-slope and therefore palaeocurrents can indicate where continents lay relative to the place where they are observed. The best evidence comes from 'flute casts', sand-filled remnants of drop-shaped scoops sculpted out of the soft seabed by the surging flow of the turbidity current. They become filled with sand when the flow begins to slow down (Figure 2.3b). The deeper, tapered end of the flute cast points in the

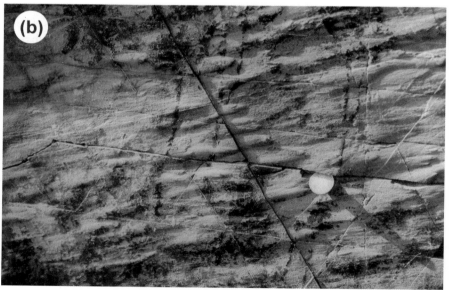

Figure 2.3 *(a) Turbidites in the Manx Group at Cass-ny-Hawin (SC298692). Sandstone beds are pale grey and mudstones are dark grey. (b) Flute casts on the underside of a bed at Pigeon Stream, Marine Drive (SC381742). The direction of flow of the turbidity current was from right to left (east to west).*

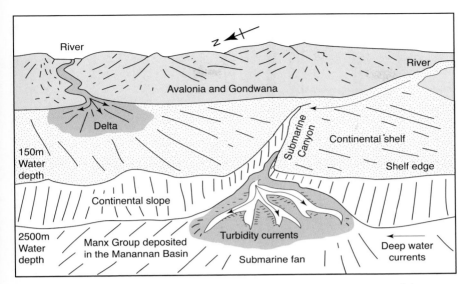

Figure 2.4 *Schematic diagram showing the environment of deposition of the Manx Group, redrafted from D.R. Prothero and F.L. Schwab (1996).*

upstream direction of the flow and the broad, shallower end points downstream. Ripples are often preserved at the top of sandstone beds and can provide an indication of the direction the sediment was transported. These ripples have an asymmetric form similar to mini sand dunes with the steep side of the ripple facing in the downstream direction of the current that formed them.

A recent study of flute casts in the Manx Group shows that flow was towards the west whereas the direction of flow indicated by ripples records flow towards the north[9]. Although such information is crucial to working out where the Manx Group sediments originally came from, the data are ambiguous in that they indicate two different directions. Woodcock and Barnes[10] explain this by invoking the presence of seabed topography partitioned into east–west trending troughs by active faults assumed to be parallel to the northern margin of Eastern Avalonia. Their interpretation is that the turbidite currents flowed westwards along these troughs, forming flute casts but occasionally spilling northwards over the sides of the troughs into deeper water to the north, where they left ripples rather than flute casts. Quirk and Burnett[11] challenge this model and instead interpret the flute casts as indicating that Avalonia lay directly to the east, from where the turbidity currents were derived, but with ripples formed by deepwater currents moving parallel to the contours of the slope. Such

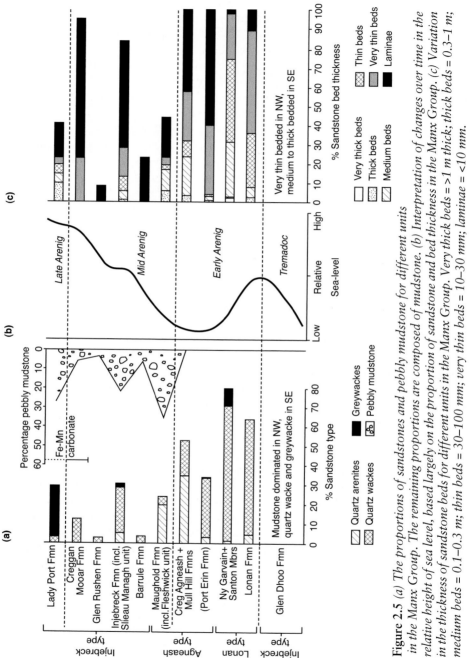

Figure 2.5 (a) _The proportions of sandstones and pebbly mudstone for different units in the Manx Group. The remaining proportions are composed of mudstone._ (b) _Interpretation of changes over time in the relative height of sea level, based largely on the proportion of sandstone and bed thickness in the Manx Group._ (c) _Variation in the thickness of sandstone beds for different units in the Manx Group. Very thick beds = >1 m thick; thick beds = 0.3–1 m; medium beds = 0.1–0.3 m; thin beds = 30–100 mm; very thin beds = 10–30 mm; laminae = <10 mm._

deep-water, contour-parallel currents are common along many modern continental slopes. Despite the difference of opinion, it is agreed that the flow pattern is consistent with the sediment being derived from Eastern Avalonia and deposited in the Iapetus Ocean.

Although turbidity currents were the cause of the majority of beds within the Manx Group, there are significant variations in bed thickness; the amount of sandstone, mudstone and other rock types; colour; the presence or absence of internal laminations and other subtleties within different parts of the succession (Figure 2.5). Some of the differences in rock type are shown in Figures 2.6, 2.7 and 2.8. These characteristics are not only used to subdivide the Manx Group but also to interpret changes in the sedimentary environment over time. The most obvious difference between rocks of the Manx Group in different parts of the island is the variation in the relative proportions of sandstone and mudstone (Figure 2.5a). For example, North Barrule and Snaefell are largely composed of dark grey mudstone whereas the cliffs at The Chasms comprise 90% white sandstone (quartz arenite). The differences in sandstone-mudstone content are usually mirrored by variations in the thickness of the beds with sandstone-dominated intervals typically thicker bedded (0.01–0.5 m) than intervals with more mudstone (e.g., 1–50 mm) (Figure 2.5c).

The proportion of sandstone and mudstone in each unit has also been used to construct a sea level curve shown in Figure 2.5b. Many Manx Group rocks consist almost entirely of mudstone and are interpreted to have been deposited during periods when sea level was rising relatively quickly, flooding the continental shelf of Eastern Avalonia. This event, called a 'marine transgression' caused coarse-grained sediment to be trapped by the rising water close to the coast. Consequently, only mud reached the deep-water environment where the Manx Group sediments were accumulating. Conversely, units in the Manx Group with high proportions of sandstone are thought to correspond to periods of falling sea level when coarse-grained sediment was flushed out into deeper water.

Another important control on the characteristics of turbidites is the distance they were deposited from the deeper-water channel or submarine canyon. Those deposited close to the mouth of a channel ('proximal' turbidites) will generally have a greater proportion of thicker beds and coarser sediments (Figure 2.6), while those deposited further away ('distal' turbidites) will tend to be dominated by thin-bedded siltstone and mudstone (Figure 2.7). Equally important is the proportion of coarse- and fine-grained sediment originally caught up in the turbidity current. This is related not only to fluctuations in the height of sea level and the size of the flow but also changes in the type of sediment supplied by rivers.

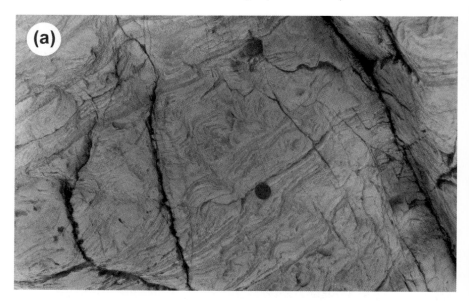

Figure 2.6 (a) Sandstone beds from the Ny Garvain Member at Port Cornaa (SC483877) showing chaotic convolute lamination formed by water escaping through the sand soon after deposition. A coin is shown for scale. Photograph by Mike Radcliffe. (b) Greywacke with ripples overlain by mudstone (dark grey) from Marine Drive (SC366729). The surface of the rock has been cut and polished to emphasise the laminations. The ripples were formed by deep-water currents at the bottom of the Iapetus Ocean 485 million years ago.

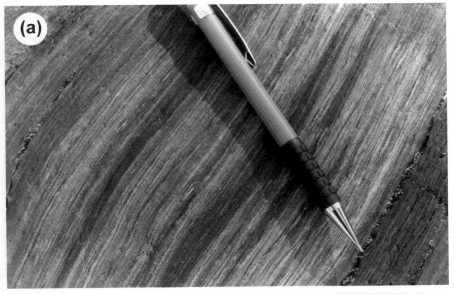

Figure 2.7 *(a) Thinly laminated mudstones and siltstones of the Maughold Formation at Maughold Head (SC495915) deposited by the slow fall-out of tiny silt and mud grains and organic matter. Photograph by Mike Radcliffe. (b) Mudstone-dominated sediments of the Injebreck Formation at Port Lewaigne (SC465933).*

Figure 2.8 *(a) Quartz arenite beds at The Chasms (SC194664). (b) Greywackes in the cliffs below Marine Drive (SC360732).*

Variations also occur in the type of grains present within sandstones in different parts of the Manx Group. The types of rock that were being eroded in the source area largely control these compositional changes and the length of time the sediment resided on the shelf. If quartz-rich rocks are being eroded from the source area, the sediment produced will already contain less feldspar and clay minerals. In addition, where sand remains in a shallow marine environment for a long period, minerals less durable than quartz tend to be destroyed and the sediment therefore becomes relatively enriched in quartz. This is probably the origin of the white sandstone at The Chasms, known as 'quartz arenite' (Figure 2.8a). Sandstones composed of quartz grains but also some mud between the grains are known as quartz wackes. Probably the majority of the mud originated from unstable fragments of clay-rich rocks, feldspar and micas that broke down to very fine-grained material during burial. Other sandstones, for example along parts of Marine Drive (Figure 2.8b), are grey-green in colour and comprise sand grains with a relatively high proportion of other fragments such as metamorphic or sedimentary rocks (Figure 2.6b). These were probably transported directly from a source area to the site of deposition and are termed 'greywackes'.

Fossils

Fossils can be used to date rock units because, through time, organisms evolve and pass into extinction. For more than 200 years geologists have used the recognition of distinctive fossils or groups of fossils to build up a relative chronology of rocks throughout the world. Fossils are also critical for determining the type of environment sedimentary rocks were deposited in. Three types of fossil have been found in the Manx Group: acritarchs, graptolites and marine trace fossils.

Evidence for life is common in the Manx Group although fossil organisms are rare. The most common life forms preserved are microscopic fossils, known as acritarchs. They are very small (typically around 0.025 mm in diameter) and are thought to be types of planktonic algae that evolved rapidly into different pollen-like shapes over time. Unfortunately they are difficult to extract and are poorly preserved in the Manx Group. They probably floated near the surface of the Iapetus Ocean but sank to the seabed as they died. Most were scavenged and consumed by other creatures or decayed, but some were preserved by being buried rapidly beneath sediment. Differences in shape, for example in the number of spines and protruberances, are used to discriminate between species and the presence or absence of certain species has been used to build a relative timescale in

Ordovician rocks in the Lake District which has since been applied to the Manx Group[12]. Another important point is that the acritarchs in the Manx Group and equivalent rocks in the Lake District are typical of those from the southern part of the Iapetus Ocean ('Avalonian affinity'). Those from the northern part of Iapetus are different ('Laurentian affinity') in the same way that different organisms are found on either side of the modern Pacific.

Graptolites have been used successfully for dating Lower Palaeozoic rocks throughout the world. They represent a now extinct animal that lived as a colony similar to modern corals. However, unlike corals, the zooids forming the colony lived in free-floating structures, often resembling thin wishbones or twigs (Figure 2.9a). Each stem appears serrated with the individual serrations (or thecae) representing the living space for one zooid. They are thought to have been preserved in a similar way to acritarchs, by slowly settling onto the seabed and being buried by sediment. However, as the structures were very delicate, they are usually found as flattened strips typically 30–50 mm long and a few millimetres wide. Unfortunately, good graptolites have been discovered at only one reliable locality in the Manx Group. These specimens were acquired from Baltic Rock, east of Port Grenaugh, within the Santon Member of the Lonan Formation (see below) and are probably of early Arenig age (485 Ma), similar to acritarchs from the same unit[13]. Rushton[14] classified the graptolites as dichograptids, *Didymograptus* and possibly *Tetragraptus*. Other specimens have been found at Cregneash (too poorly preserved to be identifiable) and in loose rock at Cronk Sumark[15].

By far the most widespread evidence of life in the Manx Group is in the form of trace fossils. These are trails left behind by organisms, which burrowed into and crawled over the sea-floor before the sediment hardened to rock. The types of organisms involved were probably mostly soft-bodied creatures such as worms but crustaceans and molluscs may have also played a part. Typical trace fossils in the Manx Group are *Phycodes*, *Planolites* and *Dictyodora* but species such as *Glockerichnus radiatus* also occur[16] (Figure 2.9b) The presence of trace fossils within most of the units provides good evidence that there was sufficient oxygen at the seabed to support life, an environment not conducive to the preservation of organisms.

Subdivision of the Manx Group

Variations in the amount and type of sandstone, variations in bed thickness and the presence or absence of other rock types such as pebbly mudstones have been used to subdivide the Manx Group into formations

Figure 2.9 *(a) Graptolite Monograptus flemingii cf.* warreni *(Barnes and Rickards [1993]) from the Dalby Group at Traie Dullish Quarry, Peel Hill. Fossil is 67 mm long. (Accession No: IOMMM:1998-0142. Photograph courtesy of Manx National Heritage). (b) Trace fossil* Glockerichnus radiatus *appearing as a series of radiating tubes on a bedding plane at Langness (SC292668).*

or units of rock with similar characteristics. The subdivisions have been constrained with several reliable acritarch ages although there is still room for significantly different interpretations.

The distribution of the formations as mapped by Quirk and Burnett[17] is shown in Figure 2.10. Previous models of the geology of the Manx Group invoked a large trough-like fold or 'syncline' running northeast through the centre of the island[18]. These models implied that rock layers on the east coast dip down under the centre of the island where they are bent upwards again to reappear on the west coast. More recent research[19] has demonstrated that this interpretation was erroneous. Instead, across most of the island, the Manx Group is tilted down to the northwest (Figure 2.11), meaning that in a general sense the oldest rocks are present in the east, and increasingly younger rocks are exposed towards the west. The exception to this is in the northwestern part of the area, around Kirk Michael, where some of the oldest rocks of the Manx Group have been faulted in.

A brief description is given below of the distribution, composition, fossil content and age of the subdivisions of the Manx Group based on the latest work by Chadwick *et al.*[20] and Molyneux[21], which incorporates interpretations and data of both Quirk and Burnett[22] and Woodcock *et al.*[23] However, it should be noted that as well as the problem of poor exposure and disruption by faults, there are also relatively few fossils present to help date the rocks. This means that there is still some uncertainty in the age relationship of the units and individual researchers often have different opinions as to the exact order of succession, hence the differences between the recent British Geological Survey map[24] and that shown in Figure 2.10.

The oldest formation, the *Glen Dhoo Formation*, is a thousand metres or more in thickness and is composed of pale mudstone with lesser amounts of siltstone and fine-grained quartz-rich sandstone together with some volcanic breccias composed of andesite. It also locally contains very thick (up to 2 m) grey sandstone beds, for instance at Glion Cam. The formation occurs at surface in a strip running northeast from Ballanayre Strand to Kirk Michael and from there eastwards to Glen Dhoo. Acritarch fossil assemblages suggest a late Tremadoc to early Arenig age. It is surrounded by younger rocks implying that it has been faulted into place.

The *Lonan Formation* outcrops along much of the east coast and consists of thin layers of fine-grained sandstone, siltstone and mudstone couplets typical of distal turbidites. It is between 1,600 and 2,500 m thick. Acritarchs indicate a late Tremadoc to early Arenig age suggesting that the age of the formation probably overlaps with the Glen Dhoo Formation. Three sand-prone units have been identified within the formation, the Keristal, Santon and Ny Garvain Members. The Keristal Member occurs

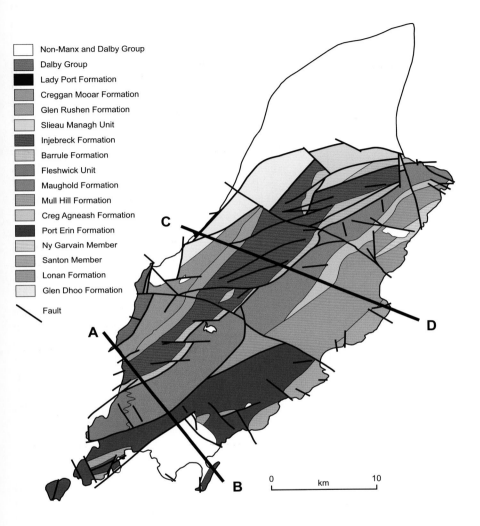

Figure 2.10 *Simplified geological map of the Manx Group. Lines of section A–B and C–D are shown in Figure 2.11.*

on the west and east sides of Keristal Bay, northeast of Port Soderick, and comprises several thick beds of quartz arenite. These are interpreted as having been deposited from the first turbidite flows associated with a period of falling sea level in the early Arenig, probably related to a period of glaciation. Two orders of magnitude thicker, the Santon and Ny Garvain

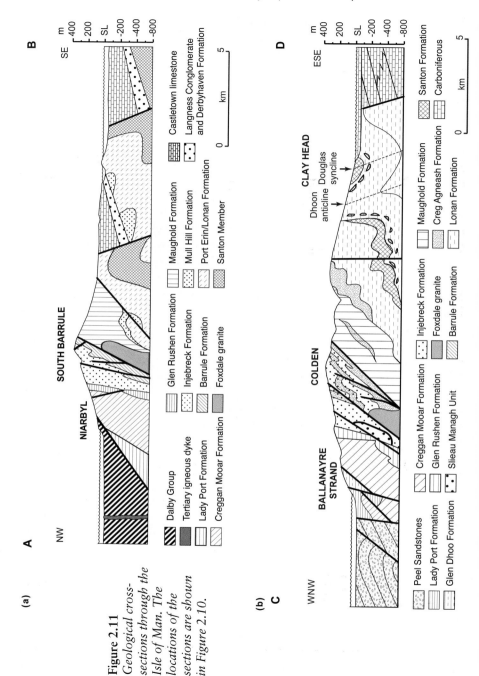

Figure 2.11
Geological cross-sections through the Isle of Man. The locations of the sections are shown in Figure 2.10.

Members almost immediately overlie the Keristal Member and are thought to represent the main part of the sea level fall. The Santon Member, well exposed in coastal sections from Onchan Head to Purt Veg, comprises thin- to medium-bedded sandstone and mudstone. A prominent, thick-bedded relatively coarse-grained sandstone unit, 50 m thick, occurs within the Santon Member at Purt Veg (SC326704) and is interpreted as the fill of a large turbidite channel[25]. Rushton[26] reported poorly preserved graptolites of probable Arenig age within this channel at Baltic Rock (SC327702). The Ny Garvain Member, lying between Gob ny Garvain and Port Cornaa, is also sandstone-dominated and displays extensive cross-lamination and convolute bedding (Figure 2.6a). The Santon and Ny Garvain Members are almost certainly lateral correlatives[27], essentially the same unit of rocks exposed in different areas of the island. Between Purt Veg and Port Erin, the rocks assigned to the Lonan Formation by Woodcock *et al.*[28] and Chadwick *et al.*[29] contain much more mudstone and are significantly thinner bedded. For this reason they have been assigned to a separate unit, the *Port Erin Formation*, by Quirk and Burnett[30] (Figure 2.10). Later work by the same authors has shown that this 1,500 m thick interval is more likely to correlate with the lower part of the Creg Agneash Formation than with the Lonan Formation[31].

The *Mull Hill Formation* overlies the Lonan Formation and is well exposed along the coast of the Cregneash peninsula, particularly at The Chasms. It is approximately 300 m thick and comprises 90% thick-bedded, quartz-rich sandstones with thin mudstone partings, typical of turbidites deposited close to the mouth of a submarine canyon. These contrast with the underlying Lonan Formation (or Port Erin Formation[32]) which in this area consists of 70% mudstone. Although acritarchs occur at Cregneash quarry (SC191674) they are not diagnostic and the formation remains undated other than by its position above the assumed Tremadoc to early Arenig Lonan/Port Erin Formation. Quirk and Burnett[33] demonstrated that the Mull Hill Formation could be the lateral equivalent of either the Santon and Ny Garvain Members or else a part of the Creg Agneash Formation. Burnett and Quirk[34] later showed, on the basis of chemical similarities, that it most likely correlates with the upper part of the Creg Agneash Formation (Figure 2.2).

The *Creg Agneash Formation* runs southwest from Maughold Head, where it is about 180 m thick, through the upper part of Laxey Glen towards Baldwin where it is as much as 750 m thick. It dies out towards Douglas but the Mull Hill Formation, which crops out along the same trend to the southwest, is probably its lateral equivalent. It consists of thin- or medium-bedded quartz-rich sandstones and laminated mudstones passing upwards into very thin-bedded mudstones. This upwards transition is interpreted as representing a change from proximal to distal turbidite deposition as sea level started to rise again (Figure 2.5b). The base of the formation is seen directly on top of the Lonan Formation below Maughold lighthouse[35] meaning that it is probably early Arenig in age. However, no fossils have been found to confirm this date.

The *Maughold Formation* is interpreted to run through the centre of the island from Maughold Head, through the eastern flanks of North Barrule, Snaefell and South Barrule to the coast at Bradda Head[36]. The formation is dominated by laminated dark grey mudstone but includes some pebbly mudstones and occasional sandstone beds in the southwest which Quirk and Burnett[37] assign to a different formation (the *Fleshwick Unit*, Figure 2.10). The sequence is at least 600 m thick and overlies the Creg Agneash Formation. Conditions were generally quiet with a gentle rain of mud particles reaching the seabed. The mud would have been carried in by distal turbidites and in suspension from shallow water. However, within the Fleshwick Unit in the southwest sediments that were originally deposited on an unstable slope have slumped and been redeposited as pebbly mudstones. Also here, quartz-rich sand was occasionally brought in by long-distance turbidity currents. The age of the Maughold Formation is poorly constrained, but it is probably early Arenig. As a whole, it probably represents the transition from the underlying quartz arenite-prone intervals to the overlying mudstones of the Barrule Formation although Quirk and Burnett[38] correlate the Fleshwick Unit with the Injebreck Formation that overlies the Barrule Formation.

The outcrop of the *Barrule Formation* forms the backbone of the island, running from The Stacks, north of Port Erin on the west coast, to Port Lewaigue on the northeast coast, and underlies the mountain summits of North Barrule, Snaefell, Beinn y Phott, the eastern flank of Colden, South Barrule and Cronk ny Arrey Laa. Its southeastern boundaries are either faulted or poorly exposed and its age relationship to adjacent formations is therefore unclear. Its thickness is also uncertain, but it is probably somewhere between 600 and 1,200 m. Where observed, its upper boundary seems to be a gradational contact with the Injebreck Formation. The formation consists of a monotonous, almost homogeneous sequence of black or grey laminated mudstone devoid of sedimentary features, thought to have been deposited from suspension. Its dark colour is due to the presence of organic carbon and this, plus the apparent absence of trace fossils, suggests that there was little or no oxygen at the seabed during deposition. The age is poorly constrained because, although acritarchs are present, they are not diagnostic and are poorly preserved, partly because the Barrule Formation is slightly more metamorphosed than the rest of the Manx Group. Its position relative to the Lonan Formation and Glen Rushen formations implies that it has an early to mid Arenig age.

The outcrop of the *Injebreck Formation* parallels that of the Barrule Formation and occupies a wide band running southwest through the Sulby Valley, between Sartfell and Injebreck Hill, between Beary and Greeba Mountains, across the Central Valley east of St Johns to meet the west coast between The Stacks and Niarbyl Bay. The formation is in the order of 1,000–2,000 m thick but in places appears thicker, probably due to the effects of folding and faulting. A gradational contact is seen with the overlying Glen Rushen Formation in the southwest. The formation bears some similarity to the Maughold Formation in that it is dominated by laminated mudstones but it also contains beds of fine-grained sandstone and pebbly mudstones. Usually the pebbly mudstones are no more than a metre thick but between Sulby and Ramsey the lower part of the formation consists of several hundred metres of pebbly mudstones. This interval was assigned to a separate formation (the *Slieau Managh Unit*) by Quirk and Burnett[39] (Figure 2.10) and probably represents an area affected by repeated submarine landslips, possibly because the seabed had a slightly steeper, more unstable slope. A sparse, low-diversity assemblage of acritarchs is not age diagnostic but its position relative to the Glen Rushen Formation indicates that the Injebreck Formation is probably early to mid Arenig. Graptolites were first recorded from the Manx Group by Bolton[40] at Cronk Sumark within what is now classified as the Injebreck Formation, but doubt was cast on their authenticity. Recent work by Rushton[41], however, has confirmed their occurrence at Cronk Sumark and indicated that they are indeed of Arenig age.

The *Glen Rushen Formation* is exposed in a narrow band of dark grey-bluish laminated mudstones running from south of Niarbyl, through Glen Rushen, Slieau Whallian and Glen Helen towards Barregarrow. It seems to represent the transition from the underlying Injebreck Formation upwards into the overlying Creggan Mooar Formation and is approximately 500–600 m in thickness. It is difficult to tell it apart from the Barrule Formation but its position relative to the Injebreck and Creggan Mooar Formations indicates that it is probably younger. The formation contains a limited acritarch fauna suggesting that the top of the formation is of mid Arenig age.

The *Creggan Mooar Formation* runs from Niarbyl Bay, northeast through Glen May and across the Central Valley eventually pinching out south of Slieau Curn. It is at least 800 m thick and its top is not seen. The formation comprises thinly bedded sandstones or siltstones and mudstones together with thin beds of a distinctive manganese-rich ironstone which weathers to a bright reddish-brown or black colour. These ironstones were probably formed by the release of volcanic fluids into the marine environment[42] some distance away from the Manannan Basin. The Creggan Mooar Formation is the most consistently fossiliferous unit in the Manx Group and yields a number of different acritarch assemblages which range in age from mid to late Arenig.

The youngest formation in the Manx Group, the *Lady Port Formation*, outcrops only on the west coast near Ladyport, between Peel and Glen Mooar, and is the most varied in terms of rock type. Numerous faults make it difficult to determine either its relationship to other formations or its thickness, but it is certainly more than 1,000 m thick and may be twice this. In different areas it resembles the Creggan Mooar, Glen Rushen, Injebreck and Glen Dhoo formations but late Arenig acritarchs have been found[43] that indicate it is, at least partly, younger. However, rather than representing a single rock unit, it is actually quite likely that it is made up of a number of separate fault blocks lying parallel to the Iapetus Suture.

Sediment composition

Microscopic examination of rock samples from the Manx Group[44] has revealed that the sandstones range from those composed almost entirely of quartz grains (quartz arenites) to others with significant quantities of less durable grains such as feldspar and rock fragments (greywackes). Sandstones with a composition intermediate between quartz arenites and greywackes (known as quartz wackes) are the most common. The greywackes and the quartz wackes also contain significant amounts of clay material between the grains whereas the quartz grains in the quartz arenites are usually cemented together by secondary quartz.

Quartz is by far the most common grain in sandstones of the Manx Group, typically comprising 80–100% of the rock. Feldspar is the next most abundant mineral and, of the feldspars, orthoclase (potassium-rich) is the most common type. Plagioclase (sodium- and calcium-rich) is the second most abundant feldspar type. After quartz and feldspar, the remaining sandstone grains are composed of broken rock fragments and fine-grained matrix that fills the spaces between the grains. In addition, other minerals such as zircon, tourmaline, pyrite and white mica are occasionally present.

The broken rock fragments that form grains within Manx Group sandstone, particularly the greywackes, are useful for interpreting from where the original sediment was derived. These fragments comprise metamorphic, sedimentary and igneous rocks, in order of decreasing abundance. The most common types are polycrystalline quartz, single grains composed of multiple crystals, such as metamorphic fragments and chert but also quartz arenite and occasional grains of the silica-rich volcanic rock called rhyolite. Other igneous grains include granite and rounded fragments of silica-rich volcanic ash. Most of these fragments would have been eroded from rocks on the continent of Gondwana and transported by rivers and turbidity currents before finally coming to rest on the Iapetus seabed.

The majority of Manx Group rocks contain matrix or very fine-grained minerals that form the groundmass of the rock and help bind the sediment together. The average sandstone comprises 79% grains and 21% matrix. The matrix is generally composed of decomposed rock fragments and feldspar, quartz, chlorite, white mica, opaque minerals and other material too fine to be identified under a geological microscope.

The chemical composition of sandstones in the Manx Group has recently been analysed[45]. Silica (SiO_2) dominates due to the high proportion of quartz. As a result of this, other elements are present in relatively low concentrations. Aluminium is the next most abundant element and is mostly related to the presence of feldspar and mica. Concentrations of iron oxide (Fe_2O_3) and magnesium oxide (MgO) are conspicuously low in the Manx Group, which is significant in that it indicates that iron-magnesium minerals, typical of basaltic-andesitic volcanic rocks, are not present. Previous models for this part of the Iapetus Ocean implied that during the early Ordovician there was a chain of volcanic islands in the area similar to the margins of the present day Pacific Ocean. Instead, this new work suggests that the region was more typical of the passive margins of the present day Atlantic.

In addition to providing descriptive information on the composition of the rocks, chemical analyses have been used in conjunction with fossil finds to aid our understanding of the order in which units of the Manx Group were deposited. Figure 2.12 shows two plots of chemical trends where it can be seen that individual rock samples from the same units tend to group together. An important observation is that different groups fall within one of three clusters or chemical fields that have been named Lonan-type, Agneash-type and Injebreck-type[46]. The Lonan-type field consists of the Lonan Formation and the Santon and Ny Garvain Members which are early Arenig (485 Ma) in age. The Agneash-type field is composed of the Mull Hill, Creg Agneash and Maughold Formations, which are younger than those of the Lonan-type field. All the units that make up the Injebreck-type field (Barrule, Injebreck, Glen Rushen, Creggan Mooar, Glen Dhoo, and Lady Port Formations) lie northwest of the Agneash-type units and are mostly mid to late Arenig (475–470 Ma) in age. However, recent analysis of acritarchs assemblages suggests that the Glen Dhoo Formation was deposited in the Tremadoc–early Arenig (495–485 Ma)[47] indicating that a fault separates them from the rest of the Injebreck-type units. In fact, in Glen Dhoo itself the sediments are similar to the sand-rich Santon and Ny Garvain Formations. The reason for the Injebreck-type chemical character may be that they were deposited in a different part of the Manannan Basin, separated from the Lonan-type and Agneash-type units. This interpreta-

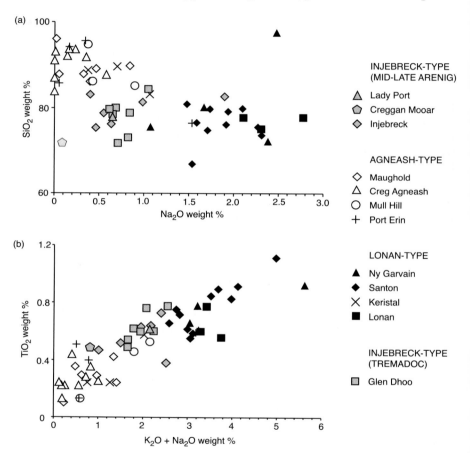

Figure 2.12 *Chemical cross-plots showing the concentration of (a) silica versus sodium oxide and (b) titanium oxide versus potassium oxide plus sodium oxide for sandstone samples from different units of the Manx Group. Note how certain units cluster together to form characteristic chemical groups, the Lonan-type and Agneash-type fields being the most distinctive.*

tion implies that the different parts of the Manx Group moved together during the Caledonian mountain-building event probably facilitated by a major fault interpreted to lie at the base of the Barrule Formation[48] (Figure 2.10).

Effect of faults on total thickness

The interpretation of the chemical data described above is actually far from straightforward. Although the rock units have been placed in date order using similarities in sediment and chemical composition, there is still considerable uncertainty in the interpretation. In particular, the implication is that the Manx Group succession is at least 7,000 m thick and possibly more than 10,000 m. This is 2,000 m to >5,000 m thicker than an equivalent interval in the Lake District (the Skiddaw Group)[49], unexpectedly large for an interval of time of no more than 20 million years[50].

Another explanation is that the Manx Group consists of more fault segments than previously recognised, comprising different panels of early to mid Arenig seabed shunted together during the Caledonian mountain-building event. This would mean that more of the sedimentary and chemical variations could be due to original spatial rather than temporal differences. For example, sand-prone sediments (e.g., Lonan-Creg Agneash Formations) are likely to have been deposited closer to the coast of Eastern Avalonia (lying southeast of the Isle of Man) whereas mud-prone sediments (e.g., Barrule-Injebreck Formations and Glen Rushen-Creggan Mooar Formations) may have been deposited in deeper water further away from (northwest of) Eastern Avalonia. In other words, the chemical composition may differentiate more proximal sediments from more distal.

The age data are really too sparse to decide to what extent the succession has been complicated by faults. However, fieldwork and geophysical data produced by techniques such as reflection seismic surveys and airborne magnetic measurements have shown that there is indeed a set of parallel faults running northeast to southwest through the centre of the island[51]. These approximately coincide with the southeast boundaries of the Barrule Formation, Slieau Managh Unit, Glen Rushen Formation and Glen Dhoo Formation suggesting that they define the bases of at least four separate Injebreck-type panels. Assuming the Lonan-Creg Agneash Formations and Lady Port Formation represent two additional fault panels, then the overall thickness of late Tremadoc–late Arenig rocks on the Isle of Man may actually be closer to 6,000 m. Quirk and Burnett[52] have illustrated some of the different possibilities but, without more fossil ages, these remain speculative.

Origin of the sediments

The high proportion of quartz and quartz-rich rock fragments and the dominance of orthoclase feldspar over the more chemically unstable plagioclase feldspar suggest that the Manx Group was derived from a land source or hinterland where the sediment had been eroded, weathered and redeposited a number of times. The quartz grains, metamorphic rock fragments and occasional granitic material from which the sandstones are composed suggest that the hinterland was similar to ancient continental areas in central parts of Africa. Rivers such as the Nile and Niger today carry large amounts of sediment to modern oceans and the same process is likely to have occurred 495–470 Ma around the northern coast of Eastern Avalonia. Turbidity currents transported the sediments out into the deep water of the Iapetus Ocean where the Manx Group accumulated. Rare volcanic fragments have also been identified and are interpreted to have been derived from ancient volcanoes extinct long before the Ordovician but exposed by erosion in the hinterland. The presence of sedimentary rock fragments in sandstones indicates that older sedimentary sequences were already present on Gondwana or Eastern Avalonia. For example, chert fragments are likely to have been originally derived from deep marine strata, but probably underwent several cycles of erosion and deposition before they were finally incorporated into the Manx Group sediment.

The interpretation of a continental source for most of the sediment in the Manx Group is consistent with low concentrations of iron and magnesium oxides that indicate very little or no contemporaneous volcanic activity. The only units showing minor indications of volcanic input are the Lonan Formation and the Lady Port Formation[53].

Direction of future research

Several criticisms can be levelled at the most recent synthesis of the Manx Group by Chadwick *et al.*[54]. For example, in the southwest part of the island, rocks ascribed by them to the Lonan Formation are significantly more muddy and have a chemical signature typical of the Creg Agneash Formation[55]. For this reason they were assigned to a separate unit (the Port Erin Formation) by Quirk and Burnett[56] (Figure 2.10). In the future it probably makes sense to resurrect this name.

The Maughold Formation has been used by Chadwick *et al.* to cover a wide variety of groups of rocks lying on the southeast side of the Barrule Formation. However, the different groups cannot be linked to one another because of poor rock exposure and cannot be dated because of a lack of fossils. To avoid the risk that different age units have been erroneously classified as one formation, Quirk and Burnett[57] instead divided them into three separate units. The pebbly mudstones and quartz arenites that lie around Bradda Head were assigned to the Fleshwick Unit (Figure 2.10) which may actually be younger than the Barrule Formation. The quartz arenites and mudstones of the Maughold Formation exposed inland, particularly in the Laxey Valley, were all interpreted by Quirk and Burnett as belonging to the Creg Agneash Formation. Only the mudstone-dominated interval in the northwest half of Maughold was assigned by Quirk and Burnett to the Maughold Formation, juxtaposed against the Creg Agneash Formation by a major east–west fault (Figure 2.10).

Other uncertainties that remain include:

- the degree to which the Injebreck Formation appears thicker than it actually is due to repetition by faulting;
- the age relationship of the Glen Rushen-Creggan Mooar Formations to the Barrule-Injebreck Formations in view of numerous large faults identified on geophysical data[58];
- the correlation between the thick interval of predominantly pebbly mudstones stretching from Glen Auldyn to Sulby River (the Slieau Managh Unit[59]) and the rest of the succession;
- the relationship of the sand-rich Glen Dhoo Formation (Tremadoc–early Arenig) to the younger, mud-dominated rocks that surround it (Injebreck, Glen Rushen, Creggan Mooar and Lady Port Formations) and the early Arenig Lonan Formation;
- whether the Lady Port Formation is composed of one unit or several separate fault panels of different ages.

These questions are fertile ground for future research, much of which will depend on carrying out additional mapping to confirm the presence or absence of faults and on discovering more fossils (acritarchs or graptolites).

Regional comparisons

Similar age rocks to the Manx Group occur in the Lake District (the Skiddaw Group)[60] and in southeast Ireland (the Ribband Group)[61]. The Skiddaw Group and the Ribband Group are thinner and contain less sandstone than the Manx Group, but all three are interpreted to have been deposited on the northern margin of Eastern Avalonia. However, while the Isle of Man/Lake District area is now regarded as a passive margin during the Arenig[62], the Ribband Group contains evidence of contemporaneous volcanic activity[63]. A volcanic centre of Tremadoc–Arenig age is present in Wales[64] but it is difficult to see how this relates to sediments further north in the Isle of Man and Lake District which contain little trace of the eruptions[65]. The most likely explanation is that large faults have shunted different parts of Avalonia together. By analogy, hundreds of kilometres of sideways motion has occurred along the present day San Andreas fault system in California.

THE DALBY GROUP

Until recently, the rocks on the west coast of the island between Niarbyl and Peel were thought to be of a similar age to the Manx Group on the east coast[66]. However, in 1997 graptolites were discovered in a quarry above Traie Dullish on the west side of Peel Hill showing that this one kilometre wide strip of rocks was 50 million years younger than the Manx Group[67]. Deposited during the Wenlock epoch (part of the early Silurian period spanning 428–423 Ma), the sediments could no longer be considered as part of the Manx Group and were therefore re-classified as the Dalby Group[68]. The Dalby Group is composed of only one unit, the Niarbyl Formation separated from the Manx Group by one large fault which runs from Niarbyl to Peel Harbour. Morris *et al.*[69] suggest that this formation is in the order of 1250 m thick.

By the time the Dalby Group was deposited, the Iapetus Ocean had narrowed from several thousand kilometres wide to perhaps only a few hundred and Eastern Avalonia would soon collide with Laurentia. The location of the join between Laurentia and Eastern Avalonia, the 'Iapetus Suture', has been constrained in southeast Ireland and is likely to run along the Solway Firth and through Northumberland. Extrapolation across the Irish Sea brings the suture very close to the Isle of Man. Fossil[70] and palaeocurrent[71] evidence show that sediments in the Manx Group were derived from Gondwana whereas the Dalby Group sediments were sourced from Laurentia, implying that the fault between them represents the Iapetus Suture. However, as the Iapetus Ocean was much diminished by the time the Dalby Group was deposited (Figure 2.13a), it is perhaps more accurate to say that it was deposited close to the line of the Iapetus Suture. Magnetic data acquired from the air suggest that the actual boundary between the two continents lies a few kilometres offshore, parallel to the northwest coast of the Isle of Man[72]. The fault separating the Dalby Group from the Manx Group (the 'Niarbyl thrust'), probably formed during the final stages of collision when the sediments lying on the floor of Iapetus were shunted together (Figure 2.13b).

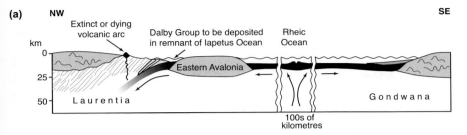

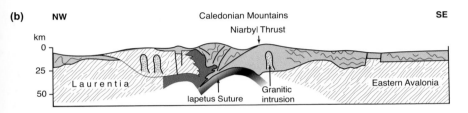

Figure 2.13 *(a) Schematic cross-section illustrating the narrow ocean between Laurentia and Eastern Avalonia in which the Dalby Group was deposited before final collision of the continents. (b) Schematic cross-section illustrating the Caledonian mountain belt after the Iapetus Ocean had closed 400 Ma.*

Environment of deposition

Like the Manx Group, the Dalby Group was deposited in marine conditions by turbidity currents. Flute casts (Figure 2.14) and ripples (Figure 2.15a) show that the direction of flow was approximately southeastwards, in contrast to the Manx Group where flow was to the west or north[73] (away from Avalonia). Detailed analysis of the flow pattern[74] suggests that the sediment was derived from the northwest, where Laurentia lay, but the currents were sometimes redirected towards the southwest, probably by deep-water currents travelling along the axis of the basin.

As with many turbidite sediments, the Dalby Group is primarily composed of alternating beds of sandstone and mudstone. The sandstones are typically fine-grained and occur in beds between 0.1 m and 0.4 m thick, although occasionally thicker beds of medium-grained sandstone are observed[75]. On the whole, the sandstones contain a greater amount of very fine-grained matrix and rock fragments than those of the Manx Group and are classified as greywackes and quartz wackes. Mudstones are interlaminated with siltstones. Also present at several locations are pale greenish-yellow layers of altered volcanic ash ('meta-bentonite') in beds of

Figure 2.14 *Flute casts on the underside of a vertical turbidite bed in the Dalby Group at Thistle Head. Flow was from bottom left to top right, equivalent to from northeast to southwest when the beds are restored to their original horizontal orientation.*

less than 0.1 m thickness. The Dalby Group also contains a type of rock known as 'laminated hemipelagite' (Figure 2.15a). This is common in the northern part of the succession and is best exposed at Traie Dullish Quarry on Peel Hill where it consists of millimetre-scale alternations of mudstone and layers with a speckled appearance. The speckled layers are of organic origin representing particles of planktonic material and mud that coalesced in the water column before descending slowly to the sea-floor. Under normal marine conditions such sediment would stand little chance of being preserved as organisms living on the seabed would soon sift and consume the organic matter. However, much of the Dalby Group was deposited under anoxic conditions, where the sea-floor environment was starved of oxygen and therefore devoid of life (trace fossils are absent in the Dalby Group). As a result of this, the laminated hemipelagite has remained undisturbed. This is a major difference with the Manx Group where burrows are widespread but animals such as graptolites are rarely preserved, indicating that the seabed was oxygenated with organic matter quickly consumed.

Sediment composition

Microscopic examination shows that sandstones in the Dalby Group are composed of a diverse range of material but quartz is the most common, occurring either as individual grains or as fragments of other rocks such as quartz-rich volcanic clasts and quartzose metamorphic rocks. Other fragments include igneous rocks like microgranite and trachyte, metamorphic mica schist, and sedimentary rocks such as shale, siltstone, quartzite and chert. In addition to quartz, mineral grains of plagioclase, potassium feldspar, white mica, green tourmaline, zircon and pyrite are present. The matrix between the sand grains contains similar material but is very fine-grained. Carbonate (probably mostly calcite) cement is also common.

The chemical composition of the Dalby Group has received little attention. What little work has been done suggests sandstones generally have a much lower silica content (61% SiO_2) than the majority of the Manx Group (70–95% SiO_2) and consequently the samples have relatively higher abundances of other major elements, particularly magnesium oxide[76].

Origin of the sediment

The limited data available on the composition of the Dalby Group suggest that it was derived from the erosion of a diverse set of rocks including those from a mountain belt and a volcanic island[77]. Therefore, it is inferred that different types of crust had already been shunted together in the source area, probably heralding the onset of the Caledonian mountain-building event when Eastern Avalonia collided with Laurentia. The presence of volcanic fragments may indicate that the Dalby Group was deposited in front (to the south) of a nearly extinct volcanic chain along the margin of Laurentia during the final stages of closure of Iapetus (Figure 2.13a). These volcanoes would have developed above the zone where crust of the Iapetus

Figure 2.15 *(a) Laminated hemipelagite beds (speckled appearance, dark coloured), very fine-grained sandstones (pale coloured), and mudstones (dark coloured) of the Dalby Group in Traie Dullish Quarry, Peel Hill. Ripples are visible in the sandstones. (b) Nautiloid from Traie Dullish Quarry, Peel Hill.*

Ocean slid beneath Laurentia. By analogy, most of the volcanoes that form the 'ring of fire' around the present-day Pacific Ocean have formed in a similar way where oceanic crust is descending beneath Asia and the Americas. The Dalby Group was later shunted southwards over the Iapetus Suture during the climax of the Caledonian mountain-building event in the late Silurian and ended up juxtaposed against the Manx Group at Niarbyl.

Fossils

Unlike the Manx Group, no acritarchs have been obtained from the Dalby Group. However, due partly to the anoxic conditions that existed on the seabed, graptolites and nautiloids have been preserved (Figure 2.15b). Most of the fossils have been found in Traie Dullish Quarry on Peel Hill and consist of cyrtograptids (fern-like graptolites), monograptids (single stem graptolites) and orthoceratid nautiloids (elongate, cone-shaped shells) of early Silurian, Wenlock (*lundgreni* Biozone) age (*circa* 428–423 Ma)[78].

Regional comparisons

The Dalby Group shows certain similarities to rocks of the same age in other parts of the British Isles. In particular, the Birk Riggs Formation in the Lake District and the Denhamstown and Clatterstown Formations, north of Dublin, which all contain hemipelagite and quartz-rich turbidites with calcite cement[79]. They probably all belong to the same narrow, linear basin that existed on the south side of Laurentia (Figure 2.13). Anoxic conditions probably existed because circulation of sea water was restricted.

SUMMARY

The Manx Group represents a sequence of deep-water, oceanic basin sediments derived from the northern Avalonian margin of the continent of Gondwana and deposited in the Iapetus Ocean in the southern hemisphere during the late Tremadoc and Arenig epochs of the Ordovician Period, some 495–470 Ma. They form a stack of sandy submarine fans formed by turbidite currents flowing towards the west, interspersed with intervals of predominantly mudstone. The mudstone intervals are thought to represent prolonged periods when sea level was high, the submerged shelf having trapped most of the sand. Variations in the amount of sand through the succession probably reflect global fluctuations in sea level caused by variations in the size of the Gondwana ice cap. The Dalby Group was deposited some 50 million years later than the Manx Group during the Wenlock epoch of the early Silurian, 428–423 Ma. They too were deposited in deep marine conditions, but were sourced from the margin of the northern continent of Laurentia at a time when the Iapetus Ocean had narrowed to a few hundred kilometres in width. Soon after this, the two continents of Avalonia and Laurentia amalgamated during the Caledonian mountain-building event.

Notes

1   G.W. Lamplugh, *The geology of the Isle of Man*, Memoir of the Geological Survey of England and Wales, (1903), 620.

2   A. Simpson, 'The stratigraphy and tectonics of the Manx Slate Series', *Quarterly Journal of the Geological Society of London*, 119 (1963), 367–400.

3   N.H. Woodcock, J.H. Morris, D.G. Quirk, R.P. Barnes, D. Burnett, D. W.F. Fitches, P.S. Kennan and G.M. Power, 'Revised lithostratigraphy of the Manx Group, Isle of Man', 45–68 in N.H. Woodcock, D.G. Quirk, W.F. Fitches and R.P. Barnes (eds), *In sight of the suture: the Palaeozoic geology of the Isle of Man in its Iapetus Ocean context*, Geological Society of London Special Publication, 160 (1999b), 370.

4   D.G. Quirk and D.J. Burnett, 'Lithofacies of Lower Palaeozoic deep marine sediments in the Isle of Man: a new map and stratigraphic model of the Manx Group', in N.H. Woodcock *et al.* (1999b), 69–88.

5   D.J. Burnett, *The stratigraphy, geochemistry and provenance of the Lower Palaeozoic Manx Group, Isle of Man*, unpublished PhD thesis, Oxford Brookes University (1999), 478.

6   J.H. Morris, N.H. Woodcock and M.P.A. Howe, 'The Silurian succession of the Isle of Man: the late Wenlock Niarbyl Formation', in N.H. Woodcock *et al.* (1999b), 189–211.

7   R.A. Chadwick, D.I. Jackson, R.P. Barnes, G.S. Kimbell, H. Johnson, R.C. Chiverrell, G.S.P. Thomas, N.S. Jones, N.J. Riley, E.A. Pickett, B. Young, D.W. Holliday, D.F. Ball, S.G. Molyneux, D. Long, G.M. Power, and D.H. Roberts, *Geology of the Isle of Man and its offshore area*, British Geological Survey Research Report, RR/01/06 (2001), 143.

8   D.G. Quirk and D.J. Burnett (1999).

9   N.H. Woodcock and R.P. Barnes, 'An early Ordovician turbidite system on the Gondwana margin: the southeastern Manx Group, Isle of Man', in N.H. Woodcock *et al.* (1999b), 89–107.

10   N.H. Woodcock and R.P. Barnes (1999).

11   D.G. Quirk and D.J. Burnett (1999).

12   S.G. Molyneux, 'A reassessment of Manx Group acritarchs, Isle of Man', in N.H. Woodcock *et al.* (1999b), 23–32.

13   P.J. Orr and M.P.A. Howe, 'Macrofauna and ichnofauna of the Manx Group (early Ordovician), Isle of Man', in N.H. Woodcock *et al.* (1999b), 33–44.

14   A.W.A. Rushton, 'Graptolites from the Manx Group', *Proceedings of the Yorkshire Geological Society*, 49 (1993), 259–262.

15   H. Bolton, 'Observations on the Skiddaw Slates of the Isle of Man', *British Association Report*, Nottinghamshire (1893), 770–771.

16   P.J. Orr and M.P.A. Howe (1999).

17   D.G. Quirk and D.J. Burnett (1999).

18   G.W. Lamplugh (1903); A. Simpson (1963).

19 D.G. Quirk and D.J. Burnett (1999); N.H. Woodcock *et al.* (1999c).
20 R.A Chadwick *et al.* (2001).
21 S.G. Molyneux, 'New evidence for the age of the Manx Group, Isle of Man', in A.L. Harris, C.H. Holland and B.E. Leake (eds), *The Caledonides of the British Isles – Reviewed*, Geological Society of London Special Publication 8 (1979), 415–421; S.G. Molyneux (1999).
22 D.G. Quirk and D.J. Burnett (1999).
23 N.H. Woodcock *et al.* (1999).
24 R.A. Chadwick *et al.* (2001).
25 N.H. Woodcock and R.P. Barnes (1999).
26 A.W.A. Rushton (1993).
27 D.G. Quirk and D.J. Burnett (1999).
28 N.H. Woodcock *et al.* (1999a).
29 R.A. Chadwick *et al.* (2001).
30 D.G. Quirk and D.J. Burnett (1999).
31 D.J. Burnett and D.G. Quirk, 'Turbidite provenance in the Lower Palaeozoic Manx Group, Isle of Man: implications for the tectonic setting of Eastern Avalonia', *Journal of the Geological Society*, 158 (2001), 913–924.
32 D.G. Quirk and D.J. Burnett (1999).
33 *Ibid.*
34 D.J. Burnett and D.G. Quirk (2001).
35 D.G. Quirk and D.J. Burnett (1999).
36 R.A. Chadwick *et al.* (2001).
37 D.G. Quirk and D.J. Burnett (1999).
38 *Ibid.*
39 *Ibid.*
40 H. Bolton (1893).
41 A.W.A. Rushton (1993).
42 P.S. Kennan and J.H. Morris, 'Manganese ironstones in the early Ordovician Manx Group, Isle of Man: a protolith of coticule?', in N.H. Woodcock *et al.* (1999b), 109–119.
43 S.G. Molyneux (1999).
44 D.J. Burnett (1999).
45 D.J. Burnett (1999); D.J. Burnett and D.G. Quirk (2001).
46 D.J. Burnett and D.G. Quirk (2001).
47 S.G. Molyneux, personal communication.
48 D.G. Quirk, D.J. Burnett, G.S. Kimbell, C.A. Murphy and J.S. Varley, 'Shallow geophysical and geological evidence for a regional-scale fault duplex in the Lower Palaeozoic of the Isle of Man', in N.H. Woodcock *et al.* (1999b), 239–257.
49 P. Stone, A.H. Cooper and J.A. Evans, 'The Skiddaw Group (English Lake District) reviewed: early Palaeozoic sedimentation and tectonism at the northern margin of Avalonia', in N.H. Woodcock *et al.* (1999b), 325–336.
50 D.G. Quirk and D.J. Burnett (1999).
51 D.G. Quirk *et al.* (1999a).
52 D.G. Quirk and D.J. Burnett (1999).
53 D.J. Burnett (1999).
54 R.A. Chadwick *et al.* (2001).
55 D.J. Burnett and D.G. Quirk (2001).
56 D.G. Quirk and D.J. Burnett (1999).
57 *Ibid.*
58 D.G. Quirk *et al.* (1999a).

59   D.G. Quirk and D.J. Burnett (1999).
60   S.G. Molyneux (1999).
61   B.J. McConnell, J.H. Morris and P.S. Kennan, 'A comparison of the Ribband Group (southeastern Ireland) to the Manx Group (Isle of Man) and Skiddaw Group (northwestern England)', in N.H. Woodcock *et al.* (1999), 337–343.
62   A.H. Cooper, A.W.A. Rushton, S.G. Molyneux, R.A. Hughes, R.M. Moore and B.C. Webb, 'The stratigraphy, correlation, provenance and palaeogeography of Skiddaw Group (Ordovician) in the English Lake District', *Geological Magazine*, 132 (1995), 185–211; D.G. Quirk and D.J. Burnett (1999).
63   B.J. McConnell *et al.* (1999).
64   P. Kokelaar, 'Tectonic controls of Ordovician arc and marginal basin volcanism in Wales', *Journal of the Geological Society of London*, 145 (1988), 759–775.
65   D.J. Burnett (1999).
66   G.W. Lamplugh (1903); A. Simpson (1963).
67   M.P.A. Howe, 'The Silurian fauna (graptolite and nautiloid) of the Niarbyl Formation, Isle of Man', in N.H. Woodcock *et al.* (1999), 177–187.
68   J.H. Morris *et al.* (1999).
69   *Ibid.*
70   S.G. Molyneux (1999).
71   N.H. Woodcock and R.P. Barnes (1999).
72   G.S. Kimbell and D.G. Quirk, 'Crustal magnetic structure of the Irish Sea region: evidence for a major basement boundary beneath the Isle of Man', in N.H. Woodcock *et al.* (1999), 227–238.
73   N.H. Woodcock and R.P. Barnes (1999).
74   J.H. Morris *et al.* (1999).
75   *Ibid.*
76   D.J. Burnett (1999).
77   J.H. Morris *et al.* (1999).
78   M.P.A. Howe (1999).
79   J.H. Morris *et al.* (1999).

3 The Caledonian Orogeny

DAVE QUIRK and DAVE BURNETT

The Ordovician Manx Group comprises deep marine sediment, several kilometres thick, derived from the northern margin of Eastern Avalonia, between 495 and 470 Ma. At this time, in the early Ordovician, the microcontinent lay on the south side of the Iapetus Ocean, but it was slowly drifting northwards as the ocean closed. Soon after deposition of the Dalby Group at the end of the early Silurian, 423 Ma, Eastern Avalonia docked with the Laurentian continent on the northern side of the relic Iapetus Ocean heralding the onset of the Caledonian mountain-building event (the 'Caledonian Orogeny') (Figure 3.1). The Manx and the Dalby Groups were compressed and deformed in the crumple zone between the two landmasses for a period of at least 10 Ma. The location of the join between Laurentia and Avalonia, termed the Iapetus Suture, runs from southwest Ireland, northeastwards towards Dublin, then through the Solway Firth towards Northumberland[1]. Extrapolation across the Irish Sea brings the near-surface expression of the suture very close to the northwest coast of the Isle of Man. The zone of suturing between the continents is thought to dip towards the northwest at an angle of approximately 20° (Figure 3.1a).

The Caledonian Orogeny was extremely complex and consisted of a number of compressional events. This complexity is mainly due to the continents colliding obliquely, rather than head on, coupled with the fact that both continental margins were uneven. The effects of the compression are seen as folds, faults, alteration of existing rocks (metamorphism) and formation of new rocks (magma-derived igneous rocks) described in this chapter. Many of the observations are technical, but their analysis is important in understanding how the Isle of Man was transformed from seabed to mountains.

STRUCTURE OF THE MANX GROUP

Considering the significance of the Caledonian Orogeny, analogous in origin and scale to the present-day Himalayas, it is perhaps surprising that the Lower Palaeozoic rocks in the Isle of Man are not more severely deformed. The reason is probably that the Manx and Dalby Groups were squeezed out as a number of fault slivers or slices. Nonetheless, evidence

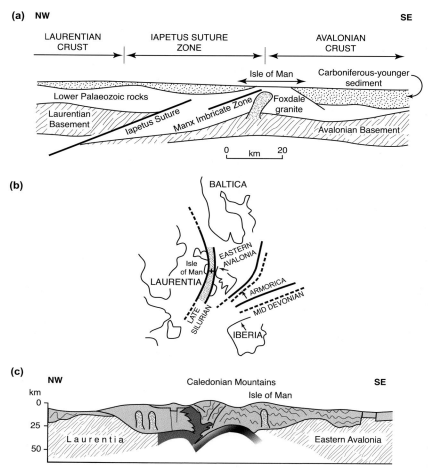

Figure 3.1 *(a) Regional cross-section through the crust of the Irish Sea area showing the probable location of the Iapetus Suture. Redrafted from Chadwick et al. (2001). (b) Schematic map illustrating the type of continental collision that led to the Caledonian Orogeny. (c) Cross-section through the Isle of Man showing major Caledonian structures.*

of the forces involved during the Caledonian Orogeny is seen in numerous folds within the slates. When layers of rock are subjected to great stresses, particularly during the collision of continents, they typically begin to bend or fold. These folds usually take the form of arch- and trough-shaped flexures, termed anticlines and synclines, respectively. If the rocks continue to be compressed, they will often break, forming a fault.

Investigation of the folds within the Manx Group rocks reveals three separate episodes of deformation, each associated with the development of folds and flat, slaty surfaces known as cleavage[2], along which the rock can be split. The earliest phase of folding (termed 'F1') formed upright folds on a wide range of scales (Figure 3.2a), with the largest up to 5 km wide. The folds are orientated northeast–southwest indicating that they were formed by northwest-southeast directed horizontal compression. F1 structures are most clearly observed on the east coast of the Isle of Man where the Douglas syncline and Dhoon anticline are well developed in the sandstone-dominated Lonan Formation and Santon Member. Such large structures also probably exist in the interior of the Isle of Man but the limited amount of rock exposure, the general lack of sandstone beds and presence of large faults mean that they are harder to discern. Smaller corrugations ('parasitic folds') have formed on the sides of the larger folds and one of the clearest examples of these is shown in Figure 3.2b, where white quartz arenite beds of the Keristal Member have been folded into a tilted S-shape on the northwest side of a large syncline known as the Douglas Syncline. The shape of this fold is thought to replicate that of a much larger anticline on the western side of the Douglas Syncline known as the Dhoon anticline. A primary cleavage (termed 'S1') is associated with these folds and is the one most strongly developed in the Manx and Dalby Groups. It commonly lies parallel to bedding showing that the beds between folds have become highly flattened, perpendicular to the direction of compression. In mudstone the cleavage is defined by aligned flakes of microscopic white mica and chlorite whereas in sandstones, which are predominantly composed of quartz, the cleavage is usually weak.

The second phase of folding ('F2') is poorly developed but does occur throughout the Manx and Dalby Groups. These folds are generally small with wavelengths rarely more than a few metres. They are best developed in mudstone-dominated units such as the Barrule Formation. Unlike F1 folds, they are flat-lying indicating that they were formed by vertical compression, probably resulting from the weight of the mountain belt as it grew in height and thickness during the late Silurian to early Devonian. The associated S2 cleavage is sub-horizontal and widely spaced. Locally it overprints the S1 cleavage in mudstone-dominated units.

A third phase of folding ('F3') is sometimes observed but is rare. These folds are upright and orientated approximately north–south, similar to the trend of folds affecting the Carboniferous limestones in the south of the island. Although most researchers believe the F3 structures are Caledonian, it is possible that they are the same age as those in the limestones, interpreted to have formed at the end of the Carboniferous (around 300 Ma)

Figure 3.2 *Folds in the Manx Group. (a) Vertical F1 fold in interbedded mudstones and fine-grained sandstones at Injebreck – the hammer is 0.4 m long. (b) S-shaped pair of F1 folds in quartz arenites at Keristal – the cliff is approximately 30 m high.*

in a later compressional event known as the Variscan Orogeny[3].

The Manx and Dalby groups are disrupted by a number of large faults (Figure 3.3). Northeast–southwest, east–west and north-northwest to south-southeast orientated faults are concentrated within a 6 km wide zone known as the Manx Imbricate Zone[4] or Barrule Thrust Zone[5] running along the central spine of the island from Niarbyl to Ramsey. This is thought to consist of a series of fault slices or segments that have been shunted together into a pile at least 1300 m thick. The faults are rarely exposed but have been identified using geophysical evidence[6]. A model for their formation suggests that the northeast–southwest faults are shallow dipping thrust faults[7], developed towards the end of the Caledonian Orogeny where rocks on the western sides of the faults were pushed up and over those on the eastern side. Sideways or 'strike-slip' movement of rocks is thought to have occurred at the same time along vertical east to west and north-northwest to south-southeast faults. One of the east–west

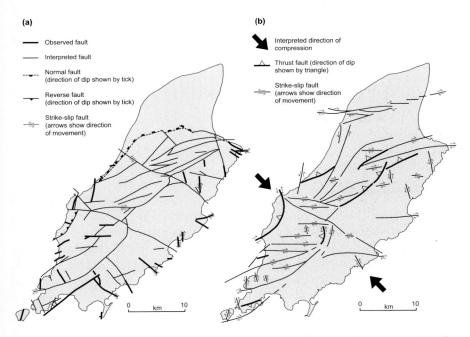

Figure 3.3 *(a) Map showing location of major faults affecting the Manx and Dalby Groups. (b) Interpretation of fault movement during the Caledonian mountain-building event, 410 Ma. Half-arrows indicate vertical fractures that have moved sideways (strike-slip faults); triangles show the direction of dip of thrust faults; large arrows indicate the direction of compression responsible for fault movement caused by continental collision between Eastern Avalonia and Laurentia.*

faults represents the fracture that was later to host the Foxdale mineral vein and similarly the Laxey vein is developed along a north-northwest to south-southeast fault. An earlier set of fault structures known as 'shear zones' are also observed at, for example, Niarbyl. Unlike the rest of the faults exposed on the island, these do not exhibit a discrete fracture surface but instead the rocks are stretched and deformed in a way that suggests that movement occurred when the rocks were relatively soft or 'ductile', probably when they were most deeply buried. Deformed igneous dykes are also found in association with these shear zones that are thought to pre-date the Caledonian Orogeny.

Quirk *et al.*[8] attempted to explain the different orientations of Lower Palaeozoic structures with a model where Eastern Avalonia was separated from Laurentia by an east-northeast to west-southwest trending plate boundary. Initially the two plates moved towards each other in an oblique direction when the shear zones were active. As contraction continued the plates locked up, causing folds, thrusts and cleavage to form parallel to the plate boundary. In the later stages of the orogeny, the direction of compression rotated anticlockwise, associated with the formation of the Manx Imbricate Zone.

STRUCTURE OF THE DALBY GROUP

F1 and F2 structures similar to those in the Manx Group are observed in the Dalby Group, proving that Caledonian deformation is younger than the early Silurian (423 Ma) when the Dalby Group was deposited. Many small faults are observed in the Dalby Group, mostly trending northeast to southwest. The most geologically interesting, however, is a major fault which separates the Dalby Group from the Manx Group. First identified by Lamplugh[9], who termed it the 'Niarbyl Shear Zone', it has been discussed by many subsequent workers[10] and its interpretation still remains a subject of discussion[11]. An intensely deformed zone of Manx Group rocks termed a shear zone is exposed at Niarbyl and is unusual in that it trends west-northwest to east-southeast, in contrast to the northeast to southwest trend of F1 structures. A shallow-dipping fault lies on top of the shear zone and marks the base of the relatively undeformed Dalby Group (Figure 3.4). In a regional sense, this fault more or less coincides with the northwest edge of the Manx Inbricate Zone. It is clear that the fault and possibly the shear zone were involved in bringing the Dalby Group (sediment derived from Laurentia) against the Manx Group (sediment derived from Eastern Avalonia) and in this respect they can be regarded as part of the Iapetus Suture, formed when the two continents collided at the end of the Silurian.

Figure 3.4 *Faulted contact between the Dalby Group (top left) and the Manx Group (bottom right) at Niarbyl. Quartz veins have developed along the plane of the fault. Photograph by Lillian Burnett.*

METAMORPHISM

Metamorphism is the process by which rocks are transformed by recrystallisation when they are subjected to high temperatures and pressures at depth within the crust. New minerals grow that not only reflect the heat and stress but also the original chemical composition of the rocks. For example, clay minerals that make up mudstone will change to chlorite and muscovite between 250 °C and 350 °C (~10 km below surface). If temperatures exceed 500 °C (~20 km depth), garnet and amphiboles become common and the rock becomes coarser grained, changing from slate to phyllite, then schist and finally gneiss in conditions where the rock may eventually begin to melt. The degree of transformation is known as metamorphic grade, slate being a low-grade metamorphic rock and gneiss being high grade.

The Isle of Man consists predominantly of low-grade metamorphic slate. The metamorphism of the Manx Group and Dalby Group is related to the Caledonian Orogeny, the minerals present in the slates recording the sorts of temperatures and pressures found at 10–15 km depth (350–400 °C)[12].

This was the depth they reached within the mountain belt as other rocks were piled on top of them, before later being removed by erosion. Chlorite and muscovite are ubiquitous, but a zone containing higher-grade metamorphic minerals (ilmenite, cordierite, chloritoid and manganese-rich garnet) runs through the centre of the island from Cronk ny Arrey Laa to North Barrule (Figure 3.5). These higher-grade minerals are confined to mudstone-dominated rocks containing relatively high amounts of iron, aluminium and manganese suggesting that the enhanced metamorphism in the central zone may reflect its chemical composition rather than deeper burial. These minerals grew in the rocks after S1 cleavage had developed but before S2.

Another metamorphic mineral, biotite, is commonly found in the Manx Group in a concentric zone or aureole, 100–200 m wide, around the Foxdale and Dhoon granites. Such metamorphic aureoles develop where recrystallisation has occurred due to heating by the magma and these are the only areas in the island where higher-grade rocks (phyllite) are known.

Thin brown sedimentary layers rich in iron and manganese occur within the Creggan Mooar Formation. Kennan and Morris[13] suggest that they may be related to unusual metamorphic rocks of similar age in the Ardennes of Belgium and in southeast Ireland where they are characterised by layers known as coticule composed of quartz and manganese-garnet. Coticule is confined to Arenig-aged rocks and may represent layers originally deposited on the seabed during periods of volcanic exhalation. Although the chemical composition of the brown bands in the Creggan Mooar Formation is similar to coticule, they do not contain garnet although this may reflect the relatively low metamorphic grade of the Manx Group.

EXTRUSIVE IGNEOUS ROCKS

Extrusive igneous rocks form at the earth's surface by the release of molten magma from vents, fissures and, more commonly, volcanoes. Many modern volcanoes lie along the margins of plates where oceanic or continental crust is being destroyed or created. Magma is often generated by the melting of ocean crust as it slides beneath lighter continental crust at what is known as a subduction zone. Thus the volcanic arcs of the Pacific 'ring of fire' are caused by subduction of Pacific and Indian Ocean crust beneath the continental plates of America and Asia.

Based on evidence of volcanic rocks of Arenig age in Wales and Ireland, until recently it had been assumed that the Manx Group had been deposited relatively close to a subduction zone. It was therefore surprising that recent chemical and microscopic analyses[14] indicate that the Manx Group sedi-

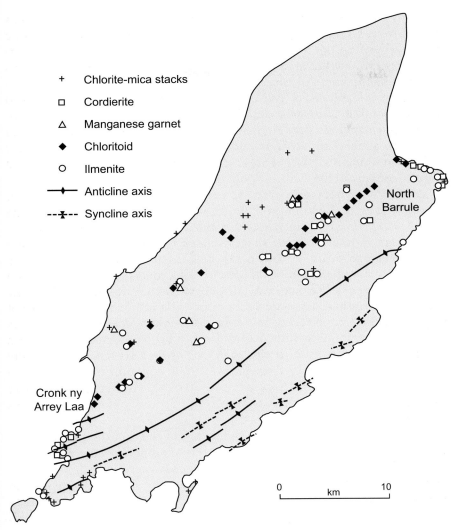

Figure 3.5 *Map showing the distribution of metamorphic minerals in the Manx Group, after G.M. Power and R.P Barnes (1999).*

ments contain little volcanic material and are instead dominated by grains derived from an old continent. Moreover, if volcanoes had been present during deposition one would expect to find thick successions of ash and lava interbedded with the sediments. In actual fact, within the several thousand metres thickness of rock that make up the Manx Group, only two intervals of volcanic rocks have been identified, consisting of highly altered ash no more than a few tens of metres thick.

Volcanic rocks assigned to the Glen Dhoo Formation[15], but previously referred to as the Peel Volcanic Formation, are exposed at two locations. Both occur along the Niarbyl Shear Zone, a major fault that separates the Manx Group from the Dalby Group. In a disused quarry southwest of Peel (SC238833) are poor exposures of volcanic material (andesitic breccia) interlayered with siltstone and mudstone. Acritarch fossils within the sequence were originally interpreted as late Arenig to early Llanvirn in age[16] but a recent re-interpretation suggests an early Ordovician, Tremadoc to early Arenig age[17]. Similar rock is exposed at Ballaquane, 2 km northeast of Dalby[18]. Samples exhibit 'trachytic' and 'autobrecciation' textures produced by freely flowing lava. A trachytic texture forms when magma begins to cool and plagioclase feldspar crystals become aligned within a matrix of finer-grained crystals and still-molten rock. If the matrix continues to flow the crystals may be broken up, producing an autobrecciation texture consisting of aggregates of broken crystals. These rocks apparently solidified at low pressures as they contain bubbles (vesicles) now filled with minerals. However, it is not clear whether the rocks were really extruded as volcanic lavas or intruded as horizontal igneous sheets or sills, close to the surface.

Chemical analysis provides an indication of the nature of the original magma that formed these volcanic rocks, even though they are altered and enriched by sodium (Figure 3.6a). They are characterised by low to intermediate amounts of silica and have chemical compositions consistent with modern-day basalts and andesites (Figure 3.6b). Relatively low ratios of the elements niobium/yttrium (<1), high zirconium/yttrium ratios (>3) and other geochemical signatures (Figure 3.7a) suggest that the rocks are similar to calcium-rich lavas produced at continental volcanic arcs such as those at the western margin of present-day South America. These sorts of volcanic rocks result from melting of oceanic crust that has been subducted beneath continental crust; in the case of the Isle of Man, where the floor of Iapetus slid beneath Eastern Avalonia. However, the altered nature of the rocks, the lack of any other evidence of volcanic activity and the proximity of the Niarbyl Shear Zone mean that their significance is highly questionable. Nonetheless, McConnell *et all*[19] tentatively correlate them with basalts and andesites of probable early Ordovician age in southeast Ireland, and together they may provide the earliest indication of subduction along this part of the northern margin of Eastern Avalonia.

It was not until the late Ordovician that a volcanic island arc became fully established, stretching across what is now the Irish Sea from southeast Ireland to northwest England[20] associated with the eruption of thick piles of ash and lava[21]. Instead, it is much more likely that during the Arenig, the Manx Group was deposited on a passive margin[22] with the continental crust of Avalonia joined directly to the oceanic crust of Iapetus with no intervening subduction zone. Such is the case around the present-day Atlantic Ocean and an analogy can therefore be made between the deposition of the Manx Group off Eastern Avalonia and the thick layers of sediment accumulating in deep water off present-day West Africa such as Nigeria. Although it is possible that the margin was in transition from passive to active, there is enough uncertainty in the age of the volcanic rocks in Ireland and the original geographic location of Wales relative to Eastern Avalonia[23] not to have to complicate the model – that of a simple passive margin. In this respect, recent research into the rocks of the Isle of Man has changed views on the nature of the earth's continental plates some 495–470 Ma.

INTRUSIVE IGNEOUS ROCKS

A number of igneous intrusions of Lower Palaeozoic age are found on the island. Intrusions form where magma originating from the mantle or lower crust cools and solidifies in the upper part of the crust. Volcanoes are formed where magma reaches the surface, but igneous intrusions are also common in the rocks deep beneath them, often acting as a reservoir for eruptions of lava and ash. Therefore, in association with volcanoes, igneous intrusions are concentrated at the margins of present-day and ancient plate margins where crust is being destroyed or created.

Poortown Basic Igneous Complex

The igneous rocks exposed at Poortown, three kilometres east of Peel, are the largest and best studied of a group of basic (silica-poor) intrusions originally identified by Lamplugh. These rocks are particularly common in the Manx Group in the northwest part of the island[24]. Although the term 'gabbro' has been used to describe the rocks[25], they are more appropriately classified as dolerite on the basis of their shape, mineral content and chemical composition. Recent investigation of the Poortown intrusion[26] shows that it consists of a number of inclined sheets separated by slabs of the Creggan Mooar Formation rather than the single, lens-like body of rock envisaged by Lamplugh. The sheets are cut by two different trends of near-vertical faults, further complicating what is now termed the Poortown Basic Igneous Complex[27]. Modelling of geophysical data indicates that the sheets occupy a limited area (0.5 km²) and extend to a depth of approximately 100 m below the present land surface[28].

Within the quarry, contacts between igneous sheets are generally parallel to the steeply dipping sedimentary beds of the Manx Group, rather than cutting across them. This type of igneous sheet, which was intruded along bedding planes, is known as a sill. The margins of the sills are characterised by zones, less than 30 mm wide, that are finer-grained than the rest of the intrusion showing that the magma cooled rapidly on contact with the sediments. The majority of the sills are coarse-grained and are zoned parallel to the margins with an outer zone of plagioclase feldspar-rich dolerite and a central zone that is more pyroxene-rich. This zonation reflects variations in composition that developed during cooling and crystallisation of the magma. Like the sediments, the dolerite is metamorphosed with chlorite defining a weak cleavage[29]. The sediments themselves are frequently silicified (enriched with silica) at the contact with the sills but other types of alteration are not observed.

Two main fault trends exist: north–south and east–west. Fault surfaces display aligned crystal fibres (slickensides) associated with deformed, elongate crystals of pyroxene in the dolerite. The faults are also mineralised with quartz, chlorite and hematite.

Rock cores from boreholes drilled to the north and east of Poortown quarry[30] support geophysical models indicating the occurrence of additional sill-like bodies. Examination of cores shows that the mineralogy of the intrusive rocks is highly variable and indicates that there were significant differences in the crystallisation history of individual sills.

Observations under the microscope reveal a range of igneous rock

Figure 3.6 *(a) Diagram showing the composition of Manx Caledonian igneous rocks as a function of their alkali metal (potassium and sodium) content. The shaded area represents compositions expected for unaltered igneous rocks. Note that many samples from the Peel Volcanic Formation and Poortown Basic Igneous Complex exhibit evidence of extensive alteration. (b) Classification scheme for volcanic and intrusive igneous rocks. The scheme uses ratios of chemical elements which are relatively unaffected by alteration processes. Virtually all samples from the Peel Volcanic Formation and Poortown Basic Igneous Complex are classified as sub-alkaline basalts and andesites. The shaded area is the transitional field between sub-alkaline and alkaline igneous rocks.*

(a)

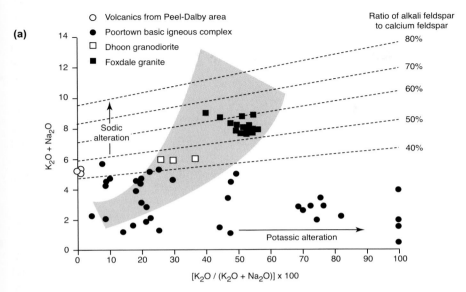

(b)

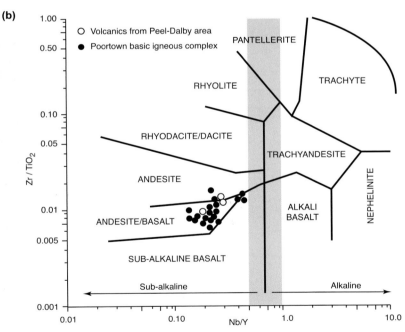

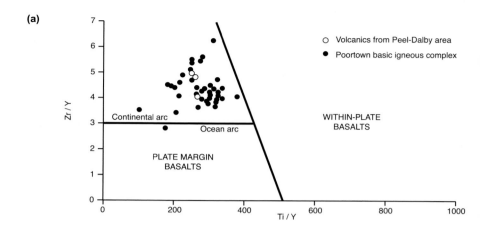

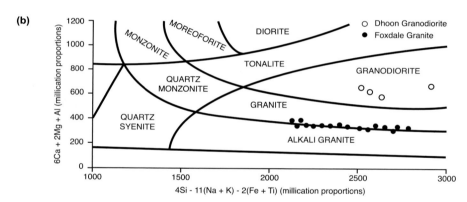

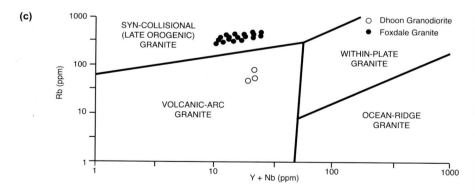

types[31]. Alteration, probably associated with regional, low-grade meta-morphism, has resulted in the extensive replacement of primary magmatic minerals by secondary minerals. Of the original minerals, only clinopy-roxenes are still common. Original calcium-rich plagioclase feldspars have now altered to sodium-rich plagioclase feldspar, while iron-magnesium rich minerals (particularly olivine) are partially to completely changed to chlorite and calcite. Secondary epidote, hornblende (actinolite), pumpel-lyite and potassium feldspar also occur in places.

Although the growth of secondary minerals has resulted in changes to their primary composition (Figure 3.6a), the chemistry of the rocks is still indicative of their origin, which was essentially basaltic or basaltic-andesitic magma (Figure 3.6b). The Poortown rocks are pyroxene-rich dolerites rather than plagioclase feldspar-rich dolerites in that they contain relatively high proportions of magnesium. This composition is often typical of magmas generated at mid-oceanic ridges (magnesium-rich tholeiitic basalts) where oceanic plates rift apart from each other. However, on most other counts, the chemistry of the Poortown dolerite bears a closer simi-larity to calcium-rich basic magmas generated in a continental volcanic arc environment (Figure 3.7a) as exists nowadays in the Andes.

Extensive alteration means that radioactive isotopes cannot be used to give a reliable age for the Poortown Basic Igneous Complex as the original concentrations of elements are not known. However, the late Arenig age of the Creggan Mooar Formation provides a limit to the maximum age of the intrusion, whilst the weak cleavage imparted by chlorite is interpreted to be related to the Caledonian Orogeny hence no younger than early Devonian[32]. The chemistry of the Poortown dolerite is fairly similar to igneous rocks in southeast Ireland[33] and northwest England[34], for example the Borrowdale volcanics which are late Ordovician in age[35]. By analogy,

Figure 3.7 *(a) Chemical diagram used to discriminate basic igneous rocks derived from different tectonic regimes. Note that all samples from the Peel Volcanic Formation and the Poortown Basic Igneous Complex appear to be associated with subduction as they plot within the destructive plate margin field, and all but one of these samples have compositions consistent with continental arc magmatism. (b) Chemical classification scheme for deep intrusive igneous rocks showing the fields for intrusions with acidic (silica-rich) to intermediate compositions. Note the distinct compositional differences between the Dhoon Granodiorite and the Foxdale Granite. (c) Chemical diagram used to discriminate granitic igneous rocks derived from different tectonic regimes. Note that samples from the Dhoon Granodiorite plot within the volcanic arc field, while all samples from the Foxdale Granite have compositions consistent with magmas produced within mountain belts.*

the Poortown Basic Igneous Complex is assumed to be the same age, approximately 450 Ma. These igneous rocks are typical of those found within volcanic arcs, indicating that by the late Ordovician the oceanic crust of Iapetus had started to subduct beneath the continental crust of Eastern Avalonia. Over the next 25 million years, the Iapetus Ocean shrank to nothing as subduction at both its southern and northern margins brought Eastern Avalonia against Laurentia, the resulting impact forming the Caledonian mountains.

The Dhoon Granodiorite

The Dhoon Granodiorite forms the high ground of Slieau Ouyr and Slieau Lhean, north of Laxey, and is well exposed in the disused quarry at Dhoon (SC459872). Geophysical modelling of the gravity response of the intrusion[36] shows that the granodiorite is a relatively small intrusive body that extends to a depth of approximately 3.5 km. It is associated with steep-dipping igneous sheets or dykes of similar composition that cut through the Manx Group outside the main intrusion.

The granodiorite is fine- to medium-grained and composed of quartz, plagioclase feldspar and biotite with only small amounts of potassium feldspar. The greater abundance of plagioclase feldspar relative to potassium feldspar and its chemical composition (Figure 3.7b) shows that the Dhoon intrusion is actually a granodiorite rather than the granite that was originally suggested by Lamplugh[37]. Xenoliths (recrystallised remnants of other rocks) are common and Nockolds[38] concluded that this was evidence that the original magma was contaminated by partial melting of surrounding rocks. Plagioclase feldspars have been extensively altered to zoisite and muscovite, and some of the quartz has undergone recrystallisation forming aggregates of polygonal-shaped crystals. These textures are consistent with the intrusion having undergone metamorphic alteration. Although contamination by xenoliths and metamorphic alteration have affected the chemical composition, analysis suggests that it was originally a calcium-enriched andesite typical of magmas generated beneath a volcanic arc (Figure 3.7c)[39].

The granodiorite is intruded into rocks of the Lonan Formation and adjacent to the igneous contact they have a spotted appearance caused by the growth of metamorphic minerals when the magma was first intruded. Power and Barnes[40] have shown that this contact metamorphism occurred prior to deformation at temperatures of around 800 °C[41]. Contamination and alteration mean that the Dhoon Granodiorite is not suitable for dating using radioactive isotopes, but the age of a biotite crystal using potassium-argon dating was determined as 377 Ma (late Devonian)[42]. However, this probably indicates the time when metamorphism ceased due to uplift and cooling rather than representing the age of intrusion. It is obviously younger than the early Arenig sediments into which it is intruded and it is at least as old as the end Silurian when Caledonian metamorphism started[43]. The Dhoon Granodiorite is similar to granitic intrusions of late Ordovician age[44] (*circa* 450 Ma) exposed in the Lake District, interpreted to have formed beneath a volcanic arc bordering the northern edge of Eastern Avalonia of similar origin but different chemical composition to the Poortown Basic Igneous Complex.

The Foxdale Granite

The Foxdale Granite crops out across Stoney Mountain, but geophysical evidence suggests that it may form part of a much larger intrusive body at depth. An area of anomalously low gravity occupies an area of approximately 50 km^2 in the south central part of the island which may correspond to the true extent of the granite in the sub-surface, and density modelling has been used to show that the granite may be as much as 10 km thick[45]. Even larger granitic bodies occur in northern England and southeast Ireland, for example the Leinster Granite[46] which is 110 km long and between 10 and 30 km wide. The contact between the Foxdale Granite and the Manx Group is currently not visible but exposures of Manx Group close to the contact contain minerals such as biotite and garnet formed as a result of the effects of heat when the magma was intruded[47]. The original top of the Foxdale Granite probably lay close to the present-day land surface at Stoney Mountain.

There is a complete absence of Manx Group xenoliths in the Foxdale Granite and little obvious deformation. At outcrop, two compositionally similar but texturally distinct granite types can be recognised. The most common is a uniformly medium-grained muscovite- and garnet-bearing granite. The second type is largely identical in mineralogy, but consists of fine-grained granite dispersed with larger crystals of quartz, feldspar and muscovite, in places containing spodumene and tourmaline. Associated with the granite are veins of very coarse-grained crystals known as 'pegmatite' that occur in three differently orientated sets. One set comprises sub-horizontal veins of quartz and microcline feldspar grown as elongate crystals perpendicular to the walls of the veins (Figure 3.8). The other two sets are near vertical veins orientated approximately north–south and east–west containing quartz, feldspar, muscovite, beryl, tourmaline and apatite[48] that were formed in the final stages when the granite began to solidify. A suite of north–south trending microgranite dykes (termed 'Foxdale elvans' by Lamplugh[49]), with a mineralogy identical to the granite, also occurs at a number of locations in the southern part of the island and these are probably related to the Foxdale Granite.

Chemical analysis shows that the granite (and associated dykes), as expected, is relatively rich in silicon, aluminium and sodium and contains very low concentrations of titanium, iron, magnesium and calcium (Figure 3.8). The mineralogy, chemistry and crystal texture suggest that it solidified from near vapour-saturated magma at temperatures of approximately 700 °C and pressures in the region of 2,000–3,000 times greater than atmospheric, typical of depths of around 20 km below surface. As it crystallised, hot fluids containing high concentrations of elements not easily incorporated into quartz, feldspar and muscovite were left circulating near the top of the granite and eventually crystallised as pegmatite.

Figure 3.8 *Pegmatite veins of quartz and potassium (microcline) feldspar within Foxdale Granite (speckled grey). The crystals have grown in an elongate fashion perpendicular to the walls of the veins. Photograph by Dave Burnett.*

Despite evidence that the granite is altered, rubidium-strontium isotopic dating of the whole rock gives a coherent and statistically significant age of 383±11 Ma[50] (Upper Devonian). This compares closely with a published potassium-argon date of 381±7 Ma[51]. Although the similarity between dates appears to provide a satisfactory estimate of intrusion age, other geological considerations suggest that the date may in fact relate to the final cooling of the intrusion and cessation of the flow of hot fluids. A more reliable age is provided by rubidium-strontium analysis of muscovite crystals in the pegmatite veins which indicates a date of intrusion of *circa* 400 Ma[52]. This age compares favourably with similar but better studied granites from southeast Ireland and northwest England which are dated as 405–390 Ma (early Devonian), intruded at the end of the Caledonian Orogeny in a very different environment to that of the older Dhoon Granodiorite (Figure 3.7c). This probably explains why F1 deformation seems to be absent.

The Oatlands Complex

Lamplugh[53] initially described a small intrusive body in a quarry at Oatlands, approximately 1 km west of Port Soderick, but it was more fully described some 30 years later by Taylor and Gamba[54]. The quarry is now filled in, and the only evidence for the presence of igneous rocks is to be found in loose quarried blocks and in drystone walls. The igneous intrusion, known as the Oatlands Complex, covers an area approximately 0.1 km² and its small size explains the absence of any obvious geophysical expression[55]. It appears to be elliptical, orientated northeast–southwest sub-parallel to the beds of the Lonan Formation into which it was intruded. These sediments have been baked close to the contact to produce a spotted, garnet-bearing metamorphic rock known as hornfels. The outer part of the intrusion is composed of gabbro and contains pyroxene, hornblende and calcium-rich plagioclase feldspar. Towards the southwest, the gabbro grades into an even more basic (silica-poor) iron-magnesium rich rock composed mostly of pyroxene and hornblende. The central part of the complex consists of granodiorite comprising quartz and plagioclase feldspar with minor potassium feldspar and biotite. The contact between the granodiorite and the gabbro is probably gradational and many xenoliths of gabbro have been found within the granodiorite, suggesting that the gabbro is older; i.e., the granodiorite was intruded up the centre of the igneous body formed by the gabbro, probably before it had completely solidified. Taylor and Gamba[56] describe the occurrence of a rock intermediate in character between the granodiorite and the gabbro, possibly indicating that the granitic magma mixed or reacted with the gabbro.

The age of intrusion of the Oatlands Complex is difficult to constrain. Taylor and Gamba[57] suggested that it has more in common with the Dhoon Granodiorite than the younger Foxdale Granite. The gabbro-granodiorite association of the Oatlands Complex is certainly to be expected in volcanic arc-related settings already interpreted for the Dhoon Granodiorite. However, unlike Dhoon and Poortown, the Oatland intrusion appears relatively undeformed and in this respect bears similarities to the Foxdale Granite which is of probable early Devonian age.

Minor igneous intrusions

Various small intrusions in the form of dykes (and occasional sills) occur throughout the Lower Palaeozoic rocks of the Isle of Man. The dykes are quite varied in composition, but it is often difficult to determine their original nature because of the effects of deformation, metamorphism and alteration by hot fluids. No absolute age determinations have been made on the dykes, but they are obviously younger than the Lower Ordovician sediments that they have been intruded into (Figure 3.9). Dykes that were formed before or during the Caledonian Orogeny have been deformed and exhibit a cleavage. They have been divided into three types. Other undeformed dykes are younger than the Caledonian Orogeny and are mostly Tertiary in age (*circa* 65 Ma); consisting of vertical, west-northwest to east-southeast trending sheets of olivine basalt.

Basic (silica-poor) dykes. Basic dykes (the 'greenstones' of Lamplugh) are common throughout the Manx Group. They are significantly altered from their original composition with chlorite forming the main alteration mineral and imparting a pale green colour to the rock. Some basic dykes show complex interfingering contacts with the local Manx Group sediments suggesting that they were intruded into the surrounding sediment while it was still soft, i.e., before it became deeply buried. Examples of these can be seen at Ladyport (SC288878) and Cass-ny-Hawin (Figure 3.9). These dykes probably represent the oldest intrusions on the island and are of probable early Ordovician age (*circa* 495–470 Ma). Those with straight contacts are interpreted to be younger, but they still pre-date metamorphism and are thought to be of late Ordovician age (*circa* 450 Ma).

Acid (silica-rich) dykes. Strongly foliated, fine-grained granite and granodiorite dykes are common in central areas of the island. They often appear to have a lenticular shape suggesting that they were intruded as a fairly viscous magma typical of granite but unlike dolerite which can flow for

Figure 3.9 *Igneous dyke in Manx Group rocks at Cass-ny-Hawin (SC298692). Note the irregular shape of the intrusion which suggests the sediment was still soft when the magma was intruded.*

tens of kilometres along narrow fissures before solidifying. The acid dykes have been deformed during the Caledonian mountain-building event and are therefore older than late Silurian, but post-date the early Ordovician Manx Group into which they are intruded.

Syn-tectonic dykes. A number of dykes in the Manx Group with dioritic to granitic compositions appear to have been only partly deformed during the Caledonian Orogeny with no evidence of F1 deformation. This suggests that they were intruded after tectonism began (late Silurian) but before the end of mountain building (early Devonian). A 15 m wide, east–west trending, dioritic dyke of this type may be seen in the old quarry above Black Hut (SC402885).

SUMMARY

The Lower Palaeozoic rocks of the Isle of Man record evidence for the destruction of the Iapetus Ocean after deposition of the Manx Group. Igneous activity typical of a volcanic arc (e.g., Poortown and Dhoon intrusions) started in the late Ordovician as oceanic crust began to subduct and melt beneath the northern margin of Eastern Avalonia. Through the late Ordovician and early Silurian, when the Dalby Group was deposited, the ocean decreased in size until Eastern Avalonia collided with the northern continent of Laurentia. The collision led to the formation of the Caledonian mountain belt, the geological effects of which are seen in the rocks as cleavage, metamorphism, folds, faults and granitic intrusions (e.g., the Foxdale Granite).

Notes

1   N.H. Woodcock, D.G. Quirk, W.F. Fitches and R.P. Barnes, 'In sight of the suture: the early Palaeozoic geological history of the Isle of Man', in N.H. Woodcock, D.G. Quirk, W.F. Fitches and R.P. Barnes (eds), *In sight of the suture: the Palaeozoic geology of the Isle of Man in its Iapetus Ocean context*, Geological Society of London Special Publication, 160 (1999), 1–10.

2   A. Simpson, 'The stratigraphy and tectonics of the Manx Slate Series', *Quarterly Journal of the Geological Society of London*, 119 (1963), 367–400.

3   W.F. Fitches, R.P. Barnes and J.H. Morris, 'Geological structure and tectonic evolution of the Lower Palaeozoic rocks of the Isle of Man', in N.H. Woodcock *et al.* (1999), 259–287.

4   D.G. Quirk, D.J. Burnett, G.S. Kimbell, C.A. Murphy and J.S. Varley, 'Shallow geophysical and geological evidence for a regional-scale fault duplex in the Lower Palaeozoic of the Isle of Man', in N.H. Woodcock *et al.* (1999a), 239–257.

5   R.A. Chadwick, D.I. Jackson, R.P. Barnes, G.S. Kimbell, H. Johnson, R.C. Chiverrell, G.S.P.Thomas, N.S. Jones, N.J. Riley, E.A. Pickett, B. Young, D.W. Holliday, D.F. Ball, S.G. Molyneux, D. Long, G.M. Power and D.H. Roberts, *Geology of the Isle of Man and its offshore area*. British Geological Survey Research Report, RR/01/06, (2001) 143.

6   D.G. Quirk *et al.* (1999).

7   D.G. Quirk and G.S. Kimbell, 'Structural evolution of the Isle of Man and central part of the Irish Sea', in N.S. Meadows, S.P. Trueblood, N. Hardman and G. Cowan (eds), *Petroleum geology of the Irish Sea and adjacent areas*, Geological Society of London Special Publication, 124 (1997), 135–159.

8   D.G. Quirk *et al.* (1999).

9   G.W. Lamplugh, *The geology of the Isle of Man*, Memoir of the Geological Survey of England and Wales (1903), 620.

10   A. Simpson (1963); C.W.K Morrison, *A study of the Anchizone-epizone metamorphic transition*, unpublished PhD thesis, St Andrew's University (1989); B. Roberts, C.W.K. Morrison and S. Hirons, 'Low grade metamorphism of the Manx Group, Isle of Man: a comparative study of white mica "crystallinity" techniques', *Journal of the Geological Society*, 147 (1990), 271–277; D.G. Quirk and G.S. Kimbell (1997).

11   D.G. Quirk *et al.* (1999a); W.F. Fitches *et al.* (1999).

12   G.M. Power and R.P. Barnes, 'Relationship between metamorphism and structure on the northern edge of eastern Avalonia in the Manx Group, Isle of Man', in N.H. Woodcock *et al.* (1999), 289–305.

13   P.S. Kennan and J.H. Morris, 'Manganese ironstones in the early Ordovician Manx Group, Isle of Man: a protolith of coticule?', in N.H. Woodcock *et al.* (1999), 109–119.

14   D.J. Burnett and D.G. Quirk, 'Turbidite provenance in the Lower Palaeozoic

Manx Group, Isle of Man: implications for the tectonic setting of Eastern Avalonia', *Journal of the Geological Society*, 158 (2001), 919–924.

15 R.A. Chadwick *et al.* (2001).

16 S.G. Molyneux, 'New evidence for the age of the Manx Group, Isle of Man', in A.L. Harris, C.H. Holland and B.E. Leake (eds), *The Caledonides of the British Isles – Reviewed*, Geological Society of London Special Publication, 8 (1979), 415–421.

17 S.G. Molyneux, 'A reassessment of Manx Group acritarchs, Isle of Man', in N.H. Woodcock *et al.* (1999), 232–254.

18 G.W. Lamplugh (1903).

19 B.J. McConnell, J.H. Morris and P.S. Kennan, 'A comparison of the Ribband Group (southeastern Ireland) to the Manx Group (Isle of Man) and Skiddaw Group (northwestern England)', in N.H. Woodcock *et al.* (1999), 337–343.

20 C.J. Stillman, 'Ordovician to Silurian volcanism in the Appalachian-Caledonian orogeny', in A.L. Harris, C.H. Holland and B.E. Leake (eds), *The Caledonides of the British Isles – Reviewed*, Geological Society of London Special Publication, 8 (1979), 275–290.

21 M.D. Max, A.J. Barber and J. Martinez, 'Terrane assemblage of the Leinster Massif, SE Ireland, during the Lower Palaeozoic', *Journal of the Geological Society*, 147 (1990), 1035–1050; A.H. Cooper, D. Millward, E.W. Johnson and N.J. Soper, 'The early Palaeozoic evolution of northwest England', *Geological Magazine*, 130 (1993), 711–724.

22 D.G. Quirk and D.J. Burnett, 'Lithofacies of Lower Palaeozoic deep marine sediments in the Isle of Man: a new map and stratigraphic model of the Manx Group', in N.H. Woodcock *et al.* (1999), 69–88.

23 *Ibid.*

24 G.M. Power and S.F. Crowley, 'Petrological and geochemical evidence for the tectonic affinity of the (?)Ordovician Poortown Basic Intrusive Complex, Isle of Man', in N.H. Woodcock *et al.* (1999), 165–175; J.D.A. Piper, A.J. Biggin and S.F. Crowley, 'Magnetic survey of the Poortown Dolerite, Isle of Man', in N.H. Woodcock *et al.* (1999), 155–163.

25 T.D. Ford, D.J. Burnett and D.G. Quirk, *The Geology of the Isle of Man*, Geologists' Association Guide, 46 (2001), 92.

26 J.D.A. Piper, A.J. Biggin and S.F. Crowley (1999); Holmes Grace Consulting Engineers Ltd, *A geological investigation of the Poortown Quarry*, unpublished report for the Department of Highways, Ports and Properties, Isle of Man (1992); M. Davies, J. Guard and A. Wright, *Poortown Quarry, Isle of Man: geological interpretive report*, unpublished report by CSA-RDL (1995).

27 G.M. Power and S.F. Crowley (1999).

28 J.D.A. Piper *et al.* (1999).

29 G.M. Power and S.F. Crowley (1999).

30 M. Davies *et al.* (1995).

31 G.W. Lamplugh (1903).

32 W.F. Fitches *et al.* (1999).

33 M.D. Max *et al.* (1990).

34 A.H. Cooper *et al.* (1993).

35 C.J. Stillman (1979).

36 J.D. Cornwell, 'A gravity survey of the Isle of Man', *Proceedings of the Yorkshire Geological Society*, 39 (1972), 93–106.

37 G.W. Lamplugh (1903).

38 S.R. Nockolds, 'The Dhoon (Isle of Man) granite', *Mineralogical Magazine*, 22

(1931), 494–509.

39   R.A Chadwick *et al.* (2001).

40   G.M. Power and R.P. Barnes (1999).

41   W.F. Fitches *et al.* (1999).

42   C.T. Harper, 'Potassium-argon ages of slates from the southern Caledonides of the British Isles', *Nature*, 212 (1966), 1339–1341.

43   W.F. Fitches *et al.* (1999); G.M. Power and R.P. Barnes (1999).

44   R.A. Hughes, J.A. Evans, S.R. Noble and C.C. Rundle, 'U-Pb chronology of the Ennerdale and Eskdale intrusions supports sub-volcanic relationships with the Borrowdale Volcanic Group (Ordovician, English Lake District)', *Journal of the Geological Society*, 153 (1996), 338–345.

45   J.D. Cornwell (1972).

46   M.A. Cooper and P.M. Brück, 'Tectonic relationships of the Leinster Granite, Ireland', *Geological Journal*, 18 (1983), 351–360.

47   G.W. Lamplugh (1903); G.M. Power and R.P. Barnes (1999); A. Simpson (1963).

48   J. Dawson, 'Beryllium in the Foxdale Granite, Isle of Man', *Bulletin of the Geological Survey of Great Britain*, 25 (1966), 55–58.

49   G.W. Lamplugh (1903).

50   S. Crowley, *personal communication* (2003).

51   P.E. Brown, J.A. Miller and R.L. Grasty, 'Isotopic ages of late Caledonian granitic intrusions in the British Isles', *Proceedings of the Yorkshire Geological Society*, 36 (1968), 251–276.

52   S. Crowley, *personal communication* (2003).

53   G.W. Lamplugh (1903).

54   J.H. Taylor and E.A. Gamba, 'The Oatland (Isle of Man) Igneous Complex', *Proceedings of the Geologists' Association*, 44 (1933), 355–377.

55   J.D. Cornwell (1972).

56   J.H. Taylor and E.A. Gamba (1933).

57   *Ibid.*

4   The Peel Sandstone

DAVE QUIRK and GEOFF THOMAS

A distinctive succession of red-coloured sediments known as the Peel Sandstone Group is exposed between the northern end of Peel Promenade and Will's Strand (Figure 4.1). They are younger than the Dalby Group (early Silurian) and are probably older than the Castletown Limestones (early Carboniferous), and are most likely Devonian in age. They comprise a succession of siltstones, sandstones and conglomerates (gravels) with calcrete[1]. Inland, thick Quaternary deposits obscure them, but two small occurrences have been recorded at Glenfaba Bridge, south of Peel[2]. The sediments are typical of those deposited in a semi-arid continental environment, such as exists nowadays over much of Arizona in the USA. These conditions are not conducive to the preservation of fossils as oxygen, high temperatures and scavenging organisms rapidly destroy organic material. As a consequence, the Peel sandstones do not contain fossils with which the rocks can be dated, so the presumed

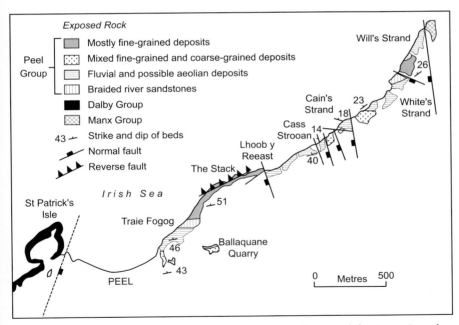

Figure 4.1 *Geological map of the Peel Sandstone based on work by Steve Crowley.*

Devonian age is based largely on comparison with similar rocks elsewhere in the British Isles.

The first subdivision of the Peel Sandstone Group was by Boyd Dawkins[3] but more recent work by Crowley[4] and the British Geological Survey[5] forms the basis of the classification used here.

TECTONIC SETTING

During late Silurian times the Iapetus Ocean closed and the collision of Eastern Avalonia and Laurentia led to the Caledonian Orogeny. The principal effect of this collision was the creation of a chain of deformed Ordovician and Silurian rocks in a wide belt running northeast to southwest across what is now most of northern and western Britain. A modern analogue is the Himalayan mountain belt, which has been created by the collision of India and Asia. When the Caledonian mountains had reached their culmination, 400 Ma before present, most of Britain lay approximately 20°S of the equator and the climate was semi-arid with sea level relatively low. Erosion of these mountains in early Devonian times shed vast quantities of sediment into basins within and around the periphery of the mountains. Uplift and erosion in mid Devonian times, associated with the final phases of the Caledonian Orogeny, removed much of the sediment, particularly south of Scotland, but remnants are preserved in the Lake District and Anglesey and probably also around Peel.

The Peel Sandstone Group dips between 15 and 50° (Figure 4.2) to the north and northwest but is otherwise fairly undeformed with an absence of cleavage or metamorphic alteration. One large-scale fold is exposed at Cain's Strand (SC263853) but otherwise the rocks show little evidence of the sort of Caledonian deformation present in the Manx and Dalby Groups.

The rocks occupy a north–south fault-bounded trough that extends offshore[6]. At the northeastern limit of exposure, the Will's Strand Fault can be observed on the foreshore and Peel sandstones are faulted against the Manx Group (SC269859). The Peel Harbour Fault, on the western margin, is not exposed but has been inferred by Boyd Dawkins[7] and Quirk *et al.*[8], following the line of the Neb River, marking the boundary between the Peel Sandstone Group and the Dalby Group (which forms Peel Hill). Vertical displacements along these boundary faults are on the scale of hundreds of metres. Whether the Peel sandstones lie directly on top of the Manx Group or Dalby Group beneath the trough is unknown. However, the absence of pebbles of either type within the Peel sandstones suggests that they were not exposed at the time of deposition. It is possible that the

Figure 4.2 *North-dipping sandstone beds between Traie Fogog and The Stack. Note lens-shaped beds typical of channels within a braided river.*

entire body of rock was emplaced by fault movement associated with plate tectonics. The folds and faults within the Peel Sandstone Group suggest that, if tectonic emplacement did occur, it was from the northwest towards the southeast. This may be related to late-stage movement on the Iapetus Suture, the join between the continental plates of Eastern Avalonia and Laurentia inferred to lie close to the west coast of the Isle of Man[9].

Neither the top nor bottom of the succession is seen at surface, but estimates of the thickness range from 520 m[10] to possibly as much as 2,000 m offshore[11]. Steeply dipping normal faults orientated north–south, offset the beds within the Peel sandstones by amounts ranging from a few centimetres to tens of metres. Most deformation is restricted to fold structures adjacent to steep-dipping normal faults or shallow-dipping thrust faults[12]. Some of the smaller-scale folds and thrusts, particularly around Will's Strand (Figure 4.3), appear to have developed when the sediment was still soft probably due to landslip caused perhaps by earthquakes or tilting of the land surface[13].

The present northwesterly dip is due to tilting after deposition, probably in association with movement on the boundary fault exposed at White Strand[14].

Figure 4.3 (above and opposite) *Anticline (a), syncline (b) and minor thrust (c) in Peel Sandstone Group at Will's Strand. These structures are thought to have developed when the sediment was relatively soft.*

DEPOSITIONAL SETTING

In a very general sense, large parts of the Peel Sandstone Group consist of beds arranged in a pattern that shows an upwards transition from coarse-grained sediments (such as sandstone) to fine-grained sediments (such as mudstone) at the top. This phenomenon, which is repetitive, is known as upwards-fining cyclicity and is typical of sediments deposited in and around rivers. The coarse-grained sediments represent river channel or flood deposits; the fine-grained sediments represent times when the river channel migrated to another part of the drainage basin or had become inactive so that only silts, muds and soils accumulate, possibly also with wind-blown sand. The exact nature of the cyclicity depends on factors such as climate, subsidence, and the type and amount of sediment available in the hinterland where the river was sourced.

The coarse-grained sediments have features that suggest they were deposited by a braided river, i.e., one with multiple channels. Braided rivers develop where rainfall and sediment supply is highly variable, reflecting seasonal changes in climate and often proximity to an upland area. The channels within this particular braided river may have been several metres deep and tens to hundreds of metres wide with ephemeral islands and sediment bars composed of gravel and sand within the channel. Evidence of flash floods and meandering channels also exist.

Some of the pebbles within the Peel sandstones were derived from the floodplain where the channels cut into earlier river sediment. The rest were derived from erosion of an upland area which, at least in part, was composed of Silurian rocks with fossil-bearing limestones. The direction of flow of the rivers appears to have been southwards based on the orientation of bed forms preserved within the sandstones. However, things are probably not this simple because palaeomagnetic data suggest that the body of rock comprising the Peel Sandstone Group may have been rotated by 45° in an anticlockwise direction from its original position[15]. In other words the source of the sediment could in fact lie to the northeast of the Isle of Man in the direction of the Lake District.

SUBDIVISION BY ROCK TYPES

Two stratigraphic schemes have previously been devised for the rock succession in the Peel Sandstone Group, by Boyd Dawkins[16] and Crowley[17]. Crowley recognised two formations and eight members, but recently the British Geological Survey[18] has proposed a new classification. This is broadly in agreement with the scheme of Crowley[19], but also includes a highly equivocal aeolian (wind-derived) component, overlain by intervals of fluvial (river-derived), lacustrine (lake-derived) and palaeosol (fossil soil) sediments.

Aeolian deposits This rock type is a minor component of the Peel Sandstone Group and the idea that it was deposited by wind is new and therefore open to question. Three classes are recognised. The most common is fine- to medium-grained, cross-bedded[20] sandstones in thick, well-defined beds best exposed at the northern end of the promenade at Peel. Ripples and frosted grains are observed. They are interpreted as the deposits of wind-generated migrating dunes drifting with a predominant wind direction from the east or northeast. Less common are thin beds of laminated fine-grained sandstone with occasional ripples found interbedded with the supposed dune deposits. These are interpreted as dry aeolian sand sheets blown across the floor of interdune areas. The third class consists of thin beds of fine-grained sandstone and thin crenulated laminae of mudstone, interbedded with the dunes and sand sheets suggested to be the product of deposition by wind of sand and mud sticking to temporarily damp surfaces. Note that it is equally possible that all three classes are products of deposition by rivers rather than wind, an interpretation favoured here.

Fluvial deposits The beds described above are overlain by a variable sequence of conglomerates and sandstones. The contact may be slightly erosional (disconformable). Two main classes can be identified. The first consists of poorly sorted conglomerates, pebbly sandstones and sandstones with erosive bases. The sandstones are up to 3.5 m in thickness and of wide lateral extent. Trough-shaped cross-bedding is common, occurring in small sets less than 30 cm thick. Occasional flakes and pebbles of mudstone (Figure 4.4a) occur within them and are derived from erosion of previously deposited beds. These sediments are interpreted to have been deposited in braided river channels several metres deep and tens to hundreds of metres wide that flowed to the southeast. The presence of pebbles within the sandstones suggests rapid deposition from sediment-loaded floodwaters on an alluvial fan or floodplain. The second class comprises fine- to medium-grained, locally coarse and pebbly sandstone in well-bedded tabular units up to a metre in thickness. They are interpreted as the deposits of high-energy unconfined flash floods in an alluvial floodplain or fan system flowing to the southeast.

Ephemeral lake deposits The flash flood sediments are overlain by up to one metre of thin alternations of mudstones and fine-grained sandstones interpreted to have formed in small ephemeral lakes. The sandstones display ripple cross-bedding (Figure 4.4b) indicative of gentle flow to the southeast and the mudstones commonly show flat laminations. Desiccation cracks formed by mud drying out (Figure 4.5a) are ubiquitous, usually associated with dewatering structures (caused by rapid escape of fluidised sand from the sediment). Much of the mudstone has been eroded and redeposited during successive flood events, leading to an abundance of mudstone flakes and pebbles within the fluvial deposits (Figure 4.4a).

Palaeosols 'Palaeosols' are the geological term for fossil soils. In the Peel Sandstone Group these consist of hard, irregular nodules of calcite ('calcrete') within siltstone or sandstone beds up to 3 m in thickness (Figure 4.5b). Calcrete nodules consist of calcite (calcium carbonate) formed just below the surface of a semi-arid alluvial plain. Modern-day calcretes typically take between 1,000 and 10,000 years to form, during which time there is little or no sedimentation.

Trace fossils Some of the soils in the Peel Sandstone Group display root-like structures encased in calcrete, indicating that primitive trees may have been growing on the alluvial plain[21] (Figure 4.6a). As trees only became established at the start of the Devonian, they suggest a maximum age for the deposits. Indications of animal life are also preserved within the sedi-

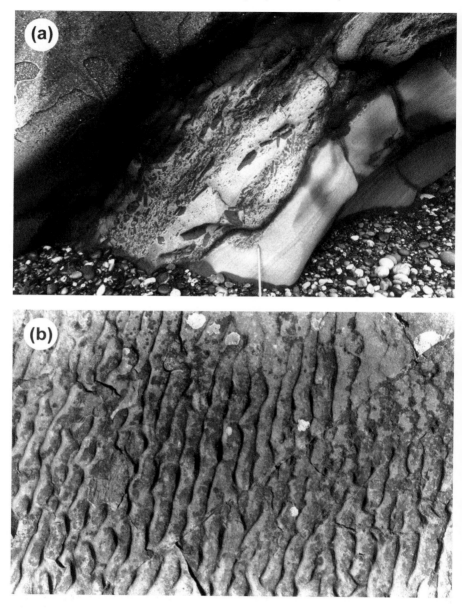

Figure 4.4 *(a) Pebbles of mudstone preserved within sandstone at the base of a channel. The pebbles were derived from erosion of beds deposited on the flood-plain. Note pencil for scale. (b) Rippled sandstone in the Peel Sandstone group. The distance between the crest of each ripple is approximately 4 cm.*

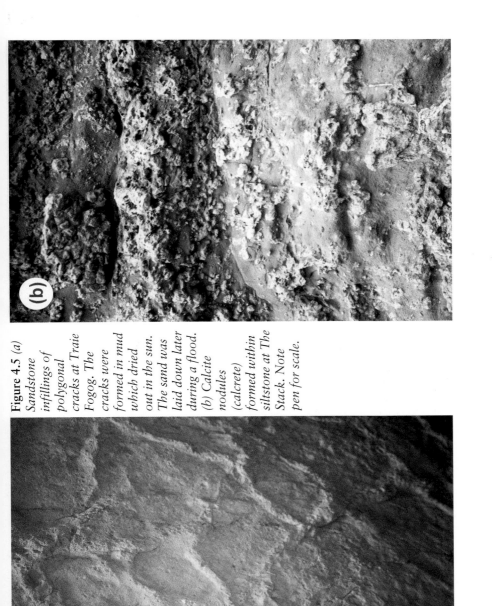

Figure 4.5 (a) Sandstone infillings of polygonal cracks at Traie Fogog. The cracks were formed in mud which dried out in the sun. The sand was laid down later during a flood. (b) Calcite nodules (calcrete) formed within siltstone at The Stack. Note pen for scale.

Figure 4.6 *(a) Root structures preserved within calcrete at The Stack indicating that trees were growing in the soil, possibly some of the earliest forms of life to colonise the land. Note pen in the middle of the picture for scale. (b) Burrow in sandstone at the northern end of Peel promenade (orientated horizontally in top centre of photograph). The crustacean or fish which formed the burrow was living within the river bed.*

ments, including some small banana-shaped burrows preserved at the north end of Peel Promenade (Figure 4.6b) and larger, calcrete-filled burrows at The Stack. These were probably formed by fish or crustaceans.

AGE OF THE PEEL SANDSTONE GROUP

Despite more than a century of investigation, determining the age of the Peel sandstones has proved contentious, due largely to the absence of contemporaneous fossils. All previous suggestions for the age of the sediments (Devonian[22], Lower Carboniferous, Upper Carboniferous[23] and Permian[24]) have been based on geological reasoning and comparison with sediments of known age from other areas of the British Isles. The lack of cleavage within the Peel Sandstone Group indicates that it must post-date the main phase of deformation in the Caledonian Orogeny placing it younger than the late Silurian, in line with the trace fossil evidence above.

Pebbles within conglomerates in the Peel sandstones contain a varied suite of rock types including quartz, quartzite, igneous rocks (including silica-rich lavas), sandstones, limestones and shales. However, most of these rocks cannot be related to outcrops elsewhere on the island. No pebbles of Manx or Dalby Group are present, indicating that these rocks were probably not exposed at the time of deposition of the Peel Sandstone Group. The limestone pebbles in the conglomerates display a diverse set of marine fossils, including corals, stromatoporoids, bryozoa, brachiopods and crinoids. Similar types of rock are exposed nowadays on the Dingle peninsula in the west of Ireland[25]. Although subject to some dispute, the fauna is dominated by corals of Lower Silurian age[26]. A more precise, Wenlockian *(circa* 428 Ma) age for the fauna has now been established by the recent identification of three new species[27]. Crowley[28] noted that the pebbles in the conglomerates at White Strand are older than those towards Peel, possibly indicating that the sediments at White Strand are younger, the source area becoming more deeply eroded over time.

An upper age limit is more difficult to define, but it can be assumed that they are no younger than the Triassic *(circa* 205 Ma) as red bed sequences such as these are absent from Jurassic, Cretaceous and Tertiary rocks in the British Isles.

Recently new evidence for the age of the Peel sandstones has come from the laboratory technique known as palaeomagnetism[29]. The inclination of the Earth's magnetic field varies according to the distance from the magnetic poles and hence is related to latitude. Palaeomagnetism attempts to measure fossilised magnetism imparted when the sediments were deposited. This magnetic signature is very weak and can be distorted by later events and therefore the interpretation is often equivocal. However, the results of palaeomagnetic analysis of the Peel Sandstone Group suggest it was deposited at a latitude of 29°S (± 6°), equivalent to the position of modern-day South Africa. Continental plate reconstructions indicate that this is where the Isle of Man lay during latest Silurian or earliest Devonian times (420–390 Ma). The implication is therefore that the Peel sandstones are the time equivalent of the Lower Old Red Sandstone, present, for example, in the Midland Valley between Glasgow and Edinburgh, and dated to between 410 and 400 Ma.

CONCLUSIONS

The latest information on the age of the Peel Sandstone Group indicates that it represents a sequence of sediments formed on land in the early Devonian, after the Iapetus Ocean had closed. The region lay south of the equator associated with a warm, semi-arid climate and variable amounts of rainfall. This was a time when uplift was occurring in many areas associated with the final stages of the Caledonian mountain-building event. Rapid erosion of these mountains shed sediment into fault-bounded basins within and around the periphery of the mountains, including one in which the Peel Sandstone Group was deposited. This basin may have finally been shunted south-eastwards by late Caledonian plate movements.

Notes

1   Calcrete is a term used for sediment with a high proportion of calcite nodules, a feature developed in many modern-day semi-arid soils.
2   W. Boyd Dawkins, 'The red sandstone rocks of Peel (Isle of Man)', *Quarterly Journal of the Geological Society of London*, 58 (1902), 633–646.
3   *Ibid.*
4   S.F. Crowley, 'Lithostratigraphy of the Peel Sandstones, Isle of Man', *Mercian Geologist*, 10 (1985), 73–76.
5   R.A. Chadwick, D.I. Jackson, R.P. Barnes, G.S. Kimbell, H. Johnson, R.C. Chiverrell, G.S.P. Thomas, N.S. Jones, N.J. Riley, E.A. Pickett, B. Young, D.W. Holliday, D.F. Ball, S.G. Molyneux, D. Long, G.M. Power and D.H. Roberts, *Geology of the Isle of Man and its offshore area*, British Geological Survey Research Report, RR/01/06 (2001), 143.
6   D.G. Quirk, and G.S. Kimbell, 'Structural evolution of the Isle of Man and central part of the Irish Sea', in N.S. Meadows, S.P. Trueblood, N. Hardman and G. Cowan (eds), *Petroleum geology of the Irish Sea and adjacent areas*, Geological Society of London Special Publication, 124 (1997), 135–159.
7   W. Boyd Dawkins (1902).
8   D.G. Quirk, D.J. Burnett, G.S. Kimbell, C.A. Murphy and J.S. Varley, 'Shallow geophysical and geological evidence for a regional-scale fault duplex in the Lower Palaeozoic of the Isle of Man', in N.H. Woodcock, D.G. Quirk, W.F. Fitches and R.P. Barnes (eds), *In sight of the suture: the Palaeozoic geology of the Isle of Man*

   in its Iapetus Ocean context, Geological Society of London Special Publication,
   160 (1999a), 239–257.

9   D.G. Quirk *et al.* (1999a).

10   W. Boyd Dawkins (1902).

11   S.F. Crowley (1985).

12   A normal fault is one caused by extension, effectively pulling the beds apart; a
     thrust or reverse fault is caused by compression, forcing the beds over one another;
     J.D.A. Piper and S.F. Crowley, 'Palaeomagnetism of the (Palaeozoic) Peel
     Sandstones and Langness Conglomerate Formation, Isle of Man: implications for
     the age and regional diagenesis', in N.H. Woodcock *et al.* (1999), 213–225.

13   T.D. Ford, 'Slump structures in the Peel Sandstone Series, Isle of Man', *Isle of
     Man Natural History and Antiquarian Journal*, 7 (1972), 440–448; T.D. Ford,
     The Isle of Man, Geologists' Association Guide, 46 (1993); T.D. Ford, D.J.
     Burnett and D.G. Quirk, *The geology of the Isle of Man*, Geologists' Association
     Guide, 46 (2001), 92.

14   D.G. Quirk, and G.S. Kimbell (1997).

15   J.D.A. Piper and S.F. Crowley (1999).

16   W. Boyd Dawkins (1902).

17   S.F. Crowley (1985).

18   R.A. Chadwick *et al.* (2001).

19   S.F. Crowley (1985).

20   Cross-bedding is where laminae dip at an oblique angle relative to the base of the
     bed. It is formed as sand moves forward in dunes, waves and ripples driven by
     either wind or water.

21   D.G. Quirk, and G.S. Kimbell (1997).

22   J.G. Cumming, 'On the geology of the Isle of Man', *Quarterly Journal of the
     Geological Society of London*, 2 (1846), 317–348; J.R.L. Allen and S.F. Crowley,
     'Lower Old Red Sandstone fluvial dispersal systems in the British Isles',
     Transactions of the Royal Society of Edinburgh: Earth Science, 74 (1983), 61–68.

23   T.D. Ford (1972); G.W. Lamplugh, *The geology of the Isle of Man*, Memoir of
     the Geological Survey of England and Wales (1903), 620; H.P. Lewis, 'The
     Avonian succession in the south of the Isle of Man', *Quarterly Journal of the
     Geological Society of London*, 86 (1930), 234–290.

24   D.G. Quirk and G.S. Kimbell (1997).

25   G.W. Lamplugh (1903); W. Boyd Dawkins (1902); E.L. Gill, 'Keisley Limestone
     pebbles from the Isle of Man', *Quarterly Journal of the Geological Society of
     London*, 59 (1903), 307–310.

26   H.P. Lewis, 'The occurrence of fossiliferous pebbles of Salopian age in the Peel
     Sandstones (Isle of Man)', *Summary of Progress of the Geological Survey*, 2
     (1933), 91–108.

27   C.T. Strutton, *personal communication.*

28   S. Crowley (1985).

29   J.D.A. Piper and S.F. Crowley (1999).

5   The Castletown Limestone

DAVE QUIRK, DAVE BURNETT and GEOFF THOMAS

CARBONIFEROUS TECTONICS

By the end of the Devonian, some 354 Ma, the Iapetus Ocean had closed, the Caledonian Orogeny was over and Avalonia had welded with Laurentia. During the Carboniferous, between 354 and 292 Ma, further plate movement saw the African portion of Gondwana continue to move northwards and collide with Europe to form the supercontinent of Pangaea (Figure 5.1). The collision produced a new mountain belt called the Variscan chain running from what is now Russia through Western Europe.

Britain lay to the north of the collision zone and was largely unaffected. The mountains formed during the Caledonian Orogeny had largely worn down by this time and during the early Carboniferous the lowland areas were slowly flooded by lakes and sea. At this time Britain and the Isle of Man lay in equatorial latitudes so that hot conditions prevailed in a seasonal but fairly arid climate. This area of Pangaea was affected by tensional stresses, and by the early Carboniferous it had started to rift apart. Where the floors of the rifts subsided below sea level, limestones began to form in an environment analogous to the present-day Red Sea basin. Modern rift basins, such as those in East Africa, are often associated with fault activity and volcanic eruptions along the margins of the basin and the early Carboniferous was no different.

As a result of rifting, a number of fault-bounded basins developed around the present-day Isle of Man (Figure 5.1b). To the north, the Solway Basin[1] runs northeast–southwest, parallel with the underlying Iapetus Suture, and is marked by parallel boundary faults; the Maryport Fault on the southeast side and the North Solway Fault on the northwest side. It extends for 200 km eastwards through the Northumberland Basin out into the North Sea and contains Lower Carboniferous sediment at least 2,500 m thick. To the west of the island, the Peel Basin[2] preserves Lower Carboniferous strata in a series of tilted fault blocks. To the south and east, the Castletown area forms the sole onshore exposure of the Eubonia Basin[3], which underlies most of the southeast Irish Sea area. The Shag Rock Fault, which runs through Port St Mary and dies out towards Silverdale, represents the western boundary of this basin. Another set of faults lying offshore, but parallel to the east coast of the Isle of Man, marks the north-

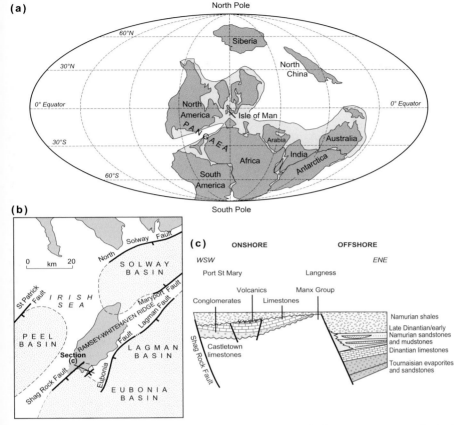

Figure 5.1 *(a) Reconstruction of the earth's continental plates approximately 360 million years ago. Note that the British Isles region lies at the equator. (b) Early Carboniferous basins in the Isle of Man area. (c) Schematic cross-section through a typical Irish Sea rift basin during early Carboniferous times based on observations in the field around Castletown and interpretation of offshore data. The tilted geometry is typical of half graben with strata thickening towards a large normal fault, active during sedimentation.*

west boundary of the Eubonia Basin and Lagman Basin further north and are partly responsible for creating the island. A northeast-trending submarine extension of the island, known as the Ramsey–Whitehaven Ridge (Figure 5.1b), links it with the Lake District. This is an up-tilted fault block that lay close to sea level for much of the early Carboniferous, separating the Lagman Basin from the Solway Basin. The southeast edge of the block is defined by a major fault known as the Lagman Fault (Figure 5.1b), which was formed by rifting, but lies parallel to older compressional faults formed during the Caledonian Orogeny.

It is worth noting that the Irish Sea area was affected by two further rifting events after the early Carboniferous (early Permian and mid Jurassic)[4]. Also, the area was subjected to significant uplift and erosion during the early Tertiary making sub-surface data in the offshore difficult to interpret at Carboniferous level. Therefore, it is often uncertain whether a fault-bounded basin containing a thick section of post-Carboniferous (mostly Triassic) sediments is actually a basin underlain by an early Carboniferous half graben (see below) or whether it is a younger structure. However, the northeast–southwest Shag Rock Fault, that comes onshore Isle of Man, the northeast–southwest Lagman Fault, bounding the Ramsey–Whitehaven Ridge, and a set of north–south faults around the Ogham Inlier (Figure 5.1b), east of the island, were clearly active during rifting in the early Carboniferous[5], suggesting that the Isle of Man started to emerge at this time.

The Carboniferous Period is divided into two eras: the Dinantian (Lower Carboniferous, 354–327 Ma) and the Silesian (Upper Carboniferous, 327–292 Ma). Dinantian rocks occur in the south of the island around Castletown at the margin of the Eubonia Basin. These rocks are informally known as the Castletown Limestones and represent the youngest solid rocks exposed at the surface on the Isle of Man.

CARBONIFEROUS ROCKS IN THE SUB-SURFACE

From Langness towards the Shag Rock Fault, the Castletown Limestones are tilted westwards (Figure 5.1c). On seismic data in the offshore[6], the interval is wedge-shaped with individual units thickening towards the fault and tapering out in the opposite direction, towards an offshore extension of Langness. This type of geometry is known as a 'half graben' and is a typical component of a rift where the floor has tilted and subsided due to downwards movement on the fault creating a depression where sediment can accumulate.

Dinantian and Silesian rocks, associated with the Solway Basin, are concealed by glacial deposits beneath the northern plain of the island and are known only from boreholes[7]. They comprise limestones and associated rocks (Dinantian) and sandstones and mudstones (Silesian). The sandstones are typical of those deposited around a river delta and in many places in Britain these Silesian rocks are associated with coal formed from vegetation collecting in lagoonal swamps. In fact, this was the reason the boreholes were drilled, to explore for potential commercially viable coal seams. These were not encountered on the island, but do exist where the sediments become thicker in the offshore. The reason for the wholesale switch from limestones in the Dinantian to deltaic deposits in the Silesian was probably due to change from a dry to a wet climate causing rivers to bring large quantities of sand and mud from rejuvenated upland areas into what were previously shallow tropical seas.

Seismic data indicate that the Solway, Eubonia-Lagman and Peel Basins may contain up to 4000 m of Carboniferous sediment and these are the source of oil (from mudstones) and gas (from coal) in the southeast Irish Sea. Jackson *et al.*[8], Quirk and Kimbell[9], Quirk *et al.*[10] and Chadwick *et al.*[11] have described the Carboniferous of the Irish Sea in detail, including the northern plain, and this book only deals with the exposed interval around Castletown.

STRUCTURE OF THE CASTLETOWN LIMESTONES

The Castletown Limestones are exposed in coastal cliffs, on the foreshore and in large quarries in the southeast of the island between Port St Mary and Cass-ny-Hawin. The beds are relatively undisturbed save for a number of small faults (e.g., northeast of Ronaldsway) and folds (e.g., east of Scarlett). The Carboniferous rocks are everywhere bordered onshore by the Manx Group; the margin is faulted at Port St Mary and Cass-ny-Hawin (Figure 5.2) but they directly overlie the Manx Group, 130 million years older, at Langness. The fault at Cass-ny-Hawin trends approximately east–west, dips very steeply to the south and is marked by a 1 to 2 m fault breccia. The amount of movement is in excess of 100 m. The fault was probably formed in the early Carboniferous, only a short time after deposition of the limestones as the Manx Group rocks have been reddened in a wide zone adjacent to the fault suggesting that the effects of tropical weathering penetrated the fault from the surface.

Several vertical east–west faults in the limestones to the south of Cass-ny-Hawin display mineral fibres and scratches on the surfaces of the faults that are near horizontal in attitude. These and the boundary fault at Cass-ny-Hawin are interpreted to have formed by left lateral (sinistral) strike-slip movement to accommodate extension on the Shag Rock Fault as the rift grew. Such transverse faults, which trend approximately 90° to the main extensional faults, are common in modern-day rifts such as the East African Rift Valley.

Figure 5.2 *Vertical fault at Cass-ny-Hawin marking the boundary between the Castletown limestones (on the left) and the Manx Group (on the right, northeast side).*

DESCRIPTION AND SUBDIVISION OF THE CASTLETOWN LIMESTONES

Limestones are rocks composed of calcium carbonate ('calcite'), which is generally of biological origin, for example derived from shells. Fossil shells present in the Castletown Limestones indicate that the environment was that of a warm, shallow sea. Calcite sometimes alters to calcium magnesium carbonate ('dolomite'), observed in the field as a change from the usual grey limestone to a brown granular rock. This 'dolomitisation' occurs in places within the Castletown Limestones.

The Castletown Limestones were first described by Cumming[12] and initially mapped by Lamplugh[13] who identified five units: the Basement Conglomerate, the Castletown Limestones, Poolvash Limestones, the *Posidonomya* beds and the Scarlett Volcanic Series. The nomenclature has been subsequently revised by Lewis[14] and Dickson *et al.*[15]. Recent investigation by the British Geological Survey[16] has partially revised the existing work (Figure 5.3), including an updated map (Figure 5.4).

Approximate age and stages				Lithostratigraphy		Approximate thickness (m)
327 Ma	BRIGANTIAN			SCARLETT VOLCANIC FORMATION		> 50 m
				CLOSE NY CHOLLAGH FORMATION		57 m
DINANTIAN	ASBIAN			POYLLVAAISH FORMATION		78 m
				BALLADOOLE FORMATION		90 m
	HOLK ERIAN			SCARLETT POINT MEMBER		14 m
				KNOCKRUSHEN & HODDERENSE LIMESTONE FORMATIONS		35 m
	COURCEYAN ARUNDIAN	DERBYHAVEN FORMATION			SKILLICORE MEMBER	21 m
					SANDWICK MEMBER	46 m
					TURKEYLAND MEMBER	25 m
354 Ma				LANGNESS CONGLOMERATE FORMATION		30 m

Figure 5.3 *Table showing subdivision of the Castletown Limestones in order of age, after R.A. Chadwick et al. (2001).*

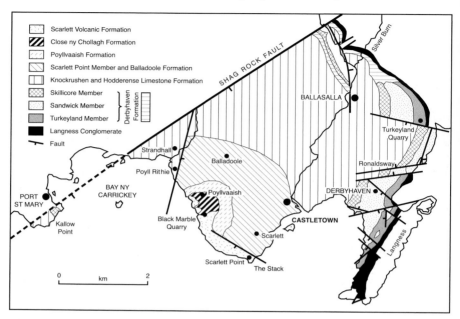

Figure 5.4 *Geological map of the limestones in the Castletown area, after R.A. Chadwick et al. (2001).*

Langness Conglomerate Formation

This is the lowest unit in the Carboniferous succession in the Castletown area and is exposed at Langness and on the foreshore at Derbyhaven. The formation has a thickness of about 30 m and is essentially a succession of red-coloured gravels ('conglomerates'), sandstones and siltstones resting at a low angle upon steeply dipping Manx Group rocks (Figure 5.5a). The irregular surface separating the two groups represents a time gap of 60 million years between the end of the Caledonian Orogeny and deposition of the conglomerate. It was formed by erosion and is a spectacular example of a geological boundary known as an 'unconformity'. The Manx Group is reddened for up to several metres below the unconformity due to weathering of the land surface in a hot climate. Similar reddening is seen in the Manx Group around Cass-ny-Hawin suggesting that, although the Langness Conglomerate Formation is not preserved there, it was probably originally present at a level not far above the present land surface.

Conglomerates deposited by flash floods and ephemeral rivers running off higher ground in a seasonally arid environment dominate the lower part of the formation (Figure 5.5b). The variable size and angular appearance

Figure 5.5 *(a) Langness Conglomerate overlying the Manx Group at The Arches on Langness (SC283656). The surface separating the two represents a gap in time of approximately 60 million years between the end of the Caledonian mountain-building event (early Devonian) and the onset of rifting in the early Carboniferous. (b) Gravel-filled channel close to the base of the Langness Conglomerate at SC283656.*

Figure 5.6 *Limestones and interbedded mudstones belonging to the Turkeyland Member at Turkeyland Quarry (SC2940694). A northwest-dipping normal fault is visible in the centre of the photograph. The height of the quarry is approximately 15 m.*

of the Manx Group pebbles in the conglomerates suggest that they were transported only a short distance from where they were eroded. The upper part of the succession contains more sandstones which may have been reworked by wave action when sea water flooded over the area ahead of limestone deposition. Being unfossiliferous, the exact age of the Langness Conglomerate is difficult to establish, but by inference it is early Dinantian (Courceyan–early Arundian, *circa* 354 to 351 Ma)[17]. In contrast to the Peel Sandstone, which is probably of early Devonian age, the Langness Conglomerate is relatively undeformed and contains pebbles of slate, indicating that the Manx Goup was exposed at the time of deposition.

North–south and east–west faults are present in the conglomerate and developed as a result of extensional forces in the crust associated with rifting (Figure 5.5a). Beds thicken towards the fault surfaces on the side that moved down indicating that the faults were active at the same time as the conglomerate was deposited, with hollows along the fault scarps becoming filled with gravel.

Derbyhaven Formation

The Derbyhaven Formation overlies the Langness Conglomerate in a 'conformable' relationship, meaning beds above and below the contact are parallel. It is approximately 90 m thick and has been subdivided into three members. The lowest, the *Turkeyland Member*, is up to 25 m in thickness and is made up of beds 0.5 m thick (Figure 5.6) composed of sand-sized shelly material. Grains in the limestones are well sorted and rounded indicating that they were deposited in shallow water affected by constant wave activity. Locally, pebbles from the underlying conglomerate are contained within the limestones. The base of the interval is marked by a thin organic-rich shale containing pyrite, which was formed when the sea first flooded over the terrestrial deposits of the Langness Conglomerate. This flooding occurred as the rift subsided below sea level.

The overlying *Sandwick Member* is best exposed on the foreshore in Sandwick Bay. It has a total thickness of some 46 m and comprises beds of dark shelly limestones, generally less than 0.5 m in thickness, with small amounts of interbedded siltstone and shale. In the lower part of the interval, the limestones contain large amounts of crinoid debris. These are typical of sediments deposited in a quiet lagoon with crinoids, a type of fossil sea lily, washed in from the edge of reefs and the shales representing periods of stagnation within the lagoon. In the upper part, formerly the Ronaldsway Member of Dickson *et al.*[18], the limestones thicken to an average of one metre and are faintly laminated. These laminations have a hummocky appearance typical of sediments affected by occasional storms, but no other current activity. The inference is that they were generated in water depths not normally influenced by waves, typically greater than 20 m, but less than 100 m, the limit of storm action. In places the bases of the beds have loaded down into underlying thin shales indicating that the sediment was deposited very rapidly onto a soft substrate, again typical of sediment moved into deep water during storms. An abundant assemblage of fossils, including the foraminifera *Glomodiscus* and *Uralodiscus*, indicates an Arundian (Middle Dinantian, 340–335 Ma) age for the Sandwick Member.

The overlying *Skillicore Member* is exposed on the foreshore northeast of Ronaldsway Airport near Lough Skillicore and has a thickness of around 21 m. The lower part shows similar hummocky laminations, but the beds are thinner (<0.5 m) and there are thicker interbeds of shale (up to 0.1 m) suggesting that there were longer periods of quiescence. One explanation for this is that the water was deeper so that shelly material was only washed in during the larger storms. Towards the top of the Skillicore Member the limestone beds become darker, finer-grained and pyrite-bearing, with some beds displaying ripples. Also, some fine-grained sandstone is present which may indicate that there was a relative fall in sea level during the later stages of deposition.

In an overall sense, the Derbyhaven Formation represents a period when sediment accumulation was unable to keep up with the effects of subsidence, so that water depths increased over time. The change in water depth is estimated to be from 1 to 2 m, when the Turkeyland Member was deposited, to something in the order of 80 m at the top of the Sandwick Member. The upper part of the Skillicore Member may record a change back to slightly shallower water, associated with a fall in the height of sea level.

A diverse assemblage of burrows and trace fossils are common throughout the Derbyhaven Formation indicating that seabed conditions were generally oxic allowing creatures such as worms, arthropods and bivalves to live within the sediment. However, the darker, pyritic beds at the top of the Skillicore Member may have been deposited in more anoxic conditions, the dark colour due to preservation of organic material and pyrite often taken as evidence for bacterial activity in the absence of oxygen.

Knockrushen Formation

Formerly the Knockrushen Member of the Castletown Formation of Dickson et al.[19], the Knockrushen Formation is best exposed on the foreshore south of Castletown Harbour. It is about 21 m thick and consists of thick, irregular beds of fine-grained limestone containing well-preserved crinoids, corals (Figure 5.7), brachiopods and traces of large burrows typical of shallow water environments. Thin beds of black, finely laminated mudstones also occur. The limestone is actually composed of carbonate mud, probably formed from the remains of foraminifera and finely ground shell debris produced by wave action. Age diagnostic fossils include the first appearance of *Archaediscus* and palaeotextulariid foraminifera, both of which suggest a Holkerian (Middle Dinantian) age (*circa* 335 Ma). Some beds have a nodular appearance resulting from either microbial action within the sediment ('concretions') or accretion of sediment by algae ('bioherms'). The Knockrushen Formation was probably deposited in a lagoon relatively sheltered from the open sea by a line of reefs lying further offshore (Figure 5.8). During the Carboniferous in many areas of Europe, colonies of algae were responsible for forming reefs. These reefs were mound-shaped bodies of carbonate mud fringed by crinoids and other shelly animals.

Figure 5.7 *(a) Solitary (non-colonial) corals within the Castletown Formation (SC259665). The hammer is 0.4 m in length. (b) Colonial corals within the Castletown Formation (SC271677). Note 50 pence piece for scale.*

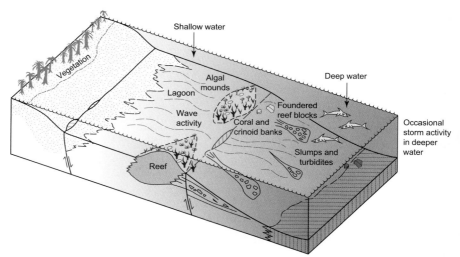

Figure 5.8 *Schematic model illustrating the sort of tropical marine environment in which the Castletown Limestones were deposited.*

Hodderense Limestone Formation

Formerly known as the Sea Mount Member of the Castletown Formation[20], this unit comprises a 14 m thickness of fairly uniform, fine-grained beds of limestone, interbedded with thin, dark coloured mudstone layers, which are laminated. The tops of many of the beds contain nodules of limestone and chert. Chert is silica that forms soon after sediment deposition, often as a result of bacterial activity. The presence of nodules and chert indicates that individual beds had probably already hardened at the seabed before burial by later sediment, possibly when the water became anoxic for a period of time. The base of the next bed is frequently muddy with shell debris suggesting that sedimentation had begun again after the waters were stirred up by storms, when oxic conditions were re-established. Some beds contain fossil-rich horizons at their base composed of broken pieces of crinoids, gastropods, ammonoids, trilobites, sponges and nodules. The interval is interpreted to have been deposited in deep water, starved of sand and mud, and represents a significant increase in the height of sea level from that during deposition of the underlying Knockrushen Formation. It is assigned a Holkerian (Middle Dinantian) age of *circa* 332 Ma and is named after similar rocks in the Craven Basin of Northern England[21].

Scarlett Point Member

The Scarlett Point Member represents the base of the Bowland Shale Formation as defined by Chadwick *et al.*[22] and the top of the Castletown formation of Dickson *et al.*[23]. It is about 14 m thick and on the whole consists of limestone similar to the underlying Hodderense Limestone Formation except that it contains darker-coloured mudstone. Also, the bases and tops of many of the limestone beds are partially dolomitised, giving it a brown, grainy appearance (Figure 5.9a). Burrows are common in the Scarlett Point Member and crinoid-rich horizons and scattered ammonoids also occur. Deposition was in a deep marine environment. Chadwick *et al*[24] suggest an early Asbian (Upper Dinantian) age. The beds are also folded (Figure 5.9a). The folds trend north–south and are asymmetric in that the east side is typically much steeper than the west side. They are thought to have formed by east–west compression during the later stages of the Variscan mountain-building event.

Balladoole Formation

The Balladoole Formation, in its unaltered state, consists of up to 90 m of fairly featureless fine-grained limestones in which crinoids, brachiopods, corals and ammonoids are common. On the coast, however, it is widely dolomitised in association with networks of quartz veins. Parallel to the walls of the quartz veins, the dolomite is often concentrically layered suggesting that the alteration worked its way outwards from the vein walls. The quartz crystallised from hot aqueous fluids flowing through fractures and it therefore seems likely that the magnesium for the dolomite was also sourced from these fluids. This type of dolomitisation is known as epithermal alteration and is often associated with ore deposits. Small quantities of metal sulphides such as chalcopyrite (copper iron sulphide) and sphalerite (zinc sulphide) occur in association with the quartz mineralisation where it is most intense at Poyll Richie (SC239679) on the east side of a north–south fault.

A general absence of bedding and the limited number of fossils within the Balladoole Formation are thought to be because it represents a reef belt accreted by algae. Behind this belt (to the north or west) lagoon conditions prevailed similar to those described for the Knockrushen Formation and in front of which (to the south or east) lay open sea analogous to the environment in which the Derbyhaven Formation was deposited (Figure 5.8).

Rare ammonoid fossils allow the age of this formation to be tightly constrained. They include *Goniatites hudsoni*, *Bollandites phillipsi*,

Figure 5.9 *(a) Partially dolomitised and folded beds of the Castletown Formation near Scarlett Point (SC258663). The beds of limestone are approximately 0.5 m thick. (b) Thin-bedded limestones at the base of the Poyllvaaish Formation overlain by thick algal reef limestones near Salt Spring Cottage (SC244678). An algal mound occurs within the thin-bedded interval several metres to the right of the person.*

Bollandites castletonesis and *Beyrichoceras vesiculiferum* that define a late Asbian age (Upper Dinantian) at *circa* 330 Ma. *Goniatites crenistria*, at the top of the formation, probably coincides with the end of the Asbian.

Late Asbian–Brigantian Formations

Unfortunately some confusion in nomenclature has arisen from the work of Chadwick *et al.*[25] who renamed some of the rock units in the upper part of the Castletown Limestones based on a limited amount of new fieldwork. Distinctive units of Brigantian age called the Poyllvaaish Formation and Close ny Chollagh Formation by Dickson *et al.*[26] have been assigned instead to the Bowland Formation by Chadwick *et al.*[27], which has at its base the Scarlett Point Member and at its top the Scarlett Volcanic Member. The Bowland Formation is also in part the same age as the Balladoole Formation, a name retained by Chadwick *et al.*[28]. To avoid unnecessary complexity, the nomenclature of Dickson *et al.*[29] will be retained here.

Poyllvaaish Formation   The base of the Poyllvaaish Formation is marked by a few metres of thin-bedded limestone and shale interspersed with algal mounds of various sizes (Figure 5.9b). The thin limestone beds comprise shelly debris (mostly crinoids and brachiopods) and pebbles that were probably washed in during storms from the sides of the larger bioherms and areas where the older Balladoole Formation was exposed at surface. Colonial corals are seen to encrust some of the smaller bioherms. This basal interval is thought to represent a small inter-reef area where lagoon conditions prevailed. Above this is another 70 m or so of algal limestone which, similar to the Balladoole Formation, is featureless except for some faint surfaces dipping to the south. These surfaces may represent the edges of individual bioherms perhaps indicating that the reef complex built outwards to the south into slightly deeper water. Unlike the Balladoole Formation, the Poyllvaaish Formation is rarely dolomitised, probably because it is impermeable due to the lack of fractures. The presence of the ammonoids *Beyrichoceras truncatum* and *Goniatites crenistria* suggests a latest Asbian (Upper Dinantian) age.

Close ny Chollagh Formation   The Close ny Chollagh Formation is separated from the Poyllvaaish Formation by an east-northeast to west-southwest trending scarp thought to represent a fault. The interval consists of broken pieces of pale-coloured limestone, resembling the Poyllvaaish Formation, within beds of dark-coloured, muddy limestone.

The sizes of the pieces of pale limestone vary from large blocks to small pebbles. The most recent interpretation is that earthquake activity along this fault caused a reef, composed of pale-coloured limestone, to collapse and slide northwards towards the scarp where dark-coloured lagoonal sediments were accumulating[30]. Collapse happened at least twice during deposition of the Close ny Chollagh Formation causing a jumble of reef material to be caught up within the beds deposited in the lagoon. On top of this interval, discrete algal reef mounds have developed (Figure 5.10), the bases of which have squashed or loaded the lagoonal sediments indicating that these reefs gained significant weight while the underlying beds were still soft.

The upper part of the Close ny Chollagh Formation consists mostly of dark-coloured, muddy limestone with only occasional isolated reefs present. At Black Marble Quarry (SC245672) the dark limestone has been recrystallised to form a relatively hard rock. The recrystallisation resulted from heating, probably from a nearby Tertiary dyke or possibly the overlying Scarlett Volcanic Formation. The rock is quarried and polished for facing and ornamental purposes. The 'marble' contains ammonoids and large bivalves together with remains of a fossil fish, *Psammodus*. A unique example of the entire bony remains of this fish has recently been discov-

Figure 5.10 *Algal mounds overlying thin-bedded limestones at the base of the Poyllvaaish Formation near Salt Spring Cottage (SC244678).*

ered in a paving stone in Castletown[31], which probably originated from the Black Marble Quarry. The ammonoid *Arnsbergites falcatus* and the bivalve *Posidonia becheri* are diagnostic of an early Brigantian (Upper Dinantian) age (*circa* 322 Ma).

Scarlett Volcanic Formation   The Scarlett Volcanic Formation consists of more than 50 m of basaltic rocks that resulted from a series of explosive eruptions at the end of the Lower Carboniferous, around 330 Ma. Durant and Grant[32] regard it as typical of Icelandic 'Surtseyan' type eruptions. The eruptions were from a number of separate vents with volcanic flows transported down-slope, mostly under water. The main rock type composes fragments or 'clasts' of rock in a finer-grained matrix of basaltic ash (Figure 5.11) given the general geological term 'volcaniclastic'. Such rocks are common where magma reaching the surface is gassy – the gas and steam escaping explosively, blowing apart the magma so that a lava does not form. Nonetheless, the resultant fragmentary ash does tend to flow downslope and forms a rock known as 'agglomerate'.

The volcaniclastic flows at the base of the Scarlett Volcanic Formation (SC245672) have a sharp contact with underlying limestones and the contact steps up and down bedding planes as a result of plucking by or injection of eruptive material. The limestone has not only been broken off and streaked out by the force of the eruptive flow, but also baked by the heat. Clasts in the agglomerate in the lower part of the succession are mainly of limestone, torn up during early eruptions. A little higher up (SC246669), a single lens of limestone, probably accreted by algae, has developed on a volcanic surface only to be buried by the next eruption.

In the main body of the Scarlett Volcanic Formation, clasts are almost exclusively basaltic indicating that the limestone had become completely engulfed by volcanic material. In a few areas unbroken basalt has survived. For example, a pile of large pillow-shaped bodies is exposed at SC245670 (Figure 5.12a). Such pillow lavas have been observed forming below water in modern volcanic areas such as Iceland. The lava emerges from fissures as if it were being squeezed from huge toothpaste tubes. The surrounding sea water rapidly cools the outer surface of each pillow so that it solidifies, but it can continue to move as the molten basalt inside the pillow continues to flow. At SC247664 only the shattered remains of pillows remain, probably due to the explosive release of gas after they began to cool and solidify. Pea-sized gas bubbles ('vesicles', Figure 5.12b) occur throughout the basalt and some of the clasts within the agglomerate are so rich in bubbles that they form pumice.

Between SC252663 and Scarlett Point thick walls, sheets and plugs of

Figure 5.11 *(a) Volcanic ash (agglomerate) within the Scarlett Volcanic Formation (SC245672). Note the pebble-sized pieces of limestone and basalt within the ash which are evidence of the explosive nature of the eruption. (b) Volcanic ash (agglomerate) overlying basaltic lava flows (SC253662). The contact is visible approximately 0.5 m below the hammer which is itself 0.4 m long.*

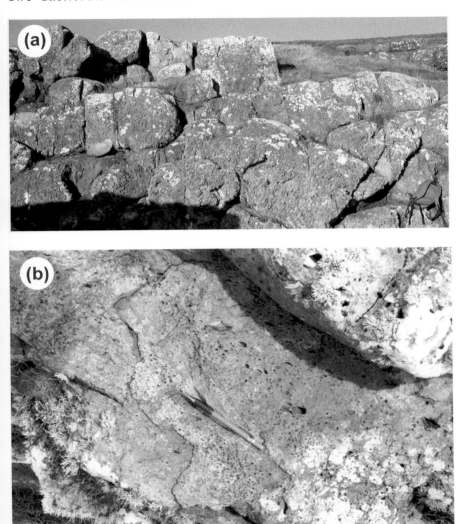

Figure 5.12 *(a) Pillow lavas in the Scarlett Volcanic Formation (SC245670). (b) Gas bubbles (vesicles) preserved within basalt lava. Note pencil for scale.*

basalt are exposed, possibly indicating that the volcano had by this time emerged above sea level as an island so that magma flowed to surface without exploding or forming pillows. Parallel layers of vesicles record the flow direction of the basalt. Undulations can be seen on the surface of one of the walls at SC252663 caused by differential movement between molten basalt flowing to surface and the partially solidified skin. In one place, one of the walls of basalt bends over to become horizontal, indicating that it was extruded up and out onto the contemporary volcanic surface.

The walls of basalt are orientated between north–south and north-west–southeast reflecting the orientation of fissures developed due to tensional stresses. This stress was probably local, resulting from settling of the volcano as the underlying magma chamber was emptied, because the trend of these fissures is different to the faults associated with formation of the rift. Most of the faults at Langness, Port St Mary and Poyllvaaish are orientated in a different direction (east–west, northeast–southwest and north–south), interpreted as indicating that regional extension was approximately northwest–southeast[33]. In contrast, the extension direction within the Scarlett Volcanic Formation appears to have been roughly east-north-east to west-southwest. The most easterly and youngest part of the Scarlett Volcanic Formation is The Stack. This dome-shaped rock probably represents a volcanic vent. The basalt that now plugs it shows columnar jointing – shrinkage cracks that develop when lava cools, similar to the Giant's Causeway in Northern Ireland.

SUMMARY

The Castletown Limestones were deposited over a period of 25 million years during the early Carboniferous, a time when the giant continent of Pangaea was slowly rifting apart. The influence of fluctuating sea levels is clearly recorded. The oldest rocks, the Langness Conglomerate, were deposited on land. However, with rising sea levels a tropical sea became established in which a variety of limestones were deposited in an environment varying from shallow-water lagoons and algal reefs to deep-water conditions. Towards the end of the early Carboniferous the area was affected by basaltic eruptions, which eventually built a volcanic island composed of ash and lava.

Notes

1   P.J. Newman, 'The geology and hydrocarbon potential of the Peel and Solway Basins, East Irish Sea', *Journal of Petroleum Geology*, 22 (1999b), 305–324.

2   D.G. Quirk, S. Roy, I. Knott, J. Redfern and L. Hill, 'Petroleum geology and future hydrocarbon potential of the Irish Sea', *Journal of Petroleum Geology*, 22 (1999b), 243–260.

3   R.A Chadwick, D.I. Jackson, R.P. Barnes, G.S. Kimbell, H. Johnson, R.C. Chiverrell, G.S.P. Thomas, N.S. Jones, N.J. Riley, E.A. Pickett, B. Young, D.W. Holliday, D.F. Ball, S.G. Molyneux, D. Long, G.M. Power and D.H. Roberts, *Geology of the Isle of Man and its offshore area*, British Geological Survey Research Report, RR/01/06 (2001), 143.

4   D.G. Quirk and G.S. Kimbell, 'Structural evolution of the Isle of Man and central part of the Irish Sea', in N.S. Meadows, S.P. Trueblood, N. Hardman and G. Cowan (eds), *Petroleum geology of the Irish Sea and adjacent areas*, Geological Society of London Special Publication, 124 (1997), 135–159.

5   D.G. Quirk and G.S. Kimbell (1997).

6   D.G. Quirk *et al.* (1999b).

7   G.W. Lamplugh, *The geology of the Isle of Man*, Memoir of the Geological Survey of the United Kingdom (1903); B. Smith, 'Borings through the glacial drifts in the northern part of the Isle of Man', *Summary of Progress of the Geological Survey*, 3 (1931), 14–23; D.G. Quirk and G.S. Kimbell (1997).

8   D.I. Jackson, A.A. Jackson, D. Evans, R.T.R. Wingfield, R.P. Barnes and M.J. Arthur, *United Kingdom offshore regional report: the geology of the Irish Sea*, HMSO, London (1995), 123.

9   D.G. Quirk and G.S. Kimbell (1997).

10   D.G. Quirk *et al.* (1999b).

11   R.A Chadwick *et al.* (2001).

12   J.G. Cumming, 'On the geology of the Isle of Man', *Quarterly Journal of the Geological Society of London*, 2 (1846), 317–348.

13   G.W. Lamplugh (1903).

14   H.P. Lewis, 'The Avonian succession in the south of the Isle of Man', *Quarterly Journal of the Geological Society of London*, 86 (1930), 234–290.

15   J.A.D. Dickson, T.D. Ford and A. Swift, 'The stratigraphy of the Carboniferous rocks around Castletown, Isle of Man', *Proceedings of the Yorkshire Geological Society*, 35 (1987), 203–229.

16   R.A. Chadwick *et al.* (2001).

17   J.A.D. Dickson *et al.* (1987); R.A. Chadwick *et al.* (2001).

18   J.A.D. Dickson *et al.* (1987).

19   *Ibid.*

20   *Ibid.*

21   R.A. Chadwick *et al.* (2001).

22   *Ibid.*

23   J.A.D. Dickson *et al.* (1987).

24   R.A. Chadwick *et al.* (2001).

25   *Ibid.*

26   J.A.D. Dickson *et al.* (1987).

27   R.A. Chadwick *et al.* (2001).

28   *Ibid.*

29   J.A.D. Dickson *et al.* (1987).

30   D.G. Quirk, T.D. Ford, J.A. King, I.L. Roberts, R.B. Postance and I. Odell, 'Enigmatic boulders and syn-sedimentary faulting in the Carboniferous limestone of the Isle of Man', *Proceedings of the Yorkshire Geological Society*, 48 (1990), 99–113.

31   P.E. Ahlberg and M.I. Coates, 'There's a ratfish in our cellar!', *Geology Today*, 13 (1997), 22–23.

32   G.P. Durant and C. Grant, 'The Scarlett Volcanic Complex, Isle of Man: a shallow-water submarine volcanic pile', *Geological Society of London Newsletter*, 14 (1985), 46.

33   D.G. Quirk and G.S. Kimbell (1997).

6 The Missing Periods

DAVE QUIRK and GEOFF THOMAS

The youngest sedimentary rocks exposed on the Isle of Man are the Lower Carboniferous limestones around Castletown, deposited between 354 Ma and 327 Ma. Thus, a significant part of the geological record since then is hidden, either (1) because younger rocks are buried beneath the surface, (2) they were never deposited in the first place, or (3) they have been removed by later erosion. Although the geological events over much of the last 330 million years cannot be observed directly on the island, the history can be inferred from rocks exposed in other areas around the margins of the Irish Sea Basin and pieced together from data acquired during oil and gas exploration offshore (Figure 6.1). This chapter briefly reviews the significant geological events of this time period and how they might have affected the island.

LATE CARBONIFEROUS (327–290 Ma)

The north of the island is almost entirely composed of unconsolidated glacial sediments deposited over the last 400,000 years during the Quaternary period. Buried beneath them in the sub-surface are solid rocks that extend outwards below the floor of the Solway Firth. Boreholes drilled in the northern plain show that the solid rocks in the sub-surface dip in a general sense to the north-east so that, moving from the edge of the uplands northwards towards the Point of Ayre, the Quaternary sediments are underlain by increasingly younger rocks; initially the Manx Group, then Carboniferous, Permian and finally Triassic (Figure 6.2).

The concealed Carboniferous rocks in the north of the island comprise Dinantian limestones, similar to those exposed around Castletown, overlain by Namurian and Westphalian[1] (Upper Carboniferous) shales and sandstones, typical of those found in and around a delta. As discussed in Chapter 5, the Dinantian limestones were deposited in relatively shallow water within newly formed rift basins. The organisms that produced the limestone depended on the existence of relatively clear water that was in part due to the relatively narrow, faulted shape of the rift basins. The change from limestone at the start of the Namurian marks the time when rifting ceased and more regional subsidence took over as the crust began to cool. The enlargement of the basins, coupled with a change to a wetter

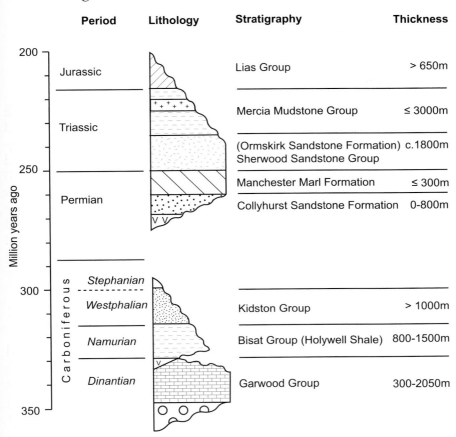

Figure 6.1 *Generalised geological column for the East Irish Sea Basin. The gap separating Carboniferous rocks from Permian-Triassic rocks represents a period of uplift in the late Carboniferous–early Permian marked by an unconformity. The Dinantian is predominantly limestones with conglomerates at the base (e.g., Langness) and occasional volcanic rocks (V) at the top (e.g., Scarlett Point). The Namurian is mudstone with occasional sandstones and contains the organic-rich Holywell Shale, the principal source rock for oil and gas in the basin. The Westphalian and Stephanian are mostly sandstone but contain coal. The Collyhurst Sandstone Formation is often conglomeratic and occasional volcanic rocks are present. The Manchester Marl comprises mudstone with some dolomite, anhydrite and salt. The Sherwood Sandstone consists of the St Bees Sandstone and the Ormskirk Sandstone, the reservoir for oil and gas in the East Irish Sea. The Mercia Mudstone contains significant amounts of salt and the Lias Group is mudstone.*

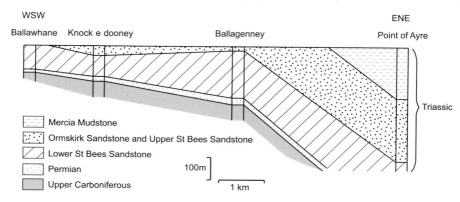

Figure 6.2 *Simplified geological cross-section through boreholes drilled along the northern coast of the Isle of Man. The Upper Carboniferous and Permian rocks consist mostly of mudstones and sandstones.*

climate, allowed major rivers to become established and thereby feed large amounts of sediments to these basins. The shallow, clear water needed by the organisms that produced limestone was lost and the reefs quickly died out. During this time it appears that the Isle of Man, and its north-eastern extension towards the Lake District, was completely submerged.

The earliest Upper Carboniferous sediments are organic-rich mudstones which have sourced much of the oil and gas in the East Irish Sea, but these are overlain by increasing amounts of sand brought in by rivers and deltas. Around much of northern Europe, Namurian (327–315 Ma) to Westphalian (315–303 Ma) sediments record an evolution from shale basin to river delta to coastal plain. In an overall sense, this means that enough sediment was brought in from the hinterland to fill the basins. Wide areas of delta and coastal plain lay close to sea level and upon them large forested swamps developed, similar to modern-day mangrove swamps. Stagnant conditions meant that layers of dead vegetation accumulated to form peat and later coal as they were buried. Although coal has not been discovered beneath the northern plain of the Isle of Man, it is present in boreholes in the East Irish Sea.

By the end of the Carboniferous (the Stephanian epoch, 303–290 Ma) the continuing influx of sediment from rivers had built the land surface in most of the basins to a height well above sea level. Continued northwards drift of Pangaea had brought the Isle of Man to a position approximately 15° north of the equator[2] where drier conditions meant that red beds developed. Although these are no longer present on the Isle of Man, the sediments were similar to those formed 110 million years earlier in the

Devonian, when the Peel Group was deposited at a similar latitude south of the equator (see Chapter 4).

THE VARISCAN OROGENY (320–290 Ma)

The Caledonian mountain belt was formed in the late Silurian when a fragment of the giant southern continent of Gondwana, known as Eastern Avalonia, moved northwards and collided with Laurentia and Baltica creating northern Europe (Chapter 3). A new mountain belt developed during the late Carboniferous when the main part of Gondwana collided with northern Europe. This event is called the 'Variscan Orogeny' and produced the giant equatorial continent of Pangaea, of which the Isle of Man formed a part. The event caused mild compression in the Irish Sea area with some folds[3] although these structures are largely overprinted by the later effects of rifting and uplift in the Permian. The Variscan Orogeny, and the Caledonian Orogeny before it, can therefore be regarded as a continuum involving the breakup of one supercontinent in the early Palaeozoic (Gondwana) and the assembly of another in the late Palaeozoic (Pangaea).

PERMO-TRIASSIC (290–206 Ma)

Continued drift northwards from the equator in early Carboniferous times meant that by the beginning of the Permian, 290 Ma, Pangaea lay at a latitude equivalent to the present-day Sahara. This change generated what has been described as 'one of the great deserts of world history'[4] across much of the south of Pangaea, including what is now Britain and western Europe. During the Permian the region began to rift again leading to uplift, fault activity and volcanism[5], similar to what happened during the early Carboniferous. Significant erosion occurred where uplift was greatest with removal of large amounts of Upper Carboniferous strata[6]. During much of this time the Isle of Man lay adjacent to a major rift system that extended from the English Channel, through Cheshire, the East Irish Sea and the North Channel to western Scotland. The rift system appears to have been partly mirrored by the current outline of the Irish Sea as this is where Permian and Triassic sediments are preserved today but it is uncertain how much, if any, have been removed in areas such as the Isle of Man by later erosion. Different fault trends were active including a new northwest to southeast set as well as the old northeast to southwest set that parallels pre-existing Caledonian and early Carboniferous structures.

By the Late Permian rifting ceased and the area around the Isle of Man began to subside again as the crust cooled. Thick Permo-Triassic sediments consisting of reddened sandstones and mudstones were deposited by rivers, sand dunes and shallow lakes with beds of salt and anhydrite (calcium sulphate) formed as a result of evaporation ('evaporites'). Such sediments indicate that the climate was hot and arid and similar to present-day Arizona. Comparable sediments developed over large parts of Pangaea at this time.

Permian and Triassic rocks are not exposed on the Isle of Man but have been found in boreholes beneath the northern plain and more particularly offshore where more than 4 km of strata are preserved in the middle of the East Irish Sea, 35 km east of Laxey[7] (Figure 6.3) and west of the island in the Peel Basin (Figure 6.4). Although much of the present-day upland area of the Isle of Man was probably exposed at the time, Permo-Triassic strata do extend into northwest England where the names used to subdivide the rocks originate: from oldest to youngest, the Collyhurst Sandstone

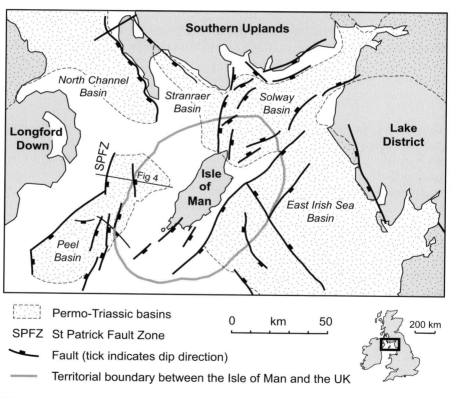

Figure 6.3 *Location map showing sedimentary basins of the Irish Sea. Redrafted from P.J. Newman (1999).*

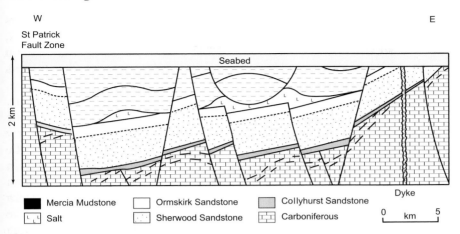

Figure 6.4 *Simplified west–east cross-section through the northern end of the Peel Basin, west of the Isle of Man, based on interpretation of seismic data. Note: the large faults offsetting the Mercia Mudstone are post-Triassic, probably late Jurassic, associated with a rifting event that affected much of northern Europe. The dyke is early Tertiary in age. The location of the cross-section is shown on Figure 6.3.*

Formation, Manchester Marl Formation, Sherwood Sandstone Group[8] and Mercia Mudstone Group[9]. Due to an absence of fossils they are hard to date, but, by comparison with other areas, the Collyhurst Sandstone and Manchester Marl are Permian in age and the Sherwood Sandstone and Mercia Mudstone are Triassic.

The Permian period represents an interval of time from 290 Ma to 248 Ma but sediments are only preserved in the latter part, initially red beds deposited on land, collectively known as the Collyhurst Sandstone, and overlain by evaporites and mudstones belonging to the Manchester Marl Formation (Figure 6.1). Some of the sandstones in the Collyhurst Sandstone Formation contain evidence that the sand was moved by a prevailing wind blowing from the east or east-northeast. Sand was also deposited by rivers originating from local sources, probably including exposed hills in the Isle of Man. The change to mudstones and evaporites of the Manchester Marl Formation reflects an intermittent rise in the water table such that at times it lay above the land surface so that an inland sea was present but at other times the sea had dried out and the water table lay below the surface. The environment was similar to the present-day coast of the United Arab Emirates, but the alternation in the height of the water table may in part reflect variations between drier and wetter climates caused by variations in the amount of ice stored at the southern pole on Pangaea.

By the start of the Triassic (248 Ma), northwest Europe had drifted northwards to approximately 25°N, but the climate remained semi-arid. Although the Triassic is often regarded as a time of continued rifting there is in fact little evidence for active extension[10]. Instead, subsidence appears to have been driven by cooling of the crust following rifting in the Permian. A major river system became established running northwards through the East Irish Sea area[11]. This 'Budleighhensis River' of Wills[12], carried considerable quantities of sediment from its source area in the Variscan mountains of Brittany into the East Irish Sea Basin via Cheshire and the West Midlands. The deposits of this river, which make up a significant part of the Sherwood Sandstone Group[13] (Figure 6.1), around 2,000 m thick to the east of the Isle of Man, forms the lower part of the Triassic. The upper part of the Sherwood Sandstone, known as the Ormskirk Sandstone, contains more wind-derived ('aeolian') sandstone beds which are highly porous due to the clean, rounded nature of air-blown sand grains. These aeolian sandstones act as excellent reservoir rocks for oil and gas in the East Irish Sea (see Chapter 10). By 242 Ma, the Budleighhensis River had almost disappeared due to a combination of rising water tables and flat topography so that evaporites and mudstones were the principal deposits. These sediments make up the Mercia Mudstone Group which is up to 3,000 m thick in the East Irish Sea.

JURASSIC (206–144 Ma)

At the start of the Jurassic (206 Ma) Britain lay approximately 30°N of the equator with a climate that was sub-tropical. The supercontinent of Pangaea, comprising almost all the land surface of the Earth, was centred about the equator. However, the Earth is constantly moving due to the effects of radioactive heating in the mantle so that Pangaea was too large to remain stable for long. Therefore, during the Jurassic rifting started to affect the central part of northwest Europe, initially leading to the formation of the North Sea in the early Cretaceous and, ultimately, to the North Atlantic in the late Cretaceous when Pangaea began to split apart fully. However, before the onset of rifting, sea water flooded across most of Britain, now reduced to a region of low relief by the effects of erosion and thermal subsidence, leading to the widespread deposition of marine mudstones. A small remnant of these mudstones is preserved in the centre of the East Irish Sea (Lias Group, Figure 6.1), the rest having been removed during uplift and erosion in the Jurassic and Tertiary. Similar to the early

Carboniferous and early Permian, the late Jurassic was a time when rifting affected much of northern Europe. Although no Upper Jurassic rocks are preserved in the Irish Sea area, major faults do appear to have been active at this time[14], suggesting that rifting occurred here also (Figure 6.4). These periods of rifting represent failed attempts to form the North Atlantic Ocean. The North Atlantic actually first opened further west in mid to late Cretaceous times.

CRETACEOUS (144–65 Ma)

Rifting probably ceased at the end of the Jurassic and was followed by renewed thermal subsidence in the Cretaceous. However, at approximately 100 Ma, at the start of the Late Cretaceous, the southern Atlantic started to open, an event which was associated with a global rise in sea level causing inundation of low-lying areas. Relatively warm waters and a general absence of river-borne sediment allowed chalk, a type of limestone sediment, to accumulate over large parts of northwest Europe, including the British Isles. Chalk consists of microscopic shells of plankton that flourished in open sea and these built up thicknesses of often hundreds of metres. Beyond the North Sea, much of the chalk has been removed by erosion, but it is still preserved along the North Antrim coast in Northern Ireland and almost certainly similar deposits once covered the Irish Sea and Isle of Man.

TERTIARY (65–1.6 Ma)

At the start of the Tertiary (65 Ma) the North Atlantic had formed and North America began to drift away from Europe. At approximately 60 Ma, during the Palaeocene, much of the British Isles was uplifted leading to widespread erosion. In the Irish Sea area, 1–3 km of sediment were stripped off[15] and the present-day topography and drainage pattern on the Isle of Man records to a greater or lesser degree the effect of this uplift and erosion.

The Palaeocene uplift event coincided with a period of high heat flow and magmatic activity in northwest Europe which was associated with the formation of Iceland and an increase in the rate of oceanic spreading in the North Atlantic[16]. Around northern Britain, numerous basalt-filled fissures ('dolerite dykes', Figure 6.5) developed in the sub-surface. These are vertical[17] and are orientated west-northwest to east-southeast and contain a glassy, green-yellow mineral known as olivine. Their chemistry is that of a type of basalt known as tholeiite which is produced in rifted oceanic areas such as Iceland. They increase in number towards Northern Ireland and

Figure 6.5 *Tertiary dolerite dyke cutting northwest to southeast across limestones at Poyllvaaish (SC244675). Here it is 75 cm wide but it continues downwards at least to the base of the crust, approximately 30 km below the surface.*

the Hebrides where fissure eruptions and volcanoes occurred at this time as the magma reached surface. A well-known example is the basalt lava of the Giant's Causeway.

Although the dykes are usually no more than a few metres wide (Figure 6.5), they can often be several tens of kilometres long and probably extend at least down to the base of the crust, approximately 30 km below surface. As they are relatively rich in iron, they are magnetic and can be mapped using magnetic detectors towed behind a low-flying aircraft[18] (Figure 6.6). The dykes have a scattered but widespread distribution in the Irish Sea region and can be mapped by their magnetic signature showing that they radiate from a volcanic centre in County Antrim, Northern Ireland, where they have been dated between 61 Ma and 53 Ma[19].

The largest dolerite dyke in the Isle of Man, the Fleetwood Dyke, comes onshore at Port Mooar (Figure 6.6) where it is 12 m wide. Further east, in the offshore, it splits into several sheets, some of which have been drilled inadvertently by Esso when exploring for oil and gas[20]. Between Port Mooar and Maughold Head, Manx Group rocks have been altered and mineralised with haematite and quartz thought to be related to hydrothermal fluids active at the same time as the dykes were formed[21].

Despite the fact that uplift in the Palaeocene seems to be related to thermal doming[22], the crust has not subsided since then as would normally be expected because of the effects of cooling. The most likely explanation is that a significant amount of magma was trapped at the base of the crust in a process known as underplating, essentially jacking up the crust[23]. An additional effect is that so much erosion occurred during uplift (see below) that sufficient load was taken off the crust to compensate, at least in part, for later cooling.

Although not present on the Isle of Man, Tertiary sediments younger than the Palaeocene are exposed in Lough Neagh in Northern Ireland and comprise lacustrine clays, sands and brown coals dated to the Oligocene (34–24 Ma). Similar sediments are scattered around the southern Irish Sea, in Tremadoc Bay in Wales and in southwest England. They are interpreted as having been deposited in lakes and swamps that formed part of a drainage system flowing to the southwest towards the Celtic Sea[24]. At the time, the climate was relatively humid.

There is evidence that the Irish Sea region was subject to a limited amount of compression between 25 Ma and 20 Ma[25], during the early Miocene, related to the formation of the Alps as Africa collided with Europe. This is thought to have caused some additional uplift around the Isle of Man.

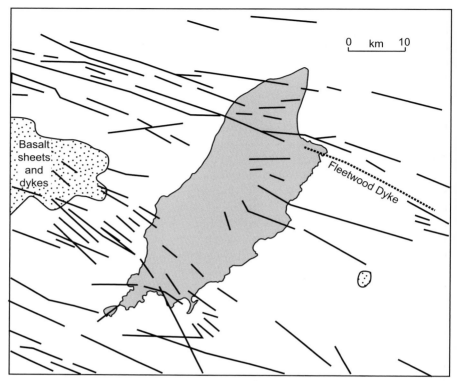

Figure 6.6 *Location of probable Tertiary igneous features around the Isle of Man identified from aeromagnetic data, after R.A.Chadwick et al. (2001).*

Tertiary Erosional History

Throughout the Tertiary, but particularly following uplift in the Palaeocene and Miocene, erosion was intense and virtually all the previous cover of Triassic, Jurassic and Cretaceous rocks was removed from onshore areas of northern Britain. Estimates of the amount of erosion have been deduced from a technique known as apatite fission track analysis which is a way of measuring the amount of time a rock has been at temperatures of less than 120 °C based on the effects of radioactivity on crystals in the rock. Lewis *et al.*[26], Holliday[27] and Green[28] have shown from apatite fission track analysis of Lower Palaeozoic, Carboniferous, Permian and Triassic rocks at outcrop and in boreholes, that much of the present-day surface around the Irish Sea was at temperatures of 70–120 °C until the early Tertiary. The interpretation is that 2–3 km of sediment have been removed by erosion during the Tertiary, therefore exposing the rocks that were previously buried to these temperatures[29]. Modern drainage patterns on the Isle of Man, notably the Central Valley, must in part reflect the influence of a geology now removed, particularly Permian and Jurassic rift-related faults[30].

Geomorphologists have long recognised that much of upland Britain displays traces of flat or gently undulating surfaces that truncate the often highly deformed rocks beneath them. The Isle of Man is no exception. Temple[31] has mapped a series of nine flat surfaces, or supposed terraces, around the margins of the uplands of the island, ranging in height from 15 m to 200 m above sea level. They are best seen as a suite of indistinct surfaces running down the eastern coastal plateau. Above 200 m, and reaching almost the highest summit on the island, is a further set of surfaces, plainly visible at Sky Hill, Gob y Volley and astride the ridge from Slieau Curn to Sartfell. In these cases the surfaces, though often indistinct, clearly truncate the complex folds of the Manx Group. It is possible, but by no means certain, that these surfaces are related to temporary erosional levels reached during progressive uplift in the Tertiary.

There is no doubt that Tertiary erosion took place, but exactly how and when and, indeed, whether Tertiary landforms can be recognised in the landscape at all, has been a matter of considerable discussion for more than a century[32]. In the nineteenth century 'exhumation' was the process in vogue with flat topographic surfaces seen as relic marine platforms caused by wave erosion during Cretaceous basin flooding. Later, largely as a reaction to the application of the Davisian model of landscape evolution to Britain[33], the surfaces were interpreted as due to subaerial fluvial activity. In the twentieth century, the explanation shifted back towards either marine erosion or a combination of marine and subaerial erosion. Thus, Temple[34] regarded the lower group of surfaces in the island, those below 200 m, as marine and the upper as subaerial. The subsequent recognition that Britain was located in relatively low latitudes during the early Tertiary led to the idea that the flat topographic surfaces were formed as a result of deep tropical weathering followed by erosion, as 'etchplains'. Another explanation was that erosion occurred in a semi-arid climate with hill slopes retreating in parallel to leave behind a flat surface known as a 'pediplain'. However, the complete lack of Tertiary sediment in the Isle of Man means that interpretations of the origin are little more than speculation. Instead it makes more sense to recognise that the Isle of Man owes its overall shape to an inheritance of Caledonian, Carboniferous, Permian and Jurassic structures such as faults and, perhaps, some of its large-scale slope form to an inheritance of Tertiary erosion surface planation, however formed. On the smaller scale, the landscape is very much a response to the subsequent effects of major cold climate processes in the Quaternary, as will be illustrated in later chapters.

Notes

1   The Namurian and Westphalian are also known collectively as the Silesian epoch.
2   P.A. Ziegler, *Evolution of Laurussia*, Kluwer Academic Publishers, Dordrecht (1989), 102.
3   D.G. Quirk and G.S. Kimbell, 'Structural evolution of the Isle of Man and central part of the Irish Sea', in N.S. Meadows, S.P. Trueblood, N. Hardman and G. Cowan (eds), *Petroleum geology of the Irish Sea and adjacent areas*, Geological Society of London Special Publication 124, (1997), 135–159.
4   D.B. Smith and J.C.M. Taylor, 'Permian', in J.C.W. Cope, J.K. Ingham and P.F. Rawson (eds), *Atlas of palaeogeography and lithofacies*, Memoir of the Geological Society of London (1992).
5   D.G. Quirk and G.S. Kimbell (1997).
6   D.G. Quirk, S. Roy, I. Knott, J. Redfern and L. Hill, 'Petroleum geology and future hydrocarbon potential of the Irish Sea', *Journal of Petroleum Geology*, 22 (1999b), 243–260.
7   R.A. Chadwick, D.I. Jackson, R.P. Barnes, G.S. Kimbell, H. Johnson, R.C. Chiverrell, G.S.P. Thomas, N.S. Jones, N.J. Riley, E.A. Pickett, B. Young, D.W. Holliday, D.F. Ball, S. Molyneux, D. Long, G.M. Power and D. Roberts, *Geology of the Isle of Man and its offshore area*, British Geological Survey Research Report, RR/01/06 (2001), 143.
8   Including the St Bees and Ormskirk sandstones.
9   Including large amounts of salt.
10   D.G. Quirk *et al.* (1999b).
11   N.S. Meadows and A. Beach, 'Controls on reservoir quality in the Triassic Sherwood Sandstone of the Irish Sea', in J.R. Parker (ed.), *Petroleum geology of northwest Europe: Proceedings of the 4th Conference*, The Geological Society of London (1993), 823–833.
12   L. Wills, 'The Triassic succession in the central Midlands in its regional setting', *Quarterly Journal of the Geological Society of London*, 126 (1970), 225–285.
13   Including the St Bees and Ormskirk sandstones.
14   D.G. Quirk and G.S. Kimbell (1997).
15   C.L.E. Lewis, P.F. Green, A. Carter and A.J. Hurford, 'Elevated K/T Cretaceous to early Tertiary palaeotemperatures throughout NW England: three kms of Tertiary erosion?', *Earth and Planetary Science Letters*, 112 (1992), 131–145; D.W. Holliday, 'Mesozoic cover over northern England: interpretation of apatite fission-track data', *Journal of the Geological Society of London*, 150 (1993), 657–660; R.A. Chadwick, G.A. Kirby and H.E. Baily, 'The post-Triassic structural evolution of north-west England and adjacent parts of the East Irish Sea, *Proceedings of the Yorkshire Geological Society*, 50 (1994), 91–102.
16   R.S. White, 'A hot-spot model for early Cenozoic volcanism in the North Atlantic', in L.M. Parsons and C.A. Morton (eds), *Early Cenozoic volcanism and the opening of the North Atlantic*, Geological Society of London Special Publication, 39 (1988), 3–13; P.A. Nadin and N.J. Kuznir, 'Palaeocene uplift and Eocene subsidence in the northern North Sea Basin from 2D forward and reverse stratigraphic modelling', *Journal of the Geological Society of London*, 152 (1995), 833–848.

17   In the Isle of Man Tertiary dykes often dip very steeply to the north-northeast suggesting the island may have been tilted slightly some time after their formation.

18   D.G. Quirk and G.S. Kimbell (1997).

19   A.E. Mussett, P. Dagley, and R.R. Skelhorn, 'Time and duration of activity in the British Tertiary Igneous Province', in A.C. Morton and L.M. Parsons (eds), *Early Tertiary volcanism and the opening of the NE Atlantic*, Geological Society of London Special Publication 39 (1988); J.A. Gamble, R.J. Wysoczanski and I.G. Meighant, 'Constrains on the British Tertiary Volcanic Province from ion microprobe U-Pb (SHRIMP) ages for acid igneous rocks from NE Ireland', *Journal of the Geological Society of London*, 156 (1999), 291–299.

20   G. Arter and S.W. Fagin, 'The Fleetwood Dyke and the Tynwald Fault Zone, Block 113/27, East Irish Sea Basin', 835–843 in J.R. Parker (ed.), *Petroleum Geology of NW Europe: Proceedings of the 4th Conference*, The Geological Society of London (1993), 835–843.

21   D.G. Quirk and G.S. Kimbell (1997).

22   R.S. White (1988); P.A. Nadin and N.J. Kuznir (1995).

23   J. Brodie and N. White, 'Sedimentary inversion caused by igneous underplating: northwest European continental shelf', *Geology*, 22 (1994), 147–150; D.G. Quirk and G.S. Kimbell (1997).

24   J.W. Murray, 'Palaeogene and Neogene', in J.C.W. Cope, J.K. Ingham and P.F. Rawson (eds), *Atlas of palaeography and lithofacies*, Memoir of the Geological Society of London (1993), 141–147.

25   P.J. Newman, 'The geology and hydrocarbon habitat of the Peel and Solway Basins', *Journal of Petroleum Geology*, 22 (1999a), 265–284.

26   C.L.E. Lewis *et al.* (1992).

27   D.W. Holliday (1993).

28   P.F. Green, I.R. Duddy and R.J. Bray, 'Variation in thermal history styles around the Irish Sea and adjacent areas: implications for hydrocarbon occurrence and tectonic evolution', in N.S. Meadows, S.P. Trueblood, N. Hardman and G. Cowan (eds), *Petroleum Geology of the Irish Sea and adjacent areas*, Geological Society of London Special Publication, 124 (1997), 73–93.

29   T.P. Bushell, 'Reservoir geology of the Morecombe field', in J. Brooks, J. Gogg and B. Van Hoorn (eds), *Habitat of Palaeozoic Gas in northwest Europe*, Geological Society of London Special Publication, 23 (1986), 189–208.

30   D.G. Quirk and G.S. Kimbell (1997).

31   P.H. Temple, *Some aspects of the geomorphology of the Isle of Man*, unpublished MA thesis, University of Liverpool (1960).

32   D. Huddart, 'Pre-Quaternary Landscape development', in D. Huddart and N.F. Glasser (eds), *Quaternary of Northern England*, Geological Conservation Review Series, 25 (2002), Joint Nature Conservation Committee, Peterborough, 10–30.

33   W.M. Davis, 'The development of certain English rivers', *Geographical Journal*, 5 (1895), 127–146.

34   P.H. Temple (1960).

7   The Ice Age

GEOFF THOMAS, RICHARD CHIVERRELL,
DAVE HUDDART, DAVID LONG and DAVID ROBERTS

INTRODUCTION

After tracing the tortured geological history of the Isle of Man over the last 500 million years, it might seem an extravagance to devote a substantial portion of this book to merely the last million years or so. This period, known as the Quaternary, or more informally as the Ice Age, is important, however, for a number of reasons. Firstly, it is the period in which our own species, *Homo sapiens*, evolved. The period is characterised by repeated fluctuations in world temperature that gave rise to the successive growth and decay of large continental icesheets, major shifts in vegetation zones, the large-scale migration of fauna and flora and continuous variation in sea level. The rapidity of these changes may, consequently, have stimulated rapid hominid evolution by a need to adapt to changing environments, and it can be argued that had the recent geological past been quieter our progress as a species may have been much slower. The effects of the Quaternary consequently provide a fundamental framework for understanding the archaeological record, the subject of volume 2 of this history.

A second, more local reason, is that most of the medium- and small-scale landforms of the island are a direct result of the effects of environmental changes during the Quaternary. The largest example is the great northern plain. Before the last glaciation the island terminated along the rock escarpment between Ramsey and Kirk Michael with the sea at its foot. During the last glaciation the island was overrun by an icesheet moving south from Scotland causing great quantities of glacial debris to be banked against the escarpment. The Plain of Ayre is thus a direct gift from Quaternary glaciation. Elsewhere almost all the smaller landforms are a result of glacial or paraglacial processes. These include the drumlin fields around Ballasalla, formed by moulding beneath a rapidly flowing icesheet; the Bride Hills, a large arcuate moraine ridge formed during retreat of the last icesheet; the Lhen trench, a winding channel created by meltwater draining from the retreating icesheet; and the large alluvial fans that drain from the northern uplands at Glen Auldyn, Sulby and Ballaugh, all a response to changing climatic conditions and river regime after the icesheet had departed. Even the general expression of Manx upland scenery, characterised by gently rolling hill slopes everywhere clothed with a smooth cover of local drift, is a consequence of a severe frost climate that lasted for some 5,000 years after the ice had gone.

A third reason is heritage. Within its small area the island displays a range of glacial phenomena barely matched elsewhere in Britain. In addition to almost every variety of glacial landform, including moraines, ice-front alluvial fans, outwash sandur, kettle holes and subglacial channel systems, it also has excellent exposure of almost every type of glacial deposit. Some of the largest and most complex glaciotectonic structures in Britain also occur, at Shellag Point. Added to these are excellent exposures of late and post-glacial organic sediments, both terrestrial and marine, containing a rich record of fossil fauna and flora including the Giant Deer. Also, beneath the northern plain, the island records one of the thickest Quaternary depositional sequences in Britain, with glacial and interglacial deposits to at least 145 m below sea level and a maximum thickness of the order of 250 m. Much of the upper part of this thickness is exposed in the 25 km of almost continuous cliff section bounding the northern plain and these sections exhibit, as Kendall[1] put it, a glacial sequence of such diverse character that it is probably unsurpassed in Britain.

This chapter begins by briefly reviewing the nature of the Quaternary climatic record in order to put the events in the Isle of Man into some context. It then examines the evidence for glaciation in various parts of the island and ends by tracing a chronological and environmental reconstruction of the events that have taken place. Although the Quaternary extends up to modern times, the chapter deals only with events up to the retreat of the last glaciation from the island, approximately 15,000 years ago. Retreat was followed by a very complex period of climatic change during which the island's environment rapidly readjusted to cold, but non-glacial conditions. This period, known as the Late Glacial, lasted from approximately 15,000 to 11,500 years ago and is dealt with in Chapter 8. The period from approximately 11,500 years ago to the present time, known as the Holocene, saw a rapid return to temperate interglacial conditions, the development of the island's natural vegetation and the ultimate advent of Man. It is dealt with in Chapter 9.

Quaternary climatic history

Although once regarded as a unique event it is now evident that large-scale glaciation is a normal part of the long-term geological cycle[2]. From a peak in the Palaeocene at approximately 55 Ma (Figure 7.1a), world temperature has slowly declined towards the present day. By 35 Ma an ice cap had formed over the Antarctica and the first evidence of large-scale glaciation in Europe and North America occurs at *circa* 2.6 Ma, a date used here to define the base of the Quaternary and separate it from the Tertiary[3]. Most of our data on glacial episodes are derived from investigations in deep ocean basins. These provide an almost continuous record of sedimentation dating back to the time of the creation of the ocean by plate tectonic movement. Variations in the ratio of the oxygen isotopes $^{16}O/^{18}O$ incorporated in foraminifera within the sediments are a response to changing environmental conditions in the overlying water column. The ^{16}O isotope is lighter and evaporates more rapidly than ^{18}O. During a cold period the evaporated ^{16}O is trapped in snow falling on icesheets and does not return to the oceans. The ocean thus becomes enriched with the remaining ^{18}O. During a warm period the ^{16}O returns to the oceans as the icesheets melt and the balance is restored. Thus, high levels of ^{18}O in fossil foraminifera indicate cold, glacial conditions at the time of deposition and low levels indicate warm, non-glacial conditions. The $^{18}O/^{16}O$ ratio therefore provides a proxy for the relative volume of glacier ice on the surface of the Earth.

Cores from ocean sediments allow the construction of isotope curves showing the volume of glacier ice over time. The volume of glacier ice in turn determines the height of global sea level because during a glacial stage water is locked up on the land surface and sea level falls; whilst during a warm stage the water returns to the oceans and sea level rises. An isotope curve is therefore an indicator of variations in the volume of glacier ice, the height of the sea and, by implication, world temperature change. Figure 7.1b shows the variations in $^{16}O/^{18}O$ from a core through oceanic sediments in the mid Pacific[4] that stretches back to the base of the Quaternary at 2.6 Ma, and it shows a strikingly regular cyclicity. Two characteristics of the curve are particularly significant. First is the general increase in the $^{16}O/^{18}O$ ratio towards the present day, suggesting that the global volume of glacier ice has increased, global temperature has decreased and the global sea level has fallen progressively over this timescale. Secondly, the amplitude of change, marked by the difference in the highs and lows of each cycle, has also increased, indicating that climatic fluctuations have become more extreme towards the present. This all suggests, despite the temporary effect of recent global warming, that if the outcome of past glaciations is prelude, then the future is climatically worse. This is consistent with the record of ice ages in the older geological record which show durations of up to 40 Ma. In this context we may be only a few million years into the current Ice Age.

The cycles of cold and warm stages provide a means of stratigraphic correlation from core to core and they have consequently been numbered

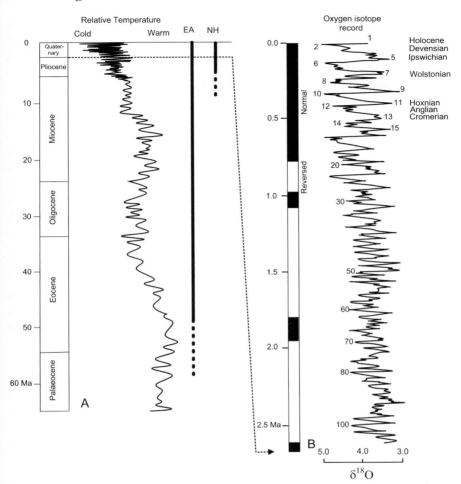

Figure 7.1 *Tertiary and Quaternary climate. (a) The slow decline of world temper-ature through the Tertiary into the Quaternary. The columns on the right indicate the date of the initiation of the East Antarctic Icesheet (EA) and icesheets in the Northern Hemisphere (NH). (b) Oxygen isotope curve from ODP site 677 showing numbering of selected stages to 2.5 Ma. The column on the left shows the palaeomagnetic timescale and the column on the right the correlation with terres-trial stage names in Britain. After N.J. Shackleton et al. (1995).*

downwards from the top. Dating is provided by the palaeomagnetic record[5]. Odd-numbered stages indicate warm periods and even-numbered stages indicate cold periods, though there are some major exceptions to this rule. The curves show more than 100 stages, or 50 warm and cold cycles, during the last 2.6 Ma. This does not necessarily indicate 50 world-wide glacial episodes, however, as variations in the amplitude of each curve, plus other climatic and tectonic factors, determine if any particular region is glaciated in any particular cycle.

Quaternary terrestrial stratigraphy

Compared to the ocean record, the terrestrial stratigraphic record is discontinuous with invariably much more gap than record. Some of the gaps represent non-deposition; other gaps occur when the deposits of an earlier glacial stage are overrun and removed by erosion in the next. Further gaps occur when sea level rise at the beginning of a warm stage erodes the deposits of the previous glacial stage. This is especially the case in shallow shelf seas, such as those surrounding Britain[6]. These problems are exacerbated because, as in the Isle of Man, successive glaciations follow essentially the same path making the deposits of separate stages often indistinguishable. The discontinuous nature of much terrestrial glacial sediment is compounded by its highly localised lithological variability, which reflects rapidly changing depositional environments as the icesheet advances or retreats. Many of these environments are so hostile to life that they contain no fossil record that can be used for dating. All these problems make the identification of the deposits of any terrestrial glacial stage, their lateral correlation with deposits of the same stage in other areas and their separation from older or younger stages, extremely difficult.

Quaternary geologists tackle these problems by using all available evidence to construct a stratigraphy, or sequence of strata. The evidence used includes lithology, sedimentology, geomorphology, soils, weathering characteristics, faunal and floral composition and relative and absolute dating methods. Once a stratigraphy has been established for one area it may be correlated with that of others and a picture built up of the sequence of events for a region. This will identify the number of glacial and inter-glacial stages, the extent of each glaciation and the climate of each stage, drawn from inferences from the fauna and flora. Only if the events recorded can be dated can a firm correlation be made with the stages identified in the oceanic oxygen isotope record.

The Quaternary of Britain

The British Quaternary is informally divided into three: the Lower, extending from 2.6 Ma to 780 ka; the Middle from 780 ka to the base of isotope stage 6 at approximately 280 ka; and the Upper, which extends to modern time. Lower Quaternary deposits are found only in East Anglia, consist mainly of marine sediments and show a number of cyclic shifts from warm to cold stages but no direct evidence of glaciation. The early part of the Middle Quaternary is marked in East Anglia by a series of marine and freshwater deposits, identified as the Cromerian Interglacial Stage, and correlated with oxygen isotope stage 13 at approximately 500 ka. These deposits are associated with the earliest evidence of hominid colonisation of southern England. Traditionally, three glacial stages have been identified following the Cromerian interglacial: the Anglian, Wolstonian and Devensian glacial stages, separated, respectively, by the Hoxnian and Ipswichian interglacial stages (Figure 7.1b). This sequence is much disputed and only two widespread glacial events, the Anglian and Devensian, are now generally recognised. Consequently, the climatic stages between the Cromerian (stage 13, *circa* 500 ka) and the Ipswichian (stage 5e, *circa* 128 ka) are seen as a complex hiatus of climatic change in which not all the cold stages necessarily generated extensive glacial phases in Britain.

The extent of the Anglian glaciation (stage 12) is well defined and it covered all of the British Isles as far south as a line from the Severn to the Thames (Figure 7.2a). At its maximum limit it diverted the River Thames south, close to its present course, and to the east it dammed up the flow of the Thames and the Rhine to form a large lake in the southern North Sea. The lowest escape for this lake were low points in the Chalk ridge between southeast England and France, forming a river down the English Channel. This began the process of separation of Britain from the continent. Because of the removal of much of the evidence by subsequent glaciation little is known of the limits of the Anglian glaciation to the west, north and east, but it probably extended across the continental shelf towards the continental slope. It also probably coalesced with the larger and more powerful Scandinavian icesheet moving westwards into the North Sea.

Between the Anglian glacial stage and the Ipswichian interglacial (stage 5e at *circa* 128 ka), the record is complex. Interglacial sites have been dated in East Anglia to correlate with stage 11 (at around 300 ka) and stages 9 and 7 (between 230 and 174 ka) but no evidence of intervening glacial deposits has been recorded[7]. In the Midlands fluvial deposits containing temperate sequences have been dated to stage 9 and stage 7 and glacial deposits to stage 6[8]. The paucity of glacial deposits recorded between stages 11 and 9, and 9 and 7, suggests that if glaciation did occur in cold stages 10 and 8 in Britain it was of limited extent. The last, Ipswichian interglacial (stage 5e) is reflected in the ocean isotope record by an abrupt shift to lighter isotopic values at around 128 ka (Figure 7.3a) and by the rapid movement of subtropical water into the North Atlantic (Figure 7.3e). Full

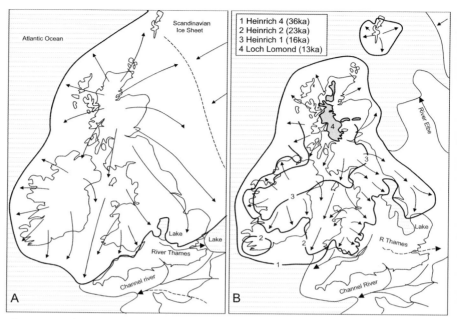

Figure 7.2 *The glaciation of Britain. (a) The palaeogeography of Britain during the Anglian glaciation (circa 400 ka), showing source areas, directions of ice flow and maximum ice limit. (b) The palaeogeography of Britain during the Devensian glaciation (circa 75–15 ka), showing source areas, flow directions and maximum limit and major retreat stages.*

interglacial conditions lasted only until 115 ka (sub-stage 5e), but the interglacial is represented in Britain by numerous organic sites that show mean annual temperatures some 2–3 °C higher and a sea level some 2–5 m higher than the present day. During the period Britain was not connected to the continent as the outflow river from the Anglian had long breached the English Channel. This may explain the apparent lack of hominid recolonisation of Britain during the Ipswichian interglacial; the Straits of Dover being too wide for Neanderthal Man with limited boat-building skills.

After 115 ka the climate deteriorated and the isotope record shows repeated, often complex shifts between cold and cool-temperate climate episodes (sub-stages 5d to 5a) up to 75,000 BP. These episodes, though originally identified as odd-numbered, warm stages, are now classified as part of the Early Devensian cold stage. Traditionally it was believed that Britain was largely ice free between the opening of stage 4 (the Middle Devensian, at *circa* 75,000 BP) and the opening of stage 2 (the Late Devensian, at *circa* 25,000 BP) and that this long period was marked by

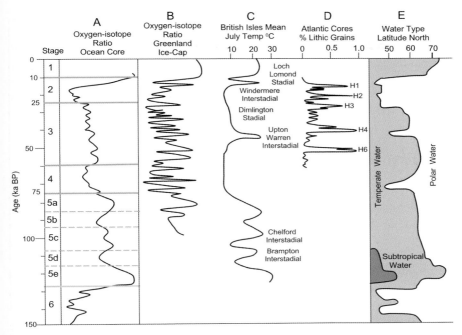

Figure 7.3 *Climate during the last 150,000 years. (a) Marine oxygen isotope curve for the last 150 ka. (b) Oxygen isotope curve from the Greenland Ice Cap. (c) Mean July temperature in Southern Britain. After G.R. Coope (1977). (d) Heinrich events in the northern Atlantic. (e) Change in foraminifera assemblages in the North Atlantic, reflecting change in water temperature.*

cold, periglacial environments, punctuated at intervals by brief warm periods (Figure 7.3c). Evidence from ice cores demonstrates, however, that the start of stage 4 is marked by a sharp increase in global ice volume, a sharp reduction in temperature and a drop in world eustatic sea level to below –60 m. This onset of pronounced cooling also marks the appearance of repeated cyclic fluctuation of temperature, called Bond cycles, lasting between 10,000 and 15,000 years. The colder part of each Bond cycle is correlated with the presence of distinct bands of ice-rafted debris, formed by major discharge of icebergs from the icesheets around the North Atlantic. These are called Heinrich[9] events and they indicate evidence for the onset of major changes in glacial conditions.

Recent work by Bowen *et al.*[10] suggests that a highly mobile and climatically sensitive icesheet existed in Britain throughout the Devensian and that it reached its maximum some time before 38,000 BP as a response to Heinrich event 4 (Figure 7.3d). At this time, all of Scotland, Ireland, most of Wales and northern England were covered by ice (Limit 1, Figure 7.2b). The maximum limit was less extensive than that of the Anglian glaciation and most of southern England remained unglaciated. On the east Scottish ice passed out onto the floor of the North Sea and a large lobe ran down the coast of England. On the west a major ice stream ran south along the floor of the Irish Sea to coalesce with ice caps in Ireland, Wales and the Lake District. South of the Isle of Man the Irish Sea ice stream diverged and sent a lobe between Wales and the Pennines to encroach into the Midlands of England[11]. As a response to Heinrich event 2 this icesheet readvanced around *circa* 23,000 BP, to limits within the previous maximum advance (Limit 2, Figure 7.2b). This was followed by extensive deglaciation until *circa* 16,000 BP when, as a response to Heinrich event 1, the icesheet surged to a limit that connected eastern Ireland with the Bride Moraine in the Isle of Man and the St Bees Moraine in Cumbria[12] (Limit 3, Figure 7.2b). After this time the icesheet rapidly disintegrated and by 14,000 BP Britain, including most of Scotland, had become deglaciated. A short interstadial episode, the Greenland Interstadial 1 between *circa* 13,000 and 12,500 BP, saw a brief return to higher temperatures. This was cut short by a further brief period of lower temperatures between *circa* 12,500 and 11,500 BP which saw the regrowth of glaciers across the Scottish Highlands in the Greenland Stadial 1 episode (Limit 4, Figure 7.2b). After this world temperature increased very rapidly with the opening of the current Holocene interglacial stage at *circa* 11,500 BP.

GLACIAL DEPOSITS AND LANDFORMS OF THE ISLE OF MAN

The Isle of Man occupies a strategic position astride successive glacial advances from major ice source areas in western Scotland, via the passage of a major ice stream down the Irish Sea passing over or around it. It has in consequence been strongly influenced by the effects of glaciation. Indeed, the original Geological Survey worker, G.W. Lamplugh[13], regarded the Isle of Man as '… an unrivalled field for the study of the conditions that ruled in the northern part of the Irish Sea basin during the Glacial Period'. In a further comment, as appropriate now as it was when it was written more than a hundred years ago, he argued that the Isle of Man was 'pre-eminently an area wherein the several theories by which the drift phenomena of the Irish Sea basin have been explained may be put to the test'. This part of the chapter outlines the history of previous research on the glacial geology of the island, the evolution of the conceptual frameworks in which it was seen and the general nature of the glacial deposits and landforms. This will provide a framework for developing a modern stratigraphic framework and a basis for interpreting some of the wide variety of glacial environments so well exposed on the island.

The evolution of ideas

The occurrence of drift in the Isle of Man was widely recognised by early workers[14] who ascribed it to deposition from catastrophic floods, marine submergence and the passage of icebergs. This view preceded the development of the Glacial Theory in the mid nineteenth century and followed the then current opinion that drift deposits[15] were a consequence of the Biblical Noachian flood. In a series of contributions in the 1840s and '50s the Rev. J.G. Cumming gave the first detailed account of the drift, devised a lithological classification, made the first distinction between the local and foreign deposits, and demonstrated that ice must have been the chief agent in its production[16]. His classification included four categories: boulder clay[17] and erratic[18] blocks; diluvium; drift gravel and alluvium. He recognised that some of the rocks in the drift originated in Scotland, observed the occurrence of shells in many of the lowland deposits and proposed that the drift was deposited by melt from icebergs carved from land-based glaciers at a time when the sea level was higher. The lowland, or 'foreign' drift of the north of the island could readily be explained by this hypothesis, but the upland, or 'insular' drift defied ready explanation as it contained boulders of Foxdale Granite at altitudes greater then the highest outcrop. Cumming devised a mechanism that involved great 'waves of translation' that carries sediment from the north, thus raising local rocks higher than their source outcrop. He also used this mechanism to explain most of the upland drift and, by subsequent redeposition after the waves had departed, the gravel fans that emanate from the mouths of many of the northward flowing upland valleys.

From his work for the Geological Survey in Lancashire in the early 1870s, Tiddeman[19] noticed that ice disregarded the local topography and, from the evidence of striae[20] and erratics, had instead flowed in a constant direction to the southeast. The only mechanism that could account for this was a land-based icesheet. Putting this evidence together with that provided by Cumming for the Isle of Man, Tiddeman introduced the concept of a large, continental-scale icesheet, emanating from Scotland, passing down the Irish Sea basin to invade parts of England. This concept was soon readily accepted. Others, however, still clung to a marine submergence origin, with Horne[21], Wright[22], Wright and Reade[23], Bell[24] and Ward[25] all arguing that the presence of shells in the lowland drift pointed to marine processes. Kendall[26] was the first to apply the new concept of a terrestrial icesheet to the Isle of Man and he showed how the pattern of upland striae and the distribution of local erratics demonstrated passage of ice right across the island. He also identified the Bride Hills as a moraine limit created during retreat or readvance of the icesheet and recognised the cluster of orientated low hills around Ballasalla as drumlins. He firmly rejected the concept of marine submergence and interpreted the shells in the lowland deposits as derived from earlier marine deposits on the sea floor north of the island and carried south as erratic clasts by the passage of ice. Perhaps his most important contribution was his explanation for the absence of foreign erratics from the uplands. He proposed that as the icesheet advanced towards the steep northern face of the island, the basal, dirt-rich layers passed around the flanks whilst the upper, dirt- and erratic-free layers sheared over the top to generate, in their passage, a suite of exclusively local glacial deposits.

If Kendall provided the conceptual framework for a modern interpretation of the glacial deposits then the prodigious work of Lamplugh[27] provided most of the detail. He devised a drift classification that distinguished between the local and foreign deposits, divided the foreign deposits into subglacial, proglacial and lacustrine components and separated the post-glacial deposits into flood gravels, alluvium and peat. In addition he described and figured most of the drift sections, mapped the distribution of striae and erratics and interpreted many of the erosional and depositional landforms. It is a testament to the accuracy of his work that the recent revision of the drift map[28] required little amendment to his boundaries. Despite the general acceptance of the concept of multiple glaciation elsewhere in Britain, Lamplugh, however, was a convinced monoglacialist and followed Kendall in regarding the entire Manx glacial sequence as the product of a single glaciation 'one and indivisible'[29].

After the publication of Lamplugh's map and memoir the glacial deposits of the island received relatively little attention. In the 1930s Smith[30] published the records of additional boreholes through the drift of the northern plain and devised a tripartite succession; the first to imply, for the Isle of Man at least, a chronology of multiple glaciation. The glacial deposits underlying the interglacial marine bed beneath the Point of Ayre, previously identified by Lamplugh, were attributed to the earliest glaciation. The deposits above this, but below the deposits exposed above sea level, were attributed to a second glaciation. The deposits above sea level were referred to the last glaciation. This tripartite view was endorsed by Cubbon[31] in the 1950s and he correlated the Manx sequence with that exposed on either side of the Irish Sea. In the 1960s Mitchell and his co-workers[32,33] examined the detail of the glacial deposits of the northwest coast, particularly the biogenic sediments, and in subsequent work[34,35] endorsed the tripartite division, but argued that the slate core of the island was exposed as a nunatak[36] during the last glaciation and was not overridden.

In a number of contributions in the 1970s, Thomas[37] devised a formal stratigraphic classification for the glacial deposits of the island and identified evidence for at least three major glacial stages within the uppermost division of the tripartite succession. Influenced by the earlier work of Mitchell he interpreted the local deposits as a product of periglacial conditions when the upland core existed as a nunatak above the level of advancing Late Devensian ice. This view was retracted in later contributions[38] when models of icesheet geometry for the Irish Sea basin[39] demonstrated that the island must have been covered by an icesheet at least 700–800 m thick in order to sustain the gradient to its southern maximum limit. In further contributions Thomas also reinterpreted the glaciotectonic structure of the Bride Moraine[40] and the sedimentology of large-scale fluvioglacial systems[41].

During the late 1980s the Isle of Man was the focus for a radical re-interpretation of the glacial conditions that pertained in the Irish Sea basin during the last glaciation. Up to that time the conventional view held that eustatic lowering of sea level[42] preceded the expansion of icesheets into shallow-water marine basins around Britain. Consequently, the Irish Sea basin would have been evacuated to a water level some 150 m below the present, and with a consequent shoreline some way out in the north Celtic Sea, some time before the Irish Sea icesheet advanced through the basin in the Late Devensian. As a result glaciation would have largely been accomplished in terrestrial margin conditions, without contact between the ice-front and the sea. Eyles and McCabe and their co-workers[43], in contrast, argued that through much of its advance and subsequent retreat history the Late Devensian Irish Sea icesheet was accompanied by an isostatically depressed marine margin caused by loading of the crust by the weight of advancing ice. Consequently, sedimentation at the margin was essentially glaciomarine rather than terrestrial. Although extended to the remainder of the Irish Sea basin, as well as the North Sea, much of the evidence for the new 'glaciomarine hypothesis' was originally obtained by reinterpretation of the glacial sediments of the Isle of Man[44]. Thus, most of the foreign deposits occurring in the island were reinterpreted either as coarse-grained subaqueous debris fans, suspension muds or iceberg 'rain out' deposited in proximal and distal marine environments immediately offshore from a grounded icesheet margin. Consequently, the Bride Moraine was reinterpreted as an ice-marginal morainal bank formed at the foot of a terminal ice cliff in relatively deep water, rather than a conventional terrestrial moraine ridge.

Although the glaciomarine hypothesis received considerable support during the 1990s it has also attracted much criticism and is now regarded as generally unsupported by the evidence. McCarroll[45] has provided a summary of the arguments against the hypothesis for the Irish Sea basin as a whole, and those particularly relevant to the Isle of Man include the lack of diagnostic sedimentary criteria for defining glaciomarine sediment, the lack of unequivocally marine micro-faunas in the supposed shallow-water marine sediments of the island, the difficulty of reconciling much of the fine-textured glacial morphology with passage through the littoral zone during isostatic rebound and subsequent sea level fall and the question of absolute sea level height. The minimum water depth required to drown out the Bride Moraine, for example, is at least 100 m above the modern. To this must be added a minimum of 75 m to account for the eustatic fall in sea level; making a total of 175 m of isostatic depression required to bring the Bride Moraine below the sea level pertaining at the time of its creation. Recent models of glacio-isostatic sea level change for the Irish Sea[46] suggest that at no time during the last 15,000 years have sea levels been above those of the modern in the area of the Isle of Man and, moreover, calculated maximum ice thicknesses, in the order of 600–700 m, are insufficient to generate the amount of isostatic depression necessary to account for the sea levels implicit in the glaciomarine model.

Local and foreign deposits

Since Cumming first described them, all subsequent workers on the island have recognised the distinction between a local, or 'insular', and a foreign, or 'extra-insular' suite of glacial deposits. The local deposits are composed exclusively of rock types exposed on the island, except at low altitude around the island margin where they are occasionally mixed with the foreign. They are made up of rock fragments derived from the Manx and Dalby Groups and, reflecting their derivation, are predominantly grey or blue in colour. Although the local deposits were originally generated by the passage of ice across the island, they have been much modified by slope processes during the Late Glacial and are consequently dealt with in more detail in Chapter 8. The foreign deposits, in contrast, are composed of rock types that do not crop out on the island and consequently include a great range of igneous, metamorphic and sedimentary rocks derived from outcrops in Northern Ireland, southern Scotland, the Lake District and the floor of the Irish Sea, by glacial erosion and transport. They comprise a great variety of glacigenic sediment types amongst which diamict, sands and gravels, laminated silts and sands, and laminated and massive muds, all dull red, brown or yellow, are the most common. They are described later in this chapter.

The local and foreign deposits were alternatively described by Lamplugh as, respectively, the 'high-level' and 'low-level' suites, and this aptly describes their geographical distribution. In general terms the local deposits are restricted to the uplands and the foreign deposits to the northern drift plain (Figure 7.4). South of Ramsey foreign deposits thin rapidly, but are exposed on the foreshore at Port Lewaigue and Port-e-Vullen, reach a height of 58 m at Carmel Mount and are exposed at Port Cornaa and Port Groudle. Foreign erratics mixed in with local deposits are common and the highest recorded are at 131 m near Ballasaig, west of Port Mooar. South of Douglas similar small patches of foreign deposits or scattered erratics occur in the low coastal lowlands towards Ballasalla. On the west coast, foreign deposits thin rapidly against the rock cliff at Gob ny Creggan Glassey, but underlie the whole of the Peel embayment and rise to 130 m on the slate hills between Kocksharry and St Johns. South of Peel little foreign deposit is seen, except as scattered erratics or discontinuous patches in low coastal areas around Dalby Point, Niarbyl, Fleshwick Bay and Calf Sound at elevations below 30 m. Along the northern margin of the slate massif, between Ramsey and Ballaugh, foreign drift is rarely exposed higher than 50 m on the steep face of the slate escarpment. Around Kirk Michael, however, where slopes are lower, a series of distinctive mounds, composed of foreign sand and gravel, sweep up the foot of the escarpment. The highest occur southeast of Kirk Michael in the upper part of the basin of Glen Wyllin at 180 m[47], with others in a line towards Bishop's Court Glen at heights between 45 and 100 m[48]. In the more open valley of Glen Dhoo similar mounds occur up to 45 m below Ravensdale. The general character of the boundary between the local and foreign deposits thus shows penetration of foreign drift to an average height of between 30 and 60 m around most of the island margin with a maximum penetration on the more exposed northwest margin to 180 m. Above these limits deposits are entirely of local composition.

Striae and erratics

The presence of striae on the Carboniferous Limestone near Castletown and Port St Mary, and on the Manx Slates at Cregneish, were first noted by Cumming[49]. Similar markings were observed by Ward[50] north of

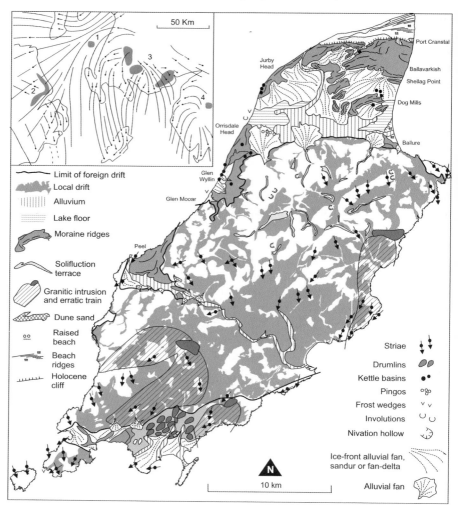

Figure 7.4 *Geomorphological map of the Isle of Man. Inset shows ice-flow directions in the northern Irish Sea derived from striae and erratics. 1: Ailsa Craig Rebeckite-eurite; 2: Chalk; 3: Southern Uplands granitic intrusions; 4: Shap Granite.*

Douglas, while others were recorded by Kendall[51] on Maughold Head and South Barrule. Lamplugh added a further 150 locations. They were observed at all heights up to the summit of Snaefell and in all areas of the island. They therefore make a singularly complete body of evidence for the movement of ice across the island. The pattern of striae on higher ground shows a dominant direction from north-northwest to south-southeast (Figure 7.4). On the flanks of hills and on lower ground the directional spread is wider and reflects the influence of local topography in diverting basal ice flow. On the low ground of the east and southeast a number of cross-cutting striae occur. These resolve into two sets; one north-northwest to south-southeast and the other east-northeast to west-southwest, indicating changing directions of ice movement. The only deduction that can be made from the distribution of striae is that the whole island has been overridden by ice at some time. This conclusion is supported by an examination of the striae pattern from areas bordering the northern Irish Sea (inset, Figure 7.4) which show a consistent pattern running south through the basin from source areas in the Firth of Clyde, the Southern Uplands and the Solway Lowlands.

Further evidence of ice override is provided by the distribution of local erratic boulders across the Manx uplands (Figure 7.4). These are derived from the igneous intrusions at Dhoon, Foxdale and Oatland. Running south from the Dhoon Granite, which is exposed over a small area north of Laxey, numerous granite boulders occur in the local drift. The major part of this train of boulders is intercepted by Laxey Bay but they can be traced, in rapidly diminishing numbers, into Douglas Bay, where they cease. The directions of transport implied are coincident with striae in the area and confirm that they were derived by ice passing over the outcrop and running south. The small boss of granite at Oatland sends a similar train south towards Ballasalla. The boulder spread of the Foxdale Granite holds a notable place in the glacial literature since it furnished a classic example of transport of erratic boulders from lower to higher ground. The Foxdale Granite is exposed on the col at the head of the Foxdale valley at an elevation of some 200 m. To the west the ground rises rapidly towards South Barrule at nearly 500 m. The great majority of boulders derived from the outcrop run south in a spread down the Santon River and Silverburn and then swing southwest towards Port St Mary, coincident with the general run of the striae in the area. A significant number, however, spread firstly westwards up the eastern slope of South Barrule to its summit and then south-westwards. This distribution caused great difficulty for the adherents of the submergence theory and we have already mentioned Cumming's imaginative idea of giant 'waves of translation' to explain it. The problem attracted the attention of Charles Darwin[52] who, though a convert to the Glacial Theory, nonetheless advocated icebergs as an explanation in this instance.

Erratics within the foreign deposits, particularly of the north, confirm the ice flow directions identified in the northern Irish Sea basin by the pattern of striae. Although no systematic study of Manx foreign glacial erratics has been undertaken, about nine-tenths[53] are derived from the uplands of southwest Scotland with the remainder from the Clyde basin, the Solway basin, the northern Lake District and offshore outcrops in the North Channel, together with some far-travelled rocks from the Western Highlands. Notable indicator rocks include pebbles of riebeckite-eurite, a micro-granite found only on the island of Ailsa Craig in the Firth of Clyde; granite and porphyry from Arran; gneiss from western Scotland; flint from the Cretaceous of Ulster; Shap Granite from the northern Lake District; and large numbers of granodiorite pebbles from the Criffel and Dalbeatie intrusions of the Southern Uplands (inset, Figure 7.4).

Sediment-landform assemblages

Glacial landforms are often better understood if they are related to the deposits that underlie them, for it is the processes of deposition that frequently determine the landforms. A modern technique is to use the concept of a sediment-landform assemblage. This is defined[54] as a mappable unit in which relatively homogeneous morphological, strati-graphic and lithological characteristics occur. A number of major sediment-landform assemblages can be identified amongst the glacial land-forms of the Isle of Man and have been used as a second order overlay to formation boundaries on the revised geological map of the island, as change in landform frequently equates with a change in the geology. The following are amongst the most notable glacial or paraglacial sediment-landform assemblages identified.

Ice-marginal moraines   These are areas of prominent linear ridges, occur-ring either singly or as en-échelon groups. The largest are the moraine ridges forming the Bride Hills. From the coast at Shellag Point, where they reach nearly 100 m in height, the moraines run westwards as a series of sub-parallel ridges, cut by a complex series of dry valleys and channels. Towards Andreas the ridges decline in height and become more subdued, but a large ridge passes from Ballakinnag southwestwards towards The Lhen and on across Jurby Head towards the Killane River. At Orrisdale Head a complex ridge, marked by a very diversified surface of minor ridges, channels and small basins, runs southwest towards Kirk Michael. Other more subdued ridges run discontinuously east–west across the area between the Bride Hills and Ramsey. All the ridges are underlain by complex sequences of diamict and sands and gravels, often tectonically deformed. The ridges represent ice-margin sedimentation and subsequent deformation during still-stand, readvance or minor snout oscillation of the ice-margin.

Ice-disintegration topography   These are areas of disorganised topography that includes small-scale ridges, mounds and basins, many water filled. They occur extensively in the area from Orrisdale Head towards Kirk Michael and locally across Jurby Head and north of Ramsey. They are underlain by complex sequences of diamict and sand and gravel, and represent the disintegration of ice-marginal topography through melt of buried ice.

Ice-front alluvial fans, subaqueous fans and sandur channels   The southern margin of many of the major moraine ridges, particularly the Bride and the Jurby, are fronted by low-angled fans often forming conjoined aprons fronting the moraine ridges. Those composed of sand and gravel are interpreted as ice-front alluvial fans draining large meltwater tunnels issuing from the ice-margin; those composed of laminated sands and silts are interpreted as subaqueous fans draining meltwater tunnels issuing from the ice-margin below the water level of fronting lake basins. Sandur channels occur as wide troughs running either at right angles to, or parallel with, moraine ridges. They are underlain by sand and gravel sequences and are interpreted as large meltwater drainage systems that have cut down through earlier fan or sandur systems. The most spectacular example is the Lhen Trench, a narrow, sinuous channel that drains directly south from the Jurby moraine ridge. Another example, the Crosby channel, in this case running parallel to the moraine ridges, occurs between the front face of the Bride moraine and a subsidiary ridge to the south.

Lacustrine basins   Extensive areas of the northern plain are essentially flat and poorly drained. Boreholes show they are underlain by recent river alluvium then laminated or massive mud, often to depths of 20 m or more. They represent former glacial lake floors, fed by meltwater streams running from successive ice-front positions across fringing alluvial fans and sandur. The largest extends from The Cronk, through the Curragh towards Ramsey. Further, smaller areas occur between Kirk Michael and Orrisdale Head.

Diamict floors   These are areas of low amplitude subdued topography underlain by thick diamict. They occur within the moraine systems in the north of the island, particularly in a linear belt running east–west on the northern side of the Bride Moraine. They also occur in small patches down the low island margin and in an extensive area running southwest of Ballasalla towards the coast at Strandhall. They represent areas of basal lodgement till deposition under thick, advancing active ice.

Drumlin fields   Within the area of diamict floor around Ballasalla are a series of small, elongated hills up to a kilometre in length and 30 to 40 m in height, all orientated towards the southwest, the regional flow direction of ice in this area. These are drumlins, a large-scale bedform generated at the base of a thick, fast moving, wet-based icesheet by moulding of under-lying diamict.

In addition to these major sediment-landform assemblages is a number of distinctive individual landform types. Pingos occur on the outer margin of the Ballaugh alluvial fan (Figure 7.4) and they form a set of large hollows, sometimes water-filled, surrounded by a subdued outer ridge[55]. They are a type of periglacial ground-ice structure, indicative of former permafrost conditions. Although cirque basins, characteristic of upland glaciation in other areas of Britain such as Snowdonia and the Lake District, do not occur in the island, a number of nivation hollows are found on the north-east slopes of North Barrule, the northwest slope of Slieau Dhoo and on the flanks of the Sulby valley. These form shallow basins of former snow accumulation, often fronted by a small pseudo-moraine caused by debris released by frost action sliding down the snow surface. They are another type of periglacial landform.

Glacial erosional landforms are rare in the island and are restricted to small-scale forms on the higher ridges of the uplands, as at Creg Bedn on the northern side of Slieau Managh, which has the character of a small roche moutonnée. Forms created by subglacial streams, however, are more common. These are rock channels that cut across rock spurs or run oblique to slopes. They carry no modern drainage, have no catchment and appear unrelated to contemporary fluvial process. The best example is the deep rock channel cut across the ridge between Glen Mooar and Glen Wyllin at Ballaleigh[56].

The Manx glacial succession

The objectives of stratigraphic classification are to identify sediment units, describe their lithological characteristics, define their boundaries, place them in depositional order, reconstruct their environments of deposition and establish a relative or absolute chronology. In summary, to provide a dated event sequence, or succession. This is often difficult to achieve because Quaternary deposits tend to be discontinuous, poorly exposed and very variable in thickness and composition. The excellence of the exposure in the Isle of Man, however, makes this task easier. Classification is done in a hierarchical framework of lithostratigraphic units based on sediment characteristics such as lithological composition, grain size and sedimentary structure. At the lowest level in the hierarchy is the *bed*. This is an informal term used to describe a sediment unit with unusual features, such as a rich fauna. At the next level is the *member*, which is defined as a homogeneous body of sediment such as a diamict, gravel or sand with identifiable vertical and lateral boundaries. Members are commonly grouped together into *formations*. Formations are defined as mappable units that relate to a specific glacial event. Thus a formation commonly includes a diamict member, overlain by a sand and gravel member; a common signature for a simple glacial advance/retreat event. This event may represent the response to one cold climate glacial stage, but more commonly it represents the response to a brief phase within it. The definition of a formation does not therefore carry chronostratigraphic significance unless supported by other evidence. Because of the nature of glacial processes, which are primarily erosive in the advancing stage, formations are frequently bounded by unconformities. As we shall see, such unconformities provide the primary criteria for the definition of glacigenic formations within the Manx Quaternary.

Lithostratigraphic classification

A formal lithostratigraphy for the island was first devised by Thomas in 1977[57] and revised in 1999[58]. Recent work for the new edition of the geological map necessitated further revision[59] and the opportunity has been taken in this volume to incorporate a number of minor changes. A brief description of each formation, its component members and evidence for its age is given below, in stratigraphic order from the base of the succession upwards. For completeness, formations of Late Glacial and Holocene age are included. A schematic diagram of the relationship between the formations across the northern plain of the island is given in Figure 7.5a. Formations are also listed, in summary form, in Figure 7.5c.

Ayre Lighthouse Formation Type-site: Borehole VI, Point of Ayre (NX440035). Known only from boreholes[60,61] at Point of Ayre it overlies Permo-Triassic bedrock at a maximum depth of −140 m O.D. and comprises about 70 m of sands, gravels and diamicts of northern origin. It is overlain by the Ayre Formation. The age of the formation is indeterminate, but on the basis of the overlying succession may be correlated with cold stage 6 or earlier.

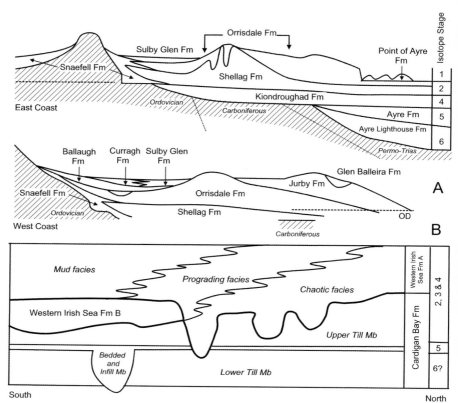

Figure 7.5 *The glacial stratigraphy of the Isle of Man. (a) Generalised cross-section north–south through the northern Isle of Man showing relationship between formations in the Manx Quaternary stratigraphy. (b) Schematic section illustrating the stratigraphic relationship, age and composition of Quaternary formations offshore the Isle of Man, after R.A. Chadwick et al. (2001). (c) A lexicon of formally defined stratigraphic units in the Quaternary of the Isle of Man.*

Ayre Formation   Type-site: Borehole IV, Point of Ayre (NX465050). Also only known from boreholes it consists of up to 8 m of shelly silts and sands at depths between –65 and –73 m O.D. and overlies the Ayre Lighthouse Formation. A shell fauna described by Lamplugh[62] as *in situ* probably represents an interglacial marine assemblage provisionally correlated with temperate stage 5e (Ipswichian) or earlier.

Kiondroughad Formation   Type-site: Borehole 16, Kiondroughad (NX395015). Known only from boreholes west of Andreas it comprises

Formation	Stratotype	Members	Lithology	Isotope Stage
Point of Ayre	Point of Ayre (NX440035)	Ayre	Beach gravel and dune sand	1
		Lough Cranstal*	Diatomite, fen peat, fresh-water lake muds and brackish-water clays	
	Phurt		Laminated silts and peats	
Sulby Glen	Sulby Glen (SC385924)		River gravel	1
Curragh†	The Curragh (SC365950)		Peat	1
Ballaugh	Ballaugh (SC348935)		Alluvial fan gravel	1 and 2
Glen Balleira††	Glen Balleira (SC314915)		Peat and organic clays and silts	2
Snaefell	Druidale (SC355 850)	Druidale	Soliflucted till, slope wash gravel, head and scree	2
		Ballure	Soliflucted till, slope wash silts and sands, head and scree	
		Mooar	Soliflucted till, slope wash silts and sands, head and scree	
Jurby	Jurby Head (SC343980)		Diamict, sand, massive and laminated mud	2
Orrisdale	Orrisdale Head (SC319930)	Orrisdale Head	Basal lodgement till	2
		Bishop's Court	Sandur sand and gravel	
		Trunk	Subaerial flow till	
		Ballaleigh	Ice-front alluvial fan	
		Ballavarkish	Subglacial lodgement till	
		Ballaquark	Subglacial lodgement till	
		Cranstal	Subglacial lodgement till	
		Kionlough	Subaerial flow till	
		The Dog Mills	Lacustrine muds and sands	
Shellag	Shellag Point (NX460000)	Bride	Basal lodgement till	2
		Cronk ny Arrey Laa	Ice-front alluvial fan	
		Wyllin	Basal lodgement till	
		Kirk Michael	Proglacial sandur	
		Ballasalla	Basal lodgement till	
		Plain of Malew	Proglacial sandur	
Kiondroughad	Borehole 16, Kiondroughad (NX395015)		Gravel, sand and diamict	4, 6 or 8
Ayre	Borehole IV, Point of Ayre (NX465050)		Shelly marine silts and sands	5, 7 or 9
Ayre Lighthouse§	Borehole VI, Point of Ayre (NX440035)		Gravel, sand and diamict	6, 8, 10 or 12

* Contains Neolithic artefacts.
† Now includes the former Bungalow Formation of G.S.P. Thomas (1999).
†† Previously identified informally as the Jurby Head and Glen Balleira Beds by G.S.P. Thomas (1999).
§ Previously named the Isle of Man Formation in G.S.P. Thomas (1999).

Figure 7.5c *A lexicon of formally defined stratigraphic units in the Quaternary of the Isle of Man.*

60 m of glacial sands, gravels and diamicts of northern origin. It rests partly on an extensive level rock platform between −41 and −53 m O.D. and partly on the Ayre Formation and is overlain by the Shellag Formation. On the basis that the underlying Ayre Formation is of temperate stage 5 age and the overlying Shellag Formation is of Late Devensian stage 2 age, its age may correspond to cold stage 4, the Early Devensian.

Shellag Formation   Type-site: Shellag Point (NX460000). A widespread, lithologically complex and frequently deformed glacigenic formation of northern origin outcropping across the northern plain and locally around the island margin. The formation probably overlies the Kiondroughad Formation but this is not proven in outcrop. It also locally overlies the Snaefell Formation at Ballure and Gob ny Creggan Glassey. The formation is divisible into a number of separate members on each coast. On the north-east coast the *Bride Member* is a massive, fine-grained basal diamict that is overlain by the *Cronk ny Arrey Laa Member*, a coarse, ice-front alluvial fan gravel. On the northwest coast, the *Wyllin Member* is a deformed, massive, fine-grained diamict correlated with the Bride Member, and succeeded by the *Kirk Michael Member*. This is composed of sand and contains a rich assemblage of *Turittella communis* either of *in situ* glaciomarine origin, or reworked into later glacial outwash sands or rafted from former sea floor. In the south of the island the *Ballasalla Member* comprises extensive basal till of mixed local and foreign composition, locally drumlinised. It is overlain by the *Plain of Malew Member*, a series of proglacial outwash deposits. The formation is locally overlain by the Orrisdale, Glen Balleira, Snaefell, Ballaugh, Sulby Glen and Curragh Formations. Two radiocarbon dates have been derived from shells occurring in the Cronk ny Arrey Laa Member at Shellag Point and give uncalibrated ages of greater than 30,300 ^{14}C yrs BP[63] and 41,688 ^{14}C yrs BP[64]. The shells are not *in situ*, as they include mixed cold and temperate species, and are clearly derived from earlier marine or glaciomarine sediments subsequently transported by the advance of ice through the northern Irish Sea basin. A further uncalibrated radiocarbon date of 36,000 ± 670 ^{14}C yrs BP[65] has been obtained from peat beneath the Ballasalla Member at Strandhall in the south of the island and clearly indicates that the island was ice-free at this time. The age of the Shellag Formation is consequently post these dates and is most probably a product of major glacial advance and retreat during the subsequent cold stage 2 of the Late Devensian.

Orrisdale Formation   Type-site: Orrisdale Head (SC319930). A widespread and lithologically complex glacigenic formation of northern origin that unconformably overlies the Shellag Formation on the northwest and northeast coasts. It is the product of major glacial readvance during stage 2 (Late Devensian). It is divisible into a number of major members. On the northwest coast, the *Orrisdale Head Member* is a coarse, stratified subglacial diamict[66] or glaciomarine density underflow or rain-out mud[67]. The *Bishop's Court Member* is a thick sequence of sands and gravels formed in a series of diachronous marginal sandurs on an unstable, ice-cored supraglacial topography[68]. The *Trunk Member* shows rapid vertical and lateral facies variation and extensive flow folding and is interpreted as a resedimented debris flow from a stagnating ice-margin[69]. On the northeast coast, to the north of the Bride Moraine, the *Ballavarkish Member*, the *Ballaquark Member* and the *Cranstal Member* all off-lap one another to the north and comprise coarse, stratified subglacial diamict. The Ballaquark and Cranstal Members were previously assigned to the Jurby Formation[70], but recent remapping identify them as older and part of the Orrisdale Formation. To the south of the Bride Moraine, the *Kionlough Member* comprises debris flow and ice-front alluvial fan sands and gravels, regarded as a breakdown product of the deformation of the moraine[71]. The member passes distally into the *Dog Mills Member*, a sequence of massive and laminated sands, silts and clays with extensive soft-sediment deformation structures, containing a rich micro-fauna that may be *in situ* or derived. The Orrisdale Formation is locally overlain by the Glen Balleira, Snaefell, Ballaugh, Sulby Glen and Curragh Formations. Between Glen Balleira and Glen Wyllin a series of radiocarbon dates from organic sediment overlying the Orrisdale Formation suggest that the formation is the product of major readvance some little time before *circa* 22,000 BP[72].

Jurby Formation   Type-site: Jurby Head (SC343980). A stratigraphically complex glacigenic formation that disconformably overlies the Orrisdale Formation across the northwest coast. It is the product of major glacial readvance during stage 2 (Late Devensian). Remapping of the area around the type-site at Jurby Head has resulted in a complete revision of the stratigraphy and the previous classifications[73] have been abandoned. The formation is not now divided into members as the sequence shows extensive lateral passage, related to sequential ice-marginal readvance into the margins of a large lake basin. Instead, it is informally divided into a number of facies assemblages including: diamict, sand, alternating sand and mud, massive mud and laminated mud. The Jurby Formation is locally overlain by the Sulby Glen and Glen Balleira Formations. Radiocarbon dates derived from organic sediment overlying the formation at Jurby Head indicate that the formation is associated with a significant readvance event between approximately 16,000 and 15,000 BP[74].

Snaefell Formation   Type-site: Druidale (SC355850). Extensive scree, head, soliflucted diamict and slope wash deposits of exclusively local origin directly overlying bedrock in the upland areas. Divisible into three members by area. The *Druidale Member* (SC355850) comprises coarse scree overlying bedrock, succeeded by units of soliflucate intercalated with redeposited diamict and occasional gravels. The lower units probably date from the Early and Mid Devensian (stages 4 and 3) but the majority are Late Devensian (stage 2) periglacially reworked local diamicts. The *Ballure Member* and *Moaar Member* comprise local head and scree that intercalate with and underlie Shellag and Orrisdale Formation glacigenic sediments at low elevations around the island margin and probably range in age from stage 4 (Early Devensian) to the opening of the Holocene (stage 1).

Glen Balleira Formation   Type-site: Glen Balleira (SC314915). The formation comprises peat, organic mud and calcareous marl deposited in kettle basins overlying the Jurby and Orrisdale Formations. Five organic kettle fill sequences have been recorded at Glen Balleira and two sequences at Jurby. The sediments range from Greenland Interstadial 1 to the beginning of the Greenland Stadial 1 (18,500–12,500 BP)[75]. Previously identified informally as the Jurby Head and Glen Balleira Beds, their palaeo-ecological significance warrants their raising to formation status.

Ballaugh Formation   Type-site: Ballaugh (SC348935). The formation comprises the large gravel-dominated mountain-front alluvial fans that fringe the northern uplands. They include fans at Glen Wyllin, Glen Balleira, Ballaugh, Sulby Glen, Glen Auldyn and Ballure, together with minor fans in the central valley and in the south of the island. All overlie the Orrisdale Formation. The Glen Wyllin and Glen Balleira fans overlie Late Glacial organic sediments and are younger than 10,500 BP[76]. The Ballaugh, Sulby and Glen Auldyn fans began accumulating earlier and the Ballure fan interdigitates with members of the Orrisdale Formation suggesting that it began accumulation immediately after the uplands were deglaciated.

Curragh Formation   Type-area: The Curragh (SC365950). Extensive peat sequences that have accumulated in lowland basins and plateaux, with

striking westwards from Shellag Point as a complex series of sub-parallel ridges. The northern slope of the moraine is largely underlain by diamict and is truncated by a distinctive raised cliff-line of early Holocene age running westwards from Blue Point towards Lough Cranstal. The southern, generally steeper, slope of the moraine, in contrast, is underlain largely by sand and gravel. From its highest point at Shellag Point, a major ridge form curves westwards towards Andreas. To the north, immediately inland from the coast, a series of subsidiary ridges strikes westwards towards Lough Cranstal. Further to the west the moraine is bisected by a large channel system at Ballakinnag running southwest and separating the Bride moraine from its western extension towards Jurby Head.

Fretting the surface of the moraine are a large number of complex channels, none of which carries current drainage (Figure 7.7). They can be divided into four main types. *Type 1* channels are flat-floored, up to 2 km long, a few hundred metres wide and either breach the moraine, as at

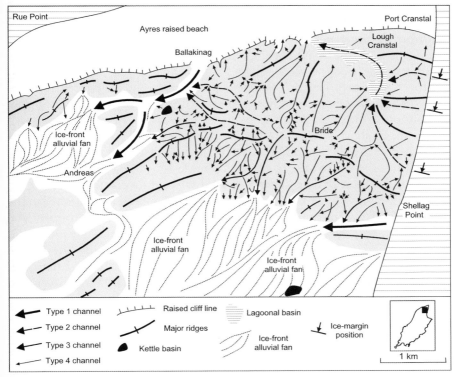

Figure 7.7 *Map of the Bride Moraine showing major ridges and types of channel. Note that the moraine ridge areas around Andreas have not been mapped in detail.*

Ballakinnag, or run parallel to its outer face, as south of Shellag Point. The channel floors are underlain by sand and gravel and feed the head of large ice-front alluvial fans sloping southwest from the moraine front. The channels represent the location of major glacial drainage exit points when the ice stood against the immediate rear of the moraine. *Type 2* channels are relatively narrow and run parallel to the trend of the moraine ridge to the rear of the crest. Where they intersect the east coast they occur immediately down-ice of the termination of thick diamict sheets, suggesting that they are proglacial meltwater channels directed to run parallel with the ice-margin. *Type 3* channels are short, narrow and deep and run directly off the forward face of the moraine to feed the head of coalescing ice-front alluvial fans. In a few cases the channels pass through the moraine crest and display a characteristically 'up and down' long-profile, suggesting that the upper parts were formed subglacially. *Type 4* channels include a very large number of small, short, often entrenched channels of all orientations that fret the forward face of the moraine. Most were probably developed as a response to local dead-ice melt.

Multiple ice-marginal oscillation – Lough Cranstal to Shellag Point

The Bride moraine is cut through at right angles to its trend by actively eroding cliff sections between Lough Cranstal and Shellag Point and a serial section is shown in Figure 7.8. The deposits of two glacigenic formations are exposed. Along much of the base of the cliffs the members of the Shellag Formation are discontinuously exposed in a series of highly deformed thrust slices, sharply truncated upwards by a marked erosional unconformity. Above are three sandy and stony diamict members of the Orrisdale Formation: the Ballavarkish, the Ballaquark and the Cranstal Members. Each has a similar body geometry and forms a sub-horizontal sheet, up to 30 m in thickness and a kilometre in length, off-lapping one another to the north and separated from the one above by an erosional unconformity The lowest member, the Ballavarkish, is the thickest and most widespread and thins some 250 m north of Shellag Point to pass out southwards into a sequence of sands, gravels and thin diamicts occupying a Type 2 marginal channel against the rear of the moraine crest. For some 400 m to the north the member lies horizontal, but then descends towards beach level to pass beneath a northward thickening sheet of Ballaquark Member. The boundary forms an erosional unconformity and to the north the underlying Ballavarkish Member is deformed into a series of open, upright folds, cut across the top by the unconformity. The relationship between the Ballaquark Member and the overlying Cranstal Member is similar though the degree of deformation beneath the separating unconformity is less.

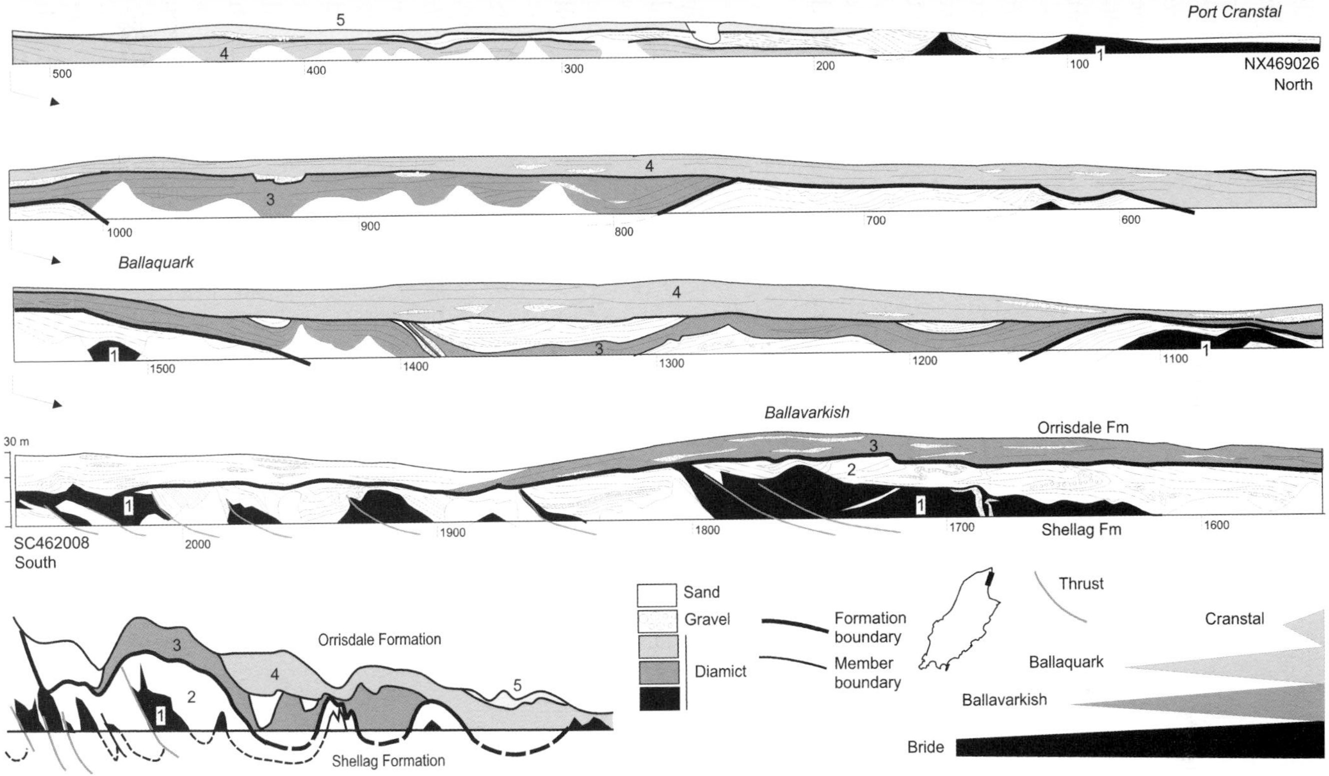

Figure 7.8 Serial stratigraphic sections between Lough Cranstal and Shellag Point. Inset at bottom left shows a summary of the stratigraphy and the inset at bottom right is a time–space diagram of the advance/readvance episodes identified in the succession. Stratigraphic units: 1 Bride Mb; 2 Cronk ny Arrey-Laa Mb; 3 Ballavarkish Mb; 4 Ballaquark Mb; 5 Cranstal Mb.

Dackombe[84] identified five major facies assemblage types in the Ballavarkish Member, in order from base to top[85]. *Assemblage A*, at the base, forms a transition from the underlying Shellag Formation and consists of a sequence of thinly bedded, matrix-rich diamict interdigitated with well-sorted fine sands. The sands are occasionally rippled and show mild deformation in the form of crenulation and overfolding of cross-beds. *Assemblage B* is a heterogeneous, matrix-rich sandy diamict containing deformed inclusions of the underlying sands. These inclusions are often streaked out into thin sand laminae or detached into blocks. *Assemblage C* is a homogeneous diamict with well-developed lamination caused by subtle variations in colour and clast composition. *Assemblage D* forms the bulk of the member thickness and is a massive, sandy and stony, matrix-supported diamict, texturally very uniform with occasional bedding. Clasts have a strong uniaxial fabric, are well striated and show evidence of collision and crushing. *Assemblage E* occurs at the top and consists of interbedded diamict and sand, similar to assemblage A but with limited evidence of deformation. Dackombe[86] interpreted the dominant assemblage D as the product of subglacial lodgement under thick ice in a terrestrial environment with the underlying assemblages A, B and C products of deformation and incorporation of underlying sediment during advance over them.

A time–space diagram showing the relationship between the three diamict members (inset, Figure 7.8) demonstrates three readvance episodes, each of which terminated to the rear of the previous. The earliest was responsible for the initial construction of the Bride Moraine. The amount of retreat that occurred between any two readvance episodes is unknown, but based on the length of exposure is a minimum of a few kilometres. The location in cliff section of the forward termination of each readvance broadly corresponds with the position of a Type 2 channel on the moraine surface and it would be convenient to consider these channels as ice-marginal indicators for each readvance limit.

Ice-front deformation – the form and structure of the Bride Moraine

At Shellag Point large-scale glaciotectonic structures are exposed and they rank amongst the largest, most complex and best exposed in Britain (Figure 7.9a)[87]. Structural disturbance is limited to the members of the Shellag Formation and occurs in a kinetostratigraphic zone (Figure 7.9c) that extends from the unconformity beneath the Ballavarkish Member to the rear of the moraine, south through the moraine ridge, to an area of a rapidly diminishing disturbance in the proglacial area to the south. In areas where it is deformed by large-scale structures the Bride Member is traversed by numerous planes of foliation, giving the appearance of a pronounced slaty cleavage. The foliation is frequently folded and the most common style is a low amplitude isocline, either upright or steeply inclined (Figure 7.9b). Major folds are found only in the moraine core which forms a tight, asymmetric anticline with an amplitude of some 100 m, slightly overturned to the north. Superimposed upon the southern limb of the main anticline is a series of four congruent, isoclinal overfolds whose axial surfaces strike approximately east to west and are steeply inclined to the south. Both members of the Shellag Formation are involved in the folding, and tectonic thinning on the limbs and thickening around the crests are considerable. High-angled reversed faults are associated with, and are the complement of, the major isoclinal folds. Four major faults occur and each dips steeply south, sub-parallel to the axial surface of the complementary isoclinal fold, and striking approximately 125–305°. Slip is of the order of 20 m with downthrow to the north. The amount of slip, however, diminishes rapidly into the roots of the moraine structure and the faults do not crop out in foreshore section (Figure 7.9b).

Overthrusts, or low angled reversed faults, occur in the areas peripheral to the moraine core. For a kilometre or so south of the moraine, a series of thrusts are exposed forming a listric fan of progressively increased dip and reduced spacing northwards towards the moraine front. Between each thrust sand is carried forward as a large, asymmetric anticline and as the spacing of the thrusts decreases northwards suites of anticlines appear stacked one behind the other. Towards the moraine front the spacing between the thrusts diminishes, the angle of northerly dip increases and the Bride Member is dragged up as slices along the plane of each of the thrusts. Similar closely spaced series of thrusts occur north of the moraine (Figure 7.9c). The geometry of the thrusts is concave upwards with dips of up to 60° at the forward end, declining to less than 10° to the rear. In plan, the thrusts are concave up-ice and are analogous to a series of stacked, or nested, spoons, dipping north. When the Bride Member is dragged up along the thrusts foliation planes within it are deformed into an elliptical pattern of dextrally overlapping, en-échelon recumbent folds, the axial traces of which run sub-parallel to the strike of the bounding thrusts.

There is general agreement that most large-scale glaciodynamic structures result from deformation at the margin of a readvancing icesheet[88]. In the case of the Bride Moraine three major arguments support this view. Firstly, the strike of structures is normal to the direction of ice movement and parallel to the ridge trend. Secondly, the upward coarsening succession from diamict, through sand into gravel in the Shellag Formation marks the general signature of a readvance episode. Thirdly, as all members of

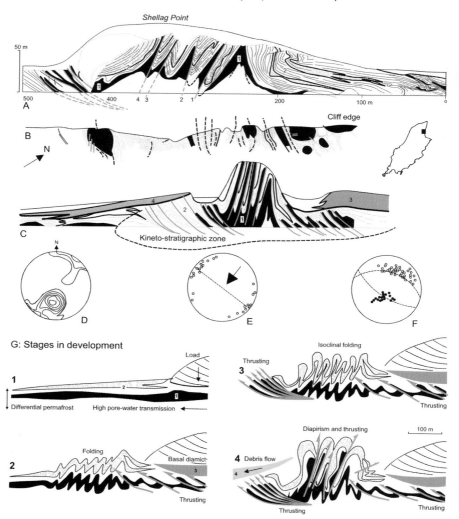

Figure 7.9 *The structure of the Bride Moraine. (a) Section through the moraine. (b) Structural map across the foreshore beneath the moraine. (c) Kinetostratigraphic zone. (d) Contour plot of poles to foliation. Contours at 1% intervals on 432 observations. (e) Plunge of fold axes. Large arrow shows inferred direction of ice advance. Broken line shows average trend of fold axes. (f) Faults. Open circles: poles to high-angled reverse faults. Solid circles: poles to low-angled overthrusts. Broken lines are projections of mean planes. (g) Stages in the development of the Bride Moraine. Stratigraphic units: 1 Bride Mb; 2 Cronk ny Arrey Laa Mb; 3: Ballavarkish Mb; 4 Kionlough Mb.*

the Shellag Formation are disturbed, deformation must have occurred after this formation was deposited, by readvance across it. Evidence that this readvance terminated at the moraine is supported by the following arguments. First is the occurrence, to the rear of the moraine, of a major unconformity separating deformed Shellag Formation below from relatively undeformed Orrisdale Formation above. Second, the basal member of the Orrisdale Formation, the Ballavarkish Member, terminates against the rear of the moraine and does not pass it. The topographic form of the Bride Moraine, its tectonic structure and parts of its lithostratigraphy are thus a function of icesheet readvance. In this respect, the moraine is a structural rather than a constructional or depositional landform and may best be classified as an ice-thrust or push moraine.

Two factors have been invoked to account for the development of glaciodynamic structures: high pore-water pressure and permafrost. The addition of an ice load during readvance will bring compression to underlying strata by the packing of grains and the expulsion of pore-water. Compression in water-saturated sediment, however, is only possible if an opportunity exists for drainage of excess water. If the overlying ice is below the pressure melting point it acts as an impermeable seal through which vertical drainage is precluded. Horizontal drainage may take place down the pressure gradient towards the ice-margin but only if a permeable sediment were available. If the permeability was low, as is the case in clay, an increase in pore-water pressure would produce a decrease in shear strength, leading to failure in the clay. The second factor, the presence of permafrost, would reduce the potential for subglacial deformation for two reasons. Firstly, the shear strength of frozen sediment is much higher than the stress imposed by glacier ice. Secondly, the transmission of pore-water pressure will be inhibited because any water between the glacial sole and the underlying permafrost is itself liable to be frozen. Despite this the development of permafrost in certain critical conditions could be expected to facilitate deformation. These conditions are where permafrost is developed in a substrate consisting of beds of highly contrasting lithologies. Grain size affects the growth of ice in the permafrost layer by influencing the freezing temperature. Thus, the amount of frozen water in a sediment varies inversely with grain size and silts and clays will remain unfrozen much longer for they freeze at lower temperature than the coarser grades. In sequences of contrasting lithologies within the permafrost zone, therefore, beds of silts and clay may remain unfrozen despite being enclosed above and below by frozen sand and gravel. Consequently, high pore-water pressure may develop within these unfrozen sediments causing reduction in shear strength and consequent failure. It is significant that in glacigenic sequences which include prominent beds of silt and clay deformation is commonly observed to be almost wholly confined to them.

Applying the above discussion to the Bride Moraine, there is evidence for both the development of high pore-water pressure and the existence of permafrost contemporaneous with its construction. Thus high pore-water pressure could be generated by the application of an ice load to the underlying substrate during the readvance responsible for the emplacement of the Ballavarkish Member. The occurrence of ice-wedge casts and the high frequency of frost-shattered clasts within the Cronk ny Arrey Laa Member indicate the presence of a contemporary permafrost layer immediately before the readvance. As the ice-margin pushed against the frozen substrate, compression, induced by ice load, was transmitted through the frozen Cronk ny Arrey Laa Member to the partially frozen Bride Member beneath (Stage 1, Figure 7.9). High pore-water pressure generated in this diamict by the application of load could not be released upwards. Only horizontal expulsion of water, towards lower-pressure areas immediately beyond the margin, would be possible. As the diamict is of low natural permeability, very high pore-water pressure would be required to produce significant horizontal expulsion. As this pressure increased the shear strength of the enclosed clay reduced, it became saturated, and failure resulted in low-angled over-thrusting beneath the sole of the ice-margin. At the same time horizontal compression of sediment in front of the ice-margin generated folding due to the reduced mobility of the clay and the presence within the multi-layered substrate of high viscosity interfaces that would facilitate buckling (Stage 2, Figure 7.9). With increased thrusting in the clay, the potential for further horizontal expulsion of high pore-water pressure became reduced and the saturated clay burst vertically out of its confining pressure along the axial surfaces of the folds to form a series of isoclinal diapiric folds. Continued compression led to thrusting along these folds, the development of the high-angled reverse faults and the generation of further thrusts planes forward of the moraine (Stage 3, Figure 7.9). A significant feature of the moraine is that the folds remained rooted and that sole thrusting did not occur across the whole of the base of the moraine, but only at its margins. As a consequence, the moraine remained relatively narrow and located close to the ice-margin. The absence of a complete basal decollement explains the intensity of the deformation, since the stress was absorbed internally rather than propagated into the proglacial area. After the release of excess pore-water pressure through the diapiric rise of the saturated Bride Member, further structural development of the moraine ceased. The ridge form created by the processes of deformation, however, continued to break down as unstable, water-saturated debris slid off the forward face as sheets of flow till. This accumulated in the immediate proglacial area as the Kionlough Member. During this process much of the upper part of the moraine structure was removed (Stage 4, Figure 7.9).

Proglacial lake sedimentation – The Dog Mills Member

From Shellag Point an almost continuously exposed cliff section runs south towards the Grand Island Hotel (Figure 7.10). The succession comprises four stratigraphic units. The two lowermost units, the Bride and Cronk ny Arrey Laa Members of the Shellag Formation are lithologically similar to their counterparts exposed at Shellag Point. The Bride Member is discontinuously exposed at the base of the cliff sections in a series of shallow structural arches whose amplitude diminishes away from the moraine. The overlying Cronk ny Arrey Laa Member, here largely comprising sand, thins progressively south from the moraine front and passes out between Kionlough and the Dog Mills. It is replaced to the south by the Dog Mills Member, a complex sequence of massive and laminated silty sands, silts and clays up to 10 m thick. This is, in turn, is disconformably overlain by the Kionlough Member which consists of a very variable sequence of massive and bedded diamicts and intercalated sands and gravels that firstly thickens rapidly off the south face of the moraine then thins south of Dog Mills. The Dog Mills Member can be divided into three major facies assemblages[89].

Facies Assemblage A occurs at the base of the sequence conformably overlying the Bride Member in a wedge thickening to the south. It is fine-grained and consists of parallel-laminated or massive silty sands, rippled sands, rapidly alternating laminae of sand and mud and massive and laminated mud (Logs 1–6, Figure 7.11). Palaeocurrent indicators show flow towards the east, southeast or south. Extensive convolute bedding, dish and pillar structures, flame and diapiric structures together with mud rip-ups and flaser bedding occur in laterally persistent horizons. Three cycle types are typically developed in the assemblage[90]. In the first, thick units of massive fine sand are succeeded by thin, parallel-laminated or massive mud; the whole cycle being commonly disrupted. The second type consists of draped laminae of fine sand, silt and clay passing upwards into massive or laminated mud. The third, less common type shows transition from rippled fine or silty sand into laminated or massive mud. These sequences all suggest basin floor sedimentation in a standing water body in which a dominant suspension fall-out regularly gave way to traction along the bed via low-flow turbidity currents. The deformed cycles may represent either periods of increased sediment supply leading to increased loading and consequent liquefaction of underlying saturated facies or rare, catastrophic

Shellag Point

Crosby Channel

SC460000 North

0 m

100

200

300

400

500

Log 8

Log 7

2

2

2

4

600

700

800

900

1000

Kionlough

Y

Y

YY

4

1

1100

1200

1300

1400

1500

250 m Gap

1700

Log 6

The Dog Mills

Log 5

1

1

4

1800

1900

2000

2100

Log 4

3

Log 3

Log 2

2200

2300

Log 1

Grand Island Hotel

SC450962 South

2400

2500

Ormsdale Formation

Shellag Formation

1

2

3

4

Frost wedge

Palaeocurrent

Dip of thrusts

high-flow turbidity currents.

Facies Assemblage B overlies assemblage A in the southern part of the sections (Logs 1–5, Figure 7.11), but thins northwards. It is coarser-grained and consists of parallel-laminated sand, rippled sand, massive sand and occasional trough and planar cross-bedded sand. Mud units are rare and deformation is uncommon. Typical facies relationships consist of an upward passage from cross-bedded sands, through horizontally laminated sands into rippled sands. The rarity of fines and the dominance of repeated current sequences suggest deposition by rapidly declining flow on a low-angle delta foreset slope. No evidence for wave action is found and bi-polar ripples, herringbone cross stratification and evidence of tidal channel scour do not occur.

Facies Assemblage C occurs north of Kionlough where assemblages A and B thin and pass rapidly northwards into sands and gravels (Logs 7 and 8, Figure 7.11). These comprise massive, granule to small pebble gravel in stacked sheets; horizontally laminated sands; low-angled cross-bedded sands; planar cross-bedded sands; trough cross-bedded sands; massive sands and thin rippled fine sands. Strong reciprocal associations occur in a simple cycle from massive gravel through planar cross-bedded sand, parallel-laminated sand into rippled sand. These are characteristic of vertical accretion in low or mid-fan glaciofluvial environments and are similar to those observed in the distal facies assemblage of the Bishop's Court Member of the Orrisdale Formation[91].

The sedimentology of the Dog Mills Member is commensurate with deposition from plumes of suspension sediment and traction carpets of turbidites on the floor of a shallow water body fed by low-angled prograding delta foresets feeding south from the toe of ice-front alluvial fans and sandar. The lack of ice-rafted debris in the sequence confirms that the water body did not abut against an ice-margin. The key question, however, is whether the water body was lacustrine or marine.

The Dog Mills Member contains a rich foraminiferal fauna and species lists have been produced by Wright[92], Haynes *et al.*[93] and Thomas *et al.*[94]. Haynes identified a dominant, well-preserved, cold-water assemblage and a meagre, poorly preserved, warm-water assemblage. The cold-water assemblage was regarded as *in situ* and indicative of proximal glaciomarine conditions dominated by *Elphidium clavatum*. In a re-examination of the fauna Thomas *et al.* identified a much larger temperate-water compo-

Figure 7.10 *Serial stratigraphic sections between Shellag Point and the Grand Island Hotel showing location of vertical log profiles and palaeocurrent pattern. Inset at lower left shows summary of stratigraphic succession. Stratigraphic units: 1 Bride Mb; 2 Cronk ny Arrey Laa Mb; 3: Dog Mills Mb; 4 Kionlough Mb.*

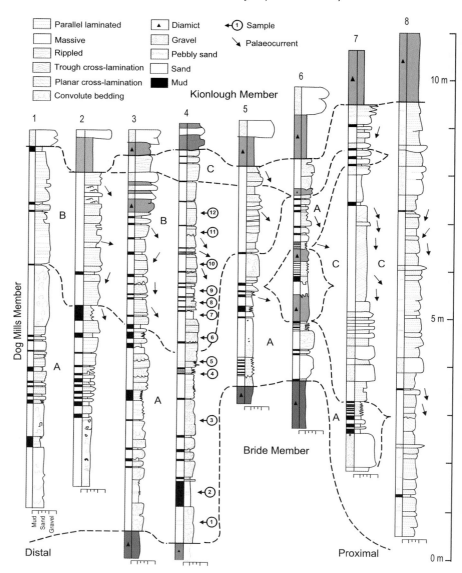

Figure 7.11 *Vertical log profiles through sections between Shellag Point and the Grand Island Hotel. For location of logs see Figure 7.10.*

nent, including significant numbers of *Elphidium selseyense*, a temperate species not identified by Haynes. The assemblage was therefore regarded as comprising two, approximately coequal, components; one characteristic of ice-proximal glaciomarine conditions dominated by *Elphidium clavatum* and the other characteristic of temperate conditions dominated by *Elphidium selseyense*.

Two interpretations of the faunal assemblages are possible. The *first interpretation* is that the fauna are wholly derived from older marine and glaciomarine sequences, subsequently transported by the passage of Late Devensian ice across them and reworked into proglacial subaqueous sediment. In this case both sets of fauna, temperate and cold, would show much the same degree of damage by transport recycling and there should be no significant change in faunal composition upwards through the sedimentary sequence. The *second interpretation* is that the temperate fauna only are derived and the cold fauna represent an *in situ* fauna living in a glaciomarine water column at the time of deposition. In this case there should be a significant difference in the degree of damage between the two sets; with the derived temperate fauna showing evidence of wear and the cold fauna relatively undamaged. In addition, the cold-water *in situ* component should show significant upward compositional change reflecting a shift in the depositional environments from dominantly deeper-water suspension at the base to dominantly shallow-water traction at the top.

Thomas *et al.*[95] have demonstrated that there was no significant difference in the degree of abrasion and breakage between the warm- and cold-water components; no change in species composition upwards through the sequence, all being dominated by coequal numbers of *Elphidium* species; and a relationship between abundance and host sediment grain-size indicative of size sorting by sedimentary process. Consequently it was concluded that the fauna were wholly derived and that the Dog Mills Member sedimentary sequences represented sedimentation in a fresh-water lacustrine basin; a conclusion originally proposed by Lamplugh[96].

West coast

The twelve kilometres of coastal cliffs between Glen Mooar and Sartfield on the northwest coast of the island show almost continuous exposure of glacial sediments. In contrast to the east coast, which displays a simple shift from subglacial, through ice-marginal to proglacial environments south through the Bride Moraine, the west coast exposures are more complex and divide into three distinctive glacigenic provinces. Between Glen Mooar and Glen Trunk they display ice-marginal sandur sedimentation, frequently deformed by the collapse of underlying dead-ice and the resultant generation of large, organic-filled kettle basins. Between Glen Trunk and The Cronk the sections cut through the Orrisdale moraine ridge and provide detail of a complex supraglacial ice-marginal environment characterised by large-scale sandur sedimentation. From Killane the sections run obliquely through the Jurby moraine ridge and reveal a complex sequence of ice-marginal sediments associated with the development of a large fronting ice-contact lake.

A summary of the west coast stratigraphy is shown in Figure 7.6b and involves the deposits of three glacigenic formations: the Shellag, Orrisdale and Jurby Formations, and two non-glacial formations. The lowest glacigenic formation, the Shellag, is divisible into two lithostratigraphic members, the Wyllin and Kirk Michael Members, correlated with and stratigraphically equivalent to the Bride and Cronk ny Array Laa Members of the east coast. The overlying Orrisdale Formation comprises four members. At the base the Orrisdale Head Member is a thick, extensively exposed diamict very similar in lithological character to the stratigraphically equivalent Ballavarkish Member of the east coast. It crops out discontinuously between Glen Mooar and Glen Balleira, progressively rises in the sections north of Glen Trunk to reach its maximum thickness at Orrisdale Head and is widely exposed at the base of the sections across Jurby Head. The member is disconformably overlain by the Bishop's Court Member, a very variable sequence of sands and gravels that crop out extensively between Glen Mooar and Orrisdale Head, where it is largely sand dominated, and between Orrisdale Head and The Cronk, where it is largely gravel dominated. The Bishop's Court Member is succeeded by a sequence of thinly bedded diamicts, the Trunk Member, that thicken off the southern face of Orrisdale Head. The Jurby Formation is exposed only across Jurby Head where it unconformably overlies the Orrisdale Head and Bishop's Court Members. Remapping of the formation has resulted in a complete revision of the stratigraphy and the previous division by Thomas[97] into members has been abandoned. Instead, the formation is informally divided into a number of major facies assemblages. The non-glacial formations along the coast comprise the Glen Balleira Formation and the Ballaugh Formation. The Glen Balleira Formation consists of organic sediment filling a series of large kettle basins in the top of the Bishop's Court Member between Glen Balleira and Glen Wyllin. It also includes the organic kettle basin fills that occur above the Jurby Formation at Jurby Head. The Ballaugh Formation comprises a series of alluvial fan gravels that issue from valleys along the upland margins and bury the organic kettle fills of the Glen Balleira Formation.

The Peel embayment

The lowland behind Peel is framed by a set of faults on its eastern, southern and western sides that downthrows an inlier of Peel Sandstone, well exposed in the low cliffs north of Peel Bay. Although little drift is exposed, boreholes indicate that the lowland is underlain by an extensive sheet of foreign glacial deposits that extends at far east as St Johns and reaches to 30 m below sea level at Glen Faba Mills[98]. By their similarity to the members of the Orrisdale Formation to the north they are included within this formation but undivided. A geomorphological map of the area is shown in Figure 7.12 and a number of distinctive landform assemblages can be identified. Most striking is the wide flood plain of the River Neb and the series of terraces that flank its margins. Three major terraces can be identified up to 15 m above the modern flood plain (Terraces T1, T2 and T3, Figure 7.12). All are of Holocene age and represent adjustment by the river Neb by excavation of its course through the cover of glacial sediments. On the southern side of the river a series of alluvial fans drain from rock gullies cut into the slate ridge of Slieau Whallian. The fans are truncated by the terraces but overlie the glacial sediment, demonstrating that they are older than the terraces but younger than the retreat of the last glacial event.

Southeast of Peel the ground is broken by a series of ridges and mounds that form a number of incomplete parallel arcs running north to northeast. The outermost arc runs northeast from Ballaharra to the large kettle basin at Close y Garey and is marked by a complex micro-relief of multiple ridges, mounds and basins. A second arc strikes northeast across Peel golf course towards a kettle basin at Ballalough then northwards through a series of connected mounds towards Knocksharry. This ridge is flanked by a narrow kame terrace banked against the rising rock slope to the east. A third ridge runs northeast from White Strand towards Knocksharry. At Lherygydhoo (SC266851) a small quarry displays a 20 m thickness of foreign parallel-laminated sands, with subsidiary channel gravels and occasional debris flows. Palaeocurrent indicators show transport to the southeast and the sequence is interpreted as a shallow delta front prograding into a small lake system trapped in front of an ice-margin. Another quarry, at Ballaharra (SC264824), shows a more complex sequence. At the base are a series of parallel-laminated sands, granule gravels and small pebble gravels passing upwards into pebble gravels and thin diamicts. This sequence is disconformably overlain by a channel fill, showing upward passage from parallel-laminated sand into rippled sand. Palaeocurrent indicators show flow directions towards the southeast. The overall sequence is consistent with deposition into the margin of another small lake basin extending to the southeast.

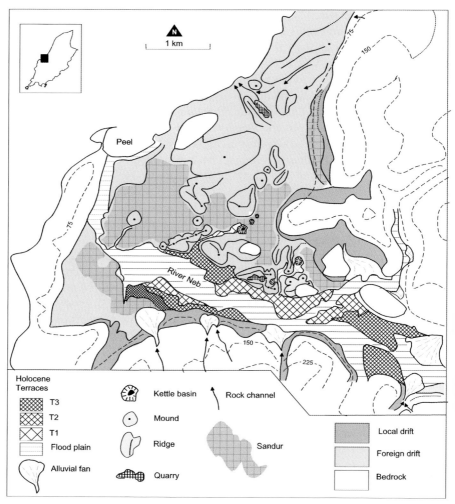

Figure 7.12 *The glacial geomorphology of the area around Peel.*

Palaeogeographic reconstruction of stages in the retreat of the ice from the Peel embayment is shown in Figure 7.13. At this time most of the uplands had been deglaciated and the Irish Sea ice-margin pressed against the west coast of the island. In an early stage of retreat the ice-margin stood at Ballaharra where irregular moraine ridges were deposited and large kettle basins, caused by the melt and collapse of buried ice, were created (Stage A, Figure 7.13). At a number of points large meltwater streams exited from the ice-margin into outwash sandur beyond it. Unlike today, where the drainage from the Neb flows west, the main flow of meltwater was eastwards, towards the central valley at St John's. A small, linear lake basin was formed by ponding of water against the reversed bedrock gradient east of Ballaharra and was fed by a fan-delta built out from the meltwater stream exit. With the uplands still covered in snow, periglacial conditions prevailed and, in summer, drainage fed alluvial fans generated at the change of gradient between the upland valley slopes and the flat floor of the proglacial sandur. As the ice-margin retreated to the west, another minor still-stand occurred and a further series of morainic mounds and kettle basins were formed (Stage B, Figure 7.13). The sandur spreads

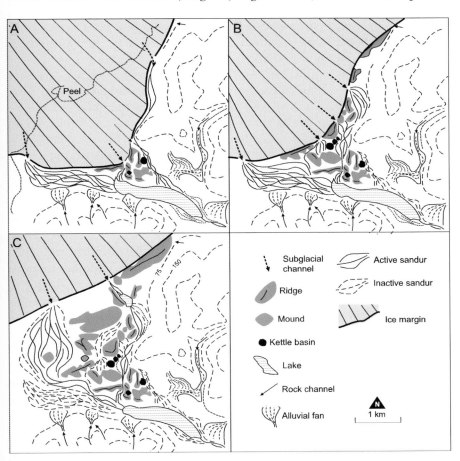

Figure 7.13 *Palaeogeographical reconstructions of stages in the retreat of ice from the area around Peel based on geomorphological mapping, palaeocurrents and interpretation of sedimentary sequences.*

expanded to occupy the ground uncovered by the retreating ice between the two moraine ridges, drainage still ran eastwards and the lake basin, though probably rapidly filling, persisted. Further retreat took the ice-margin to the position of the present coastline (Stage C, Figure 7.13). It is marked by a prominent moraine ridge northeast of Will's Strand. A major stream exit located over the site of Peel deposited large quantities of outwash sediment in the sandur that slopes south from the town. South of Will's Strand another meltwater exit fed a small lake at Lherygydhoo. The exit from this lake probably utilised the still active sandur between stages A and B and continued to feed the lake at Ballaharra.

Ice-marginal sandur sedimentation – Glen Mooar to Glen Trunk

The sections between Glen Mooar and Glen Trunk have previously been described by Lamplugh[99], Mitchell[100] and Thomas[101] and a revised serial section is shown in Figure 7.14. At the base of the sections highly deformed members of the Shellag Formation are discontinuously exposed. They locally include clay-rich, shelly diamict of the Wyllin Member, overlain by Glen Wyllin Member sands containing a rich shell fauna dominated by abundant specimens of *Turritella terebra*. The origin of these sands is problematic. Lamplugh regarded them as 'a strip of old sea bottom, dragged up and partly incorporated' into the diamict. They can also be interpreted as *in situ* glaciomarine sediment or as outwash containing a wholly derived, reworked shell fauna. The Shellag Formation is separated from the overlying Orrisdale Formation around Glen Wyllin by what Lamplugh described as 'the great unconformability'. The basal Orrisdale Head Member is discontinuously exposed between Glen Mooar and Glen Balleira, but thickens rapidly north to form much of the cliff base towards Glen Trunk. It comprises a massive, stony and sandy diamict, similar to the Ballavarkish, Ballaquark and Cranstal Members of the Orrisdale Formation of the east coast succession, and is interpreted as a basal lodgement till[102].

The Orrisdale Head Member is disconformably overlain by widespread sands and gravels of the Bishop's Court Member, locally reaching 30 m in thickness. The member can be divided into two assemblages that pass repeatedly into one another: a coarse-grained, gravel-dominated assemblage consisting of stacked sets of massive gravel and subordinate

Figure 7.14 *Serial stratigraphic sections between Glen Mooar and Glen Trunk. Stratigraphic units: 1 Wyllin Mb; 2 Kirk Michael Mb; 3 Orrisdale Mb; 4 Bishop's Court Mb; 5 Trunk Mb; 6 Balleira Fm; 7 Ballaugh Fm; 7A Ballaleigh Debris Fan; 7B Glen Wyllin Debris Fan; 7C Balleira Debris Fan.*

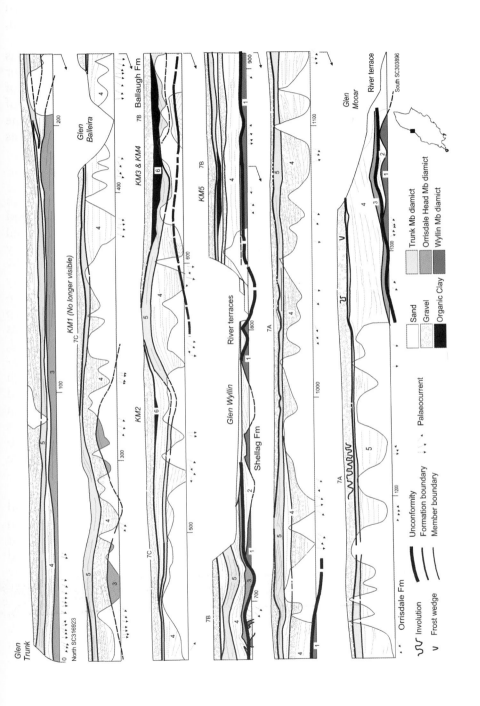

Glen Trunk

North SC316923

Glen Balleira

Ballaugh Fm

KM1 (No longer visible)

KM3 & KM4

KM2

KM5

Glen Wyllin

River terraces

Shellag Fm

Glen Mooar

River terrace

South SC303896

Orrisdale Fm

Trunk Mb diamict

Orrisdale Head Mb diamict

Wyllin Mb diamict

Sand

Gravel

Organic Clay

Involution

Frost wedge

Unconformity

Formation boundary

Member boundary

Palaeocurrent

parallel-laminated sands, and a fine-grained, sand-dominated assemblage of parallel-laminated, ripple-laminated and planar cross-bedded sand. Palaeocurrent indicators show a dominant transport direction to the southwest. The two assemblages are interpreted, respectively, as proximal and distal outwash sandur sediments deposited in an ice-marginal environment. The Bishop's Court Member is conformably overlain by the Trunk Member; a lithologically very variable sequence of thin diamicts, gravels, sands and silts displaying internal flow and slump structures, interpreted as a series of debris flows generated by movement of surface dirt off an adjacent ice-margin[103]. The member thickens off the southern slope of Orrisdale Head, reaches its maximum thickness around Glen Wyllin and then thins towards Glen Mooar. It is conformable with the top of the Bishop's Court Member and rises and falls into sag basins on its surface. Late Glacial organic sediments occupy the basins and are unconformably overlain by Late Glacial or early Holocene alluvial fan gravels of the Ballaugh Formation; at Glen Balleira, Glen Wyllin and Glen Mooar.

Supraglacial ice-marginal sedimentation – Orrisdale Head

The area around Orrisdale Head forms part of a large tract of hummocky terrain that extends as a ridge running north from Kirk Michael, through Orrisdale towards The Cronk. The ridge is cut on its northeast flank by the margin of the Ballaugh alluvial fan and at its southern end is overlain by the Glen Balleira fan. To the east the ridge falls sharply to a narrow tract of flat ground around Bishop's Court which is underlain by lake sediment. A morphological map of the area is given in Figure 7.15. The area can be described as irregular and it includes a complex assemblage of minor relief features including conical mounds, flat-top terraces, enclosed hollows, lake-filled kettle basins, subdued linear ridges, and a wide variety of shallow channels, all superimposed on a major ridge form.

The Orrisdale ridge is cut by well-exposed cliff sections between Glen Trunk and The Cronk and a serial section is shown in Figure 7.16 and a series of sedimentary logs in Figure 7.17. The stratigraphic succession is simple and consists of two members of the Orrisdale Formation. The lowest, the Orrisdale Head Member, is continuously exposed from Glen Trunk to its type-site at Orrisdale Head. Over 30 m in thickness its base is not seen, but its top is either eroded or transitional upwards into the Bishop's Court Member via a series of thin interbedded diamicts. The member is a hard, massive, sandy, matrix-rich, red-brown or grey diamict, but some distinction can be made between a lower assemblage, which displays discontinuous bedding marked by thin laminae of sand, often displaying attenuated recumbent folding, and an upper assemblage, which

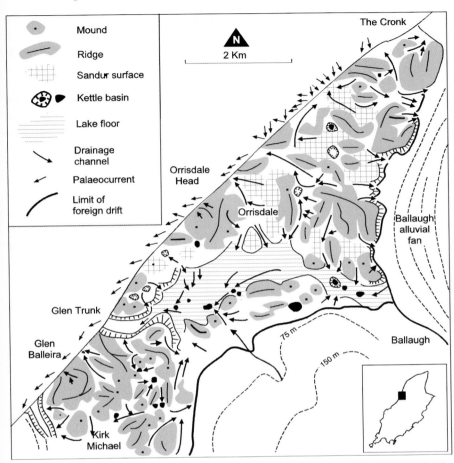

Figure 7.15 *Geomorphological map of the area between Glen Trunk and The Cronk.*

is massive. Ice-direction indicators, derived from fabrics and deformation structures, indicate flow directions from the northwest. Dackombe[104] interpreted the member as a terrestrial lodgement till, deposited under thick, temperate-based ice and identifies two depositional mechanisms. The lower assemblage is the product of thrust stacking, shearing and basal melt-out, whilst the upper assemblage is a product of subglacial lodgement. Eyles and Eyles[105], in contrast, interpret the member as glaciomarine and a product of deposition on a marine shelf by suspension, iceberg rafting and bottom traction currents.

The overlying Bishop's Court Member has been investigated in detail

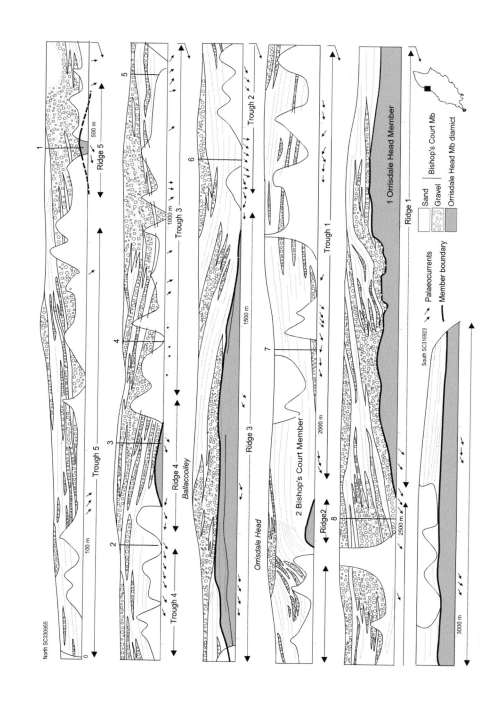

North SC330965

100 m

Trough 5

Ridge 5

500 m

Trough 4

Trough 3

Ridge 4

Ballacooiley

1000 m

Orrisdale Head

Ridge 3

1500 m

Trough 2

2 Bishop's Court Member

Trough 1

2000 m

Ridge2

1 Orrisdale Head Member

Ridge 1

2500 m

South SC316923

3000 m

Sand | Bishop's Court Mb
Gravel | Orrisdale Head Mb diamict

↗ Palaeocurrents

── Member boundary

by Thomas *et al.*[106] and two major lithofacies assemblages defined.

Assemblage A is gravel dominated and consists of either multi-storey sets of pebble to boulder gravel separated by thin sheets of parallel-laminated sands, or thinner, alternating coequal sets of granule gravel and sand (Logs 1–6, Figure 7.17). Each set represents a meltwater flood cycle. The cycle starts in a channel with transitions from trough cross-stratified sand to trough cross-stratified gravel indicating the migration of increasingly larger and coarser dune sets along the channel floor during rising flood. These pass upwards into massive gravel indicative of migrating bar cores. The internal structure of bars shows a crude sub-horizontal stratification and an upward fining from boulder or cobble gravel to pebble and granule gravel. Bar gravels pass upwards into parallel-laminated sands formed in a variety of sub-environments including bar top, bar margin and channel floor. Parallel-laminated sands pass upwards into rippled sands and thence into massive or parallel-laminated mud. This fining-upwards passage indicates a vertical accretion sub-environment formed in cut-off channel floors, in shallow scours or in hollows on bar surfaces, either during low flow or by repeated spillage of water across inactive parts of the system. This cycle is typical of proximal, gravel-dominated braided streams in the upper parts of proglacial outwash sandur[107].

Assemblage B is sand dominant and consists of planar cross-bedded and parallel-laminated sand, rippled sand and cross-laminated, parallel-laminated or massive mud in thin, but laterally extensive upward-fining sets (Logs 6 & 7, Figure 7.17). Two major sub-environments can be identified. The first is a channel sub-environment in which sand bars migrate across channel floors during rising flood and pass upwards into small dune sets formed in shallow water across stabilised bar fronts during waning flow. The second sub-environment is an overbank sub-environment, indicated by prominent upward transition from parallel-laminated sand to mud. These transitions form small-scale upward-fining successions that begin with an erosion surface. This is overlain by a parallel-laminated sand unit the base of which is often marked by small-scale cross-lamination, a slight upward coarsening and ripped-up mud clasts. This is capped by a thin mud unit with a range of small-scale structures including parallel-lamination, cross-lamination, mud-draped sinusoidal ripples, convulate lamination and flaser bedding. The upper boundary to the next parallel-laminated unit is erosional and often marked by load casting, overturned flame and ripple

Figure 7.16 *Serial stratigraphic sections across Orrisdale Head showing location of log profiles, location of former dead-ice ridges and sandur troughs and palaeocurrent pattern.*

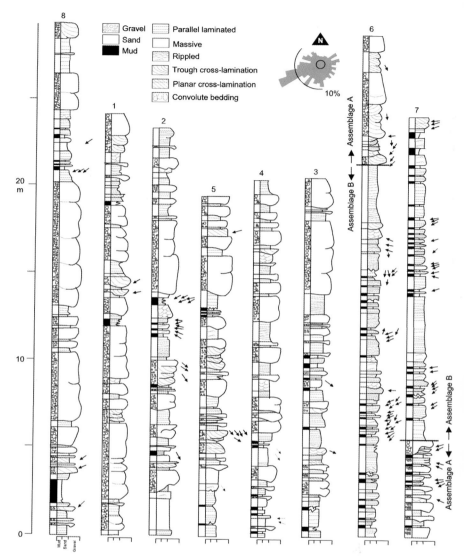

Figure 7.17 *Sedimentary logs through the Bishop's Court Member, Orrisdale Head, arranged in general coarse to fine order, after G.S.P. Thomas et al. (1985). See Figure 7.16 for location of logs. Inset top right shows palaeocurrent distribution.*

structures and small faults. This association is similar to distal, flood-generated cycles described by Steel and Asheim[108] and the sandy, distal assemblage of Rust[109], from contemporary fluvioglacial environments.

Through the sections lateral transition between one lithofacies assemblage and the other is marked, but vertically the gravel assemblages, though widening out, retain relatively fixed positions. These positions are controlled by buried ridges of Orrisdale Head Member, orientated southwest to northeast, that crop out at the base of the sections. These ridges, five in number, consequently define six adjacent troughs of sand and gravel, ranging between 100 and 500 m in width (Figure 7.16). This suggests that the principal architectural style of deposition in the Bishop's Court Member is a series of linear, vertically widening, diachronous sandur troughs running parallel to one another and to the ice-margin, deposited on an unstable, ice-cored supraglacial topography controlled by dead-ice ridges running parallel to the ice-margin. This is supported by palaeocurrent indicators which show a dominant flow direction towards the southwest. A model of this style of sedimentation is shown in Figure 7.18 and shows sediment, constrained by dead-ice ridges, rapidly filling and widening as the dead-ice ridges melted down. In the initial stages, channels cut down into the surface of the underlying Orrisdale Head Member and deposited coarse assemblage sediment during successive high-discharge meltwater flood events. As sediment accumulated it abutted against the margins of the dead-ice ridges and debris flows were released. As sedimentation continued and as the dead-ice ridges melted down, the sandur system widened. At this stage only a portion of the trough was active except in high flood. With the decline of these floods, sedimentation reverted to the lower parts of the trough where sediment accumulation was slower due to regular and repeated in-channel erosion. Thus, through much of the history of the filling of individual troughs the position of major sandur systems remained relatively stable. As the sequence built up, however, the importance of dead-ice ridge control declined and in a number of troughs abrupt upward fining in facies assemblage is indicative of the sudden abandonment of the channel system and its subsequent occupation only during peak flood events. In other cases, coarse facies assemblages shift laterally upwards to transgress adjacent troughs. This resulted from the elimination of topographic constraint by the complete melt of dead-ice ridges and the consequent coalescence of sandur surfaces.

Subaqueous ice-marginal sedimentation – Jurby Head

The extensive cliff sections across Jurby Head, from Killane to Sartfield, have received relatively little recent attention, but were figured by

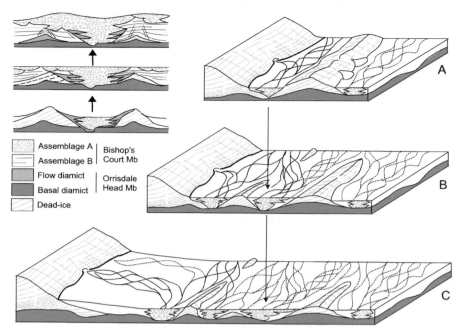

Figure 7.18 *A model for the deposition of the Bishop's Court Member. Inset top left shows development of one marginal sandur trough.*

Mitchell[110] and Thomas[111]. Remapping[112] for this volume, however, has demonstrated much greater complexity than previously recognised and a revised serial section is illustrated in Figure 7.19. Along much of the sections the Orrisdale Head Member of the Orrisdale Formation crops out at the base. Exceptionally well exposed at Jurby Head, where it reaches 25 m in thickness, it can be divided into three vertically sequential diamict assemblages. *Assemblage 1* occurs at the base and comprises a bedded diamict with individual beds, between 5 and 20 cm, separated by thin laminae of well-sorted fine sand. *Assemblage 2* is massive, but commonly displays regular boulder and cobble pavements. Many clasts show heavy striation and a significant number display characteristic subglacial 'bullet' shapes, with deeply striated upper surfaces and 'plucked' down-ice faces.

Figure 7.19 *Serial stratigraphic sections across Jurby Head between Killane and Sartfield showing palaeocurrent and structural data. Facies assemblages: Laminated Mud assemblage (LM); Massive Mud assemblage (MM); Alternating Sand and Mud assemblage (ASM); Sand assemblage (S); Diamict assemblage (D); Delta assemblage (DA).*

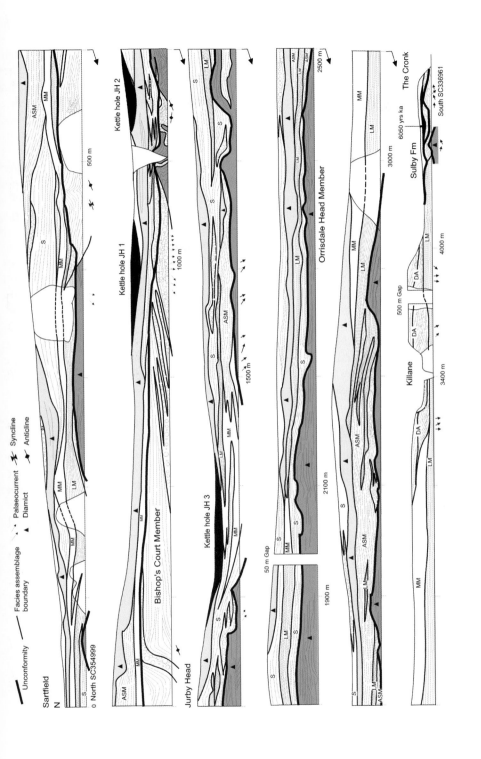

Sartfield
N

Unconformity
Facies assemblage boundary

Palaeocurrent
Diamict

Syncline
Anticline

0 North SC354999

500 m

Kettle hole JH 2

Kettle hole JH 1

1000 m

Bishop's Court Member

Jurby Head

Kettle hole JH 3

1500 m

50 m Gap

1900 m

2100 m

Orrisdale Head Member

2500 m

3000 m

MM

LM

500 m Gap

DA

DA

DA

Killane

3400 m

4000 m

Sulby Fm

The Cronk

6050 yrs ka

South SC336961

Other clasts show collision structures in which boulders have collided with another such that one or other, rarely both, are shattered or crushed. The shattered boulder often leaves a tail of streaked-out angular gravel clasts in its wake. *Assemblage 3* comprises alternating sequences of thin diamicts, separated by parallel-laminated sands, gravely sands and trough cross-bedded and massive gravels in laterally impersistent units between 5 cm and 50 cm in thickness. At its type-site at Orrisdale Head, Dackombe[113] interpreted the member as a terrestrial lodgement till and the exposure across Jurby Head is consistent with this view. Fabric evidence confirms an ice-flow direction from between north and northwest.

The Orrisdale Head Member is disconformably overlain by the Bishop's Court Member, a series of massive gravels and parallel-laminated, planar cross-bedded and rippled sands that crop out discontinuously. At the base they are cut into the upper surface of the Orrisdale Head Member in a series of wide, steep-sided channels, filled with gravel. Palaeocurrent indicators show transport direction towards the southeast. The sequence is locally deformed and structures include sharp-crested, upright and slightly over-turned folds. South of Sartfield a large-scale zig-zag fold brings up a prominent boulder gravel from below beach level to high in the cliff. The fold is sharply truncated by unconformably overlying massive muds. The clast content is exclusively Carboniferous Limestone boulders up to a metre in size and a seismic line shot across the foreshore indicates a bedrock surface less than 20 m below O.D., a depth confirmed by the positive gravity anomaly reported for the area by Cornwell[114]. This evidence of structural unconformity clearly identifies an episode of override and conse-quent deformation of the substrate caused by readvance immediately before deposition of the Jurby Formation.

The sequence of sediments overlying the Bishop's Court Member was originally identified by Thomas[115] and subsequently divided by Thomas[116] and Chiverrell *et al.*[117] into a number of members. Remapping[118], however, has demonstrated that none of these members shows stratigraphic conti-nuity. Consequently, the Jurby Formation is best left stratigraphically unclassified and instead divided into five lithofacies assemblages.

Laminated Mud assemblage (LM)   Architecturally this assemblage occurs as parallel-bounded sheets, lenses or southerly thickening wedges, up to 6 m thick and a kilometre in lateral extent. It crops out extensively north of The Cronk, to the north of Killane, around Sartfield and across Jurby Head (Figure 7.19). The basal boundary is sharp but the upper is gradational into massive mud or alternating sand and mud. Internally the assemblage consists of parallel-laminated mud in sharply bounded units a few millimetres to a few centimetres thick (Log D, Figure 7.20). Individual units can be divided into couplets with the lower component a massive clay and the upper component a finely laminated silt, separated by a sharp boundary. At regular intervals through the sequence individual units, or groups of units, are disturbed by convolution over distances of 10 to 20 m along the bedding. Occasional, low-angled intraformational disconformities also occur and are associated with small-scale roll-up structures arising from the slide of mud units down the depositional slope. The muds are generally stoneless, but north of The Cronk regular dropstone horizons occur. These show either single, well-spaced clasts up to 10 cm or clusters of smaller clasts, scattered across a lamination surface. The larger clasts display character-istic bending and penetration of units beneath the clast, bedding disruption at the margin and onlap across the top. The fine grain size and small-scale rhythmic cyclicity indicate suspension sedimentation in a standing water body in a distal location away from coarser-grained marginal input. The presence of dropstones suggests that the water body was periodically in contact with glacier ice that delivered debris-charged bergs to it.

Massive Mud assemblage (MM)   This assemblage is a massive, virtually stoneless clay occurring either in parallel-bounded sheets or large lenses up to 8 m thick and 300–400 m in lateral extent. It commonly occurs inter-calated with, passing into or overlying the laminated mud assemblage (Log D, Figure 7.20). In clean section it occurs as massive or sometimes faintly laminated units, 1 to 2 m thick, bounded by discontinuous units of fine to medium, parallel-laminated or rippled sand up to 50 cm thick. The bound-aries between the clay and sand are invariably convoluted on a scale of up to a metre or more. The characteristic fine grain size of this assemblage suggests deposition in a standing water body but in a more proximal loca-tion via heavy suspension rain-out from water with high suspended sediment concentration.

Alternating Sand and Mud assemblage (ASM)   This distinctive assem-blage occurs in southward thickening wedges up to 10 m thick and 300 m in lateral extent. It comprises rapidly alternating, sharply defined, contin-uous units of laminated mud and parallel-laminated or rippled sand in couplets ranging from a few millimetres to 20 cm in thickness (Log A, Figure 7.20). Couplet thickness and the ratio of sand to mud increase upwards. The sand component shows an upward passage from parallel-laminated sand into rippled fine sand. The sharply defined base of the mud component is draped over the topmost ripple structure in the underlying sand, but rapidly becomes horizontally laminated. Each mud unit consists

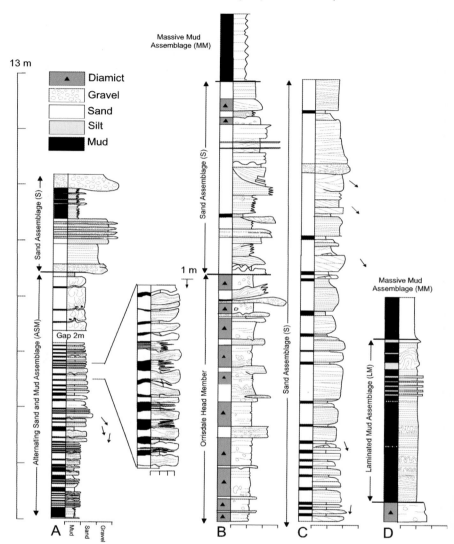

Figure 7.20 *Representative logs through facies assemblages in the Jurby Formation.* *(a) Alternating sand and mud assemblage passing up into Sand assemblage. Expanded log shows detail. (b) Passage upwards from Orrisdale Head Member, through Sand assemblage into Laminated Mud assemblage. (c) Sand assemblage. (d) Passage upwards from Laminated Mud assemblage into Massive Mud assemblage. After G.S.P. Thomas* et al. *(2004).*

of up to ten smaller couplets, usually less than 5 to 10 mm in thickness each comprising a thicker unit of massive mud grading upwards into either silt or very fine sand laminae rarely more than a few grains thick. Palaeocurrent directions show transport towards the southeast. The regular cyclicity and lateral persistence suggest deposition by rapidly fluctuating, low-velocity turbidite flow in a subaqueous fan building outwards from the exit of a subglacial meltwater stream below the waterline of a large water body.

Sand assemblage (S)   This assemblage occurs as parallel-bounded sheets, lenses or southwards thickening wedges up to 10 m thick and 800 m in lateral extent. A number of major discontinuities occur within individual units and extend to hundreds of metres but invariably pass out southwards where the upper and lower units become conformable. The assemblage consists predominantly of parallel-laminated or low-angle, cross-stratified sand, together with rippled sand, planar cross-bedded sand and thin units of laminated or massive mud (Log C, Figure 7.20), often in upward-fining sequences (Logs A and B, Figure 7.20). The assemblage is very similar to the distal facies assemblage of the Bishop's Court Member of the Orrisdale Formation at Orrisdale Head and is suggestive of distal sandur sedimentation.

Diamict assemblage (D)   This assemblage, consists of four discrete, parallel-bounded, off-lapping sheets of diamict stacked laterally one above the other. Each sheet is up to 20 m thick and extends for between 300 and 800 m. The northern end of each sheet underlies the surface, then extends south and is overlain, underlain and fronted by a thickening wedge of sand assemblage before thinning out. The next diamict sheet appears at the surface beyond the termination of the previous diamict. Except for the sand assemblage all the other lithofacies assemblages are transgressively overlain by the diamicts. The diamicts consist of relatively homogeneous mud with a low proportion of small, usually well-rounded clasts. Generally massive, some sections show diffuse lamination, sometimes marked by thin sand laminae. Many sections show well-developed vertical joints indicative of loading. They are interpreted as basal lodgement tills.

Delta assemblage (DA)   This assemblage occurs in two separate sequences at Killane and north of The Cronk. At the base, sharply overlying the laminated mud assemblage, are up to 8 m of large-scale planar cross-beds dipping at angles up to 25° to the southeast. Each foreset consists of sands and gravels either in partially graded sets averaging 1–2 m thick or as massive sands. They are interpreted as debris fall deposits formed by avalanching down the foreset slope of a simple delta or by collapse at the delta brink zone. They are unconformably overlain by flat-lying sheets of matrix-supported massive gravel and sand interpreted as representing the progradation of fluvial topsets across the delta front.

A summary of the distribution of lithofacies assemblages is shown in Figure 7.21a. Clearly, the assemblages do not form a simple layer-cake sequence, but display a number of distinctive architectural elements. First, the four diamict assemblages occur in a stacked, off-lapping sequence in the down-ice direction. In other words, each diamict extends beyond the limit reached by the one beneath it. Thus, the first appearance of each diamict starts high in the succession then descends to thin and pass out beneath the appearance of the next diamict stratigraphically above it. Second, each diamict is unconformable upon a package of lithofacies assemblages that are thickest beneath the termination of each diamict and then thin rapidly down-ice. Thirdly, each package is deposited disconformably across a common floor of Orrisdale Formation. The essential architecture is therefore of a series of off-lapping wedges of repeated lithofacies assemblage bounded downwards by an unconformity and upwards by an unconformable diamict.

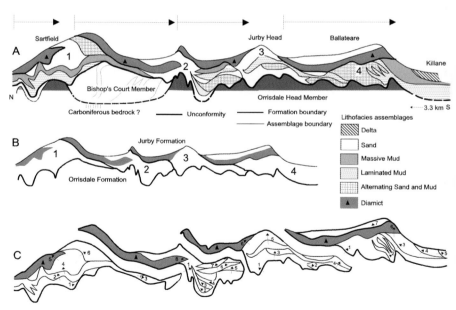

Figure 7.21 *(a) Distribution of lithofacies assemblages in the Jurby Formation. (b) Summary showing distribution of numbered packages. (c) Exploded diagram of each package showing order of deposition. After G.S.P. Thomas et al. (2004).*

The repetition of lithofacies assemblages is best analysed using sequence stratigraphy[119]. Sequence stratigraphy is the subdivision of sedimentary basin fills into packages bounded by unconformities, and a sequence is defined as a stratigraphic unit of genetically related strata bounded at their top and base by unconformities. In the context of glacial sequences, the architecture of proglacial sedimentary bodies is determined by whether the margin is advancing or retreating[120]. When advancing, the apex, or input point, extends away from the ice-margin, forming an off-lapping sequence. When retreating, the apex extends towards the ice-margin, forming an on-lapping sequence. From the summary distribution of lithofacies assemblages four off-lapping packages can be identified and are shown simplified in 7.21B. Each package is defined by an unconformity above and below it. Within each package the order of deposition of each lithofacies assemblage can be determined by counting the boundary changes from one assemblage type to the next from the lower bounding unconformity to the upper. An exploded summary of the order of sequence elements is shown in Figure 7.21c. Analysis of the order of change shows that the most common assemblage sequence is a down-ice shift from sand (S), through alternating sand and mud (ASM), then massive mud (MM) into laminated mud (LM), though considerable local variation, repetition and reversal occur.

As all lithofacies assemblages in the Jurby Formation, apart from the diamict and sand assemblages, were deposited in standing water, the sequence represents the depositional response to successive phases of read-vance off-lapping one another into the margin of a large water body. Given the lack of an *in situ* fauna in the laminated and massive mud assemblages the water body was most likely lacustrine rather than marine. This was ponded between the ice-margin and the Orrisdale moraine ridge against which the Jurby Formation thins. Considerable fluctuation in water level is indicated by lateral shifts from ice-contact to non ice-contact margins. Based on the contact height between topset and foreset components in the delta assemblage and the maximum height of laminated lake floor sediment, the lake had a minimum water level of 8 m O.D. and a maximum of 40 m O.D. Within this range, and dependent upon available accommodation space, rate of sedimentation and ice thickness, depositional environments at the margin probably shifted rapidly between ice-contact subaqueous fans, ice-contact deltas and outwash fan-deltas. Evidence for eventual draining of the lake is provided at The Cronk where laminated bottomsets underlying the foreset sub-facies are sharply incised by a steep-sided, wide channel filled with trough cross-stratified sand of probable fluviatile origin. The relationship between this lake and the lake waters identified at The Dog Mills on the east coast is considered in a subsequent section of this chapter.

The south of the island

The Plain of Malew, the lowland area at the very south of the island running between Santon Head and the Calf of Man, displays some distinctive glacial geology not otherwise seen on the island (Figure 7.22). The primary morphology of the area is controlled by the boundary of the Carboniferous Limestone basin around Castletown, which runs, as a fault, approximately northeast from Port St Mary towards Ballasalla then southeast, as an unconformity, to the coast north of the airport. This boundary serves to divide the south into three principal geomorphic areas.

Area 1 occurs to the northwest of the Carboniferous basin boundary and forms the rise of slope into the slate massif of the southern uplands towards South Barrule. The slopes are clothed by a thin veneer of local diamict reworked by periglacial processes and show limited relief. These diamicts are part of the Snaefell Formation. In a number of localities, series of narrow rock channels have been exhumed by gully erosion and show that beneath the smooth cover of local diamict the bedrock surface is frequently very irregular. These channels have unusual, up and down, long profiles and are sometimes multi-channel. They are probably subglacial, cut by meltwater streams running in tunnels beneath the ice when it over-topped the island, then subsequently filled with slope deposit upon deglaciation. Other channels feed a number of major alluvial fans that descend from the southern uplands around Colby. These were probably

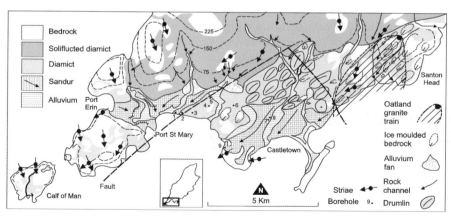

Figure 7.22 *Map of the glacial geomorphology of the south of the island.*

active, like those fringing the northern uplands, during and after deglaciation when ice had cleared the uplands.

Area 2 occurs to the northeast of the Carboniferous basin boundary, east of Ballasalla and on towards Santon Head and Port Soderick. It is characterised by a number of large, low-amplitude rock-cored ridges, up to a kilometre in length, that show a pronounced sub-parallel orientation running northeast to southwest, coincident with the direction of local striae, the flow of erratics from the adjacent Oatland Granite and the strike of the underlying Manx Group slates. They were most probably formed by intense subglacial erosion beneath thick ice passing obliquely onshore during a major ice advance episode across the island. A number of the ridges are separated by short rock channels, usually less than 500 m in length, running southwest, and include those now occupied by the Port St Mary railway and the Douglas to Castletown road. Now devoid of drainage they were probably formed subglacially by large streams in tunnels at the base of the ice.

Area 3 covers the majority of ground occupied by the Carboniferous basin around Castletown, but extends across its boundary in the west towards Port Erin. In the northeast, around Ballasalla, is a prominent field of drumlins. The drumlins are formed mainly on limestone and their up-ice boundary approximately coincides with a shift from a Manx Group to a Carboniferous Limestone substrate. Altitudes range between 30 and 70 m, amplitude is between 10 and 20 m, lengths range up to a kilometre and, with a few exceptions, orientation is predominantly northeast to southwest. Drumlin size and shape are variable though all have an ovate planform, sub-parallel to the long axis. Elongation ratios rarely exceed 3:1. Most of the drumlins appear to have rock cores mantled by diamict up to 4–5 m in thickness. The remainder of the area forms low, undulating terrain floored by limestones overlain by diamict and sand and gravel and small areas, to the southwest of Ballabeg, of ice-disintegration topography. The undulating surface can be partially attributed to the occurrence of underlying reef limestones and, in some cases, low-relief bedrock streamlining. The diamicts are primarily composed of limestone clasts together with slate and Oatland Granite erratics, derived by subglacial transport from the immediate northeast and are classified as the Ballasalla Member of the Shellag Formation. The sand and gravels, classified as the Plain of Malew Member, are associated with a series of narrow, flat-floored sandur troughs running to the southwest and are composed of clasts of both local and foreign origin. They represent deposition from the ice-margin as the icesheet thinned and retreated northwards across the island. Small sections in these sandur, showing stacked sets of planar cross-bedded sand and gravel, occur on the eastern side of Bay ny Carrickey and on the road to St Michael's Isle and show flow directions to the southwest. Further sandur surfaces, cut one into the other, occur between Port St Mary and Peel. In these cases meltwater flow direction is towards the southeast, reflecting drainage from a declining ice-margin off the west coast of the island. The sandur surfaces are cut through by shallow alluvial channels that represent post-glacial fluvial adjustment along the line of the Silver Burn and other rivers draining from the uplands to the north.

Figure 7.23 shows log profiles from a series of shallow boreholes drilled in a line running from Bay ny Carrickey east towards Ballasalla. Most boreholes record an upward passage from bedrock, through diamict into sands and gravels, though some are composed either entirely of diamict (Borehole 7) or sand and gravel (Borehole 2). Thick diamict towards the base of Borehole 4, to the rear of Strandhall, is underlain by 30 cm of banded, brown-black, completely humified organic mud, and a provisional radiocarbon date on the lowest mud unit has provided an uncalibrated age of 36,000 ± 670 ^{14}C yrs BP. This date indicates that the island was ice-free at this time and that a major expansion of ice sufficient to bury the southern part of the island occurred after deposition of the organic muds.

The relationship between the local and foreign deposits

In general terms the local deposits are restricted to the upland areas of the island and the foreign deposits to the lowland. At points on both the east and west coasts where the slates first appear from beneath the northern drift plain good exposure shows the stratigraphic relationships between the two suites. As the foreign deposits are a product of Irish Sea glaciation and the local deposits are largely a product of reworking of former locally derived glacial deposits, the stratigraphic relationship between the two suites allows the construction of an event sequence that records the varying influence of foreign glacial and local glacial and periglacial conditions. The two most significant sites are at Ballure on the east coast, and Gob ny Creggan Glassey on the west.

Ballure
On the east coast the northern drift plain terminates against the slate massif at Ballure (SC458936), south of Ramsey. Banked against a slate cliff is a very complex sequence of local and foreign glacigenic deposits previously described by Cumming[121], Horne[122], Kendall[123], Lamplugh[124] and Thomas[125]. Lamplugh described the rock in the corner of the section as an 'old cliff' that descended below modern beach level. A seismic line running

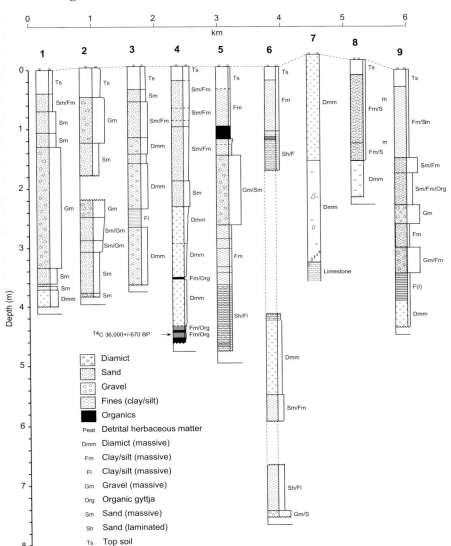

Figure 7.23 *Borehole logs from the southern part of the Isle of Man. For location of boreholes see Figure 7.22.*

20 m seaward of the cliff indicates that it is fronted by a narrow rock platform at –3 m O.D. A cave separates the main portion of the cliff from a small buried sea stack and both are buried by an apron of scree (Unit 1, Figure 7.24), up to 6 m in thickness. The scree is composed of large, very angular, broken blocks of local Manx Group slate up to a metre in diameter, tightly packed and with little matrix. It is succeeded by 5 m of stratified, dull olive-brown diamict (Unit 2) crowded with angular slate fragments, dipping north off the rock slope. This is succeeded by ~ 50 cm of laminated sandy clay, clay laminae and light brown to red sand (Unit 3), thickening as it dips off slope. Intermixed are occasional small clasts, mostly of slate but with a significant proportion of small, rounded, foreign erratics. Conformably above is a 4.5 m sequence of hard, compact, blue-grey local diamict (Unit 4) showing a crude down-slope stratification. This is succeeded sharply upwards by 7 m of contorted sands and gravels (Unit 5) broadly divisible into two upward-fining sequences. The sand is a yellow-brown, friable, well-sorted medium sand containing numerous small, broken shell fragments. The gravels are well rounded and composed predominantly of foreign erratics and a small admixture of less well-rounded Manx Slate clasts. No foreign diamict is seen directly associated with these sands and gravels, but Kendall noted 'a boss of clay' containing shell fragments and foreign boulders, between them and the underlying diamict. Foreign diamict, very similar to the Shellag Member, is exposed on the foreshore and may be equivalent to the foreign clay observed by Kendall. Together, these two units represent the first appearance of dominantly foreign sediment in the sequence.

The foreign sands and gravels are disconformably overlain by a further blue-grey local diamict (Unit 6) up to 4.5 m thick, dipping off-slope. This diamict is more massive, less well stratified and has a higher proportion of clay matrix than the otherwise similar diamict below. It is succeeded by a yellow-brown, sandy, unstratified diamict (Unit 7) thickening rapidly off-slope and containing a majority of edge-rounded and sometimes deeply striated local slate clasts, but with up to 25% foreign erratics in places. It is further exposed on the foreshore where it is overlain by foreign diamicts of the Shellag Formation. The scree and the predominantly local diamicts

Figure 7.24 *Sections showing the relationship between foreign and local deposits at Ballure. (a) Serial stratigraphic section. (b) Generalised vertical log showing major lithostratigraphic units. Based on maximum thickness of individual units. (c) Fabric directions in the local diamicts (Units 2, 4 and 6). (d) Fabric directions in the yellow diamict (Unit 7). (e) Fabric directions in the Shellag Formation diamict exposed on the foreshore. (f) Fabric directions in local gravels (Units 8, 10, 12 and 14).*

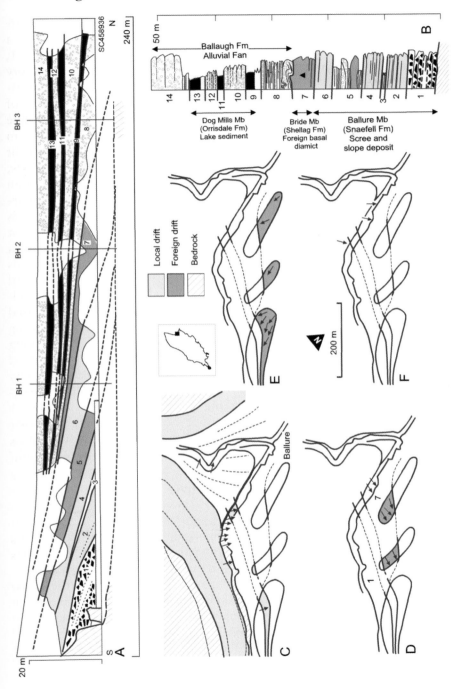

(Units 2, 4 and 6) are formally grouped together as the Ballure Member of the Snaefell Formation, as they are primarily of local origin and lithologically similar to the local deposits of the uplands. The sands and gravels and the yellow-brown diamict (Units 5 and 7) are informally grouped into the Shellag Formation, as they are of predominantly foreign origin and stratigraphically equivalent to it.

The overlying succession is repetitive with large thicknesses of local gravel, sand, silt and clay (Units 8, 10 and 12) alternating with massive, tabular sheets of foreign, red, stoneless clay and well-sorted sand (Units 9, 11 and 13). The local sequences comprise rapidly varying sets of well-sorted pebble to granule gravel, sand and thin laminated and massive silts and clays, thickening northwards. The lowest local gravel (Unit 8) is erosionally disconformable upon the Ballure Member beneath it and is disturbed at the base by either weakly developed frost wedges or load or gravitational slide structures. The intercalated red clays occur as flat-lying, tabular units with very sharply defined upper and lower boundaries. Internally, each unit consists of massive, almost stoneless red clay passing locally into laminated clay and well-sorted red sand. These clays have some considerable stratigraphic continuity as they are recorded at depths of between −6 and −8 m O.D. in a borehole a kilometre to the north at Ramsey Harbour[126]. In turn they correlate with three similar red clays units occurring within the Dog Mills Member north of the Grand Island Hotel and together identify a shallow basin under the town site of Ramsey. The succession at Ballure is completed by a 3 m thick unit of coarse, poorly sorted and dirty cobble gravel containing only locally derived clasts (Unit 14). The local gravels are informally grouped into the Ballaugh Formation, as they are of local origin and occupy the same stratigraphic position as similar fan gravels issuing from the mountain front at Sulby and Ballaugh. The red clays are referred to the Dog Mills Member of the Orrisdale Formation by virtue of their lateral correlation.

Glen Mooar

On the west coast, the foreign drift thins against the rising slate massive south of Glen Mooar. The first coastal exposure of local deposits occurs to the north of Glen Mooar and the solid makes its first appearance in the coastal cliff sections 500 m to the south, at Glen Beeg. Between these two locations, and south towards Glen Thoar, the relationship between the local and foreign deposits is well displayed. The sections have been previously described by Kendall[127], Lamplugh[128], Mitchell[129] and Thomas[130] and a revised serial section is shown in Figure 7.25. Thomas identified seven major lithological units. In contrast to Ballure, no clearly identified cliff is

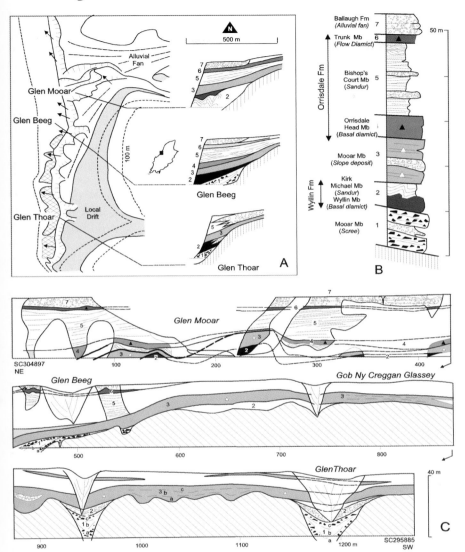

Figure 7.25 *Sections showing the relationship between foreign and local deposits in the area around Glen Mooar. (a) Map of area around Glen Mooar showing distribution of deposits, fabric directions and local variations in the stratigraphic succession. (b) Generalised vertical log showing major lithostratigraphic units. Based on maximum thickness of individual units. (c) Serial stratigraphic succession between Glen Mooar and Glen Thoar.*

seen buried beneath the local deposits and the slate surface dips gently below beach level at Glen Beeg. To the south, towards Gob ny Creggan Glassey, the bedrock rises high in the cliff sections and is capped by an attenuated thickness of mainly local drift.

At Glen Beeg the bedrock is overlain by coarse scree (Unit 1, Figure 7.25) dipping off the bedrock slope and divisible, as at Ballure, into three units. The relationship between the basal scree and the bedrock is not clear. but is in part gradational, with a downward passage from coarse scree through heavily broken and weathered bedrock into fresh bedrock. At Glen Beeg the toe of the off-slope dipping scree is overlain by a thinning wedge of dull-red, clay-rich foreign diamict, the Wyllin Member of the Shellag Formation (Unit 2). This diamict is further exposed north of Glen Mooar and in a large section up the glen. In both these locations it is highly deformed and both overlain and underlain by thick sands of the Kirk Michael Member. The Wyllin and Kirk Michael Members are, in turn, overlain by the Mooar Member (Unit 3). This was described by Mitchell[131] as 'slate-grey', 'packed with local stones' and containing blocks of the underlying Wyllin Member. It is further exposed in the section in Glen Mooar where it comprises a tabular unit of massive blue-grey diamict crowded with angular local rock clasts, dipping off the rock slope to the rear and markedly unconformable upon contorted Wyllin and Kirk Michael Members below.

On the coast to the south, the Mooar Member is almost continuously exposed from Glen Beeg, across the headland of Gob ny Creggan Glassey to Glen Thoar and beyond. Architecturally, it drapes the bedrock as a down-slope thickening wedge. Its composition is extremely variable and in places it consists of a single massive unit. Elsewhere, a crude three-fold division may be identified. The lower and upper divisions are similar and consist of faintly stratified, laterally impersistent, diamict units crowded with angular to sub-angular local clasts set in a silty-clay matrix. The middle unit, however, consists of a highly variable sequence of bedded gravels, grey sands and thin, parallel-laminated silts and clays, often separated by thin beds of diamict. Fabrics from the massive diamicts and interstratified gravels all show a pronounced off-slope orientation that parallels variation in the underlying bedrock surface. The Mooar Scree and Mooar Diamict are formally grouped together as the Mooar Member of the Snaefell Formation.

At the entrance to Glen Mooar, the Mooar Diamict is locally overlain by a foreign diamict, the Orrisdale Head Member (Unit 4). This comprises a mixed assemblage of local and foreign clasts set in a sandy clay matrix. It is in turn overlain by up to 30 m of sands of the Bishop's Court Member

(Unit 5) that thins rapidly as the bedrock surface rises south. This member consists of parallel-laminated fine to medium yellow sand, planar and trough cross-stratified coarse yellow sands and occasional massive fine gravels, showing a palaeoflow direction towards the southwest. These sands are, in turn, overlain by a thin and persistent foreign diamict, the Trunk Member (Unit 6). The succession is terminated by a flat-lying sheet of local cryoturbated gravels, the Ballaleigh Member (Unit 7), that issue as a widening, westward flowing fan from a deep gorge that crosses the watershed between Glen Mooar and Glen Wyllin.

SEQUENCE OF EVENTS

Little is known of glacial events in the Isle of Man prior to the last glaciation as the deposits associated with them are unexposed at the surface and recorded only from boreholes. It is most likely, however, that the pattern of glaciation in any of the earlier glacial episodes was similar to that of the last glaciation, as flow paths would have been dominated by passage of ice south through the basin from source areas in western and southern Scotland. The stratigraphic record suggests that the Isle of Man was overridden by ice at least once before the Devensian glaciation, but the age and duration of these glaciations remains speculative due to a lack of chronological data. The earliest episode, represented by the diamicts of the Ayre Lighthouse Formation deep beneath the Point of Ayre, may have occurred as far back as cold stage 12 (*circa* 400 ka), but equally may be assigned to the much younger cold stage 6 (*circa* 150 ka).

The last interglacial

No deposits of unequivocal interglacial age have been found exposed on the island. The Ayre Formation, sandwiched between the underlying Ayre Lighthouse Formation and the overlying Kiondroughad Formation, comprises shelly silts and sands at depths between −65 and −73 m O.D. Lamplugh[132] examined the shell fauna and considered it to be *in situ* and to represent a probable interglacial marine assemblage. If this is the case it may correspond to temperate oxygen isotope stage 5e, the Ipswichian interglacial (*circa* 125–118 ka), and may be correlated with similar fossiliferous marine clay recorded beneath diamict from a borehole at Wigton in the Solway Lowlands[133] and marine sediments occurring between diamicts in Lower Furness[134].

In the southern Irish Sea fossiliferous raised beach deposits are common and have been used as interglacial marker horizons for the lithostratigraphic succession above and below them[135]. This approach cannot be adopted in the northern basin for its coastlines are devoid of raised beach deposits overlain by glacigenic sediment. In the southern basin the apparent parallelism in height of the raised beaches implies the return of interglacial sea level to approximately the same height as the modern sea level. This does not appear to be the case in the northern basin and the limited evidence available suggests that the last interglacial marine datum now lies below modern sea level. Two explanations may account for this. The first is that isostatic rebound, arising from depression of the sea-floor during the Devensian glaciation, has not yet achieved equilibrium. The amount of depression in the northern basin is likely to have been greater than in the southern, due to thicker ice nearer the source areas, with a consequent longer rebound. There is currently little evidence to establish if rebound is complete or not and this explanation remains speculative. The second explanation concerns tectonic instability in the basin. Despite the fact that the Quaternary appears to have been a tectonically relatively quiet period in western Britain, Dobson[136] has drawn attention to the probability of movement along the boundary faults that define the graben structure of the Irish Sea basin. Loading by ice during successive glaciations may therefore have reactivated these movements and complicated the relative vertical movement of sea level between the glaciations.

The only evidence in the island for a relatively high interglacial sea level comes from Ballure. Here, the buried cliff, sea stack and fronting rock platform suggest a former temperate sea level at about 3 m below the modern. This episode pre-dates all the exposed glacial deposits of the island as the cliff underlies the lowest members of the Shellag Formation. On the basis that nowhere else in the complex cold climate record seen above the buried cliff is there evidence for any significant temperate climatic break, the buried cliff at Ballure is tentatively assigned to oxygen isotope stage 5e, the Ipswichian interglacial. If this is correct it implies that most of the great northern plain of the island did not exist during the last interglacial and that the sea lapped directly against the great rock escarpment running west from Ramsey.

The Early and Middle Devensian

Traditionally, the Devensian Cold Stage has been divided into three oxygen isotope stages. The Lower Devensian (stage 4) occurred between the end of isotope stage 5a at *circa* 75,000 BP and 50,000 BP and the Middle Devensian (stage 3)[137] between 50,000 and 25,000 BP. Although some workers have postulated an Early or Middle Devensian ice expansion into the northern Irish Sea basin as early as 75,000 BP[138], it has, until recently, been generally accepted that Britain and Ireland were largely free of extensive lowland icesheets between the end of the Ipswichian (stage 5a) at *circa* 75,500 BP and the opening of the Late Devensian (stage 2) at *circa* 25,000 BP, and that this long period was marked by cold, periglacial environments, interrupted by a number of brief interstadial episodes. The relationship between the local and foreign deposits on the island lends some support to this contention. The occurrence of scree banked against the buried fossil cliff at Ballure indicates that at the time of formation of the scree not only did frost processes prevail at the site, but also the cliff had been abandoned, presumably as a result of world-wide eustatic sea-level lowering resulting from the onset of a cold climate. The thick succession of local diamicts that succeeds the scree, at both Ballure and Glen Mooar, is indicative of a prolonged period of local deposition resulting from periglacial freeze-thaw break-up of local bedrock and its consequent transmission down-slope by solifluction processes. As these deposits occur beneath the first evidence of widespread foreign ice penetration on to the island, marked by the deposits of the overlying Shellag Formation, they must pre-date the expansion of ice into the Irish Sea basin during the Late Devensian and consequently date from a period in the Early or Middle Devensian.

The concept of an ice-free Early and Middle Devensian in Britain, however, is at variance with the behaviour of the Scandinavian and Laurentide icesheets and the ice core and oxygen isotope records[139] which all show repeated fluctuation in ice volume during these periods. In a review of this problem, Bowen *et al.*[140] argue that the British Sheet was a long-lived feature that was maintained throughout much of Devensian time and fluctuated in volume in sympathy with global ice volume. Evidence for these fluctuations may occur in the borehole record from beneath the northern plain. The Ayre Formation, identified as most probably of Ipswichian interglacial (stage 5e) age, is succeeded by the Kiondroughad Formation. This consists of sands, gravels and diamicts of northern origin, overlain by the Shellag Formation, which is of demonstrable Late Devensian (stage 2) age. The Kiondroughad Formation must, therefore, represent a glacial episode that occurred in the Early or Middle Devensian (stages 4 and 3), between *circa* 75,000 and 25,000 BP. A possible scenario for glacial events during this period would involve continuous ice-cover in the source areas of southern and western Scotland and repeated local advance and retreat of the southern margin into the northern part of the Irish Sea basin at least as far south as the Isle of Man. Whether the ice overwhelmed or partly buried the island during this period is unknown.

The Late Devensian

In the traditional view the Late Devensian glacial stage opened at *circa* 25,000 BP with rapid accumulation of ice in the source areas of Scotland and its expansion south through the Irish Sea basin to reach its maximum limits at around *circa* 22,000 BP north of Wolverhampton, in the English Midlands, and between Pembrokeshire and Wexford in the southern Irish Sea basin. Based on [36]Cl cosmogenic isotope dating, Bowen *et al.*[141] have recognised a number of phases of glacial expansion during the Late Devensian, each associated with climatically driven Heinrich events identified in the North Atlantic marine sediment record. Thus they suggest that the British Icesheet reached its maximum extent not at *circa* 22,500 BP but before *circa* 36,500 BP when the whole of Ireland was glaciated and the limit of the Irish Sea ice stream lay well out in the Celtic Sea (Figure 7.2b, stage 1). In their view rapid deglaciation of the Irish Sea basin began after this date due to icesheet collapse in response to Heinrich event 4. Between *circa* 36,000 and 25,000 BP they argue that the icesheet fluctuated several times with the traditional limits of the Last Glacial Maximum being reached at *circa* 22,000 BP, soon after Heinrich event 2. Extensive deglaciation occurred in the period to *circa* 17,000 BP, followed by subsequent readvance associated with Heinrich event 1.

Throughout these Late Devensian icesheet fluctuations the Isle of Man must have been subject to successive readvance across or around it. The principal difficulty in understanding the Devensian glaciation of the island therefore lies in matching the record of icesheet fluctuation with what is known of the stratigraphic succession on the island. In this work we have identified three Late Devensian glacigenic formations within the Manx glacial stratigraphic succession, each lithologically distinct and each separated from one another by an unconformity. Each of these unconformities demonstrates override by ice and thereby identifies an advance or readvance event. In the remaining part of this chapter we shall examine the nature of each of these events, attempt to place them in a chronology and devise a palaeogeographical reconstruction based on the detail obtained from the various sites examined around the island.

The Shellag event (*circa* 36,000–22,000 BP)

The Shellag Formation consists of a suite of predominantly red, clay-rich, clast-poor diamicts and subordinate sands and gravels extensively exposed around both northern coasts of the island. Its base is nowhere seen, but it is assumed to rest on the Kiondroughad Formation, of presumed Early

Devensian (oxygen isotope stage 4) age and is everywhere unconformably overlain by deposits of the Orrisdale Formation. The massive, clay-rich diamicts of the Shellag Formation are very similar to other 'Irish Sea Tills' exposed throughout the Irish Sea basin, particularly in the coastal lowlands of the Lake District, the Lleyn Peninsula, Pembrokeshire and southeast Ireland, but their origin has been controversial. Whilst most workers have interpreted them as terrestrial lodgement tills, others regard them as a product of glaciomarine conditions[142]. Whatever their origin the deposits of the Shellag Formation clearly represent a widespread episode of ice advance across the island to a limit well to the south. The age of this episode is constrained by the radiocarbon date of *circa* 36,000 BP recently obtained from Strandhall in the south of the island. The date occurs in organic muds overlying Carboniferous Limestone bedrock, but underlying thick diamict of the Ballasalla Member of the Shellag Formation. This relationship clearly indicates that the Irish Sea basin was ice-free at least as far north as the Isle of Man at *circa* 36,000 BP, but was subsequently overwhelmed by advancing ice sometime after this. The view is consistent with radiocarbon dates derived from shells within the Cronk ny Arrey Laa Member of the Shellag Formation at Shellag Point which indicate a major glacial expansion sometime after *circa* 41,000 BP.

During the Shellag event the island was completely buried by ice to its summit with ice thicknesses probably in excess of 800 m above sea level. In the north the basal layers of the advancing ice carried large quantities of debris, derived from northerly sources, and deposited it across what is now the northern plain. As the ice passed around the island margin it became increasingly contaminated with local debris derived from the Manx and Dalby Groups of slates. In the south, changing bed conditions, caused by differences in substrate lithology on passage of basal ice from impermeable Manx Group slates onto permeable Carboniferous Limestone, triggered thick diamict deposition and the generation of drumlins. The upper parts of the ice thickness carried little northerly debris, but as the ice passed over the island local bedrock was eroded and a discontinuous sheet of local diamicts was deposited across the upland areas. It was during this episode that most of the small erosional landforms of the upland areas, including striae, ice-moulded roche moutonnée forms and small rock channels, cut by water in subglacial tunnels, were generated.

The Orrisdale event (*circa* 22,000 BP)

From its maximum limit in the southern Irish Sea basin, the margin of the icesheet associated with the Shellag event retreated to the north of the island sometime after *circa* 23,000 BP. How far north is not known. During this episode the Isle of Man was ice-free and subject to a periglacial climate in which frost processes reworked residual local glacial diamicts left behind from the passage of the icesheet across the uplands. This is confirmed at Glen Mooar where extensive local deposits overlie foreign diamicts assigned to the Shellag Formation. At the same time runoff from the uplands transported large quantities of local sediment into a series of alluvial fans draining the northern uplands. This is confirmed by the succession at Ballure which shows the accumulation of repeated sequences of local gravel above foreign diamicts assigned to the Shellag Formation.

The Orrisdale Formation overlies the Shellag Formation with marked structural unconformity, indicating the occurrence of a substantial readvance. The stratigraphic evidence shows that, at its maximum, the Orrisdale readvance limit stood against the rear of the Bride Moraine at Shellag Point, ran west and then southwest along the moraine ridges towards Andreas, abutted against the rock margin around Ballaugh, climbed to a maximum height of some 180 m above current sea level to the rear of Kirk Michael and ran south to penetrate into the lowland embayment around Peel. From there the ice-margin ran south towards Dalby Point, along the foot of the high cliffs running southwest towards Bradda Head and southwest into what is now the Irish Sea.

As the readvancing ice slowed towards its maximum at Shellag Point, high subglacial stress deformed the underlying Shellag Formation, generated the tectonised Bride Moraine ridge at the immediate ice-margin and emplaced a sheet of basal subglacial diamict, the Ballavarkish Member, against it. Forward of the moraine extensive outwash sedimentation took place in ice-front alluvial fans, debris flows and sandur draining the margin between Andreas and the coast at Shellag Point (Figure 7.26). A major meltwater exit point was located to the west of Andreas, along the line of what is now the Lhen Trench and abutted into the northern margin of a large water body ponded between the ice-margin and the slate escarpment to the south. The balance of evidence from the Dog Mills Member suggests that the water body was lacustrine rather than glaciomarine as the contained microfauna are almost certainly derived. To the east the damming mechanism for the lake was probably provided by the extension of the ice limit from Shellag Point across Maughold Head with meltwater exiting via the low col that separates Maughold from the rock core of the island. During retreat from the maximum limit, repeated ice-marginal oscillation to the rear of the Shellag Point generated a series of basal diamict units, including the Ballaquark and Cranstal Members, each unconformably off-lapping one another, and each fronted by a moraine ridge and marginal channel system.

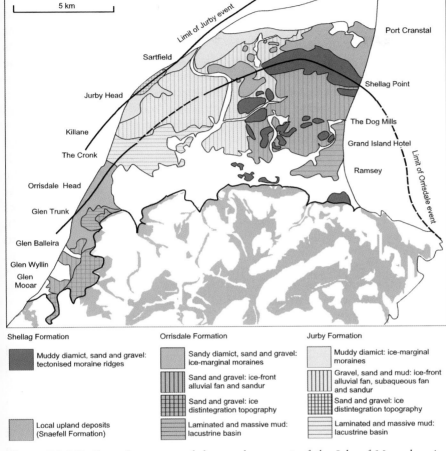

Figure 7.26 *Drift geology map of the northern part of the Isle of Man showing distribution of glacigenic formations and associated sediment-landform assemblages.*

Sufficient data are available in the Kirk Michael area to permit a detailed palaeogeographic reconstruction of events during the retreat from the maximum of the Orrisdale readvance event and are shown in Figure 7.27. The maximum limit of advance penetrated the upper parts of Glen Mooar and Glen Wyllin and the lower part of Glen Dhoo, reaching a maximum elevation of 180 m below the west face of Sartfell (Stage 1, Figure 7.27). At this time the uplands above this height were ice-free and summer drainage utilised the major valley systems to drain down to the ice-margin.

With retreat from the maximum limit of readvance, the ice surface declined and the margin moved northwest. As it did so it left behind further marginal moraine mounds (Stages 2 and 3, Figure 7.27). The origin of the deep rock channel cutting across the watershed between Glen Wyllin and Glen Mooar at Ballaleigh is enigmatic. Lamplugh[143] argued that it was cut by a marginal meltwater stream but it could equally be subglacial. Mitchell[144] suggested that it was cut by meltwater overflowing south from a lake ponded in the upper part of Glen Wyllin by the ice-margin (Stage 3, Figure 7.27).

As the ice continued to retreat it came away from the rock margin across an irregular floor of Orrisdale Head Member that it had deposited during readvance. The gap between the ice-front and the rock margin at this stage (Stage 4, Figure 7.27) provided a sink for the rapid accumulation of large volumes of outwash sediment in a wide marginal sandur draining to the southwest and the underlying Orrisdale Head Member diamict was largely buried out. As the margin retreated further, stagnation released large volumes of supraglacial dirt out across the sandur surface as a series of debris flows forming the Trunk Member. A model for the development of this sequence is given in Figure 7.28. As underlying dead-ice melted out, the outwash and debris flow surface collapsed to form a complex area of disorganised ridges, mounds and kettle basins. As the margin retreated further to the line of the Orrisdale Ridge (Stage 5, Figure 7.27) this area of stagnating ice acted as a barrier to outward flow of meltwater and a second

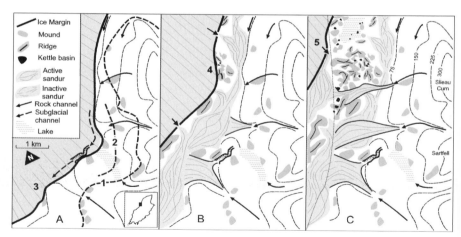

Figure 7.27 *Palaeogeographic reconstructions of stages in the retreat of ice from the area of Kirk Michael based on drift and geomorphological mapping, palaeocurrents and interpretation of sedimentary sequences. For explanation see text. Stages 1 and 2 are based on G.F. Mitchell (1965).*

sandur trough developed parallel to the ice-margin. A small ice-marginal lake system developed in front of the margin in the area around Bishop's Court and drained southwest to feed the sandur system. During the Late Glacial, sometime after the ice had departed, many of the kettle basins accumulated organic sediment. Subsequently, these basins were buried by prograding mountain-front alluvial fans issuing from Glen Wyllin and Glen Mooar and much of the original ice-stagnation topography was removed or buried.

Figure 7.29 reconstructs the palaeogeography of the adjacent Orrisdale area at the time of deposition of the Bishop's Court Member. It is based on the geomorphology, the distribution of facies assemblage types and their bounding dead-ice ridges, and on palaeocurrent and ice-direction indica-

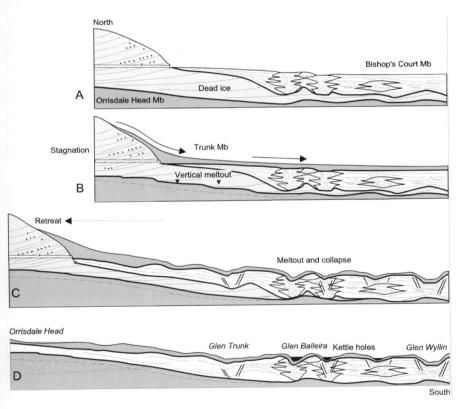

Figure 7.28 *A model for the accumulation of the Trunk Member. (a) Accumulation of outwash across a floor of buried ice in a supraglacial sandur system. (b) Release of supraglacial debris across the sandur surface. (c) Retreat of ice-margin, melt of buried ice and formation of pitted sandur surface. (d) Stratigraphic succession.*

tors. Two major stages can be identified. The first is equivalent to Stage 5 in the Kirk Michael area to the south (Figure 7.27) and is an extension northwards. At this stage the ice-margin ran southwest to northeast across Orrisdale Head with a sandur trough fronting it. The lake east of Bishop's Court, which drained into this sandur, was fed by small alluvial fans draining directly off the ice-margin. As the ice retreated from the Orrisdale ridge the sandur trough fronting it was abandoned. The ridge remained as a prominent barrier and subsequent outwash was constrained to run between it and the retreating ice-margin in a series of marginal sandur troughs. Penecontemporaneous with the development of the retreat stages remaining buried ice melted out to form an irregular, uncontrolled topography generally unrelated to conditions of deposition. Only at the very large scale, as in the overall morphological structure of the Orrisdale ridge, is some vestige of the original ridge structure preserved. Superimposed upon it is an element of reversed topography wherein the sites of marginal sandur trough-fill sedimentation now form the positive elements and the former dead-ice ridges the negative. Elsewhere, however, this relationship is less clear and the morphology provides only a general guide to sedimentary environments. On the west, as the ice retreated away from the rock margin and off the position of the current coast, large amounts of sediment were released at the ice-margin to form complex ice-disintegration topography across Orrisdale Head. Much of this caused a barrier to outward flow of meltwater which was directed southwestwards, parallel to the retreating ice-margin, to form large marginal sandur systems that generated rapid sediment accumulation. As dead-ice melted out as the margin continued to retreat kettle holes were generated in the surface of abandoned sandur and slowly began to fill with organic sediment.

Between Glen Balleira and Glen Wyllin on the west coast, organic sediment exposed in the base of kettle holes overlying the Orrisdale Formation[145] provides evidence for dating this reconstruction. The oldest radiocarbon dates from the basal organic sediment range between *circa* 22,900 and 21,900 BP[146]. These dates are out of synchrony with those for the Last Glacial Maximum in eastern England[147] and have been consequently regarded as contaminated either by incorporation of older carbon from a calcareous diamict substrate or fractionation of isotopes during subaqueous photosynthesis of *Drepanocladus revolvens*, from which the dates were derived, producing a hard water error. Taking the dates at face value, however, suggests that the Orrisdale Formation is the product of major snout oscillation during the episode of rapid retreat from the Heinrich event 2 maximum limits after *circa* 22,000 BP suggested by McCabe *et al.*[148].

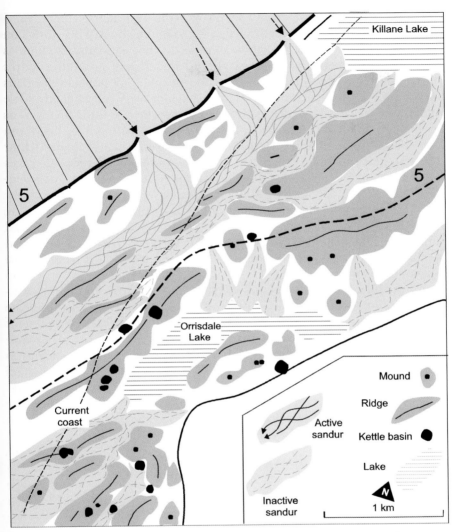

Figure 7.29 *Palaeogeographic reconstruction of stages in the retreat of ice across Orrisdale Head based on geomorphological mapping, palaeocurrents and interpretation of sedimentary sequences.*

The Jurby event (*circa* 15,000–16,000 BP)

After the Orrisdale event the Irish Sea ice-margin retreated north to clear the island, but how far north is not known. The unconformity separating the Orrisdale Formation from the Jurby Formation across Jurby Head clearly identifies a further readvance event sometime later. This readvance extended only into the far northwest corner of the island and the limit of its maximum penetration runs parallel to the current coastline. As the youngest glacigenic formation much of the morphology associated with its maximum limit has been preserved as it has not been subsequently over-ridden and destroyed by later readvances. Consequently, the formation can be mapped inland as a wide strip divisible into three sediment-landform assemblage zones running northeast to southwest at right angles to the direction of ice advance, which was from the northwest (Figure 7.26). The innermost zone forms a narrow band of linear moraines and small-scale ice-disintegration topography running parallel to the coast across Jurby Head and marks the maximum limit of the readvance. This zone passes to the southeast into an extensive area of coalescing ice-front alluvial fans, subaqueous fans and gently sloping sandur surfaces. The outermost zone forms a large, flat-floored subaqueous basin extending east from Killane and south towards Sulby.

All the lithofacies assemblages identified in the Jurby Formation, with the exception of the diamict and sand assemblages, were deposited in standing water. Consequently, the overall sedimentary sequence represents the depositional response to successive phases of readvance by an icesheet that has its margin in direct contact with a large water body. In such cases sediment is delivered by tunnels at the base of the ice out into the water body. On entry into the water, flow velocities diminish rapidly and sediment is deposited as an ice-contact subaqueous fan by turbidite flow and suspension rain-out. As the ice-margin advanced the outer part of the fan would prograde into the lake and the inner part would be overridden by

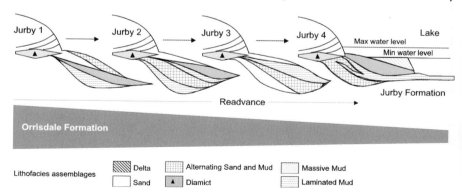

Figure 7.30 *A model to show ice-marginal sedimentation during readvance episodes in the Jurby Formation. After G.S.P. Thomas et al. (2004).*

diamict formed beneath the base of the advancing ice-margin. A model of this style of deposition is given in Figure 7.30 and is based on the distribution of lithofacies assemblage packages identified in the sections across Jurby Head. In the first stage of readvance (Jurby 1, Figure 7.30) a fan of subaqueous sediment is deposited at the immediate ice-margin. As readvance continued this fan was overidden by the ice-margin and the focus of sedimentation shifted outward to form a new fan (Jurby 2) off-lapping the previous one. Similar fans (Jurby 3 and 4) accumulated at each stage of readvance to form a series of off-lapping wedges of repeated lithofacies assemblage packages bounded downwards by an unconformity with the underlying Orrisdale Formation and upwards by an unconformable diamict. Dependent upon available accommodation space in the water body, the rate of sedimentation, the rate of ice advance and fluctuations in water level, depositional environments at the ice-margin probably shifted rapidly between ice-contact subaqueous fans, ice-contact deltas and outwash fan-deltas[149].

The lake-floor laminated mud assemblage identified in both the Jurby Formation and the Orrisdale Formation Dog Mills Member are laterally coincident with an extensive area of flat ground, mostly below 10 m O.D., that forms a shallow basin extending from Killane on the west to Ramsey on the east and bounded on the southwest by the Orrisdale ridge and on the south by the bedrock rise into the Manx uplands. The basin floor is poorly exposed, but boreholes (Figure 7.31) confirm the occurrence of thick laminated mud and sand above diamict of the underlying Shellag Formation and below local alluvial fan gravel and peat. This continuity of fine-grained lacustrine sediment between the coasts lends confirmation to the existence, originally postulated by Lamplugh, of a large ice-marginal lake, Lake Ramsey (Figure 7.31). This covered an area of up to 40 square km, had a minimum sediment infill of at least 25 m, a maximum surface height of *circa* 40 m O.D. and a maximum depth of probably 50 or 60 m. The lake was fed by ice-marginal drainage associated with both the Orrisdale and Jurby readvance episodes via ice-contact subaqueous fans, ice-contact deltas, fan-deltas and sandur, and implies that the lake existed either throughout these two episodes or reformed during the occurrence of each. The lake is therefore likely to be diachronous, with sedimentation in the eastern part significantly older than in the western. This is partially confirmed by the Lhen Trench which acted as a major distributor of ice-marginal meltwater into the lake during both the Orrisdale and Jurby events. A cartoon depicting glacial environments in the northern Isle of Man during the Jurby readvance event is shown in Figure 7.32a.

Three kettle basins overlying the Jurby Formation at Jurby Head

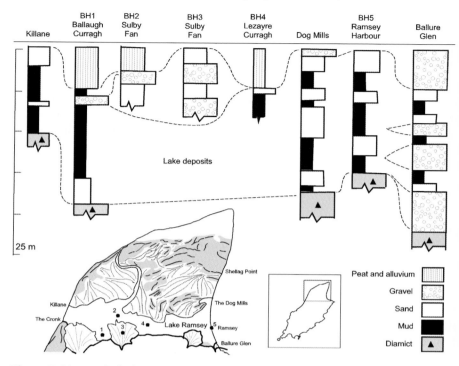

Figure 7.31 *Borehole logs through Lake Ramsey. Map at bottom shows location of boreholes and sections. After G.S.P. Thomas et al. (2004).*

provide a range of basal dates between *circa* 18,600 and 14,400 BP[150] and give a time frame for the Jurby readvance event and the deposition of the Jurby Formation. These dates broadly equate the formation with the readvance associated with Heinrich event 1 and may provide a marginal correlative for the equivalent limit reached at Killard Point, in eastern Ireland some 50 km to the west, dated to *circa* 17,000–16,500 BP[151], and possibly with the younger date of *circa* 15,500–14,300 BP at St Bees in Cumbria, some 50 km to the east. Thus, sometime between *circa* 16,000 and 15,000 BP the ice-margin associated with the regional readvance driven by the Heinrich 1 climatic event straddled the northern Isle of Man and connected Ireland to England. On retreat from this limit it was not to return again.

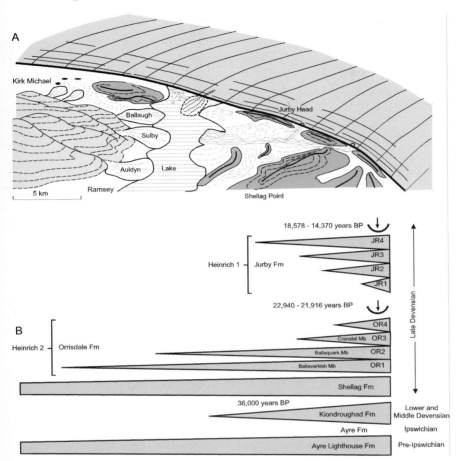

Figure 7.32 *(a) Cartoon depicting glacial environments in the northern Isle of Man at the time of deposition of the Jurby Formation, as viewed from the east. The ice-margin lay on a line from west of Orrisdale Head, through Jurby Head towards the Point of Ayre. In front of the margin large moraine ridges formed during earlier stages of retreat separate extensive areas of outwash sandur draining from the ice-margin. Much of this discharged into a large lake between Ramsey and Killane, via deltas or subaqueous fans. On the southern margin large alluvial fans, derived from reworking of upland glacial deposits, prograded into the water body. (b) Time/space diagram for glacial episodes in the Isle of Man. OR1, OR2, OR3 and OR4 represent minor ice-marginal fluctuations or still-stand episodes during retreat from the Orrisdale readvance event maximum. JR1, JR2, JR3 and JR4 represent ice-marginal fluctuations during expansion to the Jurby readvance event maximum.*

Summary

Reflecting its strategic position astride the path of successive ice advances down the Irish Sea from source areas in the highlands of western and southern Scotland, the Isle of Man records a very complex sequence of glacial deposits. Invariably, we know little of the older glacial episodes that affected the island, due to their burial or removal by later glacial stages. The earliest event, however, dates back at least 150,000 years and possibly 400,000 and is recorded in the Ayre Lighthouse Formation (Figure 7.32b). We also know little about the interglacial episodes that separate the glacials, and then only indirectly from buried sea cliffs cut to a former inter-glacial sea level or from temperate marine fauna contained in the Ayre Formation deeply buried beneath the Point of Ayre. This formation most probably relates to the last, Ipswichian interglacial between 128,000 and 115,000 years ago.

We know little of events on the island from the end of the Ipswichian interglacial at 115,000 years to 35,000 years ago, but the glacial deposits of the Kiondroughad Formation (Figure 7.32b), which overlie the Ipswichian interglacial deposits beneath the Point of Ayre and underlie the glacial deposits exposed above sea level, probably relate to this period. The global record suggests that in the period between 115,000 and 75,000 years ago climate oscillated between cold and cool temperate episodes, but with no major expansion of ice. The Isle of Man during this period was there-fore probably ice-free but subject to intermittent frost climates that resulted in the deposition of the extensive local slope deposits seen banked against the Ipswichian buried cliff-line at Ballure and elsewhere. The global record also shows that a highly mobile and climatically sensitive icesheet is likely to have existed in Britain throughout the Devensian, and a possible scenario for the period between 75,000 and 35,000 years ago might picture a large icesheet over southern Scotland which repeatedly advanced and retreated into the northern Irish Sea basin. Whether these fluctuations partly or wholly buried the island is unknown, but evidence of local slope deposits above the buried cliff at Ballure suggests that for a major portion of this time period it did not. Consequently, the island would have been subject to a very cold, perennially snow-covered periglacial climate.

Sometime after 35,000 years ago Scottish ice expanded rapidly, pushed into the southern Irish Sea basin, coalesced with the adjacent Irish and Lake District ice caps, thickened to probably 700 to 800 m in the central part of the northern Irish Sea basin and overwhelmed the island to its summit, as the Shellag event (Figure 7.32b). During its passage large quantities of glacial sediment were deposited on the northern plain and around the island margins and local deposits were generated in the uplands. From its maximum limit in the Celtic Sea this major glacial episode began to retreat rapidly in response to subsequent icesheet collapse. The retreat took the margin to the north of the island, which became completely deglaciated. Following deglaciation much of the unstable glacial debris lying on the upland slopes was reworked by periglacial processes to form extensive solifluction terraces. At the same time incision into the debris by snowmelt streams passed large volumes of sediment into the recovering upland rivers and out onto the northern plain as large alluvial fans.

At some time post *circa* 23,000 years ago, the Scottish icesheet readvanced south towards the island to reach its maximum limit at the Bride Moraine, as the Orrisdale event. At this time large volumes of sediment were deposited in ice-front alluvial fans, sandar and lake basins forward of the moraine, whilst to the rear extensive subglacial diamict was emplaced. From its maximum the icesheet progressively retreated, but was interrupted north of Shellag Point by two minor snout advances and around Orrisdale by at least four minor still-stands. Ultimately it retreated to well north of the island. Sometime before 16,000 years ago, however, it advanced again, as the Jurby event. This event was part of a regional readvance that linked limits at Killard Point in eastern Ireland and St Bees in Cumbria to the northern Isle of Man at around 15,000 to 16,000 years ago. At its maximum the Jurby event reached a limit running northeast to southwest across Jurby Head and this dammed up and reactivated Lake Ramsey, first formed as a response to the preceding Orrisdale event. On its retreat the ice did not return again as the 'Ice Age' had come to an end.

Notes

1   P.F. Kendall, 'On the glacial geology of the Isle of Man', *Yn Lioar Manninagh*, 1 (1894), 397–437.
2   For a comprehensive review of pre-Quaternary glaciation, see N. Eyles, 'Earth's glacial record and its tectonic setting', *Earth Science Reviews*, 35(2) (1984), 1–248. For a more popular overview of the topic, see B.S. John, *The Winters of the World*, David and Charles (1985).
3   In Europe the base of the Quaternary is formally defined by the first appearance of cold climate fauna and flora in marine sediments just below the top of the Olduvai magneto-subchron at Vrica in Italy at 1.905 Ma. The older date of 2.6 Ma quoted above is from the first appearance of ice-rafted debris in sediments in the North Atlantic Ocean. This date coincides with the first appearance of *Homo habilis*, the dominant genus of the Quaternary.
4   N.J. Shackelton, S. Crowhurst, T. Hagelberg, N.J. Pisias and D.A. Scheider, 'A new late Neogene timescale: application to leg 138 sites', *Proceedings of the Ocean Drilling Program*, 138 (1995), 73–101.
5   The earth's magnetic field flips from north to south polarity from time to time. This change is recorded in volcanic rocks, which can be dated using radiometric

methods. As ocean sediments contain small proportions of magnetic minerals these too can be dated.

6   The average depth of shallow shelf seas such as the Irish Sea is about 100 m. The maximum drop in world sea level recorded during the last glacial stage as a response to the amount of water locked up on the land as ice was of the order of 150–170 m.

7   S. G. Lewis, 'Eastern England', in D.Q. Bowen (ed.), *A revised correlation of Quaternary deposits in the British Isles*, Geological Society Special Report, 23 (1999), 10–27.

8   D. Maddy, 'English Midlands', in D.Q. Bowen (ed.), *A revised correlation of Quaternary deposits in the British Isles*, Geological Society Special Report 23 (1999), 28–44.

9   For a discussion of the nature and causes of Heinrich events, see R.C.L. Wilson, S.A. Drury and J.L. Chapman, *The Great Ice Age: climate change and life*, The Open University (2000).

10   D.Q. Bowen, F.M.P. Phillips, A.M. McCabe, P.C. Knutz and G.A. Sykes, 'New data for the Last Glacial Maximum in Great Britain and Ireland', *Quaternary Science Reviews*, 21 (2002), 89–101.

11   D. Maddy (1999).

12   A.M. McCabe, J. Knight and S. McCarron, 'Evidence for Heinrich event 1 in the British Isles', *Journal of Quaternary Science*, 13 (1998), 549–568.

13   G.W. Lamplugh, *The geology of the Isle of Man*, Memoir of the Geological Survey of England and Wales (1903), 620.

14   J. McCulloch, *A Description of the Western Islands of Scotland, including the Isle of Man: comprising an account of their Geological Structure, with remarks on their Agriculture, Scenery and Antiquities*, Constable, London (1819); J.S. Henslow, 'Supplementary observations to Dr Berger's account of the Isle of Man', *Transactions of the Geological Society of London*, 5 (1821), 482–505; H.E. Strickland, 'Some remarkable Concretions in the Tertiary beds of the Isle of Man', *Quarterly Journal of the Geological Society of London*, 92 (1842), 8–10.

15   Drift, a term now little used other than by the British Geological Survey, describes recent, unlithified deposits of glacial, fluvial or marine origin.

16   J.G. Cumming, 'On the geology of the Isle of Man', *Quarterly Journal of the Geological Society of London*, 2 (1846), 317–348; J.G. Cumming, 'On the superior limits of the glacial deposits of the Isle of Man', *Quarterly Journal of the Geological Society of London*, 10 (1853), 211–232. Cumming was Vice-Principal at King William's College in Castletown and made many contributions to the geology and natural history of the island.

17   Boulder clay, a term in use in the nineteenth century and until recently by the Geological Survey, has now been largely replaced by the term diamict, or till. Till is a deposit formed directly by contact with glacial ice.

18   Erratics are rock fragments transported by ice from an area where they naturally crop out to an area where they do not.

19   R.H. Tiddeman, 'On the evidence for the ice sheets of north Lancashire and adjacent parts of Yorkshire and Westmorland', *Quarterly Journal of the Geological Society*, 28 (1872), 471–489.

20   Striae, or striations, are linear scratches or shallow grooves cut into bedrock. They are caused by interaction with debris in the base of glacier ice as it passes across the bedrock. They are consequently a primary indicator of the former direction of ice movement. They also occur on rock clasts transported through ice.

21   J. Horne, 'A sketch of the geology of the Isle of Man', *Transactions Edinburgh*

Geological Society, 2 (1874), 232–247.

22 J. Wright, 'The foraminifera of the Pleistocene clay, Shellag', *Yn Lioar Manninagh*, 3 (1902), 627–629.

23 J. Wright and T.M. Reade, 'The Pleistocene clays and sands of the Isle of Man', *Proceedings Liverpool Geological Society*, 17 (1906), 103–117.

24 A. Bell, 'Tertiary Deposits in North Manxland', *British Association*, 66 (1896), 783; A. Bell, 'The Fossiliferous Molluscan Deposits of Wexford and North Manxland', *Geological Magazine*, 2 (1915), 164–169; A. Bell, 'Fossil shells from Wexford and Manxland', *Irish Naturalist*, 28 (1919), 109–114; A. Bell, 'The Cliffs of North Ramsey and their fossil contents', *Proceedings of the Isle of Man Natural History and Antiquarian Society*, 2 (1923), 383–392; A. Bell, 'On an Irish Manx Pliocene Sea', *Proceedings of the Isle of Man Natural History and Antiquarian Society*, 2 (1923), 372–383.

25 J.C. Ward, 'Notes on the geology of the Isle of Man', *Geological Magazine*, 7 (1880), 1–9.

26 P.F. Kendall (1894).

27 George Lamplugh, a self-taught geologist, worked on the island preparing the original geological map and memoir between 1893 and 1899 and examined every area, largely on horseback. His extraordinary attention to detail and his perceptive interpretation still serve as a fundamental source of information on the geology of the island. Lamplugh later became Director of the Geological Survey.

28 British Geological Survey, 'Isle of Man, Sheets 36, 45, 56 and 57', *Solid and drift geology 1:50000*, British Geological Survey, Keyworth, Nottingham (2001).

29 P.F. Kendall (1894).

30 B. Smith, 'Borings through the glacial drifts in the northern part of the Isle of Man', *Summary of Progress of the Geological Survey*, 3 (1931), 14–23.

31 A.M. Cubbon, 'The Ice Age in the Isle of Man: A Reconsideration of the Evidence', *Proceedings of the Isle of Man Natural History and Antiquarians Society*, 5 (1954), 499–512. Marshall Cubbon was, for many years, the Director of the Manx Museum.

32 G.F. Mitchell, 'The Quaternary deposits of the Ballaugh and Kirk Michael districts, Isle of Man', *Quarterly Journal of the Geological Society of London*, 121 (1965), 359–381.

33 C.A. Dickson, J.H. Dickson and G.F. Mitchell, 'The Late Weichselian Flora of the Isle of Man', *Philosophical Transactions of the Royal Society of London*, B258 (1970), 31–79.

34 G.F. Mitchell, 'The Pleistocene history of the Irish Sea', *Advancement of Science*, 17 (1960), 313–325.

35 G.F. Mitchell, 'The Pleistocene history of the Irish Sea: a second approximation', *Scientific Proceedings of the Royal Dublin Society*, A4 (1972), 181–199.

36 A nunatack is an area of land, usually including the highest mountains, that protrude through an ice cap and remain unglaciated.

37 G.S.P. Thomas, 'The Quaternary stratigraphy of the Isle of Man', *Proceedings of the Geologists' Association*, 87 (1976), 307–323; G.S.P. Thomas, 'The Quaternary of the Isle of Man', in C. Kidson and M.J. Tooley (eds), *The Quaternary History of the Irish Sea*, Geological Journal Special Issue, 7 (1977), 155–179.

38 G.S.P. Thomas, 'The Quaternary of the northern Irish Sea', in R.J. Johnson (ed.), *The geomorphology of North-West England*, Manchester University Press (1985), 143–158; R.V. Dackombe and G.S.P. Thomas, 'The glacial deposits and Quaternary stratigraphy of the Isle of Man', in J. Ehlers, P. Gibbard and J. Rose

(eds), *Glacial deposits of Great Britain and Ireland*, A.A. Balkema, Rotterdam (1991), 333–344.

39 G.S. Boulton, A.S. Jones, K.M. Clayton and M.J. Kenning, 'A British Icesheet model and patterns of glacial erosion and deposition in Britain', in F.W. Shotton (ed.), *British Quaternary Studies: Recent Advances*, Clarendon Press (1977), 231–246.

40 G.S.P. Thomas, 'The origin of the glacio-dynamic structure of the Bride Moraine, Isle of Man', *Boreas*, 13 (1984), 355–364.

41 G.S.P. Thomas, M. Connaughton and R.V. Dackombe, 'Facies variation in a Late Pleistocene supraglacial outwash sandur from the Isle of Man', *Geological Journal*, 20 (1985), 193–213.

42 Eustatic lowering of the sea level is caused by the locking up of water in icesheets. It is worldwide in its effect. Isostatic depression of the land surface is caused by the weight of ice and thereby has a regional effect on sea level.

43 C.H. Eyles and N. Eyles, 'Glaciomarine sediments of the Isle of Man as a key to Late Pleistocene stratigraphic investigations in the Irish Sea Basin', *Geology*, 12 (1984), 359–364; N. Eyles and A.M. McCabe, 'The Late Devensian (<22 000 BP) Irish Sea Basin: the sedimentary record of a collapsed icesheet margin', *Quaternary Science Reviews*, 8 (1989), 307–351; N. Eyles and A.M. McCabe, 'Glaciomarine deposits of the Irish Sea Basin: the role of Glacio-Isostatic disequilibrium', in J. Ehlers, P.L. Gibbard and J. Rose, (eds), *Glacial deposits of Great Britain and Ireland*, A. A. Balkema, Rotterdam (1991), 311–330; J.R. Haynes, A.M. McCabe and N. Eyles, 'Microfaunas from Late Devensian glaciomarine deposits in the Irish Sea Basin', *Irish Journal of Earth Sciences*, 14 (1995), 81–103.

44 C.H. Eyles and N. Eyles (1984).

45 D. McCarroll, 'Deglaciation of the Irish Sea basin: a critique of the glaciomarine hypothesis', *Journal of Quaternary Science*, 16 (2001), 393–404.

46 K. Lambeck, 'Late Devensian and Holocene shorelines of the British Isles and North Sea from models of glacio-hydro-isostatic rebound', *Journal of the Geological Society of London*, 152 (1995), 437–448; K. Lambeck, 'Glaciation and sea-level change for Ireland and the Irish Sea since Late Devensian/Midlandian time', *Journal of the Geological Society of London*, 153 (1996), 853–872; K. Lambeck, 'Sea-level change in the Irish Sea since the last Glacial Maximum: constraints from isostatic modelling', *Journal of Quaternary Science*, 16(5) (2001), 483–496.

47 G.W. Lamplugh (1903).

48 G.F. Mitchell (1965).

49 J.G. Cumming (1846).

50 J.C. Ward (1880).

51 P.F. Kendall (1894).

52 C. Darwin, 'Notes on the effects produced by the ancient glaciers of Caernarvonshire, and on the boulders transported by floating ice', *Philosophical Magazine*, 21 (1842), 180–188.

53 G.W. Lamplugh (1903).

54 G.S.P. Thomas, 'The Late Devensian glaciation along the western margin of the Cheshire-Shropshire Lowland', *Journal of Quaternary Science*, 4 (1989), 167–181.

55 E. Watson, 'Remains of pingos in Wales and the Isle of Man', *Geological Journal*, 7 (1971), 381–387.

56 G.W. Lamplugh (1903); G.F. Mitchell (1965).

57 G.S.P. Thomas (1977).

58 G.S.P. Thomas, 'Northern England', in D.Q. Bowen (ed.), *A revised correlation of Quaternary deposits in the British Isles*, Geological Society Special Report, 23 (1999), 28–44.

59 R.C. Chiverrell, G.S.P. Thomas, D. Long and D.H. Roberts, 'Quaternary', in Chadwick R.A., Jackson D.I., Barnes R.P., Kimbell G.S., Johnson H., Chiverrell R.C., Thomas G.S.P., Jones N.S., Riley N.J., Pickett E.A., Young B., Holliday D.W., Ball D.F., Molyneux S.G., Long D., Power G.M. and Roberts D.H., *Geology of the Isle of Man and its offshore area*, British Geological Survey Research Report, RR/01/06 (2001b), 143.

60 G.W. Lamplugh (1903).

61 B. Smith (1930).

62 G.W. Lamplugh (1903).

63 C.A.M. King and J.T. Andrews, 'Radiocarbon date and significance from the Bride Moraine, Isle of Man', *Geological Journal*, 5 (1967), 305–308.

64 R.C. Chiverrell and G.S.P. Thomas, unpublished.

65 D. Roberts, unpublished.

66 R.V. Dackombe and G.S.P. Thomas (eds), *Field Guide to the Quaternary of the Isle of Man*, Quaternary Research Association, Cambridge (1985).

67 C.H. Eyles and N. Eyles (1984).

68 G.S.P. Thomas *et al.* (1985).

69 R.V. Dackombe and G.S.P. Thomas (1991).

70 G.S.P. Thomas (1999).

71 G.S.P. Thomas (1984).

72 G.S.P. Thomas, R.C. Chiverrell and D. Huddart, 'Ice-marginal depositional responses to re-advance episodes in the Late Devensian deglaciation of the Isle of Man', *Quaternary Science Reviews*, 23 (2004), 85–106.

73 G.S.P. Thomas (1977); G.S.P. Thomas (1999); R.C. Chiverrell *et al.* (2001b).

74 G.S.P. Thomas *et al.* (2004).

75 M.J. Joachim, *Late-glacial Coleopteran assemblages from the west coast of the Isle of Man*, unpublished PhD thesis, University of Birmingham, (1979); R.V. Dackombe and G.S.P. Thomas (1985).

76 G.F. Mitchell (1965); C.A. Dickson *et al.* (1970).

77 G. Russell, 'The structure and vegetation history of the Manx Hill Peats', in P.J. Davey (ed.), *Man and Environment in the Isle of Man*, British Archaeological Reports, British Series, 54 (1978), 39–50.

78 G.S.P. Thomas (1999).

79 R.C. Chiverrell, G.S.P Thomas and A.M. Harvey, 'Late-Devensian and Holocene landscape change in the uplands of the Isle of Man', *Geomorphology*, 40 (2001a), 219–236.

80 M.J. Tooley, 'Sea-level changes and coastal morphology in north-west England', in R.H. Johnson (ed.) *The geomorphology of north-west England*, Manchester University Press, Manchester (1985), 94–121.

81 B.A.M. Phillips, 'The post-glacial raised shoreline around the North Plain, Isle of Man', *Northern Universities Geographical Journal*, 8, (1967), 43–48. M.J. Tooley, 'Flandrian sea-level changes and vegetational history on the Isle of Man', in P. Davey (ed.) *Man and Environment on the Isle of Man*, British Archaeological Reports, Oxford, 54 (1978a), 15–24.

82 D.I. Jackson, A.A. Jackson, D. Evans, R.T.R. Wingfield, R.P. Barnes and M.J. Arthur, *United Kingdom offshore regional report: The geology of the Irish Sea*, HMSO, London (1995), 123.

83 R.T.R. Wingfield, M.A.I. Hession and R.J. Whittington, *Anglesey, Sheet*

53°N–06°W, *Quaternary Geology 1:250,000 map*, British Geological Survey (1990).

84   R.V. Dackombe, *Aspects of the tills of the Isle of Man*, unpublished PhD thesis, University of Liverpool (1978).

85   The facies are illustrated in R.V. Dackombe and G.S.P. Thomas (1991), Plates 34–37.

86   R.V. Dackombe (1978).

87   G. Slater, 'The structure of the Bride Moraine, Isle of Man', *Proceedings of the Liverpool Geological Society*, 14 (1931), 184–96; G.S.P. Thomas (1984).

88   M.R. Bennett, 'The morphology, structural evolution and significance of push moraines', *Earth Science Reviews*, 53 (2001), 197–236.

89   G.S.P. Thomas *et al.* (2004).

90   R.V. Dackombe and G.S.P. Thomas (1985).

91   G.S.P. Thomas *et al.* (1985).

92   J. Wright (1902).

93   J.R. Haynes, A.M. McCabe and N. Eyles, 'Microfaunas from Late Devensian glaciomarine deposits in the Irish Sea Basin', *Irish Journal of Earth Sciences*, 14 (1995), 81–103.

94   G.S.P. Thomas *et al.* (2004).

95   *Ibid.*

96   G.W. Lamplugh (1903).

97   G.S.P. Thomas (1977).

98   G.W. Lamplugh (1903).

99   G.W. Lamplugh (1903).

100   G.F. Mitchell (1965).

101   G.S.P. Thomas (1977).

102   R.V. Dackombe (1978).

103   R.V. Dackombe and G.S.P. Thomas (1985).

104   R.V. Dackombe (1978).

105   C.H. Eyles and N. Eyles (1984).

106   G.S.P. Thomas *et al.* (1985).

107   B.R. Rust, 'Depositional models for braided alluvium', in A.D. Miall (ed.) *Fluvial sedimentology*, Memoir Canadian Society for Petroleum Geology, 5 (1978), 605–628.

108   R. Steel and S.M. Asheim, 'Alluvial sand deposition in a rapidly subsiding basin (Devonian, Norway)', in A.D. Miall (ed.) *Fluvial sedimentology*, Memoir Canadian Society for Petroleum Geology, 5 (1978), 597–604.

109   B.R. Rust (1978).

110   G.F. Mitchell (1965).

111   G.S.P. Thomas (1977).

112   G.S.P. Thomas *et al.* (2004).

113   R.V. Dackombe (1978).

114   J.D. Cornwell, 'A gravity survey of the Isle of Man', *Proceedings of the Yorkshire Geological Society*, 39 (1972), 93–106.

115   G.S.P. Thomas (1977).

116   G.S.P. Thomas (1999).

117   R.C. Chiverrell *et al.* (2001b).

118   G.S.P. Thomas *et al.* (2004).

119   For a review of sequence stratigraphy, see D. Emery and K.J. Myers, *Sequence Stratigraphy*, Blackwell Science, Oxford (1996), 234.

120   M.E. Brookfield and I.P. Martini, 'Facies architecture and sequence stratigraphy

in glacially influenced basins: basic problems and water-level glacier input-point controls (with an example from the Quaternary of Ontario, Canada)', *Sedimentary Geology*, 123 (1999), 183–197.

121 J.G. Cumming (1846).
122 J. Horne (1874).
123 P.F. Kendall (1894).
124 G.W. Lamplugh (1903).
125 G.S.P. Thomas (1977).
126 G.W. Lamplugh (1903).
127 P.F. Kendall (1894).
128 G.W. Lamplugh (1903).
129 G.F. Mitchell (1965).
130 G.S.P. Thomas (1977).
131 G.F. Mitchell (1965).
132 G.W. Lamplugh (1903).
133 T. Eastwood, S.E. Hollingworth, W.C.C. Rose and F.M. Trotter, 'Geology of the country around Cockermouth and Caldbeck', *Memoir of the Institute of Geological Sciences*, London (1968).
134 J.D. Kendall, 'Interglacial deposits of west Cumberland and north Lancashire', *Journal of the Geological Society of London*, 37 (1881), 29–39.
135 D.Q. Bowen, 'The Pleistocene succession of the Irish Sea', *Proceedings of the Geologists' Association*, 84 (1973), 249–273.
136 M.R. Dobson, 'The geological structure of the Irish Sea', in C. Kidson and M.J. Tooley (eds), *The Quaternary History of the Irish Sea*, Geological Journal Special Issue, 7 (1977) 13–26.
137 Although the Middle Devensian is identified as an odd-numbered isotope stage it is no longer regarded as of interglacial rank.
138 D.G. Sutherland, 'The high-level marine shell beds of Scotland and the build up of the last Scottish Icesheet', *Boreas*, 10 (1981), 247–254.
139 N.J. Shackleton and N.D. Opdyke, 'Oxygen isotope and palaeomagnetic stratigraphy of Equatorial Pacific core V28–238: oxygen isotope temperatures and ice volumes on a 10^5 and a 10^6 scale', *Quaternary Research*, 3 (1973), 39–55.
140 D.Q. Bowen *et al.* (2002).
141 *Ibid.*
142 C.H. Eyles and N. Eyles (1984); N. Eyles and A.M. McCabe (1989); N. Eyles and A.M. McCabe (1991).
143 G.W. Lamplugh (1903).
144 G.F. Mitchell (1965).
145 C.A. Dickson *et al.* (1970).
146 R.C. Chiverrell, P.J. Davey, J.A.J. Gowlett and J.J. Woodcock, in P.J. Davey (ed.) *Recent archaeological research on the Isle of Man*, Oxford, British Archaeological Reports, British Series, 278 (1999).
147 J. Rose, 'The Dimlington Stadial-Dimlington Chronozone: a proposal for naming the main glacial episode of the Late Devensian in Britain', *Boreas*, 14 (1985), 225–230.
148 A.M. McCabe *et al.* (1998).
149 I. Lønne, 'Sedimentary facies and depositional architecture of ice-contact glaciomarine systems', *Sedimentary Geology*, 98 (1995), 13–43.
150 M.J. Joachim (1978); R.C. Chiverrell *et al.* (1999).
151 A.M. McCabe *et al.* (1998).

8   Emerging from the Ice Age

RICHARD CHIVERRELL, JIM INNES,
GEOFF THOMAS, SILVIA GONZALEZ,
DAVID ROBERTS and RUSSELL COOPE

CLIMATE CHANGE AT THE END OF THE LAST ICE AGE

The Devensian Glaciation came to an end as the global climate warmed
after 16 ka and the British and Irish Icesheet declined. Cores of ice obtained
by drilling through the Greenland ice cap during the Greenland Ice core
Project (GRIP) and the Greenland Icesheet Project (GISP2) provide a very
good high-resolution and well-dated climate history for this time period
(Figure 8.1)[1]. The oxygen isotope ratios contained within these ice cores
allow the reconstruction of changes in temperature stretching back to the
start of the last interglacial at *circa* 130 ka. The Greenland ice cores have
been proposed as the stratigraphic type locality in the North Atlantic for
the termination of the Devensian (16,000–11,500 BP), a period colloqui-
ally called the 'Lateglacial', because they possess a well-dated,
representative and high-resolution palaeoclimate record. The Lateglacial
was not a continuous smooth progression towards the current post-glacial
climatic regime; it was punctuated by considerable and rapid climatic fluctuations. The Lateglacial period subdivides into the Greenland Interstadial
1 warm event (15,000–12,500 BP) and the Greenland Stadial 1 cold event
(12,500–11,500 BP), before the final warming into the Holocene epoch
circa 11,500 BP.

Greenland ice cores began to provide the stratigraphic framework for
the Devensian Lateglacial during the 1990s, but previous classifications of
the period derived from terrestrial records are still widely used[2]. Terrestrial
stratigraphic frameworks reflect regional variations in terminology, with
names derived from type localities or features within each region. The original Scandinavian scheme (Figure 8.1) subdivides the termination of the
Devensian into a sequence of climatic phases, in turn called the Bølling
Interstadial (warm: 15,000–14,500 BP), the Older Dryas Stadial (cool:
14,500–14,000 BP), the Allerød Interstadial (warm: 14,000–12,500 BP)
and the Younger Dryas Stadial (cold: 12,500–11,500 BP). In Britain
researchers refer to the Windermere Interstadial[3] (warm: 15,000–12,500
BP) and the Loch Lomond Stadial[4] (cold: 12,500–11,500 BP) to describe

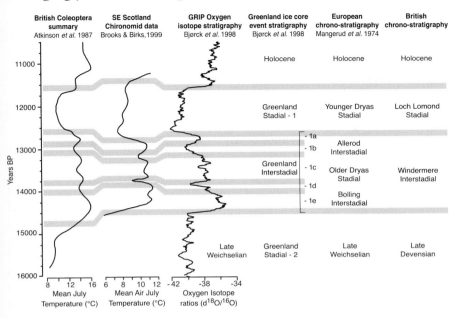

Figure 8.1 *Climate changes between 16,000–11,000 BP. The data show beetle (coleopteran) and chironomid records from the British Isles and the GRIP ice core oxygen isotope stratigraphy. Palaeoclimate data are presented against the chrono-stratigraphic framework from Greenland, Europe and the British Isles, and against timescales expressed in years BP.*

the Lateglacial period. Notwithstanding this confusing nomenclature the terrestrial record of climate change is extremely important, but perhaps the nomenclature applied to the Greenland ice cores is better suited as a stratigraphic and chronological framework[5].

There are strong similarities between the palaeo or past temperature history present within the ice cores and equivalent records derived from lake sediments in northwest Europe[6]. The insect remains present in lakes and peat bogs, particularly the Coleoptera (beetles) and the Chironomidae (non-biting midges), have provided quantitative reconstruction of climatic change, for example allowing estimation of mean July air temperatures. Beetle and midge sequences from the British Isles corroborate the pattern of climate change identified in the ice core oxygen isotope ratios from Greenland (Figure 8.1)[7]. Recent researches on carbonate sediments from lakes in Germany, Switzerland and Lancashire have also identified climate-driven d[18]O records that closely resemble the ice core isotope signature.

This is an important development, because these data allow direct comparison and correlation between the ice core record and terrestrial sediments[8].

The application of geochemical and palaeoecological techniques at finer resolution to ice core and lake sediment profiles has revealed greater complexity in the Lateglacial climate history[9]. During the early part of the Greenland Interstadial, substage 1e (15,500–14,000 BP), mean July temperatures in northwest Europe rose very rapidly (7 °C in 100 years) and reached the warmest temperatures of the interstadial. Subsequently, the climate cooled and oscillated at around 14–15 °C for the remainder of the interstadial. Conditions cooled during Greenland Interstadial 1d (13,900–13,700 BP), but warmed again during Greenland Interstadial 1c (13,700–13,100 BP), with a further pronounced cooling during Greenland Interstadial 1b (13,100–12,800 BP) followed by the warming of Greenland Interstadial 1a (12,800–12,600 BP). Mean July temperatures then declined by 4–5 °C to 10–11 °C in 500 years marking the start of Greenland Stadial 1 (12,600–11,500 BP), a cold period, when small glaciers reformed in Wales, the Lake District and Scotland. This cool period lasted until the rapid warming at the beginning of the Holocene *circa* 11,500 BP.

EMERGENCE FROM BENEATH THE ICE

That the Irish Sea Icesheet glaciated the Isle of Man to its summit during one or more glacial stages in the Quaternary was demonstrated in the last chapter. During the retreat of the Late Devensian icesheet from its maximum limit in the southern part of the Irish Sea basin after 22,000 BP, the uplands of the island were progressively uncovered as the ice thinned and wasted back. By 18,000–16,000 BP the margin of the icesheet stood along the line of the Jurby Moraine. Consequently, the area of the island south of this margin experienced some three millennia of periglacial climate before the onset of warmer conditions at the opening of Greenland Interstadial 1 at 15,000 BP. Periglacial climates are characterised by long, cold winters and short, cool summers and an average annual temperature well below zero. Much of the ground surface would be permanently frozen to depths of many metres, thawing only at the surface during the short summer period. In these conditions, vegetation would be sparse, soils thin and frost processes such as freeze-thaw breakdown, ground-ice penetration and debris flow endemic. Thus down-slope reworking, especially in the uplands where slopes are steeper, rapidly modified much of the deglaciated landscape. During the short summer, much of the reworked debris found its way into seasonally active stream systems that transferred it to large alluvial fans, especially at the gradient change at the exit of the major northern upland rivers such as the Auldyn, Sulby and Dhoo onto the northern plain. In the lowlands, where the slopes are lower, these fluvial processes were less effective, but extensive ground-ice and frost heave caused disruption of the ground surface.

PERIGLACIAL RESPONSE TO DEGLACIATION IN THE MANX UPLANDS

The uplands of the Isle of Man were too small in area and too low in altitude to nurture their own glaciers. Consequently, there is no evidence of local glaciation of the type found in similar areas of mainland Britain such as Scotland, Snowdonia or the Lake District. With the possible exception of the Laxey valley, which shows a pronounced U-shaped cross-section, none of the valleys displays large-scale glacial erosional features associated with mountain glaciation and cirque basins are absent. Similarly, evidence of glacial deposition in the form of moraines, kames or valley sandur is also absent. This evidence points to either a rapid retreat of ice from the uplands leaving behind a predominantly subdued subglacial landscape or significant periglacial reworking of the glacial sediments after deglaciation to produce a very uniform land surface.

Hill slope morphology and drift distribution

The almost ubiquitous expression of Manx upland scenery is of gently rolling hills everywhere clothed with a smooth cover of local drift and limited rock outcrop. Throughout the uplands, drift distribution and slope form are intimately related. Drift is banked thickly in the lower and deeper parts of the upland valleys but attains its greatest horizontal extent in headwater basins, from which it sweeps in smooth sheets over the wider upland cols (Figure 8.2). Through this altitudinal range three major slope elements can be distinguished (Figure 8.3).

Source slopes   These are the uppermost slope element and occupy extensive areas on the flanks of the higher ridges. They are convex in form and merge upwards from valley shoulders into flat or low-angled summit surfaces. It is within this element that most exposed rock is seen and slopes are much diversified on a small scale. Bedrock ridges are extensive, though of no great magnitude, and related to minor lithological and structural variations in the Manx Group. They are particularly pronounced on the slopes surrounding Snaefell and North Barrule. Between outcrops the surface is often obscured by an irregular cover of loose, angular rubble, usually less

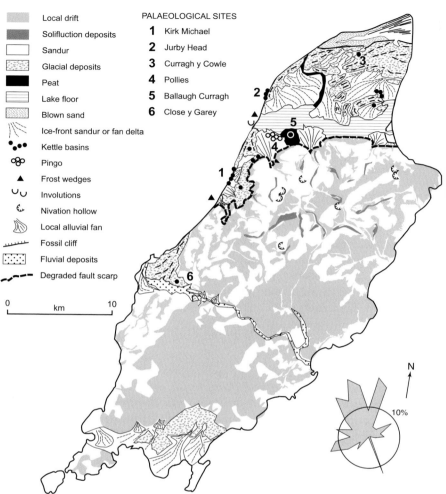

Figure 8.2 *Late Devensian geomorphology of the Isle of Man showing the distribution of nivation hollows, paraglacial slope deposits, solifluction terraces, alluvial fans, river terraces, pingos and locations yielding data on the Lateglacial flora and fauna. Inset shows rose diagram of facing direction of solifluction terraces.*

than 30 cm thick and commonly buried by thick accumulations of peat. Fabric of the rubble is poorly organised, clasts are coarse and angular, and bedrock is frequently turned down-slope, and individual clasts show an intimate relationship to underlying cleavage planes within the rock. At altitudes between 300 and 450 m on sheltered north and north-easterly facing

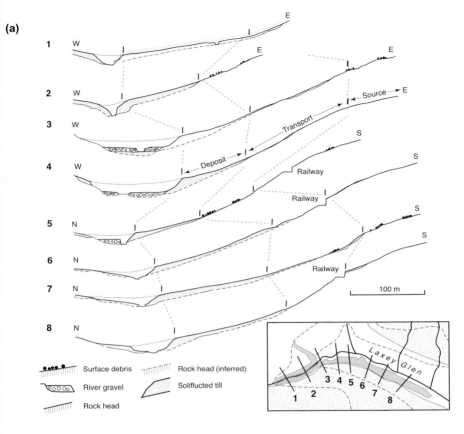

Figure 8.3 *(a) Typical slope profiles across solifluction terraces in the Manx Uplands. (b) Laxey Valley from the Veranda showing solifluction terrace. Photograph by Peter Davey.*

source slopes, there are a number of small nivation hollows, some showing enclosing pro-talus ramparts of the type encountered in central Wales[10]. Nivation or snowpatch hollows are produced by weathering and sediment transport process encouraged by late-lying snow. Curved ridges, called pro-talus ramparts, comprised of angular debris derived from the slopes above, often front nivation hollows. Examples occur on the northeast slope of North Barrule, the east flank of Snaefell, the western side of the middle Sulby valley and the western edge of Slieau Dhoo (Figure 8.2).

Transport slopes   These merge down-slope from the source slope and consist of generally rectilinear slope segments between 10° and 20°, often diversified with shallow gullies, fans, small block-streams and an irregular litter of coarse surface debris. Rock outcrop is rare. The material under-lying the transport slope is thin, usually less than a metre in thickness, and consists of coarse, angular rubble with few fines. Clasts are frequently imbricated down-slope. The element is particularly well developed on the southern side of the Laxey valley, below the line of the electric railway. In some of the deeper and narrower valleys, such as the western side of the middle Sulby valley, this slope element descends steeply to the valley floor to form an apron of now inactive scree and debris cones (Figure 8.4).

Deposit slopes   These occur below the transport slope and are distinctive, conspicuously smooth, usually rectilinear slopes at angles of between 5° and 12°, often underlain by local drift up to 20 m or more in thickness. Deposit slopes are prominently displayed in the Druidale, Laxey and middle Sulby valleys, and some distinction can be made between rather steeper slopes in the more confined valleys, such as the Sulby (Figure 8.4), and gentler slopes in the more open headwater areas, such as Druidale. Where a sharp slope break separates deposit slopes from the transport slopes above, small debris fans impinge onto the rear of the deposit slope. This is especially common on the southern flank of the Laxey valley. Apart from subsequent gullying, relief is otherwise restricted to occasional turf-banked lobes or small terraces, rarely more than a metre in frontal height, occurring in the upper parts of valleys.

   The up-slope boundary between the deposit and transport slope is often difficult to define and passage is frequently gradational over tens or some-times hundreds of metres. Where a sharp break of slope separates the two, however, it identifies the deposit slope as a sloping valley-side terrace. Such features, called solifluction terraces, are more common in the northern uplands, particularly in the valleys of the Sulby (Figure 8.4), Dhoo, Auldyn, Corrany, Laxey and Baldwin, and they form the only distinctive drift land-

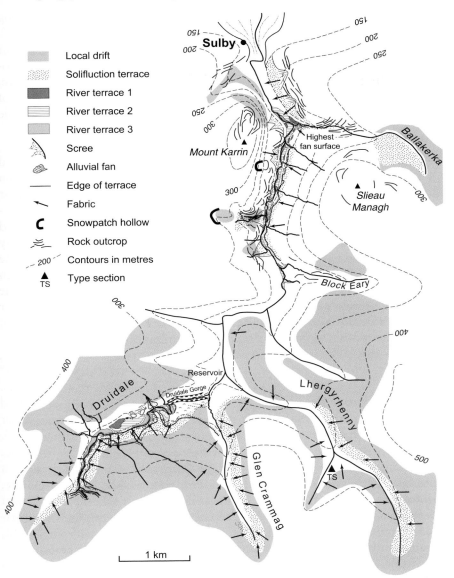

Figure 8.4 *Map of the geomorphology of Sulby Glen showing the distribution of solifluction terraces, river terraces and alluvial fans together with fabric pattern within the solifluction deposits.*

form in the upland areas. The valley-side terraces are between 50 and 300 m in width, slope at angles between 3° and 12°, and are terminated on the down-slope side by a steep bluff between 3 and 20 metres in height. The steep bluff is a function of Lateglacial and Holocene stream incision through the deposits that underlie the terraces. In this sense they are terraces only in terms of their contemporary expression, as before incision the deposit slope surface would have extended across the current valley floor.

The distribution of terraces within the northern uplands is shown in Figure 8.2, which clearly shows that the terraces have a marked preference for facing directions from west, through north to east. A plot of facing directions weighted for down-valley length confirms this (Figure 8.2). Valley slopes facing other directions have relatively limited drift development and few prominent terraces, giving rise to a pronounced drift asymmetry throughout the uplands. This is coupled with a weaker rock asymmetry, as in the middle Sulby (Figure 8.4), where east or southeast facing rock slopes are steeper and underlain by coarse, open-work scree, whilst west facing slopes are gentler and underlain by thick diamict. Similar terraces have been identified elsewhere in upland Britain including south[11] and central Wales[12], the Cheviot Hills[13], the Lake District[14] and the Howgill Fells[15], and many carry similar preferential orientation.

Sedimentology of the upland drift deposits

The local deposits are of exclusively local origin and consist of coarse, usually angular fragments of the underlying Manx Group. Three major facies types can be identified.

Diamict is the dominant component and comprises a heterogeneous assemblage of granule- to cobble-size clasts of locally derived slate set in a stiff, usually very poorly sorted, blue or grey, mud-dominated matrix. Textural variation amongst the diamicts is limited, but in the field differences in colour, degree of weathering, proportion of clasts and matrix, clast packing density, maximum size of clast and degree of stratification are evident and a general distinction can be made between stratified diamict and massive diamict. Stratified diamicts display crude bedding; either picked out by the close, parallel packing of clasts or by very thin partings of sand or silt. Bedding rarely exceeds 5 to 10 cm in thickness, is frequently discontinuous and generally dips at angles approximately parallel to the surface or bedrock slope above and below. Clast density is high and the diamict locally becomes clast supported. Clast shape is dominantly blade or rod and reflects the primary break-up shape of clasts released from the underlying Manx Group. Roundness is invariably low, few clasts exceed 15 cm and the proportion of clay in the matrix is low. Clast surface textures are rough, but some 25% show smooth, silky surfaces with faint scratch marks and occasional deeper, often intersecting striae. Massive diamicts display no internal bedding and occur as either a single internally homogeneous, matrix-supported sheet up to 6 m in thickness, or a set of stacked massive sheets each 2 or 3 m in thickness. Clast density is relatively low with infrequent large clasts up to 50 cm, or occasionally up to a metre, irregularly distributed. Compared to the stratified diamicts, clast roundness is relatively high, the proportion of clay in the matrix is nearly twice and the incidence of striated or faceted clasts is higher. Boundaries between the two diamict types are rarely sharp and most grade imperceptibly one into the other.

Gravels are rare, but are occasionally found interstratified with diamict and comprise two distinct types. The first consists of massive, poorly sorted but sometimes normally graded, clast-supported granule to cobble or occasionally small boulder gravel set in a granule gravel or sand matrix. Clasts are sub-rounded, commonly imbricated up-slope and frequently iron-stained and weakly cemented. Gravels sometimes fine upward into laterally discontinuous lenses of well-sorted, parallel-laminated sand or massive or laminated silts, and occasional channel structures occur. Generally this type of gravel shows a gradational upward passage from stratified diamict via a reduction in the proportion of matrix and an increase in clast roundness. The upward passage from gravel back to diamict is usually sharp and the uppermost gravels are commonly cemented or indurated. The second type of gravel closely resembles the stratified diamicts from which the matrix has been removed and comprises edge-rounded pebble or cobble gravel set in an open-work matrix of sand and granule gravel. Clast size is generally lower than in the first type of gravel, beds of finer sediment are absent, but thin beds of diamict frequently divide them. Upper and lower boundaries are always gradational and some difficulty arises in the field in separating this type of gravel from coarse-grained, matrix-supported stratified diamict. Discriminant analysis provides satisfactory differentiation between the two, however, and demonstrates that sorting is the most significant distinguishing parameter (Figure 8.5).

Rock Rubble occurs only at the contact between the local deposits and underlying bedrock, and its occurrence and thickness vary widely. It is composed of angular, often sharp clasts of slate up to 50 cm set in an open-work matrix of small angular rock chips. The lower boundary is gradational, usually over a metre or more, from unweathered solid rock, through deeply fractured and broken rock into the basal layers of the

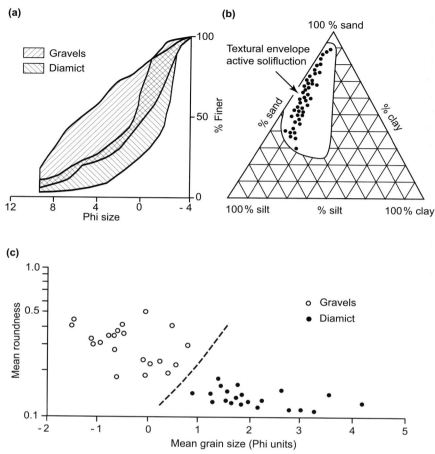

Figure 8.5 *Sedimentology of local deposits. (a) Grain size envelope for diamicts and gravels. (b) Grain size characteristics of the solifluction diamicts. (c) Grain size and clast roundness distinction between gravel and diamict.*

rubble. Individual rock beds can often be traced up through the base of the rubble where they break into individual clasts. Upwards, clasts released from the bedrock progressively rotate such that their A:B planes become orientated sub-parallel to the overall slope of the underlying bedrock. The upward transition between the rubble and overlying diamict is gradational and marked by a progressive increase in the proportion of silty matrix.

Fabric of the upland drift deposits

Fabric is the alignment of the long-axes of clasts in sediment and it provides important evidence for the direction of transport when the local deposits were laid down. Figure 8.4 shows the mean orientation of 58 macro-fabrics located throughout the drift deposits of the Sulby river basin, the largest catchment draining the uplands. All fabrics had a resultant mean orientation significantly different from random and most exhibited pronounced unimodal maxima with only a few bi- or multi-modal. Transverse peaks, normal to mean orientation, were uncommon. The overall pattern shows a close relationship between mean fabric orientation and slope direction, and the two measures change in sympathy with one another. Vertically through a sequence of deposits, mean orientation departs significantly from surface slope direction with depth. A series of seven fabrics taken vertically through a 15-metres section in the Lhergyrhenny tributary of the upper Sulby (Figure 8.6) demonstrates that only the upper units have a mean orientation consistent with the overlying slope direction. With depth, mean

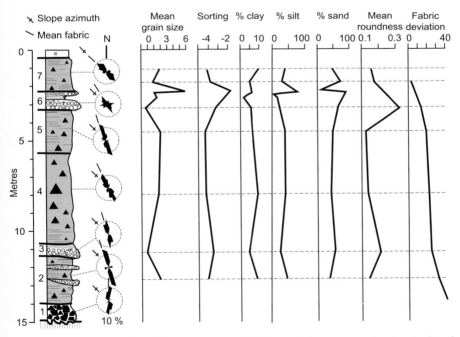

Figure 8.6 *Stratigraphy, sedimentology and fabric of the type section in the local drift deposits at Lhergyrhenny, Upper Sulby Basin. The location of the section is shown on Figure 8.4.*

orientation diverges such that at the base it is some 40° away from the surface slope direction, but is coincident with the dip-direction of a buried rock slope against which the lower part of the sequence is banked. Long axis dips typically concentrate in a narrow cone around the pole of surface slope or bedding, but where this is less than 10° clasts are imbricated down-slope. Between 10° and 20° it is parallel to slope or bedding, and where it is greater than 20° clasts are imbricated up-slope.

Landscape beneath the drift deposits

The smooth surface of the deposit slope throughout the uplands obscures considerable irregularity in the underlying bedrock surface. Figure 8.7 illustrates the rock-head relief beneath the drift terrace in Druidale, based on shallow seismic profiling and rock-head mapping in gullies[16]. Reconstruction shows that beneath the smooth surface of the central portions of the terraces, bedrock relief is often strong (for example, Figure 8.7a and d) and probably determined by structural and lithological variations in the underlying slate. Thus the general effects of the formation of the local drift sheets have been to smooth out and bury a much more irregular pre-existing bedrock relief, an observation made by others in similar areas[17]. Although there is a general tendency for drift thickness to increase gradually down-slope, thickness below the central parts of sheets is commonly less than a half or a third of that below the fronting bluff. The rock head frequently rises rapidly within the first 50 m or so up-slope from the bluff and confirms that the asymmetric filling of shallow, pre-drift rock gorges underlying the modern valley floor causes the greater thickness beneath the bluff itself. In many cases reconstruction of the buried rock surface (Figure 8.7a and b) shows that prior to Lateglacial and Holocene incision, valley floors were located towards the slopes covered with shallower drift. As incision proceeded, streams migrated towards the slope with thicker drift and, in Druidale, a buried rock gorge was exhumed. The contact between bedrock and overlying local drift is invariably gradational with an upward transition from unweathered rock, through deeply fractured and broken rock into the basal layers of the rock rubble. No sharp contacts between bedrock and drift occur and there is a marked absence of smoothed, polished or striated bedrock surfaces, even in the deepest section or in locations, such as the floor of valleys, where the preservation of bedrock surfaces scoured by the former passage of ice might be expected.

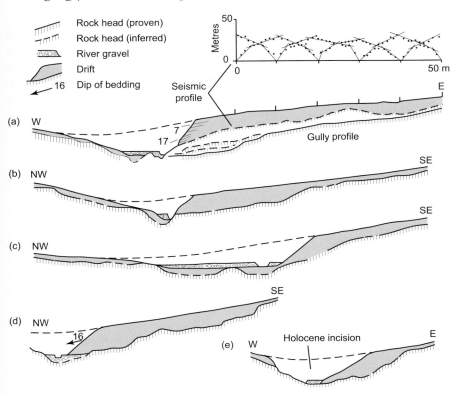

Figure 8.7 *Bedrock profiles beneath the solifluction deposits at Druidale derived from seismic data.*

Stratigraphy of the drift deposits

Figure 8.6 shows the succession through a type-site (SC384873) for the local deposits in a tributary of Lhergyrhenny in the upper Sulby river basin, together with sedimentological data obtained from each unit. Seven major lithostratigraphic units are identified. At the base broken and shattered Manx Group bedrock passes gradually upward into a rock rubble (1) comprising sharp, yellow-stained angular blocks up to 30 cm. This grades upwards into 1.8 m of olive-brown stratified diamict (2) crowded with small angular clasts up to 10 cm set in a stiff silty matrix and showing some minor alternation between coarser and finer bands. This diamict is succeeded by 0.85 m of coarse, moderately well-rounded gravel (3), either open work or set in matrix of finer gravel and sand. This passes gradually up into 5.25 m of dull brown, massive, clay-rich diamict (4) containing striated clasts up to 75 cm. This passes gradually up into a further 2 m of grey-olive, fine, stratified diamict (5) and is overlain by 1.3 m of coarse, yellow-stained, well-rounded gravel (6) that fines upwards into parallel-laminated yellow sand and laminated grey silt. The gravel sequence is terminated by a prominent band of indurated fine granule and small pebble gravel. The succession is completed by 1.8 m of olive-grey, fine, stratified diamict (7) badly weathered in its upper part by percolation from over-lying peat. A number of other sections show similar sequences, but the majority of exposures in the uplands record only partial or incomplete successions, often not laterally persistent. Where exposed, the base of all sections is marked by a variable thickness of rock rubble directly overlying shattered bedrock, and diamict, either stratified or massive, is not seen to rest on smooth, polished or striated rock surface. The rock rubble invari-ably passes upwards into stratified diamict, but from this point upwards sequences are variable and localised. Coarser, stratified diamict predomi-nates, but many sections display a distinct, often thick unit of massive diamict, similar to unit 4 in the type-site, occupying the central portion of the thickness, capped by further stratified diamict. Interstratified gravel sequences are relatively rare, but where present they invariably occur towards the base of the succession. In all cases stratification is sub-parallel to slope and fabric is down-slope.

Formation of the drift deposits

A number of arguments demonstrate that at least in terms of the last major process that acted upon them, the local deposits of the uplands of the Isle of Man achieved their present morphological and sedimentological char-acter as a result of the action of slope processes. Foremost amongst these arguments are the absence of glacial erosional and depositional landforms and the close and intimate relationship between drift distribution and slope form; a phenomenon noted by many as an indicator of former periglacial environments[18]. Thus, the zonal nature of slopes, reflecting weathering, transport and deposition in successive down-slope elements; the conse-quential down-slope thickening of the deposits; the asymmetric development of drift distribution and thickness as a function of slope facing direction; the development of preferentially facing drift terraces as a response to this; the burial of an irregular bedrock relief by a smooth drift cover; the systematic lateral shift of streams by asymmetric drift develop-ment; and the occurrence of snowpatch or nivation hollows are all indicative of slope-controlled mass-wasting processes in a frost-dominant climate. Drift asymmetry, in particular, is common in the former periglacial, non-glaciated areas of northern France and southern England[19] and also in areas within the limits of the Late Devensian glaciation, but subject to intensive or prolonged periglacial conditions, including Wales, the Lake District, the Howgill Fells and the Cheviot Hills. The sedimentological characteristics of the local deposits also lend support to a periglacial origin. Thus, the texture of the local diamicts falls well within the limits of frost susceptible soils, and also within the textural envelope of contemporaneously active solifluction deposits[20]. The organisation of the fabric also strongly supports a slope derived origin, for it has been widely reported that elongate clasts in such deposits show a preferred orientation parallel to the direction and angle of slope in both fossil and modern periglacial zones[21].

Early workers regarded the local deposits as the product of a glaciation 'one and indivisible' that swept over the island to its summit[22]. During this glaciation, basal debris-rich ice, incorporating material foreign to the island, was deposited around the island's low coastal margin whilst upper, debris-free ice sheared over the top. In its passage across the uplands this ice eroded the local Manx Group bedrock and redeposited it as sheets of locally derived glacial debris. This conception explains the marked boundary between the foreign and local drift around the island perimeter and the entire absence of foreign erratics within the local deposits, except at low altitude. Earlier workers considered that the evidence for complete glaciation related to an early glacial stage and that during the Late-Devensian cold stage the island existed as an ice-free nunatak above the limit of surrounding Devensian Irish Sea ice[23]. Consequently, the local deposits were interpreted as slope deposits, partially reworked from older glacial deposits and partially generated by *in situ* freeze-thaw breakdown and soliflucted transport of the Manx bedrock in a severe periglacial environment.

Subsequent investigations into the limits of the Late Devensian Irish Sea icesheet and reconstructions of its geometry based on numerical modelling of the behaviour of large icesheets revised this view[24]. The current conception is that the island was completely glaciated during the Late Devensian with an ice thickness of at least 200–500 m above its summit[25]. Consequently, the local deposits are now seen as a product of the reworking of local glacial deposits during and immediately after deglaciation. Lying on relatively steep, probably meltwater-saturated slopes, the local deposits were rapidly remobilised down-slope by solifluction processes acting in a cold, periglacial and ice-marginal climate. The precise age of periglacial reworking within this timeframe is not known, but probably occurred from the time of ice retreat to the north of the Isle of Man *circa* 18,000 BP to at least the pronounced warming at the opening of the Greenland Interstadial 1 *circa* 15,500 BP. Most of the periglacial reworking was accomplished rapidly in the earlier part of this period, and was accompanied by contemporaneous fluvial transport of reworked sediment down the main upland river systems and out into the accumulating fans. By the opening of Greenland Interstadial 1, vegetation colonisation had stabilised the landscape, encouraging soil development and a cover of open ground herbs and dwarf shrubs[26]. Stabilisation and increasing temperatures caused a reduction in solifluction and an increase in fluvial runoff, and so most of the fluvial incision may have occurred during the interstadial. The relationship between periglacial reworking of the local glacial deposits and their incision and removal by fluvial processes is best seen as a reciprocal, but contemporaneous process, with the former declining in significance through the time period and the latter increasing. Further periglacial reworking during Greenland Stadial 1 (12,500–11,500 BP) may be marked by the series of low, turf-banked lobes seen lying across a number of the upland deposit slopes. The final occupation of snowpatch (nivation) hollows dates from this period and the solifluction processes had ceased by the opening of the Holocene at *circa* 11,500 BP.

Two outstanding questions arise from this reconstruction. The first concerns the apparent stratigraphy within the local deposits, originally thought to represent a response to climatic change[27]. Whilst it is appealing to view the shift from solifluced diamict, through gravel and back to solifluced diamict as a response to climatic change across the various interstadial/stadial boundaries during the Devensian there is neither chronological control, nor fossil or soil evidence to support it. Consequently, the occurrence of random, laterally impersistent sorted sediment within the dominant thickness of redeposited diamict is best explained as a response to local conditions such as excess runoff, rather than a climatically induced change in slope process. The second question concerns the extent to which the local deposits represent a complete reworking of Devensian glacial deposits. In comparable sequences elsewhere in Britain, for example the Cheviots[28] or central Wales[29], solifluced diamict is commonly seen to overlie *in situ* glacial till which, in turn, overlies ice-moulded bedrock. This is not the case in the uplands of the Isle of Man as no *in situ* glacial till or ice-moulded bedrock are found. The entire sequence therefore appears to represent either *in situ* periglacial slope deposition or the reworking of glacial tills by solifluction processes.

PERIGLACIATION OF THE MANX LOWLANDS

Periglacial environments are defined as cold but non-glaciated conditions in which a number of distinctive structures and landforms are produced due to the development of permanently frozen ground or 'permafrost'[30]. Permafrost can extend to depths of 100 m below the ground surface, but is affected by summer thawing of the surface layers. The surface zone, in which thawing occurs, is called the 'active layer'. A number of periglacial structures and landforms occur in the lowlands of the Isle of Man (Figure 8.2), and they include pingos, ice-wedge casts, coversands and cryoturbated sediments.

'Pingo' is an Inuit word for contemporary ice-cored earth mounds that occur in arctic areas of North America. Closed system, or Mackenzie Delta type pingos[31], occur in current or former lake basins when the lake is sufficiently shallow for the water to freeze solid. Permafrost surrounding the lake encroaches through the unfrozen ground water beneath the lake, and excess water is forced upwards forming large ice lenses that heave the ground surface to form solitary circular hills. This freezing tends to reoccur and so the closed system process tends to produce groups of pingos. After melting, the former ice-cored mound collapses leaving basins that fill in with lake and peat sediments. A circular ridge or rampart typically surrounds pingos. Nine or ten depressions on the Ballaugh alluvial fan issuing from Glen Dhoo have been identified as pingos (Figure 8.2)[32]. The Ballaugh fan is an extensive, gently inclined gravel alluvial fan consisting of local sediments derived from the Manx uplands. These mountain-front alluvial fans began forming shortly after ice cleared the uplands. The Ballaugh fan gravels interdigitate with Jurby Formation laminated muds, which were deposited by an ice-marginal lake that existed while the ice-margin was at Jurby Head. The distal end of the Ballaugh fan would have formed a delta into this lake, and so the environment is similar in character to the Mackenzie Delta, Canada. These pingos therefore formed under a periglacial climatic regime shortly after ice retreat probably while the Killane ice-marginal lake was in existence between *circa* 18,000–16,000 BP, and the ground-ice melted leaving circular depressions (Figure 8.8) that filled with small lakes during Greenland Interstadial 1 (15,500–12,500 BP). Pollen analysis and radiocarbon dating of the organic sediment discussed later in this chapter confirm that the basal sediments date to Greenland Interstadial 1.

In severely cold, periglacial environments the ground surface is frequently cracked due to water increasing in volume as it freezes. Evidence for structures reflecting formation of ground-ice and the resultant ground

Figure 8.8 *Pingo on the Ballaugh alluvial fan, Pollies. Photograph by Richard Chiverrell.*

disturbance, which is called cryoturbation, are exposed in cliff sections around the Isle of Man. Ice-wedge casts occur in the outwash sands and gravels at Shellag Point, in outwash sands to the north of the Cronk, in the Ballaleigh ice-marginal fan gravels, in sandur deposits at the Parade overlooking the Calf of Man and in sandur gravels on Langness. Ice-wedge casts are remnant features produced when ice-wedges melt and the void left fills up with sediment. Contemporary ice-wedges form in the permafrost layer particularly where the permafrost cools rapidly in the winter. Ice-wedges form by the repeated opening of tension cracks owing to thermal contraction of sediments in the winter months. During the summer melting, the cracks or voids fill with snow and meltwater, which refreeze producing larger ice-wedges. Ice-wedges occur only when the average annual temperature is below −5 °C. On the Isle of Man ice-wedge casts occur in the permeable sand and gravel outwash sediments that were deposited during ice retreat, with formation occurring before the onset of warm conditions during Greenland Interstadial 1 between 15,500 and 12,500 BP.

Further evidence for frozen ground occurs in the upper layers of Devensian glacigenic sediments at Jurby, Orrisdale, Kirk Michael, Port

Cranstal (Phurt) and on the coast of the Calf Sound (Figure 8.2). These sediments are contorted and convoluted. Frost heave processes during seasonal thawing and freezing of the permafrost active layer produced these convoluted sediments. Frost shattered clasts in the outwash gravels at Shellag Point, Phurt and Orrisdale Head also indicate that permafrost and frost action affected glacigenic sediments after the sandur systems became inactive. Coversands are aeolian or wind-blown sands reworked from newly deposited glacigenic deposits. They are not widespread on the Isle of Man and are limited to thin exposures of well-sorted fine sand above glacigenic deposits along the east and west coasts of the northern plain. Deglaciated environments are susceptible to wind erosion and transport of recently deposited sediments owing to the absence of vegetation and soils, but clearly these aeolian processes ceased as vegetation returned as climates improved. The frost action and ground-ice structures predominantly affect outwash sands and gravels, and so indicate these proglacial environments endured a sub-aerial periglacial climate. The maturity of the periglacial landforms and structures signifies a reasonable period of periglacial activity probably before 15,500 BP.

FLUVIAL RESPONSE TO DEGLACIATION

Incision and fluvial deposition in the Manx uplands

Fluvial incision in many upland valleys has left valley-side solifluction terraces, with river terraces and alluvial fan surfaces incised into the soliflucted diamicts. These fluvial features either post-date, or at the earliest are contemporaneous with, the later stages of the substantial incision responsible for creating the valley-side solifluction terraces. The higher and oldest river terraces and upland alluvial fan surfaces in the valleys consist of very coarse clast-supported gravel that is not in keeping with the low velocity fluvial regimes of the Holocene, and are almost certainly Late Devensian in age. The lower-level river terraces and alluvial fan surfaces are younger; they consist of finer gravels and appear to be of Holocene age. The sequence of valley-floor river terraces and alluvial fan surfaces in Sulby Glen (Figure 8.4) is typical of these upland valleys. The terrace gravels have proven impossible to date independently, but a chronology for fluvial incision and gravel aggradation is suggested by the broad chronology of geomorphic change on the Isle of Man during the Late Devensian. Extensive incision into the local deposits along valley floors is matched, downstream, by the accumulation of large alluvial fans where these valleys exit into the lowlands of the north[33]. The alluvial fans were formed by deposition of vast quantities of local sediment yielded by fluvial incision into the soliflucted till that choked the upland valleys. The alluvial fan gravels overlie Late Devensian ice-marginal lake sediments that stretch from Killane on the west coast to Dog Mills on the east and are exposed in bore-holes at Ballaugh and Lezayre Curragh[34]. The alluvial fans probably became active immediately after deglaciation. At Kirk Michael distal alluvial fan gravels have buried organic sediments, which indicate the fans were still prograding after 12,000 BP. Pingos on the surface of the Ballaugh fan at Loughan Ruy and Pollies contain Greenland Interstadial 1 organic sediment. This evidence suggests that alluvial fan accumulation was active throughout the Late Devensian, perhaps slowing only as the warmer conditions of the Holocene encouraged stabilisation of the landscape. As the alluvial fan formation and incision in the uplands are inexorably linked, the intensive phase of fluvial incision is probably constrained to the period between when the Isle of Man became ice-free at *circa* 18,000 BP and the beginning of the Holocene warm period at 11,500 BP.

Fluvial sedimentation in the Manx lowlands

Paralleling solifluction of glacial sediments in the Manx uplands, vast quantities of sediment were transferred to the lowlands, but have not been retained within the valleys. As the landscape stabilised the soliflucted diamicts were incised and removed from the upland valleys by river systems transferring considerable quantities of sediment downstream. Where the river systems do not emerge from the uplands directly into the sea, large mountain-front alluvial fans have accumulated, particularly at the change in gradient at the front of the north-facing scarp slope of the northern uplands, on the coast near Kirk Michael, along the flanks of the central valley and on the northern edge of the Plain of Malew (Figure 8.2).

Northern Plain and Kirk Michael area

Alluvial fans at Glen Balleira, Glen Wyllin and Glen Mooar emerge from westwards-flowing valleys and the sediments are exposed in the sea-cliffs around Kirk Michael. These sections reveal 10–15 m of initially coarsely bedded sand and gravel that become more stratified up the sections. The gravels are predominantly composed of local Manx Group slates and the most substantial fans issue from valleys flowing onto the northern plain, producing the Sulby, Ballaugh and Auldyn alluvial fans (Figure 8.2). Sections in these mountain-front alluvial fans are rare, but there is bore-hole information from the Sulby Glen alluvial fan. A borehole at Sulby Chapel (SC381945), near the head of the alluvial fan, revealed only the uppermost 8 m of coarse local gravel set in a sandy matrix, but the total thickness of gravel is substantially more[35]. A further borehole towards the toe of the fan through thick peat deposits revealed 1.6 m of tightly packed coarse sub-angular gravel composed entirely of local Manx Group slate overlying reddish, probably glaciolacustrine, sands derived from sources north of the Isle of Man. The borehole information confirms that the alluvial fan deposits thin distally and that they prograded over Late Devensian glacigenic sediments. The accumulation of Greenland Interstadial 1 organic deposits in pingo depressions at Pollies and Loughan Ruy on the surface of Ballaugh alluvial fan indicates that sections of the alluvial fans had stabilised by 12.5 ka and that the transfer of large quantities of sediment from the uplands was slowing. Palaeobotanical evidence from these basins, reviewed later in this chapter, supports this interpretation by identifying vegetation colonisation and soil development.

Douglas to Ramsey coastline

East coast valleys dissecting the northern uplands are for the most part not fronted by alluvial fans, even though substantial quantities of sediment have undoubtedly been removed from Laxey Glen and the Corrany valley. These sediments almost certainly now rest on the floor of the Irish Sea. Ballure Glen, near Ramsey, is the exception and has been described in Chapter 7. The upper part of the succession (Figure 8.9) has been interpreted as a local alluvial fan operating at a time when a foreign ice-margin was close at hand as the sequence is repeatedly interrupted by a rapid shift in deposition from local gravel into foreign red clays and sands. These red clays can be traced via a borehole at Ramsey Harbour northwards to the Dog Mills Member, which comprises a faunally rich sequence of massive clays, laminated clays, laminated and rippled fine sands and silts that was interpreted as lacustrine deposit[36]. Recent investigations suggest that at the time the ice-margin stood at the Bride Moraine a large lake developed across the whole of the proglacial area between Ramsey and Killane[37]. In this geographical context the red clays at Ballure would be very distal and it is possible to conceive them as a response to major input events into the lake during which large quantities of fine-grained suspended sediment would be released to settle across the whole of the lake floor. In this case, they would intercalate with contemporary fan deposition from Ballure Glen. This explanation implies that the Ballure fan abutted directly into the lake. In this respect the Ballure fan is identical to other fans fringing the northern hill massif. Sections at Glen Ballure also provide exposure of proximal, earlier sediment deposited during the Late Devensian (22,000–17,000 BP), whereas at other fans there is currently only expo-

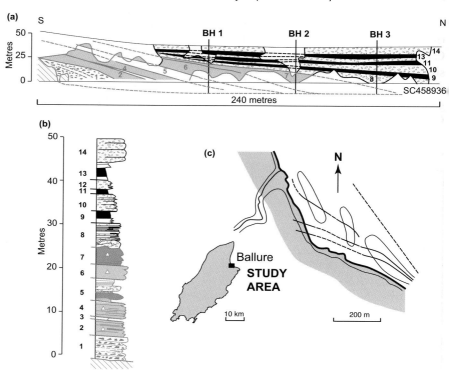

Figure 8.9 *Stratigraphy and map of the alluvial fan deposits at Ballure Glen. The section shows the interdigitation between alluvial fan gravels and proglacial lake sediments.*

sure of the distal and later sediments deposited during the Lateglacial after ice had left the island (15,000–11,500 BP).

Central valley between Peel and Douglas

Extensive early work by Lamplugh[38] and subsequent geological mapping for the recently revised geology sheet provide the current synthesis of the geomorphology of the central valley of the island (Figure 8.10)[39]. Foreign glacigenic sediments penetrate into the valley from the west coast as far as St Johns, and are intermixed with local drift across the watershed at Greeba and within flood gravels flanking the valley between Crosby and Union Mills. The terrain north of a line between Peel and St Johns is glacigenic, consisting of ice-marginal moraine ridges, sandur flats and ice-marginal deltaic sediments exposed in quarries at Ballaharra and Lherghydhoo. The deltaic sediments confirm Lamplugh's hypothesised ice-marginal lake dammed between a coastal ice-margin near Peel and either alluvial fan obstructions near St Johns or the central valley watershed at Greeba Curragh. Amongst this glaciated terrain there are organic depressions similar in character to the kettle holes of the northern plain and the depression at Close y Garey has yielded remains of the giant deer (*Megaloceros giganteus*) (Figure 8.10). The remainder of the terrain between Peel and Greeba consists of fluvial deposits of varying character and age.

Three valleys merge at St Johns and flow into the sea at Peel. The Neb drains from the northern uplands through Glen Helen, the Foxdale River

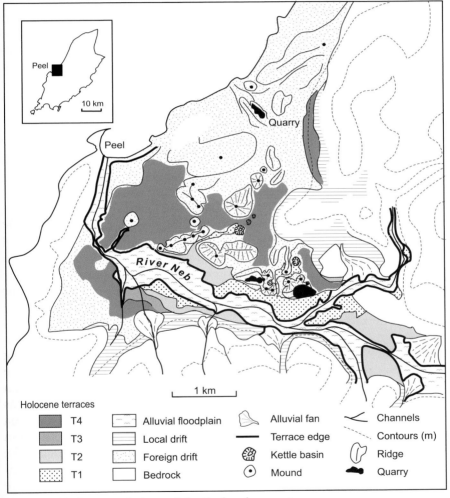

Figure 8.10 *Geomorphology of the Peel embayment.*

drains northwards out of the southern uplands and the Greeba River rises on the interfluve of the central valley at Greeba (Figure 8.10). Lamplugh identified at least four levels of fluvial surface between Peel and St Johns. The highest surfaces (T4 and T3, Figure 8.10) are likely to be glacial sandur and include the terrace at 46 m at St Johns and the extensive high terrace around Peel that extends towards Kirk Patrick and Ballamoore. Set into these sandur surfaces are two further, lower gravel terraces (T2 and T1, Figure 8.10) at 15–12 m on either side of the valley downstream from St Johns, but also extending into the Neb Valley towards Glen Helen. These terraces grade out of the Manx uplands and are probably flood gravel equivalents to the alluvial fans of the northern plain. Alluvial fans issue from many of the smaller tributaries of the central valley and these are also a response to incision in the uplands. The lowest terrace is the modern alluvium floodplain that occupies much of the floor of the lower Neb. Thick Holocene peat deposits on the watershed at Greeba Curragh grade into the modern floodplain and have been radiocarbon dated as post-dating 6,860–6,665 BP.

Plain of Malew

Sand and gravel mounds at Ballabeg and Colby along the northern edge of the Plain of Malew in the south of the island may also be gravel fans (Figure 8.2)[40], but their surface expression is not as easy to define as the alluvial fans on the northern plain. Both the Colby and Ballabeg alluvial fans have been trimmed by fluvial activity during the Holocene. Sections in the Colby fan show locally derived, slaty alluvial gravels at the ground surface and are indicative of fan formation. The presence of hollows on the upper fan slopes may reflect ice wastage contemporaneous with the formation of the alluvial fans. Consequently the Colby and Ballabeg alluvial fans could be sandur or delta complexes formed during deglaciation and not the product of sediment transfer from the uplands during the Lateglacial period. Given the magnitude of fan development in the north, the reduced scale of alluvial fan development in the south of the island is somewhat surprising. However, the two areas are characterised by contrasting topography, with the short and steep nature of the alluvial feeder valleys issuing onto the northern plain providing an ideal terrain for fan development. In the south, the river valleys responsible for the delivery of sediment to the coastal plateau have much gentler and longer profiles than their northern counterparts, and perhaps enter the coastal plateau at gradients insufficient for fan formation. Longer channel profiles also result in a loss of overall sediment load owing to deposition upstream. The Silver Burn exemplifies this, with the river passing through a drumlinoid foothill terrain before entering the coastal plateau downstream of Ballasalla. In contrast, the Colby and Ballabeg rivers are topographically more conducive to fan formation, with shorter and steeper valleys emerging on to a flat former sandur surface.

Stepped river terrace sequences are one of the most spectacular landforms to be found in the south of the island and occur along most of the lowland river valleys. The terraces are cut into the edges of the higher sandur plains and form staircases down to the alluvial spreads below them (Figure 8.2). The best examples can be seen along the lower reaches of the Colby and Silver Burn rivers and also just west of Ballachurry where fluvioglacial activity emanating from the Fleshwick system has left a clear terrace sequence. In some instances, possible braid bar remnants can be discerned on terrace surfaces. The lower river terraces are probably Holocene, but the higher terraces are Lateglacial in age probably produced during readjustment of river systems in the southern uplands of the Isle of Man.

History of Lateglacial fluvial activity

The large mountain-front alluvial fans formed between 18,000 and 11,500 BP and their sediments are grouped together as the Ballaugh Formation[41]. The fans operated from the time of recovery from glaciation in the uplands up to the opening of the Holocene. These fans thicken and prograde outwards with time, with the proximal and lower sediments older than the distal and upper sediments. The solifluction processes responsible for the slope process deposits in the upland valleys are typical of the cold periglacial conditions that occurred between initial retreat from Lateglacial Maximum limits *circa* 18,000 BP and the opening of Greenland Interstadial 1 (15,500 BP), and later during Greenland Stadial 1 (12,500–11,500 BP). The alluvial fans on the northern coastal plain formed during the main phase of fluvial incision into these solifluction deposits. Alluvial fans accumulate in a diachronous manner, which means that as sediment accumulates the fan will grow until channel avulsion forces the stream system to migrate. The migration of channels across an alluvial fan makes it difficult to discern and constrain phases of activity because away from the main channels fan surfaces can stabilise and receive little or no sediment.

Organic sediments overlying and underlying alluvial fan gravels at Kirk Michael and Ballaugh help to constrain the age of fluvial incision and fan formation. Coastal sections at Kirk Michael reveal organic sediments underlying gravels deposited by alluvial fans issuing from Glen Wyllin and Glen Balleira. Palaeoecological data (coleopteran and pollen) and radiocarbon dating reveal that these organic sediments span Greenland

Interstadial 1 (15,000–12,500 BP)[42]. That alluvial fan gravels cap these organic deposits suggests these alluvial fans were still actively prograding during Greenland Stadial 1 *circa* 12,500–11,500 BP. Pingo depressions on the surface of the large Ballaugh alluvial fan also contain organic sediments. The sequence from Pollies has yielded a pollen record that extends back into Greenland Stadial 1 (12,500–11,500 BP). An adjacent pingo at Loughan Ruy (SC353943) has yielded giant deer antler remains that have been ^{14}C dated to 13,790–12,995 BP[43]. Here alluvial fan accumulation appears to have ceased or slowed towards the beginning of the Holocene, reflecting the onset of warmer conditions and stabilisation of the landscape and allowing accumulation of organic sediments within former pingos. The formation of alluvial fans and coeval solifluction activity and fluvial incision in the uplands source areas appear to be constrained to 17,000–11,500 BP by the dating of organic sediments from above and below alluvial fan gravels at Ballaugh and Glen Balleira[44].

LATEGLACIAL ENVIRONMENTAL CHANGE

Changes in vegetation communities during the Lateglacial are recorded in organic sediments, where pollen grains and larger plant fossils (seeds, leaves and stems) are preserved in large quantities. Pollen and plant macrofossil analysis of these organic sediments reveals how plant communities recolonised the Isle of Man after the retreat of the ice. There are two particular landform types where organic sediments accumulate – kettle holes and pingos.

Kettle holes – as the margins of the icesheet retreated, stagnant blocks of dead-ice were left within moraine ridges or were buried by outwash sediment, and eventually the dead-ice blocks melt and the ground collapses leaving water-filled hollows called kettle holes. Kettle holes are common features of the ice disintegration topography at Orrisdale.

Pingos – are periglacial landforms that form in permafrost regions through the accumulation of ice beneath the ground. Initially the land surface domes over these ground-ice bodies, but collapses as the ice melts when the climate warms.

Kettle holes are widespread across the lowlands of the Isle of Man, and formed when blocks of dead-ice melted as the climate ameliorated after 15,500 BP, whereas the pingos formed under the periglacial climate that occurred between 18,000 and 15,500 BP after the ice-margin retreated to the north of the island. Both environments produced water-filled hollows, in which organic deposits accumulated. Pollen analysis of organic sediments at Kirk Michael, Loughan Ruy, Pollies, Curragh y Cowle and

Ballaugh Curragh (Figure 8.2) reveals the sequence and pattern of vegetation colonisation and succession between 15,500 and 11,500 BP. Faunal remains are also well persevered in the soft sediments, with abundant insects, ostracods and the bones of large mammals.

The Kirk Michael and Jurby Head kettle holes

The kettle hole deposits exposed in coastal cliff sections at Jurby Head and near Kirk Michael are important sites and have been much investigated. The cliffs of the northwest coast are eroded at a considerable rate and repeated investigation of the kettle holes throughout the last 30 years as the cliffs retreat demonstrates the three-dimensional architecture of the basins. Five basins occur in the cliffs at Kirk Michael (KM 1 to 5, Figure 7.14, Chapter 7), with three basins in the cliffs at Jurby (JH 1 to 3, Figure 7.19, Chapter 7). In both areas there are further basins inland, and given the rate of coastal erosion it is likely sediments will continue to be exposed. Five of the sequences at Kirk Michael have yielded pollen and plant macro-fossils[45] and KM1, KM3 and JH2 have yielded an extensive beetle fauna[46]. giant deer remains have repeatedly been uncovered from the organic deposits at Kirk Michael[47].

At Kirk Michael these organic sediments overlie a complicated former ice-marginal topography that consists of ice-disintegration terrain, moraine ridges, sandur plains and small lake basins. The sequence at Jurby Head is different because the glacial succession accumulated in front of an ice-margin that abutted directly into a large lake, and so the sediments were deposited in a subaqueous environment[48]. The thickest sequence of organic sediment at Kirk Michael exceeds 3.4 m (Figure 8.11b), whereas at Jurby Head the sequences do not exceed 1.4 m in thickness. During the last 30 years both locations have revealed extensive basins with lateral exposure extending over 100 m in length. Although the sedimentological development of the organic basins varies between sites there are features common to the stratigraphies of all the basins.

At Kirk Michael, the basal sediments are grey-blue clays interspersed with occasional moss remains (*Drepanocladus revolvens*) and sand and gravel bands. The upper sediments are more organic, culminating in a cap of peat. The succession reflects the evolution of the lake from a water body surrounded by bare ground with no vegetation or soils, through the development of soil and colonisation by plant communities to a terrestrial marsh-peat. The sequence of stratigraphic changes is repeated in the other basins, although at Kirk Michael 3 there are thick (4 m) accumulations of *Chara* marl. The sediments are called *Chara* marls owing to the large quan-

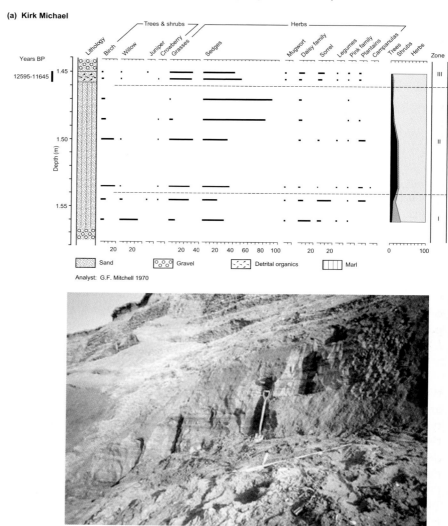

Figure 8.11 *(a) Pollen data from Kirk Michael kettle hole KM1. (b) Photograph of kettle hole KM3 between Glen Balleira and Glen Wyllin.*

tities of calcium carbonated-encrusted oogonia of Characeae, which is a macrophytic alga that utilises calcium carbonate from hard water and secretes it within the plant tissues. The calcium carbonate is derived from the underlying glacial diamicts and outwash gravels. Deposition of marl in carbonate lakes is limited to shallower waters and so often forms shelves of marl around the edges of deeper carbonate lakes. Coastal erosion since the 1970s has removed much of the marl shelf and current exposures reveal stratified carbonate muds typical of the deeper waters in the centre of a lake (Figure 8.11b). The lake was subject to repeated low energy inflow of water as the stratigraphy reveals variation in the quantity of carbonate, organic matter and mineral sand and silt. Towards the margins of the basin peat deposits accumulate as the edge of the basin filled in and terrestrialised.

Beetles[49] and plant macrofossils[50] from these basins reveal the sequence of primary succession and landscape stabilisation as plants colonised the deglaciated terrain in response to an improving climate. Both the faunal and botanical records help to explain the changes in the sedimentology and local environment. Ecological interpretation of the sequence of fossil beetles can provide reconstructions of summer temperatures and the evidence for climate change at Jurby and Kirk Michael is reviewed later in this chapter. Beetles also occupy particular habitats or niches and the species at Kirk Michael and Jurby divide into broad groups that are indicative of open water, lake margins or terrestrial ecosystems. Furthermore, certain species are sufficiently stenotopic that they are associated with particular substrate types, for example the aquatic weevils *Litodactylus leucogaster* and *Eubrychium velatus* feed on water milfoil (*Myriophyllum*) and similar plants.

Water beetles dominate the basal sediments and include species that typically inhabit shallow silty ponds with no aquatic vegetation. Terrestrial and lake-margin species are also present in the basal deposits and are typical of environments where vegetation is sparse or absent. Gradually the beetle fauna changes, indicating the ponds have expanded becoming deeper and wider. The fauna also suggests that vegetation has colonised the moraine ridges surrounding the basins and that the aquatic plants pondweed (*Potamogeton*) and water milfoil were present in the ponds. Throughout the sequence there are no species indicative of woodland and it is likely that grasslands surrounded the basins. The presence of dung beetles hints at the presence of animals browsing in the lake catchments and drinking from the lake waters. Remains of giant deer in the organic sediment confirm the presence of large herbivores around the lake basins. Towards the top of the sequences the basins terrestrialised and the numbers of water beetles and water-margin beetles decline, with species indicative of open meadows and acidic peat bogs increasing to dominate the fauna.

The plant macrofossil remains at Kirk Michael support the environmental record derived from the beetle fauna[51]. The plant fossil record suggests that there was a diverse flora in the Kirk Michael area, with 117 species of angiosperm, one gymnosperm, 9 pteridophytes and 35 bryophytes. The landscape around the kettle holes was a mosaic of species-rich grassland, dwarf shrub heathland, mire and aquatic habitats of varying trophic conditions, but little in the way of woodland. Sedges, grasses, and arctic/alpine shrubs and herbs dominate the basal sediments, with plants noted for colonising deglaciated landscape abundant. Heathland communities joined these species and birch (*Betula*) fruits indicate that trees were present probably as isolated stands or as birch scrub, but were not widespread. The upper stratigraphy indicates the terrestrialisation of the lake with lower numbers of aquatic species and abundant mire and lake-edge communities dominated by sedge (*Cyperaceae*) and rushes (*Juncus*). The uppermost stratigraphy is suggestive of a climatic downturn, with the remains of plants (e.g., *Apus glacialis* and *Polytrichum norvegicum*) associated with permanent or long-lying snow-beds.

Vegetation changes during the Lateglacial

Pollen diagrams are available from five sites on the northern plain of the island and these provide evidence of broader changes in vegetation cover during the Lateglacial (Figure 8.2). Fossil records of pollen and spores are the main source of information on the vegetation history. Pollen grains produced by the seed-producing plants (angiosperms and gymnosperms) and spores from the lower plants (cryptograms) are dispersed by a variety of methods (transported by wind, water, insect or animal). These grains are deposited and incorporated within organic sediment and are particularly well preserved when deposited under anaerobic conditions. The fossil sequence of pollen and spores from different plant species broadly reflects the plant species abundance in the environment. Moreover, the composition of the fossil assemblage reflects the composition of the pollen rain at the site in the past. Composition of the pollen rain is in turn controlled by regional and more local vegetation patterns and so the pollen stratigraphy of sediment sequences can provide records of vegetation change.

The Kirk Michael kettle holes, described in previous sections, sustained the earliest investigations of Lateglacial environments on the Isle of Man[52]. Recent investigations at Curragh y Cowle, Pollies and Ballaugh Curragh complement this early work, and Lateglacial pollen data are now available from kettle hole sediments at Curragh y Cowle (near Bride), the organic fills of pingos at Pollies and Loughan Ruy and the basal sediments from Ballaugh Curragh. Unfortunately Lateglacial pollen data have not been forthcoming from elsewhere on the island.

The pollen diagrams presented in this chapter are subdivided into biozones. Biozones are sequences of sediment that contain a uniform or similar flora, and so biozone boundaries reflect the most significant changes in the vegetation. Biozonation schemes can either be specific to an individual site or reflect changes across a region by applying a regional zonation scheme to all sites. The vegetation changes recorded at each Lateglacial site are subdivided into three biozones (I–III), with the Holocene beginning with biozone IVa[53].

Kirk Michael

At the Kirk Michael kettle holes (Figure 8.11) grasses (Poaceae), sedges, mugwort (*Artemisia*), crowberry (*Empetrum nigrum*), docks (*Rumex*) and willow (*Salix*) were the abundant taxa in biozone I[54] and reflect the initial colonisation of the landscape by sub-arctic herbs and dwarf shrubs. The end of biozone I is dated to 14,700–13,850 BP. At the opening of biozone II some of these taxa are replaced by birch, with grasses and sedges becoming more abundant. Biozone III sees reductions in birch and grass, with mugwort, docks and willow increasing in abundance and is dated to 13,110–12,435 BP, which reflects the climatic downturn into Greenland Stadial 1 (12,500–11,500 BP). Alluvial fan gravels overlie the organic sediments and truncate the later stages of the Lateglacial sequence (Figure 8.11b). Comparison of the timing of the changes in plant and beetle communities at Kirk Michael 1 and 3 reveals that beetles respond more rapidly to climate change with plant communities lagging behind[55].

Curragh y Cowle

Curragh y Cowle is a kettle hole on the Bride Moraine that contains 270 cm of turfa, detrital peats and organic limnic mud, overlying 25 cm of sand and then a marly clay sequence that extends 495 cm down to stiff limnic muds that were not penetrated (Figure 8.12a). Pollen spectra from the lower stiff limnic muds contain a biozone II assemblage, with abundant grasses and lower frequencies of sedge. Low frequencies of a wide range of open ground herbs occur, of which docks, mugwort, buttercup (*Ranunculus*), sea plantain (*Plantago maritime*) and the campions (*Silene*-type) are the more significant. Lateglacial indicator herbs including the rock roses (*Helianthemum*), saxifrages (*Saxifraga*) and meadow-rue (*Thalictrum*) also occur, and water milfoil (*Myriophyllum alterniflorum*) and the algae *Pediastrum* are important. Only sporadic shrub pollen grains occur. The pollen assemblage resembles closely the data from the Ballaugh and Kirk Michael sites, although the dominance of grasses in the Curragh y Cowle profile is much more pronounced. The upper contact of the stiff limnic mud was dated 13,135–12,435 BP (Figure 8.12a) an age for the end

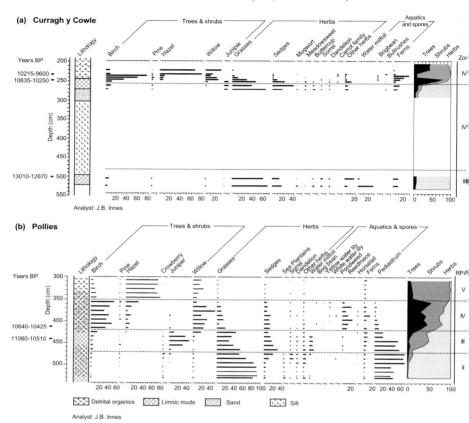

Figure 8.12 *Pollen diagrams from (a) Curragh y Cowle and (b) Pollies.*

of the Greenland Interstadial 1, and conforms to dates from elsewhere in the British Isles. Pollen was not investigated in the long clay-marl sequence (biozone III). The pollen data suggest an age immediately after the Lateglacial/Holocene transition for the base of the upper turfa, detrital peat and limnic mud sequence, which contains abundant herb pollen, dominated by grasses and sedges (biozone IVa). A wide range of open ground herbs occur, of which buttercups, docks, campions and meadowsweet (*Filipendula*) are prominent. Mugwort frequencies are low, but a little higher in the very basal sample. Juniper (*Juniperus*) is the only important shrub taxon, although low frequencies of crowberry, willow and birch also occur. In the uppermost sediment (biozone IVb and V) the Holocene succession through willow, birch and hazel (*Corylus*) takes place, with the birch rise dated to 10,635–10,250 BP.

Loughan Ruy and Pollies

Former pingos on the surface of the Ballaugh alluvial fan have yielded organic sediments and their pollen spectra cover the later stage of the Lateglacial. Early work by Mitchell near Loughan Ruy produced a 300 cm sequence of detrital peats and limnic muds and a pollen record[56] that is similar to one yielded in recent investigation of the Pollies organic fill (Figure 8.12b)[57]. At Loughan Ruy, birch, grasses and sedges dominate the basal stratigraphy (biozone II), with docks, daisy family (Asteraceae) and labiate family (*Labiatae*) less abundant but important open ground herbs. Willow and mugwort increase in abundance at the expense of birch, grasses and sedges in biozone III. Biozone IVa reverses this trend with crowberry, grasses and sedges becoming more abundant. The Loughan Ruy profile differs from the nearby Pollies sequence in lacking a distinctive juniper peak. In biozone IVb crowberry declines and birch and willow increase in abundance as tree cover increases during the early Holocene. In the uppermost sample hazel increases, denoting the start of biozone V.

Pollies yielded 5.25 m of sediment with a detrital peat and limnic sequence underlain by basal coarse sands that were not penetrated. The base of the organic limnic sediment probably dates to before the Lateglacial/Holocene transition, but not extending far into the biozone III cold phase. The basal stratigraphy, biozone III, contains a pollen succession initially dominated almost entirely by grass pollen with very low frequencies of sedges and other open ground herbs of which sea plantain and dandelion (*Taraxacum*-type) were slightly more important. A relative decline in grasses follows as sedges, docks, other herbs and crowberry increase. Water milfoil also rises. Herbaceous taxa then all decline in biozone IVa as juniper rises sharply to almost 50% of total land pollen. The peak of the juniper phase is dated to 11,155–10,425 BP. In biozone IVb juniper then falls to very low values and is replaced by willow and birch as tree cover develops at 10,690–10,290 BP. The beginning of the hazel curve and sharp declines in the suite of open ground herbs mark the base of biozone V, with only wetland herb types remaining as closed canopy conditions developed.

Ballaugh Curragh

The Curragh between Ballaugh and Sulby villages is the most extensive wetland on the Isle of Man, lying in the lowlands between the Sulby Glen and Ballaugh alluvial fans (Figure 8.2). The bulk of the Curragh stratigraphy is of Holocene age and is reviewed in the next chapter. Numerous cores sampled across the basin reveal the stratigraphy, which comprises 5 m (maximum) of Holocene limnic and detrital peats overlying deltaic sands and laminated clays that reflect the existence of an extensive ice-marginal lake during the Late Devensian. The basal stratigraphies at Ballaugh Curragh cores BC6 and BC21 (Figure 9.11, Chapter 9) have yielded palaeoecological data of Lateglacial age. The basal pollen at BC6 is dominated by grasses and sedges and also shows peaks in crowberry, docks, saxifrages and dandelion as well as a wide range of other open ground herbs. Only sporadic mugwort records occurred, signifying the stratigraphy is biozone III or late II at the earliest. Moving up the sequence open ground herb frequencies fall sharply and there is an increase in sedges followed by juniper and willow (biozone IVa), after which juniper rises steadily to consistent values of almost 60% of total land pollen. Above this pollen counts are not available. BC 6 is undated, but covers the period from Greenland Interstadial 1 pollen biozone II, through the cold phase of pollen biozone III with clastic sedimentation, into the early Holocene succession prior to the spread of birch woodland.

Some of the detail from BC6 is repeated in the 390 cm profile recovered from BC21, which contained very early Holocene pollen spectra at the base overlying coarse sands, which were not penetrated. The lowest pollen levels contain high sedges and grasses, with small peaks of docks and buttercups. Meadowsweet and crowberry are also important at the base, with juniper then rising to peak values of around 30%, followed by a rise in birch from low values. Mugwort is almost absent and it seems that the record does not extend back into the Lateglacial pollen biozone III. Lateglacial data also occurs at Ballachrink in the Lhen Trench (Figure 8.2), where very high sedge and grass occur with a wide range of open ground herbs, docks and meadow-rue being prominent, but with meadowsweet reaching almost 30% of total land pollen. There is almost no mugwort, but a low but consistent juniper curve occurs. Willow and then hazel replace this open ground assemblage. These basal pollen assemblages are probably of very early Holocene rather than final Lateglacial age.

Regional summary of the vegetation history

Notwithstanding local differences, the sequence of vegetation changes during the Devensian Lateglacial at a number of sites on the Isle of Man is broadly similar. Correlation of the biozones from the various pollen diagrams in Figure 8.13 demonstrates these similarities and identifies the geochronological control available. Willow, dock family, mountain avens, daisy family, grasses and sedges typically dominate biozone I. The pollen and plant macrofossil data point to a diverse community of arctic and subarctic plants colonising the recently deglaciated terrain. The flora reflects the amelioration of the climate. The base of biozone I is undated, but according to the ice core climate curves began *circa* 15,500 BP[58]. Before this warming and whilst the ice-margin was at or retreating from the Greenland Stadial 2 limits at Jurby Head between 18,000–15,500 BP, the island may have sustained a sparse cold arctic ice-marginal flora. The beginning of biozone II is dated to 14,700–13,800 BP and contains the expansion of birch, which shaded out some of the open ground herbs – willow, docks and mountain avens. Biozone II was a time of climate warming and is correlated with Greenland Interstadial 1 (15,000–12,500 BP). The end of biozone II is dated to *circa* 12,500 BP at Kirk Michael and to 13,140–12,640 BP at Curragh y Cowle. Biozone III sees a downturn in the climate that encouraged less continuous plant cover, with birch declining and increased occurrence of mugwort, docks, willow and other arctic to subarctic open ground herb taxa. Plant macrofossils of *Apus glacialis* and *Polytrichum norvegicum* recorded in biozone III, and these are species that typically are restricted to snow-beds and confirm the downturn in climate. The climate downturn of biozone II correlates with the Greenland Stadial 1 cold period (12,500–11,500 BP). The opening of biozone IVa sees renewed climate warming as willow, juniper and birch return and shaded out open ground herbs. The beginning of biozone IVa is dated to 11,155–10,425 BP at Pollies. Biozone IVa marks the beginning

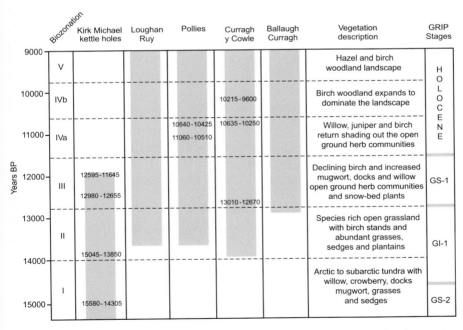

Figure 8.13 *Summary of Lateglacial vegetation history for the Isle of Man.*

of the Holocene warm epoch and subsequent pollen zones reflect the arrival of tree species during the early Holocene, with birch arrival dated to 10,690–10,290 BP at Pollies and 10,635–10,250 BP at Curragh y Cowle.

LATEGLACIAL FAUNA

Remains of giant deer (*Megaloceros giganteus*) found at Glen Balleira (near Kirk Michael), Loughan Ruy (near Ballaugh) and Close y Garey (near St Johns) are the most evocative finds in Lateglacial organic sediments from the island (Figure 8.2)[59]. However, it is the coleopteran (beetle) fauna found in the coastal cliff sections at Jurby Head and Glen Balleira that have produced the most precise reconstruction of the environmental and climatic conditions during the Lateglacial period[60].

Evidence for climate change in the beetle fauna

Reconstructing changes in climate is one of the most significant contributions made by the study of sub-fossil beetle remains. Beetle faunas have provided invaluable information about the magnitude and timing of climate change at the end of the Devensian. The reasons for this are that the geographical ranges inhabited by extant insect species are controlled by climatic parameters particularly temperature[61]. The methods used to interpret palaeoclimate information from beetle assemblages have changed during the last 30 years. Early work on the Isle of Man[62] used the distribution of stenothermic beetles (species that tolerate a narrow range of temperatures) and identified the species that occur in particular biogeographical regions, for example the seven distribution categories listed below:

- Boreal and montane species that normally occur above the tree-line
- Boreal and montane species that occur within boreal coniferous forests
- Widespread species that are distributed towards the north of the British Isles
- Species that are widely distributed
- Widespread species that are distributed towards the south of the British Isles
- Southern species that occur south of the British Isles
- Southern European species.

The mean summer temperatures that characterise these biogeographical regions allow the estimation of changes in temperature. At KM1 194 species of beetle were encountered and 81 species at JH2 and of these 37 species have restricted distributions that are climatically significant. The stratigraphies of the climatically significant species at KM1 and JH2 are displayed in Figures 8.14 and 8.15. Four distinct faunal zones (I to IV) are

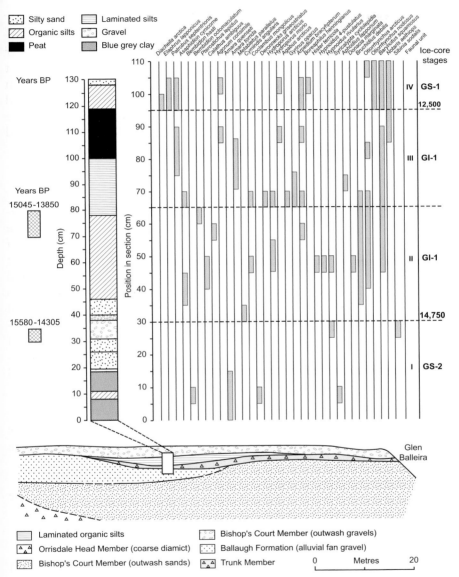

Figure 8.14 *The stratigraphy and beetle palaeoecology at Kirk Michael kettle hole KM1.*

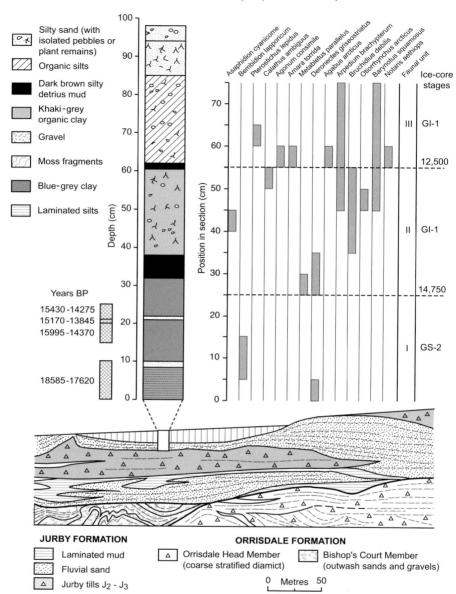

Figure 8.15 *The stratigraphy and beetle palaeoecology at Jurby Head basin JH1.*

Figure 8.16 (opposite) *Maps of the contemporary distribution of* Asaphidion cyan-icorne *and* Syncalypta cyclolepidia, *after G.R. Coope et al. (1998).*

identified in the beetle stratigraphy based upon the distribution of stenothermic species in the sediments[63].

Faunal Zone I – JH2 (0–25 cm) and KM1 (0–30 cm)   Zone I contains species indicative of a cool climate, with the occurrence of *Syncalypta cyclolepidia*, *Coelambus mongolicus*, *Bembidion hasti* and *Bembidion lapponicum* particularly significant. *Syncalypta cyclolepidia* is currently restricted to arctic Scandinavia and mountainous areas further south in Europe (Figure 8.16). *Bembidion repandum* and *Bembidion* cf. *siebkei* are also present and are typical of northern, cooler climates. The assemblage is indicative of maximum July temperatures of 10 °C, although temperatures may have been cooler than this.

Faunal Zone II – JH2 (25–55 cm) and KM1 (30–70 cm)   The fauna of zone II is radically different with all of the cold climate species declining, with the rate of change between the zones occurring very rapidly, in 5 cm of sediment accumulation. There is greater diversity in the beetle community, with species indicative of warmer climes dominating the stratigraphy. The increase in diversity need not be directly related to climate, because the expansion of extent and diversity of vegetation provides a greater range of habitat types. *Bembidion octomaculatum*, *Hister terricola*, *Asaphidion cyanicorne* (Figure 8.16) and *Metabletus parallelus* are present in zone II and are species that currently occur south of the British Isles. The stenotopic species found in zone II indicate average July temperatures of about 17 °C or even higher.

Faunal Zone III – JH2 (55–75 cm) and KM1 (70–95 cm)   The fauna of zone III differs from the previous zone, but not to the same extent as the differences between zones II and I. Species that have current distributions towards the south of the British Isles and further south on mainland Europe and provided the evidence for warm conditions in zone II decline in this zone. The most abundant beetles are species that either are currently widely distributed or have ranges limited to the north of the British Isles. This evidence suggests temperatures were cooler than in zone II, with average July temperatures perhaps of 11–12 °C.

Faunal Zone IV – KM1 (95–110 cm) and KM3/4 (75–120 cm)   The fauna in zone IV indicates the climate is similar to that encountered in zone I. The beetle community has become more restricted both in abundance and diversity, and species indicative of northern cooler climate are more abundant, including specimens of *Diacheila arctica* and *Elapherus lapponicus*. The reduced diversity of the beetle fauna parallels and may be explained by the accumulation of acidic peat at KM1. Changes in the local environment explain the variation in the beetle fauna, but it could also reflect a deteriorating climate. Cold environment fluvial gravels, solifluction deposits and cryoturbated wind-blown sands overlie the sequences at both Kirk Michael and Jurby.

The pattern of climate changes identified by the beetles is similar to that derived from sites elsewhere in the British Isles containing the warming from Greenland Stadial 2 into Greenland Interstadial 1 and the subsequent cooling into Greenland Stadial 1[64]. Four ^{14}C dates are available for the Jurby Head profile, with the basal cold stage sediments dated to 19,060–17,185 BP. There are three ^{14}C dates for the beginning of the zone II warm period that give an age range of 16,320–14,125 BP, and are in keeping with the onset of Greenland Interstadial 1 *circa* 15,000 BP. There are two ^{14}C dates available from Kirk Michael 1 for the base of zone II at 15,910–14,100 BP, with the base of zone III dated to 15,410–13,830 BP. Both these dates bracket the warmest conditions during the Late Devensian and are in keeping with the timing of Greenland Interstadial 1. The onset of zone III marks a return to cooler conditions correlated with Greenland Stadial 1 (12,500–11,500 BP) and whilst not directly radiocarbon dated, equivalent deposits contained giant deer remains radiocarbon dated to 13,110–12,435 BP. The onset of zone I typically occurs at the top of the basins at Kirk Michael, and these have been radiocarbon dated to 13,110–12,435 BP. The available radiocarbon dating evidence and the palaeoclimate data suggest the organic sediments span the period from the later stages of Greenland Stadial 2 to the onset of Greenland Stadial 1.

Climatic reconstructions using beetle faunas have been improved and refined with the advent of the Mutual Climate Range (MCR) methodology[65]. MCR uses the present-day range of climatic conditions occupied by individual species. The climate windows occupied by all the species in a fossil assemblage are overlain and the zone of overlap represents the likely climate experienced by the fossil assemblage. Application of the MCR procedure focuses upon three climatic parameters:

Tmax – Mean temperatures of the warmest month

Tmin – Mean temperatures of the coldest month

Trange – Difference between the mean temperature of the warmest and the coldest month.

The modern climate envelope for each species is generated using species distribution maps (Figure 8.16) and nearby meteorology stations. The reconstructed values are corrected to take account of the MCR overestimating Tmax and underestimating Tmin during cold periods. Applications of the MCR have focused upon producing regional syntheses of climate change using sites distributed across the British Isles. The MCR-derived climate curves compare well with the climate history inferred from the GRIP ice core[66]. Recently MCR data have been used to produce palaeotemperature maps for northwest Europe during the Late Devensian, and the Isle of Man sites were included in that dataset (Figure 8.17)[67]. Revised MCR data for the Isle of Man sites indicate mean July temperatures of 12 °C before 15,000 BP, 18 °C at the maximum of Greenland Interstadial 1, 15,000–14,000 BP and declining to 15 °C between 14,000–12,500 BP. During Greenland Stadial 1 mean July temperatures decline further to 11.5 °C between 12,500–11,500 BP. The Tmax values and patterns of climate change in the Isle of Man are in keeping with sites surrounding the Irish Sea basin in southern Scotland, Cumbria and Eire. Furthermore the pattern and timing of the climate change on the Isle of Man compare well with the climate history elucidated from the GRIP ice core.

The giant deer (*Megaloceros giganteus*)

During the transition from the Pleistocene to the Holocene, *circa* 11,500 BP, it is widely believed that a large group of animals went extinct in different parts of the world. They are referred to using the general term 'megafauna', due to their large size and include species such as woolly mammoth, giant deer, sabre-toothed cat, camel and groundsloth. The reasons for these extinctions are still strongly debated by scientists and include climatic change, human over-hunting and a combination of both. The giant deer or Irish elk (*Megaloceros giganteus*) is one of the most repre-

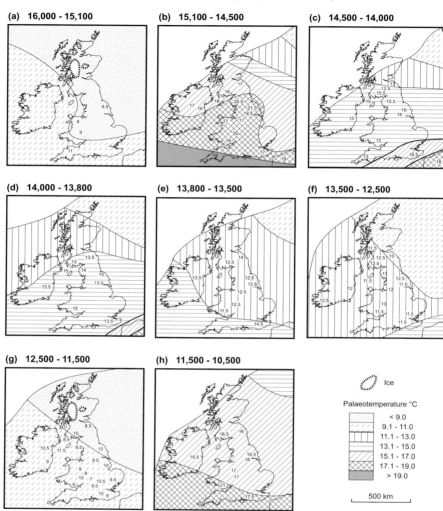

Figure 8.17 *Palaeotemperature maps of the British Isles inferred from the beetle fossil record, after G.R. Coope et al. (1998).*

sentative animals of the Late Pleistocene megafauna in northwest Europe. It had an antler span of up to 3.6 m and a maximum shoulder height of 2.1 m. First appearing *circa* 400 ka, its overall distribution during the Devensian Cold Stage (100–11.5 ka) extended across the middle latitudes of Eurasia from Ireland to the east of Lake Baikal. The name 'Irish' has been associated with the animal because of the large number of well-preserved specimens found in Lateglacial marl and peat deposits in

Ireland[68]. The giant deer is the only example of megafauna found in the Isle of Man (Figure 8.18)[69], with remains found on the island over a period of 200 years or so. The majority of the finds are in the sediments of kettle holes or pingos[70], with the bones usually embedded in marl and for that reason they are generally well preserved and ideal for radiocarbon dating. Most of the giant deer remains found on the Isle of Man are archived in the Manx Museum at Douglas.

The giant deer is believed to have become extinct during the Lateglacial, around 12,000 BP[71], an event associated with the major environmental changes around the Pleistocene/Holocene boundary. This is true for the giant deer found in western Europe, including the Isle of Man. However, recent radiocarbon dates indicate that they survived well into the Holocene (7,000 BP) in the refugia of the Ural Mountains and western Siberia[72]. Other recently published dates that indicate they were present during the Holocene in the Isle of Man and the southwest of Scotland have proved to be incorrect[73]. The reasons for the erroneous Holocene dates are uncertain, but are likely to have resulted from failure to remove contaminants during the original sample pre-treatment. Redating of the specimens by two independent radiocarbon laboratories is in good agreement and now shows that they are Lateglacial in age (Figure 8.19).

A total of 12 new accelerator mass spectrometer (AMS) radiocarbon dates for specimens from the Isle of Man are now available, more than any other area in the world[74]. They indicate that the giant deer was abundant in the island during Greenland Interstadial 1. The oldest directly dated giant deer specimen from the Isle of Man comes from a metatarsal from the Ballaugh area at 15,910–14,515 BP, showing that they reached the island at the onset of Greenland Interstadial 1, as a result of climatic improvement and vegetation recovery. Two more or less complete skeletons of giant deer have been recovered from the Isle of Man: one from a pingo structure near Ballaugh in the northern plain (Figure 8.8 and 8.18) and the other from a kettle hole basin at Close y Garey near Peel (Figure 8.18). The dimensions of these skeletons when compared against the well-known and abundant Irish specimens are small in size and in the case of the complete Ballaugh skeleton having an exaggerated head to body size ratio, showing the importance of sexual selection in maintaining large antlers, characteristics common in 'dwarfed' animals. The latest dated Irish specimen comes from Ballybetagh Bog and has an age of 13,126–11,697 BP (Figure 8.19). In contrast the oldest known Manx specimen, a metatarsal from the Ballaugh area (dated at 15,910–14,515 BP) is as large as the largest Irish specimens. These data indicate a possible size reduction, for unknown reasons, over a period of *circa* 1,500 years for the Manx specimens.

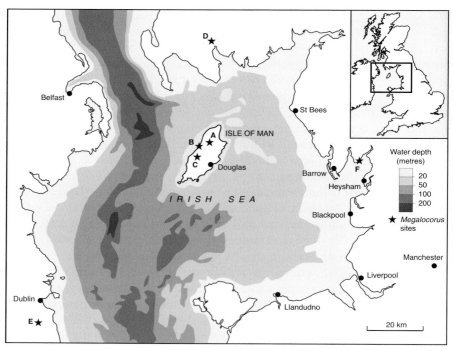

Figure 8.18 *Localities with giant deer (*Megaloceros giganteus*) remains in the Irish Sea basin with AMS dates (stars): A: Ballaugh, Isle of Man. B: Glen Wyllin, Isle of Man. C: Close y Garey, Isle of Man. D: River Cree, southwest Scotland. E: Ballybetagh Bog, Ireland. F: Kirkhead Cave, Cumbria.*

The first giant deer found in the Isle of Man, an almost complete and very well-preserved specimen, was found in 1819 within the sediments of Loughan Ruy, one of the small pingo basins on the Ballaugh gravel fan[75]. A local blacksmith reconstructed the skeleton and exhibited it for payment until the Duke of Athol gained possession through the courts and presented it to the museum of the University of Edinburgh. This was the first giant deer described in the world by the French naturalist George Cuvier in his *Ossemens fossiles* and so the specimen is of particular historical interest[76] (Figure 8.20). The specimen is today at the Royal Scottish Museum in Edinburgh (Figure 8.21a) and a small sample of the antler (Figure 8.21b) has been radiocarbon dated to 11,159 BP. The Isle of Man Natural History and Antiquarian Society recovered the other nearly complete and well-preserved specimen in 1887 from Close y Garey (Figure 8.18)[77]. It was found in a marl pit between Peel and St Johns. The specimen is currently on public display at the Manx Museum, Douglas (Figure 8.22). Also in the

	Locality	Material	Lab. I.D.	Radiocarbon Years BP	Calibrated Years BP	δ13C%	Citation
1	Ballaugh, Loughan Ruy, Isle of Man	Antler Repeat date Repeat date	AA-29744 OxA-10967 AA-51349	9,225 ± 85* 11,495 ± 65 11,159 ± 74	10245-10485 13195-13780 12995-13320	-20.3 -20.8 -22.4	1 2 2
2	Ballaugh, Isle of Man	Unspecified	OxA-10967	11,495 ± 95	13190-13790	-21.0	2
3	Ballaugh, Isle of Man	Shed antler	OxA-11596	11,550 ± 60	13405-13810	n.a.	2
4	Ballaugh, Isle of Man	Shed antler	OxA-11597	11,650 ± 55	13470-13815	n.a.	2
5	Ballaugh, Isle of Man	Unspecifed	OxA-11971	12,275 ± 50	14100-15020	-20.4	2
6	Ballaugh, Isle of Man	Metatarsal	OxA-11678	12,920 ± 120	14515-15910	-20.8	2
7	Glen Wyllin, Isle of Man	Antler	AA-30362	10,780 ± 95	12655-12980	-21.2	1
8	Glen Wyllin, Isle of Man	Femur (immature)	OxA-12118	11,130 ± 45	13005-13170	-20.5	2
9	Glen Balleira, Isle of Man	Unspecified	OxA-11685	12,130 ± 60	13840-14970	-19.9	2
10	The Cronk, Isle of Man	Unspecified	OxA-11687	12,455 ± 65	14170-15250	-20.7	2
11	Close y Garey, Isle of Man	Atlas	AA-30361	11,495 ± 95	13190-13790	-21.0	1
12	Unknown, Isle of Man	Unspecified	OxA-11688	12,020 ± 65	13820-14290	-20.3	2
13	River Cree, SW Scotland	Antler Repeat date Repeat date	AA-18513 OxA-11498 AA-51350	9,430 ± 65* 10,585 ± 65 10,257 ± 75	10560-11040 12365-12845 11705-12315	-21.4 -20.2 -21.9	1 2 2
14	Isle of Islay, SW Scotland	Skull and antlers	OxA-9040	11,985 ± 70	13675-14270	N.A.	2
15	Ballybetagh Bog, Ireland	Mandible	UB-2699	10,610 ± 495	11700-13125	-20.7	3
16	Kirkhead Cave, Cumbria, UK	Antler	HAR-1059	10,700 ± 200	12350-12985	N.A.	3

Figure 8.19 *Published radiocarbon dates obtained for giant deer (Megaloceros giganteus) remains from around the Irish Sea basin. Problematic dates are marked '*' and have been subject to repeated radiocarbon dating at independent laboratories. The citations refer to (1) S. Gonzalez et al. (2000), (2) A.J. Stuart et al. (2004) and (3) A.J. Stuart (1991).*

Manx Museum is a fragment of antler, found in 1976 at Kirk Michael in one of the kettle holes exposed on the cliffs (Figures 8.23 and 8.24a)[78]. The specimen was found at the top of the marl sequence, close to the interface with the overlying peat, and it is the latest dated Manx specimen with an age of 12,980–12,655 BP. During a field excursion to the large kettle hole between Glen Balleira and Glen Wyllin in May 2003, Tony Stuart, Adrian Lister and Silvia Gonzalez found an immature femur bone in the cliff section (Figure 8.24b), which has been radiocarbon dated to 13,005–13,170 BP.

Megaloceros were widely distributed in Ireland and the Isle of Man, where the majority are Lateglacial in age and come from deposits of Biozone II within Greenland Interstadial I[79]. However, there are some

Figure 8.20 *Drawing of the giant deer found in Ballaugh by Cuvier, 1823. It was the first time that the giant deer was described. Note that the reconstruction of the spine is wrong; it is not in a straight line, but has a curve. The specimen is currently in the Royal Scottish Museum in Edinburgh.*

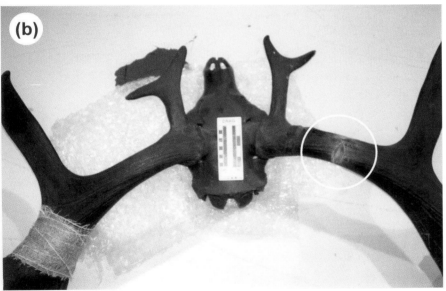

Figure 8.21 *(a) The Ballaugh antler. (b) Photograph of the radiocarbon samples taken from the Ballaugh antler.*

Figure 8.22 *Complete giant deer skeleton found in 1897 in Close y Garey near St Johns after an organised search by P.M.C. Kermode, director of the Isle of Man Natural History and Antiquarian Society. It has been radiocarbon dated to 11,495 ± 95 BP. Currently on display at the Manx Museum, Douglas.*

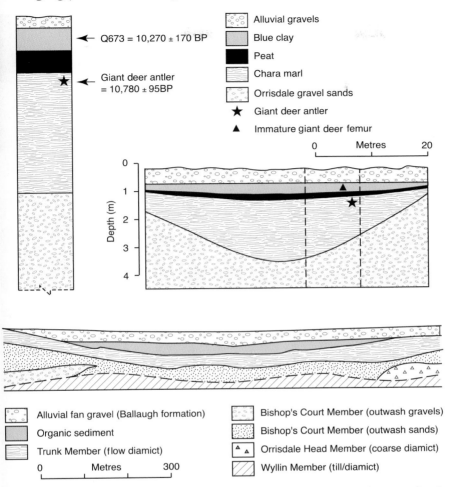

Figure 8.23 *Schematic stratigraphy of the composite Kirk Michael (KM3) kettle hole. The star indicates the position of the giant deer antler with a radiocarbon date of 10,780 ± 95 BP. The triangle indicates the position of an immature giant deer femur found* in situ. *The specimen has an AMS radiocarbon date of 11,130 ± 45 BP.*

Middle Devensian finds from Castlepook Cave, County Cork[80]. The radiocarbon dates (Figure 8.19) show that they were present on the island during Greenland Stadial 1 (pollen zone II) and went extinct from the Isle of Man and from all of western Europe in the Greenland Stadial 1 cold phase. Their extinction happened much earlier than the earliest known human occupation of the island at 10150–9780 BP[81]. Recent research in the Quaternary

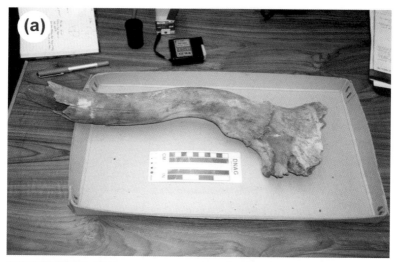

Figure 8.24 *(a) The Glen Wyllin antler found in 1976. (b) The Kirk Michael (KM3) kettle hole in May 2002, showing the excavation of the giant deer femur. The remains are now at the Manx Museum, Douglas.*

deposits of the northern plain in the Isle of Man[82] indicates that the island was isolated from Britain during the Lateglacial to early Holocene times, perhaps explaining the delayed arrival of the major tree species (Figure 8.25). The delayed rise of the Holocene forest compared with surrounding regions (southwest Scotland, eastern Ireland, Lake District, Lancashire) probably reflects severance of the land-bridge with Cumbria and provides an example of divergent island biogeography in the island ecosystem, but also could be a function of climate changes during the early Holocene and local environmental conditions. Late survival and the dwarfism of giant deer (*Megaloceros giganteus*) is another example of biogeographical divergence during the Lateglacial/early Holocene of the Isle of Man. The delayed afforestation and the absence of humans in the early Holocene of the Isle of Man offer the potential, as yet unproven, for the survival of the giant deer into the early Holocene.

The timing of the extinction of the giant deer has been the subject of some debate, where the general agreement until now was the Late Devensian. However, new radiocarbon data[83] indicate survival of the species until *circa* 7,000 BP in the Urals/western Siberia area, in a way similar to the Holocene survival of the mammoths of Wrangel Island, Siberia[84]. These two examples of the survival of megafauna into the Holocene have significance for the way extinctions have occurred in the near past. It would seem that the famous 'Late Pleistocene megafaunal extinctions' were not

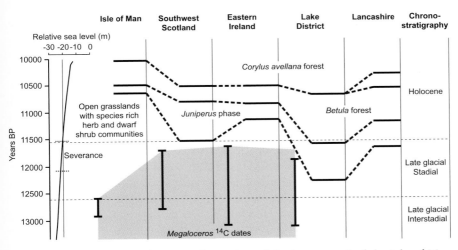

Figure 8.25 *Comparison between the timing of the 'severance' of the Isle of Man from mainland Britain, the latest radiocarbon dates for giant deer in the island and surrounding areas, together with the arrival of the main tree species in the Holocene, after J.B. Innes et al. (2004).*

as abrupt and widespread as previously believed and are instead the result of complex interactions between climatic change and human presence.

SEA LEVELS IN THE IRISH SEA BASIN DURING THE LATEGLACIAL

There has been only limited sea level research in the Isle of Man and it is not until recently that a time/altitude sea level reconstruction for the Island has been proposed[85]. Previous sea level research was concentrated in the north and established the first record of sea level rise for the island[86], which fitted broadly with the known record from northwest England (Figure 8.26)[87]. This suggested a regional sea level rising to a mid Holocene high around 7,500–6,500 BP to *circa* +5 m IOM O.D. Geomorphological evidence for Lateglacial sea levels on the island remains either ambiguous or absent. The pronounced fossil cliff-line that is intermittently present around the island at between *circa* 2–5 m O.D. relates to this Holocene high stand, of that there can be little doubt. Conversely, although older the origins of raised, rock cut 'shoreline' features at Port St Mary (*circa* 40 m O.D.) and at Niarbyl (*circa* 6 m O.D.) remain uncertain[88]. However, a record of Lateglacial sea level was not established, with earlier work to the north and south of the island suggesting sea levels never reached present levels during the Lateglacial[89]. In contrast, the much debated glaciomarine models of the mid to late 1980s, reviewed in Chapter 7, advocated high sea level stands basin wide during deglaciation.

Lambeck[90] was the first to attempt a time/altitude sea level reconstruction for the island using geophysical modelling and Holocene time/altitude relationships from around the Irish Sea basin to propose a three-phase Lateglacial and Holocene relative sea level curve (Figure 8.26). High relative sea level (*circa* +12 m O.D.) is predicted around 20,000 BP as a result of isostatic depression, falling rapidly to *circa* –25 m O.D. at 12,000 BP due to pronounced global eustatic drawdown. From 12,000 BP relative sea levels climbed rapidly as global deglaciation drove eustatic sea level rise to a Holocene high of *circa* +5 m O.D. around 6,000 BP. From this peak, relative sea level has fallen again to the present, as isostatic and eustatic sea level controls have stabilised. South of the Isle of Man initial Lateglacial sea levels were predicted to be around –90 to –80 m O.D. (20,000 and 15,000 BP) as a result of reduced isostatic depression in the southern part of the basin (Figure 8.26), and a land-bridge is thought to have connected the UK with Ireland between 20,000 and 13,000 BP. In contrast, to the north of the island the models suggested that isostatic depression may have been sufficient to elevate relative sea level to 20–30 m O.D. before 20,000

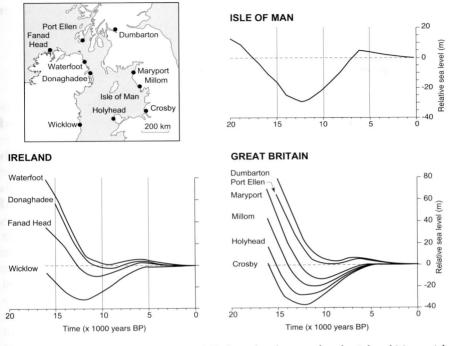

Figure 8.26 *Comparison of the modelled sea level curve for the Isle of Man with other areas around the Irish Sea.*

BP. This was then followed by a falling relative sea level between *circa* 20,000 and 15,000 BP due to rapid isostatic rebound (Figure 8.26). Importantly, Lambeck noted that despite these predicted high stands, a number of areas such as the Isle of Man remained ice covered, and thus, would not have experienced marine conditons.

Recent research in northeast Ireland has reported the occurrence of low-level glaciomarine sediments in Dundalk Bay that relate to a marine transgression up to *circa* 20 m O.D. between 16,700 and 12,700 BP[91]. These sediments, which exhibit *in situ* assemblages of cold water, arctic species of foraminifera and ostracods, indicate that the Lambeck curves require modification, as they show relative sea level to be at least 30 m too low during this period, and in some cases trending downwards rather than upwards. There are a number of reasons for this, including underestimates of ice thickness in Scotland, Ireland and Wales and bathymetric controls influencing ice streaming, stagnation and submergence along the northeast coast of Ireland[92]. The complexity of the situation is highlighted by

McCarroll[93], who notes that in the Dundalk area glaciomarine muds drape channels cut into older glacial sediments that run below present sea level, and hence record a low relative sea level before transgression between 16.7–12.7 ka; evidence that is not in phase with Lambeck's model. In spite of this the modelled time/altitude sea level reconstructions fit well with observed changes in Holocene sea level, with a number of highly accurate correlations between observed and predicted sea level trends across the British Isles[94]. The Irish findings highlight the need to understand fully the origin of water-lain sediments such as the Dog Mills Member and the Killane Member in the north of the island. Most recently, Thomas et al.[95] argue their faunal content to be derived rather than cold water, in situ assemblages, and so they appear glaciolacustrine in origin.

In conclusion, Lateglacial sea levels in the vicinity of the Isle of Man may have been as low as circa –25 m O.D. due to a rapid fall in sea level from 20,000 to 12,000 BP[96]. However, conflicting evidence suggests that between 16,700 and 12,700 BP the east coast of Ireland may have experienced elevated sea levels up to 20 m O.D., and therefore the geophysical models may need some adjustment in terms of ice thickness and the chronology of ice-margin fluctuations. The modelled sea level reconstructions have clearly demonstrated that the original high sea level stands (circa 150 m O.D.) suggested by Eyles and Eyles[97] are not feasible within the model framework. Further, even if small adjustments are made to the geophysical models, our present understanding suggests there is little sound evidence on the Isle of Man to support the occurrence of Lateglacial marine environments.

Notes

1   S. Bjørck, M.J.C. Walker, L.C. Cwynar, S. Johnsen, K.L. Knudsen, J.J. Lowe and B. Wohlfarth, 'An event stratigraphy for the Last Termination in the north Atlantic region based on the Greenland ice-core record, a proposal by the INTIMATE group', Journal of Quaternary Science, 13 (1998), 283–292.

2   J. Mangerud, S.T. Andersen, B.E. Berglund and J. Donner, 'Quaternary stratigraphy of Norden, a proposal for terminology and classification', Boreas, 3 (1974), 109–128.

3   G.R. Coope and W. Pennington, 'The Windermere Interstadial of the Late Devensian', Philosophical Transactions of the Royal Society of London, B280 (1977), 337–339.

4   J.M. Gray and J.J. Lowe, 'The Scottish Lateglacial environment: a synthesis', in J.M. Gray and J.J. Lowe (eds), Studies in the Scottish Lateglacial environment, Pergamon, Oxford (1977), 163–182.

5   S. Bjørck et al. (1998).

6   Ibid.

7   T.C. Atkinson, K.R. Briffa and G.R. Coope, 'Seasonal temperatures in Britain during the past 22,000 years, reconstructed using beetle remains', Nature, 325

(1987), 587–592; S.J. Brooks and H.J.B. Birks, 'Chironomid-inferred Lateglacial air temperatures at Whitrig Bog, southeast Scotland', *Journal of Quaternary Science*, 15 (1999), 759–764.

8   U. von Grafenstein, H. Erlenkeuser, A. Brauer, J. Jouzel and S.J. Johnsen, 'A mid-European decadal isotope-climate record from 15,500 to 5000 years BP', *Science*, 284 (1999), 1654–1657.

9   S. Bjørck *et al.* (1998).

10 E. Watson, 'Two nivation cirques near Aberystwyth, Wales', *Biutetyn Peryglacjalny*, 15 (1966), 79–101.

11 C.B. Crampton and J.A. Taylor, 'Solifluction terraces in south Wales', *Biutetyn Peryglacjalny*, 16 (1967), 15–36.

12 E. Watson, 'The Cardigan Bay area', in C.A. Lewis (ed.), *The Glaciations of Wales*, Longman, London (1970), 125–145.

13 T.D. Douglas and S. Harrison, 'Late Devensian periglacial slope deposits in the Cheviot Hills', in J. Boardman (ed.), *Periglacial processes and landforms in Britain and Ireland*, Cambridge University Press, Cambridge (1987), 237–244.

14 J. Boardman, 'The northeastern Lake District: periglacial slope deposits', in J. Boardman (ed.), *Field guide to the periglacial landforms of northern England*, Quaternary Research Association, Cambridge (1985), 23–37.

15 A.M. Harvey, R.W. Alexander and P.A. James, 'Lichens, soil development and the age of Holocene valley floor landforms: Howgill Fells, Cumbria', *Geografiska Annaler*, 66A (1984), 353–366.

16 R.V. Dackombe and G.S.P. Thomas (eds), *Field Guide to the Quaternary of the Isle of Man*, Quaternary Research Association, Cambridge (1985), 124.

17 R.W. Galloway, 'Periglacial phenomena in Scotland', *Geografiska Annaler*, 43 (1961), 348–353; T.D. Douglas and S. Harrison (1987).

18 C.K. Ballantyne and C. Harris, *The periglaciation of Great Britain*, Cambridge University Press, Cambridge (1994).

19 C.D. Ollier and A.J. Thomasson, 'Asymmetrical valleys of the Chiltern Hills', *Geographical Journal*, 123 (1957), 71–80; H.M. French, 'Asymmetrical slope development in the Chiltern Hills', *Biutetyn Peryglacjalny*, 21 (1972), 51–73.

20 C. Harris, 'Microstructures in solifluction sediments from South Wales and North Norway', *Biutetyn Peryglacjalny*, 28 (1981), 221–226.

21 E. Watson, 'The slope deposits in the Nant Iago Valley, near Cader Idris, Wales', *Biutetyn Peryglacjalny*, 18 (1969), 95–113; C. Harris, 'Solifluction and related periglacial deposits in England and Wales', in J. Boardman (ed.) (1987), 209–224.

22 P.E. Kendall, 'On the glacial geology of the Isle of Man', *Yn Lioar Manninagh*, 1 (1894), 397–437.

23 G.W. Lamplugh, *The geology of the Isle of Man*, Memoir of the Geological Survey of England and Wales (1903), 606; D. Wirtz, 'Zur Stratigraphie des Pleistocäns im Westen der Britischen Inseln', *Neues Jahrbuch für Geologie und Paläontologie*, 96 (1953), 267–303; G.F. Mitchell, 'The Quaternary deposits of the Ballaugh and Kirk Michael districts, Isle of Man', *Quarterly Journal of the Geological Society of London*, 121 (1965), 359–381; G.S.P. Thomas, 'The Quaternary stratigraphy of the Isle of Man', *Proceedings of the Geologists' Association*, 87 (1976), 307–323.

24 G.S. Boulton, A.S. Jones, K.M. Clayton and M.J. Kenning, 'A British Ice-sheet model and patterns of glacial erosions and deposition in Britain', in F.W. Shotton (ed.), *British Quaternary Studies: Recent Advances*, Clarendon Press (1977), 231–246; K. Lambeck, 'Glaciation and sea-level change for Ireland and the Irish Sea basin since Late Devensian/Midlandian time', *Journal of the Geological*

Society of London, 153 (1996), 853–872.

25　　R.A. Chadwick, D.I. Jackson, R.P. Barnes, G.S. Kimbell, H. Johnson, R.C. Chiverrell, G.S.P. Thomas, N.S. Jones, N.J. Riley, E.A. Pickett, B. Young, D.W. Holliday, D.F. Ball, S.G. Molyneux, D. Long, G.M Power and D.H. Roberts, *Geology of the Isle of Man and its offshore area*, British Geological Survey Research Report, RR/01/06, Keyworth, Nottingham (2001), 144.

26　　C.A. Dickson, J.H. Dickson and G.F. Mitchell, 'The Late Weichselian Flora of the Isle of Man', *Philosophical Transactions of the Royal Society London*, B258 (1970), 31–79.

27　　G.S.P. Thomas (1976).

28　　T.M. Douglas and S. Harrison (1987).

29　　A.S. Potts, 'Fossil cryonival features in central Wales', *Geografiska Annaler*, 53A (1971), 39–51.

30　　C.K. Ballantyne and C. Harris (1994).

31　　J.R. Mackay, 'The world of underground ice', *Annals of the Association of American Geographers*, 62 (1972), 1–22.

32　　E. Watson, 'Remains of pingos in Wales and the Isle of Man', *Geological Journal*, 7 (1971), 381–387.

33　　R.C. Chiverrell, G.S.P. Thomas and A.M. Harvey, 'Late-Devensian and Holocene landscape change in the uplands of the Isle of Man', *Geomorphology*, 40 (2001a), 219–236.

34　　G.S.P. Thomas, R.C. Chiverrell and D. Huddart, 'Ice-marginal depositional responses to probable Heinrich events in the Devensian deglaciation of the Isle of Man', *Quaternary Science Reviews*, 23 (2004), 85–106.

35　　R.V. Dackombe and G.S.P. Thomas (1985).

36　　G.W. Lamplugh (1903).

37　　G.S.P. Thomas *et al.* (2004).

38　　G.W. Lamplugh (1903).

39　　R.A. Chadwick *et al.* (2001).

40　　G.W. Lamplugh (1903).

41　　R.C. Chiverrell *et al.* (2001a).

42　　C.A. Dickson *et al.* (1970).

43　　J.B. Innes, R.C. Chiverrell, J.J. Blackford, P.J. Davey, S. Gonzalez, M.M. Rutherford and P.R. Tomlinson, 'Earliest Holocene vegetation history and Island Biogeography of the Isle of Man, British Isles', *Journal of Biogeography*, 31 (2004), 761–772; A.J. Stuart, P.A. Kosintsev, T.F.G. Higham and A.M. Lister, 'Pleistocene to Holocene extinction dynamics in giant deer and woolly mammoth', *Nature*, 431 (2004), 684–689.

44　　R.C. Chiverrell *et al.* (2001a).

45　　C.A. Dickson *et al.* (1970).

46　　M.J. Joachim, *Lateglacial Coleopteran assemblages from the west coast of the Isle of Man*, unpublished PhD thesis, University of Birmingham (1979).

47　　G.M. Reeves, 'On the remains of a skeleton of *Cervus Giganteus* (Irish Elk) in a Late-glacial kettle hole deposit near Kirk Michael, Isle of Man', *Proceedings of Isle of Man Natural History and Antiquarian Society*, New Series VIII, 4 (1982), 416–422; S. Gonzalez *et al.* (2000); A.J. Stuart *et al.* (2004).

48　　G.S.P. Thomas *et al.* (2004).

49　　G.R. Coope, 'The fossil coleoptera from Glen Balleira and their bearing upon the interpretation of Lateglacial environments', in G.S.P. Thomas (ed.), *Isle of Man Field Guide*, Quaternary Research Association, Liverpool (1971), 13–15; M.J. Joachim (1979).

50   C.A. Dickson *et al.* (1970).
51   *Ibid.*
52   *Ibid*; G.F. Mitchell (1965).
53   H. Godwin, *The History of the British Flora: a factual basis for phytogeography*, Cambridge University Press, (1956), 383.
54   C.A. Dickson *et al.* (1970).
55   M.J. Joachim (1979).
56   G.F. Mitchell (1965).
57   J.B. Innes *et al.* (2004).
58   S. Bjørck *et al.* (1998).
59   S. Gonzalez *et al.* (2000).
60   G.R. Coope, G. Lemdahl, J.J. Lowe and A. Walking, 'Temperature gradients in northern Europe during the last glacial-Holocene transition (14–9 ^{14}C kyr BP) interpreted from coleopteran assemblages', *Journal of Quaternary Science*, 13 (1998), 419–433.
61   T.C. Atkinson *et al.* (1987).
62   M.J. Joachim (1979).
63   *Ibid.*
64   G.R. Coope *et al.* (1998).
65   T.C. Atkinson *et al.* (1987).
66   S. Bjørck *et al.*, (1998).
67   G.R. Coope *et al.* (1998).
68   S.H. Reynolds, *A Monograph on the British Pleistocene Mammalia: The Giant Deer or Megaloceros*, The Palaeontographical Society, London (1927), 1–62; G.F. Mitchell and H.M. Parkes, 'The giant deer in Ireland', *Proceedings of the Royal Irish Academy*, 52B (1949), 291–314.
69   G.W. Lamplugh (1903).
70   G.F. Mitchell (1965); E. Watson (1971); R.C. Chiverrell, S. Gonzalez, J.B. Innes, M. Marshall, J. Marshall, G.R. Coope and G.S.P. Thomas, 'Glen Balleira: evidence for late glacial environmental change', in R.C. Chiverrell, A.J. Plater and G.S.P. Thomas (eds), *The Quaternary of the Isle of Man and Northwest England Field Guide*, Quaternary Research Association, London (2004a), 73–93.
71   A.J. Stuart, 'Mammalian Extinctions in the Late Pleistocene of Northern Eurasia and North America', *Biological Reviews*, 66 (1991), 453–562.
72   A.J. Stuart *et al.* (2004).
73   S. Gonzalez *et al.* (2000).
74   A.J. Stuart *et al.* (2004).
75   S. Hibbert, 'Notice of the remains of an animal resembling the Scandinavian Elk, recently discovered in the Isle of Man', *Edinburgh Journal of Science*, 3 (1825), 15–28; H.R. Oswald, 'Observations relative to the Fossil Elk of the Isle of Man', *Edinburgh Journal of Science*, 3 (1825), 28–31.
76   G. Cuvier, *Recherches sur les Ossemens fossiles de Quadrupedes, ou l'on Rétablit les Caractères de Plusieurs Espèces d'Animaux que les Révolutions de Globe Paroissent Avoir Détruites*, Paris, Deterville, nouv. ed. IV (1823), 70–88.
77   P.M.C. Kermode, 'The Irish Elk in the Isle of Man', *Geological Magazine*, N.S. Decade IV, Vol. V (1898), 116–119.
78   G.M. Reeves (1982).
79   C.A. Dickson *et al.* (1970).
80   R.E.M. Hedges, P.B. Pettitt, C. Bronk Ramsey and G.J. Van Klinken, 'Radiocarbon dates from the Oxford AMS System: Archaeometry Datelist 23', *Archaeometry*, 39 (1997a), 247–262; R.E.M. Hedges, P.B. Pettitt, C. Bronk

Ramsey and G.J. Van Klinken, 'Radiocarbon dates from the Oxford AMS System Archaeometry Datelist 24', *Archaeometry* 39 (1997b), 445–471.

81 S.B. McCartan, 'The Manx early Mesolithic: a story in stone. Recent Archaeological Research on the Isle of Man', in P.J. Davey (ed.), *Recent archaeological research on the Isle of Man*, Oxford, British Archaeological Reports British Series 278 (1999), 5–11; S.B. McCartan, 'Mesolithic hunter-gatherers in the Isle of Man: adaptations to an island environment?', in L. Larsson, H Kindgren, K. Knutsson, D. Loeffer and A. Akerlund (eds), *Mesolithic on the Move*, Oxford, Oxbow (2003), 331–339.

82 J.B. Innes *et al.* (2004).

83 A.J. Stuart *et al.* (2004).

84 S.L. Vartanyan, V.E. Garutt and A.V. Sher, 'Holocene dwarf mammoths from Wrangel Island in the Siberian Arctic', *Nature*, 362 (1993), 337–340.

85 K. Lambeck (1996).

86 B.A.M. Phillips, 'The post-glacial raised shoreline around the North Plain, Isle of Man', *Northern Universities Geographical Journal*, 8 (1967), 43–48; M.J. Tooley, 'Sea-level changes and coastal morphology in north-west England', in R.H. Johnson (ed.), *The geomorphology of north-west England*, Manchester University Press, Manchester (1985), 94–121.

87 M.J. Tooley, 'Sea-level changes during the last 9000 years in N.W. England', *Geographical Journal*, 140 (1974), 18–42.

88 B.A.M. Phillips (1967).

89 G.R. Coope and J.A. Brophy, 'Lateglacial environmental changes indicated by a coleopteran succession from North Wales', *Boreas*, 1 (1972), 97–142; R.T.R. Wingfield, 'The Late Devensian (<22 000BP) Irish Sea basin: the sedimentary record of a collapsed ice sheet margin; discussion and reply', *Quaternary Science Reviews*, 11 (1992), 377–379.

90 K. Lambeck (1996).

91 A.M. McCabe and J.R. Haynes, 'A Late Pleistocene intertidal boulder pavement from an isostatically emergent coast, Dundalk Bay, eastern Ireland', *Earth Surface Processes and Landforms*, 21 (1996), 555–572.

92 D. McCarroll, 'Deglaciation of the Irish Sea basin: a critique of the glaciomarine hypothesis', *Journal of Quaternary Science*, 16 (2001), 393–404; N.F. Glasser and G.H. Sambrook-Smith, 'Glacial meltwater erosion of the mid-Cheshire ridge: implications for ice dynamics during the Late Devensian glaciation of northwest England', *Journal of Quaternary Science*, 14 (1999), 703–710; C. O'Cofaigh and D.J.A. Evans, 'Sedimentary evidence for deforming bed conditions associated with a grounded Irish Sea glacier, southern Ireland', *Journal of Quaternary Science*, 16 (2001), 435–454; J. Knight, 'Glaciomarine deposition around the Irish Sea Basin: some problems and solutions', *Journal of Quaternary Science*, 16 (2001), 405–418.

93 D. McCarroll (2001).

94 I. Shennan, W.R. Peltier, R. Drummond and B.P. Horton, 'Global to local scale parameters determining relative sea-level changes and post-glacial isostatic adjustment of Great Britain', *Quaternary Science Reviews*, 21 (2002), 397–408; I. Shennan and B. Horton, 'Holocene land- and sea-level changes in Great Britain', *Journal of Quaternary Science*, 17 (2002), 511–526.

95 G.S.P. Thomas *et al.* (2004).

96 K. Lambeck, (1996).

97 C.H. Eyles and N. Eyles, 'Glaciomarine sediments of the Isle of Man as a key to late Pleistocene stratigraphic investigations in the Irish Sea Basin', *Geology*, 12 (1984), 359–364.

9 The Holocene

RICHARD CHIVERRELL, JIM INNES,
JEFF BLACKFORD, DAVID ROBERTS, GEOFF THOMAS,
PHILIPPA TOMLINSON, ED POOLEY, MIKE FULLEN,
MICHAEL HALLETT and JOHN HARRIS

The British Isles emerged from the last Ice Age at approximately 11,500 BP as the climate improved rapidly into the subsequent warm period, which is called the Holocene. Temperatures inferred from sequences of fossil beetles (coleoptera) and midges (chironomid) within lake and peat deposits suggest that temperatures rose rapidly, by around 8 °C in 500–100 years, and shortly after 11,500 BP temperatures reached levels similar to those experienced today (Figure 9.1). Subsequently the Isle of Man has experienced a temperate climate and although there have been changes in climate during the Holocene these changes are reflected in varying levels of precipitation and temperature of no more than 2–3 °C. Climate change during the Holocene has been of lower magnitude than that experienced during the preceding Ice Ages. Nevertheless, climate changes have affected both ecosystems and land-forming processes. Whilst the climate affects the environment, during the Holocene the most important driver of environmental change has been people, and increasing human impact upon the landscape distinguishes the Holocene from previous times. This chapter reviews the Holocene environmental history of the Isle of Man and discusses environmental changes in the context of both climate and the history of human occupation. The history of people will be addressed in later volumes of the *New History of the Isle of Man*; here the focus is upon the response of the natural landscape to changing climates and human activity.

CLIMATE CHANGE DURING THE HOLOCENE
RICHARD CHIVERRELL

Biological archives like tree rings and ice cores from Greenland, together with geomorphological records, peat bogs, speleotherms (e.g., stalactites), and the isotope and chironomid records from lakes, have been widely used to provide evidence for climate change during the Holocene. These varied sources of information show that temperatures have varied during the

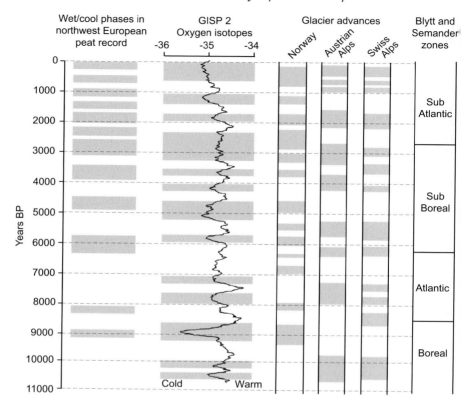

Figure 9.1 *Summary of palaeoclimate reconstructions for the Holocene derived from ice advance histories, ice cores and peat bogs.*

Holocene, but in northwest Europe summer temperatures have varied by no more than 2 or 3 °C. The Greenland ice cores, in particular, are an invaluable record of temperature change, revealing the warming into the Holocene and a climatic optimum between 8,600–4,200 BP. Temperatures have subsequently declined, with the later part of the Holocene, the past 4,000 years, cooler. The GRIP and GISP2 ice core data (Figure 9.1) also identify shorter duration climatic variation, with significant colder periods around 11,300, 9,300, 8,200 and 500–100 BP. A strong record of cyclic climatic variability is superimposed upon these larger events, and this is the subject of ongoing ice core research[1].

The oxygen isotope signature recorded in carbonate lake sediments at Ammersee, southern Germany appears to reflect changes in temperature, and identifies significant colder events *circa* 9,300 and 8,300 BP. Research on carbonate lakes in northwest England (e.g., Hawes Water, North Lancashire) have revealed similar records[2]. Unfortunately, beetle (coleopteran) analyses have not been carried out in sufficient detail to produce a temperature history for the Holocene and scientists have had to rely upon other archives to reconstruct the history of climate change. Glaciers in the mountains of Scandinavia and Central Europe have advanced and retreated in response to climate, and the evidence for fluctuation of the glacier margins provides information about climate change (Figure 9.1). During the Holocene glaciers have for the most part been in a state of retreat, but periods of significant ice advance in Scandinavia and the Alps occurred *circa* 8,500–7,900, 7,500–7,300, 6,300, 5,800–5,300, 4,500–4,200, 3,700–3,500, 3,000–2,000, 1,800–1,400 and after 500 BP.

Tree rings offer the opportunity to examine climate variability as individual tree rings reflect favourable and unfavourable growth conditions on a year-by-year basis. Favourable growth conditions are controlled to some extent by climate, with wide rings in Scandinavia, Central Europe and Ireland believed to reflect a warmer climate. However, favourable growth conditions reflect a number of factors including both temperature and precipitation. Tree ring sequences clearly offer annually resolved palaeoclimate information and so are extremely valuable resources. Overlapping sequences from mature living trees (100–250 years old) with dead wood preserved in old buildings, archaeological sites and buried within peat bogs extend the tree ring palaeoclimate record. The longest tree ring series are the Scandinavian[3] pine record and the 'bog oak' records from temperate Europe (Northern Ireland, Germany and the Netherlands)[4]. Both the Scandinavian and temperate European tree ring records extend back through the past 8,000 years and reveal numerous variations in summer temperatures, including cooler periods 3,600–3,400, 2,500–2,200, 2,100–2,000, 1,500–1,000 and 500–80 BP.

Some of the earliest research on Holocene climate history used the stratigraphic horizons within peat bogs to identify climate shifts, with highly decomposed peat reflecting drier or warmer climatic conditions and poorly decomposed peat produced under cooler or wetter conditions. This climate framework, known as the Blytt and Sernander scheme, became a cornerstone of understanding the Holocene climate history and identified five broad climatic periods; the Pre-Boreal with an indeterminate climate (before 9,000 BP), the warm and dry Boreal (9,000–7,000 BP), the maritime and mild Atlantic (7,000–5,000 BP), the warm and dry Sub-Boreal (5,000–2,600 BP), and the cool and humid Sub-Atlantic (2,600–0 BP). Early research used peat stratigraphy to elucidate climate history through the identification of features called recurrence surfaces, which are stratigraphic changes where highly decomposed peat is succeeded by poorly decomposed peat dominated by the remains of the bog mosses (*Sphagnum*). Recurrence surfaces reflect an ecological and diagenetic response to increased availability of water on the mire surface. Reconstruction of past climates using peat deposits depends on the sensitivity of mire systems to changes in effective precipitation, which is defined as precipitation minus losses through evapotranspiration. Clearly a climate-driven moisture signal will be best preserved in peat bogs that receive their moisture solely as rainfall, from peat bogs that are called ombrotrophic. Climate is the fundamental control upon the hydrology of ombrotrophic peat bogs, unless there has been substantial natural or anthropogenic drainage of the bog.

In recent years there has been renewed attention to the finer detail in the sedimentary record of ombrotrophic peat bogs[5] producing a substantial volume of research from sites across the British Isles and northwest Europe. This work uses the decomposition stratigraphy of the peat alongside the plant remains and the shells of microscopic Protozoa (testate amoebae) preserved within peat to infer a history of surface wetness conditions. The distribution of both the plants and testate amoebae are strongly affected by water table, with certain species preferring dry conditions and others wet. Peat bogs provide a regional synthesis of climate change, with similarities in the palaeoclimate data recorded in peat sequences distributed across northwest Europe. Similar histories of surface wetness are present at a large number of sites[6], with shifts to a wetter or cooler climate recorded *circa* 8,300–7,900, 6,200–5,800, 5,400–5,200, 4,400–4,200, 3,500, 2,800–2,600, 2,300–2,200, 1,500–1,300 and 500–400 BP (Figure 9.1).

CLIMATE CHANGE: THE EVIDENCE FROM BEINN Y PHOTT   RICHARD CHIVERRELL

Unlike most areas of the British Isles, there is no tree ring or peat-based climate reconstruction for the island. This is a function of scarcity of wood remains and appropriate peat sequences, and a lack of research activity. Ombrotrophic peat deposits are not widespread on the island, with the thickest deposits of blanket peat on watersheds in the northern uplands. The comparative absence of ombrotrophic peat from the Isle of Man is largely a function of peat cutting, which has denuded the stratigraphy of Ballaugh Curragh, the major wetland on the Isle of Man. The climate of the island is certainly suitable for the formation of lowland raised and upland blanket mires. The only widespread blanket peat deposits are on

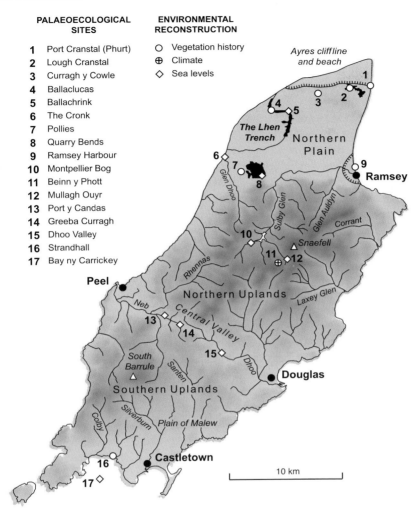

Figure 9.2 *Holocene sites of importance on the Isle of Man.*

the northern flanks of Beinn y Phott (Figure 9.2), which in Manx means 'Turf Mountain'. Not surprisingly Beinn y Phott has been significantly affected by peat cutting, with only remnants of the former peat bog remaining.

Ombrotrophic peat provides evidence for climate from the record of hydrological change recorded in the stratigraphy. Peat stratigraphy provides a somewhat ambiguous record of past climate, because a shift to a wetter mire surface could be either a response to cooler or wetter climatic conditions. Careful interpretation of changes in sedimentary characteristics of peat allows reconstruction of mire palaeohydrology. For example, the degree to which the peat is decomposed or humified is controlled by surface wetness. Peat deposits consist of two layers with radically different aerobic conditions; the upper aerobic zone is called the acrotelm and comprises the surface layers of peat above the minimum summer water table. The remainder of the peat sequence is beneath the water table, anaerobic and called the catotelm. Most of the decay experienced by peat takes place in the acrotelm. Consequently the amount of time that it takes for organic matter freshly accumulated on the surface mire to be buried and pass through the acrotelm controls the degree of humification. This means that fluctuations in the minimum summer water table are an important control upon peat humification. In the case of ombrotrophic mires the minimum summer water table is controlled by the climate. The plant remains preserved within peat deposits allow reconstruction of changes in the mire vegetation and can also provide climate information, because surface moisture conditions are a critical factor controlling the distribution of plants. Certain plant species prefer specific environmental habitats, for example heather (*Calluna vulgaris*) prefers drier locations like the tops of hummocks whereas the species of bog moss, for example *Sphagnum cuspidatum*, prefer wetter locations like pools or hollows. Variations in the abundance of plant species in the fossil record allow the moisture tolerances of certain species to be used to identify changes in hydrology.

Peat deposits at Beinn y Phott have been analysed for the degree of humification and for the plant macrofossil remains preserved within the peat stratigraphy. The humification profile (Figure 9.3) contains short-term variability that reflects fluctuations of the water table, with shifts to poorly humified peat in particular denoting higher water tables. Mineral matter is abundant towards the base of the peat profile and reflects the early stages of peat inception, when the site received mineral input from surface flow. The cotton-grass (*Eriophorum vaginatum*) and unidentifiable organic matter dominate throughout the plant macrofossil profile (Figure 9.3). There are bands of peat with *Sphagnum* remains that formed 3,500–3,300 and 2,900–2,700 BP, and these bands possibly signify wetter conditions, but *Sphagnum* never really dominates the stratigraphy; remaining a minor component within an essentially well-humified *Eriophorum vaginatum* peat. The plant remains reveal little about changes in surface wetness, whereas the humification stratigraphy of Beinn y Phott provides a clear record of changes in mire surface wetness. Surface wetness inferences in the stratigraphy at Beinn y Phott support research on peat bogs elsewhere in Europe (Figure 9.1), with the humification changes signifying a move to wetter or cooler climate conditions at 3,600–3,400, 2,800–2,500, 1,600–1,400 (the 'Dark Ages') and 800–500 (the Little Ice Age) BP.

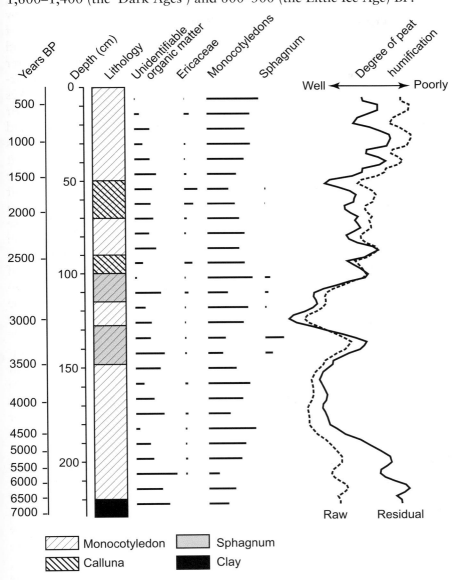

Figure 9.3 *The peat humification and plant macrofossil stratigraphy from Beinn y Phott.*

COASTAL AND SEA LEVEL HISTORY

JIM INNES, DAVID ROBERTS and RICHARD CHIVERRELL

Compared with elsewhere in the British Isles there has been only limited sea level research in the Isle of Man and only recently have time/altitude sea level reconstructions been proposed for the island[7]. Lambeck[8] used geophysical modelling and established time against sea level altitude relationships for the Irish Sea basin[9] to produce a relative sea level curve (Figure 9.4), which identifies that relative sea level rose rapidly from 12,000 BP as global deglaciation drove eustatic sea level rise to a Holocene high of *circa* +5 m O.D. around 6,000 BP. From this peak, relative sea level has fallen to the present day as isostatic and eustatic sea level controls have stabilised.

There is a wealth of both submerged and raised shoreline features around the Isle of Man (Figure 9.2) that could test the accuracy of Lambeck's modelled sea level curve. These include several submerged forest beds that demonstrate that sea levels were once lower than at present and that they have subsequently risen during the Holocene. The altitudinal maximum of such a post-glacial relative sea level rise is reflected in the extensive Ayres raised beach complex and the marked raised cliff-line cut into glacial sediments between 2–5 m above O.D. (Figure 9.5). The clearest indicator of a Holocene sea level high occurs in the sediments of Lough Cranstal, which is a relict lagoon situated at the base of the raised cliff-line on the northeast coast (Figure 9.6). Radiocarbon dating constrains the marine incursion at Lough Cranstal to between 8,930–8,430 and 8,330–8,040 BP. This fits broadly with the known and modelled Holocene sea level record from northwest England, which suggests regional sea level rising to a mid Holocene high of approximately 5 m above O.D. (Figure 9.4)[10].

Submerged and nearshore forest beds and peat deposits have also been reported from Ramsey harbour, Port Cranstal (previously referred to as Phurt) and Bay ny Carrickey[11]. Their occurrence offshore suggests a Holocene sea level rise over a previously more extensive landscape. The 'Strandhall peat' and other peat deposits at Kentraugh and Poyllvaaish in the south of the island (Figure 9.2) have a maximum elevation within 1–2 m of the present high water mark and could indicate a slightly elevated past relative sea level, but as yet the deposits have not been dated. Tooley identified a wave cut platform (+2.4 to +3.5 m O.D.) at Strandhall, which is presently being exhumed from the beach[12]. He suggests the feature is polycyclic in age and a function of interglacial/glacial inheritance. However, the feature is not clear in the field and the bedding structure of

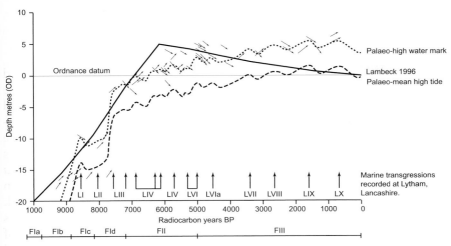

Figure 9.4 *Sea level curve (solid line) for the Isle of Man for the last 20,000 years, after K. Lambeck, (1996). Relative sea level changes in northwest England, after M.J. Tooley (1978), with the dotted line showing palaeo – high water mark and the dashed line palaeo-mean high tide. A point and associated arrow shows the age and altitude of a sea level index point, with upwards pointing arrows showing a transgressive overlap and a downwards pointing arrow a regressive overlap. L–I to L–X denote marine transgressions recorded at Lytham, Lancashire.*

Figure 9.5 *The Ayres early Holocene raised cliff-line at Blue Point. Photograph by Richard Chiverrell.*

the limestone in the area may have been a strong influence on any platform formation. Phillips identified cemented beach deposits at Strandhall, which has a surface that ranges in altitude between +6.0 to +9.0 m O.D.[13].

The raised beaches and fossil cliff-lines around the Isle of Man are convincing evidence of high sea levels during the Holocene. Whilst these features provide an indication of the altitudinal limits of past sea levels, morphological shoreline features cannot be directly dated. It is also uncertain as to whether such features represent past mean sea level, high tide level or storm levels. In order to test the models of sea level history proposed for the island and the central Irish Sea area (Figure 9.4)[14] research data are

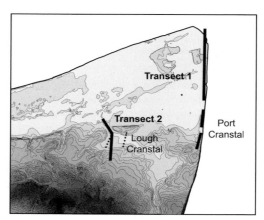

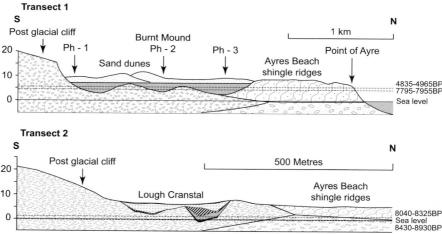

Figure 9.6 *The coastal stratigraphy and sea level evidence from Lough Cranstal and Port Cranstal.*

required with much more precise altitudinal and chronological information about coastal change and the position of past sea levels. The fine-grained sediment sequences of intercalated peat, mud, silts and clays that form in the inter-tidal and immediate supra-tidal zones are ideal for this purpose. In these settings, stratigraphic changes in sedimentary sequences represent past changes in depositional environment that are related directly to changes in relative sea level. Description and radiocarbon dating of the organic-inorganic boundaries thus reveal the nature and timing of a change, for example a shift from salt-marsh peat to mudflat can be related to a past water level in the tidal cycle such as Mean High Water of Spring Tide (MHWST). Levelling of the altitude of these boundaries relative to present sea level provides a time against altitude measure of sea level. Microfossils found within the sediments, such as pollen, diatoms and foraminifera, which have known ecological requirements, can be used to prove their marine, inter-tidal, salt-marsh or freshwater origin and to indicate their formation at a particular water level within the tidal cycle. Data of this type are critical given that the tidal range may be many metres, as it is today. Samples with such high-precision palaeoecological data, such as those mentioned above from Lough Cranstal, are termed sea level index points (Figure 9.6). A set of several such index points allows the reconstruction of past trends in relative sea level and helps to separate local coastal factors operating at individual sites from the more regional factor of sea level change.

Evidence for sea level change: the northern plain of the Isle of Man

The low-lying area of the northern plain has a number of coastal sites that preserve soft sediments with the potential to contain a sea level record. The single marine incursion recorded at Lough Cranstal[15] provides two sea level index points; one transgressive with marine clay resting upon freshwater organic deposits, and one regressive with the marine clay overlain by freshwater peat, together representing a relative rise then relative fall of sea level. Coastal barriers, perhaps associated with the formation of the Ayres gravel complex, presumably protected the lagoon at Lough Cranstal from marine inundation thereafter.

The coastal sections at Port Cranstal have recently been reinvestigated[16] and a compact basal peat bed resting upon glacial till containing tree stumps has been dated to 7,950–7,725 BP. The peat bed contained indications of inter-tidal environments in its upper levels, with foraminifera test linings present as well as the pollen of salt-marsh plants. The top of the peat was dated 7,740–7,550 BP. This peat appears to be a lagoonal facies formed in a small basin and either directly influenced by, or very close to, brackish water conditions under rising sea level. Above the basal peat lies clayey sand, then sandy clay, then an upper more clayey peat deposit and finally terrestrial sands. Although the sands and clays between the two peat layers contain no direct evidence of marine conditions, there are high values of salt-marsh pollen, particularly the Goosefoot family (Chenopodiaceae) just below and into the upper peat, declining towards the top. The upper peat has lower and upper contacts dated 5,570–5,100 BP and 5,020–4,830 BP and may have formed in an upper salt-marsh, becoming more terrestrial under falling sea level influence. Port Cranstal therefore records a rising sea level tendency from about 7,000 BP and then a falling tendency starting before 5,600–5,100 BP. The site contributes four sea level index points to the dataset for the northern plain (Figure 9.9).

At Ramsey a 25 cm thick submerged peat bed is exposed near the low water mark to the north of the harbour wall. Birch (*Betula*) wood remains dominate this compressed peat, which overlies poorly exposed glacial sediments. Contemporary beach sands overlie the peat deposits. Pollen data reveal a typical early Holocene vegetation sequence with little coastal influence. Basal and uppermost samples have been radiocarbon dated to 11,055–10,560 BP at –1.75 m O.D. and 9,910–9,635 BP at –1.72 m O.D. respectively. The sequence provides a lower limiting point for terrestrial environments during the early Holocene, with no marine influence at altitudes of –1.75 to –1.72 m O.D. between *circa* 11,000 and 9,635 BP (Figure 9.9).

Cores taken near the coast within the valley of the Lhen Trench (Figure 9.2) have also revealed organic sediments, which contain multiple lenses of blue-grey silty clay. The most seaward core, Lhen Trench 5 (LT5) near Ballaclucas, includes four such silty clay layers, each of which contains estuarine and marine diatoms (Figures 9.7 and 9.8). The altitudes of these silty clay layers range between +3.04 and +5.19 m O.D. and indicate the recurrent direct incursion of brackish water inter-tidal conditions into the valley. The silty clays are separated by mostly freshwater organic sediments reflecting periods when marine influence was withdrawn from the site, although the pollen data, which include some indicator halophyte types like goosefoot and sea plantain (*Plantago maritima*), show that some of the intervening organic sediments were deposited under salt-marsh environments or very near to them. This repeated reduction in marine influence could have occurred because of periodic lowering of sea level as part of a fluctuating sea level tendency, or because of the opening and closing of local sand-dune barriers across the mouth of the valley. The upper and lower boundaries of the four marine clays have been radiocarbon dated

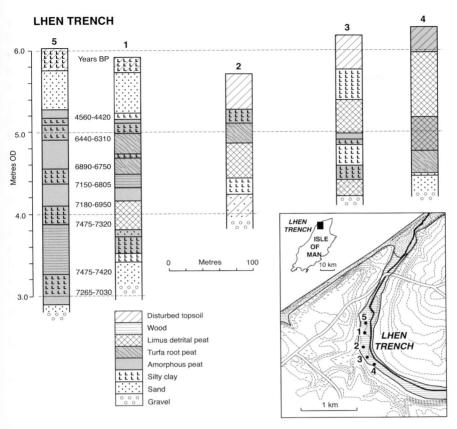

Figure 9.7 *Stratigraphy of the Lhen Trench around Ballaclucas.*

and provide a series of sea level index points (Figure 9.9). The lowest silty clay boundary provided an erroneously young date out of sequence with the rest, probably due to contamination, which has been disregarded. The pollen data suggest an age for that contact of about 7,800 BP. The site therefore provides a sea level history between *circa* 7,800 and 4,600 BP[17].

Sea level research in the south

In the south of the island a number of sites offer the opportunity to expand present knowledge of the sea level history of the area. The most important of these is the drift cut, raised fossil cliff-line stretching intermittently from Gansey Point to Langness. At Gansey it has cut a slate bedrock platform,

Figure 9.8 *The pollen diagram from the Lhen Trench core (LT5) at Ballachucas,.*

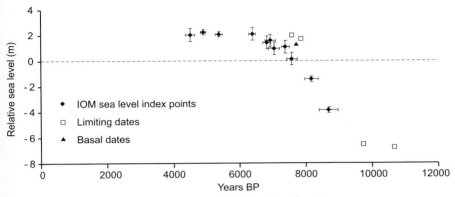

Figure 9.9 *Sea level index points and curve for the Isle of Man.*

giving a minimum altitudinal control on the post-glacial sea level maximum. Other sites, for example at Kentraugh and Langness, while similar in altitude, may have aggradational foreland complexes obscuring the exact altitude of the base of the cliff, and hence require further investigation before they can be utilised as altitudinal controls on the post-glacial sea level maximum. Extensive research[18] on sea levels around the island suggests the base of the post-glacial cliff-line in the south lies between +5 to +7 m O.D. (e.g. Kentraugh at 5.73 m O.D.; Poyllvaaish to Scarlett from 5.48 to 5.79 m O.D.; Derbyhaven at 6.15 m O.D.; Port Grenaugh at 6.09 m O.D.). Furthermore, the Bay ny Carrickey area has a number of organic deposits associated with and in close proximity to the raised cliff-line which may relate to former changes in relative sea level and potential could provide a chronological framework. The peat found at the base of the Kentraugh cliff, behind the Shore Hotel and at Strandhall, is most likely back barrier sediment, formed behind an offshore barrier complex situated in Bay ny Carrickey. Without a barrier the shore would have been subjected to a high-energy wave regime negating the establishment of low-energy environments where peats would have formed. Indeed, it is likely that the present gravel barrier situated onshore intermittently between Strandhall and the Shore Hotel is a remnant of the original offshore barrier driven onshore by a rising Holocene sea level. The concept of an offshore barrier is not new, Cumming having proposed such an environment when describing the origin of submerged peat in the Strandhall area[19].

The raised beach sediments between Strandhall and Poyllvaaish and near Kentraugh are also worthy of further close investigation. In the Strandhall case their stratigraphic context is particularly critical. At this locality cemented, shelly, sandy gravels occur at approximately 1 to 2 m above the high water mark. The faunal composition of the deposit is very well preserved and intact, and virtually identical in faunal assemblage to the adjacent modern beach. At the southern end of the section (SC 240683) this cemented shelly gravel appears banked against limestone bedrock, possibly an older cliff-line. However, only *circa* 50 to 100 m further north the cliff section increases in height to 5 m and the stratigraphic relationship between the shelly gravels at the base of the cliff and overlying sands and gravels becomes somewhat more complex. In the first instance the shelly gravels lack a major faunal component, although stratigraphically it is feasible to correlate them with the shelly gravels just to the south. Secondly, the overlying sands and gravels appear to be glaciofluvial in origin, and not a beach facies. These sands and gravels form a broad flat plain immediately to the east of the section, which is interpreted as a former glacial outwash surface. However, at this locality where the cliff has been preferentially eroded and cemented to form chaotic calcrete pillars, the shelly gravels appear in places stratigraphically to underlie the overlying sands and gravels. Thus, the shelly gravels could be the first interglacial sediments reported from the Isle of Man. Unfortunately this stratigraphic relationship is heavily obscured by calcrete and requires coring investigation inland to confirm its stratigraphic context. It should be stressed however, that the sediments are more likely to be post-glacial beach sediments recently cemented on to the cliff face and relating to the mid Holocene sea level high. The shelly gravels at the base of the Kentraugh cliff are similar to those described.

The raised cliff-lines on both the east and west sides of the Langness peninsula also require closer investigation. Altitudinally, the base of the cliffs appears similar to others described along the south coast, but as yet no organic sediments have been found associated with them. A well-preserved beach plain approximately 1 to 3 m above high water fronts the western raised cliff-line. Beyond this are the remains of a salt-marsh, thinly developed (50 cm in depth) over the underlying Carboniferous Basal Conglomerate and it may hold some palaeoenvironmental information.

It is most likely that the raised shoreline features so far described in the south relate to the mid Holocene sea level rise pointing to a relative sea level high of 2 to 3 m O.D. around 7,000 BP[20]. However, there are other raised features that may pre-date this period, including a rock cut cliff-line (5–10 m high) at approximately 40 m O.D. along the western edge of Port St Mary. The Niarbyl raised platform sequence described by Phillips[21] is also worthy of further consideration, because the wave cut platform at 5–6 m O.D. probably also pre-dates the Holocene sea level maximum. The other easily identifiable platforms at Niarbyl are within the present tidal zone[22].

The Holocene relative sea level record

Sites on the coast of the northern plain have provided 16 sea level index points, and the ages and altitudes are shown in Figure 9.9. Unfortunately, there are no radiocarbon dated sea level index points from the south of the island. The sea level index points were defined following standard relative sea level methodologies[23] to the data. This sea level dataset shows a clear trend of rising relative sea level from –4 m O.D. in the early Holocene up to a sea level mid Holocene maximum that occurs between *circa* 6,600 and 4,300 BP at 2 m O.D., after which there are limited data. The trend of relative sea level is constrained by limiting dates obtained from terrestrial environments at Port Cranstal and Ramsey. At Ramsey these date to between 9,700 and 10,700 BP and limit sea level to below –6.55 m O.D., while at Port Cranstal they limit sea level to below 2.04 m O.D. between 7,600–7,900 BP. The overall rate of relative sea level rise between 8,700 and 6,400 BP is 2.6 mm per year, but this slows very quickly to *circa* 0.3 mm per year between 6,400 and 4,500 BP.

In addition to eustatic and isostatic controls upon relative sea level a number of local factors must also be considered, particularly site morphology and coastal processes. The pronounced raised shoreline around the north of the island at 5–8 m O.D. appears too high to correspond with the reconstruction for the Holocene relative sea level maximum proposed in Figure 9.9. However, these altitudes are for raised beach gravel ridges aggraded under storm conditions and not the result of low-energy marine inundation. Consequently a direct altitudinal relationship between the cliff and relative sea level is difficult to ascertain. Indeed, raised beach or barrier complexes may have influenced the timing and extent of low-energy inundation of basins at Port Cranstal, Lough Cranstal and the Lhen Trench, as they are all fronted by the Ayres raised beach complex, and the repeated introduction and withdrawal of marine influence throughout a period of steadily rising sea level (Figure 9.9) may have been influenced by barrier stability. Marine inundation of the Lhen Trench may also have been altitudinally amplified by the narrow morphology of the valley.

The rising relative sea level to the mid Holocene maximum does conform, however, to a broad regional trend regarded mainly as a response to eustatic sea level rise due to the continued melting of icesheets. The mid Holocene high sea level of *circa* 2 m O.D. on the island suggests that there is also a residual glacio-isostatic component in the sea level record resulting from delayed rebound of the land surface after the removal of Devensian ice loading. Previous research[24] suggests a north to south regional isostatic gradient in the Irish Sea basin in response to increased ice loading in northern Britain, with the northwest of England lying in a pivotal zone between subsidence in the south and isostatic uplift in the north. Comparison of the Isle of Man data with Morecambe Bay, Cumbria, the northern Solway Firth and the north of Ireland[25] suggests there is a more pronounced isostatic signal to the north with mid Holocene relative sea level in Solway approaching *circa* 4 m O.D. To the south the records from Morecambe Bay and Cumbria are mainly eustatically driven. The residual uplift on the island is also greater than that encountered in the north of Ireland. This regional pattern of residual uplift is difficult to reconcile with reconstructed icesheet thickness and residence times in the central Irish Sea basin, which point to ice thicknesses of *circa* 500 m over the island, *circa* 600 m over Ireland and *circa* 700 m over the Lake District[26], and rapid loss of ice mass in the central basin during deglaciation[27]. Consequently the Isle of Man should record a more subdued isostatic response to loading. These differences in residual uplift between the centre and the peripheries of the Irish Sea basin could reflect the close proximity of the island to the centre of British Icesheet loading in Scotland, but may also relate to incorrect estimates of ice thickness in Ireland and the Lake District, or more complex differential crustal responses to loading across the basin[28].

Comparison between observed sea level data and the geophysical models[29] shows that the observed sea level record for the island differs from the Lambeck curve for the Isle of Man. There is neither a pronounced mid Holocene inflexion from submergence to emergence, nor a very steep and rapid early Holocene rise demonstrated in the Manx data (Figures 9.4 and 9.9). Lambeck's rate of eustatic rise is also very fast and there appears to be too much residual uplift in the model. Peltier's model[30] provides a better fit for the Isle of Man data. Both models create a number of conceptual difficulties in relation to relative sea level in the Irish Sea basin, however, particularly in relation to the existence and duration of land-bridges between the Isle of Man and Cumbria. Water depths in the northern Irish Sea are too deep for a direct land-bridge between the Isle of Man and Ireland, even given maximum isostatic depression. In contrast, the shelf between Cumbria and the Isle of Man does not exceed 40 m water depth and Lambeck and Peltier's models suggest the presence of a land-bridge between 13,000 to 10,500 BP and 10,000 to 9,000 BP respectively. Discrepancies between the models though bring into question the spatial extent and longevity of the land-bridges, as the vertical offset in sea level between the models approaches 20 m between 13,000 and 10,000 BP, effectively hindering land-bridge development. The precise location and timing of the opening of the land-bridge thus remains poorly understood.

HISTORY OF THE NATIVE VERTEBRATE FAUNA
PHILIPPA TOMLINSON and ED POOLEY

Severance, and the subsequent insular status that developed during the latter part of the Lateglacial (12,500–11,500 BP)[31] prevented immigration of new non-avian species and the replacement of any species that declined during the Holocene. The sudden onset of the warmer Holocene period and the rapid development of closed canopy woodland by 8,000 BP encouraged the fauna to change markedly. Crucially for the non-avian element of the vertebrate fauna, the onset of insular status established the first distinctive faunal assemblages. Insular status meant that some species, especially large ones, could not survive for long because of an absence of sufficient habitat to maintain a viable population. It also meant that when subsequent climate and associated vegetation change produced conditions which were no longer what particular species required, they eventually died out and that there was no free migration of 'replacement' individuals. During the later Holocene human settlement and the effect of an increasingly managed landscape were important controls upon the native fauna. The contemporary fauna is therefore the product of a combination of remnant survivors from the initial post-glacial colonisation, supplemented by the human-mediated introduction of new species to the island. Evidence of the vertebrate fauna before any documentary record relies entirely upon the identification and dating of animal bones and teeth uncovered from natural sediments. Only positive evidence of presence can be used in interpreting the mammalian fossil record; the absence of a fossil record does not necessarily mean the absence of species. Evidence from either archaeological contexts or in sediments post-dating the arrival of people, and especially after the advent of farming, must be treated with caution unless radio-carbon dating of specimens has taken place.

The fauna of the Lateglacial period, discussed in the last chapter, is completely absent today. The most extensive zooarchaeological record in the British Isles as a whole during the late Devensian, that of the giant deer (*Megaloceros giganteus*), includes representatives from the Isle of Man. Based on the wider evidence[32] other members of the Lateglacial fauna of the Isle of Man might have included the ungulates – reindeer, aurochs, saiga (*Saiga tatanica*) and elk (*Alces alces*) and also mountain hare, wolf, lynx, arctic fox, lemming (*Lemmus lemmus* and *Dicrostonyx torquatus*) and vole (*Microtus gregalis*). It seems possible that, if present, a few of these may have survived into the early Holocene, but they never formed insular populations. For the Holocene, there is little hard evidence for the evolving record. Garrad[33] discusses the bone and place name evidence for the history of Manx mammals. Bone records are mainly from archaeological sites and the specimens are either no longer available or are difficult to verify, with several specimens of deer bone in the Manx Museum unprovenanced. Place name evidence is not strong enough on its own to confirm the presence of particular species. A recent re-examination of the mammal bones in the Manx Museum failed to find any promising candidates for a radiocarbon dating programme. Although red deer (*Cervus elaphus*) was certainly present in the later Holocene and is confirmed by good archaeological and documentary evidence[34], the only apparently early Holocene specimen is from an undated peat deposit in the Lhen Trench (at the Guilcagh)[35]. The deer bone from Strandhall found in 1889 is from an uncertain context[36] and therefore has to be discounted. The very few bones of cat from Port St Mary and Perwick Cave can only be described as domestic cat as there is probably not enough evidence for these to be wildcat as Garrad suggests[37]. The *Sus* sp. tusk from Port St Mary[38] is the size and shape of any domestic pig found on an archaeological site, so may not be wild boar.

Recent reviews of the evidence for the origin of the native fauna of Ireland provide an invaluable comparison for the Manx record. A number of smaller vertebrates including bank vole, water vole, field vole, common shrew, water shrew and mole never naturally colonised either Ireland or apparently the Isle of Man. It is perfectly plausible that some of the other species present in Ireland today for which a continuous population is evident, such as red fox and badger, simply did not survive the onset of human settlement in the Isle of Man. In contrast, a few 'relict' species from the Lateglacial have been shown to colonise Ireland from the ice-free areas in the south. Recent sea level research[39] concluded that not only was the land-bridge between Ireland and Britain lost about 1,000 years before that between Britain and continental Europe, but also the Britain–Ireland link migrated northwards in the early Holocene providing a more variable land-bridge than has hitherto been postulated. Some of the larger mammals may never have established populations in the area of the Isle of Man. It appears highly likely that the conclusion[40], from the radiocarbon dating of an assemblage of Irish Museum specimens from a variety of natural and archaeological sites, that red deer became extinct in the Lateglacial before reintroduction by Neolithic settlers much later on, could be extended to the Isle of Man.

Amongst Lateglacial survivors in the present Manx fauna, there is one compelling candidate for a southwestern origin, the stoat (*Mustela ermina*). The present-day population of this species bears an exactly similar pelage to the Irish sub-species[41] which, in Ireland, has been shown to have been present south of the Devensian ice advance[42] and can be considered certain to have survived continuously, thereafter allowing subsequent migration northeastwards to the Isle of Man. There is, however, no evidence for the continuous survival of the mountain hare (*Lepus timidus*), which would have been another potential migrant of similar origin from southern Ireland by this route. The mountain hares that occur on the island today, mainly on the northern hills, were introduced about 100 years ago[43]. The origin of the few species suspected to have maintained a continuous presence since unaided colonisation is more likely to have been from the east. In the case of the pygmy shrew (*Sorex minutus*), recently completed research which examined mitochondrial DNA from a large number of specimens' tails taken in 1994 from a range of sites including the Isle of Man, has shown that the current Manx population of this species is derived from specifically British rather than Irish stock, with the Irish stock indicating a southwest European origin[44]. Bat species are potentially a slightly different case insofar as over water flight is a possibility in some cases. It appears very likely, based on known present-day bat ecology, that all the current breeding bat species have been present since severance of the land-bridge.

Other current land species are mainly human mediated introductions by intent or accident since the beginning of human settlement. The only significant degree of doubt as to natural colonisation followed by population survival is in the case of the brown hare, for which there is documentary evidence of their presence in AD 1417[45]. The house mouse (*Mus musculus*) is likely to have arrived by human mediation during the Iron Age, but now barely survives; whilst the early initial introduction of rabbits is likely to have been as much as a means of developing the warrens on the Calf of Man for shearwater nesting as for their direct use[46], with rabbits for meat at other warrens including the Ayres being a later development. Arrival of the wood mouse (*Apodemus sylvaticus*) appears to have been human mediated; probably arriving in the twelfth century, early enough to yield bones in the Peel Castle excavations[47]. Polecat-ferrets were introduced in medieval times to manage the rabbit warrens already created and, in this case, human mediation appears to have selected feral ferrets for the purpose, and a recent genetic and morphometric examination of a representative selection of present-day survivors has concluded without equivocation that they are pure feral ferrets[48]. There is no documentary or other evidence of the historical status of grey seals, but it is at least possible that they were present during much of the Holocene; unlike common seals, which are a very recent arrival as a breeding species. Equally, there is no evidence of the origin of the sole current reptile species, the common lizard, and all current amphibian species except the common frog are definitely recent introductions. In common with the general picture for the British

Isles, Late Devensian and early Holocene colonisation by freshwater fish populations is likely to have been achieved by many euryhaline species[49], with some surviving to the present including: brown trout, Atlantic salmon, river lamprey, sea lamprey, European eel and three-spined stickleback. The historical development of the faunal record in more recent times is included in the review of the current vertebrate fauna in Chapter 11.

VEGETATION HISTORY OF THE ISLE OF MAN
RICHARD CHIVERRELL, JIM INNES and JEFF BLACKFORD

Before 1995 only a small amount of palaeoecological research had been carried out on the Isle of Man compared with elsewhere in the British Isles. Understanding of the history of vegetation change was based upon radio-carbon dated pollen diagrams from Lough Cranstal, Port Cranstal, Mullagh Ouyr and Dhoo Valley (Figure 9.2). Research associated with the production of this volume has radically changed this situation and in five years our knowledge of Holocene palaeoecology has moved the Isle of Man from one of the poorest to one of the better-known vegetation histories around the British Isles.

Holocene vegetation changes in the northern lowland

The pollen profiles from Lough Cranstal[50] and lagoonal sediments at Port Cranstal[51] were the only published radiocarbon dated information on the Holocene vegetation history of the northern coastal plain. Recent research[52], summarised below, has produced pollen diagrams from a further nine sites (Figure 9.2). Furthermore, a large number of radiocarbon dates provide a chronology for these pollen records. Individually, none of these sites spans the entire Holocene, but there is considerable chronological overlap between sites (Figure 9.10) and correlation of the pollen data allows reconstruction of vegetation changes throughout the Holocene.

Palaeoecological sites
Ballaugh Curragh is the most extensive wetland on the island nestling between two large mountain-front alluvial fans at Sulby and Ballaugh. Peat deposits accumulated over a formerly extensive proglacial lake that existed while the Devensian ice-margin was near Jurby. This former lake basin provided a flat terrain ideal for the development of a substantial wetland, with impeded drainage producing blue-grey lacustrine clays and encouraging subsequent peat inception during the early Holocene (Figure 9.11). Pollen analysis has been carried out at the sites identified in Figure 9.11,

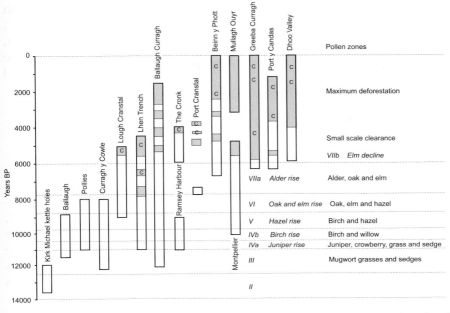

Figure 9.10 *Duration and span of organic sediments from sites across the Isle of Man. Shading shows woodland clearing. 'C's denote presence of cereals.*

with the sequences at BC21, Quarry Bends and Close Sartfield, radio-carbon dated. Ballaugh Curragh displays evidence that there is a hiatus or truncation to the stratigraphy; the fresh surface turfa peat reflects regrowth after cutting, although an original turfa peat probably survives in places. The Lhen Trench is a long flat-floored channel that flows in a broad curve from south of Blue Point on the north coast to Close e Kewin to the north of Ballaugh Curragh (Figure 9.2). The channel is either a former outwash channel or a feature related to the drainage of the ice-marginal lake between Killane and Ramsey. In the Lhen Trench peat inception occurred during the early Holocene, with *circa* 3 m of peat and organic silts accumulating during the last 9,000 years. The Lhen Trench sediments provide an impor-tant record of sea level changes during the Holocene, containing seven sea level index points within the stratigraphy[53]. Curragh y Cowle is a kettle hole basin on the southern flanks of the Bride Moraine with a 5.4 m thick sequence of early Holocene limnic muds. Pollies is a large basin on the surface of the alluvial fan issuing from Glen Dhoo near Ballaugh, adjacent to the Loughan Ruy basin that yielded giant deer remains. The basin is a former pingo formed by the accumulation of periglacial ground-ice during the late Devensian and 5.5 m of limnic mud sediment began accumulating after the ice had melted in the basin around 11,000 BP. The Cronk is a sequence of floodplain peat, 0.4 m in thickness, intercalated within fluvial gravels that are exposed in coastal cliff sections.

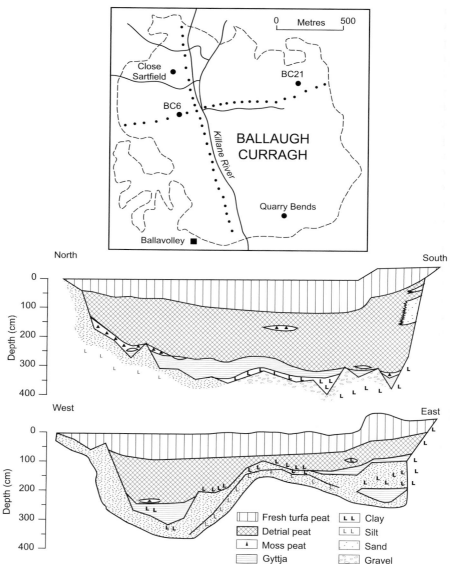

Figure 9.11 *Ballaugh Curragh: stratigraphic sections and the distribution of core sites.*

Vegetation history

Climatic amelioration at the transition from the Lateglacial to the Holocene allowed stabilisation of soil profiles and the rapid replacement of an open ground, tundra-type herb flora with successional plant communities evidenced in pollen profiles from Pollies, Curragh y Cowle, Ballaugh Curragh and Loughan Ruy. Complete ground cover by rich grassland took place with tall herb associations dominated by docks and sorrels (*Rumex*), but including several other taxa like buttercup (*Ranunculus*), meadow-rue (*Thalictrum*) and meadowsweet (*Filipendula*). This rich grassland was gradually invaded and supplanted by seral crowberry (*Empetrum*), dwarf heath and taller juniper (*Juniperus*) shrub communities as stages in the classic succession towards post-glacial woodland. The radiocarbon dated pollen record from Pollies, located near to the original Ballaugh profile, suggests that pre-woodland grass and shrub communities persisted as the dominant vegetation type on the northern coastal plain for a long period of time in the early Holocene[54]. The main peak in juniper percentages, the clear transitional pollen marker between earlier rich grass-heath and later, established willow (*Salix*)-birch (*Betula*) dwarf woodland, is radiocarbon dated at Pollies as 11,060–10,500 BP with the rise to importance of tree birches probably significantly after that time (Figure 9.12a). The earliest birch and willow woodland would have included dwarf-shrub forms of these species normally regarded as trees (birch and willow). The birch rise is dated to 10,635–10,250 BP and pre-dates the main hazel (*Corylus avellana*) rise, dated at Curragh y Cowle to 10,215–9,600 BP, and so the establishment of closed birch woodland occurred in the northern plain at or a little before 10,000 BP (Figure 9.12b). It appears that for several centuries, perhaps most of the first Holocene millennium, parts of the northern plain of the island supported rich grassland and latterly low shrub vegetation rather than woodland.

The eventual establishment of closed woodland conditions caused the shading out and suppression of the early Holocene open herb-heath-shrub communities by continuous tree cover. Birch and willow woods were ubiquitous in the lowlands, with the latter probably more favoured in wetter areas, until 10,215–9,600 BP when pollen data from Curragh y Cowle identify the immigration and rise to co-dominance of hazel. The addition of hazel to the woodland would have increased the density of the canopy and finally shaded out any surviving lowland juniper. Willow also would have declined although surviving in wetland situations. The thermophilous deciduous trees oak (*Quercus*) and elm (*Ulmus*) were the next major components of the Holocene forest to rise to prominence. In most pollen diagrams oak is easily the more abundant of the two, but in the Lhen

Trench at Ballachrink (core LT12) elm is present in consistently higher frequencies (Figure 9.12). Here the immigration of oak and elm occurs together at 8,510–8,130 BP. More dates are required to show whether this age is representative of the Manx lowland as a whole. Significant variation occurs in the frequencies of these major forest trees from site to site, and it appears that their importance in lowland forest composition showed considerable spatial differences. This is particularly true of pine (*Pinus*), which does not become important in the lowlands until after oak and elm have become fully established in the forest. A short-lived period of high pine frequencies is a consistent feature of lowland woodland history between about 7,500 and 7,000 BP. There are major differences in relative percentages at the pine maximum over relatively small distances, with pine reaching 30% of total land pollen at Pollies, less than 10% of total land pollen at Ballaugh Curragh (BC21, Figure 9.11), yet at Quarry Bends in the Curragh it briefly attains almost 80%. Pine percentages of 20–30% at Ballachrink (LT12, Figure 9.2) and Port Cranstal[55] perhaps point to the more average pine representation across the area as a whole. In general, however, a forest mosaic with substantial spatial differences in all tree abundances across the northern plain seems to be demonstrated by the pollen data. At the Curragh and the Lhen Trench alder (*Alnus*) is recorded for the first time, increasing sharply, and at Quarry Bends and BC21 in Ballaugh Curragh it appears to replace pine. The spread of alder within the woodland is dated 8,060–7,700 BP at Ballachrink (Figure 9.13). Increased climatic wetness in the mid Holocene may well have led to the direct replacement of pine by alder in the lowland wetlands, although at Ballachrink moderate pine frequencies are little affected by the increase in alder, hazel being the main declining curve when alder rises.

A major decline in elm pollen frequencies around 5,700 BP defines the end of the mid Holocene phase of maximum extension of forest cover in most areas of the British Isles and elsewhere in northwest Europe. Examples of the classic late mid Holocene elm decline are uncommon on the island, in many cases because erosion, peat cutting or marl digging have removed the relevant sediments, as at Pollies and Curragh y Cowle. The only securely dated lowland Manx example is from The Cronk (Figure 9.14). The date of 6,175–5,950 BP agrees well with many elm decline dates from lowland Britain and Ireland. Indications of small-scale forest opening accompany the elm decline at The Cronk, which may indicate the role of early farmers in this vegetation change, although the death of elm trees through natural causes may also create conditions of temporary canopy opening[56]. Although hunter-gatherer communities may have caused small and localised changes, the Holocene history of the lowland vegetation on the

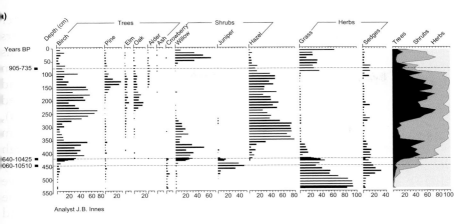

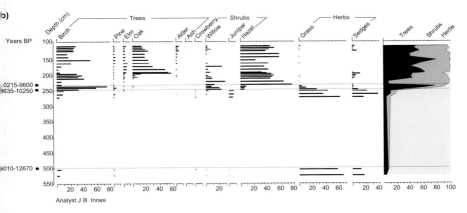

Figure 9.12 *Selected taxa pollen diagrams from (a) Pollies (near Ballaugh) and (b) Curragh y Cowle showing the arrival of tree species during the early Holocene.*

island before the elm decline was dominantly that of the natural spread and development of forest. Other natural vegetation communities existed in specialised habitats, however, of which the early Holocene rich grass-lands have already been discussed. Lowland dry heaths may have existed if sandy or gravel soils remained unstable, but this community may have been restricted to the coastal fringes. Coastal dune environments may have favoured the persistence of pine and heather (*Calluna vulgaris*), while coastal salt-marsh communities preserved opportunities for specialised herbaceous vegetation, as shown at Port Cranstal[57] and at Ballaclucas near the mouth of the Lhen Trench (Figure 9.8). Wetland vegetation provided

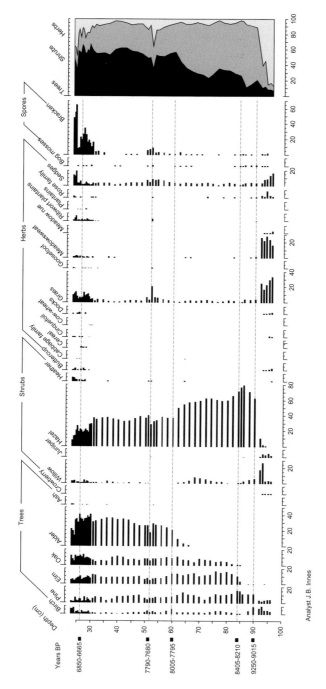

Figure 9.13 Pollen diagram from Ballachrink, Lhen Trench core (LT12), showing evidence for Neolithic and later woodland disturbance.

the main element of non-woodland diversity in the lowland landscape, however, and while the present distribution of wetland environments is small because of long-term land drainage they must have been of far greater extent in the past. Lagoon, marsh, fen and carr habitats must have been common in valley locations throughout the Holocene and provided alternative vegetation successions with rich herbaceous floras and long-term maintenance of willow and alder communities[58]. More acid mire systems would also have provided islands of diversity within the generally wooded Manx lowlands.

There are few indications of human interference with the vegetation prior to the regional decline in elm pollen frequencies; only in the Lhen Trench near Ballachrink[59] does a convincing phase of disturbance occur which may result from human activity in the Mesolithic period. The deciduous forest canopy around that site was broken at 7,920–7,590 BP with oak, elm, hazel and alder pollen values declining and plants indicating more open conditions appearing in the pollen record. Small quantities of charcoal at this level suggest that fire may well have caused this small forest clearing. Many analogous examples in Britain have been attributed to Mesolithic hunting activities[60]. A larger-scale woodland disturbance occurs high in the same profile at 6,890–6,770 BP when reductions in tree pollen are accompanied by high values for bracken (*Pteridium*), plantains (*Plantago* spp.) and other weeds. Cereal-type pollen is also recorded and this phase may be a very early example of Neolithic farming in the Isle of Man, within a still heavily wooded landscape. Certainly of Neolithic age are a number of small woodland clearances which occur in the millennium after the elm decline and which are alike in containing increased frequencies of plantain and other grassland and disturbed ground weeds and heliophyte shrubs like heather and hazel. Falls in tree pollen values at these levels suggest the creation of small open areas within woodland, perhaps for pasturing of livestock. Such clearings have been recorded in the eastern Ballaugh Curragh, at Lough Cranstal[61] and Port Cranstal on the northeast coast and in the Lhen Trench near Ballaclucas. They range in date from about 5,700 to 4,600 BP and may well represent the localised effects of small-scale Neolithic farming. Cereal-type pollen has been recognised in the phases at Lough Cranstal and Ballaclucas and in a Neolithic cultural soil at Port Cranstal[62], showing that some arable cultivation formed part of the Neolithic economy in this area. The decline in elm pollen frequencies itself may have resulted from Neolithic farming practices and at The Cronk, where it is dated to 6,175–5,950 BP, this feature is accompanied by slight evidence of woodland opening which may be human in origin.

During the Bronze Age, between about 4,000 and 2,700 BP, forest clear-

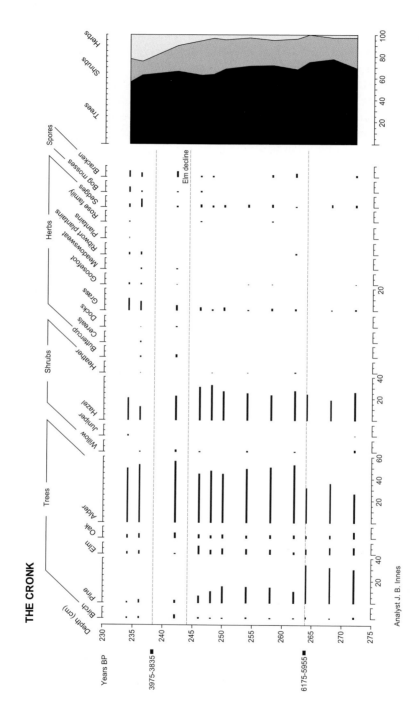

Figure 9.14 *Pollen diagram from the Cronk coastal section showing the mid-Holocene Elm Decline.*

ance increased considerably in intensity and distribution[63], although the latter perhaps reflects the greater number of pollen records of this age available for study. Periodic woodland clearance occurs from 4,500–4,150 to 3,210–2,850 BP at Quarry Bends at the edge of the Ballaugh Curragh near the foot of the northern uplands with cereal-type pollen commonly present (Figure 9.15). Bracken spores, plantain and cereal-type pollen occur with other open ground indicators at The Cronk around 3,750–3,400 BP, although without major reductions in tree pollen, and similar evidence of cleared land and local cultivation has been reported from the fill of a Bronze Age burnt mound feature at Port Cranstal[64]. Local abundance of wetland trees and shrubs like alder, willow and birch at most of these sites makes it difficult to calculate the degree of dry land tree cover reliably, but a major increase in human impact on the vegetation seems to have occurred in the Bronze Age. On the northern plain few sites exist from which environmental evidence for the impact of Iron Age (2,700–1,500 BP) and later communities on the landscape has been reported, but those that are available show that forest clearance continued to alter the composition of the Manx vegetation. The only radiocarbon dated pollen diagram that is of Medieval Age (1,500–500 BP) from the north of the island is from Pollies near Ballaugh (Figure 9.12a). The pollen data there record a well-cleared landscape dominated by open ground and mixed farming, with the regional dry land signal from Pollies suggesting that on the northern plain almost complete removal of woodland for agriculture had taken place by that date. The late Holocene history of human impact on the vegetation of the northern coastal plain is therefore one of deforestation from the beginning of farming settlement and perhaps even earlier, becoming increasingly widespread and intensive in later prehistoric and more recent times.

Holocene vegetation changes in the central valley

The central valley of the island runs northwest to southeast from Peel towards Douglas. Two rivers drain the valley, the Dhoo flowing southeast and the Neb flowing northwest. The valley floor is narrow in most places, intersected by alluvial fans of post-glacial age. At various points along the valley peat deposits are found; some buried or concealed by agricultural activity, but in other places found with a characteristic curragh wetland vegetation type[65], with areas of standing water and dense tree cover. Other peat deposits have accumulated in small kettle basins in the glacial deposits north of the Peel to St Johns road, such as those to the north and south of Ballalough. Pollen data have been collected from Greeba Curragh and Port y Candas, supplemented by radiocarbon dates (Figure 9.2). These,

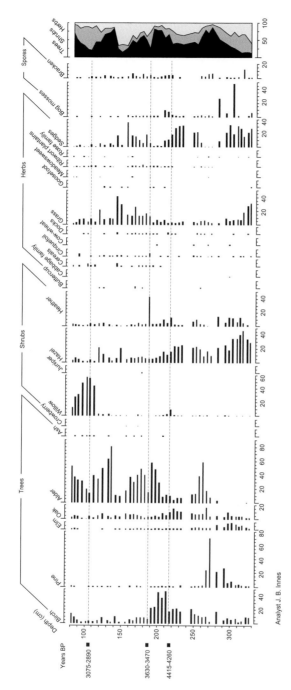

Figure 9.15 *Selected taxa pollen diagram from Quarry Bends (Ballaugh Curragh) showing the early Holocene Pine rise and later Holocene woodland clearances.*

Analyst J. B. Innes

combined with work from the Dhoo Valley[66], allow a picture of peat accumulation and vegetation history in the central valley to be compiled.

Palaeoecological sites

Greeba Curragh is an extensive area of curragh wetland on the watershed of the central valley. Peat depths of around 3 m occur towards the centre of the valley, within 20 m of the River Neb, and these were sampled for pollen analysis. The peat is largely fibrous, consisting of sedge and grass remains but with wood fragments. A radiocarbon date of 6,860–6,665 BP at the base suggests that 6,500 years of palaeoecological record should be available at this site. Port y Candas is a small area of curragh wetland near St Johns that has considerable archaeological significance. Centrally located shallow cores of 1.1 m were sampled for detailed pollen analysis and yielded basal radiocarbon dates indicating that peat accumulation began *circa* 7,000 BP. Further east in the Dhoo Valley between Glen Vine and downstream towards Union Mills there are further extensive organic sediments of a former peatland currently buried beneath agricultural soils. Detailed coring revealed peat deposits not exceeding 2 m in thickness. The deposits overlie Lateglacial flood gravels over which a mixture of sand, silt and clay and mineral to organic peat has accumulated during the Holocene. Two cores from the Dhoo Valley have produced pollen diagrams supported by radiocarbon dates that indicate peat accumulation began *circa* 6,000 BP. Pollen data from Greeba Curragh, Port y Candas and the Dhoo Valley are the basis for the following discussion of the vegetation history of the central valley.

Vegetation history

Peat accumulation in the central valley appears to have begun later than in the north of the island, and so there are no palaeovegetation data available for the earliest stages of the Holocene. Potential early Holocene vegetation records could exist in the kettle holes located to the north of the Peel to St Johns road near Ballalough. The Close y Garey kettle hole has yielded giant deer remains radiocarbon dated to 13,825–13,160 BP, however *in situ* and undisturbed organic sediments of equivalent age have proven difficult to find. The peat deposits at Greeba Curragh and Port y Candas provide the earliest palaeovegetation data for the central valley. The basal deposits at both sites are radiocarbon dated to *circa* 7,000 BP, when trees and shrubs such as hazel dominated the pollen assemblages suggesting a wooded environment that was dominated by alder, probably growing on and around the valley bottom wetlands. The arrival on the island of the tree species that make up the mixed deciduous woodlands of early Holocene times were complete some 1,500 years before peat started accumulating at either Greeba Curragh or Port y Candas. The decline in elm pollen frequencies, a well-known feature of pollen diagrams across northwest Europe, is clearly evidenced at Greeba Curragh and Port y Candas. The elm decline occurs just beneath a radiocarbon date of 5,840–5,620 BP at Port y Candas, which supports the interpolated chronology at Greeba Curragh indicating that in the central valley the elm decline occurred *circa* 5,700 BP. The elm, along with other dry land trees, was probably growing on the better-drained valley sides. In the central valley there is no evidence for a wide-scale forest clearance at this time and the overall percentage of trees and shrubs remains high enough to suggest the persistence of woodland, but the first cereal pollens are recorded and the pollen of grasses increases. At Port y Candas a fall in the oak and hazel pollen curves is radiocarbon dated to Neolithic times *circa* 5,700 BP, and is associated with increased grasses, cow-wheat (*Melampyrum*), tormentil (*Potentilla*), docks and sorrels (*Rumex*), which all suggest an increase in woodland disturbance particularly by pastoral agriculture. This evidence in combination suggests that Neolithic farmers did not clear the central valley of woodland, but that they were present, using arable and pastoral farming. The pollen indicators of this activity continue to the top of both peat profiles that is through to the present day, suggesting that the mixed woodland and farmland landscape is essentially 5,700 years old.

In the intervening millennia considerable variation in the proportion of the landscape under either agricultural use or woodland has occurred. At Greeba (Figure 9.16), the woodland survived through the Bronze Age, although a drop occurred in some tree pollen percentages, notably of oak, ash, alder and hazel, and increased frequencies of cereal-type pollen occurred shortly after a dated horizon of 4,510–4,300 BP. At this time there is a layer of grey silt in the valley bottom peat, which given the proximity to the steep southern slopes of the valley could represent an erosion event. Erosion events need not be directly related to human disturbance of the soils on the slope; alternatively the river may have flooded at this time with a high sediment load, but this seems less likely given that Greeba Curragh is close to the river's source. This pattern of mineral inwash deposits in peat has been shown elsewhere in the UK, for example in southern Scotland[67] and in North Yorkshire[68], where they have also been linked to increased human activity. At Port y Candas there is clear evidence of an intensification of agricultural land use, including a clearance of the curragh wetland trees themselves, radiocarbon dated to 3,550–3,380 BP. Further south at Dhoo Valley, from 3,980–3,840 BP the vegetation was still dominated by alder, with oak, hazel and birch. Declines in local tree pollen

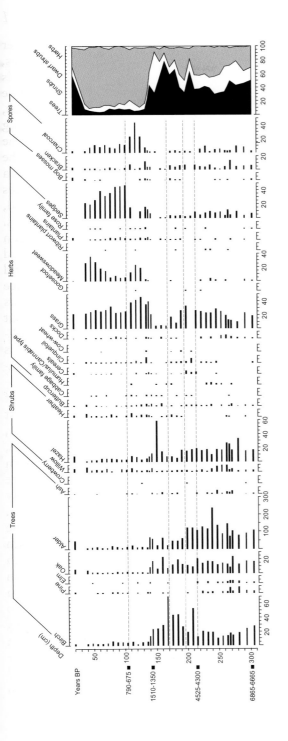

Analyst: J. J. Blackford

Figure 9.16 *Selected taxa pollen diagram from Greeba Curragh in the central valley.*

and increased abundance of plantains and other grassland or pastoral type weeds from 3,980–3,840 BP onwards identifies that a shift towards more open ground occurred, including cultivated cereals and weeds of arable fields. Subsequent more significant changes are undated at Dhoo Valley; however the interpolated chronology suggests they occurred after *circa* 1,800 BP. In fact wholesale clearance of woodland, reducing the tree and shrub cover in the central valley to almost nothing, is recorded *circa* 1,800 BP at Port y Candas, a little later at Greeba Curragh (Figure 9.16) and from *circa* 1,400 BP in the Dhoo Valley. The clearances are associated with increases in plants indicative of farming activity, plus microscopic charcoal, generally considered an indicator of burning in the area. Further silt deposits were recorded at Greeba Curragh shortly after this clearance (Figure 9.16), which suggests an increase in soil erosion or flooding. From then on, at Greeba Curragh the peat grew much more rapidly, perhaps due to a rise in the water table after the loss of trees. At Port y Candas and at Greeba Curragh, where the current environment is still wetland, the uppermost pollen horizons record a return of trees and shrubs, an impression confirmed by the current ecology, and consist of most notably alder carr woodland at Greeba Curragh and willow carr woodland at Port y Candas.

Holocene vegetation changes in the northern uplands

This synthesis of the vegetation history of Manx uplands is based upon a small number of pollen diagrams compared with other upland areas within the British Isles. The lack of palaeoecological data stems from the paucity of appropriate sites, with the Manx uplands lacking any lakes and only a few peat sequences. Until recently the only pollen diagram was from extensive but thin blanket peat deposits on Mullagh Ouyr (Figure 9.2)[69]. The Mullagh Ouyr pollen diagram is of limited value because the profile is poorly dated with one basal radiocarbon date. It only covers the last 3,000 years and presents only a limited number of species. Recent research has added pollen diagrams from blanket peat on the flanks of Beinn y Phott and the Montpellier Bog valley mire in Druidale (Figure 9.2). Between them these two pollen profiles span the entire Holocene and both are radiocarbon dated. Pollen diagrams from Beinn y Phott and Montpellier Bog, and earlier research at Mullagh Ouyr provide the vegetation history of the Manx upland.

Palaeoecological sites
Beinn y Phott is a formerly extensive area of blanket peat that forms the

headwater watershed of Llergyrhenny (Figure 9.2). Peat, some 2.5 m in thickness, blankets the northern flank of Beinn y Phott near Brandywell, but does not cover the summit. During the early stages of peat accumulation the entire site would have received water as surface flow, but as peat accumulated the water-shedding nature of the ridge is enhanced and influence of surface flow reduced. Unfortunately the blanket mire has been damaged by cutting peat for fuel. Intact sequences are preserved beyond the cuttings, but the most recent history may be affected by the disturbance at the site. Chronology for the pollen record is provided by five radiocarbon dates. Further evidence is provided by peat deposits at Montpellier Bog, a small valley mire within Druidale (Figure 9.2). Geomorphological interpretation of Druidale suggests that during the Late Devensian the river followed a path across the mire, whilst the adjacent gorge was filled with glacial and solifluction sediments. Fluvial erosion excavated the gorge during the Late Devensian capturing the river and allowing 3 m of peat to accumulate upon the former floodplain. Again there is evidence of disturbance of the mire surface and so the recent pollen record may not be intact. Chronology for the pollen analysis is provided by four radiocarbon dates. Mullagh Ouyr is another extensive area of blanket peat that forms the headwaters of Llergyrhenny and Laxey Glen (Figure 9.2). Peat blankets the northern flank of Mullagh Ouyr and a pollen profile exists for this 2 m thick sequence[70].

Vegetation history

Montpellier Bog (Figure 9.17) provides the only record of early Holocene vegetation changes in the Manx uplands, but the arrival of thermophilous trees at the beginning of the Holocene was already under way at the onset of peat accumulation. Birch, hazel and pine were already present at 10,500–10,190 BP, with oak and elm reaching their rational limit *circa* 9,235–9,005 BP. The alder rise occurs later and is dated at *circa* 7,605–7,505 BP. Pollen data from Beinn y Phott (Figure 9.19) do not contradict this history, with basal pollen data revealing that by 7,250–7,030 BP oak, elm, alder and hazel were abundant in the uplands. All the components of the mixed deciduous forest were present in the Manx uplands by 7,250–7,030 BP and the only areas not forested were probably the large expanses of peat at Beinn y Phott, localised clearings and the rocky summits. The low values of pine encountered at Beinn y Phott are interesting, because at Montpellier Bog, only 2 km away, pine is abundant between *circa* 8,000 and 5,400 BP. The proximity of the two sites and the quantity of pine pollen possibly reflect local Scots Pine woodlands in Druidale. Montpellier Bog (Figure 9.17) shows a pine decline dated to after

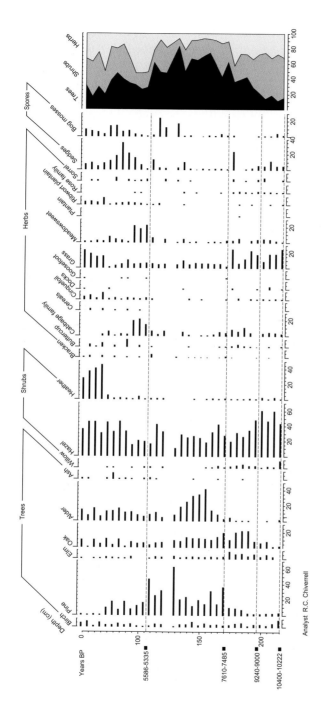

Figure 9.17 *Early Holocene pollen diagram from Montpellier Bog in the northern uplands.*

5,610–5,330 BP, with a further decline after *circa* 4,000 BP.

Beinn y Phott (Figure 9.18) provides the only well-dated mid to late Holocene record of vegetation change for the Manx uplands. Heather, sedges and bog mosses (*Sphagnum*) are the most abundant pollen taxa, almost certainly derived from local mire and moorland communities. Sedges and the bog mosses were particularly abundant between 3,800–3,300 and 2,000–500 BP, but heather was abundant throughout the profile indicating that moorland was a significant component of the upland landscape throughout the last 6,500 years. Beinn y Phott also records three phases with declining tree pollen. The reductions in tree pollen parallel increases in herb taxa, particularly the plantains, buttercups, cinquefoils (*Potentilla*), bracken and other indicators of pastoral farming or open ground. The absence of elm pollen frequencies at Montpellier Bog mire above a radiocarbon date of 5,610–5,330 BP provides the only evidence from the Manx uplands for an event equivalent to the 'Elm Decline', but unfortunately the elm record at Beinn y Phott is far from clear. The earliest woodland clearance recorded is clearly represented at Beinn y Phott. It is small-scale, affects alder and oak frequencies *circa* 3,320–2,955 BP, and is coincident with increases of grasses, plantains, meadowsweet, buttercups and bracken. These vegetation changes signify the creation of open spaces perhaps produced by agricultural activity during the Bronze Age[71]. Frequencies of the pioneer tree taxa (birch and ash) also increase, probably exploiting the open spaces created by woodland clearance.

Tree pollen frequencies recover between 2,800–2,300 BP after the Bronze Age and into the early Iron Age, with oak, elm, alder and ash recovering to the levels present before clearance. A more significant woodland clearance starts during the mid Iron Age and is radiocarbon dated to 2,350–2,120 BP. The clearance affects oak, elm, alder, ash and hazel, with total tree pollen declining to 20% of non-mire pollen. Pollen data from Mullagh Ouyr post-date 3,075–2,890 BP and identify a cleared landscape, with low frequencies of tree species, and abundant moorland and herbaceous taxa. Coincidently, at Beinn y Phott during this clearance phase, grasses, plantains, plants in the rose family and bracken are significantly more abundant, and cereal pollen appears for the first time. During the subsequent period, 2,350–1,250 BP, tree pollen frequencies remain low, after which, between *circa* 1,290–1,180 BP and the top of the pollen profile, oak, alder and birch recover. However, frequencies of herbaceous pollen remain high implying that this woodland recovery may be somewhat limited in spatial extent. Peaks in environmental magnetic parameters identify increased loading of magnetic minerals perhaps reflecting increased transport of airborne particulate matter owing to heightened soil erosion or more open and windswept landscapes in the wake of woodland clearance (Figure 9.18). Peaks in lead and titanium curves for the Beinn y Phott peat profile also coincide with clearance phases (Figure 9.18). The most obvious explanation for these changes in magnetic and geochemical stratigraphy are as follows: woodland clearance increasing the efficiency of transport of airborne particulate matter by wind; land use pressure encouraging heightened erosion and availability of particulate matter; and local mining or smelting activities increasing the levels of atmospheric pollution.

Relatively high frequencies of tree pollen throughout the last 7,000 years imply a continuous and substantial presence of woodland in the uplands. Fluctuations in tree pollen frequencies in the Manx uplands during the last 2,300 years reflect variations in the intensity of human activity manifested as clearance and regrowth of woodland on lands marginal for agricultural exploitation. The Manx uplands would not have been prime agricultural land, but was perhaps exploited as population pressure necessitated the use of upland landscape for summer grazing and so the Manx uplands may not have been actively clear-felled of trees. Clearance of steep valley slopes and mountain tops may have been achieved by browsing of young trees by livestock, and so the history of pastoral farming on the island is critical for understanding the upland vegetation history.

Vegetation succession and the 'wildwoods' of the early Holocene

The beginning of the Holocene epoch *circa* 11,500 BP is marked by climatic warming, when willow, juniper and birch returned and shaded out open ground herbs. The immigration of tree species to and expansion on the island are events that cannot be reviewed in an insular manner, and benefit from comparison with pollen-derived vegetation histories from Lancashire, Cumbria, southern Scotland and Northern Ireland. Palaeovegetation maps assimilated from numerous Holocene pollen diagrams from across the British Isles are an invaluable resource in this regard, allowing the newly derived Manx data to be placed in a regional context (Figure 9.19)[72]. Pollen data are particularly important because, until recently, there has been no radiocarbon dated information on the arrival of tree species on the island during the early Holocene and these isochrone maps (Figure 9.19) only estimate the timing of tree spreading on the island. The existence, tenure and character of the land-bridge connecting Britain with the Isle of Man during the Lateglacial and early Holocene are important issues that must be considered when discussing the immigration of plant species as it provided a route-way for plants to migrate onto the island.

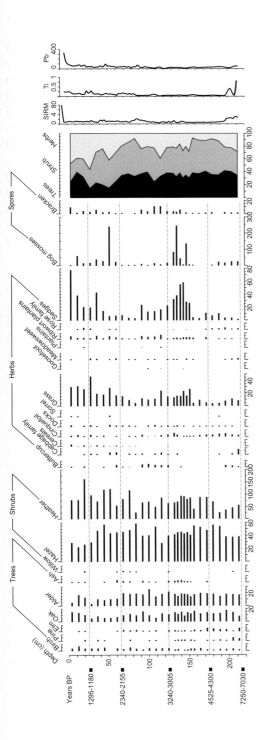

Analyst R.C. Chiverrell

Figure 9.18 *Pollen diagram from Beinn y Phott (northern uplands) showing Bronze and Iron Age woodland clearances.*

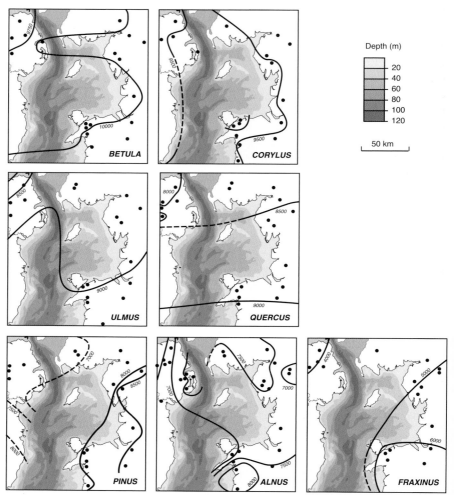

Figure 9.19 *Pollen isochrone maps showing the timings of the expansion of tree species in the regions around the Irish Sea basin during the early Holocene, after H.J.B. Birks (1989).*

Pre-woodland grass and shrub communities appear to have persisted as the dominant vegetation types on the Isle of Man for a long period of time in the early Holocene, as is shown by detailed pollen data from Pollies, Curragh y Cowle[73] and Ballaugh[74]. In north Lancashire[75], Cumbria[76] and the Southern uplands[77], birch and willow woodland was swiftly established *circa* 11,400–11,200 BP, certainly on glacial till soils and even in comparable areas of sandy outwash soils, but the arrival and expansion of birch-willow woodland on the Isle of Man appears to lag behind (Figure 8.25)[78]. Grassland environments on the Isle of Man, in persisting until 11,100–10,400 BP, have lasted significantly longer than in the adjacent Irish Sea coastal areas of Britain. The earliest forms of birch and willow may also have been dwarf forms on the exposed windswept northern coastal plain of the Isle of Man. The environment may have provided a permissive context for the as yet unproven survival of the giant deer into the earliest Holocene. Hazel became established in both the northern lowlands and uplands of the Isle of Man around or before 10,200–9,600 BP, but again, as with almost all of the main vegetation changes, was probably diachronous across the area depending upon local edaphic and other environmental factors. The radiocarbon date from Curragh y Cowle of 10,200–9,600 BP is quite late when compared with the range of dates recorded elsewhere around the Irish Sea for this event (10,900–10,700 BP), a view confirmed in the Manx uplands where hazel was abundant at 10,500–10,200 BP. Hazel propagates through the dispersal of nuts, which are transported by a variety of mechanisms including by animals (birds, rodents, etc.), deliberate or accidental spreading by humans and by water[79]. There is considerable debate amongst palaeoecologists over the role people have played in the expansion of hazel, but there is as yet no archaeological evidence that early human populations influenced the spread of tree and shrub taxa in the island, as perhaps was also the case in Britain or Ireland[80].

The thermophilous deciduous trees oak and elm were the next species to dominate the Holocene forests. Increases in the occurrence of oak and elm are dated in the lowlands and uplands to around 8,500–8,130 BP. These dates are comparable to those from regions surrounding the north Irish Sea basin, if somewhat towards the later end of that range, with the increases *circa* 8,850 BP in the Southern uplands of Scotland[81], 9,000–8,500 BP in Cumbria[82] and 9,400–9,000 BP in Northern Ireland[83]. The delays in reaching the Isle of Man reflect migration routes either northwards through Lancashire and across from Cumbria or northeastwards across Northern Ireland. The arrival and expansion of pine is variable in character on the Isle of Man, with extremely high frequencies encountered *circa* 8,500–7,500 BP at Quarry Bends on the edge of Ballaugh Curragh adjacent to the Sulby Glen alluvial fan. The location of the Quarry Bends near to the uplands may account for its very high peak values, as pine frequencies of 30% total land pollen with peaks above 60% occur between 8,500 and 5,500 BP at Montpellier Bog in the northern uplands. These data extend the known rational limits of pine in the British Isles (Figure 9.19), because pine appears not to have been a significant component of the forests in southwest Scotland, did not reach northeast Ireland until

8,700–8,500 BP and expanded into south Cumbria around 9,500–8,900 BP. One of the most significant elements of Manx vegetation history is the mid Holocene rise of alder pollen, which often occurs sharply and a short period after its first appearance in the pollen record. In large lowland wetlands such as the Ballaugh Curragh alder rises to dominance, whereas around smaller wetland sites its increase is less spectacular, perhaps reflecting more diverse woodlands on the surrounding drier soils of moraine ridges and sandur surfaces. The arrival of alder occurred *circa* 8,050–7,700 BP on the Isle of Man, an age which is in close agreement with the mean dates for the feature around the Irish Sea province, for example *circa* 8,000–7,800 BP at Red Moss, Lancashire, *circa* 7,700–7,200 BP in southwest Scotland and 7,600 BP in northeast Ireland[84].

After the spread of alder through the woodland, the assembly of the mid Holocene mixed forest was complete on the Isle of Man. Sporadic single grains of lime (*Tilia*) have been recognised in the pollen assemblages, but are not secure evidence that the tree may have been native to the island. Lime is by nature a low producer of pollen and the grains are transported by insect and not by wind like birch or pine, and so lime pollen grains are often poorly represented in sediments. Isochrone pollen maps (Figure 9.19) show that the Isle of Man was on the outer limits of the spread of lime across the British Isles, reaching the shores of Lancashire *circa* 6,300 BP. Pollen grains of less common tree taxa – ash (*Fraxinus*), maple (*Acer*), yew (*Taxus*) and beech (*Fagus*) – also occur in very low numbers, but rarely before the late Holocene disturbance of the woodland by humans. As the pollen percentages of these trees would be very low in any case, it is as yet not possible to say whether they were natural members of the Manx flora, although of these ash is the most likely to have been so. Ash is present in percentages similar to those encountered in regions surrounding the Irish Sea basin, arriving at Montpellier Bog after 5,000–4,500 BP and is present albeit sparsely at Quarry Bends after 4,000 BP, with the clearest evidence at Greeba Curragh in the central valley, where ash is reasonably abundant *circa* 5,800 BP. Isochrone maps of tree expansion suggest that ash reached the coasts of the Lake District and Lancashire around 6,000–5,500 BP and extended into Scotland after 5,500 BP, dates that are not dissimilar to the earliest occurrences of ash in Manx pollen records. Isochrone maps of the expansion of beech across the British Isles show that beech did not occur in the woodlands surrounding the Irish Sea basin and beech pollen is not present in large quantities on the Isle of Man.

Human impact and forest removal during the later Holocene

The vegetation history of the Isle of Man during the latter half of the Holocene has been profoundly influenced by human activity, in particular by forest clearance and by increasingly intensive agricultural land use. The conversion of the mainly wooded post-glacial environment shown by the pollen diagrams to the almost completely open landscape of recent centuries has almost entirely been the cumulative result of human land clearance. This activity may even have been the trigger for further environmental change, such as soil acidification or the spread of blanket bog in the uplands, by exposing such environmentally vulnerable areas to the effects of deteriorating late Holocene climate. While the cultural impact on the environment will be dealt with in detail in Volume 2, here we present a summary of the main evidence for vegetation change caused by human activity. There are few indications of human interference with the vegetation before the regional decline in elm pollen, which occurs at about 5,800 BP in the Isle of Man. Only in the Lhen Trench near Ballachrink[85] does a convincing phase of disturbance occur which may result from human activity in the Mesolithic period. The deciduous forest canopy around that site was broken at 7,920–7,590 BP, with oak, elm, hazel and alder pollen values reduced and plants indicating more open conditions appearing in the pollen record. Small quantities of charcoal at this level suggest that fire may well have caused this small forest clearing. Many analogous examples in Britain have been attributed to Mesolithic hunting activities[86]. A larger-scale woodland disturbance occurs high in the same profile at 6,890–6,770 BP when reductions in tree pollen are accompanied by high values for bracken, plantains and other weeds. Cereal-type pollen is also recorded and this phase may be a very early example of Neolithic farming in the Isle of Man, within a still heavily wooded landscape.

The mid Holocene elm decline forms a pollen stratigraphic marker horizon that signals the start of the later Holocene period of increasing diminution of tree cover. The surviving woodland changes in both composition and character towards a more open, secondary type, which eventually leads to the creation of an almost entirely open landscape. The impact of human activity was increasingly the prime cause of deforestation, but deterioration of climate and soils was also an important factor. All of these influences may well have contributed to the major fall in elm frequency, as well as a possible outbreak of a pathogen similar to that of the recent Dutch elm disease that greatly reduced elm populations in Britain in only a few decades. Dates in the Isle of Man for the mid Holocene elm decline tend to cluster in the few centuries before 5,800 BP, which equates with dates in the lowlands surrounding the Irish Sea basin. Dates for the elm decline from upland areas tend to be a little later than 5,800 BP and evidence from the Manx uplands at Montpellier Bog seem to confirm this dichotomy. More dated profiles are required from the Isle of Man before any secure conclusions can be reached about the timing and causes of the elm decline, but at present the Manx pattern appears to conform well to that of the rest of the Irish Sea region. Also of Neolithic age are a number of small woodland clearances which occur in the millennium after the elm decline and which are alike in containing increased frequencies of plantain and other grassland and disturbed ground weeds and heliophyte shrubs like heather and hazel. Falls in tree pollen values at these levels suggest the creation of small open areas within woodland, perhaps for pasturing of livestock. Such clearings have been recorded at Port y Candas, the eastern Ballaugh Curragh, at Lough Cranstal[87] and Port Cranstal on the northeast coast, in the Lhen Trench near Ballaclucas and in the northern upland at Montpellier Bog. They range in date from about 4,900–4,000 BP and may well represent the localised effects of small-scale Neolithic farming. Cereal-type pollen has been recognised in these phases at Lough Cranstal and Ballaclucas and in a Neolithic cultural soil at Port Cranstal[88], showing that some arable cultivation formed part of the Neolithic economy in this area. The decline in elm pollen frequencies itself may have resulted from Neolithic farming practices and at The Cronk, where it is dated to 6,175–5,950 BP, this feature is accompanied by slight evidence of woodland opening which may be human in origin.

Elm is not the only tree to decline during the mid Holocene, with pine declining after a period of abundance at Quarry Bends briefly between 7,500–7,000 BP and at Montpellier Bog between 8,000–5,330 BP. Declines in pine frequencies have been recorded in macrofossil and pollen records across the northwest British Isles around 5,000–4,000 BP[89]. The timing and rate of the pine decline do vary across the British Isles, however, and some of the apparent asynchrony stems from dates of pine stumps not coinciding with dated pollen records. The distribution of pine around the northern fringes of the British Isles is close to its northern climatic limits, to the extent that the virtual extinction of pine *circa* 4,000 BP in the far north of Scotland has been attributed to climatic deterioration[90]. Damage to pine populations by people, mammals, insects and pathogens is also a possible cause for the declines in pine. It is difficult to place the pine decline recorded at Montpellier Bog within this debate, but the Isle of Man is close to the northern limits for pine. However it is possible that the concentrations of pine pollen at Montpellier Bog reflect intensive local stands sheltered within Druidale. At Montpellier Bog local fires are an unlikely explanation for the reductions in pine given the absence of microscope charcoal fragments. The impact of volcanic aerosols from the Icelandic Hekla 4 eruption (3,820 BP) has also been linked with the pine declines in Scotland[91], with acidic pollutants stressing trees that were already affected by climatic change. The degree to which volcanic aerosols could affect environments this distal can be questioned. The timing of pine declines in the Manx uplands is in keeping with either a climatic deterioration or Hekla 4 volcanic aerosols triggering the reductions in pollen frequencies. Perhaps the most convincing explanation of the pine decline is that it coincides with increases in birch and ash, tree species suited to exploiting open spaces, and greater frequencies of cereals, arable and pastoral weeds, perhaps indicating that human activity is the most likely cause of the reduction in pine pollen.

During the Bronze Age, between 4,000 and 2,800 BP, forest clearance increased considerably in intensity and distribution, although the latter perhaps reflects the greater number of pollen records of this age available for study from the Isle of Man. Major woodland clearance occurs at this time at sites in the Central Valley. Cores in the Dhoo Valley[92] record declining local tree pollen and the presence of plantains and other grassland or pastoral type weeds from 3,980–3,840 BP. Similarly dated but larger-scale events occur at Port y Candas, which include cereal-type pollen, while forest clearance is also apparent at nearby Greeba Curragh at this time. Periodic woodland clearance occurs from 4,100 to 2,900 BP at Quarry Bends at the edge of the Ballaugh Curragh near the foot of the northern uplands, with cereal pollen commonly present. Bracken spores, plantain and cereal pollen occur with other open ground indicators at The Cronk around 3,750–3,400 BP, although without major reductions in tree pollen. Similar evidence of cleared land and local cultivation has been reported from the fill of a Bronze Age burnt mound feature at Port Cranstal[93]. In the uplands low-scale disturbance of woodland begins at Beinn y Phott around 3,320–2,955 BP. The local abundance of wetland trees and shrubs like alder, willow and birch at most of these sites makes it difficult to calculate the degree of dry-land tree cover reliably, but a major increase in human impact on the vegetation seems to have occurred in the Bronze Age[94]. Towards the end of the Bronze Age, recovery of woodland populations is recorded at Quarry Bends in the north and at Beinn y Phott in the northern uplands, reflecting a reduction in human activity around these sites during the late Bronze Age.

Fewer sites exist from which environmental evidence for the impact of Iron Age (2,800–1,500 BP) and later communities on the landscape has been reported, but those that are available show that forest clearance continued to alter the composition of the Manx vegetation. Increased activity took place in the northern uplands, with phases of clearance at Beinn y Phott at 2,350–2,120 BP with cereal-type pollen present. Peat inception at Mullagh Ouyr[95] began at *circa* 2,900 BP also in association with evidence of local vegetation disturbance. Evidence of woodland clearance at Beinn y Phott continues with cereal-type pollen and other agricultural indicators until a woodland recovery phase starting 1,290–1,180 BP. Further major pollen evidence of woodland clearance and replacement by mixed farming occurs *circa* 1,800 BP at Port y Candas, a little later at Greeba Curragh and from *circa* 1,400 BP in the Dhoo Valley.

There are only four radiocarbon dated episodes of vegetation history which are of medieval age in the Isle of Man. These dates average *circa* 800 years and are from Druidale in the northern uplands, Pollies near Ballaugh in the north, and Dhoo Valley and Greeba Curragh in the Central Valley. All record a well-cleared landscape dominated by open ground and mixed farming, although at the two valley sites local wetland shrub vegetation was sufficiently important to obscure the dry land record. The more regional dry land signal from the Pollies site suggests that at least in the northern plain the almost complete removal of woodland for agriculture had taken place by that date. Recent sediments from Druidale indicate that during the last 500 years the uplands were a cleared landscape dominated by pastoral lands and open moorland[96]. Other, undated, pollen records from Beinn y Phott, Port y Candas and Peel Castle that may also be of this recent age record a very well-cleared landscape. The history of human impact on the vegetation of the Isle of Man is therefore one of deforestation from the beginning of farming settlement in the island and perhaps even earlier, becoming increasingly widespread and intensive in later prehistoric and more recent times.

GEOMORPHOLOGY　　Richard Chiverrell, Geoff Thomas and David Roberts

In comparison with proceeding glacial times the magnitude of landform development during the Holocene appears quite subdued. Nevertheless geomorphological research across the British Isles identifies that, albeit on a smaller scale, the Holocene has seen considerable changes in the landscape. Investigation of upland and lowland river systems demonstrates considerable landform development during the Holocene. The dominant land-forming processes in temperate mid latitude countries during the Holocene are fluvial and so much research has focused upon the behaviour and development of river systems. The scale of climate change during the Holocene is significantly reduced compared to glacial times and the densely vegetated and soil-covered land surface appears less susceptible to fluvial erosion. Even so, observations in the Isle of Man reveal the landscape is far from inactive. There are freshly cut sections in river banks, the Sulby River regularly floods and gullies are eroded on the steeper slopes of the uplands. In recent years landslides have threatened the roads on the flanks of North Barrule and in Sulby Glen. In summary land-forming processes have occurred throughout the Holocene and the results are there to see in the landscape.

Increased scale of human activity, changes in the climate and individual high magnitude climatic events are the most likely triggers for phases with increased geomorphic activity during the Holocene. Research in the Howgill Fells[97], the Forest of Bowland[98], the Pennines[99], Wales[100] and southern Scotland[101] has attributed switches between incising and aggrading river systems to either human activity or climate change or a combination of the two[102]. River terraces are important features because they provide evidence of changes in the dynamics of fluvial systems, and for a river to alter from floodplain aggradation to incision clearly there must have been changes in the parameters controlling the system. People can affect changes to fluvial systems by changing the intensity and nature of land use, through woodland clearance, by using larger numbers or different livestock species and introducing new ploughing technologies. Climate affects river systems through changes in the precipitation and temperature regime, but the importance of short-lived high magnitude events should not be overlooked because large floods can radically alter the fluvial geomorphology. Given that people and climate exercise such control over the landscape, uncovering the sequence of changes within the geomorphological record provides important information about environmental change during the Holocene and earlier times[103].

The Isle of Man possesses well-defined sequences of Holocene landforms and research has focused upon the geomorphological record in the northern uplands and southern lowlands of the island. In the northern uplands well-developed fluvial depositional landforms only occur in the valleys of the Sulby, Druidale, Auldyn, Rhennas, East Baldwin and West Baldwin rivers (Figure 9.2)[104]. Fluvial landforms in the southern uplands are not as well developed as their counterparts in the north. Upland valleys on the Isle of Man only contain depositional landforms where stream gradients are sufficiently shallow. The catchments draining onto the northern coastal plain and into the Central Valley contain sequences of river terraces, with well-developed sequences in Sulby Glen, Glen Auldyn, Rhennas Valley and Druidale (Figure 9.2). There are no river terraces in Laxey Glen and Corrany Valley because these rivers are currently eroding into bedrock and any sediment has been flushed directly into the sea. Three main river systems flow out from the southern uplands onto the Plain of Malew: the Santon, Silverburn and Colby catchments. They all have relatively narrow alluvial spreads constrained closely by the present-day channel systems.

Unfortunately, extensive sections through the various river terraces revealed no wood or organic sediments and so it has not been possible to radiocarbon date directly materials within the fluvial sediments. However, radiocarbon dates on organic channel fills overlying the river terraces and optically stimulated luminescence (OSL) dates on fluvial sands provide a tentative outline chronology for the Holocene geomorphology. Two ^{14}C dates were obtained for the base of organic channel fills in Druidale and constrain the timing of abandonment of these fluvial surfaces. Radiocarbon dating is a familiar technique, whereas OSL dating is perhaps less so. This sediment dating procedure analyses individual grains of quartz or feldspar and works by measuring the amount of natural radiation to which the sample has been exposed. The duration of exposure to radiation corresponds to the luminescence of the quartz or feldspar grains under a light stimulus. The amount of radiation and resultant luminescence signal is time dependent; the greater the length of exposure to natural environmental radiation, the greater the luminescence signal. This procedure works as a dating technique because the luminescence signal can be zeroed by heating the sample or by exposure to sunlight. Luminescence dating estimates the length of time since the quartz or feldspar grains were last exposed to sunlight. Inadequate exposure to sunlight before burial means that only three of the luminescence dates obtained for river terrace sands and gravels can be used with a degree of confidence.

The sequence and timing of landform development can also be inferred from i) the topographic relationships between landforms and ii) the maturity of soils overlying landforms. The comparative maturity of soil profiles overlying landforms is used as an approximate guide to the age of landforms. Soils on older features are mature podzols or brown earths that have been accumulating for several thousand years, and imply these surfaces were abandoned by incision during the mid to early Holocene. Younger surfaces are covered with either less well-developed podzols demonstrating horizon development probably abandoned 1,000–500 years ago or more recent, very thin skeletal soils.

The northern uplands

Solifluction terraces provide the earliest evidence of geomorphic activity, and they formed immediately after the retreat of the Devensian icesheet.

Subsequently rivers have incised into the solifluction sediments and transported large quantities of sediment to the lowlands where it was deposited
as large mountain-front alluvial fans. The formation of the large alluvial
fans and the contemporaneous fluvial incision into the soliflucted tills
occurred between 15,000 and 10,500 BP and was reviewed in Chapter 8.
The solifluction terraces and mountain-front alluvial fans are the most
substantial geomorphological features in and around the Manx uplands
and they were already in place by the beginning of the Holocene. Only the
landforms in the Sulby, Auldyn and Rhennas river systems have been investigated in any detail on the Isle of Man.

Sulby river system

The Sulby is the largest drainage basin on the island, with a dramatic steep-
sided valley in the lower reaches and more subdued drift-mantled valley
sides in the headwaters; the catchment encapsulates the character of the
Manx upland landscape. River terraces occur within two reaches of the
Sulby, in the headwaters of Druidale and in the main valley downstream
of Tholt y Will. Confluences with major tributaries in upland streams often
produce alluvial fans. The confluences between the major Druidale,
Llergyrhenny and Crammag tributaries are in the tightly confined reach of
Tholt y Will Gorge and Lamplugh recorded no fluvial landforms[105];
however the presence or absence of large alluvial fan surfaces cannot be
ascertained owing to the construction of the Sulby reservoir.

The headwater reach of Druidale rises on the flanks of Slieau Maggle
and has incised a reach into Late Devensian solifluction sediments.
Originally these solifluction sediments would have filled the valley, but
currently there is a broad reach within which three river terraces are set
(Druidale 1 to 3, Figure 9.20). The highest fluvial landforms include a
channel buried beneath the peat deposits of Montpellier Mire and a meandering channel incised into bedrock, both 10 m above the current stream.
The morphology of these channels is typical of proglacial or subglacial
fluvial erosion, and so the channels pre-date solifluction. These higher
surfaces imply that the early post-glacial river did not utilise Druidale
Gorge, but occupied a valley floor currently buried by Montpellier Mire.
The excavation of Druidale Gorge caused a substantial change in the post-
glacial evolution of Druidale. During the early post-glacial period either
glacial or soliflucted sediment blocked the gorge. Tributaries on the
northern valley side began to excavate this sediment and head-ward incision uncovered the gorge back to the current waterfall, capturing a further
tributary and the main Druidale stream, and radically altered the drainage
pattern. Radiocarbon dating of the basal peat at Montpellier Mire indi-

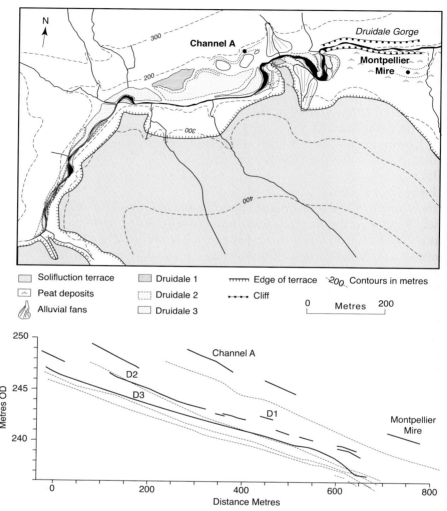

Figure 9.20 *Geomorphology and height range relationships between the river terraces in Druidale, after R.C. Chiverrell et al. (2001).*

cates that the high fluvial surface was abandoned before 10,500–10,190 BP. The river has then aggraded the deposits of three river terraces that grade to the waterfall at the head of the gorge. Druidale 1, the highest terrace, is covered by a very mature podzol, and dates to at least the mid Holocene. Organic sediments in a channel fill on the surface of Druidale 2 contain plant remains. Pollen recovered from the organic sediment identifies a predominantly grassland and moorland landscape punctuated by occasional stands of hazel, but the vegetation cover reveals little about the age of the sediments. A radiocarbon date for the base of the organic deposits signifies Druidale 2 was abandoned before 625–500 BP. The lowest suite of terraces, Druidale 3, is set into the middle terrace and essentially consists of recently abandoned floodplain. Druidale 3 terrace fragments vary in age from recently vegetated point-bars to small terraces covered with thin skeletal soils.

In the lower Sulby fluvial landforms are set incised into the soliflucted till deposits that flank the eastern edge of Sulby Glen and include valley floor river terraces and alluvial fans at confluences with tributary streams (Figure 9.21). There are three levels of river terrace (Sulby 1 to 3) as identified when the relative heights of the terrace fragments are plotted as a height-range diagram (Figure 9.21). The highest terrace (Sulby 1) occurs as isolated fragments, with the middle terrace (Sulby 2) the most extensive surface and widespread throughout the valley. The lowest terrace (Sulby 3) is also fragmentary and is incised into the other terraces. Sulby 1 and Sulby 2 consist of coarse downstream-imbricated alluvial gravel composed of locally derived Manx Group slates and quartz. Sulby 1 gravels locally overlie stratified solifluction deposits and are the oldest river terrace deposits, formed not long after the solifluction activity. Sulby 2 is probably also a Lateglacial and early Holocene terrace; which the OSL chronology indicates was abandoned during incision after 2,410–1,230 BP[106].

Road construction, mining, building works and conifer afforestation have affected alluvial fans at most of the tributary confluences on the western flank of the Sulby Glen. However, the Ballakerka alluvial fan is well preserved and is a complex multiple-phase landform with four distinct surfaces (Figure 9.21). The higher two fan surfaces consist of very coarse imbricated alluvial gravels, probably formed shortly after solifluction activity ceased and may be contemporaneous with river terraces Sulby 1 and Sulby 2. There are lower surfaces incised into these two higher alluvial fan surfaces that are probably equivalent to Sulby 3 river terrace. The coarse fluvial sediments that form the higher fan surfaces and river terraces are typical of high-energy streams and of a catchment where there is a large quantity of sediment available for erosion, which would have been the case during the Lateglacial, but not during much of the Holocene.

Glen Auldyn

Glen Auldyn rises on the flanks of Clagh Ouyr (Figure 9.22) and has a flat valley floor confined by steep, 300 m slopes and cliffs. Late Devensian solifluction terraces flank the eastern edge of the valley. There are two levels

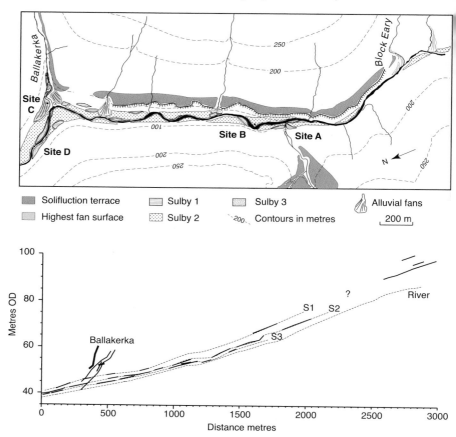

Figure 9.21 *Geomorphology and height range relationships between the river terraces in Sulby Glen, after R.C. Chiverrell et al. (2001).*

of river terrace, Auldyn 1 and Auldyn 2, in the main valley and both consist of coarse imbricated alluvial gravels, but the oldest alluvial landform is a complex multiple-phase alluvial fan with three surfaces. The highest alluvial fan surface is the oldest fluvial surface in Glen Auldyn, and the second highest alluvial fan surface grades into and is of equivalent age to the Auldyn 1 river terrace. Sections through the two higher fan surfaces reveal thick, 10 and 5 m sequences of imbricated and clast-supported alluvial gravel, which are overlain by mature podzols. Auldyn 1 and the higher two alluvial fan surfaces are incised into solifluction sediments and in places directly overlie soliflucted tills, providing evidence of early fluvial activity perhaps immediately post-dating the solifluction activity. Throughout

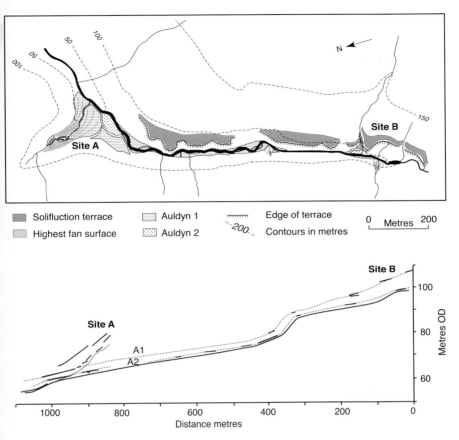

Figure 9.22 *Geomorphology and height range relationships between the river terraces in Glen Auldyn, after R.C. Chiverrell et al. (2001).*

most of the reach Auldyn 1 consists of 2–3 m of very coarse imbricated gravel overlain by a thick stony brown earth. It probably began forming during the Late Devensian and an OSL date on the uppermost sands indicates the terrace was abandoned following incision after 4,760–3,240 BP. There are several lower surfaces that form a terrace, Auldyn 2, and these younger features are often no more than recently abandoned floodplain.

Rhennas and the Neb catchment

Rhennas is a headwater tributary of the Neb and is part of one of the largest catchments on the Isle of Man. The Neb has river terraces in its lower reaches near Peel and a further sequence in the headwater reaches. The

Rhennas river rises on the flanks of Sartfell and Slieau Maggle (Figure 9.23) and is confined on both sides by steep slopes. Late Devensian solifluction terraces flank both sides of the valley. There are four river terraces, Rhennas 1 to 4 (Figure 9.23). The highest terrace, Rhennas 1, is covered by mature well-developed podzols, which implies the surface was abandoned during the early Holocene. Rhennas 2 is a more extensive terrace filling much of the valley and is covered by a less mature podzol no more than a couple of thousand years old. The lower surfaces, Rhennas 3 and Rhennas 4, are incised into the middle terrace and vary from recently vegetated point-bars to more substantial features covered by thin, immature, probably less than 500-year-old soils. At the confluence between the two most substantial tributaries in the Rhennas Valley there is a multiple-phase alluvial fan. The highest surface of the fan is equivalent to terrace Rhennas 1 and the middle alluvial fan surface grades into Rhennas 2. The lower alluvial fan surfaces appear to be equivalent to Rhennas 3 and Rhennas 4. Downstream the Rhennas flows through Glen Helen and into the central valley, joining with the Greeba and Glen May rivers to form the River Neb. The Neb contains the most impressive sequence of river terraces on the island (Figure 8.10). The highest two Neb terraces are almost certainly Devensian outwash or sandur surfaces, but the third terrace Lamplugh categorised as similar to the flood gravels of the large alluvial fans on the northern plain, and so is probably of late Devensian age. Set incised into these terraces is a sequence of Holocene fluvial terraces that includes the current floodplain. On the catchment watershed at Greeba Curragh organic sediment began accumulation 7,000 BP, and the surface of the peat deposits grades into the current floodplain, which indicates that the floodplain sediments probably span the Holocene.

The southern lowlands

The main contemporary river systems entering the south of the island, the Silverburn and Colby, both have relatively narrow alluvial spreads close to the present-day channel within reaches incised into surrounding higher glacial outwash gravel terraces. Both the Silverburn (Silverburn 3 to Silverburn 1, Figure 9.24a) and Colby (Colby 3 to Colby 1, Figure 9.24b) display a sequence of three Holocene terraces, with the higher two terraces (3 and 2) composed of coarse gravel 3–1.5 m above the current river. In the Colby these deposits are undated, but there are two OSL dates for the Silverburn 2 terrace, which date the uppermost gravels and suggest that terrace aggradation occurred before 2,710–1,290 years ago after which there was a phase of incision abandoning the terrace surface. The dates for

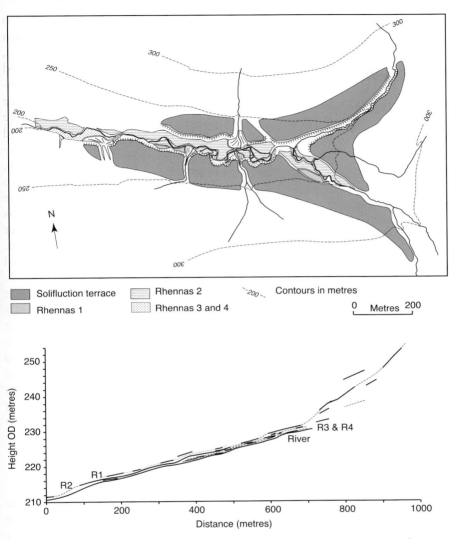

Figure 9.23 *Geomorphology and height range relationships between the river terraces in Rhennas Valley, after R.C. Chiverrell et al. (2001).*

the Silverburn 2 terrace imply that the Silverburn 1 terrace dates to the earlier Holocene or late Devensian. The lowest terraces (Colby 1 and Silverburn 1) comprise fine-grained alluvium with reaches incised into the higher two terraces and probably have aggraded during the last 1,500 years. The sequence of depositional fluvial landforms associated with the

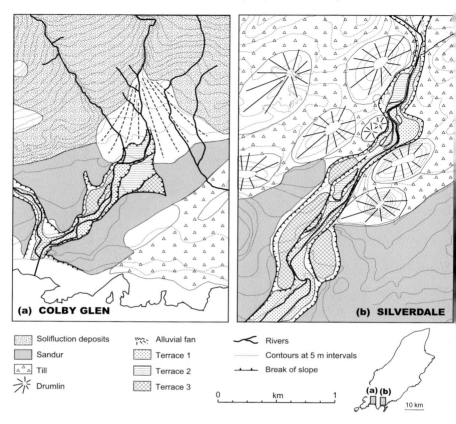

Figure 9.24 *Geomorphology of the south. (a) Colby Glen. (b) Silverdale.*

third river system, the Santon, that enters the south of the island is not as well developed with only poorly discernible terrace fragments.

The alluvial fills associated with the Dumb river and Strandhall/ Cronkmooar areas (Figure 9.2) are much wider in expanse and reflect either a wider floodplain development and/or standing water bodies in the past[107]. There are historical records of standing water in the Dumb system and frequent flooding of the Strandhall/Cronkmooar area by the Colby river[108]. Lamplugh divided the Strandhall/Cronkmooar alluvium into a westerly spread of gravelly or silty alluvium distinguished from easterly blue, stony clay deposits, which he termed the 'Colby Wash' and inter- preted derived from storm or flood washing of glacial till and not strictly riverine alluvium. Given the altitude of the Strandhall/Cronkmooar allu- vial basin (10–20 m O.D.), it seems unlikely to have been inundated by marine waters at any time since deglaciation. The Dumb river system is below O.D., and hence a Holocene sea level high of +3 to +5 m O.D. may have led to a degree of marine incursion.

Both the Dumb river and Strandhall/Cronkmooar alluvial plains display subtle channelled features suggestive of relict fluvial activity. The Strandhall/Cronkmooar system provides examples of clearly visible palaeochannels, meandering in some instances. The Dumb river exhibits similar, if not more complex, fluvial systems. The most complex of these lies directly south of Lower Ballanorris where the fluvial system has indistinct channel edges and relict bars. Further to the east, there also appear to be relict channel and bar features; these reoccur further south, along with a clear palaeo-meander scar alongside the present river. Despite the historical evidence for standing water in these systems the surface geomorphology suggests that river channel systems operated in these areas.

Holocene geomorphological history of the Isle of Man

The fluvial geomorphology of the Isle of Man is constrained by the tentative nature of the chronologies. Nevertheless, dated phases of fluvial incision and terrace aggradation identify some of the most significant changes to have occurred in the upland landscape during the last 11,500 years. The timing and correlation of periods of river terrace formation and fluvial incision are summarised in Figure 9.25. Solifluction activity and the bulk of the substantial incision into the till-choked valleys were complete by the beginning of the Holocene. Some of the higher terrace gravels that aggraded during this early incision may have formed the floodplain during the early to mid Holocene. During the mid Holocene many of the Manx rivers incised and abandoned terraces Auldyn 1, Sulby 1, Druidale 1, Rhennas 1, Colby 1 and Silverburn 1. Correlation of these terraces is at best tentative and is based upon the calibre of the coarser sediment and the maturity of the soils on them. Only Auldyn 1 sediments have been absolutely dated, with an OSL assay on the uppermost sands indicating that incision took place after 4,760–3,240 BP. Gravel aggradation followed this mid Holocene incision and produced Auldyn 2, Sulby 2 Druidale 2, Rhennas 2 and Silverburn 2. There are strong similarities between these terraces with the sediment consisting of gravels and overlain by moderately mature soils at most 2,000 years old. Luminescence dating on the uppermost gravels constrains fluvial aggradation of Sulby 2 to 2,410–1,230 BP and the subsequent incision to the late Holocene. Radiocarbon dating of organic sediments overlying Druidale 2 constrains the aggradation of this terrace and the ensuing phase of incision to before 625–500 BP. Later alluvial sedimentation in Sulby Glen, Glen Auldyn, the Colby and Silverburn produced lower terraces composed of finer-grained sediments. In Druidale and Rhennas Valley the sequence is more complicated, because the reach incised into the middle terrace contains suites of younger terraces – Druidale 3, Rhennas 3 and Rhennas 4. The younger fluvial landforms are mainly vegetated point-bars and abandoned channels; but there is a more substantial low terrace in Rhennas Valley. Cycles of incision and aggradation during the last 500–200 years are clearly responsible for these more recent terraces.

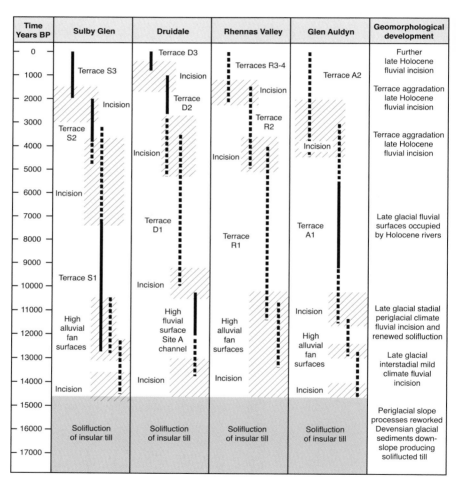

Figure 9.25 *Interpretation and chronology of post-glacial landforms in the Manx uplands.*

In summary, during the early Holocene rivers on the Isle of Man either aggraded or occupied floodplains inherited from the Lateglacial. The evidence for this is a calibre of material in the terrace deposits that is clearly not in keeping with fluvial transport of sediment during the Holocene. Three phases of fluvial activity are tentatively identified:

1. During the early Holocene rivers occupied surfaces that formed during the late Devensian and the rivers gradually modified and incised into the higher river terraces. Mid Holocene incision is recorded in Glen Auldyn.
2. After the early to mid Holocene incision, a series of river terrace deposits have aggraded. For example Sulby 2 is set incised into Sulby 1 and was deposited after the system switched to aggradation. This phase of aggradation (Sulby 2) ends after 2,410–1,230 BP, with further incision abandoning the Sulby 2 terrace.
3. Further phases of aggradation occurred during the late Holocene, with a sequence of low terraces in Druidale. The suite of low terraces in Druidale and Rhennas Valley reflects phases of incision and aggradation that have occurred during the last 500 years.

The sequence of events identified for the Isle of Man has similarities with fluvial records elsewhere in upland Britain. Fluvial records from the eastern Pennines and southern Scotland identify phases of incision and then increased alluviation during the late Holocene, which are attributed to a combination of human impact and changes in the regional climate[109]. The Manx sequence differs from the Pennine and Scottish records in that the fluvial system appears to have been quiescent or incising during the early Holocene. Heightened geomorphic activity during the late Holocene also occurred in the Howgill and Bowland Fells, with increased human activity around AD 1,000 regarded as the trigger[110].

The Isle of Man has been utilised by people for hunting and to graze livestock since the Mesolithic (9,000–5,100 BP), but the chronology of the archaeological record is poorly resolved[111]. There is little evidence for large-scale exploitation of the Manx uplands before the Bronze Age (3,800–2,600 BP), after which the archaeological record is particularly rich and provides a possible explanation for phases of incision and terrace aggradation. Removal of woodland from the uplands renders hill slopes susceptible to erosion and gullying, of which there is widespread evidence in the Manx hills. Erosion of slope deposits transferred quantities of material to the valley floor and encouraged streams to aggrade. Pollen diagrams from Beinn y Phott, reviewed in this chapter, identify two phases of woodland clearance, with small-scale clearances during the Bronze Age dated to

3,400–3,100 BP and a more substantial massive clearance during the Iron Age *circa* 2,350–2,120 BP. Woodland clearance and increased farming in the uplands during the Bronze Age and Iron Age is clearly a potential trigger for fluvial aggradation. The most concerted attempts to exploit the Manx uplands have involved field enclosures and ploughing of upland soils and this scale of activity during the last 300 years is a potential trigger for the most recent cycle of fluvial incision and aggradation.

The Beinn y Phott peat sequence also provides the only evidence for climate change during the late Holocene on the Isle of Man, recording changes in mire surface wetness during the last 5,000–4,000 years. There is evidence for several shifts to wetter conditions present within these peat deposits, with the most significant *circa* 2,500 BP and 1,500 BP. The timing of these wet shifts agrees with data from other peat sequences from the British Isles, and so climate change is another possible cause of fluvial incision during the late Holocene. However, a combination of climate change and woodland clearance is the more likely explanation for heightened rates of geomorphic activity during the late Holocene.

SOILS OF THE ISLE OF MAN   MIKE FULLEN, JOHN HARRIS and MICHAEL HALLETT

The soils of the Isle of Man exemplify many of the important contrasting soil types within the British Isles and are illustrative of broader patterns and processes of soil formation[112]. Manx soils also have an applied interest, as the nature and properties of soils fundamentally influence agricultural activities (cropping, grazing or forestry) and their intensity, sustainability and likely success[113]. Soils are also of considerable interest for planning activities, including urban development and nature conservation. Brian Kear carried out most of the initial soil surveys and soil mapping for the Isle of Man[114]. This research produced the 1:63,360 scale Soil Association Map of the Isle of Man and tentatively correlated the soil series identified on the island with those in England and Wales[115]. The Soil Survey and Land Research Centre (SSLRC), which also investigated relationships between soil properties and groundwater resources, has recently performed detailed soil mapping of the island at the soil series scale[116].

The soil forming factors

Soils are dynamic systems, both influenced by and interacting with their environment. The environmental conditions which influence the nature and properties of soils are described as 'the soil forming factors'. The Russian soil scientist Vasilli Dokuchaev initially identified these factors and investigated relationships between soils and environmental factors on the Russian Steppes. In 1883 he identified five soil forming factors, namely parent material, biota (flora and fauna), relief, climate and time. Although the model has been subject to modification, Dokuchaev's concepts remain at the core of pedology. The Isle of Man provides a suitable environment to study the soil forming factors, their dynamic interaction and environmental consequences. The island is quite small and diverse, with relatively varied parent materials, relief and mesoscale climates. On the world map of soils, the soils of the Isle of Man are classified as Dystric Cambisols[117]. Dystric means the soils have low fertility and has its origins in the Greek 'dys' meaning ill. On the Isle of Man, this dystric status is mainly due to intense leaching, which causes soil acidity. Cambisols are soils with properties (colour, structure and consistence) resulting from weathering *in situ*. The FAO-UNESCO Map scale is 1:5,000,000 and so only one soil type can be shown, but on a local scale Manx soils are extremely varied.

The Isle of Man exemplifies many of the important contrasts in soils between the uplands and lowlands of the British Isles. In the Manx lowlands, parent material tends to be the dominant soil-forming factor, with climate becoming progressively more important with increasing altitude. The upland/lowland distinction is clearly evident in the reconnaissance soil map produced by Kear (Figure 9.26)[118]. There are two main areas of upland soils, the larger on the northern upland massif and the smaller upland area to the south of the Central Valley between Douglas and Peel. The most extensive area of lowland soils is developed on the glacial deposits of the northern plain. On a local scale, soils have been mapped as series. The oceanic and mountainous nature of the island produces many parallels with the soil patterns of the Lake District, the Southern uplands of Scotland and especially upland North Wales. A total of 25 soil series with equivalents in England and Wales were identified. Some 77 series were identified by the SSLRC, using the established nomenclature in England and Wales. The most extensive are typical brown earths of the Denbigh series and typical brown podzolic soils of the Manod series. However, the consistency of soil series between England and Wales and the Isle of Man remains to be verified[119].

Soil parent materials

The main rock type on which pedogenesis occurs is the Manx slate, which occupies some 80% of the island. The slates are siliceous and base defi-

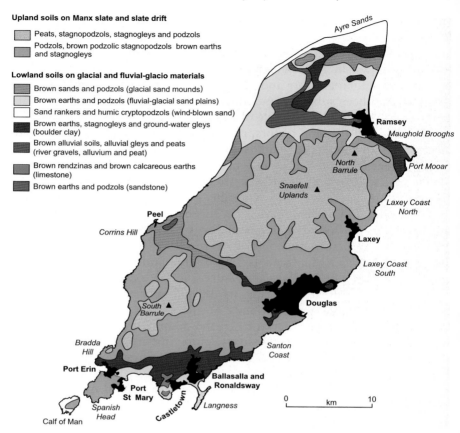

Figure 9.26 *Simplified soil map of the Isle of Man, after B. Kear (1976).*

cient and in the cool, humid and temperate Manx climate result in the development of acid soils. Acidity is a dominant characteristic of the island's soils and soil pH values are typically between 5 and 6[120]. The main soils associated with these conditions are podzols (Figure 9.27a) and brown podzolic soils (Figure 9.27b).

Calcareous soils have developed on the Carboniferous limestones near Castletown. Since limestone is slowly soluble in water, relatively pure calcareous parent materials are slowly dissolved, leaving minimal amounts of insoluble residues. Consequently the process produces shallow soils, which often consist of topsoil with quite a high organic matter content (Ah horizon), resting directly on calcareous bedrock (Cr horizon). On pure limestones these soils are rendzinas. They occur on the outcrops of

Figure 9.27 *(a) Podzol profile on Ballaugh Plantation (SC370911). (b) A brown sand soil from the Orrisdale Hills. Photographs by M.A. Fullen.*

Carboniferous limestone around Castletown and have neutral to alkaline pH values (7 or above). Impure calcareous rocks can weather to a thicker calcimorphic soil, which possesses B-horizons. Surface additions of sediments (colluvium, alluvium, aeolian materials or till) can be significant sources of mineral matter in these soils. Calcimorphic soils are thicker than rendzinas and consequently have better moisture retention. Together with pH levels of 6 to 7, these soils are suitable for arable crops and many are used for arable agriculture. On the Isle of Man, calcimorphic soils are derived mainly from calcareous till and are concentrated north of the limestone outcrop, in the vicinity of Ballasalla. On the coast, shells are significant sources of calcium carbonate, especially on the Ayres, and form calcareous, immature sandy soils (sand-pararendzinas). On steep, upland slopes, soils are often shallow and stony, with a predominance of slate fragments. These rankers[121] consist mainly of skeletal material. Devonian sandstones form localised parent materials in the Peel area, leading to the development of reddish soils with sandy loam textures.

Glacial till is an important soil parent material throughout the island, especially on ground below 180 m altitude. The spatially variable nature of Manx tills is an important factor explaining the variety of Manx soils. Sands and gravels derived from glaciofluvial sediments are the main parent materials in the north of the island. Sediment parent materials also include fluvial gravels, alluvium, glaciolacustrine deposits and, at the Ayres, aeolian sand over a raised beach. Since the pattern of glacial deposition was very complicated, the soils are very varied and so have been mapped on the northern plain as a soil complex[122]. Generally, soils developed on sandy deposits are dominated by brown sand soils, which are relatively light and easily cultivated. These sandy soils are frequently both 'hungry and thirsty', requiring liming for soil acidity correction and often irrigation in summer.

Biotic factors

Fauna and flora play important and complex roles in soil formation. Soils and biota are interactive and mutually adjusting dynamic systems. The dynamic interrelationships between soils and biota are termed edaphic relationships. The Manx slates are ecologically suitable for calcifuge plant communities. In turn, these communities alter the soil environment. Pedogenesis on Manx slates in a cool, oceanic climate has made the Manx uplands suitable for heath vegetation, characterised by such species as common heather (*Calluna vulgaris*) and bell heather (*Erica cinerea*). The island is noted for the extensive tracts of gallic heath, consisting mainly of mixtures of heathers and western gorse (*Ulex gallii*). These communities in turn influence soil development. Calcifuge communities tend to produce a raw, acidic and fibrous mor[123] humus. Mor humus topsoils on the Isle of Man have pH values generally in the range 3.2–3.8. Needle litter from coniferous woodlands tends to produce distinct mor humus topsoils. Therefore, afforestation with coniferous species may be contributing to topsoil acidification. Afforestation is occurring up to an altitude of *circa* 270 m, using mainly Sitka spruce (*Picea sitchensis*), Norway spruce (*Picea abies*) and Scots pine (*Pinus sylvestris*). In contrast, many of the lower sections of Manx glens have a mature cover of deciduous woodland. Here, the humus is mor-like mull[124] or moder[125] humus. Due to the prevalent soil acidity, mull humus is generally absent on the Isle of Man. Human effects on soil systems could be included in the biotic factors. These are manifested in many ways and all Manx soils are influenced by human agency. These influences include sterilisation by urban construction and modifications induced by farming, drainage, fertiliser application, liming, livestock grazing and forestry.

Topography

Topography plays an important role in the development of Manx lowland peats (the Curraghs, Lough Cranstal and Greeba). Water entrapment on the undulating northern plain and Central Valley led to the development of marshy conditions, in which site wetness decreased rates of plant tissue decomposition, thus leading to peat accumulation. The lowland fen, sedge or carr peats tend to be highly decomposed and amorphous. Moreover, fen peats tend to have higher pH values than upland peats and have greater faunal activity, which causes pedoturbation. Topography plays an important role in influencing patterns of soil drainage, particularly producing gley soils. Site wetness can impede decomposition of organic matter and gleys frequently have a humose topsoil (A horizon with high organic matter content, imparting a dark colour). Profile wetness can also mobilise manganese, producing soft black concretions in the zone of water table fluctuation. Gleys develop due to rising and falling water tables, as on floodplains, and are designated as belonging to the ground-water gley soils major group by the Soil Survey of England and Wales[126]. Gleys also develop due to impeded drainage, encouraging surface waterlogging and belong to the surface-water gley soils major group. These can be divided into two groups, the stagnogley soils, with a distinct mineral topsoil and the stagnohumic gley soils, with a humose or peaty topsoil[127]. The stagnogleys are particularly associated with the lowlands and the more extensive stagnohumic gleys with the uplands.

Climate

Climatic variation within the Isle of Man is very much altitudinally controlled. The change from sea level to the 621 m peak of Snaefell within seven kilometres means the island experiences many of the climatic variations encountered within the British Isles. Increased altitude changes a whole range of climatic factors, including decreased air and soil temperatures, solar radiation values and growing season. It is estimated that the growing season decreases on average by one day for each 15 m increase in altitude. Precipitation generally increases with altitude, as does the amount and frequency of snowfall. With altitude, the frequency and duration of frost, humidity, cloud cover and wind velocity generally increase and evapotranspiration rates decrease. These combined effects produce a cool, wet upland climate. Consequently, steep climatic gradients exist across the island, which profoundly influence the nature of pedological processes. The climate of the exposed uplands is particularly suitable for peat formation, due to the combined conditions of site wetness, acidity and low temperatures. Systematic topographic relationships are evident, with upland peats progressing down-slope, firstly into podzols and then into brown podzolic soils, each transition being at a lower elevation in the wetter west than the drier east. Thus, the island has an upper core of peat, above *circa* 230 m. These peats are surrounded by peaty soils, with between 7 and 40 cm of peat, which in turn are surrounded by mineral acid soils at lower elevations. Thicker peats, exceeding 3 m, are located above 355 m; the thickest are to the southwest of Snaefell, at Beinn y Phott.

The contrast in the nature and properties of peats between Beinn y Phott and the Curraghs is representative of general contrasts between upland and lowland peats in the British Isles. Most upland peats belong to the raw peat soils group, tending to be raw, ombrotrophic, fibrous and acidic (pH values usually less than 4.5). In contrast, most lowland peats belong to the earthy peat soils group and tend to be more humified, eutrophic and semi-fibrous to amorphous. They are enriched by inflows of nutrients from adjacent areas and consequently, they tend to have higher pH values. The peats of the Curraghs are enriched with nutrients from water draining from Sulby Glen and, although still acid (mean soil pH 6.4), they are much less so than peats in the uplands (e.g., Beinn y Phott, mean pH 3.8)[128]. Changes in climate produced much of the raw material for subsequent pedogenesis.

Time

Soil systems change through time. Generally, soils in the British Isles are relatively young, many having only developed in the 17,000 to 11,500 years since deglaciation and landscape stabilisation. To illustrate the effect of time, it is possible to examine the changing nature of pedogenesis in a transect across the Ayres. On the older dunes, profile horizons of humus stained 'grey sand' (Ah horizons) alternate with unconsolidated dune sand parent material (Cu horizons). The Cu horizons are indicative of periods of dune instability, with influxes of aeolian sand. The Ah horizons reflect periods of relative stability, in which humus derived from the ecosystem accumulated. The complex pattern of soils on the Ayres illustrates that soil forming factors cannot be simply separated. The nature and properties of parent materials, biota, topography and climate interact with the soil system and each other. These dynamic systems interact through time, to produce the complex array of soil types.

Soils and agriculture

Agriculture is the main land use on the island and is intimately related to the nature and properties of soils. John Harris[129] surveyed the agricultural soils, and visited and classified the soils of most fields on the island. In this context, agricultural soils are defined as soils of enclosed fields used for pastoral or rotational farming, but not including unimproved hill or coastal land used solely for extensive sheep farming and upland forestry. Recently a reconnaissance agricultural soil map of the Isle of Man was produced which attempts to synthesise the pedological and agricultural soil information[130]. However, the map had some uncertainties, including the extent of calcareous soils in the south of the island, the extent of sandy soils around Peel and the boundaries in the soil complex around Cooil, southwest of Douglas. Consequently, John Harris investigated these areas between 1996 and 1999, developing a classification system for potential of land in agricultural use, based essentially on the nature and properties of parent materials[131]. The soils were divided into five categories, each of which was divided into a number of sub-categories, based mainly on soil textural characteristics. Some sub-categories were further subdivided into phases, which were differentiated on the basis of slope, stoniness, depth or other criteria significant for land use. In the first version of the map, 25 map units were recognised, but further soil survey has suggested another seven, and these 32 map units (consisting of 27 sub-categories and 10 phases) are described below[132]. The five categories are:

Category A Soils associated with slates, flagstones and shales (11 mapping units, 11 sub-categories);

Category B Soils associated with limestone (4 mapping units, 3 sub-categories and 2 phases);

Category C Soils associated with Peel Sandstone and Neb gravels (3 mapping units, 3 sub-categories);

Category D Soils associated with glacial deposits (8 mapping units, 6 sub-categories and 4 phases);

Category E Soils associated with peat deposits (6 mapping units, 4 sub-categories and 4 phases).

Each soil category (A–E) was matched with the soil subgroup on the 1:250,000 Soil Association Map of England and Wales[133] with which it was considered to have the closest affinity. The categories, comparable soil subgroups and subgroup codes are:

Category A soils Typical brown podzolic soils (6.11);
Category B soils Typical brown calcareous soils (5.11);
Category C soils Typical brown sands (5.51);
Category D soils Typical brown earths (5.41);
Category E soils Earthy oligo-fibrous peat soils (10.21).

Soil sub-categories were numbered on a scale, based on a qualitative evaluation of the relative extent and agricultural importance of each sub-category (i.e., A1 is the most extensive Category A sub-category). The sub-categories within each of the five categories were then classified according to soil texture, using a scale from 1 (heaviest or most clay-rich or argillaceous) to 11 (light sandy or arenaceous soils). Soil textures were assessed by field survey, supported by laboratory determinations of the particle size distributions of selected soil samples[134]. Soil categories A–E were allocated different colours and the textural classes within each were distinguished by different colour intensities, the lighter colours for the lighter textural classes and darker for the heavier textural classes.

On completion of the field survey in March 1999, the data have been collated with a GIS (Figure 9.28) and 'draped' over a digital elevation model (DEM) of the island using the Isle of Man Government's digital mapping data (MANNGIS) and DEM data as the base. Land quality can be evaluated by the 'Land Use Capability Classification' system[135]. Little Manx agricultural land is Grade 1 or 2 and most is Grade 3 and 4. This is partly a result of the relatively short history of intensive farming and low soil nutrient levels, though there are also climatic, relief and soil limitations

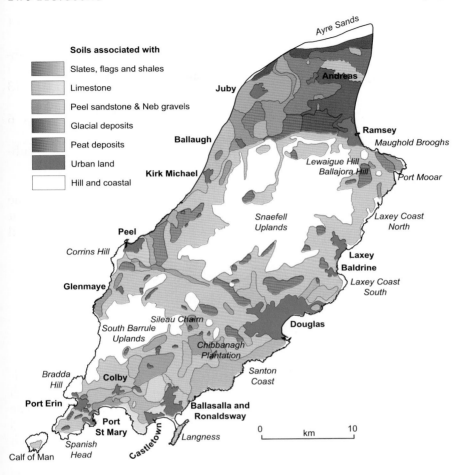

Figure 9.28 *Agricultural soil classification map of the Isle of Man.*

to land use in these categories[136]. Each of the 32 map units was assessed in terms of Land Use Capability Classes and only nine units were classified as belonging to one class. Due to the variability of Manx soils, most units include two classes, and these have been divided into those having a dominant class (13 units) or an approximately equal mixture of two classes (10 units) on the Land Use Capability Map (Figure 9.29).

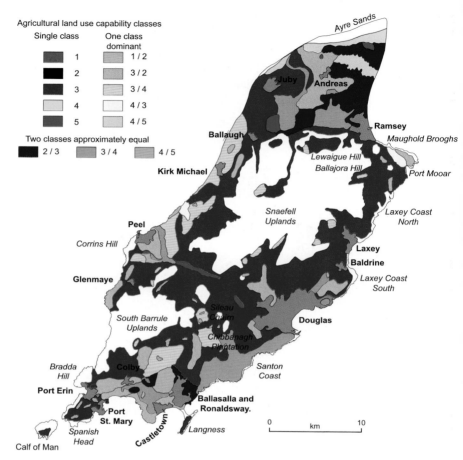

Figure 9.29 *Agricultural land use capability map of the Isle of Man.*

Notes

1   S.J. Johnsen, D. Dahl-Jensen, N. Gundestrup, J.P. Steffensen, H.B. Clausen, H. Miller, V. Masson-Delmotte, A.E. Sveinbjørnsdottir and J. White, 'Oxygen isotope and palaeotemperature records from six Greenland ice-core stations: Camp Century, Dye-3, GRIP, GISP2, Renland and NorthGRIP', *Journal of Quaternary Science*, 16 (2001), 299–307.

2   J.D. Marshall, R.T. Jones, S.F. Crowley, F. Oldfield, S. Nash and A. Bedford, 'A high resolution Lateglacial isotopic record from Hawes Water, Northwest England Climatic oscillations: calibration and comparison of palaeotemperature proxies', *Palaeogeography Palaeoclimatology Palaeoecology*, 185 (2002), 25–40.

3   H. Grudd, K.R. Briffa, W. Karlen, T.S. Bartholin, P.D. Jones and B. Kromer, 'A 7400-year tree ring chronology in northern Swedish Lapland: natural climatic variability expressed on annual to millennial timescales', *Holocene*, 12 (2002), 657–666.

4   H.H. Leuschner, U. Sass-Klaassen, E. Jansma, M.G.L. Baillie and M. Spurk, 'Subfossil European bog oaks: population dynamics and long term growth depressions as indicators of changes in the Holocene hydro-regime and climate', *Holocene*, 12 (2002), 695–706.

5   B. Aaby, 'Cyclic climatic variations in climate over the past 5,500 years reflected in raised bogs', *Nature*, 263 (1976), 281–284.

6   K.E. Barber, F.M. Chambers and D. Maddy, 'Holocene palaeoclimates from peat stratigraphy: macrofossil proxy climate records from three oceanic raised bogs in England and Ireland', *Quaternary Science Reviews*, 22 (2003), 521–539.

7   K. Lambeck, 'Glaciation and sea-level change for Ireland and the Irish Sea since Late Devensian/Midlandian time', *Journal of the Geological Society of London*, 153 (1996), 853–872; D.H. Roberts, R.C. Chiverrell, J.B. Innes, S. Gonzalez, S. Turner and B.P. Horton, 'New data on Holocene sea level changes on the Isle of Man', in R.C. Chiverrell, G.S.P. Thomas and A.J. Plater (eds), *Quaternary of the Isle of Man and Northwest England: a field guide*, Quaternary Research Association, Cambridge (2004), 112–124.

8   K. Lambeck, (1996).

9   M.J. Tooley, 'Sea level changes and coastal morphology in north-west England', in R.H. Johnson (ed.), *The geomorphology of north-west England*, Manchester University Press, Manchester (1985), 94–121.

10 *Ibid.*

11 G.W. Lamplugh, *The geology of the Isle of Man*, Memoir of the Geological Survey of England and Wales (1903), 606.

12 M.J. Tooley (1985).

13 B.A.M. Phillips, 'Effective levels of marine planation on raised and present rock platforms', *Review Geography Montreal*, 24 (1970), 227–240.

14 K. Lambeck (1996).

15 M.J. Tooley, *Sea level changes: north-west England during the Flandrian stage*, Oxford University Press, Oxford (1978b), 227.

16 S. Gonzalez, J.B. Innes, D. Huddart, P.J. Davey and A.J. Plater, 'Holocene coastal change in the north of the Isle of Man: stratigraphy, palaeoenvironment and archaeological evidence', in K. Pye and J.R.L. Allen (eds), *Coastal and Estuarine Environments: sedimentology, geomorphology and geoarchaeology*, Geological Society Special Publication, 175 (2000), 343–363.

17 D.H. Roberts *et al.* (2004).

18 B.A.M. Phillips, *Cliff and shore platform development in the Isle of Man*, unpub-

lished PhD thesis, University of Wales (1969).

19 J.G. Cumming, 'On the geology of the Isle of Man', *Quarterly Journal of the Geological Society of London*, 2 (1846), 317–348.

20 M.J. Tooley (1985); K. Lambeck (1996).

21 B.A.M. Phillips (1969).

22 *Ibid.*

23 I. Shennan, 'Interpretation of Flandrian sea level data from the Fenland, England', *Proceedings of the Geologists' Association*, 93 (1982), 53–63; I. Shennan, 'Flandrian sea-level changes in the Fenland II. Tendencies of sea-level movement, altitudinal changes and local and regional factors', *Journal of Quaternary Science*, 1 (1986), 155–179.

24 K. Lambeck (1996); I. Shennan and B. Horton, 'Holocene land- and sea-level changes in Great Britain', *Journal of Quaternary Science*, 17 (2002), 511–526.

25 D.H. Roberts *et al.* (2004).

26 K. Lambeck (1996); N.F. Glasser and G.H. Sambrook-Smith, 'Glacial meltwater erosion of the mid-Cheshire ridge: implications for ice dynamics during the Late Devensian glaciation of northwest England', *Journal of Quaternary Science*, 14 (1999), 703–710.

27 N. Eyles and A.M. McCabe, 'The Late Devensian <22,000 BP Irish Sea Basin: the sedimentary record of a collapsed ice sheet margin', *Quaternary Science Reviews*, 8 (1989), 307–351; K. Lambeck (1996); A.M. McCabe and P.U. Clark, 'Ice sheet variability around the North Atlantic Ocean during the last deglaciation', *Nature*, 392 (1998), 373–377.

28 D.H. Roberts *et al.* (2004).

29 K. Lambeck (1996); I. Shennan, W.R. Peltier, R. Drummond and B.P. Horton, 'Global to local scale parameters determining relative sea-level changes and post-glacial isostatic adjustment of Great Britain', *Quaternary Science Reviews*, 21 (2002), 397–408.

30 I. Shennan *et al.* (2002).

31 K. Lambeck (1996); I. Shennan and B. Horton (2002); D.H. Roberts *et al.* (2004).

32 D.W. Yalden, *The History of British Mammals*, Poyser Natural History, London (1999).

33 L.S. Garrad, 'Evidence for the history of the vertebrate fauna of the Isle of Man', in P.J. Davey (ed.), *Man and Environment in the Isle of Man*, British Archaeological Reports, British Series 54, Oxford (1978), 61–76; L.S. Garrad, 'Nature conservation', in V. Robinson and D. McCarroll (eds), *The Isle of Man: Celebrating a Sense of Place*, Liverpool University Press, Liverpool (1990b), 84–98.

34 L.S. Garrad, 'The history of mammals', in V. Robinson and D. McCarroll (eds), *The Isle of Man: Celebrating a Sense of Place*, Liverpool University Press, Liverpool (1990a), 74–76.

35 L.S. Garrad (1990a).

36 L.S. Garrad (1978).

37 L.S. Garrad, *The Naturalist in the Isle of Man*, David and Charles, Newton Abbot (1972a), 234.

38 F. Swinnerton, 'Early Neolithic Cists and Refuse Heap at Port St Mary', *Yn Liaor Manninagh*, 1 (1890), 137–139.

39 R.T.R. Wingfield, 'A model of sea level changes in the Irish and Celtic seas during the end-Pleistocene to Holocene transition', in R.C. Preece (ed.), *Island Britain: a Quaternary perspective*, Geological Society Special Publication, 96 London (1999).

40 P.C. Woodman and N. Monaghan, 'From mice to mammoths: dating Ireland's earliest faunas', *Archaeology Ireland*, 7 (1993).

41 C.M. King, *The natural history of weasels and stoats*, Christopher Helm, London (1989).

42 A.J. Stuart and L.H. van Wijngaarden-Bakker, 'Quaternary vertebrates', in K.J. Edwards and W.P. Warren (eds), *The Quaternary history of Ireland*, Academic Press, London (1985), 221–249.

43 E.J. Pooley, 'Non-avian vertebrates and the implications of habitat change', in T. Hopson and J. Lamb (eds), *Proceedings of the Manx Hill-lands seminar*, Manx Nature Conservation Trust, Douglas (1997), 39–50.

44 S. Mascheretti, M.B. Rogatcheva, I. Gündüz, K. Fredga and J.B. Searle, 'How did pygmy shrews colonize Ireland? Clues from a phylogenetic analysis of mitochondrial cytochrome b sequences', *Proceedings of the Royal Society London: Series B Biological Sciences*, 270, 1524 (2003), 1593–1599.

45 L.S. Garrad (1978).

46 K. Williamson, 'Ornithology on the Calf of Man', *Proceedings of the Isle of Man Natural History and Antiquarian Society*, 7 (1941), 419–439.

47 C. Crellin, 'The small mammal bones', in M.A. Cubbon, P.J. Davey and M. Gelling (eds), *Excavations on St Patrick's Isle, Peel, Isle of Man: Prehistoric, Viking, Medieval and later, 1982–88 by David Freke*, Liverpool University Press, (2002), 251.

48 J.D.S. Birks and A.C. Kitchener, *The distribution and status of the Polecat Mustela putorius in the 1990s*, The Vincent Wildlife Trust, London (1999).

49 P.S. Maitland and R.N. Campbell, *Freshwater Fishes of the British Isles*, Harper Collins, London (1992).

50 M.J. Tooley (1985).

51 S. Gonzalez *et al.* (2000).

52 R.C. Chiverrell, J.B. Innes, J.J. Blackford, J.J. Woodcock, P.J. Davey, P.R. Tomlinson, M.M. Rutherford and G.S.P. Thomas, 'Palaeoecological and archaeological evidence for Bronze Age human activity on the Isle of Man', *Holocene*, 14 (2004b), 346–360; J.B. Innes, R.C. Chiverrell, J.J. Blackford, P.J. Davey, S. Gonzalez, M.M. Rutherford and P.R. Tomlinson, 'Earliest Holocene vegetation history and Island Biogeography of the Isle of Man, British Isles', *Journal of Biogeography*, 31 (2004), 761–772; J.B. Innes, J.J. Blackford and P.J. Davey, 'Dating the introduction of cereal cultivation to the British Isles: early palaeoecological evidence from the Isle of Man', *Journal of Quaternary Science*, 18 (2003), 603–613.

53 D.H. Roberts *et al.* (2004).

54 C.A. Dickson, J.H. Dickson and G.F. Mitchell, 'The Late Weichselian Flora of the Isle of Man', *Philosophical Transactions of the Royal Society of London*, B258 (1970), 31–79; J.B. Innes *et al.* (2004).

55 S. Gonzalez *et al.* (2000).

56 I. Perry and P.D. Moore, 'Dutch elm disease as an analogue of Neolithic Elm Decline', *Nature*, 326 (1987), 72–73.

57 S. Gonzalez *et al.* (2000).

58 P.J. Davey, J.J. Blackford, R.C. Chiverrell, J.B. Innes and P.R. Tomlinson, 'The curragh and other lowland wetlands of the Isle of Man', in M.A. Atherden (ed.), *Wetlands in the landscape: archaeology, conservation, heritage*, People Landscape and Cultural Environment (PLACE) Research Centre, York, (2001), 12–40.

59 J.B. Innes *et al.* (2003).

60 I.G. Simmons, *The Environmental Impact of Later Mesolithic Cultures*,

Edinburgh University Press (1996).

61 M.J. Tooley (1985).

62 S. Gonzalez *et al.* (2000).

63 R.C. Chiverrell *et al.* (2004b).

64 S. Gonzalez *et al.* (2000).

65 P.J. Davey *et al.* (2001).

66 J.B. Innes, *The Dhoo Valley, Isle of Man: a palaeo-environmental assessment*, Research Report 2, Centre for Manx Studies, Douglas (1995).

67 K.J. Edwards, K.R. Hirons and P.J. Newell, 'The palaeoecological and prehistoric context of minerogenic layers in blanket peat: a study from Loch Dee, southwest Scotland', *Holocene*, 1 (1991), 29–39.

68 I.G. Simmons, M.A. Atherden, P.R. Cundill and R.L. Jones, 'Inorganic layers in soligenous mires of the North Yorkshire Moors', *Journal of Biogeography*, 2 (1975), 49–56.

69 G. Russell, 'The structure and vegetation history of the Manx Hill Peats', in P.J. Davey (ed.), *Man and Environment in the Isle of Man*, British Archaeological Reports, British Series, 54 (1978), 39–50.

70 G. Russell (1978).

71 R.C. Chiverrell *et al.* (2004b).

72 B. Huntley and H.J.B. Birks, *An atlas of past and present maps for Europe: 0–13000 BP*, Cambridge University Press (1983); H.J.B. Birks, 'Holocene isochrone maps and patterns of tree-spreading in the British Isles', *Journal of Biogeography*, 16 (1989), 503–540.

73 J.B. Innes *et al.* (2004).

74 C.A. Dickson *et al.* (1970).

75 R.W. Cowell and J.B. Innes, *The Wetlands of Merseyside: North West Wetlands Survey 1*, English Heritage and Lancaster University, Lancaster (1994).

76 H.J.B. Birks (1989).

77 N.T. Moar, 'Late Weichselian and Flandrian pollen diagrams from south-west Scotland', *New Phytologist*, 68 (1969), 433–467; R.M. Tipping, 'Holocene evolution of a lowland Scottish landscape: Kirkpatrick Fleming. Part II, regional vegetation and land-use change', *Holocene*, 5 (1995a), 83–96.

78 J.B. Innes *et al.* (2004).

79 H.J.B. Birks (1989).

80 A.G. Smith, 'The influence of Mesolithic and Neolithic man on British vegetation: a discussion', in D. Walker and R.G. West (eds), *Studies in the vegetational History of the British Isles*, Cambridge University Press, London (1970), 81–96.

81 R.M. Tipping (1995a).

82 H.J.B. Birks (1989).

83 A.G. Smith and I.C. Goddard, 'A 12,500 year record of vegetational history at Sluggan Bog, Co. Antrim, N. Ireland (incorporating a pollen zone scheme for the non-specialist)', *New Phytologist*, 118 (1991), 167–187.

84 F.A. Hibbert, V.R. Switsur and R.G. West, 'Radiocarbon dating of Flandrian pollen zones at Red Moss, Lancashire', *Proceedings of the Royal Society of London: Series B Biological Sciences*, 177 (1971), 161–176.

85 J.B. Innes *et al.* (2003).

86 I.G. Simmons (1996).

87 M.J. Tooley (1985).

88 S. Gonzalez *et al.* (2000).

89 K.D. Bennett, 'The post-glacial history of *Pinus sylvestris* in the British Isles', *Quaternary Science Reviews*, 3 (1984), 133–155; M.C. Bridge, B.A. Haggart and

J.J. Lowe, 'The history and palaeoclimate significance of subfossil remains of *Pinus sylvestris* in blanket peats from Scotland', *Journal of Ecology*, 78 (1990), 77–99; A.J. Gear and B. Huntley, 'Rapid changes in the range limits of Scots pine 4000 BP', *Science*, 251 (1991), 544–547; J.J. Blackford, K.J. Edwards, A.J. Dugmore, G.T. Cook and P.C. Buckland, 'Icelandic volcanic ash and the mid-Holocene Scots pine (*Pinus sylvestris*) pollen decline in northern Scotland', *Holocene*, 2 (1992), 260–265.

90 A.J. Gear and B. Huntley (1991).

91 J.J. Blackford *et al.* (1992).

92 J.B. Innes (1995).

93 S. Gonzalez *et al.* (2000).

94 R.C. Chiverrell *et al.* (2004b).

95 G. Russell (1978).

96 R.C. Chiverrell, G.S.P. Thomas and A.M. Harvey, 'Late-Devensian and Holocene landscape change in the uplands of the Isle of Man', *Geomorphology*, 40 (2001a), 219–236.

97 A.M. Harvey, F. Oldfield, A.F. Baron and G. Pearson, 'Dating of post-glacial landforms in the central Howgills', *Earth Surface Processes and Landforms*, 6 (1981), 401–412.

98 A.M. Harvey and W.H. Renwick, 'Holocene alluvial fan and terrace formation in the Bowland Fells, Northwest England', *Earth Surface Processes and Landforms*, 12 (1997), 249–257.

99 A.J. Howard, M.G. Macklin, S. Black and K.A. Hudson-Edwards, 'Holocene river development and environmental change in Upper Wharfedale, Yorkshire Dales, England', *Journal of Quaternary Science*, 15 (2000), 239–252.

100 M.G. Macklin and J. Lewin, 'Terraced fills of Pleistocene and Holocene age in the Rheidol Valley, Wales', *Journal of Quaternary Science*, 1 (1986), 21–34.

101 R.M. Tipping, 'Holocene evolution of a lowland Scottish landscape: Kirkpatrick Fleming. Part III, fluvial history', *Holocene*, 5 (1995b), 184–195.

102 M.G. Macklin and J. Lewin, 'Holocene river alluviation in Britain', *Zeitschrift für Geomorphologie (Supplement)*, 88 (1993), 109–122.

103 M.G. Macklin, 'Holocene river environments in prehistoric Britain: human interaction and impact', in K.J. Edwards and J.P. Sadler (eds), *Holocene environment of prehistoric Britain*, Quaternary Proceedings No. 7, Wiley, Chichester (1999), 521–530.

104 R.C. Chiverrell *et al.* (2001a).

105 G.W. Lamplugh (1903).

106 R.C. Chiverrell *et al.* (2001a).

107 G.W. Lamplugh (1903).

108 *Ibid.*

109 R.M. Tipping (1995b).

110 A.M. Harvey, 'Holocene hillslope gully systems in the Howgill Fells, Cumbria', in S.M. Brooks and M.G. Anderson (eds), *Advances in Hillslope Processes*, Volume 2, Wiley, Chichester (1996), 731–752.

111 A. Johnson, 'Sulby', in P.J. Davey (ed.), *Recent Archaeological Research on the Isle of Man*, British Archaeological Reports: British Series 278, Oxford (1999), 153–170.

112 M.A. Fullen, J. Harris and B.S. Kear, 'Soil forming processes on the Isle of Man', *Geography Review*, 13 (1999), 22–26.

113 J. Harris, M.A. Fullen and M.D. Hallett, *Agricultural Soils of the Isle of Man*, Centre for Manx Studies, Research Report 9 (2001), 24.

114 B.S. Kear, *Agriculture Soil Survey. Report on the examination of soils in the first phase areas of development around the main urban centres in the Isle of Man*', Department of Town and Country Planning, Isle of Man Local Government Board (1971); B.E. Davies and B.S. Kear, 'Environmental factors and the soil pattern on the Isle of Man', *Transactions of the 10th International Congress of Soil Science*, Moscow, Volume VIII: *Soils of the World* (1974), 93–100.

115 B.S. Kear, 'Soils of the Isle of Man', *Isle of Man Natural History and Antiquarian Society*, 8 (1976), 38–50; B.S. Kear, *The Isle of Man: its soils and their significance*, North of England Soils Discussion Group Special Publication No. 18 (1982), 53 (including 1:63,360 'Soils of the Isle of Man' Soil Association Map).

116 R.C. Palmer, G.R. Beard, R.I. Bradley, R.G.O. Burton, T.R. Harrod, J. Hazeldon, J.M. Hollis and I.P. Holman, *Soil Survey of the Isle of Man*, Soil Survey and Land Research Centre, Cranfield University (2000).

117 FAO-Unesco, *Soil Map of the World (1:5,000,000)*, Volume I (Legend) and Volume V1 (Europe), Unesco, Paris (1974).

118 B.S. Kear (1982).

119 R.C. Palmer *et al.* (2000).

120 M.A. Fullen, J. Harris and B.S. Kear, *Soils of the Isle of Man*, Centre For Manx Studies, Research Report 5 (1996), 29.

121 A 'ranker' is a poorly developed soil that occurs on steep slopes.

122 B.S. Kear (1982).

123 'Mor' is a term used to describe the organic matter in the surface soil horizon with limited decomposition and pH < 5.5.

124 'Mull' is a term used to describe the organic matter in the surface soil horizon with extensive decomposition and pH > 5.5.

125 'Moder' is a term used to describe the organic matter in the surface soil horizon with limited decomposition and pH of around 5.5.

126 B.W. Avery, *Soil Classification for England and Wales [Higher Categories]*, Soil Survey Technical Monograph No. 14, Lawes Agricultural Trust, Harpenden (1980).

127 *Ibid.*

128 M.A. Fullen *et al.* (1996).

129 Formerly of the Manx Department of Agriculture, Fisheries and Forestry, where he worked as an agricultural advisory officer for 24 years (1969–1993).

130 M.A. Fullen *et al.* (1996).

131 J. Harris *et al.* (2001).

132 *Ibid.*

133 Soil Survey of England and Wales, Legend for the *1:250,000 Soil Map of England and Wales*, Lawes Agricultural Trust, Harpenden (1983).

134 Undertaken by Dr T. Batey, University of Aberdeen.

135 J.S. Bibby (ed.), *Land Use Capability Classification for Agriculture*, Macaulay Land Use Research Institute, Aberdeen (1991).

136 M.A. Fullen *et al.* (1996).

10   Economic Geology

TREVOR FORD, DAVE QUIRK and GEOFF THOMAS

INTRODUCTION

Historical records of mineral extraction in the Isle of Man date back to at least the thirteenth century and the island shows evidence of Bronze Age mining[1]. Although mineral extraction on the island today is confined to bulk minerals such as sand, gravel, crushed rock and small amounts of building stone, the island was an important mining area for lead, zinc, copper and a small amount of silver from the late eighteenth to the early twentieth century. Between 1845 and 1938 recorded production of metal ores was 268,000 tons of lead, 256,000 tons of zinc, 14,000 tons of copper and 25,000 tons of iron concentrates[2]. During this period, the Isle of Man contributed 5% of the total British output of lead ores and 20% of the total output of zinc ores. The ores were contained in veins (mineralised fissures) in three main areas, Laxey–Snaefell, Foxdale–Glen Rushen and Bradda Head (Figure 10.1). Altogether, there were about 100 other small mines and trials scattered throughout the island.

Previous literature on mining includes Smyth's list of minerals[3], Lamplugh's memoir[4], Carruthers and Strahan's lead ores memoir[5], Dewey and Eastwood's copper ores memoir[6], Skelton's review of the mines[7], Pearce and Rose's review of mining[8], Von Arx's accounts of Snaefell and Kirk Michael mines[9], Dobson and Hollis's account of the mines of Glen Auldyn[10], Warriner and Gilling's survey of the Great Laxey mine[11] and unpublished reports by Wilson[12] and Mackay and Schnellmann[13]. In addition, Hollis provided historical notes on uranium, iron and gold[14]. A general overview is given in Ford *et al.*[15] and in Ford's analysis of the Laxey mines[16]. The recent revision of the British Geological Survey memoir provides further detail[17].

LEAD, ZINC AND COPPER MINERAL DEPOSITS

The principal ore minerals extracted were lead sulphide (galena), zinc sulphide (sphalerite) and copper iron sulphide (chalcopyrite). Other copper minerals were found including chalcocite and cuprite, but these are rare. Silver was found only as a constituent of galena. Traces of gold were recorded from adits around Douglas, but not in economic quantities. Pyrite

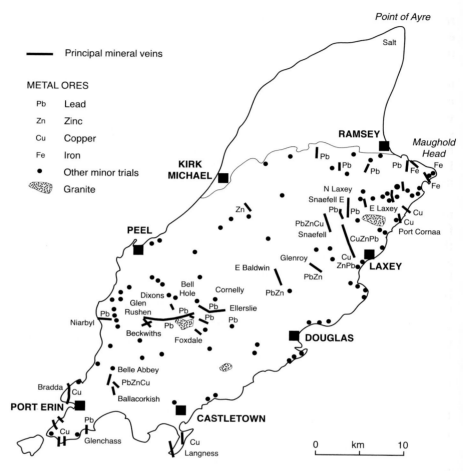

Figure 10.1 *Map showing important mineral veins in Manx Group rocks of the Isle of Man.*

(iron sulphide) and minor amounts of pyrrhotite, marcasite and pyromor-phite occur as well as traces of other metals including bismuth, antimony, titanium and molybdenum. Oxidation products of the ore minerals such as cerussite (lead carbonate) and malachite (copper carbonate) are present, but not in great quantities. Iron in the form of hematite (iron oxide) was mined in the northeast of the island around Maughold. A by-product of mining metal ores was large quantities of non-ore minerals, mainly quartz, calcite, dolomite, siderite and barite. Quartz is by far the commonest, often known as 'spar' on the Isle of Man. Although there were some older, small-scale smelting operations, by the nineteenth century, when the major expansion in mining on the island occurred, most of the ores were shipped to Liverpool or South Wales for smelting.

The mined minerals are confined to veins typically a few kilometres long, dipping 65–90° to the horizontal. They occur in metamorphosed sediments of the Manx Group except for some of the veins around Foxdale, which entered granite. The Cornelly mine was worked in the halo of altered slates around the Foxdale Granite. Traces of both lead and zinc sulphides have been found in veinlets in the Carboniferous rocks of the Castletown Limestone, for example near Ronaldsway airport, but these have not been mined on a commercial scale.

Although little of the vein material is now visible, they were originally mineral-filled fractures cutting through the folded slates and granite. The fractures appear to represent faults that have moved in a sideways rather than vertical sense (strike-slip instead of dip-slip), although the direction and amount of movement cannot be easily determined. Two main trends have been mined – north–south veins including the Laxey, Snaefell and Bradda mines; and east–west veins including the Foxdale–Glen Rushen and Cornelly mines. Quirk *et al.*[18] suggest that east–west faults have moved in a right lateral (dextral[19]) sense and north–south faults in a left lateral (sinistral[20]) sense during the latter stages of the Caledonian mountain-building event in the early Devonian, before their becoming mineralised, probably in the early Carboniferous[21].

Laxey mine

Lead, zinc and copper ores were raised at Laxey from a north–south vein about 2 km long inclined eastwards at about 80° to the horizontal. The vein was reported to have been offset by several small east–west faults known locally as 'slides', although preserved mine plans show only limited displacement (Figure 10.2). The vein reached widths of up to about 8 m but averaged 2 m. In places it tightened to a fissure ('leader') no more than a few millimetres wide. The host rocks are the Lonan and Creg Agneash formations of the Manx Group and the vein obliquely crosses the Dhoon Anticline[22], a northeast–southwest trending arch-shaped fold. It was worked to a final depth of 526 m below sea level. Based on incomplete production records, over a million tons of ore and waste were extracted, yielding 3–8% lead, 5–15% zinc and 2–5% copper. The non-ore minerals were quartz with lesser amounts of calcite, dolomite, siderite and barite. A search for an extension to the Laxey vein south of Laxey village proved fruitless but, to the north in the Cornaa Valley, a few small mines (East

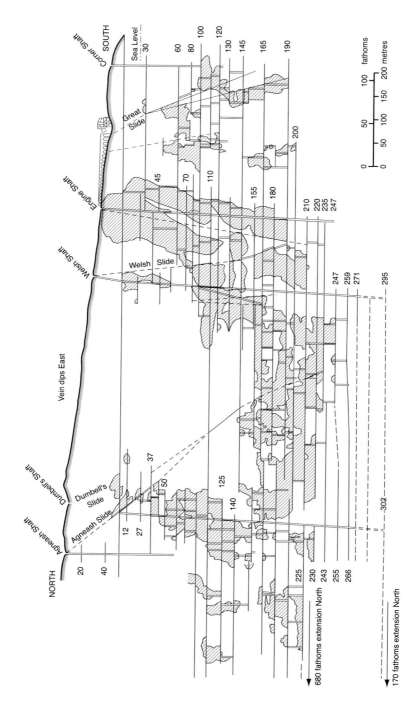

Figure 10.2 *Section through the Laxey mine. Worked areas are shown with diagonal hatching.*

Snaefell, North Laxey and Glen Cherry) worked what may be offshoots from the Laxey vein. These extracted lead ore but none was particularly productive.

Mining in Laxey commenced at least as early as 1780. It reached peak production in the 1850s and the mine closed in 1919 after a strike. The vein was worked from six deep shafts sunk at an inclined angle down the vein and linked by a haulage adit level with the valley bottom. As the workings went far below sea level, water influx was a constant problem, leading to the construction of the Lady Isabella water-wheel in 1854 which still turns today as a tourist attraction. A water-pressure-powered 'man engine' conveyed miners to the lower workings.

Snaefell mine

Lying about 3 km west of Laxey, the Snaefell mine worked a vein beneath the eastern flank of Snaefell. The vein has a north-northwest to south-south-east trend (160°) inclined eastwards at 75° from the horizontal. Workings were carried to a depth of about 400 m below surface. Both zinc and lead ores were raised, but the mine was never very profitable. It was worked from 1856 to 1898, closing when a large slab of rock fell from the side of the shaft. Unsuccessful attempts were made for another 10 years to reopen the mine and the waste heaps were removed for reprocessing in the 1950s.

The Foxdale mines

The Foxdale–Glen Rushen vein is shown on most maps as a single vein approximately 5 km long trending east–west. However, as it was only worked in places along its length (Figure 10.3), it may actually comprise a number of parallel veins offset from one another by fractures containing no or limited amounts of ore. Another east–west vein lies a little more than 2 km to the north at Cornelly mine. Also a short north–south vein was worked at Bell Hole mine to the north of Foxdale village[23].

Old Foxdale mine was sunk in the village around 1724 into the Foxdale Granite although the mine extended east and west into the Manx Group. The mine was worked from two main shafts, Bawden's and Beckwith's, with Pott's Shaft further east (Figure 10.4). Workings reached a total depth of *circa* 650 m below surface before closure in 1911. The vein was up to 3 m wide, but in places closed to a few millimetres. Two parallel veins branch off from the main vein near Beckwith's shaft in a direction of 155° inclined to the southwest. The ore was almost exclusively galena, locally argentiferous (alleged to yield 350 ounces of silver to a ton of lead). Some

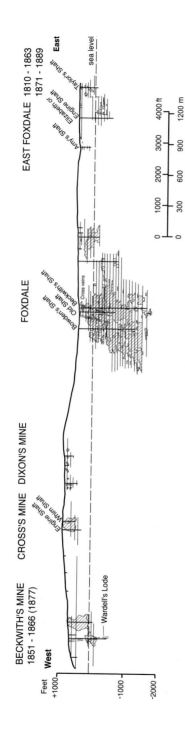

Figure 10.3 *Section through the Foxdale–Glen Rushen mines. Worked areas are shown with diagonal hatching.*

Figure 10.4 (opposite) *Section through the Foxdale mine. Worked areas are shown with diagonal hatching.*

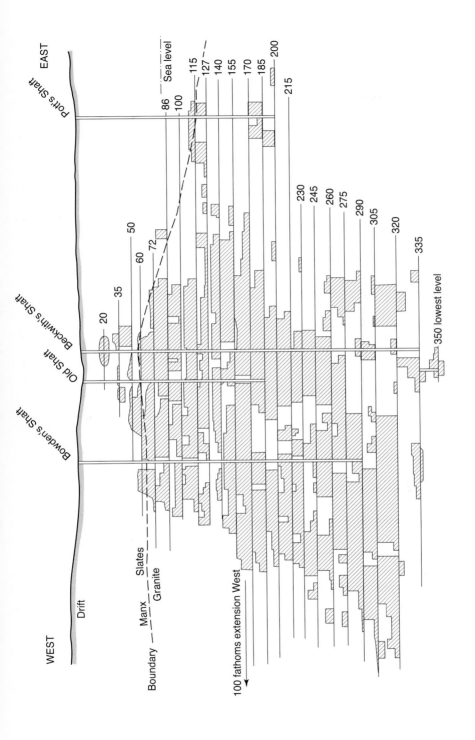

antimony minerals were recorded, but it is not clear whether these were separated for sale. The non-ore mineral was mostly quartz but minor amounts of carbonates such as calcite can be found on the waste-heaps.

The East Foxdale mines worked a group of east–west veins around Ellerslie separated from the Foxdale vein by a distance of approximately 1 km. Here the ore was mainly galena. Similar to the East Foxdale mines, the Glen Rushen mines lie on the same trend as the main Foxdale vein, but are separated by a gap of about 1 km of unworked ground on the north-east slopes of South Barrule. Cross's and Dixon's mines formed part of the Glen Rushen mines and were worked in the 1830s. Neither went deeper than about 100 m and production was limited. Beckwith's mine, about 0.5 km further west, was more productive. Although the vein at Beckwith's mine is aligned with the Foxdale vein, it splits into a west-southwest to east-northeast branch and a west-northwest to east-southeast branch, both inclined to the south. The workings are reputed to have penetrated the granite at depth. There were shafts on both branches and an adit from Glen Rushen served to pump out water. The main vein is crossed by the north–south Wardell's vein, which dips steeply east. Beckwith's mine was in production from 1837 to 1866 and the ore was almost entirely galena. The main vein was up to 6 m wide with highly variable ore content. A barren east–west vein composed of only quartz lies to the north of the main vein. The shaft on the west-southwest to east-northeast branch went to a depth of 333 m, about 100 m below sea level, and therefore required elaborate pumping arrangements. Remains of these and dressing floors with wooden buddles for concentrating the ore survive at the mine site. Despite the good rock exposure provided by several old slate quarries on the west side of Glen Rushen, no westward extension of the vein has been found. However, a trial on the same trend in Niarbyl Bay is said to have yielded some antimony ore.

Cornelly mine worked from 1845 to 1884, and is located about 2 km northeast of Foxdale on the margin of Archallagan Plantation. The ore was mainly galena with a little sphalerite and the non-ore mineral was chiefly quartz. The host rock is micaceous slate. At a depth of around 100 m the mine entered granite where the vein was followed to a final depth of about 250 m. Workings were concentrated in the northern of two parallel east–west veins, with the inclination of the vein changing from south near the surface to north at depth. Steeply curved fractures such as this are typical of strike-slip faults that have later become mineralised[24].

Separate production figures for East Foxdale, Cross's, Beckwith's and Cornelly mines are not available as their yields were amalgamated with those from the Foxdale mines. The total from 1845 to 1911 was recorded as approximately 180,000 tons of lead concentrates, probably equating with more than a million tons of ore and waste, broadly comparable to the production from Laxey mine. Apparently zinc and copper were not separated at Foxdale and probably only occurred in minor quantities.

Bradda mines

The vein at Bradda lies northwest of Port Erin, crossing the headland in a north–south direction. Archaeological relics suggest copper was worked here as early as the Bronze Age. Historical records cover mining from 1656 to 1874. Various adits and shafts penetrate the cliff face north of the headland. Spittal's shaft was sunk from the hilltop whilst South Bradda shaft began at the beach below the southern cliff (Figure 10.5). Workings were carried to a depth of around 120 m below sea level with pumping required

Figure 10.5 *South Bradda shaft and vein. The vein is the dark fissure running up the cliff to the right of the tower.*

Figure 10.6 *Mineralised breccia composed of broken pieces of Manx Group (grey) cemented by quartz (white) in the wall of Bradda vein at South Bradda shaft.*

to prevent flooding. The Bradda vein occurs in two parts where it is observed in the southern cliff – a quartz-filled fracture with little visible ore, adjacent to a broken mass (breccia) of slate, quartz and ore (Figure 10.6). Underground these form a vein up to 20 m wide surrounded by deformed slates and quartz veins. Production figures are incomplete but a yield of 817 tons of copper concentrates and 2,000 tons of lead concentrates has been deduced.

Ballacorkish mines

Lying in the south of the island, two mines at Ballacorkish worked intermittently in the eighteenth and nineteenth centuries and closed in 1894. The veins trend north-northwest to south-southeast and dip steeply to the west in the Maughold Formation. The veins appear to follow a Tertiary dyke, although it is likely that the dyke (65–60 million years old) is younger than the veins. The veins were each about 2 m wide and lead, zinc and copper ores were produced. Yields of 3,693 tons of lead ore, 2,869 tons zinc ore and 138 tons of copper ore were recorded from 1854 to 1894.

Other mines

Few records survive of the numerous small mines and trials on the Isle of Man. Notes are included in Lamplugh's memoir[25] and there is a list in Mackay and Schnellmann's unpublished report[26]. Some of the more important trials were at Glen Chass near Port St Mary, on the Langness peninsula, in Baldwin Glen, at Ballaglass, at Kerrowmooar near Sulby, in Glen Auldyn and at Cornaa. Adits have also been driven for minor quantities of lead and iron ore on Douglas Head and at Onchan where traces of gold were produced[27].

Several small mines were worked for iron ore around Maughold Head[28]. The iron occurred in the form of earthy hematite in quartz and carbonate minerals and may represent a phase of mineralisation separate to the vein deposits on the island[29], bearing similarities to the iron ore deposits on the margins of the Lake District. There are adits and shafts on both sides of the headland, the most accessible being at Port Mooar. Up to 200 tons per annum of ochre and umber were produced from 1854 to 1883.

In a search for possible new ore deposits, the modern techniques of stream sediment and soil sampling for chemical analysis were tried in the 1950s together with a limited number of boreholes[30]. However, the chemical data were difficult to interpret because of contamination from waste material and exploration activity soon ceased.

MECHANISMS OF MINERALISATION

The processes by which metalliferous ores are emplaced in fractures in sedimentary rocks are complex. Broadly, the mineral veins in the Isle of Man fall within the category of hydrothermal deposits, that is, they crystallised from hot, water-based fluids. Since the veins cut straight through deformed Manx Group strata and through the Foxdale Granite, they must be younger than early Devonian. Analysis of radioactive isotopes is equivocal but may point to a Carboniferous age – a time of widespread mineralisation in northwest Europe.

The source of the metals may have been the Manx Group sediments themselves. Clay minerals in particular carry small traces of metals and these are released into solution when the chemistry of the minerals changes, for example, due to burial or, as is more likely in metamorphosed rocks such as the Manx Group, because of interaction with hydrothermal fluids. Together with their high temperature, the fluids themselves are usually strongly saline, allowing higher concentrations of metals, sulphur and silica to be dissolved than would be the case with fresh water. The temperature of hydrothermal fluids is typically 100–300 °C, similar to the temperature of rocks at 3–10 km below surface, depths to which the Manx Group was buried in the Lower Palaeozoic. Such fluids do not boil because of the effects of high pressure caused by the overlying rocks. They do, however, move preferentially towards areas of lower pressure such as fissures. Over time a circulation system is likely to develop within the fissures due to changes in the density of the fluids as they cool down or heat up. Variations in temperature and the chemistry of the rocks and other co-mingling fluids can lead to changes in the solubility of dissolved elements such that minerals like lead sulphide (galena), zinc sulphide (sphalerite), copper iron sulphide (chalcopyrite) and silica (quartz) crystallise on the walls of the fissures.

The Carboniferous (354–292 Ma) is known to be a period of tectonic upheaval and high heat flow throughout northwest Europe with active faults and volcanic eruptions affecting the land surface and extensional stresses causing fissures to develop within the sub-surface. Similar conditions exist today in the East African rift valley and in such settings hydrothermal fluids escape to the surface to form hot springs. Large lead, zinc and silver ore deposits were formed in Lower Carboniferous limestones and mudstones in Ireland at this time and it is possible that these are underlain by vein deposits in older rocks similar to the Isle of Man. Significant amounts of metalliferous minerals may also have been deposited in the Castletown Limestones, but have since been removed by erosion. Minor amounts of mineralisation do occur in the conglomerate at Langness (Figure 10.7a) and in hydrothermally altered limestone near Ronaldsway and Strandhall (Figure 10.7b) supporting this idea. The origin of the uranium-bearing thucolite in the Laxey vein (see below) may also be from Carboniferous sediment that once overlay the area. A model of the processes that probably led to mineralisation in the Isle of Man is shown in Figure 10.8.

MISCELLANEOUS MINERALS

In addition to lead, zinc and copper, the Manx and Dalby Groups yield a number of other metalliferous minerals, none of which, however, has had, or is likely to have, economic importance. They include antimony, found in a small but unworkable pocket at Niarbyl Bay; traces of vein gold in Sulby Glen, Onchan and Maughold[31]; free gold from slate at Langness[32]; small quantities of molybdenite as a coating on joints in the Dhoon granodiorite[33] and traces of millerite (nickel iron sulphide) in the Rhennas area[34]. The high uranium content of locally abundant solid hydrocarbons, known as thucholite, in veins at Laxey and Snaefell attracted attention in

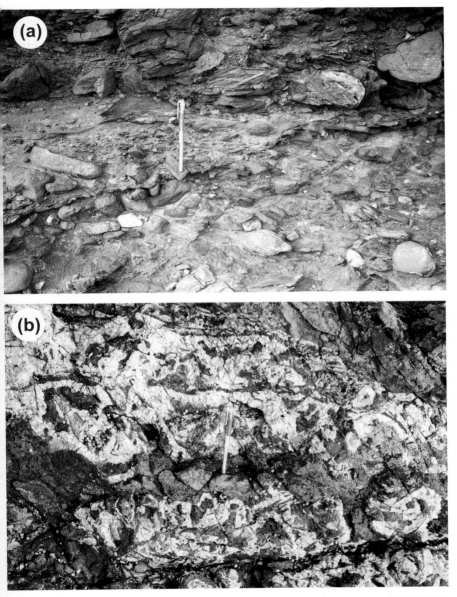

Figure 10.7 *(a) Veinlet at the base of the Langness Conglomerate at SC283652, running horizontally across the photograph at the level of the top of the pen. It is 2.4 mm wide and consists of pyrite, chalcopyrite and galena. (b) Mineralised breccia composed of dolomitised limestone (grey) cemented by quartz (white) exposed at Strandhall (SC239683). A pen is shown for scale.*

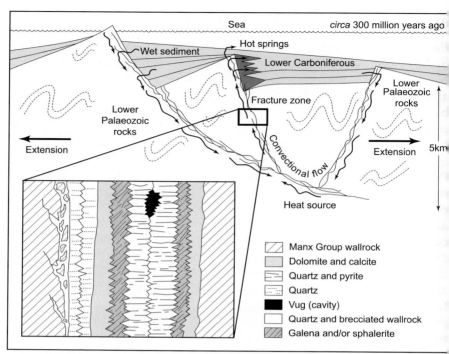

Figure 10.8 *Schematic cross-section illustrating the sort of geological processes that may have caused mineralisation in the Isle of Man and Ireland during the Carboniferous. An inset shows the appearance of a typical mineral vein where crystals have grown on the walls of a widening fissure.*

the 1950s[35], but no commercially workable deposits were found.

Amongst the non-metalliferous minerals Lamplugh[36] noted the working of asbestos for the manufacture of polishing powder from veins in the Dhoon granodiorite and the localised occurrence of graphite, both within graphitic slates and metalliferous veins at Beary[37]. Dawson[38] reported the presence of significant amounts of beryl in two pegmatite veins associated with the Foxdale granite and Lamplugh[39] commented on the working of vein quartz for ornamental rock at Foxdale and Kerrowgarroo, near St Johns. At the time of Lamplugh's survey[40], ferruginous deposits of ochre and umber (impure iron and manganese oxides), used as yellow and brown pigments, were locally extracted at Bradda and Ballacorkish mines, from decomposed and dolomitised Carboniferous Limestone at Ballasalla and weathered dolerite dykes at Maughold Head. Lamplugh[41] also referred to the use of glacial clay at Glen Wyllin as a fulling agent, probably the calcareous *Chara* marl currently exposed in the floor of kettle basins at this locality.

BULK AND INDUSTRIAL MINERALS

Building stone   Although most of the island's rocks have been used for building at some time, good quality building stone is rare and most modern building uses imported or locally manufactured blocks. Flaggy sandstones and blocks of laminated mudstone and siltstones from the Manx Group have been widely used for domestic buildings where it occurs at surface, especially in Douglas, Port Erin and Port St Mary, as well as in most farm buildings and the walls of fields. The Peel Sandstone Group was formerly quarried at Creg Malin, northeast of Peel, and used in the construction of Peel Castle and other buildings around the town. However it has poor resistance to weathering. The Carboniferous Limestone, used both as rough and dressed blocks, was used in the construction of Castle Rushen and many houses and public buildings in the vicinity of Castletown. Dark, organic-rich limestone exposed east of Poyllvaaish is still worked as an ornamental stone, marketed as a 'black marble', and has been used for chimney-pieces, mantel-pieces and tombstones. The granitic rocks have also been quarried for building stone, as well as paving setts and formerly for agricultural rollers. Granite is quarried today at Stoney Mountain to provide crushed aggregate, ornamental building stone and rock-armour for sea defences. Rotten granite was worked in the 1960s where it was crushed and washed to separate mica (for roofing felt) and feldspar (for use in the Potteries). In the north of the island, where no solid rock crops out, large erratic blocks from the glacial drift deposits have been utilised as building stone and may be seen in the walls of many of the older thatched cottages.

Bricks   Despite having to import coal for the kilns, bricks have been made intermittently on the island since the late seventeenth century[42]. Most of the clay used was glacial in origin, extracted from areas such as the northern plain and the Neb river valley[43]. An exception to this was the Glenfaba brickworks close to Peel where crushed mudstone from the Dalby Group was used.

Roadstone   Crushed rock aggregate, used for building foundations and roadstone, is currently worked from a variety of sources including sandstones from the Manx Group at Dreemskerry, granite from Stoney Mountain and Dhoon, dolerite from Poortown (near Peel) and Carboniferous Limestone from Turkeyland and Billown.

Slate   Although informally known as the 'Manx Slates', the Manx Group yield little good-quality roofing slate because it is difficult to split thinly as most of the thick mudstone intervals have more than one simple, flat cleavage. The Barrule and Glen Rushen Formations within the Manx Group have provided the main source of slate but competition from the better quality Cambrian slates of North Wales in the nineteenth century and manufactured roofing tiles in the twentieth century diminished the market for Manx Slate. Some slate is worked today for building stone and hardcore around South Barrule and Maughold.

Limestone   Limestone has been extensively used in the island, both as a building stone, for example in Castle Rushen, and to produce agricultural lime. The majority of limestone has been quarried from the Carboniferous Limestone of the Castletown area, but Lamplugh[44] noted the use of erratic boulders of limestone from the north of the island and calcrete layers in the Peel Sandstone Group at The Stack for agricultural use. Limestone working is now restricted to quarries at Turkeyland and Billown, both of which produce agricultural lime and aggregate, but little building stone.

Salt   Triassic rocks buried beneath the northern plain contain layers of salt (halite) originally deposited from playa lakes when the Isle of Man lay in a desert environment. Brine from these beds was extracted through boreholes at the Point of Ayre in the late nineteenth century and sent by pipeline along the foreshore to an evaporation plant in Ramsey. Production was short-lived as the pipeline was destroyed by storms[45].

Sand and gravel   The extensive glacial deposits of the island, especially in the north, provide local sources of sand and gravel for use in building and as aggregate. Extraction is small-scale, sufficient to meet island demand, and includes sand and gravel from the Holocene raised beach deposits at the Point of Ayre (now partly used for disposal of rubbish), Holocene dune sand from Ballagarraghyn, near Jurby, and sand from two small glacial deltas near Peel (Lhergydhoo and Ballaharra).

Coal   Exploration for coal on the Isle of Man dates back to at least 1699 when the then Lord of Mann, Charles, 8th Earl of Derby, initiated an unsuccessful search for workable deposits. At the end of the nineteenth century a number of boreholes[46] were drilled through the drift plain of the north in an attempt to find an extension of the Whitehaven coalfield to the east in Cumbria. Although similar rock successions were found in the Carboniferous sequences no workable coal was found. At the end of the twentieth century further boreholes at Shellag Point also failed to find coal[47]. However, exploration for oil and gas to the east of the Isle of Man has proven that coal exists where Upper Carboniferous (Westphalian) sediments are preserved[48].

OIL AND GAS

Origin

In the East Irish Sea oil and gas originates from the Holywell Shale, a dark, organic-rich mudstone ('source rock') of Upper Carboniferous (Namurian) age[49]. This contains kerogen, the fossilised remains of planktonic material such as algae. If kerogen is heated to temperatures of 85 °C or more for a long period of time, typically as a result of burial to around 3 km, it slowly cooks to produce oil. At higher temperatures and greater depths of burial gas rather than oil is formed. If enough hydrocarbons are generated within the source rock, the oil or gas may become mobile and rise into overlying permeable beds such as sandstone. Up to 35% of sandstone by volume may comprise pore space between grains. In the sub-surface, these pores are generally saturated with water. However, if hydrocarbons flow into the sandstone, they tend to displace the water. As these are less dense than water they will rise to the highest part of the layer of sandstone where they can become trapped. In the case of the East Irish Sea, oil began to flow from the underlying Holywell Shale into the Sherwood Sandstone of Triassic age during the early Jurassic, with gas flowing later in the Cretaceous[50]. The formation of hydrocarbons stopped when uplift and erosion occurred in the early Tertiary as this had the effect of cooling the source rock, equivalent to switching off the 'cooker'.

Ultimately oil and gas will escape to surface unless a barrier in the subsurface traps it. Such a barrier is generally an impermeable layer known as a seal. The Triassic Mercia Mudstone directly overlying the Sherwood Sandstone provides the seal in the East Irish Sea (Figure 10.9). Hydrocarbons, mainly gas, have therefore been trapped in the highest parts of the Sherwood Sandstone, in an interval known as the Ormskirk Sandstone Formation. The Ormskirk Sandstone is the reservoir for all the commercial fields in the East Irish Sea and is fortunately more porous and permeable than the underlying St Bees Sandstone Formation, which makes up the majority of the Sherwood Sandstone. The best reservoir consists of very round grains of sand originally deposited by wind as sand dunes in a desert environment. The relatively large amount of pore space and the high permeability of the Ormskirk Sandstone Formation allow large quantities of gas to be extracted relatively quickly from boreholes used to develop the fields.

The traps for oil and gas in the East Irish Sea comprise up-faulted and tilted blocks bounded by north–south and east–west faults (Figure 10.9) of late Jurassic and, possibly, early Tertiary age. These highs in the subsurface are identified using reflection seismic data. These data are

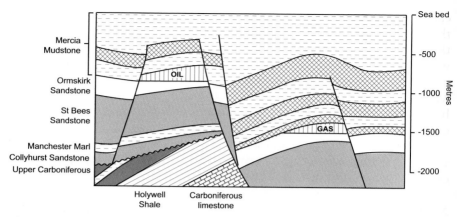

Figure 10.9 *Idealised cross-section illustrating how oil and gas is trapped in sandstone reservoirs in the East Irish Sea Basin. The source of the hydrocarbons is the organic-rich Holywell Shale. From there, oil and gas have migrated upwards due to buoyancy through water-bearing Permian-Triassic sandstones until reaching the impermeable Mercia Mudstone which forms the seal. The hydrocarbons collect in the highest parts of the Ormskirk Sandstone bounded by north-south and east-west normal faults.*

essentially echo soundings of the sub-surface, with measurements taken of the strength of the signal and the time it takes for sound energy to travel down, reflect off a rock layer and travel back to surface. Although the technique is nowadays highly advanced, it is still difficult to get an accurate image of the sub-surface with seismic data, as the signal is very weak. Even where a potential trap is identified using seismic data, its true depth is not known directly and has to be calculated from assumptions made on the speed that sound travels through rocks. Also some of the highs contain no hydrocarbons, either because the source rock has not been buried deep enough or because the high was formed after the oil and gas had already flowed through the system or because the seal was slightly permeable, allowing hydrocarbons to escape slowly to the seabed during the Tertiary.

Exploration history

Exploration for hydrocarbons in Manx territorial waters was encouraged by the discovery and successful exploitation of commercial oil and gas fields in the East Irish Sea[51]. The giant Morecambe Bay gas field, 50 km southeast of the Isle of Man, was identified in 1974 by British Gas and came on stream in 1985. Volumetrically it is the second largest gas find on the UK continental shelf, providing 12% of UK proven reserves. One of the satellite fields, the Millom field, lies just outside Manx territorial waters, 20 km east of the island. These fields lie at the northern end of a prolific area of oil and gas production, stretching from offshore Morecambe Bay to Liverpool Bay. Within the basin 16 commercial fields have been discovered to date with reserves prior to production of 8 trillion cubic feet of gas and 200 million barrels of oil.

The first hydrocarbon discovery close to the Isle of Man was in 1982 when BP drilled well 112/25–1, offshore of Maughold. Unfortunately, the company were unable to get the gas to flow to the surface and the well was sealed off as an intriguing but disappointing failure. In 1992, the Isle of Man Government extended its territorial waters to 12 miles, including the area where 112/25–1 was drilled. A Manx exploration round soon followed where oil companies were allowed to apply for licences to search for hydrocarbons. Consequently, in 1996 two boreholes were drilled within sight of the Manx coast, one by Elf and partners (well 112/19–1), a short distance northeast of the Point of Ayre, and the other by Marathon (well 112/29–1), east of Douglas. Neither well encountered hydrocarbons and, although they originally planned to drill another two boreholes, Elf were let off their remaining commitments by the Manx Government having demonstrated that the chance of finding a commercial field was now minimal due to the fact that the Holywell Shale was absent, having been eroded during late Carboniferous to early Permian times[52]. Two other boreholes (111/25–1 and 111/29–1) were drilled by Elf in 1994 and 1996 in the UK part of the Peel Basin, west of the Isle of Man, and Esso drilled well 112/15–1 in the UK part of the Solway Firth. No hydrocarbon accumulation was encountered in any of these wells.

Future potential

Although no commercial finds have so far been discovered within Manx territorial waters, it should be noted that, even in areas where hydrocarbons are known to occur, the majority of boreholes fail to find any oil or gas. For example, in the East Irish Sea basin, 63 exploration wells have been drilled, of which 18 have discovered gas, four oil and one oil with gas. Of the 23 discoveries, only 70% have been large enough to support the cost of developing a field. In other words, 47 exploration wells (three out of four) have been commercial failures. With a typical exploration well in the Irish Sea costing many millions of pounds it might seem that hydrocarbon exploration is an expensive form of gambling. However, a commercial oil or gas field is often worth hundreds of millions of pounds so that the value of the one in four successes generally far outweighs the cost of the failures. Assuming that the geological and geophysical work is good and provided a company is prepared to drill enough times to beat the statistical chance of bad luck, exploration can prove to be a good investment.

Oil companies are allowed to explore once the Government has granted them a licence. These licences are divided into blocks with a full block defined as a rectangular area covering 10° of latitude by 12° of longitude, equivalent to approximately 250 km². Several blocks in the UK part of the East Irish Sea basin have never been licensed, particularly in the north. Here there is a risk that the porosity and permeability of the reservoir are poorer than elsewhere in the basin, but the chance of discovering at least one commercial gas field is still high. Until recently, environmental concerns in the Liverpool Bay area led the UK Government to discourage exploration for oil, but the search for gas continues, particularly in the northern part of the East Irish Sea. Potential for oil also exists in older sandstones in the Carboniferous on the margins of the East Irish Sea[53].

SUMMARY

Geological resources have played an important role in the industrial history of the Isle of Man, particularly the mining of veins containing lead, zinc and copper sulphides. Nowadays, Manx rocks can be seen throughout the island in buildings, walls, roads, paths and even Viking crosses. Although it is unlikely that commercial oil or gas will be found within Manx territorial waters, new fields are likely to be found in the future to the east of the island in the UK part of the Irish Sea.

Notes

1   T.D. Ford, D.J. Burnett and D.G. Quirk, *The geology of the Isle of Man*, Geologists' Association Guide, 46 (2001).
2   T.D. Ford, *The Isle of Man*, Geologists' Association Guide, 46 (1993).
3   W.W. Smyth, 'List of minerals found in the Isle of Man', *Transactions of the Isle of Man Natural History and Antiquarian Society*, 1 (1888), 143–147.
4   G.W. Lamplugh, *The geology of the Isle of Man*, Memoir of the Geological Survey of England and Wales (1903), 606.
5   R.G. Carruthers and A. Strahan, 'Notes on lead and zinc mining in the Isle of Man' in *Lead and Zinc Ores of Durham, Yorkshire, Derbyshire and the Isle of Man*, Geological Survey Special Report on Mineral Resources, 26 (1923), 89–91.
6   H. Dewey and T. Eastwood, 'Copper ores of the Midlands, Wales, the Lake District and the Isle of Man', *Geological Survey Special Report on Mineral Resources*, 30 (1925), 78–87.
7   R.H. Skelton, 'The Manx mines', *Mining Magazine*, 92 (1955), 9–18.

8   A. Pearce and G.M. Rose, 'Mining in the Isle of Man', *Bulletin of the Peak District Mines Historical Society*, 7 (1979), 216–230.

9   R. Von Arx, 'East Snaefell Mine', *British Mining*, 50 (1994), 158–160; R. Von Arx, 'A glimpse of Snaefell Mine', *British Mining*, 57 (1996), 34–46; R. Von Arx, 'Kirk Michael Mine in the Isle of Man', *British Mining*, 61 (1998), 74–90.

10   M. Dobson and D.B. Hollis, 'Lead mines and trials in Glen Auldyn, Isle of Man', *Bulletin of the Peak District Mines Historical Society*, 12 (1993), 31–37.

11   D. Warriner and A. Gilling, 'Exploration and survey of the Great Laxey Mine, Isle of Man', *Bulletin of the Peak District Mines Historical Society*, 8 (1983), 373–381.

12   W.H. Wilson, *Exploration for mineral deposits in the Isle of Man*, unpublished report, Island Exploration Co. Ltd. (1957).

13   L. Mackay and G.A. Schnellmann, *The Mine and Minerals of the Isle of Man*, submitted to the Industrial Officer for the Government of the Isle of Man, Isle of Man Government (1963).

14   D.B. Hollis, 'Uranium in the Isle of Man', *British Mining*, 34 (1987a), 44–45; D.B. Hollis, 'The forgotten iron mines of Kirk Maughold, Isle of Man', *British Mining*, 34 (1987b), 46–54; D.B. Hollis, 'The Kirk Maughold iron mines, Isle of Man', *British Mining*, 37 (1988), 4–15; D.B. Hollis, 'The search for iron, lead and gold in Douglas Bay, Isle of Man: old mining trials and new insight into the geology', *Bulletin of the Peak District Mines Historical Society*, 10 (1989a), 291–304.

15   T.D. Ford et al. (2001).

16   T.D. Ford, 'The Geology of the Laxey Vein, Isle of Man', *Mercian Geologist*, 14 (1998), 125–134.

17   R.A Chadwick, D.I. Jackson, R.P. Barnes, G.S. Kimbell, H. Johnson, R.C. Chiverrell, G.S.P.Thomas, N.S. Jones, N.J. Riley, E.A. Pickett, B. Young, D.W. Holliday, D.F. Ball, S.G. Molyneux, D. Long, G.M. Power and D.H. Roberts, *Geology of the Isle of Man and its offshore area*, British Geological Survey Research Report, RR/01/06, Keyworth, Nottingham (2001), 143.

18   D.G. Quirk, D.J. Burnett, G.S. Kimbell, C.A. Murphy and J.S. Varley, 'Shallow geophysical and geological evidence for a regional-scale fault duplex in the Lower Palaeozoic of the Isle of Man', in N.H. Woodcock, D.G. Quirk, W.F. Fitches and R.P. Barnes (eds), *In sight of the suture: the Palaeozoic geology of the Isle of Man in its Iapetus Ocean context*, Geological Society of London Special Publication, 160 (1999a), 239–257.

19   The opposing wall of the fault has moved to the right relative to the near wall.

20   The opposing wall of the fault has moved to the left relative to the near wall.

21   D.G. Quirk and G.S. Kimbell, 'Structural evolution of the Isle of Man and central part of the Irish Sea', in N.S. Meadows, S.P. Trueblood, N. Hardman and G. Cowan (eds), *Petroleum geology of the Irish Sea and adjacent areas*, Geological Society of London Special Publication, 124 (1997), 135–159.

22   D.G. Quirk and D.J. Burnett, 'Lithofacies of Lower Palaeozoic deep-marine sediments in the Isle of Man: a new map and stratigraphic model of the Manx Group', in N.H. Woodcock, D.G. Quirk, W.F. Fitches and R.P. Barnes (eds), *In sight of the suture: the Palaeozoic geology of the Isle of Man in its Iapetus Ocean context*, Geological Society of London Special Publication, 160 (1999), 69–88.

23   D.B. Hollis, 'Bell Hole – the history and geology of a small lead mine near Foxdale, Isle of Man', *Bulletin of the Peak District Mines Historical Society*, 10 (1989b), 291–304.

24   T.D. Ford and D.G. Quirk, 'Mineralization of the South Pennines', *Geology*

Today, 11 (1995), 177–182.

25   G.W. Lamplugh (1903).
26   L. Mackay and G.A. Schnellmann (1963).
27   D.B. Hollis (1989a).
28   *Ibid.*
29   D.G. Quirk and G.S. Kimbell (1997).
30   L. Mackay and G.A. Schnellmann (1963).
31   D.B. Hollis (1989b).
32   G.W. Lamplugh (1903), 549.
33   *Ibid.*, 550.
34   *Ibid.*, 547; W.W. Smyth (1888).
35   C.F. Davison and S.H.U. Bowie, 'Thucolite-pitchblende, hydrocarbon and moisture – at Laxey lead mine', *Bulletin of the Geological Society of Great Britain*, 3 (1951), 4; D.B. Hollis (1987a).
36   G.W. Lamplugh (1903), 556.
37   R.P. Greg and W.G. Lettsom, *Manual of the mineralogy of Great Britain and Ireland*, John Van Voorst, London (1977).
38   J. Dawson, 'Beryllium in the Foxdale Granite, Isle of Man', *Bulletin of the Geological Survey of Great Britain*, 25 (1966), 55–58.
39   G.W. Lamplugh (1903), 557.
40   C.F. Davison and S.H.U. Bowie (1951).
41   G.W. Lamplugh (1903), 556.
42   L.S. Garrad, T.A. Bawden, J.K. Qualtrough and W.J. Scatchard, *The Industrial Archaeology of the Isle of Man*, David and Charles, Newton Abbot (1972).
43   G.W. Lamplugh (1903), 557.
44   G.W. Lamplugh (1903), 653.
45   T.D. Ford (1993).
46   G.W. Lamplugh (1903); B. Smith, 'Borings through the glacial drifts in the northern part of the Isle of Man', *Summary of Progress of the Geological Survey*, 3 (1931), 14–23.
47   R.A Chadwick *et al.* (2001).
48   D.G. Quirk and G.S. Kimbell (1997).
49   P.J. Newman, 'The geology and hydrocarbon habitat of the Peel and Solway Basins', *Journal of Petroleum Geology*, 22 (1999a), 265–284; P.J. Newman, 'The geology and hydrocarbon potential of the Peel and Solway Basins, East Irish Sea', *Journal of Petroleum Geology*, 22 (1999b), 305–324; J.P. Armstrong, J. Smith, V.A.A. D'Elia and S.P. Trueblood, 'The occurrence and correlation of oils and Namurian source rocks in the Liverpool Bay–North Wales area', in N.S. Meadows, S.P. Trueblood, N. Hardman and G. Cowan (eds), *Petroleum Geology of the Irish Sea and adjacent areas*, Geological Society of London Special Publication, 124 (1997), 195–211.
50   G. Cowan, S. Burley, N. Hoey, P. Holloway, P. Bermingham, N. Beveridge, M. Hamborg and Ø. Sylta, 'Oil and gas migration in the Sherwood sandstone of the East Irish Sea Basin', in A.J. Fleet and S.A.R. Boldy (eds), *Petroleum Geology of northwest Europe: Proceedings of the 5th Conference* (1999), 1383–1398.
51   D.G. Quirk, S. Roy, I. Knott, J. Redfern and L. Hill, 'Petroleum geology and future hydrocarbon potential of the Irish Sea', *Journal of Petroleum Geology*, 22 (1999b), 243–260.
52   *Ibid.*
53   D.G. Quirk and G.S. Kimbell (1997).

11 Contemporary Environment

PHILIPPA TOMLINSON, KATE HAWKINS,
LARCH GARRAD, ELIZABETH CHARTER,
STELLA THROWER, ED POOLEY, PAT CULLEN and
CHRIS SHARPE

The natural factors that have shaped the Manx landscape over the past millennia have been described in the foregoing chapters. Here, before moving on to discuss the impact of human activity on the landscape in prehistory[1], the contemporary natural environment and ecology will be briefly described. An introduction to the history of biological recording, research and conservation on the island is followed by an examination of the present-day land use and descriptions of the surviving areas of semi-natural vegetation. Even though virtually the entire landscape of the island has been affected by human activity from early prehistoric times and some of the more biodiverse and interesting habitats are a direct result of use of the land for agriculture or other activities, the remaining areas of semi-natural habitat are one of the island's most valuable assets, not only in terms of biodiversity, but also as part of its varied landscape. Finally, the plants and animals themselves are discussed with special reference to particularly well-studied groups, to the effects of insularity and to recent research. It is not intended to provide a detailed description of the island's natural history and reference is given to relevant published works where appropriate. The concluding paragraphs examine areas where future conservation and research are most needed.

RECORDING AND CONSERVING THE NATURAL ENVIRONMENT PHILIPPA TOMLINSON, KATE HAWKINS, ELIZABETH CHARTER and LARCH GARRAD

History of recording and research

The main early influences on the study of Manx natural history have been the Isle of Man Natural History and Antiquarian Society, founded in 1879, the Manx Museum[2], which had its beginnings in an Act of Tynwald in 1886[3] and the Marine Laboratory at Port Erin, which started publishing reports in 1892. Edward Forbes, one of the first to study the marine ecology with a monograph on Manx molluscs in 1838[4], made a major contribution to knowledge of the Manx flora. Sir William Herdman, who in 1885 formed the Liverpool Marine Biological Committee in order to study the Irish Sea, realising that the waters off the Isle of Man were the cleanest and biologically richest he had ever seen, transferred the Marine Laboratory, initially established in North Wales, to Port Erin. The success of the two original custom-built laboratories on Port Erin Bay encouraged sponsorship from the Isle of Man Government for a new, much larger laboratory built in 1902 on the south side of the bay. This was the kernel of Liverpool University's Marine Biological Station, which since 1919 has developed into one of the most successful research departments carrying out pioneering studies of the Irish Sea, the local fishing industry and effects of industrial activities. *Marine Fauna of the Isle of Man* first published in 1937 and revised in 1963 still provides the definitive species list for the island's coasts and neighbouring waters[5].

P.M.C. Kermode, the polymath founder, outstanding Manx scholar and first curator of the Manx Museum, did much to foster the study of natural history, and from the start he worked with William Herdman on many projects. Even before the Museum was provided with a permanent home in the former Noble's Hospital in 1922 he had begun to build up collections of such things as moths, butterflies and mounted birds, and had started to publish his findings[6]. He formalised a system for collecting bird records under which recording forms and stamped, addressed envelopes were sent annually to all the Manx lighthouses and other people who expressed an interest. In the 1930s an active Field Club evolved and the Museum acquired an Assistant, Kenneth Williamson, who went on to do superb work with the British Trust for Ornithology. With the aid of Field Club members, especially W.S. Cowin, he created an index of all accessible published records of the Manx fauna and also set out to collect new voucher specimens of Manx insects. The Field Club was later amalgamated with the Natural History and Antiquarian Society and then lapsed completely although the Bird Club, later Manx Ornithological Society, continued to flourish. During the 1960s, the Manx Museum made considerable input into the various mapping schemes run from the Nature Conservancy's already computerised mapping centre at Monks Wood. Among the groups covered were bats, spiders, grasshoppers, woodlice, ants, bees and wasps, non-marine molluscs, reptiles and amphibians.

Larch Garrad, Assistant Keeper in the Manx Museum from 1964 to 1996, brought together all the available information in her 1972 publication *The Naturalist in the Isle of Man*[7], which provided a detailed and thorough description of the flora, fauna and habitats of the island and remains the only volume of its kind.

Botanical recording

The history of botanical recording on the island, described in detail by Allen[8] shows that it started remarkably early with notables such as J. Ray, W. Wilson, H.C. Watson and E. Forbes. In more recent times, an intensification of fieldwork carried out during the 1950–70s, including excursions from the Botanical Society of the British Isles and annual visits by David Allen, combined with regular fieldwork by residents Larch Garrad and Marjorie Devereau, culminated in publication of *Flora of the Isle of Man* in 1984, and also ensured Man was well represented in the *Atlas of the British Flora*, published in 1962 and in the *New Atlas* project in 2000[9].

Bird recording

Despite various early sightings on the island[10], P.M.C. Kermode published the first list in 1880[11]. F. Craine started bird ringing in 1926 while K. Williamson with W.S. Cowin helped to establish the Manx Field Club and, in 1941 the journal *Peregrine (Yn Shirragh ny Ree)*. In 1959 it was Williamson's idea to set up the Calf Bird Observatory[12], which has continued[13] as an important bird ringing station linked to the British Trust for Ornithology ever since. Perhaps not surprisingly, more books have been published on Manx birds than any other group, the most significant being *Birds of the Isle of Man*[14]. The Manx Bird Atlas was established in 1997 to carry out a detailed survey on the status of bird life and to establish the distribution, abundance and population of each species over a five-year field study. A new methodology for bird recording, which is likely to become a standard for future atlas research elsewhere, has been developed. The outcome of this research, the most comprehensive of its kind yet undertaken, will be a breeding bird survey and a winter bird atlas. The detailed level of recording, to 100 m squares, has also opened up the possibility of research based on spatial modelling and habitat mapping techniques.

Conservation and land management

The Manx Museum has played a major role in the conservation of the landscape, particularly since it became responsible for the National Trust lands in 1951[15]. More than 800 hectares of land are in the care of the Trust (Figure 11.1), including the low intensity farmland at Cregneash, coastal heath and tall cliffs of the Meayll Peninsula, Spanish Head and Marine Drive, the Calf of Man with its Bird Observatory, parts of the coastal dune system at the Ayres, and the extensive wetland of the Ballaugh Curraghs[16].

Today, with a greater understanding for the need for wildlife conservation, National Trust lands are managed and monitored by a countryside warden, together with two wardens on the Calf of Man whose records are published in the *Calf of Man Annual Reports*. Long-term conservation management is guided by detailed plans, which have been prepared for the Calf, Ballaugh Curraghs and Maughold Head[17]. The discovery of nesting Manx Shearwater (*Puffinus puffinus*) on the Calf, proved in partnership with the Manx Bird Atlas in 2000–3, will influence modifications to the management plan to give these highly symbolic birds the best chance of success. Biological reference collections are maintained by Manx National Heritage, which has also recently reaffirmed its responsibility as the Isle of Man Biological Records Centre.

Conservation policy and legislation have generally followed, but in some cases lagged behind, other countries in the British Isles. Certain breeding birds have been protected since the Seagull Preservation Act of 1867 and the Bird Protection Acts in 1932 and 1955. The Manx Museum and National Trust Acts 1959–86 enabled areas of land in Trust ownership to be conserved (as described above). The Curraghs Acquisition Act 1963 effectively compulsorily purchased the core area of Ballaugh Curragh as a wildlife refuge. This has largely reverted to willow carr over an area of formerly agricultural land and is now managed by Manx National Heritage. Under a Tynwald scheme 16 hectares of Ballaugh Curragh were set aside for the establishment of the Curraghs Wildlife Park, which opened to the public in 1965. An emphasis on wetland species began in the late 1980s when the Park formally moved closer to conservation and education as its aims rather than leisure and recreation. It houses a variety of exotic and wetland species and includes a curragh interpretation nature trail.

In the 1970s an island-wide ecological survey produced a list of 34 sites of special ecological importance[18]. A Phase 1 ecological survey carried out by the Manx Department of Agriculture, Fisheries and Forestry between 1991 and 1994[19] has provided important baseline data that enable a description of proportions of the different land use on the island (Figures 11.12a and b). This was followed by Phase 2 survey work between 1995 and 1999, which has been incorporated into the database of vegetation held by the Department in the Government's geographic information system (Figures 11.3 and 11.4). These surveys did not include the shoreline, which was surveyed in 1999 under the auspices of the Port Erin Marine Laboratory and the Manx Wildlife Trust[20]. Since the Manx Government passed the 1993 Tree Preservation Act, the Isle of Man has been ahead of other countries because, in addition to issuing orders on individual speci-

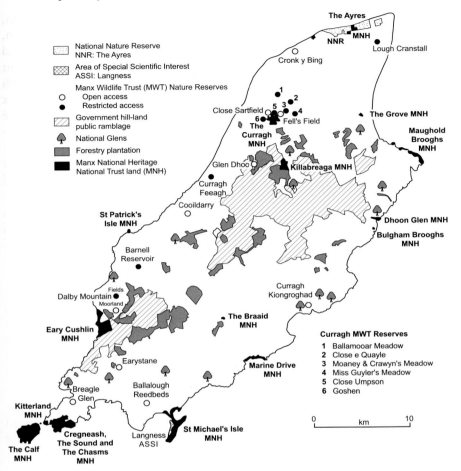

Figure 11.1 *Location of statutory designated areas and nature reserves on the Isle of Man.*

mens, a licence from the Forestry Division is required before *any* mature tree on the island is felled.

In the UK, site protection for general conservation started in 1949 with the National Parks and Protection of the Countryside Act. The island did not follow this path until the 1990 Wildlife Act was passed which prescribed the policy for the protection of areas for conservation. This was broadly modelled on the 1981 UK Wildlife and Countryside Act. The first Area of Special Scientific Interest, some 272 hectares of coastal grassland heath and dune habitats in the central Ayres, was designated in 1996 and declared a National Nature Reserve in 2000. In 2003 10 hectares of coastal habitats at Langness, Derbyhaven and Sandwick were similarly designated[21]. During the 1990s the island agreed to be included in the UK's ratification of the RAMSAR, BERN, BONN, OSPAR and CITES conventions, which provide specific protection for a wide range of wildlife and habitats[22].

The 1992 European Agri-environment Directive initiated countryside management schemes on farms throughout Europe, as voluntary support for environmentally friendly farming. These schemes include habitat management, habitat creation and organic farming. In 1997 the Department of Agriculture, Fisheries and Forestry decided to introduce an equivalent scheme in the island, after much campaigning by the Farming and Wildlife Advisory Group. A new Wildlife and Conservation Office was established within the Department in 1998. It has responsibility for the Wildlife Act of 1990, which empowers it to designate Areas of Special Scientific Interest, National Nature Reserves, Marine Nature Reserves and Areas of Special Protection for birds, plants and animals. More recently it has undertaken the implementation of the Manx pilot Agri-environment Scheme, passed by Tynwald in February 2002. In addition, there is a registration scheme for the keepers of birds of prey, and the sales of certain stuffed birds and animals are controlled.

In 1971, with the growing realisation of the loss of habitats, particularly marginal ones such as wetlands and hay meadows, and intensification of arable farming, the Manx Conservation Council was formed, following the European Conservation year in 1970. This pressure group led to the foundation of the Manx Nature Conservation Trust in 1973[23]. Since acquiring its first nature reserve, Barnell Reservoir, in 1974, it went on to become the Manx Wildlife Trust with 20 nature reserves across the island covering over 80 ha (Figure 11.1). The Trust provides an important role in pressing for the application of statutory protection of areas for conservation. Its concerns about the expansion of forestry plantation on the hill-lands and loss of heathland habitats were well publicised with two publications and a seminar during the 1990s[24] and led eventually to a change in government policy in 2000. The Trust's conviction in favour of the preservation of the heathlands was opposed by Friends of the Earth, who argued for the planting of native broadleaved species in these areas. More recently, a Manx Woodland Trust has been proposed.

The Wildlife Trust also has a role in research. It has developed management plans for its reserves and produced surveys of sensitive areas such as river corridors and road verges. In the last decade several projects initiated by the Trust have been carried out in conjunction with the Port Erin Marine Laboratory and the Marine Biologists' Sub-aqua Club. A three-year sub-

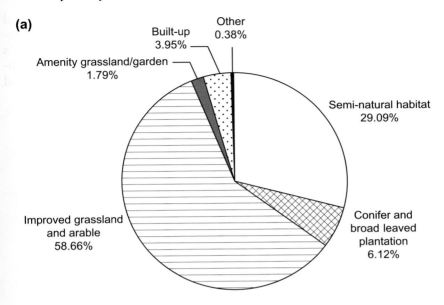

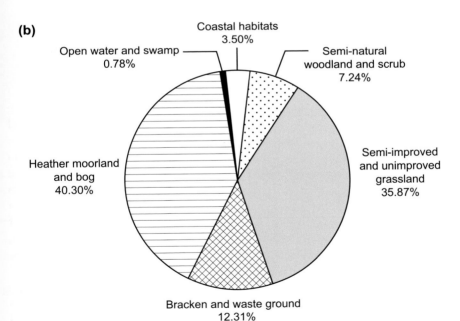

Figure 11.2 *(a) Proportions of major land-use types. (b) Proportions of semi-natural habitats.*

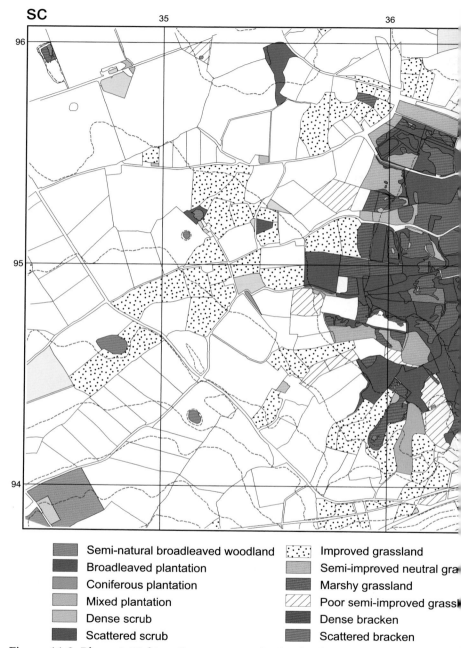

SC

Semi-natural broadleaved woodland   Improved grassland
Broadleaved plantation   Semi-improved neutral gra
Coniferous plantation   Marshy grassland
Mixed plantation   Poor semi-improved grassl
Dense scrub   Dense bracken
Scattered scrub   Scattered bracken

Figure 11.3 *Phase 1 Habitat Survey map of a lowland area around Ballaugh Curragh. Drawn from the Isle of Man Government Department of Agriculture, Fisheries and Forestry GIS dataset.*

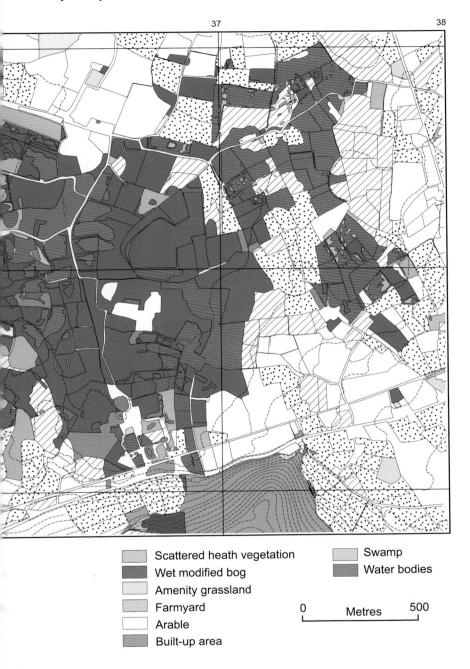

Scattered heath vegetation

Wet modified bog

Amenity grassland

Farmyard

Arable

Built-up area

Swamp

Water bodies

0   Metres   500

littoral survey was undertaken around the island, with local divers and visitors undertaking a total of 162 survey dives to a set format to produce a report detailing the main habitats just off the island's shoreline. The habitats on both sides of the Point of Ayre were mapped in detail, showing a rich and interesting diversity. Two other surveys, one on land use immediately inshore of the coastline[25] and another on the inter-tidal region[26] were completed. The result of this work has provided baseline data from immediately inland of the shoreline to about a kilometre offshore all around the island. Research on the waters around the Calf of Man provided data for a Calf of Man marine reserve proposal[27]. The Wildlife Sites System, initiated by the Wildlife Trust, sets out to prioritise the terrestrial sites of ecological and geological importance (Figure 11.1). It is felt that nature reserves on their own are too small and isolated and therefore a network of wildlife sites should be established to supplement and act as a buffer for the reserves[28]. In broad terms, the Wildlife Trust, with its nature reserves and visitor centres, plays a major role in raising public awareness about nature conservation. It now has over 1,100 members and carries out a variety of educational and fund-raising activities.

In recent years, a partnership approach has proved to be the best way forward in utilising the still relatively scarce resources available for nature conservation. Manx National Heritage, for example, co-ordinates management of its land at the Ayres National Nature Reserve with the Department of Agriculture, Fisheries and Forestry and contributes towards the cost of a seasonal warden. Similarly, management of St Michael's Isle and other archaeological sites within the Langness Area of Special Scientific Interest (Figure 11.1) and elsewhere on the peninsula involves careful liaison with the Department to satisfy all needs. The Manx Wildlife Trust initiated the Biodiversity Action Plan with support from Manx National Heritage and the Department of Agriculture, Fisheries and Forestry. Manx National Heritage is leading a joint approach in developing the Biological Records Centre to provide an information service of the highest standard, which is a vital tool for the planning process. In addition, Manx National Heritage and the Department of Agriculture, Fisheries and Forestry sponsor a range of survey work that is undertaken on the island. A new landscape designation, termed National Heritage Area, is being developed for the island, and is intended to include all the significant natural and cultural heritage elements, such as ASSI[29] and Ancient Monuments, within specified protected areas in an integrated approach to conservation. Two National Heritage Areas have also been proposed; in Sulby Glen and the Meayll Peninsula. The principles of how these areas will be defined and protected are addressed in the Isle of Man *Draft Strategic Plan*[30].

CLIMATE   P H I L I P P A T O M L I N S O N

The island's temperate climate is predominantly influenced by the close proximity of the sea – nowhere is more than 8 km from the coast – and by its varied topography. The prevailing southwesterly winds bring high levels of precipitation, which fall with increased intensity on the hills. The general temperatures, ameliorated by the sea, vary considerably with altitude. The rugged topography means that local effects of shelter and exposure are very variable. Hence, some areas of the island are markedly drier and sunnier than others whereas heavy rainfall and exposure to wind are also key elements. All these factors affect the soils and hence the vegetation patterns. In winter, snowfall and frost are infrequent. Even when snow does occur, it rarely lies on the ground for more than a day or two. February is normally the coldest month, with an average daily temperature of 4.9 °C, but it is often relatively dry. In summer, April, May and June are the driest months whilst May, June and July are the sunniest. July and August are the warmest months, with an average daily maximum temperature around 17.6 °C. The highest temperature recorded at the island's weather centre at Ronaldsway is 28.9 °C. Thunderstorms are rare. With altitude, the frequency and duration of frost, humidity, cloud cover, snow and wind velocity generally increase. The effects of topography are illustrated by comparing measurements at Ronaldsway, the Point of Ayre and mountain recording stations[31]. The variation in local climate has a profound influence on soil types and their distribution.

The Isle of Man, relatively unpolluted and poised in such a maritime situation, may be a good place to study climate change. Some hints are coming from the weather records, from trials of new crops such as maize and the fodder crop, typhon, which may do better as summers become warmer or the growing season lengthens, and from introduced species which begin to set seed and colonise.

CURRENT ENVIRONMENTAL THREATS
P H I L I P P A T O M L I N S O N and E L I Z A B E T H C H A R T E R

Coastal erosion

The northern coastline of the island, from Ramsey to the Point of Ayre on the east and from the Point of Ayre to Glen Mooar on the west, consists either of soft glacial gravel, sand and clay or recent dune sands and is subject to intense erosion. Of the 37 km of coastline 84% is eroding and only 16% is accreting. Erosion is sporadic and can occur along stretches that have previously been either stable or accreting. A 2 m wide, 2 km strip of cliffs north of Port Cranstal, for example, was eroded by a single storm in 1946. Most of the eroded material is transported by long-shore drift caused by the prevailing southwesterly winds. On the west coast sand and gravel are moved northeast and progressively accrete as successive prograding beach ridges towards the Point of Ayre. On the east coast sand and gravel are moved directly north to erode the eastern end of the beach ridges and transport it further north as a series of large sand banks off the northeastern tip of the island. The erosion of the coastal cliffs, by as much as 1.2 m per annum in some stretches, provides an excellent opportunity to study the exposed glacial stratigraphy, but also causes significant problems of coastal management and protection of properties.

Following the report by Jolliffe in 1981[32], Rouse published a full summary of the evidence for coastal erosion in the north of the island in 1990[33]. Since then several further studies have been completed[34] and the most recent, by Duvivier[35], was commissioned by the Department of Transport in order to enable them to consider a coastal management strategy for the northern shoreline of the island. Duvivier estimated that, assuming the historic rates of erosion continue unchanged, approximately 15 properties would be lost over the next 50 years. Following consultation with several government departments and other bodies, the Department of Transport report in Tynwald[36] October 2000 recommended that a Coastal Lands and Rivers Bill be drafted, for introduction into the House of Keys during 2001/2 to provide the necessary organisation within Government to co-ordinate or deal specifically with coastal management issues.

Two alternative options to inaction in the face of continued erosion are available: a 'managed retreat' versus a 'hold the line' approach involving large-scale construction of sea defences. The latter is not likely to be considered because of the high costs involved. The proposal for the new bill was a form of 'managed retreat' where the authorities would 'be ready to do something if required but only with the proper environmental assessment and planning consents'. It was proposed that the Department of Local Government and the Environment would be responsible for monitoring and safeguarding works on coastal lands in any place in the island where there is a justifiable and sustainable case. It is very likely that the discussions on this issue will continue and the recent *Draft Strategic Plan*[37], for example, suggests that 'the final management plans (for coastal protection work) ... should seek to develop, wherever possible, environmentally acceptable soft engineering solutions and long term strategic solutions whilst taking account of the possible impacts of sea level changes' and that coastal development should not be permitted in areas threatened with erosion.

Since the recommendations in October 2000 no further progress has been made. As no funds have been allocated, the Department of Local Government and the Environment has refused to take responsibility for coastal monitoring and remedial work. New housing continues to be proposed within areas of Kirk Michael that are predicted to start eroding in *circa* 30 years[38]. Nowhere in the recommendations is there any suggestion that there should be planning regulation for the private, or local authority construction of coastal defences to protect individual dwellings. Protection of the cliffs with short lengths of boulders, as at Glen Wyllin, or with a granite and concrete revetment, as at Carlan Mill, Killane, can only provide short-term solutions. The promontory effect of increased erosion on either side can already be seen at Carlan Mill, which will be an unsightly and dangerous scar on the coastline for many years as the rounded concrete blocks are themselves eroded and roll away from the cliff. Consideration should be given to the removal of the materials once they cease to perform any protective function. In the future, perhaps within 100 years from now, the Wright's Pit East rubbish tip at the Point of Ayre will be eroded, potentially causing a major marine pollution hazard.

Recent changes in land use

The increased intensity of land use on good agricultural land, caused by modernisation and intensification of agricultural practices as well as demographic changes[39], follows a period when the rural economy and population declined and large areas, which had once been intensively occupied and managed, were abandoned. This section describes some of the changes in the past 200 years.

Agricultural development in the island was perhaps not quite as rapid as elsewhere but the nineteenth century saw the change from subsistence to commercial farming[40] with the introduction of mechanisation and land management techniques. The impetus behind this commercialisation was largely the growth of the tourist industry from around the middle of the nineteenth century. Conversely, agricultural fields on steeper slopes on the margins of upland areas have been less intensively managed or abandoned and subsequently colonised by scrub.

There have been changes in farm size over the past 200 years. At the beginning of the nineteenth century the main farms were between 20–60 hectares, with many smaller holdings and very few larger than 80 hectares[41]. At the beginning of the twentieth century 63% of farms were less than 20 hectares, but by 2000 this figure had decreased to 49% and the number of farms bigger than 120 hectares had increased from one in

1910 to 11 in 2000[42]. Recent changes in agricultural practice, such as the increase in silage production, are discussed below.

A major feature of the twentieth century was the spread of conifer plantations, which by 1994 constituted over half of the total woodland as opposed to broadleaved plantation and semi-natural woodland. A large proportion of the conifers were planted onto upland heather moor. Local pressure persuaded the Government to rethink its policy so that by 2000 conifer planting was halted and the emphasis was placed on increasing the cover of broadleaved species.

Housing development has been very rapid in recent decades when the Government has encouraged the use of greenfield sites around the existing major settlements and in the rural parishes. The effect on the natural landscape may appear slight because it is usually agricultural land not semi-natural habitats that are developed. The gradual destruction of natural field boundaries and roadside trees, the introduction of alien species and the increased pressure of traffic urgently suggest that the long-term changes need to be monitored and assessed. Conversely, the increase in the creation of garden lakes may have partially made up for the loss of nineteenth-century millponds and dubs.

HABITAT SURVEY   PHILIPPA TOMLINSON and ELIZABETH CHARTER

Description of the main semi-natural habitats

The island, despite its small size, an area of 572 square kilometres, contains a very wide range of habitats. Some of them, such as salt-marsh and open still water, cover only small areas but are nevertheless important for biodiversity. The 120 km of coastline and large area of acidic-soiled upland are the dominant features. There follows a very brief description of the main semi-natural habitats based on the Phase 1 Survey[43]. The percentages given in brackets after the name of the habitat type are the proportion of the total of the semi-natural habitats which themselves make up 29% of the island (Figures 11.2, 11.3 and 11.4).

Heathland (36.2%)

The nature of the geology of the uplands and the high rainfall and relative mild temperatures cause considerable leaching. This, combined with the use of the hills in the past for cattle and in more recent times for sheep grazing, which has continued since at least the Bronze Age[44], produces highly acidic soils and, in the wettest northern slopes, areas of blanket bog. The two main semi-natural heathland habitats in the uplands are 'dry dwarf shrub heath' (34.3%) and 'wet dwarf shrub heath' (1.9%), both dominated by Heather (*Calluna vulgaris*), Bell Heather (*Erica cinerea*) and Bilberry (*Vaccinium myrtillus*). Together these two communities cover 10.54% of the whole island forming a significant habitat (Figure 11.3). In the hill-lands the wet heath often grades into areas of mire or may form a mosaic with acid grassland where heather is co-dominant with Purple Moor Grass (*Molinia caerulea*). In areas where sheep grazing and heather burning cause the dry heath vegetation to be partly replaced by grasses, a mosaic of dry heath and acid grassland is formed. This occurs a little in the periphery of the heath in the southern hills but in quite large areas in the northern hills. Typical species include Mat Grass (*Nardus stricta*), Heather, Bilberry and Wavy Hair Grass (*Deschampsia flexuosa*). Western Gorse (*Ulex gallii*) grows with the dry heath in many areas, including the characteristic 'lichen heath' found in The Ayres coastal strip (see below).

Heather-dominated dwarf shrub heath is limited in its geographical extent to northwest Europe and is centred on the British Isles. Its landscape and diverse plant and animal communities are therefore considered to be of major scientific and conservation importance[45]. The heathland is maintained by grazing and burning, which encourages young growth for sheep grazing and grouse shooting. The southern hills, with a more extensive area of heather, may have been less intensively grazed in the past. Some heathland edge habitats may also be invaded by Bracken (*Pteridium aquilinum*) or European Gorse (*Ulex europaeus*) and should be monitored.

Semi-improved and unimproved grassland and marsh (35.8%)

Acid grassland (19.2%) and semi-improved acid grassland (6.1%)   Acid grassland, dominated by Mat Grass, Heath Rush (*Juncus squarrosus*), Heath Grass (*Danthonia decumbens*) and Bilberry, is normally found in unenclosed hill-land, nowadays grazed by sheep. Because of acidity, the species diversity is low, but the heath is interspersed with more diverse patches such as wet flushes, springs and bogs. It is thought that much of this grassland was originally dry dwarf shrub heath now modified by grazing and burning. Transition of heathland to grassland has occurred elsewhere in the British Isles where grazing by sheep is heavy. Semi-improved acid grassland is generally enclosed land around the flanks of the hills and may quickly become invaded by gorse and bracken if management is reduced. This habitat is good for bryophytes and birds such as Snipe (*Gallinago gallinago*) and Curlew (*Numenius arquata*), but is otherwise species poor.

Neutral grassland (0.1%) and semi-improved neutral grassland (3.8%)
The very small amount of unimproved neutral grassland has floristic
interest, particularly in two areas on the northern plain. Conservation, with
co-operation from landowners, is important because changes in management, such as reseeding the sward, will cause a rapid loss of species richness.
Although agricultural improvement has altered the composition of the
semi-improved neutral grassland it has rarity value. Grassland that has
been grazed to a low sward may conceal some of its diversity. Another category of poor semi-improved grassland was included in the survey, in areas
where management has ceased and tall rank grasses and herbs have
colonised, often where land use is changing to building development.
Remnant areas of semi-improved neutral grassland may be found along
hedges, road verges, tracks and disused railways. Sod hedges and verges
are particularly important in preserving relict meadowland species in areas
of predominantly agricultural land, but their management needs to be
closely monitored and assessed over time. The Manx Wildlife Trust carried
out a thorough survey of road verges[46] and in conjunction with the
Department of Transport designated a series of 'conservation verges',
which are managed to maintain species diversity[47]. Species-rich grasslands
cut for hay in the traditional way are particularly scarce. The Phase 1 survey
did not separate these from grazed semi-improved grassland. The largest
area of this grassland type is Jurby airfield.

At the other end of the spectrum, but not a semi-natural habitat, is
improved grassland, which has generally been ploughed, drained, reseeded
and fertilised. The rapid trend away from hay to silage leys over the past
50 years has caused a dramatic loss of semi-improved grassland to what is
effectively arable land[48]. Although this change has perhaps not been as
dramatic as, for example in the UK, the effect on ground-nesting birds such
as Skylark (*Alauda arvensis*) is certainly evident. Changes in semi-improved
grassland are difficult to evaluate as it is being farmed at varying levels of
intensity. Unimproved and semi-improved grassland may be lost to arable
but, conversely, reversion of improved grasslands to low-diversity wet
grassland with rushes occurs when drainage channels are no longer maintained or field drains become blocked.

Marshy grassland (6.7%)   Marshy grassland is a varied habitat depending
on altitude, drainage conditions and soil types. In the lowlands, often called
garey, it is characterised by Rush (*Juncus*) species and Meadowsweet
(*Filipendula ulmaria*) with a diversity of herbs such as Whorled Caraway
(*Carum verticillatum*), various orchids including the Northern Marsh
Orchid   (*Dactylorhiza   purpurella*)   and   Greater   Butterfly-orchids

(*Platanthera chlorantha*), Yellow Iris (*Iris pseudocorus*), Purple Loosestrife (*Lythrum salicaria*) and Ragged Robin (*Lychnis flos-cuculi*). Many invertebrates, particularly Damselflies, and Dragonflies (Odonata), Butterflies and Moths (Lepidoptera), as well as common frog (*Rana temporaria*) and birds like Curlew and Lapwing (*Vanellus vanellus*) are found on poorly drained land in the margins of curragh that is lightly grazed or cut for hay. Often the botanical diversity has developed over a long period where the fields have been managed for hay, mown in late summer and grazed in the autumn and winter. These hay meadows are important for wildlife, but they have been fast disappearing with agricultural improvement. The wildlife value of maintaining hay meadows using traditional farming methods is clearly evident at Close Sartfield nature reserve where the recent reappearance of Corncrake (*Crex crex*) and the abundance of meadow flowers and insects show what can be achieved. Upland marshy grassland is relatively species poor with Purple Moor Grass and Mat Grass, and *Nardus stricta*, sedges (*Carex* spp), rushes and mosses (Musci) and Cotton Grass (*Eriophorum angustifolium*) in the wetter areas.

Tall herb and fern communities (12.3%)

Bracken (12.0%)
Dense bracken forms extensive areas in valleys, for example Laxey, Sulby and Agneash; coastal areas, for example Fleshwick to Cronk ny Arrey Laa and Bulgham; and in The Ayres. Its presence suggests areas of abandoned arable and also indicates that the soil may be suitable for the regeneration of woodland. It is likely that bracken forms the first stage in the succession to woodland as shown by those dense areas which are presently developing scrub and trees, such as in the Sulby and Glen Auldyn valleys where there is reduced grazing pressure and Hawthorn (*Cratageus monogyna*), Rowan (*Sorbus aucuparia*), Holly (*Ilex aquifolium*) and Ash (*Fraxinus excelsior*) are all able to colonise. A limitation of such natural recolonisation is the lack of a local seed source for shrubs and trees in many areas. Although bracken is an unwanted nuisance from the farmer's viewpoint, preventing the growth of grass by its dense summer shade, in areas where changing agricultural practices have allowed abandonment, it provides a good habitat for shade tolerant early spring flowers such as Bluebell (*Hyacinthoides non-scripta*), Heath Bedstraw (*Galium saxatile*), Pignut (*Conpodium majus*) and Primrose (*Primula vulgaris*). Scattered bracken also occurs frequently with other habitats, generally as an intermediate stage in a transition to dense bracken, where it spreads quite rapidly by underground rhizomes and suppresses other plants by its dense summer shade and slowly decaying litter.

Tall herbs of disturbed ground (0.3%)
The percentage of tall ruderal (disturbed ground) habitats mapped in the Phase 1 survey is likely to be an underestimate because isolated patches often occur in, for example, neglected field corners that were too small to map. Component species include Common Nettle (*Urtica dioica*), Thistles (*Circium* spp.) and Brambles (*Rubus* spp.), and are often dominated by Hogweed (*Heracleum sphondylium*). Other species, such as Rosebay Willowherb (*Chamerion angustifolium*), and Common Ragwort (*Senecio jacobaea*), often occur in patches such as along riverbanks and paths. This can be an important habitat for insects and small birds and provides structural diversity, both important for wildlife.

Semi-natural woodland (1.0%), dense scrub (6.2%) and plantations

Woodland: general introduction

As recent pollen analysis has shown, the island was once covered in dense and varied woodland that was gradually removed from early prehistoric times and by clearance for agriculture during later prehistory[49]. Chaloner[50] described in 1653 a land 'now destitute of wood', but said there were 'plantations, which some few have made about their houses, as well as fruit trees' and yet there was no shortage of 'fewel' because there was 'great plenty of Turf and Pete; and, of Pete, the best that I ever saw'. Garrad and Allen[51] have discussed the evidence from the historical record as to the treeless nature of the island in earlier periods and it is clear that only a tiny remnant of the earlier woodland survived. William Blundell wrote in 1648–56 that 'there hath been no woods in Man this 140 years', that is, since *circa* 1500[52].

Broadleaved woodland   Broadleaved woodland occurs throughout the island but represents only 3.6% of its *total* woodland, including forestry. The largest areas are on the edges of the central massif. Much of it has been disturbed, felled and replanted although there are indications of ancient woodland in the presence of indicator species and there is some early literary evidence of woodland survival[53]. The commonest tree species are Ash (*Fraxinus excelsior*), Sycamore (*Acer pseudoplatanus*) and Wych Elm (*Ulmus glabra*). Oak (*Quercus robur*) and Hazel (*Corylus avellana*) also occur, the latter probably planted for use in the mines in the Laxey valley. The ground flora tends to be very consistent in species composition; Sanicle (*Sanicula europaea*), Great Woodrush (*Luzula sylvatica*), Wood Anemone (*Anemone nemorosa*), Wood Sage (*Teucrium scorodonia*) and Wood Sorrel (*Oxalis acetosella*) are typical[54]. The largest area of semi-natural woodland is at Narradale where Common Cow Wheat (*Melampyrum pratense*) is found. There is also a little evidence of former woodland management represented by coppiced trees[55]. Small groups of trees, remnants of the native woodland, can be found in ungrazed upland gullies and cliff edges[56]. Herbs, such as bluebells on cliff tops and the Great Woodrush that occurs in patches on the slopes of some of the northern hills, perhaps represent woodland relicts[57].

Dense scrub and natural regeneration   There are two main types of dense scrub: gorse and willow carr. European Gorse was planted on sod hedges to provide shelter, fuel and fodder and is thought to be an introduced species[58], which spreads rapidly onto semi-improved acid grassland where management has ceased. Areas of impeded drainage, such as curragh margins and *garey*, if left ungrazed, regenerate with Grey Willow (*Salix cinerea* ssp. *oleifolia*)[59], and dryer curragh with Silver Birch (*Betula pendula*), Sycamore and Ash, spreading from neighbouring field boundaries. Other scrub species include Broom (*Cytisus scorparius*), which was probably more widespread in the past, and Bramble, Hawthorn and Blackthorn (*Prunus spinosa*). Dense scrub provides a valuable wildlife habitat especially when it occurs in a mosaic with grassland and wetland. The area under scrub is increasing in some areas as it spreads onto upland semi-improved grassland and undergrazed areas of wet grassland and lowland wet heath. In the case of the curragh this change has the effect of reducing species diversity and wetland habitats may be lost. Management to reduce this has been carried out on a small scale in recent years but consideration should be made to increasing this in certain areas[60].

Forestry plantation and the National Glens   The process of redeveloping the island's woodland began in the eighteenth century when landowners, most notably Bishops Wilson and Hildesley, began planting in the many glens and in private gardens[61]. Neither the rent Rolls of 1508 and 1511[62] nor the 1540 Court of Augmentation Returns mention woodland and in the latter the Nunnery is shown to have brought timber from Ireland for building[63]. By the Victorian period the glens were planted with a wide variety of ornamental trees and shrubs and opened to the public. Their management was taken over by the Forestry Board in the 1950s. The Forestry Division of the Department of Agriculture, Fisheries and Forestry now owns and manages the hill-lands, plantations, parkland, amenity sites and 15 National Glens; in total about 18% of the area of the island.

Afforestation begun in the 1880s with three plantations, Archallagan, South Barrule and Greeba, increased slowly until the 1950s when the Crown plantations and unenclosed land were vested in the Forestry, Mines and Lands Board[64]. In 1985 a rapid expansion was initiated which would have doubled the area of plantation, this in part, to help the local economy. This was modified, and by 2000 halted, because it became clear that conifer plantation in the hill-lands would severely threaten the moors[65] and the initial market of pit props had been lost due to mine closure in the UK. Recent forestry policy has also led to the planting of broadleaved trees rather than conifers. The overall rate of conifer planting by the Forestry Division is expected to fall, but the natural regeneration of conifers may lead to extension of woodland where the land is free of grazing, such as the pines in the trial forestry plot on The Ayres.

A wider variety of species of trees and shrubs are planted in towns and gardens now than ever before and a small proportion do naturalise. Climatic change may lead to the success of different species and a few may become invasive. Government foresters have planted a variety of non-native species such as the Southern Beech (*Nothofagus antarctica*) in Glen Maye.

Of the total woodland on the island, 58.5% is coniferous plantation grown for timber and 16.0% is broadleaved plantation or mixed. Although the conifer plantations themselves are dense, dark and low in species diversity there are some positive aspects. Open spaces in some of the well-established plantations such as Archallagan and Stoney Mountain enable semi-natural vegetation to thrive free of grazing which in turn has allowed the establishment of the Hen Harrier (*Circus cyaneus*) as a breeding species. On the drier moors the planted conifers regenerate creating patchy, mixed age stands and areas of failed plantation also provide diversity. Within the forestry fencing, where tree growth is poor, dense, tall heather, Cranberry (*Vaccinium oxycoccus*) and associated species thrive – an ideal area for Short-eared Owls (*Asio flammeus*) to breed.

Mire (4.9%)

Flushes, blanket bog, wet modified bog, dry modified bog, valley and basin mires and raised bog are only relatively minor habitats, but they form an important part of the island's diversity.

Flushes (2.8%)   Flushes, acid or neutral, often found in association with marshy grassland and wet dwarf shrub heath, mainly in the northern hills, are dominated by Moss (*Sphagnum* spp.) with Rush and Sedge species.

Blanket bog (0.6%) and dry modified bog (0.4%)   Blanket bog occurs mainly on the north-facing hill slopes and is dominated by Mosses with Cottongrasses (*Eriophorum* spp.) and Deergrass (*Trichophorum cespitosum*). The bog becomes modified with heavy grazing, burning and drainage or where recent cutting for fuel has occurred, sometimes resulting in patches of bare peat and erosion to the rock surface.

Wet modified bog (0.2%)   The largest area in Ballaugh Curragh (Figure 11.3) may once have developed into a raised bog, but has been extensively affected by human activity in the past[66]. Drained in the seventeenth and eighteenth centuries and subdivided as 'intack'[67], it was used for both arable and pastoral agriculture as well as extensive peat cutting. The least affected central area, overlying a considerably depth of peat, was soon disused and left unmanaged, and since 1963 has been maintained as a wildlife refuge. Some small-scale management has seen the removal of colonising birch and willow to maintain the diverse bog surface vegetation and, in the 1990s, the opening up to the public by the creation of paths along the tops of the old sod hedges which once formed the boundaries of the agricultural land. Two factors may particularly be affecting this habitat, which is expected to qualify as a RAMSAR site, and urgently require monitoring. The intensification of the farmland in the marginal areas around Ballaugh Curragh, including drainage and reclamation, and the runoff from the Wildlife Park may be changing the pH affecting particularly the invertebrates[68]. There is also loss of marshland and reed-bed to scrub invasion by willow. The feral colony of Red-necked Wallaby (*Macropus rufogriseus*) that resulted from an escape in the 1960s may also be having an impact on the vegetation.

Where there is shallow peat, Bogbean (*Menyanthes trifoliate*), Pondweed (*Potamogeton* sp.), Cross-leaved Heath (*Erica tetralix*), Bog Myrtle (*Myrica gale*) and Common Cottongrass (*Eriophorum angustifolium*) make up the ground flora while Grey Willow is increasingly covering these areas. Royal Fern (*Osmunda regalis*) is quite abundant in places, particularly along the lines of abandoned sod hedges and intack roads. The hedges, being slightly drier than the surrounding areas, provide an ideal habitat for the fern, which appears to grow in preference on the raised areas with its roots in the wet bog.

Valley and basin mires (0.9%)   These types of fen are formed of peat that is dependent on ground water runoff rather than precipitation, which makes them richer in minerals and less acidic. They occur in small river valleys such as Druidale (Figure 11.4), Laxey and the head of Glen Roy or small, waterlogged basins and are usually associated with wet flushes.

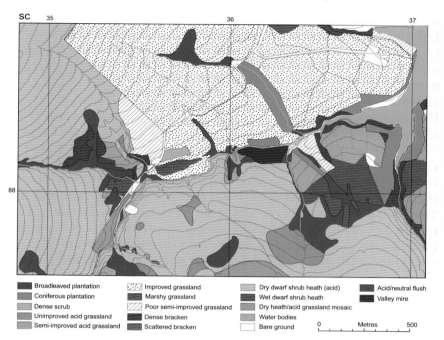

SC 35 36 37

88

■ Broadleaved plantation	Improved grassland	Dry dwarf shrub heath (acid)	■ Acid/neutral flush
Coniferous plantation	Marshy grassland	Wet dwarf shrub heath	Valley mire
Dense scrub	Poor semi-improved grassland	Dry heath/acid grassland mosaic	
Unimproved acid grassland	Dense bracken	Water bodies	
Semi-improved acid grassland	Scattered bracken	Bare ground	

0 Metres 500

Figure 11.4 *Phase 1 Habitat Survey map of an upland area around Druidale. See Figure 11.3 for key. Drawn from the Isle of Man Government Department of Agriculture, Fisheries and Forestry GIS dataset.*

Raised bog (0.002%)   Classic raised bog, which forms into a domed shape of deep peat only fed by rainwater, is only found where human activity has not modified the surface and is extremely rare. Some of the lowland bogs would probably have developed into raised bog had they not been cut for turf and otherwise disturbed by human activity.

Coastland (3.4%)

Dunes (3.0%)   The dunes have the full range of successional habitats from open dune, dune grassland, dune heath, dune slack and dune scrub, increasing with age and stability with distance from the sea. These habitats are found most extensively in The Ayres and also in isolated patches along the northwest coast round to Ballaugh Cronk. The Ayres has the most extensive area of dunes. It is very rich botanically, with Early-purple and Pyramidal Orchids (*Orchis mascula* and *Anacamptis pyramidalis*), as well as a range of shore species, Portland and Sea Spurge (*Euphorbia port-landica* and *E. paralias*), Sea Holly (*Eryngium maritimum*), Sea Bindweed (*Calystegia soldanella*) and the rare but spectacular Oysterplant (*Mertensia maritima*). The lichen heath on The Ayres coastal strip is unique in having the lichen *Usnea articulata*, which is usually found on trees, but here has adapted to growing on stones and sand. Heather, Bell Heather, Burnet Rose (*Rosa pimpinellifolia*) and Sand Sedge (*Carex arenaria*) are other characteristic species.

Cliff tops (0.37%) The cliff tops have coastal grassland (0.3%) with Red Fescue (*Festuca rubra*), Sea Plantain (*Plantago maritima*), Spring Squill (*Scilla verna*), Thrift (*Armeria maritima* ssp. *maritima*) and Bird's-foot Trefoil (*Lotus corniculatus*) and coastal heathland (0.07%) with maritime species within the heather including the characteristic Western Gorse. Cattle or sheep grazing on the cliff tops provide an important habitat for the Chough (*Pyrrhocorax pyrrhocorax*).

The rocky cliffs themselves are one of the main wildlife features of the island especially on the limestone where there are lime-rich wet flushes and a variety of communities notably at Scarlett and Kallow Point where there is slightly less exposure. The flora here is characteristic of calcareous conditions and includes Purple Milk Vetch (*Astragalus danicus*), which is unusual in western Britain, Black Bog-rush (*Scheonus nigricans*) and Field Mouse-ear (*Cerastium arvenset*)[69]. There are several sea caves, some below the tide, which provide an unusual habitat for the rare Maidenhair Fern (*Adiantum capillus-veneris*) and in the permanently submerged parts of the caves invertebrates such as Sea-Squirts (Tunicata), Sponges (Porifera), Corals and Anemones (Anthoza)[70].

Rocky shores support species such as Rock Samphire (*Crithmum maritimum*), Sea Kale (*Crambe maritima*), Greater Sea-spurry (*Spergularia media*) and Sea Spleenwort (*Asplenium marinum*).

Salt-marsh (0.04%) Small areas of salt-marsh occur in a few locations. Where there is shelter and a build-up of marine sediments, salt-marsh vegetation develops, for example in the estuaries of the Sulby, Neb and Silverburn, behind the shingle bank at Cornaa and around Langness and Poyllvaaish. Like the unstable dune habitats, salt-marsh can occur ephemerally in places along the eroding northern coast. The full range of salt-tolerant vegetation can be found with some fluctuation in occurrence as might be expected in tide-dispersed communities. The rich invertebrate fauna is important for bird-life. Cornaa and Langness salt-marshes were formerly grazed.

Open water (0.6%)

The standing water on the island is found in the nine reservoirs, in flooded quarries and only small areas of natural water bodies. The reservoirs are relatively poor in plants and invertebrates having mainly upland catchments and acid water. Given time, species do colonise these water bodies, such as Kerrowdhoo reservoir with Creeping Yellow-cress (*Rorippa sylvestris*)[71] and the draw-down zone of the Injebreck reservoir with a variety of smaller plants such as Shoreweed (*Littorella uniflora*), Water Purslane (*Lythrum portula*) and Common Water Starwort (*Callitriche stagnalis sens. lat.*).

The natural open waters include the rivers, the ponds of glacial origin (kettle holes and pingos, which are often rich habitats) and in the hills peaty pools that are sometimes ephemeral and devoid of aquatic vegetation. There are also ponds[72], which were dug for marl to provide lime-rich fertiliser, as farm ponds or for retting flax. The natural flora of the northern kettle holes and dubs includes Yellow Water-lily (*Nuphar lutea*), Greater Spearwort (*Ranunculus lingua*), the rather rare Northern Yellow-cress (*Rorippa islandica*), Trifid Bur-marigold (*Bidens tripartita*) and many others. A number of invasive alien aquatics have been recorded recently including New Zealand Pigmy-Weed (*Crassula helmsii*) and to a lesser extent Water Fern (*Azolla filiculoides*), Parrot's Feather (*Myriophyllum aquaticum*) and Floating Pennywort (*Hydrocotyle ranunculoides*). Fairy Shrimps (*Chirocephalus* spp.) have also been found in one pond[73].

The rivers are mainly upland in character, fast flowing and stony with few submerged species. Several introduced species such as Japanese Knotweed (*Fallopia japonica*), Giant Hogweed (*Heracleum mantegazzianum*) and Indian Balsam (*Impatiens glandulifera*) are spreading vegetatively and by seed along rivers such as the Sulby, Neb and Auldyn and may cause problems. Until recently the rivers have been little studied, but work on river quality by assessing invertebrates is now carried out by the Government Analyst's Laboratory[74] and the Manx River Improvement Association is doing practical work to monitor fish, invasive plants and pollution from farms and old mine spoil and to improve riverbanks and structures to encourage diversity.

Although open water and water margin habitats are being lost through dubs being infilled or ploughed, elsewhere, larger ornamental lakes in private gardens and worked-out gravel pits provide new habitats for aquatic species. The water-filled pits at the Point of Ayre are now recognised as an Area of Special Protection for Birds.

Swamp, marginal and inundation vegetation (0.15%)

Swamp vegetation represents the transition zone between open water and dry land. Dominated by tall grasses such as Common Reed (*Phragmites australis*) and sedges such as Bottle Sedge (*Carex rostrata*), the largest example is around Lough Cranstal. This must have been a habitat much more common in the past before drainage took place and would be an excellent one to try to encourage wetland wildlife. Marginal wetland habitats occur around dubs and edges of ditches. Inundation vegetation includes unstable communities, for example around the margins of reservoirs and dubs. These are small communities, but botanically interesting and diverse habitats and therefore important for wildlife.

Lowland farmland and other man-made habitats

Prominent features of the landscape are the small grassland fields surrounded by sod hedges, which are often topped with shrubs, such as European Gorse, Hawthorn (*Crataegus monogyna*), wild Roses (*Rosa* sp.) and trees. A variety of species of unimproved well-drained soils, previously much more widespread throughout the fields, are preserved on the hedges. These include Field Scabious (*Knautia arvensis*), Devil's Bit Scabious (*Succisa pratensis*), Wild Thyme (*Thymus polytrichus* ssp. *britannicus*), Pignut (*Conopodium majus*), Primrose (*Primula vulgaris*) and Common Dog Violet (*Viola riviniana*).

Road verges, the largest resource of remaining unimproved grassland, often display a wide variety of introduced species, either deliberately or accidentally spread by man. These include garden escapes such as Spanish Bluebell (*Hyacinthoides hispanica*), now hybridising in some areas with the widespread native, more delicate and scented Bluebell (*H. non-scripta*), Italian Lords-and-Ladies (*Arum italicum*) and Montbretia (*Crocosmia* x *crocosmifolia*). A very few verges have been sown with commercial wildflower mixes which only occasionally persist, such as Salad Burnet (*Poterium sanguisorba* spp. *minor*) at Poortown and Quarry Bends (Sulby). Some of these introduced species or foreign variants of native species do not survive very long here. Others cross with local types.

Recent changes in farming practices　Thrower has summarised the results from the annual returns for 1945–2000[75]. In the twentieth century there was a transfer from spring grown cereals to winter cereals on certain soils. The acreage of oats grown has declined compared with barley and wheat. By the turn of the century the decline in the diversity of crops and livestock, associated with increased specialisation, is less marked than in much of the UK.

At the lower margins of the uplands where now only sheep graze, there are numerous signs of more active and varied farming in the past; ruined farm buildings, low field boundaries, lines of trees and old fields now invaded by bracken and gorse. All these indicate more diverse and extensive arable farmland in the nineteenth and early twentieth centuries[76]. The nature and dating of this activity will be discussed in later volumes but it has certainly had its effect on the present-day vegetation and requires consideration when management of these areas is planned.

Urban railways, walls and gardens   The pavements, waste ground and roadsides in towns are known for an interesting mix of naturalised garden species and native colonisers. Dry-stone and mortared walls support a range of Ferns (Pteropsida) – Wall-rue (*Asplenium ruta-muraria*), Maidenhair Spleenwort (*Asplenium trichomanes*), Hart's Tongue (*Phyllitis scolopendrium*) and Rustyback (*Ceterarch officinarum*). Fairy Foxglove (*Erinus alpinus*) may colonise walls near gardens.

Plants found mainly on railway tracks include rarities such as Prickly Poppy (*Papaver argemone*), Sharp-leaved Fluellen (*Kickxia elatine*), Small Cudweed (*Filago minima*) and Dwarf Spurge (*Euphorbia exigua*). Berry-bearing garden shrubs such as Cotoneaster are quick to colonise bare ground and the many other species, which become weeds in gardens, are sometimes deposited with other garden waste in back lanes and parking areas, as well as in the wider countryside. All this variety, especially where gardens include wild areas and ponds, provides additional habitats for a range of wildlife.

Inter-tidal and sub-tidal habitats[77]

The rocky shores on the steeper parts of the western coasts of the island, such as the exposed promontory of Niarbyl, are colonised by Barnacles (Cirripedia), wracks such as Bladder Wrack (*Fucus vesiculosus*) and Common Limpet (*Patella vulgata*) with Thongweed (*Himanthalia elongata*) and a turf of red algae on the lower shore giving way to kelp beds. In areas of localised shelter such as the coves at Derbyhaven there are beds of Knotted Wrack (*Ascophyllum nodosum*) and a rich under-storey of other algae. In the Calf Sound the current-swept lower inter-tidal area supports a diverse community of sessile animals such as Sea Firs (Hydroids), Sea Squirts (Tunicates) and many Anemones. Good examples of rocky shores are the limestone of Kallow Point and Scarlett Point, the

Sugar Loaf caves with sub- and inter-tidal zones and rich fauna, and Wart Bank, a submerged shelly bank.

The soft sediment shores, such as mobile gravel and cobbles, tend to be relatively poor in species diversity. The more sheltered beaches such as Ramsey Bay, Laxey Bay, Derbyhaven and the inner harbour of Port St Mary have dense populations of Sandhoppers (amphipods) and Sea-slaters (isopods), the Sandmason Worm (*Lanice conchilega*) and the Ragworm (*Arenicola marina*). Peel Harbour has a small estuary and a sandy bay with inter-tidal flats. Salt-marsh occurs at Cornaa behind the shingle bank at Derbyhaven and along the banks of the Sulby River at Ramsey. Port Erin Bay is a classic example of an exposed sandy bay with sub-littoral sediments of gravel grading to fine sand towards the shore.

Bedrock and boulders dominate the shallow sub-littoral zone immediately adjacent to the island[78]. This is more extensive around the south where there are vertical walls, ledges, reefs, gullies, caves and boulder slopes. Here there are kelp forests with a rich diversity of Anemones, Sea Squirts, Dead Men's Fingers (*Alcyinium digitatum*) and an abundance of crustaceans and fish. Other shallow sub-littoral communities include the Brittle-star (Ophiuroidea) beds that are common off Spanish Head, maerl beds[79] at Niarbyl and in Ramsey Bay, an Edible Mussel (*Mylitus edulis*) bed off the Point of Ayre, patches of the Horse Mussel (*Modiolus modiolus*) and exceptionally diverse communities in and around the tidal rapids of Calf Sound. In the bays the sub-tidal communities on the sands include burrowing worms and bivalves, juvenile flatfish, Weever Fish (Trachinidae), Gobies (Gobiidae) and small crustaceans. Two seagrass beds, which may include Eelgrass (*Zostera marina*) and Tasselweed (*Ruppia* spp.), have recently been recorded at Langness and in Ramsey Bay[80].

Further offshore, there are four different types of seabed community[81]. Off the bays of Ramsey and Castletown, the 'shallow Venus' community[82] is found, where the bed is generally sandy and may be subject to strong currents. This grades into the 'deep Venus' communities to the east and west of the island, which are found on coarse sand, gravel and shell between 40–100 m. To the north and south are mixed grounds of 'deep Venus' and hard ground. The fourth community, beds of Horse Mussel, is found in two areas overlying mud or sandy/stony ground; one to the south has become patchy and mainly composed of shell debris but another, to the north, has recently been found. These beds form reefs that provide important habitats for a diverse fauna of Sea Firs (Hydroids), Sea Squirts, Sponges (Porifera) and anemones and mobile species such as Starfish (Asteroidea), Sea Urchins (Echinoidea), Spider Crabs (Majidae) and Brittlestars.

A review of sites of marine nature conservation importance around the island was carried out for the Manx Wildlife Trust in 2000[83]. This report identifies 13 of the best examples of areas rich in habitats and species using selection criteria developed for the whole of Europe and confirming which areas are important or rare in the Manx context.

BIODIVERSITY

Vascular plants   PHILIPPA TOMLINSON, ELIZABETH CHARTER and LARCH GARRAD

Questions that are often asked about the flora of the Isle of Man are: what are the differences from or similarities with surrounding areas, what are the 'island' effects and why in some respects do a few species appear to 'behave' slightly differently than they might do, for example, in southern England. Species are defined as native if they have colonised the island naturally and without human intervention and arrived by a process of natural succession. It seems very likely that the majority of native flowering plant species arrived on the Isle of Man well before the severance[84]. The very early fossil flora from the kettle holes was notably rich and diverse, reflecting climatic constraints, but also already representing a wide range of habitats[85]. The presence of plant macrofossils, such as leaves and fruits, provides more specific identifications than the pollen record and allows a fascinating comparison with the present-day flora.

There are indications that the grassland of the north of the island survived somewhat later than in the neighbouring islands because of a delay in the natural succession to Birch woodland[86], very possibly because of continued grazing by giant deer. Similarly, some grassland species such as Purple Milk Vetch (*Astragalus danicus*) and Field Mouse-ear (*Cerastium arvense*) were able to continue growing in this region in coastal, unshaded, grassland, although their present distribution is mostly confined to the eastern side of Britain today[87].

Another question is whether any species arrived across a land-bridge from Britain but did not make it to Ireland before its severance. Allen gives four possibilities, but Marsh Valerian (*Valeriana dioica*) with a European-temperate distribution going up into southern Scotland, which used to grow in Ballaugh Curraghs, is perhaps the only unassailable contender. The other three are: Isle of Man Cabbage (*Coincya monensis* ssp. *monensis*) which has a localised distribution around the Irish Sea, probably has seed dispersal by sea; Yellow Vetch (*Vicia lutea*) has seeds which may well be carried on gulls' feet (the plants are found near gulls' nests); and Dyer's Greenweed (*Genista tinctoria*) could well have been introduced and planted for its yellow dye. Others may have become extinct before modern records began. A thorough search through the *New Atlas*[88] has revealed three further species that are native on Man but not in Ireland.

Although islands often have a reduced diversity of natural flora than larger adjacent landmasses, the *New Atlas* shows that the number of species reduces from south to north across the whole British Isles and if most species arrived before severance the island effect may not be significant. Allen reckoned that Man has approximately two-thirds of the Irish total and some two-fifths of the British in every well-worked plant and animal order[89]. Certain groups, although perhaps not flowering plants, may remain under-recorded and thus bias the data. An analysis of the numbers of native species listed in the *New Atlas* in several islands and comparable land areas shows that Man lies within the expected trend. Apart from the possible effect of severance, the difference in land area and the distance from the nearest landmasses, the main reason for the relative paucity of native species is the lack or very small representation of several habitats, notably salt-marsh and expanses of natural freshwater. Most of the species that do not occur on Man either require specific habitats, such as limestone or freshwater, are climatically limited, or have a patchy distribution elsewhere. More significantly, there have been extinctions in the past. Beaked Tasselweed (*Ruppia maritima*) for example, a plant that occurs in brackish waters such as coastal lakes near the sea and occurred at Lough Cranstal in the mid Holocene, no longer has suitable brackish habitats on Man. The earliest of these extinctions, such as some of the 46 taxa listed by Dickson *et al.*[90], were probably due to climatic amelioration and natural succession of habitats such as wetland and woodland, but subsequently the effects of human activity, particularly woodland clearance for agriculture, grazing and the gradual spread of arable land even further into the hills than today. More recently habitat loss caused by agricultural reclamation, drainage and intensification has been the most significant. Over the years there have been losses, but the gains of non-native species have also been dramatic, as will be discussed below. Although there are no endemic or island-specific varieties of flora on Man as far as is known, suggesting insufficient length of insularity, the Isle of Man Cabbage is a strong contender for an endemic because it must have developed somewhere in the Irish Sea area.

Despite the paucity in certain habitats, the island has wide geographical representation in its flora, with elements from temperate, oceanic and polar Europe[91]. A recent study divides the British Isles into ten bio-climatic zones based on the plant species present[92]. Three of these zones are represented in the Isle of Man. 'Cool Oceanic Lowland/Upland' covers probably 90% of the island and also occurs in the coastal parts of western Scotland

and the Isles. 'Mild Sub-Oceanic Upland' is centred on the northern hills in Man, and occurs in much of upland Cumbria, the Pennines and upland Wales. 'Mild Oceanic Lowland' is represented on the island's south and southeastern coast; it covers the whole of Anglesey and a narrow coastal strip of Wales and the whole southwestern peninsula of England. Thus the majority of the island has a botanical composition most comparable with coastal and island western Scotland.

At the highest altitudes a very few arctic-alpine species occur – Dwarf Willow, protected when a new mast was built on Snaefell summit, Cowberry (*Vaccinium vitis-idaea*) and a montane sub-species of Wavy Hair Grass (*Deschampsia flexuosa* ssp *Montana*). Other species such as Mountain Pansy (*Viola lutea*), Mountain Everlasting (*Antennaria dioica*) and Yellow Saxifrage (*Saxifraga aizoides*) once occurred, the loss of which Allen[93] puts down to pressure of grazing. There are two particular northern species, the Lesser Twayblade (*Listera cordata*), which may still occur, well hidden, on the northern hills but has not been seen since the 1880s and the Lesser Butterfly-orchid (*Platanthera bifolia*), which is still present in lowland wet heaths and boggy pastures.

The flora of the island has strong elements of western and oceanic influence and in many instances it is the western sub-species or variety that is found, on close inspection, to be the native. For example the ivy is Atlantic Ivy (*Hedera helix* ssp *hibernica*) and the Harebell is the hexaploid variety of *Campanula rotundifolia* (*C. giesekiana* Vest) that has also been found in peripheral areas in western Scotland, Ireland and Cornwall[94]. The climate is also very suitable for Mosses and Liverworts (Bryophytes) and Ferns (Filicopsida). Prothalli[95] of the Killarney Fern (*Trichomanes speciosum*) were recently refound[96].

Some species are close to the edge of their range and their occurrence on the island is only rare where they would be very common further south and east. The native populations of Cow Parsley (*Anthriscus sylvestris*), for example, are restricted to some of the northern glens but along the road-sides and field margins Hogweed (*Heracleum sphondylium*) is usually to be found. Cow Parsley is also a good example of the care that has to be taken in distinguishing native and introduced populations; the variety introduced from southern England occurs in restricted roadside locations.

Native trees and shrubs   PHILIPPA TOMLINSON

The area of native woodland is now limited to small groups of trees, such as Alder (*Alnus glutinosa*), Hazel (*Corylus avellana*), Sessile Oak (*Quercus petraea*), Downy Birch (probably the relict northern race *Betula pubescens* ssp. *odorata*), Wych Elm (*Ulmus glabra*), Aspen (*Populus tremula*), and Rowan. It is clear from the pollen record that they were common before human colonisation began, but it is not necessarily certain whether any of the remaining trees are descended from this early stock. Plantations using foreign and different genetic stock[97] may also have subsequently interbred with existing trees.

The Native Oak Group has encouraged the use of local, native species and also collected specimens of oak buds from a large number of relict oak trees growing on cliffs and steep valley sides around the island[98]. These specimens went towards a Europe-wide study, which looked at the distribution of variation in genetic material from oaks in order to understand the effects of post-glacial colonisation and human management[99]. The majority of oaks sampled from Britain (98%) possessed three genetic characteristics from a lineage commonly found in Spain and western France. The findings support the hypothesis that most British native Sessile and Pedunculate (*Quercus robur*) Oaks originate from a Pleistocene refugium in the Iberian Peninsula. These three characteristics are found in both species, but in different geographical areas of Britain. Of the oak woods sampled from the Isle of Man, all except one strongly resembled oaks in Cumbria, north Wales, Cornwall and western Scotland. This distribution may be the result of the nature of colonisation of oak trees, that is, single long-distance dispersal events, probably by birds carrying acorns, which in the case of Man may have been strengthened by its island situation. In contrast the specimens from Traie de Halsall were much closer to trees in south Wales and central England, still from Iberian lineage, but very likely to have been imported to Man.

Changing floristic diversity   Larch Garrad

The attractive Common Wintergreen (*Pyrola minor*) took advantage of the spread of the willow thickets resulting from the Manx government's purchase of the Ballaugh Curraghs, which converted this superb wetland into a wildlife reserve. In the last few years, management has attempted to halt the spread of the willow and birch to maintain the Bog Myrtle (*Myrica gale*) areas and the diversity of smaller lovers of wet ground. The Manx orchid flora is quite diverse but often sadly transient. A surprising addition was Dense-flowered Orchid (*Neotinea maculata*), which the first major myxomatosis outbreak in Man in 1965–66 allowed to flower freely. It has been suggested that the colony, which died out in 1985 or 1986, derived from an Irish source brought down by the vapour from transatlantic jets. When John Ray (1627–1705) and his young patron Francis Willoughby

(1635–72) landed at Ramsey in July 1660[100] they encountered a small, yellow crucifer, which has ever since been known as Isle of Man Cabbage. It still grows on Ramsey north shore and other coastal sands in the north.

The plants associated with varying water levels in ponds are quite commonly erratic in their appearance, such as Golden Dock (*Rumex maritimus*). Uniquely in the British Isles, Pennyroyal (*Mentha pulegium*) appears to have maintained the same range it enjoyed in the 1820s, occurring in mineral-rich northern ponds. It also appeared in the 1990s as a street weed, seeded from a supermarket herb pot. This more robust alien variant may well be on the increase in Britain[101].

Shore plants are particularly ephemeral. Recently Sea Kale (*Crambe maritima*) and Oyster Plant (*Mertensia maritima*) have done well in Man. As elsewhere in the British Isles, inter-tidal Eelgrass was affected by disease, but has recovered on the evidence of plants washed up at Derbyhaven and Port Erin and found by scuba divers between Fort Island and Langness. Common Cord-grass (*Spartina anglica*) apparently did not arrive until the 1970s and several colonies have proved to be transient. Maidenhair Fern survives in a few virtually inaccessible sea caves and was recently seen by an excursion of the British Pteridological Society[102].

Introduced species   L A R C H   G A R R A D

Plant species are introduced into the wild by a number of different routes, for example as arable weeds, garden escapes, and nursery weeds or from birdseeds or packaging. They may then become naturalised and grow within the wild flora, such as Sycamore (*Acer pseudoplatanus*). Alternatively, they may be restricted to a small area or grow only for one or two seasons, such as Thorn-apple (*Datura stramomium*) that occasionally appears from birdseed. Only species able to replicate themselves in the wild should be counted as established aliens. The creeping pink-brown leaves of New Zealand Willow Herb (*Epilobium brunnescens*) are now widespread along tracks in the plantations.

A project initiated to record the recent introduction and spread of species on the island is also hoping to spot potential escapees 'in the act'[103]. This requires an examination of historical records as well as careful fieldwork to distinguish the established aliens from the short-term casuals that may never become established or species deliberately planted in the wild. The results of this work are well shown in the *New Atlas*, with an unusually large number of alien plant records for the island compared to other areas[104]. A preliminary list of *circa* 460 known introduced flowering plant species has been drawn up.

Arable weeds have declined in diversity and abundance as elsewhere. Before seed was so thoroughly cleaned and herbicides developed, a range of annual weeds would have been regularly brought in and dispersed in the countryside. Archaeological records from excavations such as Peel Castle and Billown have produced a number of weed records. Many of these grow widely today, such as Corn Marigold (*Chrysanthemum segetum*), Fat Hen (*Chenopodium album*), Scarlet Pimpernel (*Anagallis arvensis* ssp. *arvensis*), Corn Chamomile (*Anthemis arvensis*), Black Bindweed (*Fallopia convolvulus*) and Redshank (*Persicaria maculosa*)[105].

Others are no longer a feature of the Manx flora, such as Nettle-leaved Goosefoot (*Chenopodium murale*), which latterly was virtually confined to upper shores in Castletown and Peel until development eliminated it. According to historic, as opposed to archaeological, botanical records, arable weeds would have included Corncockle (*Agrostemma githago*), which was very common in Forbes's time, Small-flowered Buttercup (*Ranunculus parviflorus*), Corn Buttercup (*Ranunculus arvensis*), probably now extinct, and Cornflower (*Centaurea cyanus*), extinct by *circa* 1925[106]. Recent records of Corncockle and Cornflower have mainly been the result of planting ill-sourced wild plant seeds. An illustration of this was Austrian Chamomile (*Anthemis austriaca*) supplied to Ramsey Commissioners as Corn Chamomile, of which there are only three records on cultivated ground with light soils.

When it was decided to create a car park on Fort Island, St Michael's Isle, seed was collected on site and spread over the soil-filled plastic cells. By 2001 the transplanted vegetation was fully established. This contrasts very pleasingly with the curious 'amenity' selection, which was supplied for emergency soil erosion control at the Gob-ny-Rona car park. This included such birdseed ingredients as Niger (*Guizotia abyssinica*) and the tall, coarse grass Cockspur (*Echinochloa crus-gallii*). It is hoped that the Manx Wildlife Trust's Wildflowers of Man seed bank of natives can be called on if similar emergencies occur, as well as in other habitat restoration and creation projects.

Survivals, or relicts, from former herbal use are conspicuous. Among the more noteworthy are Elecampane (*Inula helenium*) in Rushen Sheading and Masterwort (*Peucedanum ostruthium*) a 'cow doctor's herb' in Andreas and Bride[107].

During the twentieth century a considerable number of additions to the Manx flora became established from garden escapes. Red Valerian (*Centranthus ruber*) was first noticed in Douglas about 1900 and is now common and widespread on roadsides, walls and structures in all its colour forms – white, pink and red. Three-cornered Garlic (*Allium triquetrum*) was first discovered as an escape at Poyllvaaish in 1946. Initially its spread was concentrated in the Sheading of Rushen, but after 1960 its range expanded and it was mapped in virtually every kilometre square for the *New Atlas*. Butterfly-bush (*Buddleja davidii*) was noticeably uncommon in the 1950s in comparison with its post-war status in London and south-west England. Its opportunities in Man did not come until the demolition of older structures in Castletown, Douglas and Ramsey. It consolidated rapidly and is now found as a street weed, on every part of dwellings from wall bases to chimney tops, and far out in the countryside in scrub and on hedge banks. At least six different Cotoneaster and Hedge Veronica (*Hebe*) species have become commonplace as escapes from gardens.

Among those plants that now behave as wildings the more conspicuous include Purple Toadflax (*Linaria purpurea*) – now much commoner than that relic of the railway age, Common Toadflax (*L. vulgaris*) – and Pink-Sorrel (*Oxalis articulata*). At least six other exotic *Oxalis* are known, including one, seemingly unique in the British Isles, Ten-leaved Pink-Sorrel (*O. decaphylla*), in the Douglas Promenade gardens. The hybrid Monbretia (*Crocosmia* x *crocosmiiflora*) is widespread and abundant. It forms a fascinating association with Sea Bindweed (*Calystegia soldanella*) on the Ayres fore dunes. New Zealand willow herb was unknown in Man until 1961, but did not expand its territory much before the 1980s.

Bulrush (*Typha latifolia*) was, on evidence from the pollen record, present in antiquity but vanished until reintroduced about 1900. It is now quite widespread in garden ponds, distributed by gardeners and wind-blown seed. One of the oddest locations for a colony was for some years the roof of a public convenience in upper Douglas.

Lichens   STELLA THROWER

Historically, the Isle of Man's lichen flora has been recorded largely by visiting lichenologists here for periods of a few days or weeks. Earland-Bennett[108] produced a preliminary assessment and included a survey of the studies made up to that date. At no time has there been a local lichenologist involved in making a complete survey of the lichen flora of the island. The most comprehensive study to date has been made on the very small Santon churchyard (0.28 hectare) where a total of 102 species in 46 genera was recorded[109].

All 344 species in 108 genera recorded from the island also occur in Great Britain predominantly in the northwest, west and southwest counties; many also occur in continental Europe. In contrast the British Isles has over 1,700 species, in 262 genera[110]. It has been suggested that a probable total of some 500 species could be achieved for the Isle of Man with a thorough investigation[111]. Records for the island are incorporated into the British Mapping Scheme, which was inaugurated in 1964. They are held in the data banks of the Biological Records Centre at Monks Wood, England, and distribution maps are regularly published in the British Lichen Society's journal *Lichenologist*.

The factors that determine the distribution of lichens include climate, topography, management practices with respect to woodland and heathland and human activity. Lichens grow on trees, rocks and soil and their distribution is also determined by their specificity with reference to the substrate. If a particular rock type or tree species is absent from an area, then the lichens associated with that substrate will also be absent. Threats to the lichen flora arise primarily from threats to their substrates. Stone walls, infrequent only on the northern plain, carry possibly the richest lichen flora in the Isle of Man. Many are deteriorating when no longer maintained. Others may be lost through developments or road-widening activities. With removal of the walls the lichen flora also disappears. The other important substrate is the mature tree, and where such trees are taken down, again their lichen flora is lost.

Human activities can have both positive and negative effects. Many species, often rare, which occur on natural rock outcrops in upland areas have now become widespread, as their range of substrates is increased by brick and concrete structures, tombstones and new walls. City environments tend to become lichen deserts as they succumb to air pollution caused by sulphur dioxide emissions and automobile fumes. In Douglas only 12 species of lichen can be found in St George's churchyard compared with 102 species in Santon churchyard, situated in the countryside some 9 km away.

Invertebrates   KATE HAWKINS

Much recent knowledge of invertebrates in the Isle of Man derives from ecological survey, focused on practical goals rather than distribution mapping and building species inventories, although these are often by-products. Boyce and Fowles' survey[112] provided much needed information about the invertebrate conservation value at selected coastal and woodland sites around the island. A major survey of riverine invertebrates was commissioned for the IRIS (Integration and Recycling of the Island's Sewage) project[113] as a baseline for measuring subsequent effects of the removal of raw sewage effluent. It found a restricted fauna, attributed partly to the island situation and lack of mature rivers, but also to the legacy of heavy metal pollution from the mining industry. Freshwater invertebrates are important indicators of water quality. A scoring system, based on families of invertebrates, is used in standard, river-quality monitoring by Government analysts[114].

The usefulness of the information gained by invertebrate survey has to be placed in the context of limited collecting periods, with standard, but not always comprehensive collecting techniques, such as ground fauna biased pitfall traps. This is compounded by the, often huge, task of species identification. Nevertheless, surveys at The Ayres[115], Langness[116] and Druidale[117] have provided a valuable insight into the invertebrate component of the faunas and contributed towards a broader understanding of their habitat management needs. Detailed biodiversity information is available in a case study of Santon churchyard[118], which tackles the complete range of invertebrates.

Annual reports are another good source of records; the Manx Bird Atlas produces a list of 'non-avian' sightings from its annual returns[119], the Calf of Man Bird Observatory reports include invertebrate records when expertise is available, and the recent appointment of a seasonal warden for the Ayres National Nature Reserve has produced useful observations on Butterflies and Moths, Dragonflies and Damselflies and others[120].

Amateur recording of invertebrates continues, though some groups are better covered than others. The checklist of spiders increased rapidly to more than 200 species, thanks to a series of visits by Wright between 1989 and 1996[121]. A short visit by Huxley in 2000 gave a long overdue boost to knowledge of Manx aquatic bugs (Hemiptera-Heteroptera), although the number of new species found was offset by the apparent disappearance of others previously recorded, suggesting worrying ecological change[122]. Dragonflies and Damselflies are rather poorly represented in the Isle of Man, with only five common species. However the Emerald Damselfly (*Lestes sponsa*) has made a welcome reappearance and there have been recent reports of new additions to the Manx list, although these need to be confirmed by more systematic survey. The latest checklist of Beetles (Coleoptera) included many contributors[123] and concluded that some families such as Ladybirds (Coccinellidae) are fairly well covered, whereas others like the Scarab and Dung Beetles (Scarabaeoidea) would repay more work.

Butterflies and Moths are well recorded, mostly by light trapping. Local specialities such as Dew Moth (*Setina irrorella*), The Grey (*Hadena caesia*), Black-banded (*Polymixis xanthomista*) and the rare 'micromoth' Scarce Crimson and Gold (*Pyrausta sanguinalis*) are monitored[124] and new records are added regularly[125]. Craine produced an updated checklist in

1998, assembled with contributions from a number of recorders[126]. Manx records were included in the Butterflies for the New Millennium atlas project, and two of the species from the island's meagre list, Grayling (*Hipparchia semele*) and Dark Green Fritillary (*Argynnis aglaja*) have since been identified as candidate Species of Conservation Concern due to declines in their populations elsewhere[127].

Although the Isle of Man has yet to sign the Convention on Biological Diversity some detailed single species work is being done towards Biodiversity Action Plans for locally vulnerable invertebrates. A number of insect species here are known to be at the extremities of their range in the British Isles. In this respect The Ayres continues to be important for sting-bearing Bees, Wasps and Ants (Aculeate Hymenoptera), with *Oxybelus mandibularis* and *Smicromyrme rufipes* of recent note[128]. The stronghold of the Manx Robber Fly (*Machimus cowini*), known only from a few localities around the Irish Sea, now appears to be on the soft cliffs along the northeast coast[129]. At Langness the theory of a glacial refugium origin for the Lesser Mottled Grasshopper (*Stenobothrus stigmaticus*) is still debated[130]. Crellin has reported on the behaviour and distribution at The Ayres of the Beefly (*Bombylius minor*) for which the only other known sites are on the Dorset heaths[131].

Over 100 years of existence the Port Erin Marine Laboratory has built up a considerable body of scientific knowledge about the marine environment, guiding amongst other things the process towards sustainable exploitation of the fisheries. Marine habitats and communities have been systematically recorded, with particular emphasis in recent years on conserving the rich biodiversity of Manx waters *per se*. Invertebrates figure heavily: a dive survey around the Calf of Man in 1991–2 found over half the total number of Sea Slug (nudibranch) species recorded in the UK[132]. Recently a rare Sea-mat (Bryozoan) Ross Coral (*Pentapora fascialis*) was rediscovered off the islet[133], reinforcing the report's assessment of the area's 'exceptional diversity'. A later sub-littoral survey around the whole island identified a number of important invertebrate-dominated communities such as Brittlestar and Mussel beds[134] and dominant invertebrates are noted in the inter-tidal habitat survey carried out on behalf of the Manx Wildlife Trust[135].

Terrestrial non-avian vertebrates   ED POOLEY

The numbers of species
The island is presently home to resident, confirmed breeding populations of 37 species of non-avian vertebrates. This is two more than the total

reported in 1997[136]. The breeding status of the Flounder (*Platichthys flesus*) in the north of the island and of the Common Seal (*Phoca vitulina*) on the Calf has since been confirmed[137]. The Common Pipistrelle Bat (*Pipistrellus pipistrellus*) has recently been identified as two separate species, one with the original name and one as *Pipistrellus pygmaeus*. Both are resident and breeding on the Isle of Man. The Red Fox (*Vulpes vulpes*) was provisionally assessed in 1997 as established and breeding, but this has not been the outcome.

It is interesting to note that, excluding introductions, it was not until the 1990s that Leisler's and Daubenton's Bats (*Nyctalus leiseri* and *Myotis daubentonii*), which are likely to have been here for as long as any other bats, were formally recorded. A number of species introductions, which have subsequently become established with apparent ease are either known or believed to have occurred within the last 100 years. These include Red-necked Wallaby (*Macropus rufogriseus*), which currently sustains the longest-surviving free-living population in the British Isles, and repeated, but now illegal, introductions of Common Toad (*Bufo bufo*), Smooth Newt (*Triturus vulgaris*) and Palmate Newt (*Triturus helveticus*). Rainbow Trout (*Oncorhynchus mykiss*), Tench (*Tinca tinca*) and Minnow (*Phoxinus phoxinus*) have also been imported directly or indirectly for sport fishing purposes. Two recent illegal attempts to introduce the Red Fox have not resulted in viable free-living populations and the initial success of the 1987 introduction was subsequently overstated[138]. A spotlit transect survey in 1999 failed to locate any individuals[139].

A comparison of the resident terrestrial breeding species in the Isle of Man with the lists for Britain and Ireland shows that the Manx list totalling 37 species is largely a sub-set of the Irish list of 61 species. Britain, by comparison, has 127 species on the same definition. Whilst human-mediated additions and losses to the fauna since settlement began have significantly altered the natural colonisation, this still underlies current similarities and differences. In some cases, such as reptiles, Ireland and Man share the same native species. Many small mammals are missing from both: Water Vole (*Arvicola terrestris*), Field Vole (*Mictrotis agrestis*), Common Shrew (*Sorex araneus*), Water Shrew (*Neomys fodiens*) and Mole (*Talpa europaea*) for example. That some larger species such as Badger (*Meles meles*) and Red Fox have survived in Ireland but not in the Isle of Man can reasonably be attributed to a combination of habitat differences and constraints on species populations imposed by the relatively small size of the Isle of Man. The fact that the totals for a restricted insular area are so relatively high in Man can be attributed in significant part to the surprising variety of habitats still found.

Some significant points on current species   Some species have declined because of loss of habitat. For example, some bats have suffered roost interference and feeding habitat loss, and fish numbers have been affected both by a succession of acute water pollution incidents during the 1980s and 1990s arising from both industrial and agricultural sources, and by loss of riverine habitat following the impounding of the Sulby River in the early 1980s. There has been a significant reduction in the rural Common Frog (*Rana temporaria*) population because of a loss of farm ponds, partially balanced by an increase in suburban garden ponds. More direct human activity has contributed to the decline of other species such that the losses caused by increasing levels of road traffic and the positive management of the Brown Rat (*Rattus norvegicus*), Feral Ferret (*Mustela furo*)[140] and Rabbit (*Oryctolagus cuniculus*) populations based on the status of all three as pest species. The domestic Cat (*Felis catus*), along with apparently rising numbers of feral cats, is a major predator of small mammals, birds and lizards. Against this can be set the apparent stability and health of the small population of Red-necked Wallabies dating from a 1976 release in Ballaugh at around the time the Wildlife Park was first established.

'Threatened species'   A number of species are present in very small numbers. For example, the continuing breeding status of the Common Seal is not yet assured, Leisler's Bat has only a single confirmed and persistent breeding roost and while both River Lamprey (*Lampetra fluviatilis*) and Sea Lamprey (*Petromyzon marinus*) are still present in the Sulby River, despite permanent reduction in water flows since the Sulby Dam was built, their status is uncertain, as is that of the Nine-spined Stickleback (*Pungitius pungitius*). It is not known whether any stock of native Brown Trout (*Salmo trutta*) survives, but isolated headwaters are probable locations. Even the House Mouse (*Mus musculus*), a small and dispersed population exclusively commensal to humans, appears to be in decline and is subject to increasing levels of pest control.

'Potentially threatened'   Relatively few breeding roosts of the Natterer's Bat are known and currently no clear understanding of the species' insular ecology exists. Research is also urgently needed to ensure that habitat change does not prejudice the future viability of the Stoat (*Mustela erminea*), which is almost certainly the longest-surviving native mammal. The Common Frog is in danger of in-breeding of dispersed populations with reduced mixing, but this trend is balanced by localised human redistribution of spawn. The well-established breeding populations of Feral Goat (*Capra hircus*) and Red-necked Wallaby are potentially threatened by human intervention.

Had Foot and Mouth disease arrived on the island in 2001 every attempt would have been made to exterminate the goats, and should the Ballaugh Curraghs be designated a RAMSAR site, the small but persistent population of wallabies may yet be rounded up and returned to captivity.

Avifauna   PAT CULLEN and CHRIS SHARPE

A historical review of Manx ornithology, descriptions of principal avian habitats and details of individual species up to 1985 can be found in *Birds of the Isle of Man*[141]. One of the early historical records of Manx birds is the illustration of the extinct Great Auk and the Gannet by Daniel King around 1652[142]. Based on the accounts of fishermen handed down a generation, Cullen and Jennings suggest that the Great Auk was perhaps a summer visitor to the island up to about 1790 and it probably became extinct not long after then.

The Isle of Man has a closer affinity to Ireland than to Britain in its avifauna, thus the commonest owl is the Long-eared (*Asio otus*), while, as in Ireland, the Tawny Owl (*Strix aluco*), as well as the Woodpeckers (*Picus viridis* and *Dendrocopos major*), Redstart (*Phoenicurus phoenicurus*) and Pied Flycatcher (*Ficedula parva*) are absent as breeding birds. Conversely, Nuthatch (*Sitta europaea*) and Marsh Tit (*Parus palustris*), absent in Man, are virtually absent from Scotland too. Inexplicably, Bullfinches (*Pyrrhula pyrrhula*) and, to a lesser extent, Jays (*Garrulus glandarius*), are widespread in the surrounding isles but absent from Man. The many rocky streams would appear tailor-made for the Dipper (*Cinclus cinclus*), which is also plentiful in Britain and Ireland, yet the minute Manx population was lost early in the last century and has never become re-established.

The Isle of Man is particularly rich in four species which have a westerly distribution in the British Isles, namely Hen Harrier, Peregrine (*Falco peregrinus*), Chough and Raven (*Corvus corax*). Significant recent developments have been the establishment in the Ballaugh Curragh of the largest communal roost of Hen Harriers in western Europe, as well as another sizeable roost on Stoney Mountain; the colonisation of the island by Siskins (*Carduelis spinus*) and Eiders (*Somateria mollissima*), both reflecting a general southerly extension of breeding range; and the arrival of the Ruddy Duck (*Oxyura jamaicensis*) following its expansion from its stronghold in the English Midlands to Cheshire, Anglesey and Northern Ireland. Not unexpected was the recent location of a pair of Golden Plover (*Pluvialis apricaria*), apparently breeding in the northern Manx hills.

Habitat changes have, to some extent, had an impact on the avifauna, but cannot explain the loss of the Corn Bunting (*Miliaria calandra*) and the severe decline of the Grey Partridge (*Perdix perdix*), Lapwing, Snipe, and, to a lesser degree, Yellowhammer (*Emberiza citrinella*). The increasingly early cutting of grass for silage has contributed to the demise of the Corncrake, and the preservation of traditional hay meadows at for example Close Sartfield on the margin of the Ballaugh Curragh has demonstrated that sympathetic land management may be the first step in restoring this species' fortunes as a breeding bird. Low-intensity farming is considered to have contributed to the prosperity of the Chough, which benefits from the short turf of the coastal pasture grazed by sheep and the presence of dung fauna. Although afforestation has deprived the island of considerable areas of moor, the infant plantations provide an attractive, though short-term, habitat for Hen Harrier and Short-eared Owl. Equally, failed plantations confer the same advantages.

The Manx Wildlife Trust, through its thoughtful land management and Manx National Heritage, by measures such as the introduction of loughtan sheep to its land, are making important contributions to the preservation of the island's threatened avifauna. Other bodies whose work must benefit the bird life include the Manx Bird Atlas, which is currently conducting a breeding bird survey of all the island's one kilometre squares, and the Manx Chough project, which undertakes population monitoring and nest-site conservation and, through colour ringing, monitoring the movements of Chough.

CONSERVATION MANAGEMENT AND FUTURE RESEARCH   PHILIPPA TOMLINSON

Trends

The main pressures on the countryside today are the rapidly increasing human population with its insatiable housing and leisure demands, together with economically led changes in agricultural land use that are as complex as in the past. Some arable and semi-improved land is reverting to semi-natural habitat, often through changes in ownership. A proportion of semi-natural habitat is also being improved agriculturally. An increase of built-up land, amenity grassland and gardens is reducing the improved grassland and arable as well as a small part of the semi-natural habitat. Other developments are an increase in horse-grazing meadows and plantation of lowland broadleaved woodland as land goes out of direct agricultural use. In order that these changes should be managed effectively for the benefit of wildlife, both governmental policies and structures need to be founded on a continuing programme of primary research.

Government policy and its implementation

The passing of the Wildlife Act in 1990 and the Manx Government's acceptance of a number of international conventions have given welcome protection for a wide range of species, and the establishment of a new Wildlife and Conservation Office within the Department of Agriculture, Fisheries and Forestry in 1998 has provided the administrative structure for the implementation of a raft of conservation measures. Despite these positive developments, there is still a great deal of catching up to do, which will require a strong and continued commitment from the Government. For example, it took six years from the passing of the 1990 Act before a single Area of Special Scientific Interest was designated and since then only one more has been created. No RAMSAR sites have been defined over 10 years after the Convention. The Isle of Man also needs to agree to follow the Rio Convention on Biological Diversity. The Manx Wildlife Trust has made progress with a Biodiversity Action Plan, but this still needs to be implemented.

The problem remains that, apart from the several charitable organisations, such as the Wildlife Trust, the Farming and Wildlife Advisory Group, the Manx Rivers Improvement Association and the Manx Bird Atlas, all the professionals dealing with conservation and wildlife are within a number of government departments none of whose primary concerns is nature conservation. There is a very strong need, as there has been ever since the Manx National Trust was combined with the Manx Museum, for the creation of an independent, government-funded, agency, such as English Nature which could have overall responsibility for nature conservation. It would deal with major planning decisions, co-ordinate information and decision making between government departments, liaise with non-government organisations and promote nature conservation to the general public. This would remove the problems of self-regulation, separate the task of prosecution and enforcement from government departments and establish a transparent line of responsibility for action.

Research

The present faunal and floral assemblage is a complex mix of native species and human-mediated introductions, moderated by both direct and indirect management. The pace of both habitat change and species management and introduction has been increasingly evident over the last 100 years. There is an increasing recognition that understanding all the ramifications of these changes is an important prerequisite for a sound environmental management strategy. The necessary degree of understanding of the status of Manx species and their potential vulnerability is still some way off.

The genetic status of many existing Manx populations is uncertain. It is often impossible to know whether a given species is a direct descendant of an original early Holocene coloniser or the result of much more recent introduction. Research of the kind carried out on the 'Polecat Ferret' and the 'native' Oaks should be undertaken on many more species. A serious attempt should be made to identify pollen reservoirs dating to the last 1,000 years or so in order to fill the gap between the existing palaeobotanical record, normally truncated by peat digging, and the present. When, for example, did the uplands become heather moor? What was the effect of the 1860 Disafforesting Act? The recovery of much more dated fossil material from archaeological excavations throughout the island would also be advantageous.

In order to ensure that Manx conservation policies are based on sound information and a good understanding of the complex ecosystems that form the basis of the island's natural environment, it is essential that overall research priorities are established. There are large gaps in the records; certain groups of invertebrates and some of the lower plants, for example, require detailed scientific study. Others, such as terrestrial molluscs[143], were well catalogued in the past, but need to be reappraised in light of modern recording requirements. This, combined with a unified, up-to-date biological records centre, is an essential basis for future research and planning.

Although habitat mapping, in conjunction with computerised geographic information systems, will enable future changes in land use to be closely monitored, it is important to remember that the scale of existing mapping may have missed many of the smaller areas of semi-natural habitat, which may provide refuges for a range of rare or under-recorded species and could easily disappear without being accounted for. Further detailed fieldwork is needed to establish the precise status and ecology of a number of rare and possibly threatened species such as Sea Lamprey, Nine-spined Stickleback, Flounder, Robber Fly and Natterer's Bat, which would all benefit from the kind of study being applied to the Chough. The ecological effects of more common species such as Bracken, the Stoat or Hen Harrier would be of interest, as would an assessment of the impact of such non-native species such as Red-necked Wallaby.

In many cases the recording and ecological contribution of invertebrates will be essential to the study of specific plants and vertebrates[144]. Not only are they relatively poorly recorded, but also they have different conservation needs. Their life cycles demand consistent, often specialised niche conditions, such as structural rather than species diversity in vegetation, and they frequently have limited powers of dispersal.

The effects of alternative management policies, for example on heather moor, or the Manx wetlands, need detailed research, as do the more mundane but geographically much more significant implications of a range of agricultural and forestry practices. Much more work of the type carried out on alternative management of the headlands of arable fields in the north of the island needs to be done[145]. Similarly, in the uplands, studies of the effects on biodiversity, species composition and long-term viability of grazing regimes of differing intensity and timing should be attempted. At a time when environmental change is likely, with or without human involvement, the survival or otherwise of a number of Manx species will depend on the implementation of appropriate conservation measures that are founded on the best available scientific knowledge.

Conclusion

In conclusion, whilst recent trends of improved resources for wildlife management are welcome, there is a need to establish effective structures within a framework of a focused programme of research in order to ensure that there are no further losses of established species and that the biodiversity of the Manx environment will be maintained for the benefit of future generations.

1   See P.J. Davey (ed.), *A New History of the Isle of Man*, Volume 2, *Prehistory*, Liverpool University Press, (forthcoming).
2   Since 1992 the Manx Museum has been a part of Manx National Heritage.
3   The Act established the Museum and Ancient Monuments Trustees.
4   E. Forbes, *Malacologia Monensis: a catalogue of the Mollusca inhabiting the Isle of Man*, Edinburgh (1838).
5   J.R. Bruce, J.S. Colman and N.S. Jones, *Marine Fauna of the Isle of Man*, Liverpool University Press (1963), 307.
6   P.M.C. Kermode, 'Contributions to a vertebrate fauna of the Isle of Man', *Zoologist*, 17 (1893), 61–70.
7   L.S. Garrad, *The Naturalist in the Isle of Man*, David and Charles, Newton Abbot (1972a), 234.
8   D.E. Allen, *Flora of the Isle of Man*, The Manx Museum and National Trust, Douglas (1984), 29–42.
9   C.D. Preston, D.A. Pearman and T.D. Dines, *New Atlas of the British and Irish Flora*, Cambridge University Press (2002), 910.
10   J.P. Cullen and P.P. Jennings, *Birds of the Isle of Man*, Bridgeen Publications, Douglas, Isle of Man (1986), 39.
11   P.M.C. Kermode, 'List of birds of the Isle of Man', *Proceedings of the Isle of Man Natural History and Antiquarian Society*, 1 (1888), 15–23.

12 K. Williamson, 'Ornithology on the Calf of Man', *Proceedings of the Isle of Man Natural History and Antiquarian Society*, 7 (1941), 419–439.

13 Under Manx National Heritage management.

14 J.P. Cullen and P.P. Jennings (1986).

15 Now known as Manx National Heritage. See S. Harrison, *100 Years of Heritage*, Manx Museum and National Trust, Douglas (1986), 207.

16 L. Garrad, 'Nature Conservation', in V. Robinson and D. McCarroll (eds), *The Isle of Man: Celebrating a Sense of Place*, Liverpool University Press (1990b), 90–98.

17 J. Fairhurst, *Calf of Man Management Plan*, unpublished report, Manx National Heritage, Properties Section (1996); J. Fairhurst, *Ballaugh Curragh Management Plan*, unpublished report, Manx National Heritage, Properties Section (1998); J. Callister, *Maughold Brooghs and Gob ny Rona Site Management Plan*, unpublished report, Manx National Heritage, Properties Section (2002).

18 L. Garrad (1990b); D.F. Perkins and A. Buse, *A report on an ecological survey of the Isle of Man*, Nature Conservation Council and Institute of Terrestrial Ecology report to the Isle of Man Government (1974).

19 T. Sayle, J. Lamb, A. Colvin and B. Harris, *Isle of Man Habitat Survey Phase 1 Report 1991–1994*, Department of Agriculture, Fisheries and Forestry, Isle of Man Government, Douglas (1995).

20 L. Veale, R. Thompson and M. Bates, *Isle of Man sublittoral survey 1974–1977*, Port Erin Marine Laboratory, unpublished report (1998a); J. Lamb, *A terrestrial survey of the coast of the Isle of Man*, Report to Manx Wildlife Trust (1999); S. Gubbay, *A Review of sites of marine nature conservation importance around the Isle of Man*, Report to Manx Wildlife Trust (2000). For more detailed descriptions of habitats see: L.S. Garrad (1972a); D.E. Allen (1984); J.P. Cullen and P.P. Jennings (1986).

21 Designated areas, including Manx Wildlife Trust reserves and National Trust land, cover 2% of the total land area.

22 RAMSAR – Convention on Wetlands of International Importance, especially as wildfowl habitat; BERN – Convention on the Conservation of European Wildlife and natural Habitats; BONN – Convention on the Conservation of Migratory Species of Wild Animals; OSPAR – Convention on hazardous Substances in the Marine Environment (extended to the northeast Atlantic); CITES – Convention on International Trade in Endangered Species of Fauna and Flora.

23 J. Lamb, 'The Manx Nature Conservation Trust in the 1990s and beyond', *Proceedings of the Isle of Man Natural History and Antiquarian Society*, 10 (1995), 149–160.

24 T. Hopson and J. Lamb (eds), *Manx Hill-land*, Report to Manx Nature Conservation Trust (1995); Manx Nature Conservation Trust, *Proceedings of the Manx Hill-land seminar* (1997).

25 J. Lamb (1999).

26 T.J. Holt, *An intertidal survey of the Isle of Man 1996–1999*, Port Erin Marine Laboratory, Manx Wildlife Trust (1999).

27 C.C. Morrow, B.E. Picton and J.D.D. Bishop, *A sublittoral survey of the Calf of Man*, Report prepared for the Calf Marine Trust, (1993).

28 B. Keehan, *Manx Wildlife Sites Handbook: a handbook describing the practical implementation of the Manx Wildlife Sites System*, Manx Wildlife Trust (2002), (revised by Peter Dullaghan).

29 Area of Special Scientific Interest.

30 Isle of Man Government, Department of Local Government and the

Environment, *Draft Strategic Plan* (2001).

31   M.A. Fullen, J. Harris and B.S. Kear, *Soils of the Isle of Man*, Centre for Manx Studies Research Report, 5 (1996), 8–11.

32   I.P. Jolliffe, *An investigation into coastal erosion problems in the Isle of Man: causes, effects, and remedial strategies*, Report to the Isle of Man Harbour Board and Isle of Man Government (1981), 149.

33   C. Rouse, 'The Isle of Man's unstable coast', in V. Robinson and D. McCarroll (1990), 77–83.

34   Isle of Man Government, Harbour Board and Board of Agriculture, Fisheries and Forestry, *Report on erosion of the coasts of the north of the Isle of Man*, Report to Tynwald (1983); Isle of Man Government, Department of Highways, Ports and Properties and the Department of Agriculture, Fisheries and Forestry to the Executive Council, *Coast Erosion Policy* (1990); Posford Duvivier International, *Coastal erosion study at Kirk Michael*, Report to Isle of Man Department of Transport in Tynwald (1999).

35   Posford Duvivier International, *Coastal management options for the northern shoreline of the Isle of Man (Kirk Michael to Ramsey)*, Report to the Isle of Man Department of Transport (2000).

36   Isle of Man Government, Department of Transport, *Report into coastal erosion on the northern coasts of the Isle of Man*, Report to Tynwald (2000).

37   Isle of Man Government, Department of Local Government and the Environment (2001).

38   *Isle of Man Examiner*, 14 January 2003, 17.

39   V. Robinson, 'Social demography', in V. Robinson and D. McCarroll (1990), 133–162.

40   C. Page, 'Manx farming communities and traditions: an examination of Manx farming between 1750 and 1900', in P.J. Davey and D.F. Finlayson (eds), *Mannin Revisited: twelve essays on Manx culture and environment*, Scottish Society for Northern Studies (2002), 117–135.

41   T. Quayle, *General view of the agriculture of the Isle of Man*, London (1812) (reprinted W. Bulmer, Douglas 1992).

42   L.B. Thrower, *Manx agriculture 1945–2000: a review of the June census*, Centre for Manx Studies Research Report, 10 (2002).

43   T. Sayle *et al.* (1995). Latin names of plants are given on their first occurrence and follow C. Stace, *New Flora of the British Isles*, Cambridge University Press (1997), 1226. There has been no attempt to use the Manx Gaelic names of the plants mentioned in the text as these have been the subject of recent, as yet unpublished, research and would require additional linguistic explanation not of direct relevance here, but see D.E. Allen (1984).

44   R.C. Chiverrell, J.B. Innes, J.J. Blackford, J.J. Woodcock, P.J. Davey, P.R. Tomlinson, M.M. Rutherford and G.S.P. Thomas, 'Palaeoecological and archaeological evidence for Bronze Age human activity on the Isle of Man', *Holocene*, 14 (2004b), 346–360.

45   T. Hopson and J. Lamb (1995).

46   A. Scott, *Road verge survey project report*, Report to Manx Nature Conservation Trust (1997).

47   J. Lamb (1995).

48   L.B. Thrower (2000).

49   R.C. Chiverrell *et al.* (2004b).

50   J. Chaloner, 'A short treatise on the Isle of Man' [originally published in 1656 as an appendix to 'King's Vale Royal of England'], in J.G. Cumming (ed.), *Manx*

Society, 10 (1864), 57.

51 L.S. Garrad, 'Some thoughts on Manx woodland', *Proceedings of the Isle of Man Natural History and Antiquarian Society*, 7 (1974), 666–685; D.E. Allen, 'The vanished forests', *Peregrine*, 2 (1956), 7–9.

52 W. Blundell, 'History of the Isle of Man' [manuscript written between 1648 and 1657], in W. Harrison (ed.), *Manx Society*, 25 (1876), 135.

53 R. Bohan, 'Manx woodland history and vegetation', in K.J. Kirby and C.Watkins (eds), *The ecological history of European Forests*, CAB International (1998), 155–166.

54 L.S. Garrad (1972a), 155–156, 645; L.S. Garrad, 'Plants and people in the Isle of Man, AD 800–1800', *Botanical Journal of Scotland*, 46 (1994), 644–650.

55 R. Bohan (1998).

56 The native woodland trees are discussed in more detail below.

57 D.E. Allen (1984).

58 *Ibid*.

59 The common Manx species 'Common Sallow' is sub-species *oleifolia*, c.f. D.E. Allen (1984).

60 J. Fairhurst (1998).

61 L.S. Garrad, 'A history of Manx gardens', *Collector's Choice* (1985), 20–22.

62 T. Talbot, *The manorial roll of the Isle of Man 1511–1515*, Oxford University Press, London (1924), 118.

63 P.J. Davey and J. Roscow, 'Rushen Abbey and the dissolution of the monasteries on the Isle of Man', *Isle of Man Natural History and Antiquarian Society Monograph 1* (in press).

64 R.G. Pollard, *The role of the Department of Agriculture, Fisheries and Forestry (Forestry Division) in the Management of the Manx Hill Lands* (1997).

65 T. Hopson and J. Lamb (1995); Manx Nature Conservation Trust (1997).

66 L. Garrad (1990a); P.J. Davey, J.J. Blackford, R.C. Chiverrell, J.B. Innes and P.R. Tomlinson, 'The curragh and other lowland wetlands of the Isle of Man', in M. Atherden (ed.), *Wetlands in the landscape: archaeology, conservation and heritage*, PLACE Research Centre, York (2001), 12–40; J.A. Wheldon and J.W. Hartley, 'The flora of the Manx curraghs', *Lancashire Naturalist* (1910), 271–304.

67 Manx-English word meaning enclosure by agreement, normally after AD 1500.

68 L.S. Garrad (1990a), 90–94; J. Fairhurst (1998).

69 Referred to by Allen as a preglacial relic. See D.E. Allen (1984).

70 B. Sanderson, B. McGregor and A. Brierley, *Dive sites and marine life of the Calf of Man and neighbouring area*, Immel Publishing Ltd, London (1994), 46.

71 No longer present.

72 Manx-English 'dubs'.

73 L. Sampson, *Ponds and Dubs Survey*, Report to Manx Government, Department of Agriculture, Forestry and Fisheries (2002).

74 Isle of Man Government, Analyst's Laboratory, *River Quality Report* (2000).

75 L.B. Thrower (2002).

76 The first edition OS map gazetteer shows that 51% of the plots were arable in 1868/70; in 2000 16% of farmland was arable although a quarter of the grassland would have been ley for silage, L.B. Thrower (2002).

77 S. Gubbay (2000); A.J. Geffen, S.J. Hawkins and E.M. Fisher (eds), 'The Isle of Man', in Irish Sea Study Group, *The Irish Sea: an environmental review. Part 1: Nature Conservation*, Liverpool University Press (1990), 133–168; T.J. Holt (1999); L. Veale *et al*. (1998a).

78   R.A. Irving *et al* (1996); L. Veale *et al.* (1998a).

79   Hard knobbly particles of chalk with a thin outer layer of a reddish pink algae.

80   L. Veale, R. Thompson and M. Bates, *Isle of Man Sub-littoral Survey 1994–1997*, Port Erin Marine Laboratory, unpublished report (1998b).

81   A.S.Y. Mackie, 'Offshore benthic communities of the Irish Sea', in Irish Sea Study Group (eds), *The Irish Sea: an environmental review. Part 1: Nature conservation*, Liverpool University Press (1990), 169–218.

82   Named after the genus of bivalves called *Venus* which characterise this habitat.

83   S. Gubbay (2000).

84   See Chapter 9.

85   C.A. Dickson, J.H. Dickson and G.F. Mitchell, 'The Late Weichselian Flora of the Isle of Man', *Philosophical Transactions of the Royal Society of London*, B258 (1970), 31–79.

86   J.B. Innes, R.C. Chiverrell, J.J. Blackford, P.J. Davey, S. Gonzalez, M.M. Rutherford and P.R. Tomlinson, 'Earliest Holocene vegetation history and Island Biogeography of the Isle of Man, British Isles', *Journal of Biogeography*, 31 (2004), 761–772; J.B. Innes, 'Radiocarbon (AMS) dating of the *Betula* and *Alnus* pollen rises and Holocene woodland history in the Isle of Man', *Bulletin of the British Ecological Society*, 34 (2003), 37–38.

87   D.E. Allen (1984).

88   C.D. Preston *et al.* (2002).

89   D.E. Allen (1984).

90   C.A. Dickson *et al.* (1970).

91   C.D. Preston and M.O. Hill, 'The geographical relationships of British and Irish vascular plants', *Botanical Journal of the Linnean Society*, 124 (1997), 1–120.

92   H.R. Arnold, T.D. Dines, D.A. Pearman and C.D. Preston, 'Vascular plant diversity in Britain and Ireland', in C.D. Preston *et al.* (2002), 27–34.

93   D.E. Allen (1984).

94   H.A. McAllister, '*Campanula rotunifolia*: a local race in south-west Scotland', *Glasgow Naturalist*, 1 (1973), 66.

95   Small plates of tissue derived from a spore and bearing male and female reproductive structures.

96   R. Cooke and A. Paul, 'Isle of Man 6–11 August', *Bulletin of the British Pteridological Society*, 5 (1999), 153–155.

97   For example, *Alnus glutinosa*, D.E. Allen (1984), 142.

98   L.S. Garrad, 'Oak woodland in the Isle of Man', *Watsonia*, 9 (1972c), 59–60; L.S. Garrad (1972a).

99   J.E. Cottrell, R.C. Munro, H.E. Tabbener and A.C.M. Gillies, 'Distribution of cDNA variation in British oaks, *Quercus robur* and *Quercus petraea*, in the influence of post-glacial colonisation and human management', *Forestry Ecology and Management*, 156 (2002), 181–195.

100 D.E. Allen (1984).

101 C.D. Preston *et al.* (2002).

102 R. Cooke and A. Paul (1999), 155.

103 L.S. Garrad, 'The spread of introduced plants into the wild in the Isle of Man', *Proceedings of the Isle of Man Natural History and Antiquarian Society*, 10 (1992b), 145–160;   L.S. Garrad, 'Denizen or natives?', *Proceedings of the Isle of Man Natural History and Antiquarian Society*, 10 (1992a), 163–165.

104 C.D. Preston *et al.* (2002).

105 A more detailed discussion of archaeological evidence for weeds and past crop species will be given in Volume 2.

106 D.E. Allen (1984).

107 L.S. Garrad (1994).

108 P.M. Earland-Bennett, 'A preliminary survey and assessment of the Lichen Flora of the Isle of Man', *Proceedings of the Isle of Man Natural History and Antiquarian Society*, 8 (1979), 139–155.

109 S.L. Thrower, *Biodiversity in a Manx churchyard*, unpublished report (2001).

110 O.W. Purvis, B.J. Coppins, D.L. Hawksworth, P.W. James and D.M. Moore, *The lichen flora of Great Britain and Ireland*, Natural History Museum, London (1992).

111 M.R. Seaward, the official Lichen Recorder of the British Lichen Society, personal communication.

112 D.C. Boyce and A.P. Fowles, *Invertebrate Conservation in the Isle of Man: an assessment of selected sites of ecological interest, 30 April–5 May 1989*, unpublished report (1989).

113 J.E. Eaton, T.J. Holt, G.W. Hopkin, K.W. White and N.J. Wilby, *IRIS Project: Baseline Environmental Survey Report, volume 3, Freshwater Ecology*, Report to the Isle of Man Government (1994).

114 P.D. Styles, *Isle of Man Freshwater Invertebrate Family Checklist*, Isle of Man Government Laboratory, Department of Local Government and the Environment (2001).

115 M.L. Luff, *A pitfall survey of the Ayres*, unpublished report (1992).

116 M.L. Luff, 'An entomological survey of the Langness peninsula, Isle of Man', *Proceedings of the Isle of Man Natural History and Antiquarian Society*, 9 (1990), 565–586.

117 T. Hopson and J. Lamb (1995).

118 S.L. Thrower (2001).

119 C.M. Sharpe, *Non-avian records*, Annual reports to Isle of Man Biological Records Centre, The Manx Museum, Douglas (1999–2002).

120 C. Wormwell, *Warden's Report for Ayres A.S.S.I.*, Report to Department of Agriculture, Fisheries and Forestry, Isle of Man Government (1999); B. Jones, *Warden's Report for Ayres National Nature Reserve*, Report to Department of Agriculture, Fisheries and Forestry, Isle of Man Government (2000).

121 J.E. Dalingwater and J. Wright, 'Spiders of the Isle of Man: Provisional List to 1990', *Proceedings of the Isle of Man Natural History and Antiquarian Society*, 10 (1992), 141–144; J. Wright, 'Additions to the spiders of the Isle of Man: Provisional List 1991 to June 1995', *Proceedings of the Isle of Man Natural History and Antiquarian Society*, 10 (1996), 294–295.

122 T. Huxley, *Aquatic bugs (Hemiptera – Heteroptera) of the Isle of Man*, Report to Manx Museum (2000).

123 M.L. Luff, S. Crellin and M.V.L. Barclay, 'Coleoptera of the Isle of Man updated', *Entomologist's Monthly Magazine*, 137 (2001), 59–64.

124 G.D. Craine, 'Isle of Man report', *Atropos* 12 (January 2001), 65–66.

125 T. Bagworth, *Calf of Man Bird Observatory*, Annual Report for 2000, Manx National Heritage (2000); T. Bagworth, *Calf of Man Bird Observatory*, Annual Report for 2001, Manx National Heritage (2001).

126 G.D. Craine, *Records and status of the larger moths and butterflies of the Isle of Man*, unpublished report (1998).

127 J. Asher, M. Warren, R. Fox, P. Harding, G. Jeffcoate and S. Jeffcoate, *The Millennium Atlas of Butterflies in Britain and Ireland*, Oxford University Press (2001), 208–211, 224–227.

128 S. Crellin, 'Some aculeate hymenoptera new to the Isle of Man', *Entomologist's*

Monthly Magazine, 123 (1987), 35–36.

129 S. Crellin, personal communication (2001).
130 A.J. Cherrill, *A survey of the grasshoppers of the Isle of Man, with particular reference to the distribution, biology and conservation of Stenobothrus stigmaticus (Rambur) on Langness Peninsula*, unpublished report, Department of Agricultural and Environmental Science, University of Newcastle upon Tyne (1990); J.F. Burton, 'The mystery of the Isle of Man's endangered grasshopper', *British Wildlife*, 2 (1990), 37–42.
131 S.R. Miles, *Heathland Flies – UK Biodiversity Action Plan, 1st Report* (1999); S.R. Miles, *Heathland Flies – UK Biodiversity Action Plan, 2nd Report* (2000).
132 C.C. Morrow *et al.* (1993).
133 M. Bates, 'Life under the Ocean Waves – Sublittoral Surveying', *Manx Nature*, Newsletter of the Manx Wildlife Trust (2001).
134 L. Veale *et al.* (1998b).
135 T.J. Holt (1999).
136 E.J. Pooley, 'Non-avian vertebrates and the implications of habitat change', in T. Hopson and J. Lamb (1995), 39–50.
137 T. Bagworth, *Calf of Man Bird Observatory*, Annual Report for 2000, Manx National Heritage (2000).
138 D.W. Macdonald and E.C. Halliwell, 'The rapid spread of red foxes, *Vulpes vulpes*, on the Isle of Man', *Global Ecology and Biogeography Letters*, 4 (1994), 9–16.
139 E.J. Reynolds and M.J. Short, 'The status of Foxes (*Vulpes vulpes*) on the Isle of Man in 1999', *Mammal Review*, 33 (2003), 69–76.
140 Often referred to as polecat-ferrets, but genetically equivalent to ferrets.
141 J.P. Cullen and P.P. Jennings (1986); for archaeological records see C. Fisher, 'Past human exploitation of birds on the Isle of Man', *International Journal of Osteoarchaeology*, 7 (1997), 292–297.
142 The illustrations were prepared for but not used in J. Chaloner (1864).
143 L.S. Garrad, 'Non-marine molluscs of the Isle of Man', *Peregrine*, 3 (1998), 184–188; L.S. Garrad, 'Non-marine molluscs of the Isle of Man II', *Peregrine*, 4 (1972b), 41–44; L.S. Garrad, 'Non-marine molluscs of the Isle of Man III', *Peregrine*, 4 (1973), 71–72; P. Tattersfield, *A preliminary checklist of the terrestrial mollusca of the Isle of Man*, unpublished list (1987).
144 UK Biodiversity Group, *Tranche 2 Action Plans, Vol. IV – Invertebrates*, English Nature (1999), 9–10; D.C. Boyce and A.P. Fowles, (1989).
145 P. Longworth, *An investigation into the relative importance of agricultural operations on arable field boundary vegetation in the Isle of Man including management recommendations*, unpublished MSc dissertation, University of Stirling (2000).

References

Aaby B., 'Cyclic climatic variations in climate over the past 5,500 years reflected in raised bogs', *Nature*, 263 (1976), 281–284.

Ahlberg P.E. and Coates M.I., 'There's a ratfish in our cellar!', *Geology Today*, 13 (1997), 22–23.

Allen D.E., 'The vanished forests', *Peregrine*, 2 (1956), 7–9.

—— *Flora of the Isle of Man*, Manx Museum and National Trust, Douglas (1984), 29–42, 142.

Allen J.R.L. and Crowley S.F., 'Lower Old Red Sandstone fluvial dispersal systems in the British Isles', *Transactions of the Royal Society of Edinburgh: Earth Science*, 74 (1983), 61–68.

Armstrong J.P., Smith J., D'Elia V.A.A. and Trueblood S.P., 'The occurrence and correlation of oils and Namurian source rocks in the Liverpool Bay–North Wales area', in Meadows N.S., Trueblood S.P., Hardman N. and Cowan G. (eds), *Petroleum Geology of the Irish Sea and adjacent areas*, Geological Society of London Special Publication, 124 (1997), 195–211.

Arnold H.R., Dines T.D., Pearman D.A. and Preston C.D., 'Vascular plant diversity in Britain and Ireland', in Preston C.D., Pearman D.A. and Dines T.D. (eds), *New Atlas of the British and Irish Flora*, Cambridge University Press (2002), 27–34.

Arter G. and Fagin S.W., 'The Fleetwood Dyke and the Tynwald Fault Zone, Block 113/27, East Irish Sea Basin', in Parker J.R. (ed.), *Petroleum Geology of NW Europe: Proceedings of the 4th Conference*, The Geological Society of London (1993), 835–843.

Asher J., Warren M., Fox R., Harding P., Jeffcoate G. and Jeffcoate S., *The Millennium Atlas of Butterflies in Britain and Ireland*, Oxford University Press (2001), 208–211, 224–227.

Atkinson T.C., Briffa K.R. and Coope G.R., 'Seasonal temperatures in Britain during the past 22,000 years, reconstructed using beetle remains', *Nature*, 325 (1987), 587–592.

Avery B.W., *Soil Classification for England and Wales [Higher Categories]*, Soil Survey Technical Monograph No. 14, Lawes Agricultural Trust, Harpenden (1980).

Bagworth T., *Calf of Man Bird Observatory*, Annual Report for 2000, Manx National Heritage (2000).

—— *Calf of Man Bird Observatory*, Annual Report for 2001, Manx National Heritage (2001).

Ballantyne C.K. and Harris C., *The periglaciation of Great Britain*, Cambridge University Press, Cambridge (1994).

Barber K.E., Chambers F.M. and Maddy D., 'Holocene palaeoclimates from peat stratigraphy: macrofossil proxy climate records from three oceanic raised bogs in England and Ireland', *Quaternary Science Reviews*, 22 (2003), 521–539.

Barnes J.H., Robson C.F., Kaznowska S.S., Doodey J.P. and Davidson N.C., *Coasts and Seas of the United Kingdom, Region 13 Northern Irish Sea: Colwyn Bay to Stranraer, including the Isle of Man*, JNCC Coastal Directories Project 8 (1996).

Bates M., 'Life under the Ocean Waves – Sublittoral Surveying', *Manx Nature*, Newsletter of the Manx Wildlife Trust (2001).

Bell A., 'Tertiary Deposits in North Manxland', *British Association*, 66 (1896), 783.

—— 'The Fossiliferous Molluscan Deposits of Wexford and North Manxland',

Geological Magazine, 2 (1915), 164–169.

—— 'Fossil shells from Wexford and Manxland', *Irish Naturalist*, 28 (1919), 109–114.

—— 'The Cliffs of North Ramsey and their fossil contents', *Proceedings of the Isle of Man Natural History and Antiquarian Society*, 2 (1923), 383–392.

Bennett K.D., 'The post-glacial history of *Pinus sylvestris* in the British Isles', *Quaternary Science Reviews*, 3 (1984), 133–155.

Bennett M.R., 'The morphology, structural evolution and significance of push moraines', *Earth Science Reviews*, 53 (2001), 197–236.

Bibby J.S. (ed.), *Land Use Capability Classification for Agriculture*, Macaulay Land Use Research Institute, Aberdeen (1991).

Birks H.J.B., 'Holocene isochrone maps and patterns of tree-spreading in the British Isles', *Journal of Biogeography*, 16 (1989), 503–540.

Birks J.D.S. and Kitchener A.C., *The distribution and status of the Polecat Mustela putorius in the 1990s*, The Vincent Wildlife Trust, London (1999).

Bjørck S., Walker M.J.C., Cwynar L.C., Johnsen S., Knudsen K.L., Lowe J.J. and Wohlfarth B., 'An event stratigraphy for the Last Termination in the north Atlantic region based on the Greenland ice-core record, a proposal by the INTIMATE group', *Journal of Quaternary Science*, 13 (1998), 283–292.

Blackford J.J., Edwards K.J., Dugmore A.J., Cook G.T. and Buckland P.C., 'Icelandic volcanic ash and the mid-Holocene Scots pine (*Pinus sylvestris*) pollen decline in northern Scotland', *Holocene*, 2 (1992), 260–265.

Blundell W., 'History of the Isle of Man' [manuscript written between 1648 and 1657], in Harrison W. (ed.), *Manx Society*, 25 (1876), 135.

Boardman J., 'The northeastern Lake District: periglacial slope deposits', in Boardman J. (ed.), *Field guide to the periglacial landforms of northern England*, Quaternary Research Association, Cambridge (1985), 23–37.

Bohan R., 'Manx woodland history and vegetation', in K.J. Kirby and C.Watkins (eds), *The ecological history of European forests,* CAB International (1998), 155–166.

Bolton H., 'Observations on the Skiddaw Slates of the Isle of Man', *British Association Report*, Nottinghamshire (1893), 770–771.

Boulton G.S., Jones A.S., Clayton K.M. and Kenning M.J., 'A British Ice-sheet model and patterns of glacial erosions and deposition in Britain', in Shotton F.W. (ed.), *British Quaternary Studies: Recent Advances*, Clarendon Press (1977), 231–246.

Bowen D.Q., 'The Pleistocene succession of the Irish Sea', *Proceedings of the Geologists' Association*, 84 (1973), 249–273.

—— Phillips F.M.P., McCabe A.M., Knutz P.C. and Sykes G.A., 'New data for the Last Glacial Maximum in Great Britain and Ireland', *Quaternary Science Reviews*, 21 (2002), 89–101.

Boyce D.C. and Fowles A.P., *Invertebrate Conservation in the Isle of Man: an assessment of selected sites of ecological interest, 30 April–5 May 1989*, unpublished report (1989).

Boyd Dawkins W., 'The red sandstone rocks of Peel (Isle of Man)', *Quarterly Journal of the Geological Society of London*, 58 (1902), 633–646.

Bridge M.C., Haggart B.A. and Lowe J.J., 'The history and palaeoclimate significance of subfossil remains of *Pinus sylvestris* in blanket peats from Scotland', *Journal of Ecology*, 78 (1990), 77–99.

British Geological Survey, 'Isle of Man, Sheets 36, 45, 56 and 57', *Solid and drift geology 1:50000*, British Geological Survey, Keyworth, Nottingham (2001).

British Museum, *British Palaeozoic Fossils*, British Museum, London (1975), 203.

Brodie J. and White N., 'Sedimentary inversion caused by igneous underplating: northwest European continental shelf', *Geology*, 22 (1994), 147–150.

Brookfield M.E. and Martini I.P., 'Facies architecture and sequence stratigraphy in glacially influenced basins: basic problems and water-level glacier input-point controls (with an example from the Quaternary of Ontario, Canada)', *Sedimentary Geology*, 123 (1999), 183–197.

Brooks S.J. and Birks H.J.B., 'Chironomid-inferred Lateglacial air temperatures at Whitrig Bog, southeast Scotland', *Journal of Quaternary Science*, 15 (1999), 759–764.

Brown P.E., Miller J.A. and Grasty R.L., 'Isotopic ages of late Caledonian granitic intrusions in the British Isles', *Proceedings of the Yorkshire Geological Society*, 36 (1968), 251–276.

Bruce J.R., Colman J.S. and Jones N.S., *Marine Fauna of the Isle of Man*, Liverpool University Press (1963), 307.

Burnett D.J., *The stratigraphy, geochemistry and provenance of the Lower Palaeozoic Manx Group, Isle of Man*, unpublished PhD thesis, Oxford Brookes University (1999), 478.

—— and Quirk D.G., 'Turbidite provenance in the Lower Palaeozoic Manx Group, Isle of Man: implications for the tectonic setting of Eastern Avalonia', *Journal of the Geological Society*, 158 (2001), 913–924.

Burton J.F., 'The mystery of the Isle of Man's endangered grasshopper', *British Wildlife*, 2 (1990), 37–42.

Bushell T.P., 'Reservoir geology of the Morecombe field', in Brooks J., Gogg J. and Van Hoorn B. (eds), *Habitat of Palaeozoic Gas in NW Europe*, Geological Society of London Special Publication, 23 (1986), 189–208.

Callister J., *Maughold Brooghs and Gob ny Rona Site Management Plan*, unpublished report, Manx National Heritage, Properties Section (2002).

Carruthers R.G. and Strahan A., 'Notes on lead and zinc mining in the Isle of Man', in *Lead and Zinc Ores of Durham, Yorkshire, Derbyshire and the Isle of Man*, Geological Survey Special Report on Mineral Resources, 26 (1923), 89–91.

Chadwick R.A., Jackson D.I., Barnes R.P., Kimbell G.S., Johnson H., Chiverrell R.C., Thomas G.S.P., Jones N.S., Riley N.J., Pickett E.A., Young B., Holliday D.W., Ball D.F., Molyneux S.G., Long D., Power G.M. and Roberts D.H., *Geology of the Isle of Man and its offshore area*, British Geological Survey Research Report, RR/01/06, Keyworth, Nottingham (2001), 143–144.

—— Kirby G.A., and Baily, H.E., 'The post-Triassic structural evolution of north-west England and adjacent parts of the East Irish Sea, *Proceedings of the Yorkshire Geological Society*, 50 (1994), 91–102.

Chaloner J., 'A short treatise on the Isle of Man' [originally published in 1656 as an appendix to 'King's Vale Royal of England'], in Cumming J. G. (ed.), *Manx Society*, 10 (1864), 57.

Cherrill A.J., *A survey of the grasshoppers of the Isle of Man, with particular reference to the distribution, biology and conservation of Stenobothrus stigmaticus (Rambur) on Langness Peninsula*, unpublished report, Department of Agricultural and Environmental Science, University of Newcastle upon Tyne (1990).

Chiverrell R.C., Davey P.J., Gowlett J.A.J. and Woodcock J.J., in Davey P.J. (ed.), *Recent archaeological research on the Isle of Man*, Oxford, British Archaeological Reports, British Series, 278 (1999).

—— Gonzalez S., Innes J.B., Marshall M., Marshall J., Coope G.R. and Thomas G.S.P., 'Glen Balleira: evidence for Late Glacial environmental change', in Chiverrell R.C., Plater A.J. and Thomas G.S.P. (eds), *The Quaternary of the Isle of Man and Northwest England Field Guide*, Quaternary Research Association, London (2004a), 73–93.

—— Innes J.B., Blackford J.J., Woodcock, J. Davey P.J., Tomlinson, P.R., Rutherford M.M. and Thomas G.S.P., 'Palaeoecological and archaeological evidence for Bronze Age human activity on the Isle of Man', *The Holocene*, 14 (2004b) 346–360.

—— Thomas G.S.P. and Harvey A.M., 'Late-Devensian and Holocene landscape change in the uplands of the Isle of Man', *Geomorphology*, 40 (2001a), 219–236.

——Thomas G.S.P., Long D. and Roberts D.H., 'Quaternary', in Chadwick R.A., Jackson D.I., Barnes R.P., Kimbell G.S., Johnson H., Chiverrell R.C., Thomas G.S.P., Jones N.S., Riley N.J., Pickett E.A., Young B., Holliday D.W., Ball D.F., Molyneux S.G., Long D., Power G.M. and Roberts D.H., *Geology of the Isle of Man and its offshore area*, British Geological Survey Research Report, RR/01/06 (2001), 107–116.

Cocks L.R.M., 'The Early Palaeozoic geography of Europe', *Journal of the Geological Society, London*, 157 (2000), 1–10.

Cooke R. and Paul A., 'Isle of Man 6–11 August', *Bulletin of the British Pteridological Society*, 5 (1999), 153–155.

Coope G.R., 'The fossil coleoptera from Glen Balleira and their bearing upon the interpretation of Lateglacial environments', in Thomas G.S.P. (ed.), *Isle of Man Field Guide*, Quaternary Research Association, Liverpool (1971), 13–15.

—— and Brophy J.A., 'Lateglacial environmental changes indicated by a coleopteran succession from North Wales', *Boreas*, 1 (1972), 97–142.

—— and Pennington W., 'The Windermere Interstadial of the Late Devensian', *Philosophical Transactions of the Royal Society of London*, B280 (1977), 337–339.

—— Lemdahl G., Lowe J.J. and Walking A., 'Temperature gradients in northern Europe during the last glacial-Holocene transition (14–9 ^{14}C kyr BP) interpreted from coleopteran assemblages', *Journal of Quaternary Science*, 13 (1998), 419–433.

Cooper A.H., Millward D., Johnson E.W. and Soper N.J., 'The early Palaeozoic evolution of northwest England', *Geological Magazine*, 130 (1993), 711–724.

—— Rushton A.W.A., Molyneux S.G., Hughes R.A., Moore R.M. and Webb B.C., 'The stratigraphy, correlation, provenance and palaeogeography of Skiddaw Group (Ordovician) in the English Lake District', *Geological Magazine*, 132 (1995), 185–211.

Cooper M.A. and Brück P.M., 'Tectonic relationships of the Leinster Granite, Ireland', *Geological Journal*, 18 (1983), 351–360.

Cornwell J.D., 'A gravity survey of the Isle of Man', *Proceedings of the Yorkshire Geological Society*, 39 (1972), 93–106.

Cottrell J.E., Munro R.C., Tabbener H.E. and Gillies A.C.M., 'Distribution of cDNA variation in British oaks, *Quercus robur* and *Quercus petraea*, in the influence of post-glacial colonisation and human management', *Forestry Ecology and Management*, 156 (2002), 181–195.

Cowan G., Burley S., Hoey N., Holloway P., Bermingham P., Beveridge N., Hamborg M. and Sylta Ø., 'Oil and gas migration in the Sherwood sandstone of the East Irish Sea Basin', in Fleet A.J. and Boldy S.A.R. (eds), *Petroleum Geology of northwest Europe: Proceedings of the 5th Conference* (1999), 1383–1398.

Cowell R.W. and Innes J.B., *The Wetlands of Merseyside: North West Wetlands Survey 1*, English Heritage and Lancaster University, Lancaster (1994).

Craine G.D., *Records and status of the larger moths and butterflies of the Isle of Man*, unpublished report (1998).

—— 'Isle of Man report', *Atropos*, 12 (2001), 65–66.

Crampton C.B. and Taylor J.A., 'Solifluction terraces in south Wales', *Biutetyn Peryglacjalny*, 16 (1967), 15–36.

Crellin C., 'The small mammal bones', in Cubbon M.A., Davey P.J. and Gelling M. (eds), *Excavations on St Patrick's Isle, Peel, Isle of Man: Prehistoric, Viking, Medieval and later, 1982–88 by David Freke*, Liverpool University Press (2002), 251.

Crellin S., 'Some aculeate hymenoptera new to the Isle of Man', *Entomologist's Monthly Magazine*, 123 (1987), 35–36.

Crowley S.F., 'Lithostratigraphy of the Peel Sandstones, Isle of Man', *Mercian Geologist*, 10 (1985), 73–76.

Cubbon A.M., 'The Ice Age in the Isle of Man: A reconsideration of the evidence', *Proceedings of the Isle of Man Natural History and Antiquarian Society*, 5 (1954), 499–512.

Cullen J.P. and Jennings P.P., *Birds of the Isle of Man*, Bridgeen Publications, Douglas, Isle of Man (1986), 39.

Cumming J.G., 'On the geology of the Isle of Man', *Quarterly Journal of the Geological Society of London*, 2 (1846), 317–348.

—— 'On the superior limits of the glacial deposits of the Isle of Man', *Quarterly Journal of the Geological Society of London*, 10 (1853), 211–232.

Cuvier G., *Recherches sur les Ossemens fossiles de Quadrupedes, ou l'on Rétablit les Caractères de Plusieurs Espèces d'Animaux que les Révolutions de Globe Paroissent Avoir Détruites*, Paris, Deterville, nouv. ed. IV (1823), 70–88.

Dackombe R.V., *Aspects of the tills of the Isle of Man*, unpublished PhD thesis, University of Liverpool (1978).

—— and McCarroll D., 'The Manx landscape', in Robinson V. and McCarroll D. (eds), *The Isle of Man: Celebrating a Sense of Place*, Liverpool University Press (1990), 10–17.

—— and Thomas G.S.P. (eds), *Field Guide to the Quaternary of the Isle of Man*, Quaternary Research Association, Cambridge (1985), 124.

—— 'The glacial deposits and Quaternary stratigraphy of the Isle of Man', in Ehlers J., Gibbard P. and Rose, J. (eds), *Glacial deposits of Great Britain and Ireland*, A.A. Balkema, Rotterdam (1991), 333–344.

Dalingwater J.E. and Wright J., 'Spiders of the Isle of Man: provisional list to 1990', *Proceedings of the Isle of Man Natural History and Antiquarian Society*, 10 (1992), 141–144.

Darwin C., 'Notes on the effects produced by the ancient glaciers of Caernarvonshire, and on the boulders transported by floating ice', *Philosophical Magazine*, 21 (1842), 180–188.

Davey P.J. (ed.), *Recent archaeological research on the Isle of Man*, British Archaeological Reports: British Series, 278, Oxford (1999).

—— (ed.), *A new history of the Isle of Man, Volume 2, Prehistory*, Liverpool University Press (in press).

—— and Roscow J., 'Rushen Abbey and the dissolution of the monasteries on the Isle of Man', *Isle of Man Natural History and Antiquarian Society Monograph 1* (in press).

—— Blackford J.J., Chiverrell R.C., Innes J.B. and Tomlinson P.R., 'The curragh and other lowland wetlands of the Isle of Man', in Atherden M. (ed.), *Wetlands in the landscape: archaeology, conservation and heritage*, People, Landscape and Cultural Environment (PLACE) Research Centre, York (2001), 12–40.

Davies B.E. and Kear B.S., 'Environmental factors and the soil pattern on the Isle of Man', *Transactions of the 10th International Congress of Soil Science*, Moscow, Volume VIII: *Soils of the world* (1974), 93–100.

Davies M., Guard J. and Wright A., *Poortown Quarry, Isle of Man: geological inter-*

pretive report, unpublished report by CSA-RDL (1995).

Davis, W.M., 'The development of certain English rivers', *Geographical Journal*, 5 (1895), 127–146.

Davison C.F. and Bowie S.H.U., 'Thucolite-pitchblende, hydrocarbon and moisture – at Laxey lead mine', *Bulletin of the Geological Society of Great Britain*, 3 (1951), 4.

Dawson J., 'Beryllium in the Foxdale Granite, Isle of Man', *Bulletin of the Geological Survey of Great Britain*, 25 (1966), 55–58.

Dewey H. and Eastwood T., 'Copper ores of the Midlands, Wales, the Lake District and the Isle of Man', *Geological Survey Special Report on Mineral Resources*, 30 (1925), 78–87.

Dickson C.A., Dickson J.H. and Mitchell G.F., 'The Late Weichselian Flora of the Isle of Man', *Philosophical Transactions of the Royal Society of London*, B258 (1970), 31–79.

Dickson J.A.D., Ford T.D. and Swift A., 'The stratigraphy of the Carboniferous rocks around Castletown, Isle of Man', *Proceedings of the Yorkshire Geological Society*, 35 (1987), 203–229.

Dobson M.R., 'The geological structure of the Irish Sea', in Kidson C. and Tooley M.J. (eds), *The Quaternary History of the Irish Sea*, Geological Journal Special Issue, 7 (1977) 13–26.

—— and Hollis D.B., 'Lead mines and trials in Glen Auldyn, Isle of Man', *Bulletin of the Peak District Mines Historical Society*, 12 (1993), 31–37.

Douglas T.D. and Harrison, S., 'Late Devensian periglacial slope deposits in the Cheviot Hills', in Boardman J. (ed.), *Periglacial processes and landforms in Britain and Ireland*, Cambridge University Press (1987), 237–244.

Durant G.P. and Grant C., 'The Scarlett Volcanic Complex, Isle of Man: a shallow-water submarine volcanic pile', *Geological Society of London Newsletter*, 14 (1985), 46.

Earland-Bennett P.M., 'A preliminary survey and assessment of the Lichen Flora of the Isle of Man', *Proceedings of the Isle of Man Natural History and Antiquarian Society*, 8 (1979), 139–155.

Eastwood T., Hollingworth S.E., Rose W.C.C. and Trotter F.M., 'Geology of the country around Cockermouth and Caldbeck', *Memoir of the Institute of Geological Sciences*, London (1968).

Eaton J.E., Holt T.J., Hopkin G.W., White K.W. and Wilby N.J., *IRIS Project: Baseline Environmental Survey Report, Volume 3, Freshwater Ecology*, Report to the Isle of Man Government (1994).

Edwards K.J., Hirons K.R. and Newell P.J., 'The palaeoecological and prehistoric context of minerogenic layers in blanket peat: a study from Loch Dee, southwest Scotland', *Holocene*, 1 (1991), 29–39.

Emery D. and Myers K.J., *Sequence Stratigraphy*, Blackwell Science, Oxford (1996), 234.

Eyles C.H. and Eyles N., 'Glaciomarine sediments of the Isle of Man as a key to late Pleistocene stratigraphic investigations in the Irish Sea Basin', *Geology*, 12 (1984), 359–364.

Eyles N., 'Earth's glacial record and its tectonic setting', *Earth Science Reviews*, 35 (2) (1984), 1–248.

—— and McCabe A.M., 'The Late Devensian (<22,000 BP) Irish Sea Basin: the sedimentary record of a collapsed ice sheet margin', *Quaternary Science Reviews*, 8 (1989), 307–351.

Fairhurst J., *Calf of Man Management Plan*, unpublished report, Manx National

Heritage, Properties Section (1996).

—— *Ballaugh Curragh Management Plan*, unpublished report, Manx National Heritage, Properties Section (1998).

FAO-Unesco, *Soil Map of the World (1:5,000,000)*, Volume I (Legend) and Volume VI (Europe), Unesco, Paris (1974).

Fisher C., 'Past human exploitation of birds on the Isle of Man', *International Journal of Osteoarchaeology*, 7 (1997), 292–297.

Fitches W.F., Barnes R.P. and Morris J.H., 'Geological structure and tectonic evolution of the Lower Palaeozoic rocks of the Isle of Man', in Woodcock N.H., Quirk D.G., Fitches W.F. and Barnes R.P. (eds), *In sight of the suture: the Palaeozoic geology of the Isle of Man in its Iapetus Ocean context*, Geological Society of London Special Publication, 160 (1999), 259–287.

Forbes E., *Malacologia Monensis: a catalogue of the Mollusca inhabiting the Isle of Man*, Edinburgh (1838).

Ford T.D., 'Slump structures in the Peel Sandstone Series, Isle of Man', *Isle of Man Natural History and Antiquarian Journal*, 7 (1972), 440–448.

—— *The Isle of Man*, Geologists' Association Guide, 46 (1993).

—— 'The Geology of the Laxey Vein, Isle of Man', *Mercian Geologist*, 14 (1998), 125–134.

—— Burnett D.J. and Quirk D.G., *The geology of the Isle of Man*, Geologists' Association Guide, 46 (2001), 92.

—— and Quirk D.G., 'Mineralization of the South Pennines', *Geology Today*, 11 (1995), 177–182.

—— Wilson E. and Burnett D.J., 'Previous ideas and models of the stratigraphy, structure and mineral deposits of the Manx Group, Isle of Man', in Woodcock N.H., Quirk D.G., Fitches W.F. and Barnes R.P. (eds), *In sight of the suture: the early Palaeozoic geology of the Isle of Man in its Iapetus Ocean context*, Geological Society of London Special Publication, 160 (1999), 11–21.

French H.M., 'Asymmetrical slope development in the Chiltern Hills', *Biutetyn Peryglacjalny*, 21 (1972), 51–73.

Fullen M.A., Harris J. and Kear B.S., *Soils of the Isle of Man*, Centre For Manx Studies, Research Report 5 (1996), 29.

—— Harris J. and Kear B.S., 'Soil forming processes on the Isle of Man', *Geography Review*, 13 (1999), 22–26.

Galloway R.W., 'Periglacial phenomena in Scotland', *Geografiska Annaler*, 43 (1961), 348–353.

Gamble, J.A., Wysoczanski R.J. and Meighant, I.G., 'Constrains on the British Tertiary Volcanic Province from ion microprobe U-Pb (SHRIMP) ages for acid igneous rocks from NE Ireland', *Journal of the Geological Society of London*, 156 (1999), 291–299.

Garrad L.S., *The Naturalist in the Isle of Man*, David and Charles, Newton Abbot (1972a), 155–156, 234, 645.

—— 'Non-marine molluscs of the Isle of Man II', *Peregrine*, 4 (1972b), 41–44.

—— 'Oak woodland in the Isle of Man', *Watsonia*, 9 (1972c), 59–60.

—— 'Non-marine molluscs of the Isle of Man III', *Peregrine*, 4 (1973), 71–72.

—— 'Some thoughts on Manx woodland', *Proceedings of the Isle of Man Natural History and Antiquarian Society*, 7 (1974), 666–685.

—— 'Evidence for the history of the vertebrate fauna of the Isle of Man', in Davey P.J. (ed.), *Man and Environment in the Isle of Man*, British Archaeological Reports, British Series, 54, Oxford (1978), 61–76.

—— 'A history of Manx gardens', *Collector's Choice* (1985), 20–22.

—— 'The history of mammals', in Robinson V. and McCarroll D. (eds), *The Isle of Man: Celebrating a Sense of Place*, Liverpool University Press (1990a), 74–76.

—— 'Nature conservation', in Robinson V. and McCarroll D. (eds), *The Isle of Man: Celebrating a Sense of Place*, Liverpool University Press (1990b), 84–98.

—— 'Denizen or natives?', *Proceedings of the Isle of Man Natural History and Antiquarian Society*, 10 (1992a), 163–165.

—— 'The spread of introduced plants into the wild in the Isle of Man', *Proceedings of the Isle of Man Natural History and Antiquarian Society*, 10 (1992b), 145–160.

—— 'Plants and people in the Isle of Man, AD 800–1800', *Botanical Journal of Scotland*, 46 (1994), 644–650.

—— 'The non-marine molluscs of the Isle of Man', *Peregrine*, 3 (1998), 184–188.

—— Bawden T.A., Qualtrough J.K. and Scatchard W.J., *The Industrial Archaeology of the Isle of Man*, David and Charles, Newton Abbot (1972).

Gear A.J. and Huntley B., 'Rapid changes in the range limits of Scots Pine 4000 BP', *Science*, 251 (1991), 544–547.

Geffen A.J., Hawkins S.J. and Fisher E.M., 'The Isle of Man', in Irish Sea Study Group (eds), *The Irish Sea: an environmental review. Part 1: Nature conservation*, Liverpool University Press (1990), 133–168.

Gill E.L., 'Keisley Limestone pebbles from the Isle of Man', *Quarterly Journal of the Geological Society of London*, 59 (1903), 307–310.

Glasser N.F. and Sambrook-Smith G.H., 'Glacial meltwater erosion of the mid-Cheshire ridge: implications for ice dynamics during the Late Devensian glaciation of northwest England', *Journal of Quaternary Science*, 14 (1999), 703–710.

Godwin H., *The History of the British Flora: a factual basis for phytogeography*, Cambridge University Press (1956), 383.

Gonzalez S., Innes J.B., Huddart D., Davey P.J. and Plater A.J., 'Holocene coastal change in the north of the Isle of Man: stratigraphy, palaeoenvironment and archaeological evidence', in Pye K. and Allen J.R.L. (eds), *Coastal and Estuarine Environments: sedimentology, geomorphology and geoarchaeology*, Geological Society of London Special Publication, 175 (2000), 343–363.

—— Kitchener A.C. and Lister A.M., 'Survival of the Irish Elk into the Holocene', *Nature*, 405 (2000), 753–754.

Gradstein F.M. and Ogg J., 'A Phanerozoic time scale' *Episodes*, 19 (1996), 3–4.

Gray J.M. and Lowe J.J., 'The Scottish Lateglacial environment: a synthesis', in Gray J.M. and Lowe J.J. (eds), *Studies in the Scottish Lateglacial environment*, Pergamon, Oxford (1977), 163–182.

Greg R.P. and Lettsom W.G., *Manual of the mineralogy of Great Britain and Ireland*, John Van Voorst, London (1977).

Green P.F., Duddy I.R. and Bray R.J., 'Variation in thermal history styles around the Irish Sea and adjacent areas: implications for hydrocarbon occurrence and tectonic evolution', in Meadows N.S., Trueblood S.P., Hardman N. and Cowan G. (eds), *Petroleum geology of the Irish Sea and adjacent areas*, Geological Society of London Special Publication, 124 (1997), 73–93.

Grudd H., Briffa K.R., Karlen W., Bartholin T.S., Jones P.D. and Kromer B., 'A 7400-year tree-ring chronology in northern Swedish Lapland: natural climatic variability expressed on annual to millennial timescales', *Holocene*, 12 (2002), 657–666.

Gubbay S., *A Review of sites of marine nature conservation importance around the Isle of Man*, Report to Manx Wildlife Trust (2000).

Harper C.T., 'Potassium-argon ages of slates from the southern Caledonides of the British Isles', *Nature*, 212 (1966), 1339–1341.

Harris C., 'Microstructures in solifluction sediments from South Wales and North

Norway', *Biutetyn Peryglacjalny*, 28 (1981), 221–226.

—— 'Solifluction and related periglacial deposits in England and Wales', in Boardman J. (ed.), *Periglacial processes and landforms in Britain and Ireland*, Cambridge University Press (1987), 209–224.

Harris J., Fullen M.A. and Hallett M.D., *Agricultural Soils of the Isle of Man*, Centre for Manx Studies, Research Report 9 (2001), 24.

Harrison S., *100 Years of Heritage*, Manx Museum and National Trust, Douglas (1986), 207.

Harvey A.M., 'Holocene hillslope gully systems in the Howgill Fells, Cumbria', in Brooks S.M. and Anderson M.G. (eds), *Advances in Hillslope Processes*, Volume 2, Wiley, Chichester (1996), 731–752.

—— Alexander R.W. and James P.A., 'Lichens, soil development and the age of Holocene valley floor landforms: Howgill Fells, Cumbria', *Geografiska Annaler*, 66A (1984), 353–366.

—— Oldfield F., Baron A.F. and Pearson G., 'Dating of post-glacial landforms in the central Howgills', *Earth Surface Processes and Landforms*, 6 (1981), 401–412.

—— and Renwick W.H., 'Holocene alluvial fan and terrace formation in the Bowland Fells, Northwest England', *Earth Surface Processes and Landforms*, 12 (1997), 249–257.

Haynes J.R., McCabe A.M. and Eyles N., 'Microfaunas from Late Devensian glaciomarine deposits in the Irish Sea Basin', *Irish Journal of Earth Sciences*, 14 (1995), 81–103.

Hedges R.E.M., Pettitt P.B., Bronk Ramsey C. and Van Klinken G.J., 'Radiocarbon dates from the Oxford AMS System: Archaeometry Datelist 23', *Archaeometry*, 39 (1997a), 247–262.

—— 'Radiocarbon dates from the Oxford AMS System: Archaeometry Datelist 24', *Archaeometry*, 39 (1997b), 445–471.

Henslow J.S., 'Supplementary observations to Dr Berger's account of the Isle of Man', *Transactions of the Geological Society of London*, 1 (1821), 482–505.

Hibbert F.A., Switsur V.R. and West R.G., 'Radiocarbon dating of Flandrian pollen zones at Red Moss, Lancashire', *Proceedings of the Royal Society of London: Series B Biological Sciences*, 177 (1971), 161–176.

Hibbert S., 'Notice of the remains of an animal resembling the Scandinavian Elk, recently discovered in the Isle of Man', *Edinburgh Journal of Science*, 3 (1825), 15–28.

Holliday D.W., 'Mesozoic cover over northern England: interpretation of apatite fission-track data', *Journal of the Geological Society of London*, 150 (1993), 657–660.

Hollis D.B., 'The forgotten iron mines of Kirk Maughold, Isle of Man', *British Mining*, 34 (1987a), 46–54.

—— 'Uranium in the Isle of Man', *British Mining*, 34 (1987b), 44–45.

—— 'The Kirk Maughold iron mines, Isle of Man', *British Mining*, 37 (1988), 4–15.

—— 'The search for iron, lead and gold in Douglas Bay, Isle of Man: old mining trials and new insight into the geology', *Bulletin of the Peak District Mines Historical Society*, 10 (1989a), 291–304.

—— 'Bell Hole – the history and geology of a small lead mine near Foxdale, Isle of Man', *Bulletin of the Peak District Mines Historical Society*, 10 (1989b), 291–304.

Holmes Grace Consulting Engineers Ltd, *A geological investigation of the Poortown Quarry*, unpublished report for the Department of Highways, Ports and Properties, Isle of Man (1992).

Holt T.J., *An intertidal survey of the Isle of Man 1996–1999*, Port Erin Marine

Laboratory, Manx Wildlife Trust (1999).

Hopson T. and Lamb J. (eds), *Manx Hill-land,* Report to Manx Nature Conservation Trust (1995).

Horne J., 'A sketch of the geology of the Isle of Man', *Transactions Edinburgh Geological Society,* 2 (1874), 232–247.

Howard A.J., Macklin M.G., Black S. and Hudson-Edwards K.A., 'Holocene river development and environmental change in Upper Wharfedale, Yorkshire Dales, England', *Journal of Quaternary Science,* 15 (2000), 239–252.

Howe M.P.A., 'The Silurian fauna (graptolite and nautiloid) of the Niarbyl Formation, Isle of Man', in Woodcock N.H., Quirk D.G., Fitches W.F. and Barnes R.P. (eds), *In sight of the suture: the Palaeozoic geology of the Isle of Man in its Iapetus Ocean context,* Geological Society of London Special Publication, 160 (1999), 177–187.

Huddart, D., 'Pre-Quaternary Landscape development', in Huddart D. and Glasser N.F. (eds), *Quaternary of Northern England,* Geological Conservation Review Series, No 25 (2000), Joint Nature Conservation Committee, Peterborough, 10–30.

Hughes R.A., Evans J.A., Noble S.R. and Rundle C.C., 'U-Pb chronology of the Ennerdale and Eskdale intrusions supports sub-volcanic relationships with the Borrowdale Volcanic Group (Ordovician, English Lake District)', *Journal of the Geological Society,* 153 (1996), 338–345.

Huntley B. and Birks H.J.B., *An atlas of past and present maps for Europe: 0–13000 BP,* Cambridge University Press (1983).

Huxley T., *Aquatic bugs (Hemiptera – Heteroptera) of the Isle of Man,* Report to Manx Museum (2000).

Innes J.B., *The Dhoo Valley, Isle of Man: a palaeo-environmental assessment,* Research Report 2, Centre for Manx Studies, Douglas (1995).

—— 'Radiocarbon (AMS) dating of the *Betula* and *Alnus* pollen rises and Holocene woodland history in the Isle of Man', *Bulletin of the British Ecological Society,* 34 (2003), 37–38.

—— Blackford J.J. and Davey P.J., 'Dating the introduction of cereal cultivation to the British Isles: early palaeoecological evidence from the Isle of Man', *Journal of Quaternary Science,* 18 (2003), 603–613.

—— Chiverrell R.C., Blackford J.J., Davey P.J., Gonzalez S., Rutherford M.M. and Tomlinson P.R., 'Earliest Holocene vegetation history and Island Biogeography of the Isle of Man, British Isles', *Journal of Biogeography,* 31 (2004), 761–772.

Irving R.A., Jones D.R., Holt T.J. and Hawkins S.J., 'The sea bed', in Barnes J.H., Robson C.F., Kaznowska S.S., Doodey J.P. and Davidson N.C., *Coasts and Seas of the United Kingdom Region 13 Northern Irish Sea Colwyn Bay to Stranraer, including the Isle of Man,* JNCC Coastal Directories Project 8 (1996).

Isle of Man Government, Analyst's Laboratory, *River Quality Report* (2000).

Isle of Man Government, Department of Highways, Ports and Properties and the Department of Agriculture, Fisheries and Forestry to the Executive Council, *Coast Erosion Policy* (1990).

Isle of Man Government, Department of Local Government and the Environment, *Draft Strategic Plan* (2001).

Isle of Man Government, Department of Transport, *Report into coastal erosion on the northern coasts of the Isle of Man,* Report to Tynwald (2000).

Isle of Man Government, Harbour Board and Board of Agriculture, Fisheries and Forestry, *Report on erosion of the coasts of the north of the Isle of Man,* Report to Tynwald (1983).

Jackson D.I., Jackson A.A., Evans D., Wingfield R.T.R., Barnes R.P. and Arthur M.J., *United Kingdom offshore regional report: The geology of the Irish Sea,* HMSO,

London (1995), 123.

Joachim M.J., *Lateglacial Coleopteran assemblages from the west coast of the Isle of Man*, unpublished PhD thesis, University of Birmingham (1979).

John B.S., *The Winters of the World*, David and Charles, Newton Abbot (1985).

Johnsen S.J., Dahl-Jensen D., Gundestrup N., Steffensen J.P., Clausen H.B., Miller H., Masson-Delmotte V., Sveinbjørnsdottir A.E. and White J., 'Oxygen isotope and palaeotemperature records from six Greenland ice-core stations: Camp Century, Dye-3, GRIP, GISP2, Renland and NorthGRIP', *Journal of Quaternary Science*, 16 (2001), 299–307.

Johnson A., 'Sulby', in Davey P.J. (ed.), *Recent Archaeological Research on the Isle of Man*, British Archaeological Reports, British Series, 278, Oxford (1999), 153–170.

Jolliffe I.P., *An investigation into coastal erosion problems in the Isle of Man: causes, effects, and remedial strategies*, Report to the Isle of Man Harbour Board and Isle of Man Government (1981), 149.

Jones B., *Warden's report for Ayres National Nature Reserve*, Report to Department of Agriculture, Fisheries and Forestry, Isle of Man Government (2000).

Kear B.S., *Agriculture Soil Survey. Report on the examination of soils in the first phase areas of development around the main urban centres in the Isle of Man*, Department of Town and Country Planning, Isle of Man Local Government Board (1971).

—— 'Soils of the Isle of Man', *Isle of Man Natural History and Antiquarian Society*, 8 (1976), 38–50.

—— *The Isle of Man: its soils and their significance*, North of England Soils Discussion Group Special Publication, 18 (1982), 53.

Keehan B., *Manx Wildlife Sites Handbook: a handbook describing the practical implementation of the Manx Wildlife Sites System*, Manx Wildlife Trust (2002) (revised by Peter Dullaghan).

Kendall J.D., 'Interglacial deposits of west Cumberland and north Lancashire', *Journal of the Geological Society of London*, 37 (1881), 29–39.

Kendall P.F., 'On the glacial geology of the Isle of Man', *Yn Lioar Manninagh*, 1 (1894), 397–437.

Kennan P.S. and Morris J.H., 'Manganese ironstones in the early Ordovician Manx Group, Isle of Man: a protolith of coticule?', in Woodcock N.H., Quirk D.G., Fitches W.F. and Barnes R.P. (eds), *In sight of the suture: the Palaeozoic geology of the Isle of Man in its Iapetus Ocean context*, Geological Society of London Special Publication, 160 (1999), 109–119.

Kermode P.M.C., 'List of birds of the Isle of Man', *Proceedings of the Isle of Man Natural History and Antiquarian Society*, 1 (1888), 15–23.

—— 'Contributions to a vertebrate fauna of the Isle of Man', *Zoologist*, 17 (1893), 61–70.

—— 'The Irish Elk in the Isle of Man', *Geological Magazine*, N.S. Decade IV, Vol. V (1898), 116–119.

Kimbell G.S. and Quirk D.G., 'Crustal magnetic structure of the Irish Sea region: evidence for a major basement boundary beneath the Isle of Man', in Woodcock N.H., Quirk D.G., Fitches W.F. and Barnes R.P. (eds), *In sight of the suture: the Palaeozoic geology of the Isle of Man in its Iapetus Ocean context*, Geological Society of London Special Publication, 160 (1999), 227–238.

King C.M., *The natural history of weasels and stoats*, Christopher Helm, London (1989).

Knight J., 'Glaciomarine deposition around the Irish Sea Basin: some problems and solutions', *Journal of Quaternary Science*, 16 (2001), 405–418.

Kokelaar P., 'Tectonic controls of Ordovician arc and marginal basin volcanism in

Wales', *Journal of the Geological Society of London*, 145 (1988), 759–775.

Lamb J., 'The Manx Nature Conservation Trust in the 1990s and beyond', *Proceedings of the Isle of Man Natural History and Antiquarian Society*, 10 (1995), 149–160.

—— *A terrestrial survey of the coast of the Isle of Man*, Report to Manx Wildlife Trust (1999).

Lambeck K., 'Late Devensian and Holocene shorelines of the British Isles and North Sea from models of glacio-hydro-isostatic rebound', *Journal of the Geological Society of London*, 152 (1995), 437–448.

—— 'Glaciation and sea-level change for Ireland and the Irish Sea since Late Devensian/Midlandian time', *Journal of the Geological Society of London*, 153 (1996), 853–872.

Lamplugh G.W., *The geology of the Isle of Man*, Memoir of the Geological Survey of England and Wales (1903), 549–550, 606, 620.

Leuschner H.H., Sass-Klaassen U., Jansma E., Baillie M.G.L. and Spurk M., 'Subfossil European bog oaks: population dynamics and long term growth depressions as indicators of changes in the Holocene hydro-regime and climate', *Holocene*, 12 (2002), 695–706.

Lewis C.L.E., Green P.F., Carter A. and Hurford A.J., 'Elevated K/T palaeotemperatures throughout NW England: three kms of Tertiary erosion?', *Earth and Planetary Science Letters*, 112 (1992), 131–145.

Lewis H.P., 'The Avonian succession in the south of the Isle of Man', *Quarterly Journal of the Geological Society of London*, 86 (1930), 234–290.

—— 'The occurrence of fossiliferous pebbles of Salopian age in the Peel Sandstones (Isle of Man)', *Summary of Progress of the Geological Survey*, 2 (1933), 91–108.

Lewis S.G., 'Eastern England', in Bowen D.Q. (ed.), *A revised correlation of Quaternary deposits in the British Isles*, Geological Society Special Report 23 (1999), 10–27.

Longworth P., *An investigation into the relative importance of agricultural operations on arable field boundary vegetation in the Isle of Man including management recommendations*, unpublished MSc dissertation, University of Stirling (2000).

Lønne I., 'Sedimentary facies and depositional architecture of ice-contact glaciomarine systems', *Sedimentary Geology*, 98 (1995), 13–43.

Luff M.L., 'An entomological survey of the Langness peninsula, Isle of Man', *Proceedings of the Isle of Man Natural History and Antiquarian Society*, 9 (1990), 565–586.

—— *A pitfall survey of the Ayres*, unpublished report (1992).

—— Crellin S. and Barclay M.V.L., 'Coleoptera of the Isle of Man updated', *Entomologist's Monthly Magazine*, 137 (2001), 59–64.

Macdonald D.W. and Halliwell E.C., 'The rapid spread of red foxes, *Vulpes vulpes*, on the Isle of Man', *Global Ecology and Biogeography Letters*, 4 (1994), 9–16.

Mackay J.R., 'The world of underground ice', *Annals of the Association of American Geographers*, 62 (1972), 1–22.

Mackay L. and Schnellmann G.A., *The Mine and Minerals of the Isle of Man*, report submitted to the Industrial Officer for the Government of the Isle of Man (1963).

Mackie A.S.Y., 'Offshore benthic communities of the Irish Sea', in Irish Sea Study Group (eds), *The Irish Sea: an environmental review. Part 1: Nature conservation*, Liverpool University Press (1990), 169–218.

Macklin M.G., 'Holocene river environments in prehistoric Britain: human interaction and impact', in Edwards K.J. and Sadler J.P. (eds), *Holocene environment of prehistoric Britain*, Quaternary Proceedings No. 7, Wiley, Chichester (1999), 521–530.

Macklin M.G. and Lewin J., 'Terraced fills of Pleistocene and Holocene age in the Rheidol Valley, Wales', *Journal of Quaternary Science*, 1 (1986), 21–34.

Macklin M.G. and Lewin J., 'Holocene river alluviation in Britain', *Zeitschrift für Geomorphologie (Supplement)*, 88 (1993), 109–122.

Maddy D., 'English Midlands', in Bowen, D.Q. (ed.), *A revised correlation of Quaternary deposits in the British Isles*, Geological Society Special Report 23 (1999), 28–44.

Maitland P.S. and Campbell R.N., *Freshwater Fishes of the British Isles*, Harper Collins, London (1992).

Mangerud J., Andersen S.T., Berglund B.E., and Donner J., 'Quaternary stratigraphy of Norden, a proposal for terminology and classification', *Boreas*, 3 (1974), 109–128.

Manx Nature Conservation Trust, *Proceedings of the Manx Hill-land seminar* (1997).

Marshall J.D., Jones R.T., Crowley S.F., Oldfield F., Nash S. and Bedford A., 'A high resolution Lateglacial isotopic record from Hawes Water, Northwest England climatic oscillations: calibration and comparison of palaeotemperature proxies', *Palaeogeography Palaeoclimatology Palaeoecology*, 185 (2002), 25–40.

Mascheretti S., Rogatcheva M.B., Gündüz I., Fredga K. and Searle J.B., 'How did pygmy shrews colonize Ireland? Clues from a phylogenetic analysis of mitochondrial cytochrome b sequences', *Proceedings of the Royal Society London: Series B Biological Sciences*, 270, 1524 (2003), 1593–1599.

Max M.D., Barber A.J. and Martinez J., 'Terrane assemblage of the Leinster Massif, SE Ireland, during the Lower Palaeozoic', *Journal of the Geological Society of London*, 147 (1990), 1035–1050.

McAllister H.A., '*Campanula rotundifolia*: a local race in south-west Scotland', *Glasgow Naturalist*, 1(1973), 66.

McCabe A.M. and Clark P.U., 'Ice sheet variability around the North Atlantic Ocean during the last deglaciation', *Nature*, 392 (1998), 373–377.

—— and Haynes J.R., 'A Late Pleistocene intertidal boulder pavement from an isostatically emergent coast, Dundalk Bay, eastern Ireland', *Earth Surface Processes and Landforms*, 21 (1996), 555–572.

—— Knight J. and McCarron S., 'Evidence for Heinrich event 1 in the British Isles', *Journal of Quaternary Science*, 13 (1998), 549–568.

McCarroll D., 'Deglaciation of the Irish Sea basin: a critique of the glaciomarine hypothesis', *Journal of Quaternary Science*, 16 (2001), 393–404.

McCartan S.B., 'The Manx early Mesolithic: a story in stone. Recent Archaeological Research on the Isle of Man', in Davey P.J. (ed.), *Recent archaeological research on the Isle of Man*, Oxford, British Archaeological Reports, British Series, 278 (1999), 5–11.

—— 'Mesolithic hunter-gatherers in the Isle of Man: adaptations to an island environment?', in Larsson L., Kindgren H., Knutsson K., Loeffer D. and Akerlund A. (eds), *Mesolithic on the Move*, Oxbow, Oxford (2003), 331–339.

McConnell B.J., Morris J.H. and Kennan P.S., 'A comparison of the Ribband Group (southeastern Ireland) to the Manx Group (Isle of Man) and Skiddaw Group (northwestern England)', in Woodcock N.H., Quirk D.G., Fitches W.F. and Barnes R.P. (eds), *In sight of the suture: the Palaeozoic geology of the Isle of Man in its Iapetus Ocean context*, Geological Society of London Special Publication, 160 (1999), 337–343.

McCulloch J., *A Description of the Western Islands of Scotland, including the Isle of Man: comprising an account of their Geological Structure, with remarks on their Agriculture, Scenery and Antiquities*, Constable, London (1819).

Meadows N.S. and Beach, A., 'Controls on reservoir quality in the Triassic Sherwood Sandstone of the Irish Sea', in J.R. Parker (ed.), *Petroleum geology of NW Europe:*

Proceedings of the 4th Conference, The Geological Society of London (1993), 823–833.

—— Trueblood S.P., Hardman N. and Cowan G. (eds), *Petroleum geology of the Irish Sea and adjacent areas*, Geological Society of London Special Publication, 124 (1997), 447.

Miall A.D., 'A review of the braided river depositional environment', *Earth Science Reviews*, 13 (1977), 1–62.

Miles S.R., *Heathland Flies – UK Biodiversity Action Plan, 1st Report* (1999).

—— *Heathland Flies – UK Biodiversity Action Plan, 2nd Report* (2000).

Mitchell G.F., 'The Pleistocene history of the Irish Sea', *Advancement of Science*, 17 (1960), 313–325.

—— 'The Quaternary deposits of the Ballaugh and Kirk Michael districts, Isle of Man', *Quarterly Journal of the Geological Society of London*, 121 (1965), 359–381.

—— 'The Pleistocene history of the Irish Sea: a second approximation', *Scientific Proceedings of the Royal Dublin Society*, A4 (1972), 181–199.

—— and H.M. Parkes, 'The giant deer in Ireland', *Proceedings of the Royal Irish Academy*, 52B (1949), 291–314.

Moar N.T., 'Late Weichselian and Flandrian pollen diagrams from south-west Scotland', *New Phytologist*, 68 (1969), 433–467.

Molyneux S.G., 'New evidence for the age of the Manx Group, Isle of Man', in Harris A.L., Holland C.H. and Leake B.E. (eds), *The Caledonides of the British Isles – Reviewed*, Geological Society of London Special Publication, 8 (1979), 415–421.

—— 'A reassessment of Manx Group acritarchs, Isle of Man', in Woodcock N.H., Quirk D.G., Fitches W.F. and Barnes R.P. (eds), *In sight of the suture: the Palaeozoic geology of the Isle of Man in its Iapetus Ocean context*, Geological Society of London Special Publication, 160 (1999), 23–32, 232–254.

Mook W.G., 'Recommendations/resolutions adopted by the Twelfth International Radiocarbon Conference', *Radiocarbon*, 28 (1986), 799.

Morris J.H., Woodcock N.H. and Howe M.P.A., 'The Silurian succession of the Isle of Man: the late Wenlock Niarbyl Formation', in Woodcock N.H., Quirk D.G., Fitches W.F. and Barnes R.P. (eds), *In sight of the suture: the Palaeozoic geology of the Isle of Man in its Iapetus Ocean context*, Geological Society of London Special Publication, 160 (1999b), 189–211.

Morrison C.W.K., *A study of the Anchizone-epizone metamorphic transition*, unpublished PhD thesis, St Andrew's University (1989).

Morrow C.C., Picton B.E. and Bishop J.D.D., *A sublittoral survey of the Calf of Man*, report prepared for the Calf Marine Trust (1993).

Murray, J.W., 'Palaeogene and Neogene', in Cope J.C.W., Ingham J.K. and Rawson P.F. (eds), *Atlas of Palaeogeography and lithofacies*, Memoir of the Geological Society of London (1992), 141–147.

Mussett A.E., Dagley P. and Skelhorn R.R., 'Time and duration of activity in the British Tertiary Igneous Province', in Morton A.C. and Parsons L.M. (eds), *Early Tertiary Volcanism and the opening of the NE Atlantic*, Geological Society of London Special Publication, 39 (1988).

Nadin P.A. and Kuznir N.J., 'Palaeocene uplift and Eocene subsidence in the northern North Sea Basin from 2D forward and reverse stratigraphic modelling', *Journal of the Geological Society of London*, 152 (1995), 833–848.

Newman P.J., 'The geology and hydrocarbon habit of the Peel and Solway Basins', *Journal of Petroleum Geology*, 22 (1999a), 265–284.

—— 'The geology and hydrocarbon potential of the Peel and Solway Basins, East Irish Sea', *Journal of Petroleum Geology*, 22 (1999b), 305–324.

Nockolds S.R., 'The Dhoon (Isle of Man) granite', *Mineralogical Magazine*, 22 (1931), 494–509.

O'Cofaigh C. and Evans D.J.A., 'Sedimentary evidence for deforming bed conditions associated with a grounded Irish Sea glacier, southern Ireland', *Journal of Quaternary Science*, 16 (2001), 435–454.

Ollier C.D. and Thomasson A.J., 'Asymmetrical valleys of the Chiltern Hills', *Geographical Journal*, 123 (1957), 71–80.

Orr P.J. and Howe M.P.A., 'Macrofauna and ichnofauna of the Manx Group (early Ordovician), Isle of Man', in Woodcock N.H., Quirk D.G., Fitches W.F. and Barnes R.P. (eds), *In sight of the suture: the Palaeozoic geology of the Isle of Man in its Iapetus Ocean context*, Geological Society of London Special Publication, 160 (1999), 33–44.

Oswald H.R., 'Observations relative to the Fossil Elk of the Isle of Man', *Edinburgh Journal of Science*, 3 (1825), 28–31.

Page C., 'Manx farming communities and traditions: an examination of Manx farming between 1750 and 1900', in Davey P.J. and Finlayson D.F. (eds), *Mannin Revisited: twelve essays on Manx culture and environment*, Scottish Society for Northern Studies (2002), 117–135.

Palmer R.C., Beard G.R., Bradley R.I., Burton R.G.O., Harrod T.R., Hazeldon J., Hollis J.M. and Holman I.P., *Soil Survey of the Isle of Man*, Soil Survey and Land Research Centre, Cranfield University (2000).

Pantin H.M., 'Quaternary sediments of the northern Irish Sea', in Kidson C. and Tooley M.J. (eds), *The Quaternary history of the Irish Sea*, Geological Journal Special Issue, 7 (1977), 27–54.

—— 'Quaternary sediments from the north-east Irish Sea: Isle of Man to Cumbria', *Bulletin of the Geological Survey of Great Britain*, 64 (1978).

Pearce A. and Rose G.M., 'Mining in the Isle of Man', *Bulletin of the Peak District Mines Historical Society*, 7 (1979), 216–230.

Perkins D.F. and Buse A., *A report on an ecological survey of the Isle of Man*, Nature Conservation Council and Institute of Terrestrial Ecology report to the Isle of Man Government (1974).

Perry I. and Moore P.D., 'Dutch elm disease as an analogue of Neolithic Elm Decline', *Nature*, 326 (1987), 72–73.

Phillips B.A.M., 'The post-glacial raised shoreline around the North Plain, Isle of Man', *Northern Universities Geographical Journal*, 8 (1967), 43–48.

—— *Cliff and shore platform development in the Isle of Man*, unpublished PhD thesis, University of Wales (1969).

—— 'Effective levels of marine planation on raised and present rock platforms', *Review Geography Montreal*, 24 (1970), 227–240.

Piper J.D.A. and Crowley S.F., 'Palaeomagnetism of the (Palaeozoic) Peel Sandstones and Langness Conglomerate Formation, Isle of Man: implications for the age and regional diagenesis', in Woodcock N.H., Quirk D.G., Fitches W.F. and Barnes R.P. (eds), *In sight of the suture: the Palaeozoic geology of the Isle of Man in its Iapetus Ocean context*, Geological Society of London Special Publication, 160 (1999), 213–225.

—— Biggin A.J. and Crowley S.F., 'Magnetic survey of the Poortown Dolerite, Isle of Man', in Woodcock N.H., Quirk D.G., Fitches W.F. and Barnes R.P. (eds), *In sight of the suture: the Palaeozoic geology of the Isle of Man in its Iapetus Ocean context*, Geological Society of London Special Publication, 160 (1999), 155–163.

Pollard R.G., *The role of the Department of Agriculture, Fisheries and Forestry (Forestry Division) in the Management of the Manx Hill Lands* (1997).

Pooley E.J., 'Non-avian vertebrates and the implications of habitat change', in Hopson T. and Lamb J. (eds), *Proceedings of the Manx Hill-lands seminar*, Manx Nature Conservation Trust, Douglas (1997), 39–50.

—— 'Non-avian vertebrates and the implications of habitat change', Hopson T. and Lamb J. (eds), *Manx Hill-land Report*, Manx Wildlife Trust (1995), 39–50.

Posford Duvivier International, *Coastal erosion study at Kirk Michael*, Report to Isle of Man Department of Transport in Tynwald (1999).

—— *Coastal management options for the northern shoreline of the Isle of Man (Kirk Michael to Ramsey)*, Report to the Isle of Man Department of Transport (2000).

Potts A.S., 'Fossil cryonival features in central Wales', *Geografiska Annaler*, 53A (1971), 39–51.

Power G.M. and Barnes R.P., 'Relationship between metamorphism and structure on the northern edge of eastern Avalonia in the Manx Group, Isle of Man', in Woodcock N.H., Quirk D.G., Fitches W.F. and Barnes R.P. (eds), *In sight of the suture: the Palaeozoic geology of the Isle of Man in its Iapetus Ocean context*, Geological Society of London Special Publication, 160 (1999), 289–305.

—— and Crowley S.F., 'Petrological and geochemical evidence for the tectonic affinity of the (?)Ordovician Poortown Basic Intrusive Complex, Isle of Man', in Woodcock N.H., Quirk D.G., Fitches W.F. and Barnes R.P. (eds), *In sight of the suture: the Palaeozoic geology of the Isle of Man in its Iapetus Ocean context*, Geological Society of London Special Publication, 160 (1999), 165–175.

Preston C.D. and Hill M.O., 'The geographical relationships of British and Irish vascular plants', *Botanical Journal of the Linnean Society*, 124 (1997), 1–120.

—— Pearman D.A. and Dines T.D., *New Atlas of the British and Irish Flora*, Cambridge University Press (2002), 910.

Prothero D.R. and Schwab F.L., *Sedimentary geology: An introduction to sedimentary rocks and stratigraphy*, W.H. Freeman and Company, New York (1996), 575.

Purvis O.W., Coppins B.J., Hawksworth D.L., James P.W. and Moore D.M., *The lichen flora of Great Britain and Ireland*, Natural History Museum, London (1992).

Quayle T., *General view of the agriculture of the Isle of Man*, London (1812) (reprinted W. Bulmer, Douglas, 1992).

Quirk D.G. and Burnett D.J., 'Lithofacies of Lower Palaeozoic deep marine sediments in the Isle of Man: a new map and stratigraphic model of the Manx Group', in Woodcock N.H., Quirk D.G., Fitches W.F. and Barnes R.P. (eds), *In sight of the suture: the Palaeozoic geology of the Isle of Man in its Iapetus Ocean context*, Geological Society of London Special Publication, 160 (1999), 69–88.

—— and Kimbell G.S., 'Structural evolution of the Isle of Man and central part of the Irish Sea', in Meadows N.S., Trueblood S.P., Hardman N. and Cowan G. (eds), *Petroleum geology of the Irish Sea and adjacent areas*, Geological Society of London Special Publication, 124 (1997), 135–159.

—— Burnett D.J., Kimbell G.S., Murphy C.A. and Varley J.S., 'Shallow geophysical and geological evidence for a regional-scale fault duplex in the Lower Palaeozoic of the Isle of Man', in Woodcock N.H., Quirk D.G., Fitches W.F. and Barnes R.P. (eds), *In sight of the suture: the Palaeozoic geology of the Isle of Man in its Iapetus Ocean context*, Geological Society of London Special Publication, 160 (1999a), 239–257.

—— Ford T.D., King J.A., Roberts I.L., Postance R.B. and Odell I., 'Enigmatic boulders and syn-sedimentary faulting in the Carboniferous limestone of the Isle of Man', *Proceedings of the Yorkshire Geological Society*, 48 (1990), 99–113.

—— Roy S., Knott I., Redfern J. and Hill L., 'Petroleum geology and future hydrocarbon potential of the Irish Sea', *Journal of Petroleum Geology*, 22 (1999b),

243–260.

Reeves G.M., 'On the remains of a skeleton of *Cervus Giganteus* (Irish Elk) in a Late-glacial kettle hole deposit near Kirk Michael, Isle of Man', *Proceedings of Isle of Man Natural History and Antiquarian Society*, New Series VIII, 4 (1982), 416–422.

Reynolds E.J. and Short M.J., 'The status of Foxes (*Vulpes vulpes*) on the Isle of Man in 1999', *Mammal Review*, 33 (2003), 69–76.

Reynolds S.H., *A Monograph on the British Pleistocene Mammalia: The Giant Deer or Megaloceros*, The Palaeontographical Society, London (1927), 1–62.

Roberts B., Morrison C.W.K. and Hirons S., 'Low grade metamorphism of the Manx Group, Isle of Man: a comparative study of white mica "crystallinity" techniques', *Journal of the Geological Society*, 147 (1990), 271–277.

Roberts D.H., Chiverrell R.C., Innes J.B., Gonzalez S., Turner S. and Horton B.P., 'New data on Holocene sea level changes on the Isle of Man', in Chiverrell R.C., Thomas G.S.P. and Plater A.J. (eds), *Quaternary of the Isle of Man and Northwest England: a field guide*, Quaternary Research Association, Cambridge (2004), 112–124.

Robinson V., 'Social demography', in Robinson V. and McCarroll D. (eds), *The Isle of Man: Celebrating a Sense of Place*, Liverpool University Press (1990), 133–162.

Rose J., 'The Dimlington Stadial-Dimlington Chronozone: a proposal for naming the main glacial episode of the Late Devensian in Britain', *Boreas*, 14 (1985), 225–230.

Rouse C., 'The Isle of Man's unstable coast', in Robinson V. and McCarroll D. (eds), *The Isle of Man: Celebrating a Sense of Place*, Liverpool University Press (1990), 77–83.

Rushton A.W.A., 'Graptolites from the Manx Group', *Proceedings of the Yorkshire Geological Society*, 49 (1993), 259–262.

Russell G., 'The structure and vegetation history of the Manx Hill Peats', in Davey P.J. (ed.), *Man and Environment in the Isle of Man*, British Archaeological Reports, British Series, 54 (1978), 39–50.

Rust B.R., 'Depositional models for braided alluvium', in Miall A.D. (ed.), 'Fluvial sedimentology', *Memoir Canadian Society for Petroleum Geology*, 5 (1978), 605–628.

Sampson L., *Ponds and Dubs Survey*, Report to Manx Government, Department of Agriculture, Forestry and Fisheries (2002).

Sanderson B., McGregor B. and Brierley A., *Dive sites and marine life of the Calf of Man and neighbouring area*, Immel Publishing Ltd, London (1994), 46.

Sayle T., Lamb J., Colvin A. and Harris B., *Isle of Man Habitat Survey Phase 1 Report 1991–1994*, Department of Agriculture, Fisheries and Forestry, Isle of Man Government, Douglas (1995).

Scott A., *Road verge survey project report*, Report to Manx Nature Conservation Trust (1997).

Shackelton N.J., Crowhurst S., Hagelberg T., Pisias N.J. and Scheider D.A., 'A new late Neogene timescale: application to leg 138 sites', *Proceedings of the Ocean Drilling Program*, 138 (1995), 73–101.

—— and Opdyke N.D., 'Oxygen isotope and palaeomagnetic stratigraphy of Equatorial Pacific core V28–238: oxygen isotope temperatures and ice volumes on a 10^5 and a 10^6 scale', *Quaternary Research*, 3 (1973), 39–55.

Sharpe C.M., *Non-avian records*, Annual reports to Isle of Man Biological Records Centre, The Manx Museum, Douglas (1999–2002).

Shennan I., 'Interpretation of Flandrian sea-level data from the Fenland, England', *Proceedings of the Geologists' Association*, 93 (1982), 53–63.

—— 'Flandrian sea-level changes in the Fenland II. Tendencies of sea-level movement, altitudinal changes and local and regional factors', *Journal of Quaternary Science*, 1 (1986), 155–179.

—— and Horton B., 'Holocene land- and sea-level changes in Great Britain', *Journal of Quaternary Science*, 17 (2002), 511–526.

—— Peltier W.R., Drummond R. and Horton B.P., 'Global to local scale parameters determining relative sea-level changes and post-glacial isostatic adjustment of Great Britain', *Quaternary Science Reviews*, 21 (2002), 397–408.

Simmons I.G., *The Environmental Impact of Later Mesolithic Cultures*, Edinburgh University Press, Edinburgh (1996).

—— Atherden M.A., Cundill P.R. and Jones R.L., 'Inorganic layers in soligenous mires of the North Yorkshire Moors', *Journal of Biogeography*, 2 (1975), 49–56.

Simpson A., 'The stratigraphy and tectonics of the Manx Slate Series', *Quarterly Journal of the Geological Society of London*, 119 (1963), 367–400.

Skelton R.H., 'The Manx mines', *Mining Magazine*, 92 (1955), 9–18.

Slater G., 'The structure of the Bride Moraine, Isle of Man', *Proceedings of the Liverpool Geological Society*, 14 (1931), 184–196.

Smith A.G., 'The influence of Mesolithic and Neolithic man on British vegetation: a discussion', in Walker D. and West R.G. (eds), *Studies in the vegetational history of the British Isles*, Cambridge University Press, London (1970), 81–96.

—— and Goddard I.C., 'A 12,500 year record of vegetational history at Sluggan Bog, Co. Antrim, N. Ireland (incorporating a pollen zone scheme for the non-specialist)', *New Phytologist*, 118 (1991), 167–187.

Smith B., 'Borings through the glacial drifts in the northern part of the Isle of Man', *Summary of Progress of the Geological Survey*, 3 (1931), 14–23.

Smith D.B. and Taylor J.C.M., 'Permian', in Cope J.C.W., Ingham J.K. and. Rawson P.F. (eds), *Atlas of Palaeogeography and lithofacies*, Memoir of the Geological Society of London (1992).

Smyth W.W., 'List of minerals found in the Isle of Man', *Transactions of the Isle of Man Natural History and Antiquarian Society*, 1 (1888), 143–147.

Soil Survey of England and Wales, *Legend for the 1:250,000 Soil Map of England and Wales*, Lawes Agricultural Trust, Harpenden (1983).

Stace C., *New Flora of the British Isles*, Cambridge University Press (1997), 1226.

Steel R. and Asheim S.M., 'Alluvial sand deposition in a rapidly subsiding basin (Devonian, Norway)', in Miall A.D. (ed.), *Fluvial sedimentology*, Memoir Canadian Society for Petroleum Geology, 5 (1978), 597–604.

Stillman C.J., 'Ordovician to Silurian volcanism in the Appalachian-Caledonian orogeny', in Harris A.L., Holland C.H. and Leake B.E. (eds), *The Caledonides of the British Isles – Reviewed*, Geological Society of London Special Publication, 8 (1979), 275–290.

Stone P., Cooper A.H. and Evans J.A., 'The Skiddaw Group (English Lake District) reviewed: early Palaeozoic sedimentation and tectonism at the northern margin of Avalonia', in Woodcock N.H., Quirk D.G., Fitches W.F. and Barnes R.P. (eds), *In sight of the suture: the Palaeozoic geology of the Isle of Man in its Iapetus Ocean context*, Geological Society of London Special Publication, 160 (1999), 325–336.

Strickland H.E., 'Some remarkable Concretions in the Tertiary beds of the Isle of Man', *Quarterly Journal of the Geological Society of London* 4, pt.1, 92 (1842), 8–10.

Stuart A.J., 'Mammalian Extinctions in the Late Pleistocene of Northern Eurasia and North America', *Biological Reviews*, 66 (1991), 453–562.

—— and van Wijngaarden-Bakker L.H., 'Quaternary vertebrates', in Edwards K.J. and Warren W.P. (eds), *The Quaternary History of Ireland*, Academic Press, London (1985), 221–249.

—— Kosintsev P.A., Higham T.F.G. and Lister A.M., 'Pleistocene to Holocene extinction dynamics in giant deer and woolly mammoth', *Nature*, 431 (2004), 684–689.

—— Kosintsev P., Higham T. and Lister A.M., 'Holocene extinction of "Pleistocene" megafauna: new evidence on the Irish Elk', *Nature* (in press).

Styles P.D., *Isle of Man Freshwater Invertebrate Family Checklist*, Isle of Man Government Laboratory, Department of Local Government and the Environment (2001).

Summerfield M.A., *Global geomorphology*, Longman, New York (1991), 537.

Sutherland D.G., 'The high-level marine shell beds of Scotland and the build up of the last Scottish Ice-sheet', *Boreas*, 10 (1981), 247–254.

Swinnerton F., 'Early Neolithic Cists and Refuse Heap at Port St Mary', *Yn Liaor Manninagh*, 1 (1890), 137–139.

Talbot T., *The manorial roll of the Isle of Man 1511–1515*, Oxford University Press, London (1924), 118.

Tattersfield P., *A preliminary checklist of the terrestrial mollusca of the Isle of Man*, unpublished list (1987).

Taylor J.H. and Gamba E.A., 'The Oatland (Isle of Man) Igneous Complex', *Proceedings of the Geologists' Association*, 44 (1933), 355–377.

Temple, P.H., *Some aspects of the geomorphology of the Isle of Man*, unpublished MA thesis, University of Liverpool (1960).

Thomas G.S.P., 'The Quaternary stratigraphy of the Isle of Man', *Proceedings of the Geologists' Association*, 87 (1976), 307–323.

—— 'The Quaternary of the Isle of Man', in Kidson C. and Tooley M.J. (eds), *The Quaternary History of the Irish Sea*, Geological Journal Special Issue, 7 (1977), 155–179.

—— 'The origin of the glacio-dynamic structure of the Bride Moraine, Isle of Man', *Boreas*, 13 (1984), 355–364.

—— 'The Quaternary of the northern Irish Sea', in Johnson R.J. (ed.), *The geomorphology of North-West England*, Manchester University Press (1985), 143–158.

—— 'The Late Devensian glaciation along the western margin of the Cheshire-Shropshire Lowland', *Journal of Quaternary Science*, 4 (1989), 167–181.

—— 'Northern England', in Bowen, D.Q. (ed.), *A revised correlation of Quaternary deposits in the British Isles*, Geological Society Special Report, 23 (1999), 28–44.

—— Chiverrell R.C. and Huddart D., 'Ice-marginal depositional responses to probable Heinrich events in the Devensian deglaciation of the Isle of Man', *Quaternary Science Reviews*, 23 (2004), 85–106.

—— Connaughton M. and Dackombe R.V., 'Facies variation in a Late Pleistocene supraglacial outwash sandur from the Isle of Man', *Geological Journal*, 20 (1985), 193–213.

Thrower L.B., *Manx agriculture 1945–2000: a review of the June census*, Centre for Manx Studies Research Report, 10 (2002).

Thrower S.L., *Biodiversity in a Manx churchyard*, unpublished report (2001).

Tiddeman R.H., 'On the evidence for the ice sheets of north Lancashire and adjacent parts of Yorkshire and Westmorland', *Quarterly Journal of the Geological Society*, 28 (1872), 471–489.

Tipping R.M., 'Holocene evolution of a lowland Scottish landscape: Kirkpatrick Fleming. Part II, regional vegetation and land-use change', *Holocene*, 5 (1995a), 83–96.

—— 'Holocene evolution of a lowland Scottish landscape: Kirkpatrick Fleming. Part III, fluvial history', *Holocene*, 5 (1995b), 184–195.

Tooley M.J., 'Sea-level changes during the last 9000 years in N.W. England', *Geographical Journal*, 140 (1974), 18–42.

—— 'Flandrian sea-level changes and vegetational history on the Isle of Man', in Davey

P. (ed.), *Man and Environment on the Isle of Man*, British Archaeological Reports, Oxford, 54 (1978a), 15–24.

—— *Sea level changes: north-west England during the Flandrian stage*, Oxford University Press, Oxford (1978b), 227.

—— 'Sea-level changes and coastal morphology in north-west England', in Johnson R.H. (ed.), *The geomorphology of north-west England*, Manchester University Press, Manchester (1985), 94–121.

Tucker R.D. and McKerrow W.S., 'Early Palaeozoic chronology: a review in light of new U-Pb zircon ages from Newfoundland and Britain', *Canadian Journal of Earth Sciences*, 32 (1995), 368–379.

UK Biodiversity Group, *Tranche 2 Action Plans, Vol. IV – Invertebrates*, English Nature (1999), 9–10.

Vartanyan S.L., Garutt V.E. and Sher A.V., 'Holocene dwarf mammoths from Wrangel Island in the Siberian Arctic', *Nature*, 362 (1993), 337–340.

Veale L., Thompson R. and Bates M., *Isle of Man sublittoral survey 1974–1977*, Port Erin Marine Laboratory, unpublished report (1998a).

Veale L., Thompson R. and Bates M., *Isle of Man sub-littoral Survey 1994–1997*, Port Erin Marine Laboratory, unpublished report (1998b).

Von Arx R., 'East Snaefell Mine', *British Mining*, 50 (1994), 158–160.

—— 'A glimpse of Snaefell Mine', *British Mining*, 57 (1996), 34–46.

—— 'Kirk Michael Mine in the Isle of Man', *British Mining*, 61 (1998), 74–90.

von Grafenstein U., Erlenkeuser H., Brauer A., Jouzel J. and Johnsen S.J., 'A mid-European decadal isotope-climate record from 15,500 to 5000 years BP', *Science*, 284 (1999), 1654–1657.

Ward J.C., 'Notes on the geology of the Isle of Man', *Geological Magazine*, 7 (1880), 1–9.

Warriner D. and Gilling A., 'Exploration and survey of the Great Laxey Mine, Isle of Man', *Bulletin of the Peak District Mines Historical Society*, 8 (1983), 373–381.

Watson E., 'Two nivation cirques near Aberystwyth, Wales', *Biutetyn Peryglacjalny*, 15 (1966), 79–101.

—— 'The slope deposits in the Nant Iago Valley, near Cader Idris, Wales', *Biutetyn Peryglacjalny*, 18 (1969), 95–113.

—— 'The Cardigan Bay area', in C.A. Lewis (ed.), *The Glaciations of Wales*, Longman, London (1970), 125–145.

—— 'Remains of pingos in Wales and the Isle of Man', *Geological Journal*, 7 (1971), 381–387.

Wheldon J.A. and Hartley J.W., 'The flora of the Manx curraghs', *Lancashire Naturalist* (1910), 271–304.

White R.S., 'A hot-spot model for early Cenozoic volcanism in the North Atlantic', in Parsons L.M. and Morton C.A. (eds), *Early Cenozoic volcanism and the opening of the North Atlantic*, Geological Society of London Special Publication, 39 (1988), 3–13.

Williamson K., 'The puffins of the Calf Isle', *Journal of the Manx Musuem*, 62 (1940), 178–180.

—— 'Ornithology on the Calf of Man', *Proceedings of the Isle of Man Natural History and Antiquarian Society*, 7 (1941), 419–439.

Wills L., 'The Triassic succession in the central Midlands in its regional setting', *Quarterly Journal of the Geological Society of London*, 126 (1970), 225–285.

Wilson R.C.L., Drury S.A. and Chapman J.L., *The Great Ice Age: climate change and life*, The Open University (2000).

Wilson T., 'A new survey and description. An account of the Isle of Man', in Cruttwell

C. and Cruttwell R. (eds), *The works of Bishop T. Wilson*, Cruttwell, Bath (1772).

Wilson W.H., *Exploration for mineral deposits in the Isle of Man*, unpublished report, Island Exploration Co. Ltd. (1957).

Wingfield R.T.R., 'The Late Devensian (<22 000BP) Irish Sea basin: the sedimentary record of a collapsed ice sheet margin; discussion and reply', *Quaternary Science Reviews*, 11 (1992), 377–379.

—— 'A model of sea level changes in the Irish and Celtic seas during the end-Pleistocene to Holocene transition', in Preece R.C. (ed.), *Island Britain: a Quaternary perspective*, Geological Society of London Special Publication, 96 (1999).

—— Hession M.A.I. and Whittington R.J., *Anglesey, Sheet 53°N–06°W, Quaternary Geology 1:250,000 map*, British Geological Survey (1990).

Wirtz D., 'Zur Stratigraphie des Pleistocäns im Westen der Britischen Inseln', *Neues Jahrbuch für Geologie und Paläontologie*, 96 (1953), 267–303.

Woodcock N.H. and Barnes R.P., 'An early Ordovician turbidite system on the Gondwana margin: the southeastern Manx Group, Isle of Man', in Woodcock N.H., Quirk D.G., Fitches W.F. and Barnes R.P. (eds), *In sight of the suture: the Palaeozoic geology of the Isle of Man in its Iapetus Ocean context*, Geological Society of London Special Publication, 160 (1999), 89–107.

—— Morris J.H., Quirk D.G., Barnes R.P., Burnett, D., Fitches W.F., Kennan P.S. and Power G.M., 'Revised lithostratigraphy of the Manx Group, Isle of Man', in Woodcock N.H., Quirk D.G., Fitches W.F. and Barnes R.P. (eds), *In sight of the suture: the Palaeozoic geology of the Isle of Man in its Iapetus Ocean context*, Geological Society of London Special Publication, 160 (1999a), 45–68.

—— Quirk D.G., Fitches W.F. and Barnes R.P. (eds), *In sight of the suture: the Palaeozoic geology of the Isle of Man in its Iapetus Ocean context*, Geological Society of London Special Publication, 160 (1999b), 153–163, 370.

—— 'In sight of the suture: the early Palaeozoic geological history of the Isle of Man', in Woodcock N.H., Quirk D.G., Fitches W.F. and Barnes R.P. (eds), *In sight of the suture: the Palaeozoic geology of the Isle of Man in its Iapetus Ocean context*, Geological Society of London Special Publication, 160 (1999c), 1–10.

Woodman P.C. and Monaghan N., 'From mice to mammoths: dating Ireland's earliest faunas', *Archaeology Ireland*, 7 (1993).

Wormwell C., *Warden's Report for Ayres A.S.S.I*, Report to Department of Agriculture, Fisheries and Forestry, Isle of Man Government (1999).

Wright J., 'The foraminifera of the Pleistocene clay, Shellag', *Yn Lioar Manninagh*, 3 (1902), 627–629.

—— and Reade T.M., 'The Pleistocene clays and sands of the Isle of Man', *Proceedings Liverpool Geological Society*, 17 (1906), 103–117.

Wright J., 'Additions to the spiders of the Isle of Man: Provisional List 1991 to June 1995', *Proceedings of the Isle of Man Natural History and Antiquarian Society*, 10 (1996), 294–295.

Yalden D.W., *The History of British Mammals*, Poyser Natural History, London (1999).

Ziegler P.A., *Evolution of Laurussia*, Kluwer Academic Publishers, Dordrecht (1989), 102.

Index

of the Manx and Dalby groups 57–8,
    57, **59**, 62
and mineral extraction 359
and oil and gas 373
of the Peel Sandstone Group 78–9,
    80–1
fauna 16
    contemporary 413–19
    fossils 247, 256–72, 297–300
        see also giant deer (*Megaloceros
        giganteus*)
feldspar 29, 38, 39, 42, 64, 69, 70, 328,
    371
    plagioclase 62, 67, 68, 71
    potassium 47, 67, 68, **70**, 71
feral ferret (*Mustela furo*) 299, 417
feral goat (*Capra hircus*) 417–18
fern 404, 408
Field Club 380
field mouse-ear (*Cerastium arvense*) 401,
    406
field scabious (*Knautia arvensis*) 403
field vole (*Mictrotis agrestis*) 298, 416
Firth of Clyde 141
fish 300, 416, 421
    fossil 106–7
Fleetwood Dyke 121, **121**
Fleshwick 245, 395
Fleshwick Bay 139
Fleshwick Unit **33**, 36, 43
flint 142
floating pennywort (*Hydrocotyle
    ranunculoides*) 402
floods 123, 135
    flash 81, 83, 96
    meltwater flood cycles 177, 179
    sea 98, 99
flora 16
flounder (*Platichthys flesus*) 416, 421
flushes 398
flute casts 21–3, **22**, 45, **46**
fluvial deposits, Peel Sandstone Group
    82–3, **84**
fluvial responses, to deglaciation 239–46
fluvial sedimentation, lowland 240–5
folds 115
    of the Bride Moraine 159, **160**, 162
    of Castletown Limestone 93, 103, **104**
    Dalby Group
        folding phase 1 (F1) 58
        folding phase 2 (F2) 55, 58
    isoclinal 159
    Manx Group 54–5, **56**
        folding phase 1 (F1) 55, **56**
        folding phase 2 (F2) 55
        folding phase 3 (F3) 55
    parasitic 55, **56**

Peel Sandstone Group 79
    see also anticlines; synclines
foliation 159
foot and mouth disease 418
foraminifera 99, 100, 128, 165–7, 273,
    289
Forbes, Edward 379–80, 381, 411
Ford, T.D. 357
forestry 349
    plantations 397–8
    see also woodland
Forestry Board 397
Forestry, Mines and Land Board 397–8
formations, glacial 145–51
Fort Island 41, 411
fossil cliffs 14, 272, 288, 291–4, 295
    buried 198, 199, 212
fossils 7, 246–72
    acritarchs 29–30, 32, 35, 36–7, 38, 40,
        62
    of Castletown Limestone 94, 99, 100,
        101, 102, 103–5, 106–7
    of the Dalby Group rocks 46–7, **48**, 49
    fauna 247, 256–72, 297–300
    foraminifera 99, 100, 128, 165–7, 273,
        289
    Holocene 279
    of the Manx Group rocks 29–30, **31**,
        32, 35, 36–7, 38, 40, 47
    marine trace 29, 30, **31**
    Peel Sandstone Group 77–8, 82, 83,
        85–6, 87
    plant 246–56
    Quaternary markers 197–8
    see also giant deer (*Megaloceros
    giganteus*); graptolites
Fowles, A.P. 413
Foxdale 141, 359, 370
Foxdale Granite 9, 60, **65–6**, 69–71, **70**,
    135, 367
    garnet-bearing 69
    muscovite-bearing 69
Foxdale mineral vein 58
Foxdale River 13, 243–4
Foxdale-Glen Rushen mines 357, 359,
    361–5, **362–3**
    Bawden's Shaft 361, **362–3**
    Beckwith's Shaft 361, **362–3**, 364–5
    Cross's mine **362**, 364–5
    Dixon's mine **362**, 364
    Pott's Shaft 361, **363**
    Wardell's vein 364
France 131, 235
Friends of the Earth 384
frost climate 127

gabbro 63, 71, 72